Jesus in Art and Literature

ACKNOWLEDGMENTS

I wish to thank in particular:

Jean de Saint-Chéron, the talented editor of the original French edition of this book, who patiently brought it to completion;
Aude Mantoux, Marie-Amélie Clercant, and Claire Lemoine for kindly rereading and critiquing my texts;
Isabelle Mascaras, for the quality of her iconographic research;
Marine Bezou for the beautiful graphic design.

And also:

Maciej Leszczynski, Father Frédéric Curnier-Laroche, Fleur Nabert, and Sophie Mouquin, who kindly shared with me their way of looking at the masterpieces of Christian art;
my father-in-law, the painter Gérard Ambroselli (1906–2000), who taught me to appreciate in works of art what makes them appreciable as works of art.

Pierre-Marie Dumont

The spiritual and theological positions presented in this book are primarily those of the artists who painted the works or the authors of the texts reproduced and not those of the authors of the book or the publisher.

Excerpts from the Bible appearing in the margins are cited from the Revised Standard Version, Second Catholic Edition (RSV–2CE).

Citations from the Bible that appear during the course of the Prologue and in the commentaries on the works of art are given in the author's version, which is often a freer rendering.

The other citations, particularly of artists, were collected by the author over a lifetime. Whenever possible a currently verifiable reference is given.

All the text blocks entitled *In Art History* are by Mario Choueiry.

COVER : *Christ*
Cima da Conegliano (*ca.* 1459-1517/1518)
Oil on poplar wood, 13.6 x 10 in
Dresden, Gemäldegalerie Alte Meister

Jesus in Art and Literature

Pierre-Marie Dumont

WITH THE COLLABORATION OF
MARIO CHOUEIRY

PREFACE BY **EDWART VIGNOT**

TRANSLATED BY **MICHAEL J. MILLER**

MAGNIFICAT

Paris • New York • Oxford • Madrid

“Yes, I say my prayers when everything goes badly.
You do, too, as you well know.
We plunge into prayer and rediscover
the atmosphere of our First Communion.
You do this, too.”

Henri Matisse to Picasso

Table of Contents

PREFACE

Jesus Christ in art

EDWART VIGNOT

In 1995, one of my very first jobs, at the Museum of Fine Arts in Strasbourg, was to tell the story of Jesus during the Christmas season to children aged five through seven, through four episodes from his life illustrated by works exhibited in its permanent collection. This visit, which never went over forty-five minutes, the maximum attention span that one could expect from such a young audience, invariably started with *The Visitation*, a small-size painting by Peter Paul Rubens (1577–1640), followed by an exquisite *Adoration of the Shepherds* by Carlo Crivelli (*ca.* 1430/1435–*ca.* 1493/1500), then an immense *Adoration of the Magi* painted on canvas by Bartolomeo Biscaino (*ca.* 1632–*ca.* 1657), only to conclude with a delicate *Flight into Egypt* by Claude Gellée, also called Le Lorrain (1600–1682). Besides this simple yet evocative anecdote, what struck me at the time was to see how the figure of Jesus, his physical representation, had little importance, because all that mattered was the story. The Christ Child might have been chubby or skinny, and have had blond, brown, or even red hair, and that would not have affected at all the emotions felt by the viewers. To my great astonishment, this idea was reinforced one day when I asked a small group of children what strategy the painter Biscaino had found to make us recognize immediately the Child Jesus surrounded by his famous relatives and one of them exclaimed, “That’s easy: he has a light-bulb head!” After his initial surprise, by reflecting carefully on it, the very young spectator had immediately understood that that luminous halo symbolized in an incandescent way Christ’s holiness!

Thus, from the oral traditions to the Scriptures and then to the literary texts, the image of Jesus was carried and formed by an enormous number of artists whose imaginations nourished each other, in order to design but also to produce these countless portraits and other emblematic scenes from the Savior’s life.

After the fourth century A.D. the artistic representation of Christ often reflected idealized typologies; the result was an infinitesimal number of physiognomies, always close to an Oriental type, and historians today agree in describing the physique of these *Christs* as of a “Syro-Palestinian” type. Not until the Renaissance was the convention of a Caucasian type of Jesus Christ established, which today we would even describe as “European.”

What a delicate mission it is to give an image of Christ! How ambitious! How can anyone depict God? God made man, yes, but God after all. Our Jewish brethren, and also Muslims, took a path without icons: God cannot be depicted, therefore he must not be. This question is posed in different terms for Christians who adore an incarnate God. By this very incarnation, doesn't God give us an image of himself? What are we to do, then, about the Second Commandment of the Decalogue, uttered twice in the Old Testament? *You shall not make for yourself a graven image, or any likeness of anything that is in heaven above, or that is in the earth beneath, or that is in the water under the earth* (Ex 20:4; Dt 5:8).

These questions legitimately perturbed the theorists of the first era of Christianity. A painted or sculpted image was in effect an aid to devotion and an essential instructional tool for the early Christian communities even before the establishment of written sources, which for a long time would remain difficult for most believers to access. The image was also a valuable vehicle for spreading this new faith.

Before depicting Christ under his human appearance, artists drew his name in the form of a fish, *ichthus*, a Greek acronym for "Jesus Christ, Son of God, Savior." Very soon the first Christian iconographic sources were devoted to the figure of Christ, the heart of the Gospel message. Nevertheless, artists represented Christ and not the life of Christ. He is shown as a philosopher, clothed in a toga, without any particular scenery, or as the Good Shepherd. This approach, which focused above all on the human nature of Jesus Christ, did not prevent the emergence of depictions of Christ the Pantocrator, in other words, Christ in glory, in Byzantine mosaics. The emphasis is then on the divine nature of Christ, represented in his glorified body. As the iconography budded spontaneously, the new developments would quickly be called into question and their legitimacy would be debated.

The violence of the iconoclastic quarrel that perturbed the Byzantine Empire starting in the year 726 testifies to the crucial matter at stake in this question. The very existence of depictions of God-made-man gave rise to confrontations between Christians within the Eastern Roman Empire. The iconodules, who advocated the depiction of the divinity, were opposed by the iconoclasts, who condemned it. The century was scarred by the repeated destruction of images and by successive and reciprocal persecutions. The question was partly resolved during the Second Council of Nicaea in 787, which reestablished the devotional use of images and officially authorized the veneration of sacred images.

Until around the 13th century, artists developed the image of a powerful, triumphant Christ, whose face is calm even on the cross. Then works appeared that let the faithful see the image of a suffering, emaciated Christ on the cross, his body deformed by the ill treatment of the Passion. The humanity of the Son of God takes flesh in human weaknesses, in our fears and sufferings. His face, lowered, sometimes goes so far as to take on the appearance of a death mask. These works echo a medieval theological sensibility, in which questions of death and suffering occupy a central place.

The Renaissance that came from Italy transposed ancient settings and physical rules into religious scenes. The development of this profane beauty impassioned artists, perhaps to the point of exceeding the bounds of devotion and losing itself in aesthetic delight. Indeed, in the 16th century, the Protestant Reformation again posed the question about graphic representations of the Divine Persons and about their role in popular piety. The use of images clashed, once more, with accusations of idolatry. This produced great distrust of images, particularly of divine representations which were thought to encourage superstition. The Church made a new pronouncement on this thorny subject during the Council of Trent, which was convened in 1545. The assembled bishops affirmed that one can "draw great benefit" from the "legitimate use of images" that can "instruct and strengthen the people in the articles of faith" and be "useful to uninstructed people." This didactic role of the image also concerned the depiction of Christ. Consequently, complete freedom was given to artists and to those who commissioned them to produce painted or sculpted images representing Christ, the saints, and the Blessed Virgin, whose cult had just been reaffirmed. This explains the multiplication, from the late 16th century on, of depictions of the Christ Child on his Mother's knees: Nativity, Adoration of the Magi or of the Shepherds, Holy Family, Virgin with Child, Rest during the Flight into Egypt.

From the four canonical Gospel artists took episodes from the life of Christ, sometimes supplemented by accounts from the apocryphal gospels, which have the peculiar feature of emphasizing the childhood of Christ and feed one stream of the Christian imagination. We owe to them, for example, the presence of the ox and the ass that warm the Infant Christ with their breath in Nativity scenes. These iconographic sources are combined of course with the artist's own inventiveness and the patron's preference.

This turbulent history can be glimpsed through the depictions of Christ that centuries of art history have made available to us. They are legion and are reproduced in all mediums. Mosaics, paintings, sculptures, engravings, and stained-glass windows, from the first eras of Christianity down to the present, though uniformly material, suggest the many subtle tones of the human vision of an incarnate God. These images of Christ, whether he is powerful, suffering, or a child, carry believers and non-believers into the depths of an intimate reflection. They are also the historical testimony of more than twenty centuries of artistic creation relying on the biblical account. The Church, the chief patron of artists and a powerful one, thus assured the vivacity of Christ's image; its permanence did not keep it from being reimagined perpetually.

Our contemporary society has a bulimic relation to images; they can sometimes tire our eyes or blunt our ability to admire them. This in no way detracts, I think, from the power of these images. This book collects an admirable *florilegium* of them.

The Carrying of the Cross
El Greco (1541–1614)
Ca. 1602
Oil on canvas, 42.5 x 31 in
Madrid, Prado Museum

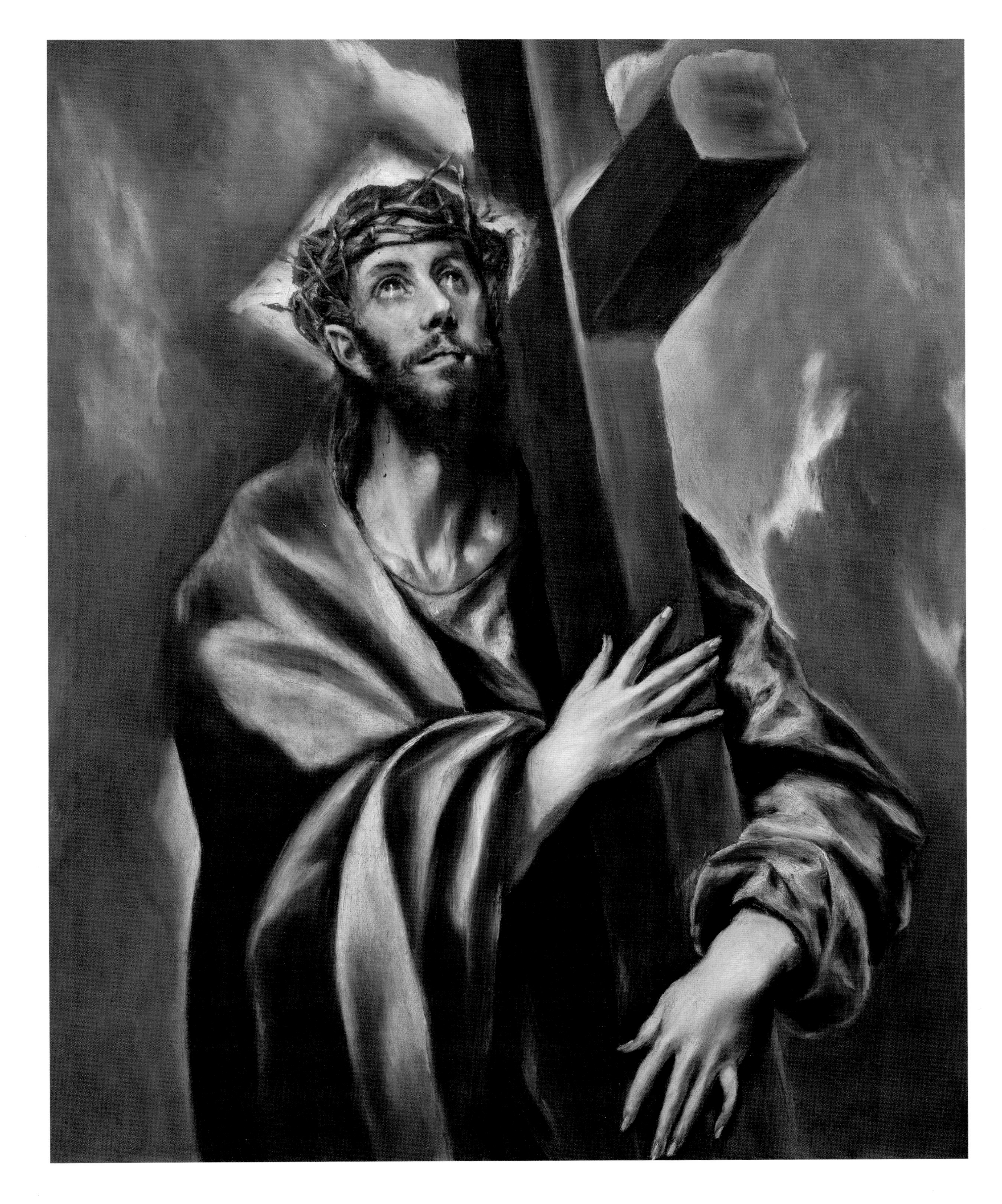

"In art, only one thing has worth:
what cannot be explained."
Georges Braque

PROLOGUE

But who is this man, *Jesus*?

PIERRE-MARIE DUMONT

In our culture, for almost twenty centuries, the principle subject and motif chosen by artists and writers has indisputably been a Jewish prophet named Jesus of Nazareth (referring to his geographical origin). He was the founder of Christianity, and believers prefer to call him Jesus Christ to signify the divine mission of the Savior of the world, which he claimed as his own. The "life" and the message of this Jesus have been handed down to us mainly by four distinct accounts collected under the name of the Gospels.

The great geniuses whose masterpieces this book presents for your admiration had a deep, even intimate knowledge of the Gospels. Moreover, most of them faithfully practiced the Christian religion and maintained with this historical personage a relation of veneration and love.

In our post-modern era, knowledge about Jesus and his message has generally become superficial, or insignificant. It seems necessary therefore to revisit rapidly his "story," his deeds, and the essentials of his teaching before getting to the mysteries that the artworks reproduced in this book present for our contemplation.

Jesus was born around the year 6 before the Common Era[1] in the heart of the Greco-Roman Orient, specifically in the kingdom of Judea, during the reign of Herod I, called the Great.

At that time, Herod was nearing the end of a brilliant reign that had started around thirty years earlier. He suffered from an incurable ailment that would soon carry him off. The question about his succession obsessed him, and he strove to frustrate intrigues and plots, real or imagined, hatched by those close to him. His work left its mark on his era: did he not go so far as to restore the Olympic Games that had fallen into disuse, so as to be named their president for life?

As a stern, sensible monarch, and often at the expense of sacrificing some subjects of his kingdom, he contributed decisively to the passage of the land of the Jewish nation to Greco-Roman modernity. Its language and administration had become Greek, and many new or rebuilt towns rivaled the Hellenic cities in splendor: paved roads for communication, porticos and aqueducts, theaters and palaces, hippodromes and circuses, even amphitheaters testified to an accelerated transition to the pagan civilization.

The Roman Empire, ruled then by Augustus, appreciated the unfailing "friendship" of Herod the Great. The Jewish memory of him preserves above all the image of the one who rebuilt the grandiose Temple in Jerusalem, their ancestral capital, which then performed the duties of the royal shrine.

According to the Gospel accounts, this was the context in which Mary, the wife of Joseph, brought into the world her first-born son in Bethlehem, in Judea, a few kilometers south of Jerusalem. Following the Jewish tradition, eight days later, on the occasion of his circumcision, his parents gave the newborn the name of Jesus, *Yéshûâ* in Aramaic (the local Semitic language), which means "God saves." After a short exile imposed by the persecutions of Herod, which the Gospel situates in Egypt, Joseph and Mary returned to live in northern Palestine, in Nazareth of Galilee, their town of origin. The unassuming market town is located six kilometers from the mighty, sumptuous Sepphoris which Herod Antipas, succeeding his father in A.D. 4, had decided to rebuild so as to make it his first capital. Thus the child Jesus would be an eyewitness to how this second-generation Herod pursued his father's policy of openness to the Greco-Roman culture.

We know little about the acts and deeds of the child Jesus. He followed the developments of growing up like all other children. In a land imbued with the Greek, so-called "Hellenistic" culture, he was raised according to the traditions of the popular Jewish milieu to which he belonged, which nourished him with the ancestral sap of his family tree.

1 Our era, also referred to as "A.D.," *anno Domini*, "the year of Our Lord," begins on the presumed date of Jesus' birth, as it was fixed, with accuracy to within a few years, by a learned monk in the 6th century. Today historians date the birth of Jesus somewhere between the year 9 and the year 3 V$7 $

Most certainly the young Jesus attended the regular assemblies that were held in the family circles and in the synagogues, where the people prayed, chanted the psalms, read, and commented on the Scriptures.[2] His future talents as a preacher and his profound knowledge of the Torah,[3] the prophetic books, and the wisdom literature may suggest that he received instruction from the reputable scribes and masters, who were well-versed in the subtle debates about Scripture. However, the Gospel accounts, reporting the words of the firsthand witnesses of his childhood, lead us to suppose rather that this was not the case: *Where did this man learn all this? Where does his knowledge come from?* they exclaimed in astonishment (Mk 13:54).

AT THE AGE OF THIRTY, JESUS LEFT HIS CARPENTER'S SHOP

Having reached his full maturity, around the age of thirty, Jesus left both Galilee and the carpenter's shop that he had taken over from his father, so as to withdraw to the desert of Judea. Many ascetics had gone there before him, and some were living in communities near the western shores of the Dead Sea. Further to the north, on the bank of the Jordan, Jesus found a renowned preacher, his cousin John, nicknamed the Baptist, who repeated the warnings of the great prophets of Israel and proclaimed the imminent coming of the kingdom of God, "the kingdom of heaven." John practiced an unheard-of ritual of individual baptism, administered as a sign of cleansing from sin to anyone who had resolved to make a radical conversion of life by way of repentance.

For Jesus, the desert experience did not stop there. In the same spirit as the "crossing of the desert" accomplished by the Hebrews[4]—his ancestors liberated from slavery in Egypt under the leadership of Moses, whose wanderings lasted for forty years before they entered into the Promised Land—he stayed there for forty days, praying and fasting. He also went through a series of trials that made him endure the sum total of human temptations in a moving combat against all the forces of evil mobilized against him in the name of Satan, the "devil" or the "tempter." Foreseeing the end of his power over humanity because one man brushed off all his seductions, the tempter finally retreated so as to prepare the final battle, this one to the death, with authority over the world at stake.

At the conclusion of his retreat in the desert, Jesus returned to Galilee. Definitively setting aside his professional tasks, he gathered a few disciples and started to travel through the region, preaching "the Gospel of God" (*evaggelion* in Greek, in other words, "Good News"). Speaking to audiences that soon grew as his reputation spread, he developed the major theme of the kingdom of heaven; John the Baptist, his precursor, had correctly grasped its pivotal function.

Jesus, for his part, no longer spoke of imminence but of actual presence: *"The kingdom of heaven is in your midst,"* he repeated wherever he went.

Blessed are the poor in spirit, for theirs is the kingdom of heaven.
Blessed are the meek, for they shall conquer the earth.
Blessed are the sorrowing, for they shall be comforted.
Blessed are those who hunger for righteousness, for they shall be satisfied.
Blessed are those who forgive, for they shall be forgiven.
Blessed are the pure of heart, for they shall see God.
Blessed are the peacemakers, for they shall be called children of God.

With this proclamation (cf. Mt 5:3-12), in which all is paradox yet there is no contradiction, Jesus opened a programmatic discourse addressed to an immense crowd that had flocked to him from all parts to this high place in Galilee.

The building up of the kingdom of heaven advocated by Jesus is fundamentally interior. In order to change the world, it must first take place in the heart of man, on the ruins of everything that causes his unhappiness: the desire for riches, power, and pleasure, with their corollaries: theft, deceit, injustice, violence, murder. "Wretched man that I am! Who will deliver me from the law of sin that drags

2 "Scripture" or "the Scriptures" designate for the Jews and on the lips of Jesus himself "the Law and the Prophets," in other words, the set of books of Jewish traditions reputed to have been inspired by God. Composed by human beings, these books reveal that history has a direction and a meaning: this is Revelation. This meaning would be defined by the Covenant between God's plan and human freedom. When Christians added the books of the New Testament to this corpus, which from then on was called the Old Testament, they constituted the Bible, usually called "Sacred Scripture."

3 For the Jews, the Torah, the Law, is not only the Decalogue (the Ten Commandments) but the entirety of the first five books that would make up the Bible: Genesis, Exodus, Leviticus, Numbers, and Deuteronomy. Thus the Torah collects not only hundreds of laws and commandments, but also historical accounts that make up the inspired history of the Covenant between God and his people, Israel.

4 Name of the "chosen people" made up of the descendants of Abraham, Isaac, and Jacob, which they kept until around the sixth century V$7 $ Then others started to call them "the Jewish people."

me down into death?" (cf. Rom 7:24), we cry to heaven! *"Blessed are you,"* Jesus responds. In order to make all humanity share in this promised happiness, he does not only lay down precepts, the fulfillment of which would suffice to make a man righteous. He comes to change hearts, not the Law.

Jesus limited his travels at first to a territory marked out by three towns: Nazareth, Nain, and Cana. Then he headed east, reaching the western shores of the Sea of Galilee, or the Lake of Gennesaret, and made Capernaum, at the far north, the base from which he set out unceasingly. The lake, called "of Tiberias" after Herod Antipas made the city of Tiberias his new capital, was attractive. It was easy to cross by boat, giving access to the eastern shores which had been won over to the pagan culture and morals; Jesus did not hesitate to venture even there.

Within the limits of this expanded triangle, with its opening toward the lake, Jesus called to follow him the men whom he soon chose as his twelve apostles (*apostolos*, "envoys" in Greek), whom he would describe also as *diakonos*, "servants." These men, of very different ages and social backgrounds, would be his close companions and his accredited collaborators for three years, then the missionaries of the Gospel and "the servants of the servants of God" until the end of their lives. Besides the apostles, an important group of disciples, including both men and women, followed him, in particular providing for his needs. Gradually a genuine brotherhood was organized, which very soon was affiliated with a new movement within the Jewish people, causing enthusiasm and admiration among many, irritation and hostility in others.

COMPANION OF DRUNKARDS AND GLUTTONS

Surrounded or preceded by his disciples, Jesus soon extended his mission field; for long months, starting from Galilee, he would take the major roads running from east to west and back. These routes ended at the Mediterranean ports, Tyre among others, in the far north, where he stayed. They also led, east of the Jordan, to the Greek cities of Caesarea Philippi, of Syria, and of the Decapolis (a network of ten towns), among other areas. Foreigners themselves, whether Greco-Roman or oriental, took these roads, on which the use of Greek was often required. Jesus traveled therefore in the same way as the merchants, the businessmen, and the idea-mongers did. He went far, as much as nearly two hundred miles, in all directions. In all these places his teaching penetrated like a powerful seed, and his community—for there really was a community—spread.

The many "signs"—often described as miraculous—that Jesus performed enhanced his reputation as a wonder-worker with versatile gifts. And so he was welcomed as one of those "divine men," itinerant magicians or inspired prophets, figures that were not foreign to the eastern Mediterranean populations of that time.

Despite all that, as soon as the contemporaries of Jesus were confronted with him, directly as hearers of his words and witnesses of his works, it seems that they lost their bearings. For the Jesus who was revealing himself in surprising ways was unlike the models previously experienced or foretold. Those who expected a mortified ascetic discovered a man who enjoyed the good things in life and was denounced as *a companion of drunkards and gluttons* (Lk 7:34); those who expected an exemplar of purity discovered *a friend of publicans* [collectors of the Roman tax and therefore very unpopular] *and sinners* (Mt 11:19); those who expected a scrupulous interpreter of the Mosaic Law discovered an observant believer who nonetheless could behave as a scandalous transgressor, going so far as to teach that the Law is made for man, and not man for the Law (cf. Mk 2:27); those who expected a spiritual master discovered an inspired guide who nevertheless refused to manipulate his disciples in any way; those who expected a royal Messiah called to reign and to kick the pagan invader out of the land of Israel discovered a *meek and humble* servant (Mt 11:29) reluctant to take power over others.

His adversaries, who were recruited mainly from among the religious authorities and the Jewish leaders, took every opportunity to prove that this man had to be either an imposter or possessed by a demon. But the people continued to follow Jesus in a crowd that increased in number every day. For *no man ever spoke like this man* (Jn 7:46). The four Gospel accounts agree in presenting a charisma emanating from Jesus that was more than human yet capable of touching hearts.

After three years of fruitful preaching, Jesus left Galilee and the surrounding areas to go to Judea. He knew Judea and Jerusalem, its religious capital, with its Temple and its pilgrimages. He had family and friends there, particularly Lazarus, whom he raised from the dead, as the Gospel relates. From Galilee, regular incursions led him toward the province that was now governed directly by Rome. Two authorities—administrative and religious—were exercised there in two distinct capitals, Caesarea and Jerusalem respectively.

Since the year 26, the Roman governor, called the "procurator" or "prefect," had been Pontius Pilate. He resided in Caesarea, a new city that Herod the Great had ordered built on the Mediterranean to rival the Athenian port of Piraeus. All the military, administrative, and cultural services were located there, and of course the games. Jerusalem, for its part, with its Temple, was the city of the high priest and the priestly profession, and also of the Sanhedrin, the supreme Jewish authority for official studies of the Scriptures and debates on the Law; in short, it was the institutional center responsible for the smooth running of the wheels of the Jewish social and religious system that Christians would later designate by the name "Judaism." Jerusalem was also the focal point for Jews who flocked from all Palestine and the diaspora during the major feasts—which sometimes became turbulent. In Judea, there was no lack of conflicts, and most often they were severely repressed. The balance of the two powers was not automatic, but it was firmly maintained.

IS JESUS "THE MESSIAH"?

These are the complex circumstances in which Jesus appeared in Judea, accompanied by his apostles. He was preceded by a solid reputation of being a highly successful leader. The proclamation of the coming of the kingdom of heaven was always the point of his teaching. It was not neutral with regard to the two coexisting authorities. Among the Jewish leaders principally—since the Roman authority intervened only in cases of serious disturbances—suspicion would develop into opposition and then into hostility. It must be noted that the moral doctrine advocated by Jesus, as an accomplishment of the prophetic texts of Scripture, drew positive lessons from the fact that the political jurisdiction of the national land was under foreign domination. This situation had value as a parable. The innovative message of Jesus tolerated the distinction of roles between God on the one hand and Caesar on the other, with their respective rights. Jesus' message was universal, insofar as he addressed every conscience, starting of course with the conscience of each member of the Jewish people, but without making that group exclusive or even privileged.

Thus Jesus was, in fact, a serious competitor of the Pharisees, influential promoters of a doctrine elaborated for the Jewish people considered as a holy, sovereign entity. For these Pharisees, the practice of interpreting the Scriptures, traditionally the prerogative of the priests in Jerusalem, must expand everywhere, into the residence of every subject of the Mosaic Law. The necessary act of sanctification becomes possible far from the Temple and without the priests, since every family table purified according to the rules has a function analogous to that of the altar of sacrifices. In many of its aspects, the "new and eternal" Law that Jesus proposed coincided with this ideal. But it also surpassed it, being open to all human beings, wherever they are and whatever they are; and it raises it to the highest power by setting as its criterion not external attitudes that are often marked by hypocrisy, but the disposition *to love in deed and in truth* (1 Jn 3:18).

Another factor worked against Jesus: the ever stronger influence that he had on the crowds and, far more importantly, the character of it. They were inclined to acknowledge him as the Messiah, the descendant of King David who would liberate Israel from pagan occupation, as many hoped. According to the Gospel accounts, the titles "Messiah" and "son of David" were proclaimed repeatedly in the presence of Jesus or in reference to him. This fame gave rise to demonstrations of enthusiasm on the occasion of major religious feasts, in Jerusalem and its environs, but also to controversies that were sometimes vehement.

Within Jewish society under Roman occupation, the expectation of the Messiah was most often imprecise, hesitant, and timid. Around Jesus it assumed a resolute, full, and dynamic form. The people who had been edified by Jesus found themselves increasingly won over by the idea that he personally combined all the so-called messianic virtues. In Greek, *messias*, in other words, "one consecrated by the divine anointing," is pronounced *christos*, "Christ," and the term "messianic," *christianos*, would soon mean "Christian." Wasn't the multitude of men and women who acclaimed Jesus in this way already, in potency, the "Christian" community?

Except in the secrecy of one particular conversation, Jesus nevertheless avoided declaring that he was the Messiah, a term that would signify too restrictively "messiah of Israel." His attitude as well as his formulations, in his prayers and even more in his unfathomable mystical experiences, started to make it evident that everything was at work for him in the altogether unique character of his filial relation to God.

Our Father: so begins the prayer that Jesus taught to his disciples. These two affectionate words addressed to God have transformed humanity. The Jewish people had long since glimpsed the fact that God is Father for all human beings; although often *demanding and terrible* (Dt 7:21), isn't God also *slow to anger and full of love* (Ex 34:6)? But the "sons of Israel" jealously claimed God's tenderness as theirs exclusively, and they would have been afraid to demean the Almighty by addressing him with the confident familiarity of a child who knows that his father is nothing but love, because he has experienced it. Jesus, for his part, addressed God as "Father," *Abba* in Aramaic.

Claiming to be so close to God *the Father* as to *be one with him* (Jn 10:30), thus declaring himself the only-begotten Son of the Father (cf. Jn 1:18), Jesus invited all men and all women of all times to recognize that they were his brothers and his sisters so that through him, with him, and in him, they might address God in truth by calling him "Our Father."

With this end in view, the three Gospels according to Saint Matthew, Saint Mark, and Saint Luke, as well as a letter by Saint Paul, report that on the eve of his death, Jesus gathered his disciples to have a Last Supper with them in the Cenacle. During this meal he offered them the opportunity to become in some way members of his body. Taking bread, he broke it and distributed it to them saying: *"This is my body which will be given up for you"* (cf. Lk 22:19). And taking the cup of wine, he shared it with them saying: *"This is my blood, which will be poured out for the multitude"* (Mt 26:28).

Then, according to the fourth Gospel, at the end of the meal, Jesus entrusted to them his testament:

My little children,
I give to you a new commandment:
Love one another as I have loved you....
If you love me,
you will keep my commandments....
He who loves me will be loved by my Father,
And we will come to him
and make our home with him. (Jn 13:33-34; 14:15-23)

Christ's disciples are called to recite and to live the *Our Father* and to put into practice the *new commandment*; from this will arise a community of brothers and sisters, the "assembly" (in Greek *ekklēsia*, "Church") of the "children of God," who are recognized as such not by their human descent, nor by their membership in an ethnic group, but because they are truly born of God through Jesus, with him, and in him.

This grace of a new and everlasting divine filiation [sonship] for all human beings is addressed first and naturally to the Jews, the heirs of the primordial promise made to Abraham. Would they agree to make up the original nucleus of this nascent people who from then on would be the authentic people of God? And would they acknowledge in Jesus the prophet of the new times, appointed directly by God as his only Son, having come into history to bring the grace of salvation to the multitude of people, with no distinction as to sex, origin, race, or social status, nor of personal abilities and faculties?

LIABLE TO THE DEATH PENALTY

Here, now, we see that the call of Jesus would be received by the authorities of the Jewish people as a challenge, and the gratuitous gift—as a provocation. Grace, which is meant to be offered as the most authentic and long-awaited ratification of the divine election claimed by Israel, would be understood as an attempt to dispossess them of a heritage that they had already received. Then, Jesus' pretention to divinity appeared as the worst of blasphemies, liable to the death penalty.

When Jesus was in Jerusalem for the yearly feast of the Passover, some of the religious dignitaries and Jewish leaders seized the occasion to coordinate a campaign against him. Exploiting as many grievances against him as they could and cleverly taking advantage of the complexity of the political situation, they would ask the supreme jurisdiction of the Roman occupying force to punish him for being a troublemaker, a potential conspirator against the authority of the Emperor in Rome. Jesus was judged swiftly. The procurator, Pontius Pilate, the only official authorized to make such life-or-death decisions, confirmed the death penalty for the man who was ironically pointed out to him as a pretender to be the king of the Jews.

At that time, fugitive slaves, soldiers who had deserted, and criminals who were not Roman citizens were often condemned to be fastened to a cross in view of everyone so as to die there slowly of asphyxiation in the most unspeakable sufferings. This extremely cruel pillory was meant to serve as an object lesson, and it was a familiar spectacle then even for the Jews. More than a century earlier, the high priest of Israel himself, Alexander Jannaeus, had resorted to it to put down the major rebellion of the Pharisees against him for taking the title of King of Judea; he had several hundred Jews, his co-religionists, crucified.

Sentenced to death, Jesus was denied and abandoned by his disciples, particularly by the apostles who had shared his life for three years. Terrorized by the prospect of suffering the same fate as their Lord, they were discouraged because of the evident failure of his promise of a kingdom, which they had believed so firmly, however, that they had left everything to follow him. Only his mother, Mary, two of his aunts, Mary of Cleophas and Mary Salome, Mary Magdalene, and the one whom the Gospel according to Saint John calls "the disciple whom Jesus loved" accompanied him to the place of execution, a hill called Golgotha ("place of the skull," or "Calvary"), located within plain view of the entrance to Jerusalem. There, at around noon, on the eve of the feast of Passover in the year 33,[5] Jesus was nailed naked to the wood of the cross. At three o'clock, sated with sufferings and humiliations, he gave up his spirit.

That same evening, his mortal remains were placed in a tomb, after being embalmed and covered with a shroud according to the Jewish custom observed at that time. Having managed in time to escape lynching, the disciples of Jesus now had only one thought in mind: to be forgotten while waiting for the affair to settle down. Many had already left to return to Galilee. The only ones still hiding in Jerusalem were the appointed deputies of the Crucified, who were liable to be pursued as his notorious accomplices.

According to the Gospel accounts, at dawn on the Sunday following the feast of Passover,[6] the tomb of Jesus was found open and empty by three of the women who had accompanied him to his death. "Passover" means "passage": very quickly the death of Jesus was understood by his disciples as a passage. The tomb was found empty: wasn't this emptiness a space opening onto a new life, beyond death?

The disciple whom Jesus loved, who had remained faithful to the end, was confronted with the empty tomb, where there was nothing to see: *He saw and he believed,* the Gospel according to Saint John states paradoxically **(Jn 20:8)**. Standing by the tomb also was Mary Magdalene. She thought she saw a gardener, but when he spoke, she recognized the voice of Jesus calling her by her first name: "Mary." She threw herself down at his feet and tried to embrace him: *Noli me tangere,* "Do not touch me," Jesus says in response to her lunge toward him: the absence of his cadaver opens onto infinity and expresses his very real bodily presence, but under another form, with another untouchable, ungraspable, inconceivable nature; and yet still his own body, which the heart of Mary Magdalene recognized as the real, personal presence of her beloved Master.

DEATH IS ONLY A PASSAGE

On that same evening and over the course of the following days, other disciples too said that Jesus, "alive again," had appeared to them, spoken to them, and even eaten with them. But they also testified that upon meeting him, no one had recognized him at first.

And behold, fifty days after the death of Jesus, on the day of the feast of Pentecost, his apostles, having regained their assurance, dared to go out in broad daylight to address the crowd, proclaiming: *"You Israelites, listen: You had this Jesus killed by nailing him to a cross, but God raised him up, and we are his witnesses"* **(Acts 2:22, 32)**. They were soon arrested and hauled before the same Jewish authorities who had

5 A probable date. Historians situate the death of Jesus between 26 and 36.

6 Passover is the Jewish feast commemorating the divine establishment of the people of the Covenant at the time of their liberation from slavery in Egypt and their passage through the Red Sea toward the Promised Land. For Christians, Passover prefigures the feast of Easter, in which the risen Jesus passed from death to life, opening for all humanity the way to eternal life.

condemned Jesus to death. But now they feared nothing. When they were released, they would never cease proclaiming the resurrection of Jesus, despite the persecutions against them. Between five and thirty years after that, they would all be tortured and die, without ever having wavered in their testimony.

Thus the truth—"to be believed"—about the Resurrection of Jesus appears to be settled from the very origin of Christian preaching. Twenty years later (around 55), the apostle Paul—a leading Pharisee who had converted—wrote to the Christians in Corinth, who were already very numerous: *"For I delivered to you what I myself received, that Christ died and that he was raised on the third day"* **(cf. 1 Cor 15:3-4)**. And he added: *"If Christ has not been raised, our faith is in vain"* **(1 Cor 15:14)**.

Fundamentally, the teaching of Jesus about the meaning of human life is intelligible only from the perspective of death which is merely a passage to life regained, *welling up abundantly* in an infinite space. According to Jesus, every human being, together with his body and everything that constitutes the proper identity of his person, is destined, after death, to infinitely augmented conditions of life and existence, under new forms that are inconceivable to us because they are divine. For Jesus, death is the supreme baptism, the passage toward a rebirth.

The earthly existence, teaching, and passion of Jesus are facts that the historian can claim to manage to reconstitute to a great extent, with more or less accuracy, of course. The Resurrection is a historical event that belongs to the truth of the faith, which is a subjective act of adherence. "And the faith would not be faith if someone succeeded in 'proving' that it speaks accurately rather than that it 'sees' the truth. For faith has eyes before it has words, and its words emanate from its eyes."[7] The Resurrection of Jesus, and consequently the resurrection of every human being, is the inexhaustible challenge that unceasingly rings out when the question is asked: "But who was that man, then?"

THE REASON FOR BEING OF EACH ONE OF US

The Gospels are not works by historians, in the modern sense of the term. However, in many respects, they can be likened to the classical *vitae*, "biographies" according to the current idea that people had of them in Antiquity. There is an essential difference, however: in taking up a pen to write, the authors of the final versions of the Gospels intended to make of them much more than "biographies." The first intention of the evangelists was to reveal to human beings in all times and in all places the ideal objective of life to which everyone unceasingly aspires, often without knowing it and sometimes without willing it. An objective whose name is "beatitude," in other words, "a life of happiness for eternity." For this purpose, their authors structured the Gospels, not primarily to relate the life of a famous man, but to deliver a dramatic instruction about the reason for being of the human race. It was a matter of creating in each reader an intimate dialogue between "existence," on the one hand, which is subject to all its vicissitudes and which will end in death, and, on the other hand, the "Life" revealed by Jesus Christ and in Jesus Christ in all the potential of its eternal prospects. Thus the Gospels claim to offer to every human being the power to open himself to the infinite dimension of his own destiny.

"Behold the man!" Pontius Pilate had shouted while showing Jesus to the crowd as a man condemned to death. "Behold the man!" the greatest artistic geniuses of humanity proclaim graphically in this book. Most of them were believers, and so they invite us not only to admire their own vision of the exceptional man that Jesus was, but also to follow after them and to enter into contemplation of the mysteries[8] of the One who is forever the Risen Lord, the firstborn to eternal life of a multitude of brothers and sisters.

7 André Paul, *Croire aujourd'hui dans la résurrection* (Paris: Salvator: 2016). The present prologue also owes much to the book by the same author, *Jésus Christ, la rupture: Essai sur la naissance du christianisme* (Paris: Bayard, 2001).

8 This word refers not only to a reality inaccessible to human knowledge, but also to infinite realities that are the essential component of the human being, what he tends toward, what he is ordered to, his reason for being. Every human person is therefore open to the mysteries and is himself or herself a mystery.

"That which we call 'a work of art' is the result of an action whose final goal is to provoke infinite development in someone."

Paul Valéry

The Cathedral of Chartres, detail
Gaston de La Touche (1854–1913)
1899
Oil on canvas, 24 x 24 in
Beauvais, MUDO – Oise Museum (*Musée de l'Oise*)

Jesus prefigured

Where did we come from? What are we? Where are we going? This is the title of a painting by Gauguin (cf. page 284). The Bible claims to answer these three questions by articulating the whole history of the world and the destiny of humanity around a historic figure named Jesus of Nazareth. Christians believe that the authors who set the Bible down in writing, over the course of almost a millennium (from 800 B.C. to A.D. 120), were inspired by divine revelation. Most admit that this inspiration does not always pertain primarily to factual accuracy, but to the meaning to be given to human history. The Bible begins with the book of Genesis, an account of the creation of the world. J.R.R. Tolkien said that truth is expressed in mythical history and in symbolism.

The origin of the world

Ivan Konstantinovich Aivazovsky (1817–1900) was a Russian painter of Armenian origin, contemporary with Aleksandr Pushkin and Nikolai Gogol. Admired by Eugène Delacroix and William Turner, he enjoyed considerable fame during his lifetime in his homeland and throughout the world. His exhibitions in Paris and New York were a real triumph. Unlike contemporary painters of seascapes—Johan Barthold Jongkind, Gustave Courbet, or Eugène Boudin—he did not paint on site but from memory, in an essentially emotional recreation of natural reality. His romantic soul, exalted by Mount Ararat, where Noah's ark is said to have run aground after the Flood, drove him to celebrate the great myths of Armenian culture. His work can be understood as a deep contemplation of water in all its states: source of life illuminated by creative light, waves of death mingling their blades with ink-black skies. When, in 1841, Aivazovsky painted the commotion of the primordial waters at the moment of Creation, Charles Baudelaire, another Romantic contemptuous of secular rationalism, echoed it in writing:

Free man, you'll always love the sea—for this,
That it's a mirror, where you see your soul
In its eternal waves that chafe and roll;
Nor is your soul less bitter an abyss. ("Man and the Sea")

And the poet articulates what the painter presents to the viewer:

The breakers, rolling the reflected skies,
Mixed, in a solemn, enigmatic way,
The powerful symphonies they seem to play
With colours of the sunset in my eyes. ("Former Life")

THE BIBLE - GN 1:1-4

In the beginning God created the heavens and the earth. The earth was without form and void, and darkness was upon the face of the deep; and the Spirit of God was moving over the face of the waters. And God said, "Let there be light"; and there was light. And God saw that the light was good; and God separated the light from the darkness.

Chaos, or The Creation
Ivan Konstantinovich Aivazovsky (1817–1900)
1841
Oil on paper, 29 x 42.5 in
Venice, Monastery San Lazzaro of the Armenians, Armenian Museum

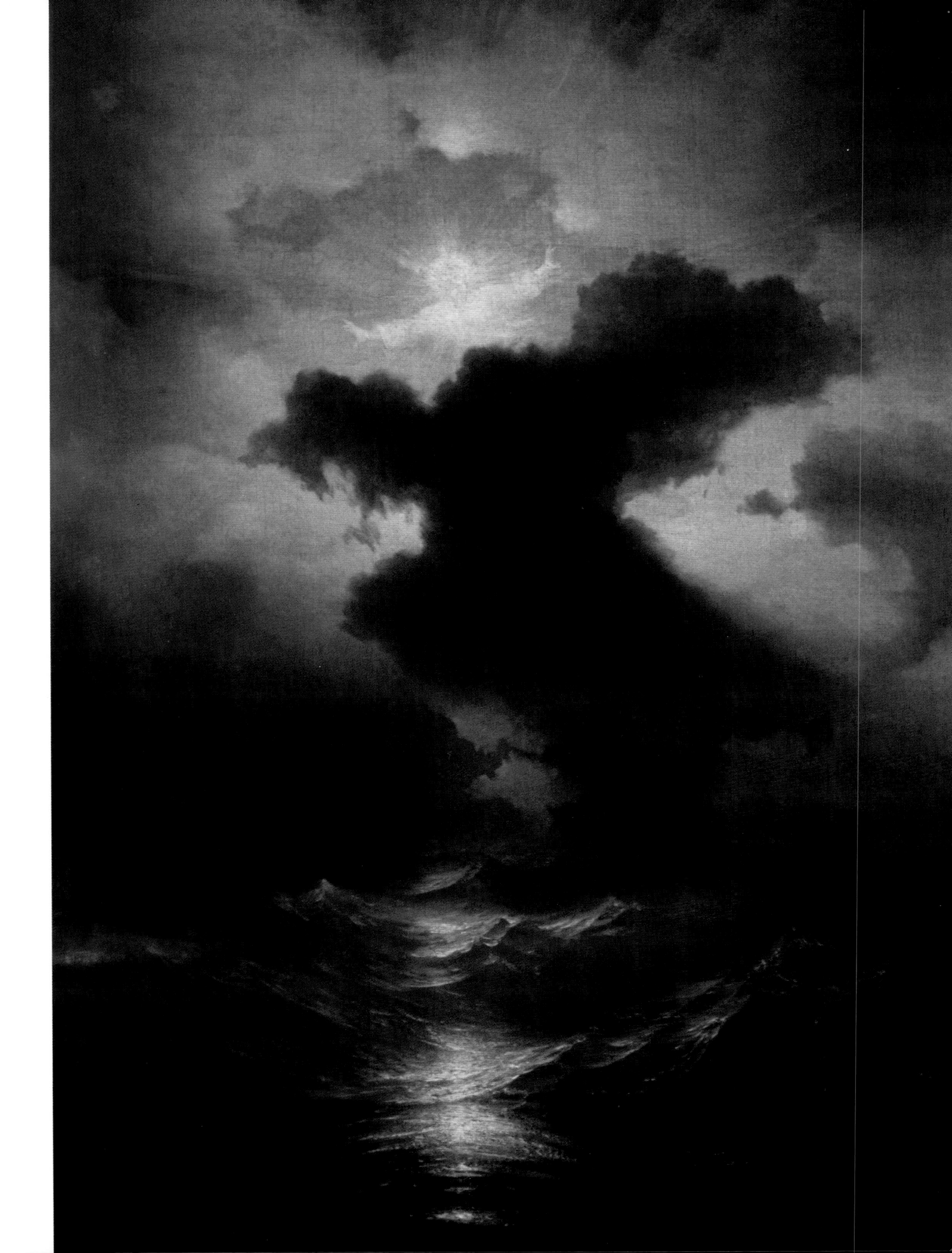

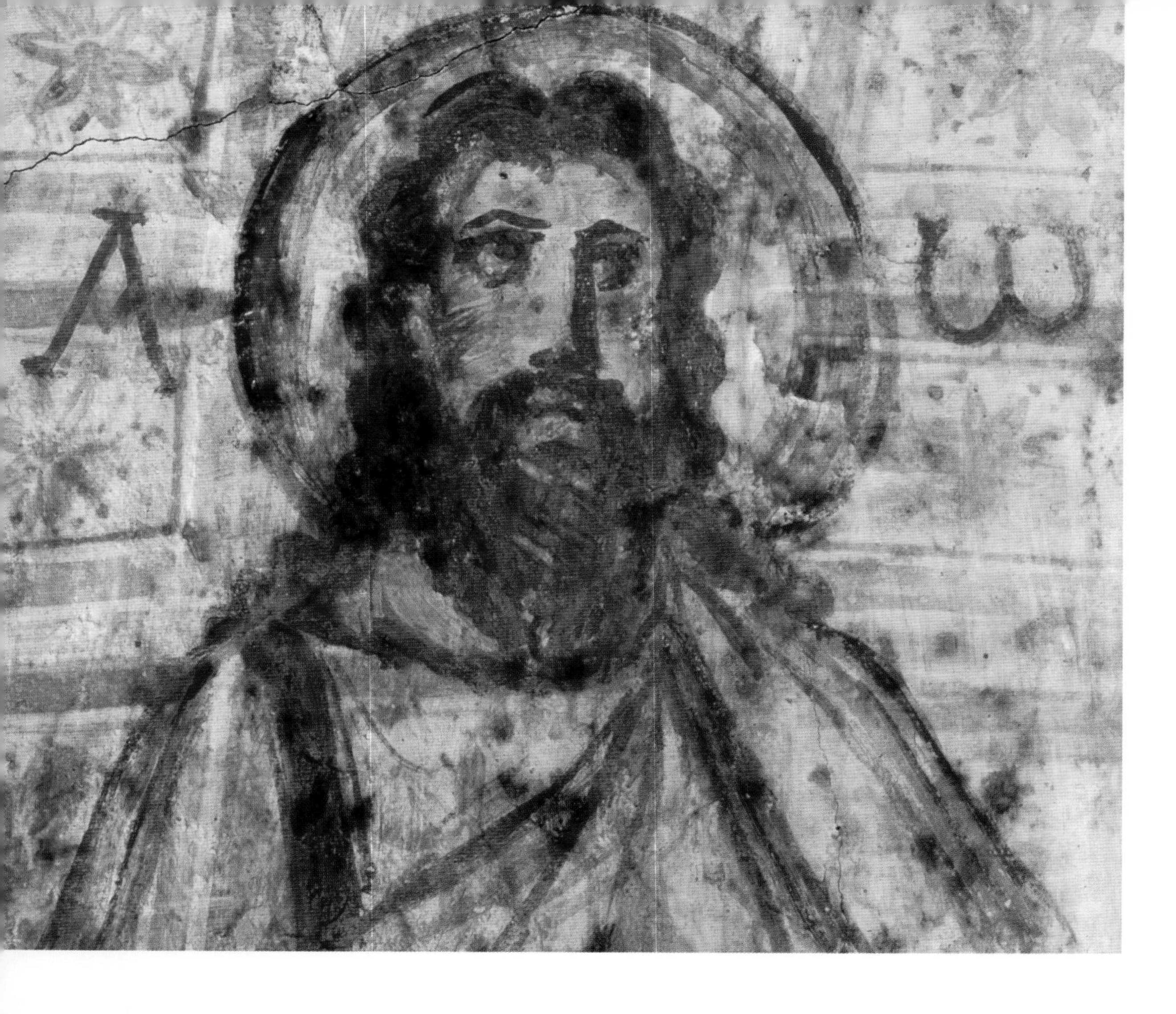

Christ, the Alpha and the Omega
ca. 350
Fresco, 24 x 28 in
Rome, Catacombs of Commodilla

This paleo-Christian fresco is one of the very earliest representations of Jesus, the first "institutional" front view, framed. The message transmitted by the first and last letters of the Greek alphabet—Alpha and Omega—announces Jesus as the beginning and the accomplishment of human history. Saint Paul evokes how Jesus is the Alpha of our history: *He is the image of the invisible God, the first-born of all creation; for in him all things were created, in heaven and on earth, visible and invisible, whether thrones or dominions or principalities or authorities—all things were created through him and for him. He is before all things, and in him all things hold together* (Col 1:15-17).

However, here, borrowing their hues from those of the parousia promised at the end of time, the colors are those of the original dawn, the first sunrise of the light on the creation of life.

This grandiose and moving work is intended to be contemplated like a divine liturgy which, according to the Orthodox soul of Aivazovsky, is a celebration of the holy mysteries. To those who take the trouble to enter into it, it comes to reveal what will be the manifesto of the symbolist movement in art and literature: the essential dimension of the visible is the invisible, is The Invisible. Artist, "you contemplate your soul," testifies Baudelaire: in these "bitter chasms," beyond the foam of the hatred with the dark clouds of evil overhanging them, you discern in yourself the image of the Creator; you reflect his light and you forever speak his benevolent design according to the expressions of the Beautiful, the Good, and the True. ■

Anthony Esolen is a professor of humanities, and writer in residence, at Magdalen College of the Liberal Arts. He has written or translated twenty-five books on language, literature, culture, and the Christian faith, including a three-volume translation and edition of Dante's *Divine Comedy* and a collection of original religious poetry, *The Hundredfold: Songs for the Lord.* The excerpt is from his recent poetic commentary on the Prologue to the Gospel according to Saint John.

The sheer comprehensive power of the Word

ANTHONY ESOLEN

How might we render John's words, then, to illuminate the sheer comprehensive power he attributes to the Word [*Logos*]? By him, all things came to pass (*egeneto*), and nothing that came to pass (*egeneto*) did so without him. All things happened through him, and no happening came to happen without him. All things were begotten through him, and without him nothing was begotten, that was begotten.... What does the evangelist mean, however, when he says that all things came to pass *through* the Word? The King James translation, almost always sensitive to figurative meanings and suggestions made present in and through the literal, here is a bit weak: "All things were made by him." John's preposition, *dia*, is the strongest possible for what he wants to express. It means *through*, suggesting motion all the way through to the end. It is not the most common word for mere instrumentality or agency. So God "spake by [*dia*] the mouth of his holy prophets, which have been since the world began," says Zacharias the father of the Baptist (Lk 1:70). The prophet is not some inanimate trumpet to be played and then set aside. He is fully himself and fully energized by the Lord; most fully himself, because most filled with God. Or, for a terrible alternative, even a sinner may be wholly taken up in God's providential plan. "Truly the Son of man goeth," says Jesus to his apostles at the Last Supper, "but woe unto that man by [*dia*] whom he is betrayed!" (Lk 22:22).

So Milton in *Paradise Lost* describes the Son as being in himself the fullness of the Father's creative power:

> And thou my Word, begotten Son, by thee
> This I perform, speak thou, and be it done. (7.163–64)
> So spake th'Almighty, and to what he spake
> His Word, the Filial Godhead, gave effect. (7.174–75)

... The Word of God [Milton] portrays in action here in creating world upon world is much closer to the Word as revealed to us in the words of Saint John than he is to a mere teacher, or to any man we might appreciate and patronize. Let us never reduce Christ to mere greatness.

To say that all things were made, or come to pass, or are begotten not merely by but *through* the Word, the Speaking, is to rule out any opposition between Creator and Redeemer.

Anthony Esolen, *In the Beginning was the Word: An annotated reading of the Prologue of John* (Brooklyn: Angelico Press, 2021), 24-25.

In light of the whole Bible, from Genesis to the Book of Revelation, and first and foremost from the words of Jesus reported by the Gospels, Christian tradition understands the act of the creation of the world as God's work, inasmuch as he is "Trinity," in other words, one God in three Persons (Father, Son, and Holy Spirit). The Son, who is the Second Person of the Trinity, is also called the *Logos*, that is, the "Word" of God. His intervention is primordial at the moment of Creation, since God creates by speaking: "And God said...." Christians believe that "in the fullness of time" this Son, or Word of God, became man in the person of Jesus, so that man might become God.

The hand that speaks

Master Bertram (*ca.* 1345–*ca.*1415) had the most important workshop in Hamburg (Germany). His masterpiece is the monumental altarpiece on the high altar of the Church of Saint Peter. Installed in 1383, it remains impressive in its dimensions: 23.8 feet wide and 9 feet high. Its three inner panels are decorated with seventy-nine sculpted polychrome figures, its four outer panels contain twenty-four painted scenes. One of these tableaux, *The Creation of the Stars,* is shown here.

God the Creator is represented in human form. He is clothed in a red toga, the divine color *par excellence,* symbol of the empire of his omnipotence over the visible and invisible universe, but also a proof of the divine love. The artist was inspired by the First Letter of Saint John (1 Jn 4:16-19): *God is love,* an overflowing love, and this is why God is Creator: *God...first loved us.* The Creator also wears a long blue tunic, the color of the heaven where he dwells and the color of eternity.

To express symbolically the Biblical text: *God said: "Let there be lights in the firmament of the heavens".... And God saw that it was good* (Gn 1:14,18) the artist attributes to the Creator a hand gesture. In the Old Testament, the expression "the hand of God" accounts for the sovereign will, the omnipotence, and the invincible might which are his divine attributes. The creative hand is recorded in the space-time continuum where his attributes are displayed. Ultimately, this hand that speaks signifies the Word who is act, and who produces the effect. Now the New Testament will reveal that the Word is a distinct Divine Person, the only-begotten Son of God the Father, who became man so that humanity would be not only saved from the power of evil, but also divinized. Thus the artist reveals the mystery of the Incarnation at the heart of his vision of the mystery of Creation.

Finally, the artist represents here God in action, inasmuch as he is what Christian tradition calls the "Holy Trinity," three Persons in one God. Creation was made in the name of the Father, and of the Son, and of the Holy Spirit: the bearded face evokes the "Ancient of Days," the Father; the red cloak the fire of the Holy Spirit; the creative hand the Word, the only-begotten Son. By his Word, according to the will of the Father and with the power of the Holy Spirit, God speaks and it is done.

The Creation of the Stars, detail of the altarpiece of Grabow
Master Bertram (*ca.* 1345–*ca.* 1415)
1379–1383
Tempera on wood, 105 x 286 in
Hamburg, Kunsthalle

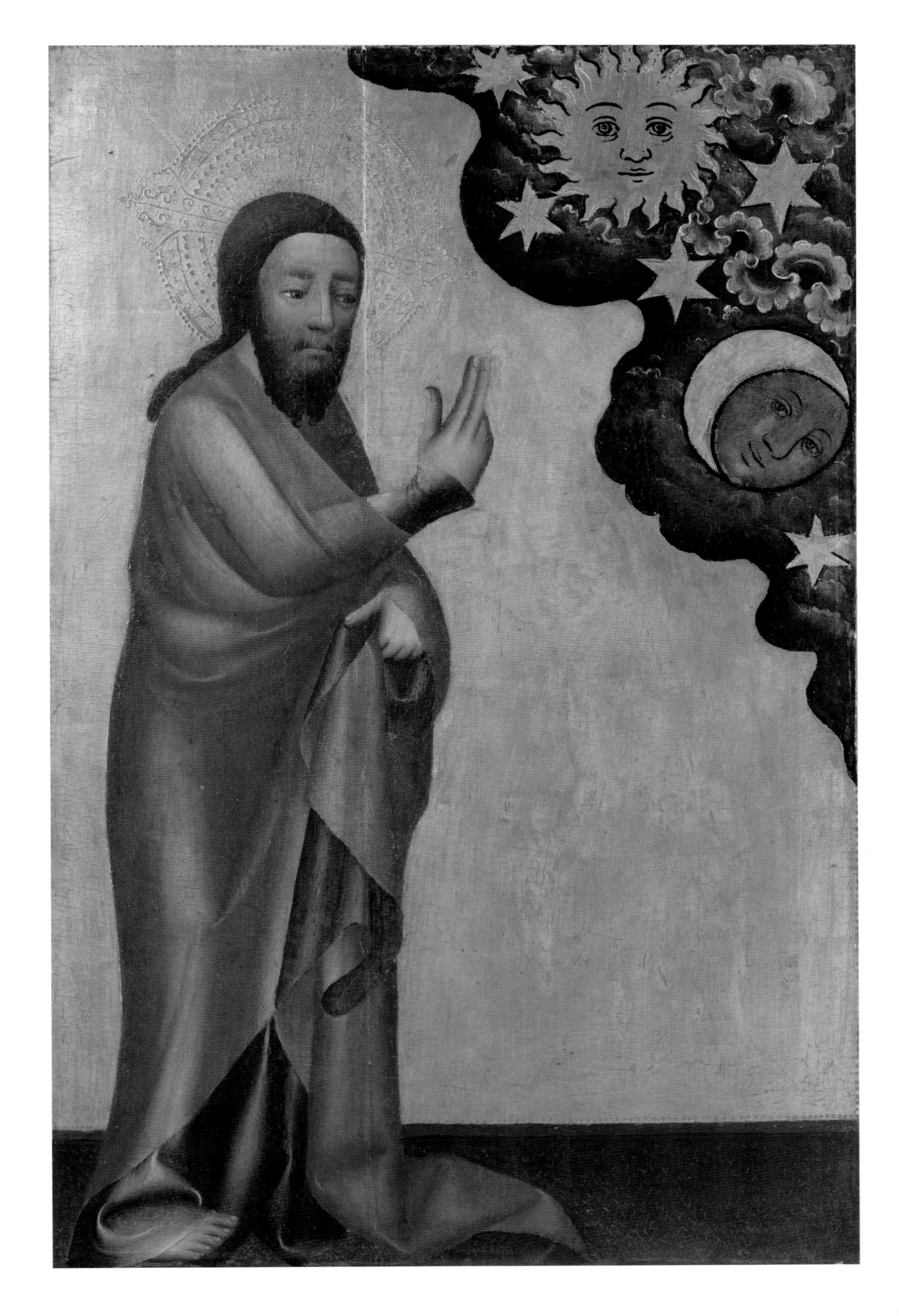

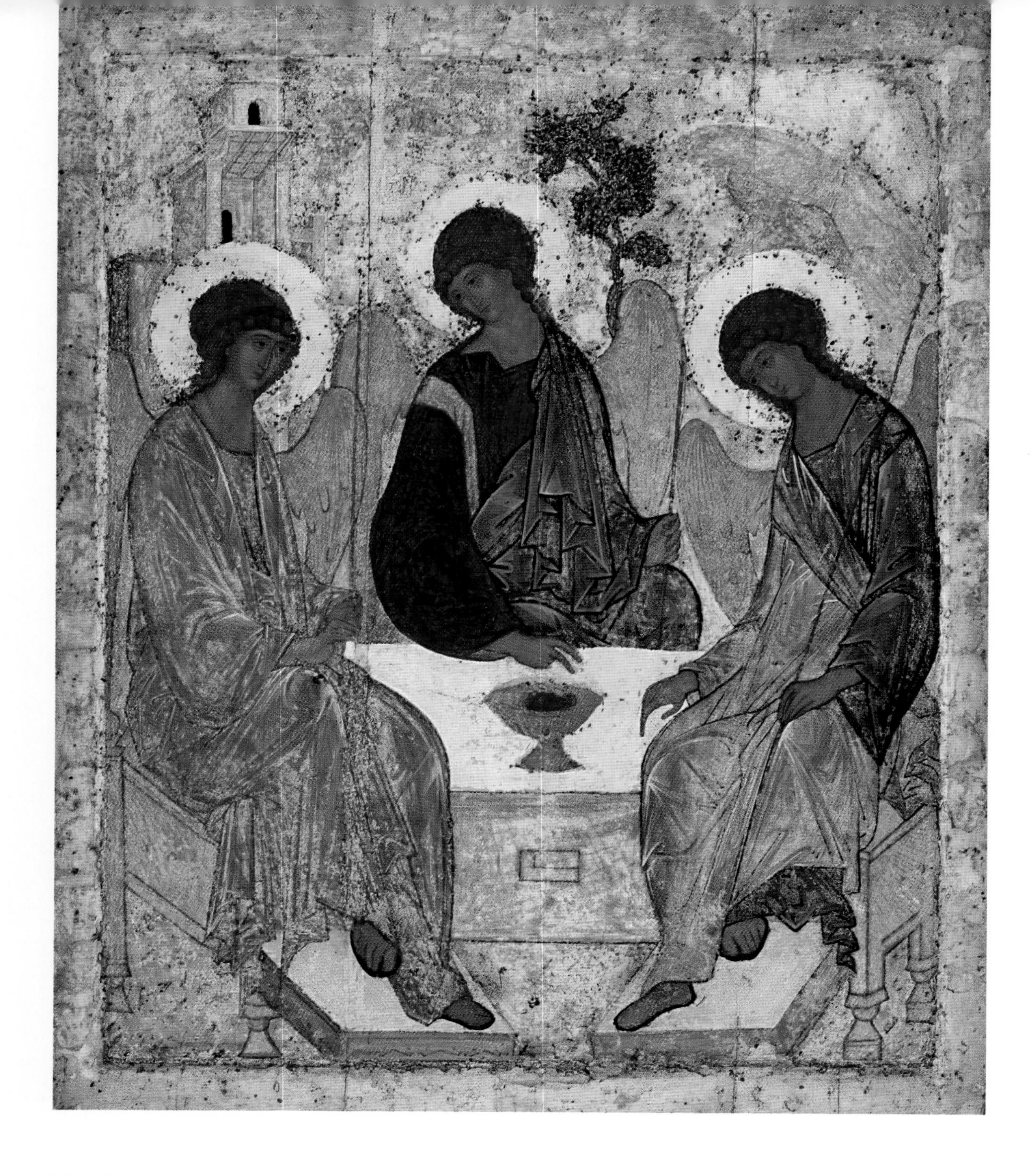

The Trinity
Andrei Rublev (*ca.* 1360–1427/1430)
Around 1410–1427
Tempera on wood, 56 x 45 in
Moscow, Tretyakov Gallery

In order to depict the Trinity, one God in three Persons, Andrei Rublev represents the three mysterious visitors welcomed by Abraham beneath the oaks of Mamre (*cf.* Gn 18:1-16).

In a way bordering on abstraction, Master Bertram depicts the sky in a corner of the invisible, gilded universe in which God stands. The stars, the moon, and the sun are depicted poetically in a way that recalls the *Canticle of Brother Sun* by Francis of Assisi:

Praised be You my Lord with all Your creatures,
especially Sir Brother Sun,
Who is the day through whom You give us light....
Praised be You, my Lord, through Sister Moon and the stars,
In the heavens you have made them bright, precious and fair. ■

The 17th-century English poet John Milton, a stern Puritan by conviction, chose *Paradise Lost* as the theme of his epic poem. The title refers to the fall of the wicked angels and also to original sin. Amid the fanciful descriptions of divine consultations and celestial battlefields, there are lyrical passages deeply informed by the Christian faith.
The passage quoted is from Book VII, in which the Archangel "Raphael at the request of Adam relates how and wherefore this world was first created."

John Milton, *Paradise Lost* (1667), Book VII, verses 163-191

"Speak thou, and be it done"

JOHN MILTON

"And thou my Word, begotten Son, by thee
This I perform, speak thou, and be it done:
My overshadowing Spirit and might with thee
I send along, ride forth, and bid the Deep
Within appointed bounds be Heav'n and Earth,
Boundless the Deep, because I am who fill
Infinitude, nor vacuous the space.
Though I uncircumscrib'd myself retire,
And put not forth my goodness, which is free
To act or not, Necessity and Chance
Approach not mee, and what I will is Fate."

So spake th'Almighty, and to what he spake
His Word, the Filial Godhead, gave effect.
Immediate are the Acts of God, more swift
Than time or motion, but to human ears
Cannot without process of speech be told,
So told as earthly notion can receive.
Great triumph and rejoicing was in Heav'n
When such was heard declar'd the Almighty's will.
Glory they sung to the most High, good will
To future men, and in their dwellings peace.
Glory to him whose just avenging ire
Had drive out th'ungodly from his sight
And th'habitations of the just; to him
Glory and praise, whose wisdom had ordain'd
Good out of evil to create, instead
Of Spirits malign a better Race to bring
Into their vacant room, and thence diffuse
His good to Worlds and Ages infinite.

The allegory of an artist God who, with clay, models the human being as a couple—Adam and Eve—does not stop at matter. The Bible narrative insists on the sense of the otherness of man and woman, emphasizing their vocation to unity in love. Love presupposes an *other* who loves and is loved. In this respect, the Bible reveals, the human being was created in the image of God: *for God is love* (1 Jn 4:8). "Who are we?" In mythical and mystical language, the Bible answers that humanity is not just an accidental product of random evolution.

Adam and Eve

"Art is contemplation.... It is the joy of the intellect which sees clearly in the universe and re-creates it by illuminating it with consciousness.... There is only one beauty, that of the truth which is revealed." Thus spoke Auguste Rodin (1840–1917) when he lavishly proposed, through his sublime *The Hand of God,* to give "an initiation into the infinite splendor of eternal things."

The artist shows before the foundation of the world only a huge block of marble scarcely roughed out. It is the invisible universe of the divine eternity: it is not accessible to the artist's vision. To show anything of it would be a lie, the product of imagination and not of contemplation. This eternal block generates by itself a space-time. This outgrowth of the infinite, so to speak, changes nothing of its immutability; it creates outside of eternity a matrix in which the embryo of a finite reality begins to be shaped. This "work in creation" is called to develop in passing time, until, at the end of time, it is "brought into the invisible world" and is born to eternity. Now what emerges from the invisible universe to create the visible universe is a hand and, what is more, a hand that speaks. It is the Word of God, the only-begotten Son. And what does this hand of God say? *Let us fashion the human being in our image and likeness!* (Gn 1:26)

Thus, the Word of God becomes an artist's hand to shape a man and a woman, as a sculptor models clay to make out of it a masterpiece, a true image of God, inasmuch as their vocation is to be united by love into "one being."

Have you not read that he who made them from the beginning made them male and female, and said, "For this reason a man shall leave his father and mother and be joined to his wife, and the two shall become one"? So they are no longer two but one. What therefore God has joined together, let no man put asunder.

THE BIBLE – MT 19:4-6

But the most extraordinary thing about Rodin's vision, nourished by Pauline theology, is that to create the human being man and woman, the Word of God has indeed come out of eternity and has resolutely entered time (already!) to become *the first-born of all creation* (Col 1:15). Not that he himself was a creature (we see clearly that the divine hand remains part of the eternal marble block), but because all things were created in him and for him (cf. Col 1:16-17), so that through him, at the end of humanity's temporal gestation, *God may be everything to everyone* (1 Cor 15:28).

According to this vision of Rodin, humanity is said to have been created, certainly, but from the beginning it communed in the Word—God the Son—and thus it bore within itself a trace of divine begetting which makes the human

The Hand of God
Auguste Rodin (1840–1917)
Ca. 1896–1902
White marble, 29 x 23 x 25.2 in
New York, The Metropolitan Museum of Art

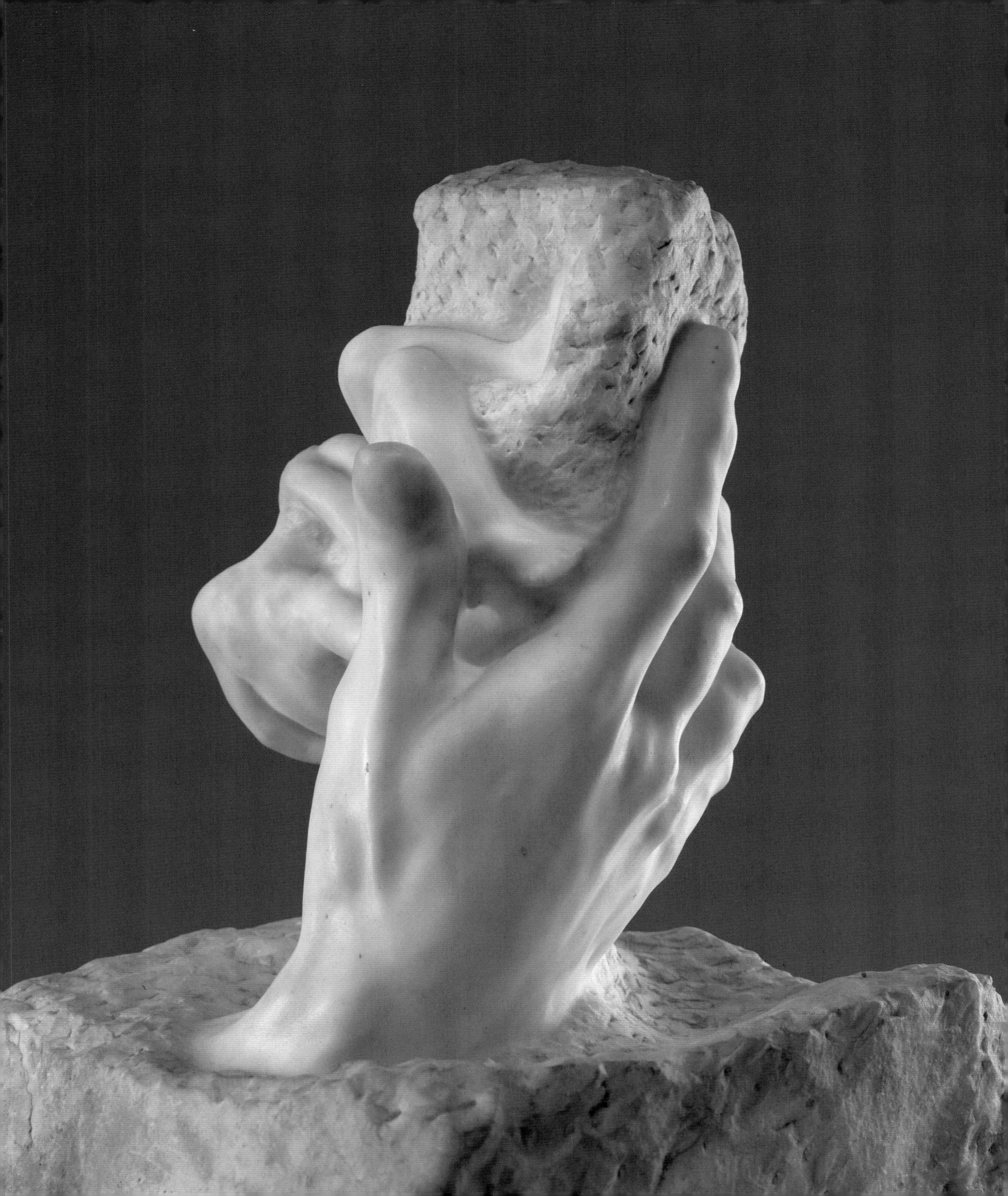

IN ART HISTORY

THE MARBLES OF RODIN: A STUDIO PRACTICE

The Hand of God, a metaphor for divine creation as well as for the act of sculpting by a creative artist, dates from the turn of the twentieth century, when Rodin was at the peak of his art and of his fame in France and abroad.

Auguste Rodin (1840–1917), famous for modeling in clay, nevertheless placed marble at the forefront of his concerns as a sculptor, with the resulting paradox that would sometimes earn him criticism: he entrusted this physical labor to specialists in the art of carving. He himself stopped carving in 1874, while orders for his marble sculptures continued to increase. His success ensured that he could support a consistent number of collaborators.

A long list of the assistants who worked for Rodin, and literally acted as his own hands, became famous sculptors themselves: Victor Peter (1840–1918), Léon Fourquet (1841–1939), Jean Escoula (1851–1911), Louis Mathet (1853–1920), François Pompon (1855–1933), Medardo Rosso (1858–1928), Antoine Bourdelle (1861–1929), Aristide Maillol (1861–1944), Lucien Schnegg (1864–1909), Camille Claudel (1864–1943), Gaston Schnegg (1866–1953), Séraphin Soudbinine (1867–1944), Charles Despiau (1874–1946)...

Rodin appreciated the freedom this way of working gave him, and as the years went by he entrusted to them not only finished plaster models but also sketches, without even worrying about the differences that would result from the marble adaptation of his small-scale models.

This production method involved some risk for Rodin but preserved a degree of creativity for the assistant. However, the confidence that the master willingly granted had limits.

Indeed, Rodin reserved for himself the right to intervene every day until the end of a project to ratify or to contradict his assistant's execution of the idea. The master then marked with black pencil on the marble the places to hollow out further, and sometimes, when dissatisfied, he used a hammer and chisel to make the chips fly. If the work did not seem finished enough, he sometimes delayed a delivery or refused a payment.

When his assistants became confused and asked older colleagues for advice, Rodin would declare that such an approach was useless, since his works, he said, could be interpreted in different ways depending on the sensibility of one collaborator or another. On the other hand, it was not uncommon for Rodin to assert that he could not authenticate a marble sculpture on which his collaborator had left a little too much of the imprint of his own genius for stone cutting.

It was therefore legitimate for Rodin, the sole designer but not the executor of his marble sculptures, to sign the finished works, since he had followed and guided the sculpting of them with the utmost care.

Many of Rodin's marble sculptures were then replicated. There were, for example, three *Kisses*, four *Sirens*, five *Fugit Amors*, six *Danaïds*, and ten *Eternal Springs*. It sometimes happened that Rodin had the first version modeled in marble and was satisfied with it, which added a new source for the later production of bronze replicas.

The esthetic of the *non finito* ["unfinished"] culminated in his later marbles executed for his museum at the Hôtel Biron in Paris. Like *The Hand of God*, the subjects scarcely detach themselves from the block, as if a work was never completed but on the contrary was marked above all by a continuous development, that of life itself.

There are four known versions of *The Hand of God* in marble, one of which was commissioned at the very end of the master's life and is now kept in the Rodin Museum. It refers back to several hand studies and anticipates *The Cathedral*, in which the sculptor evokes the whole of Gothic architecture and ribbed vaults by two hands joined together.

M. C.

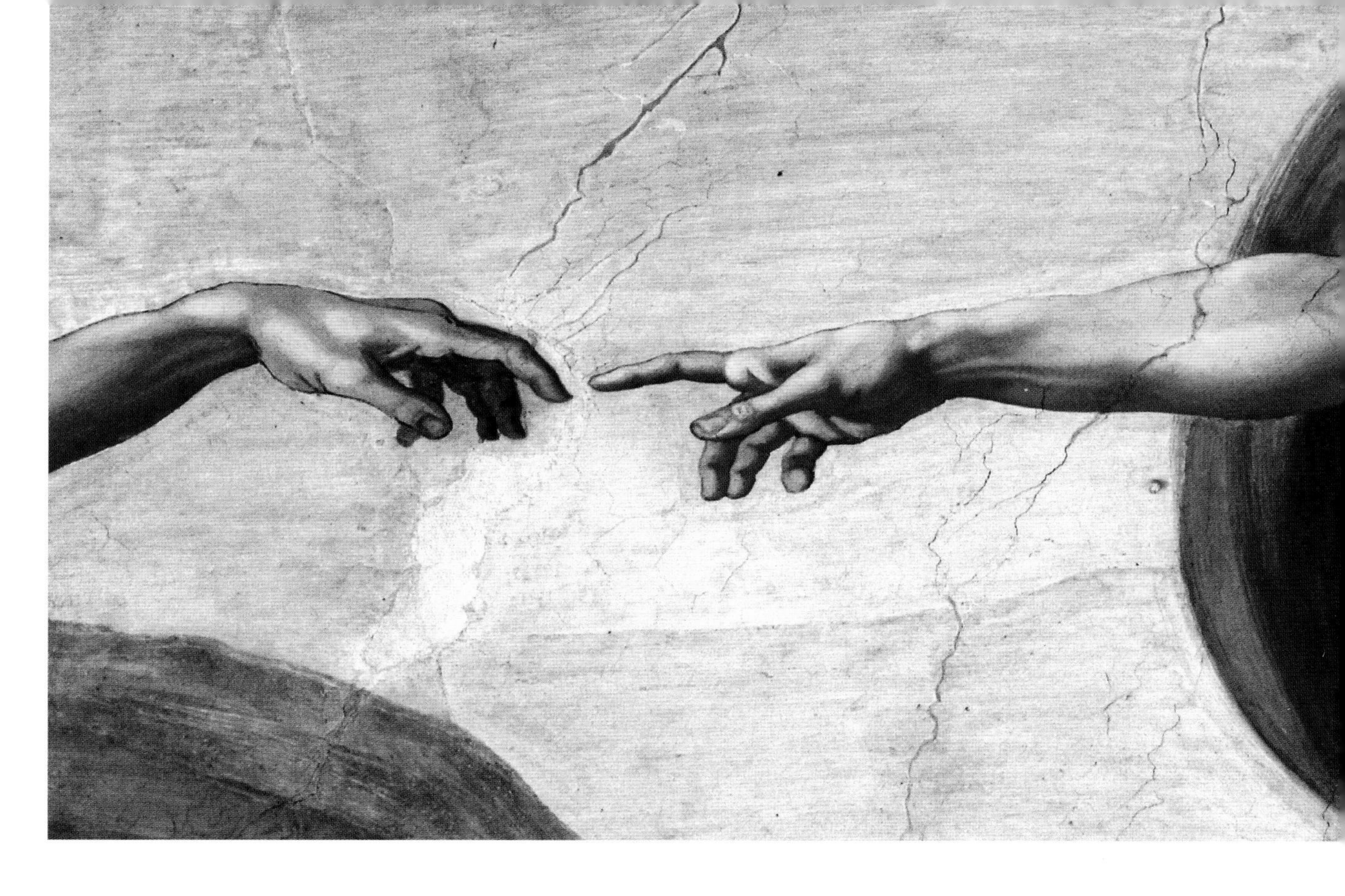

being a little less than God (cf. Ps 8). Rodin expresses this vision by giving the same polish, the same high patina to the skin of the divine hand that shapes and to the skin of man and woman that are shaped: in his sculpture, the human presence and the divine presence have the same relationship to the light that generates the form.

A psalm puts on the lips of God these words addressed to human beings: *I say, "You are gods, sons of the Most High, all of you"* (Ps 82:6). In the Gospels, Jesus himself repeated this verse from Scripture, warning that it cannot be nullified (Jn 10:34-35). Rodin's genius managed to reveal in the genesis of the human being the mysterious dimension of a divine sonship, begotten, in human nature, which is created.

The artist is not a theologian, he is a visionary. With his *Hand of God,* Rodin claims to guide our contemplation toward a mystery of which Judeo-Christian tradition claims to be the guardian. What mystery? The one which alone can account for the fact that human sin originally caused such a cosmic cataclysm; the one which alone can account for the fact that *in the fullness of time* (Gal 4:4) human nature was able to unite so perfectly with the divine nature in the womb of Mary, the Mother of Jesus; the mystery which alone can account for God's determination to save humanity, to redeem it, and—whatever it might cost him—to be united with it forever:

What is man, O Lord,
that you make so much of him,
and that you set your mind upon him? (Jb 7:17) ■

The Creation of Adam, detail
Michelangelo (1475–1564)
1508–1512
Fresco
Vatican, Sistine Chapel

In creating him, God the Father communicated to the human being his image and likeness, and made of him the true icon of his dearly beloved Son.

The story of Creation in the Bible ends with the tragic episode in which, tempted by Satan—the devil—Adam and Eve commit the "original sin." It is a matter of accounting for the incomprehensible fact that in the creation willed and made by an "almighty and all-loving" God, the life of his creatures proves to be subject to suffering, evil, and death. Worse, the creatures themselves, though created in the image of God (Gn 1:27), are inclined to do harm to each other (Cain, the elder son of Adam and Eve, kills his brother Abel). The deluge of evil having finally submerged the Creation, the meaning of history is changed: humanity will have to wait for God to save it. In this sense, in the Christian tradition, Noah is interpreted as a prefiguration of Jesus, the future Savior, and the ark as an image of the Church that will gather within it all who are saved.

The flood and Noah's ark

Here is Notre Dame de Chartres, so dear to Charles Péguy, with its "perfect spire that cannot fail" (*Presentation de la Beauce à Notre-Dame de Chartres*). Like Noah's ark surviving the flood under the rainbow's wing, it seems to emerge from "the heavy fog bank and the deep swell and the ocean of wheat."

Here the cathedral is the symbol of the Church battered by the waves of the world. She gathers within her the immense crowd of those who will forever be saved from the flood of sins and the abyss of death. In the sky, separating light from darkness, the rainbow then appears as a transfiguration in reverse: it is the divinity that makes his humanity visible as a sign of the new and eternal Covenant.

The biblical rainbow is composed of six colors: the three primary colors, red, yellow, and blue, and the three colors resulting from the association of the primary colors two by two, green, orange, purple. In biblical tradition each symbolizes a human virtue: red, Love; blue, Fortitude; yellow, Wisdom; orange, Justice; purple, consecration to one's own vocation; green, Piety. These human qualities, united in Edenic harmony, clothed Adam and Eve with their admirable resemblance to God. Six is, in fact, the number that represents the original beauty and goodness of created humanity (according to the Bible, God created man on the sixth day). Thus, when the rainbow shares the heavens, it is because the divine light, of a whiteness that is unknowable to our eyes, diffracts into six colors to show itself in the

THE BIBLE - GN 9:8-15

Then God said to Noah and to his sons with him, "Behold, I establish my covenant with you and your descendants after you, and with every living creature that is with you, the birds, the cattle, and every beast of the earth with you, as many as came out of the ark. I establish my covenant with you, that never again shall all flesh be cut off by the waters of a flood, and never again shall there be a flood to destroy the earth." And God said, "This is the sign of the covenant which I make between me and you and every living creature that is with you, for all future generations: I set my bow in the cloud, and it shall be a sign of the covenant between me and the earth. When I bring clouds over the earth and the bow is seen in the clouds, I will remember my covenant which is between me and you and every living creature of all flesh; and the waters shall never again become a flood to destroy all flesh."

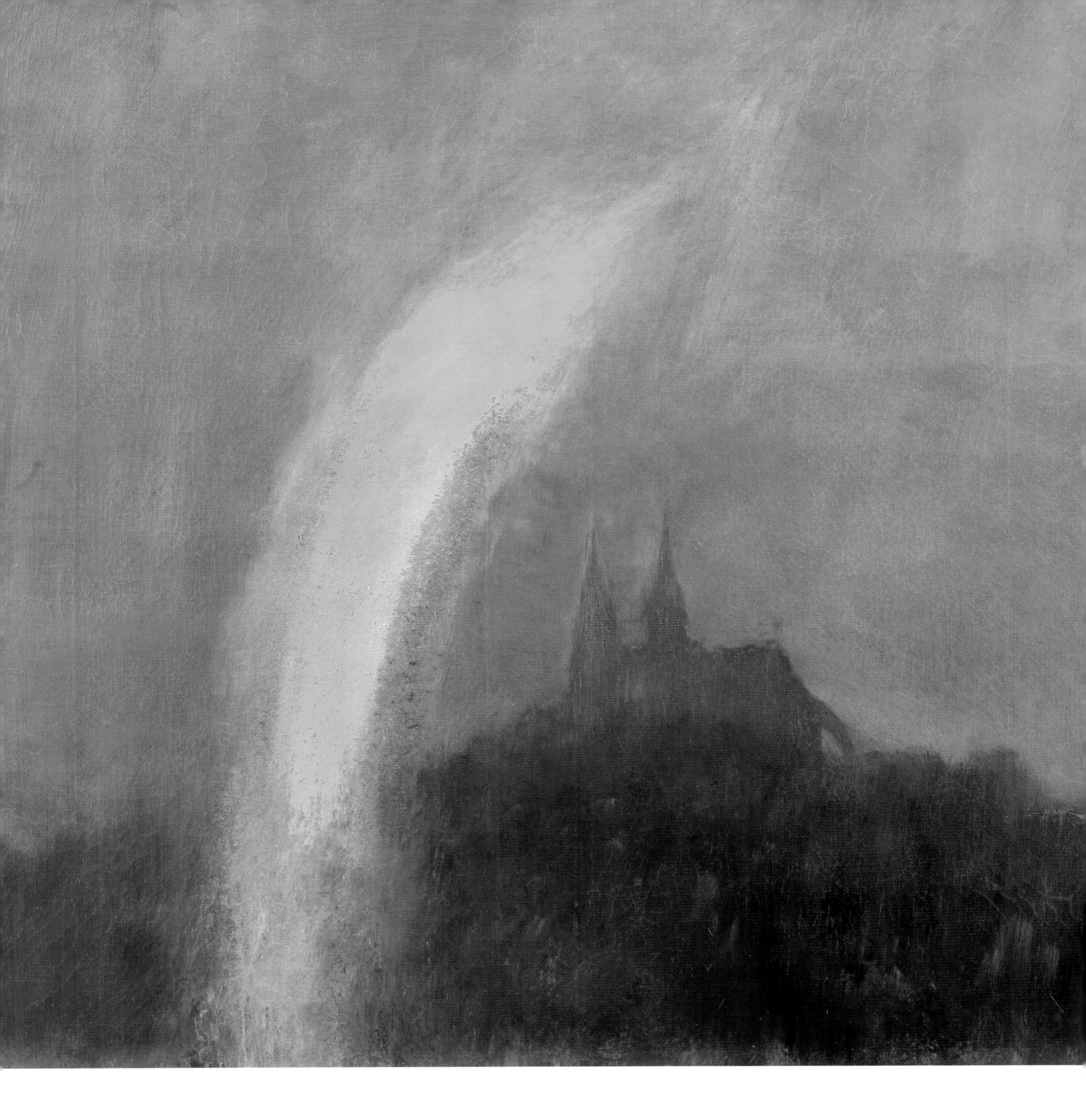

The Cathedral of Chartres
Gaston de La Touche (1854–1913)
1899
Oil on canvas, 24 x 24 in
Beauvais, MUDO – musée de l'Oise

fullness of its humanity. Six plus one (the white light) equals seven: the rainbow was placed by Gaston de la Touche (1854–1913) like a crown above the cathedral in order to show divinity assuming humanity despite original sin and actual sins, and, by this act of infinite mercy, glorifying its own perfection.

And so, as in the biblical account of the Flood, the rainbow represents here the symbolic figure of the Savior of the world, Jesus, surrounding his Church with an aura of holiness. Johann Wolfgang von Goethe dared to say: "Colors are the expressions of the suffering of light." As though echoing this thought, Gaston de La Touche seems to transcribe pictorially the warning of Blaise Pascal: "Jesus will be in agony until the end of the world; we must not sleep during this time" (*Pensées*). ■

Noah's Ark
12th century
Mosaic
Venice, Basilica San Marco, narthex

Noah releases the dove to make sure that dry land has emerged.

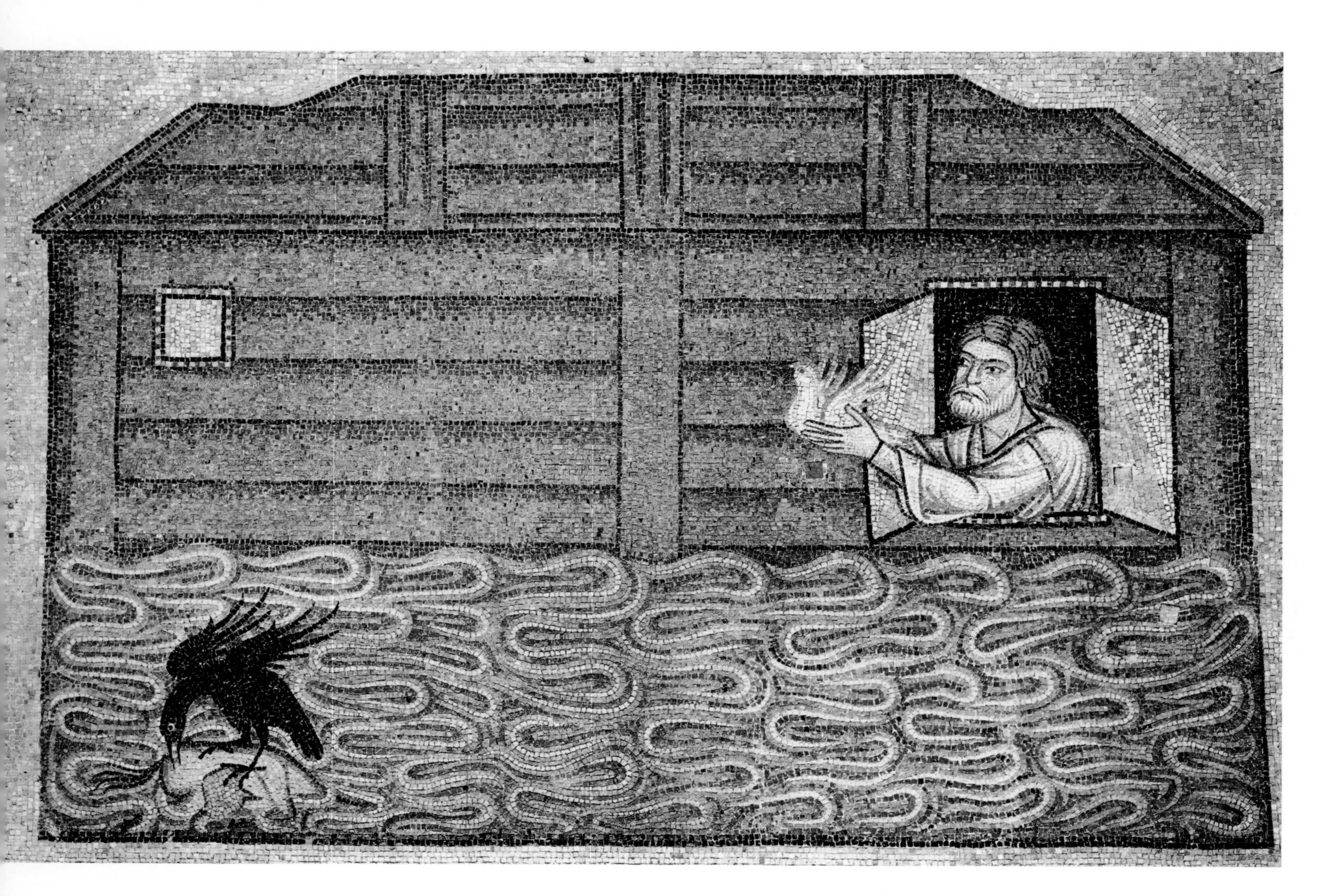

Marcel Proust (1871–1922), one of the most important writers in all of literature, is especially famous for his immense fresco of memory and society and love: *In Search of Lost Time* [originally translated into English as *Remembrance of Things Past*], in which God, though discreet, is not absent.
In this passage from Proust's first book, *Pleasures and Days* (1896), the author explores in terms of the figure of Noah something that will be a major theme of his work: the love of his mother and the anguish of separation.

Marcel Proust, "To my friend Willie Heath," dedication of *Pleasures and Days, and "Memory," Short Stories by Marcel Proust*, translated and edited by Edward Ousselin (Mineola, NY: Dover Publications, Inc., 2014).

To see the world from the Ark

MARCEL PROUST

When I was a small child, no other Biblical character's fate seemed to me as miserable as Noah's, because of the Flood that kept him cooped up in the ark for forty days. Later, I was often sick, and I, too, had to spend long days in the "ark." I then understood that Noah never could see the world as well as from the ark, even though it was enclosed and night had fallen over the earth. When my convalescence started, my mother, who had not left me, and who even stayed by my bedside at night, "opened the door of the ark" and left. However, like the dove, "she came back that evening." Then I was fully cured, and like the dove "she did not come back again." I had to start living again, to turn away from myself, to hear harsher words than those of my mother; furthermore, her words, so perpetually gentle up to that point, were no longer the same; they were marked with the severity of life and of duty, which she had to teach me. Gentle dove of the Flood, upon seeing you leave, how could one not think that the patriarch Noah felt some sadness blend with the joy of a world being reborn? Sweetness of the suspension of life, of the real "Truce of God" that interrupts work and evil desires; "Grace" of sickness that brings us closer to the realities beyond death—and its graces, too, graces of "those vain ornaments and those heavy veils," of the hair that an intrusive hand "has taken care to gather"; gentle faithfulness of a mother and a friend who so often appeared to us as the very face of our sadness, or like the protective gesture implored by our weakness, and which will end at the threshold of our convalescence, I have often suffered from feeling you to be so far away from me, all of you exiled descendants of the dove of the ark.

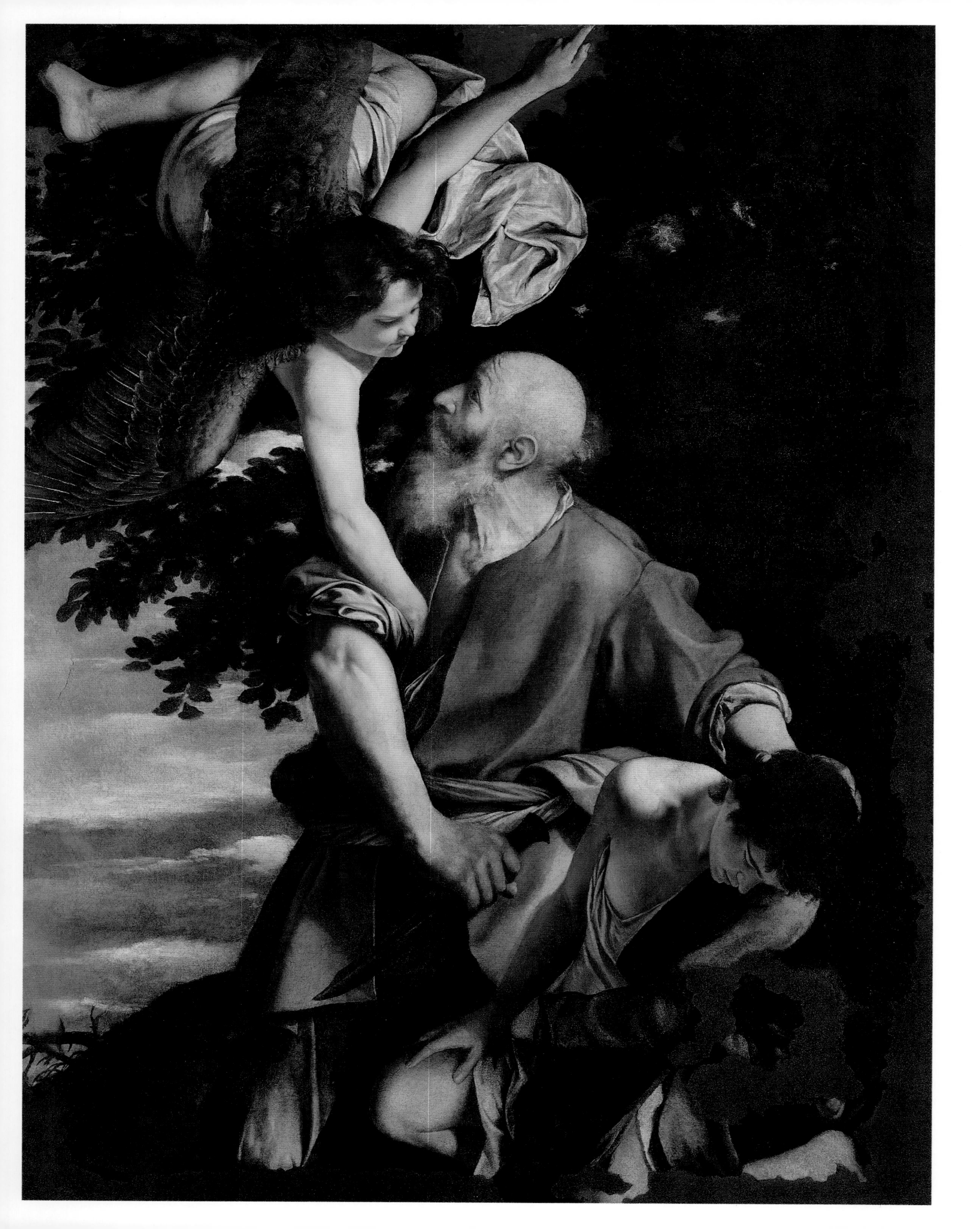

The sacrifice of Isaac

Abraham was born in Ur, in Chaldea, in present-day Iraq, about two thousand years before Jesus Christ. Responding to a call from God, he left to settle his tribe in the region of Canaan (west of Palestine) in order to found there a people who would become "the chosen people." Abraham is called the "father of believers" because he believed in God's promises, against all hope. Abraham had so much faith in his God that he was ready to sacrifice to him what he held dearest, his only son, the only one who could fulfill the divine promise. Mount Moriah, the place of sacrifice in the story, probably refers to Mount Zion (Jerusalem).

Until 1612, Orazio Gentileschi (1563–1639) worked in Rome with Caravaggio, with whom he was a close friend. From 1624 on, he could be found in France, where he socialized with Philippe de Champaigne and Laurent de La Hyre, who led him to downplay his Caravaggesque manner—naturalism, brutal realism, tenebrism—for a more classical technique in keeping with the French taste—purity of form, restraint of expression, harmony of colors. Seduced by Gentileschi's new manner, King Charles I invited him to England, where Gentileschi would work as a court painter until his death. His *Sacrifice of Isaac* was painted in Genoa between 1621 and 1623.

Many philosophers have exhausted themselves trying to get at the "true meaning" of Chapter 22 of Genesis—where God asks Abraham to sacrifice his only son, Isaac—even some modern thinkers, such as Immanuel Kant and Søren Kierkegaard, and then post-moderns, like Jacques Derrida and Jean-Luc Marion. For Gentileschi, a faithful interpreter of the Church teaching that had just been made explicit by the Council of Trent (1545–1563), divine pedagogy, through the episode of Isaac's sacrifice, began to reveal the mystery of faith in the sacred history of Israel, that mystery which Jesus, the Anointed of God, would manifest perfectly, in the fullness of revelation, in a supreme and definitive sacrifice, a sacrifice which the Church offers in an unbloody manner at every Mass for the glory of God and the salvation of mankind.

Gentileschi proposed to enter into the contemplation of this mystery of the Christian faith prefigured by the sacrifice of Isaac, by interpreting it on several levels. At the first level, that of the First Covenant, the angel abruptly stops Abraham's horrible deed of infanticide. His expression is severe and, with his left arm raised towards heaven, he points out, in a sort of anticipation of the gift of the Tables of the Law to Moses at Sinai, the law of God: *You shall not kill!* (Dt 5:17). The God of Israel,

THE BIBLE - GN 22:1-2, 9-12

After these things God tested Abraham, and said to him, "Abraham!" And he said, "Here am I." He said, "Take your son, your only-begotten son Isaac, whom you love, and go to the land of Moriah, and offer him there as a burnt offering upon one of the mountains of which I shall tell you." When they came to the place of which God had told him, Abraham built an altar there, and laid the wood in order, and bound Isaac his son, and laid him on the altar, upon the wood. Then Abraham put forth his hand, and took the knife to slay his son. But the angel of the LORD called to him from heaven, and said, "Abraham, Abraham!" And he said, "Here am I." He said, "Do not lay your hand on the lad or do anything to him; for now I know that you fear God, seeing you have not withheld your son, your only son, from me."

The Sacrifice of Isaac
Orazio Gentileschi (1563–1639)
1621–1623
Oil on canvas, 78 x 58 in
Genoa, Galleria Nazionale di Palazzo Spinola

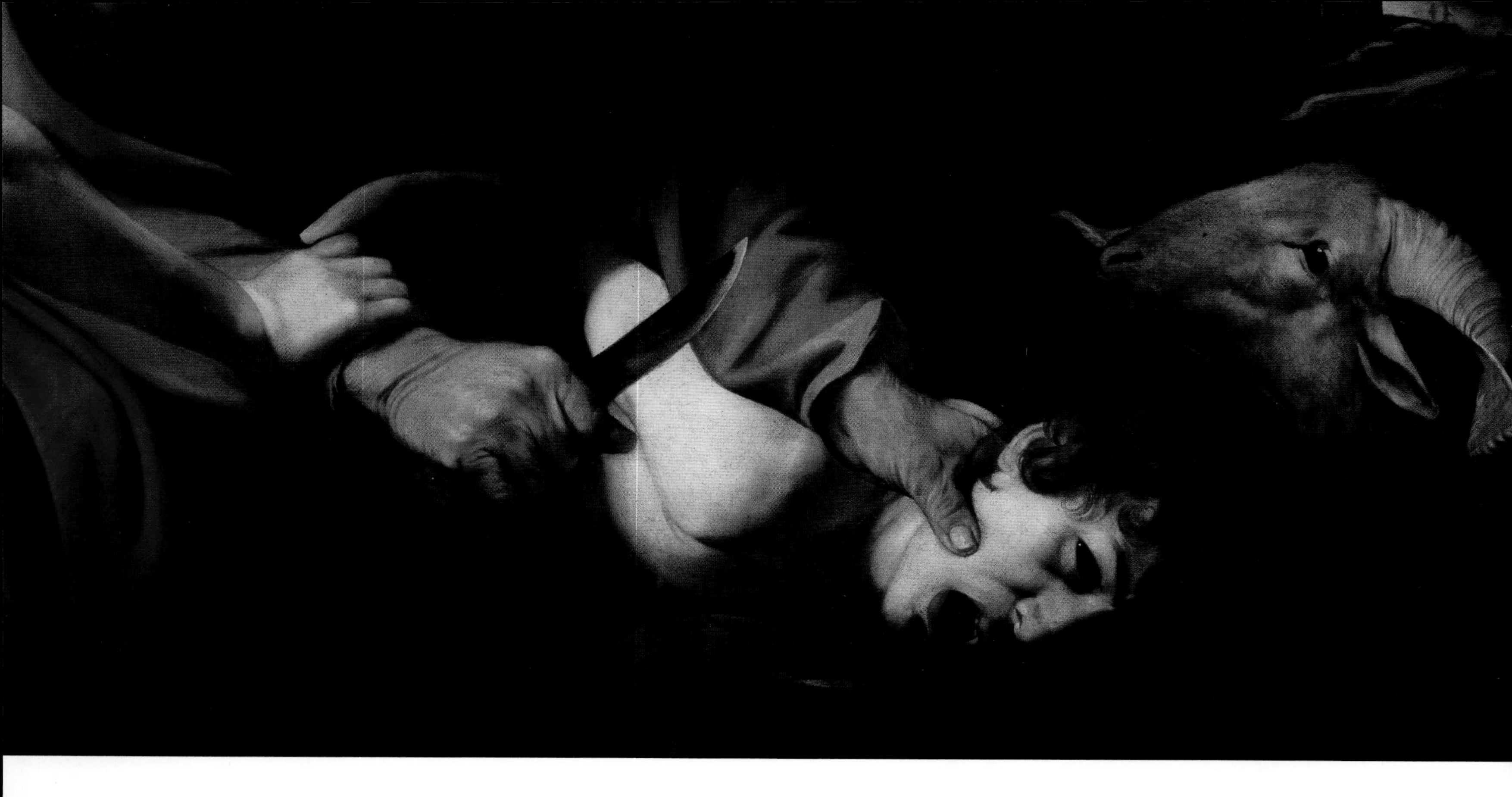

The Sacrifice of Isaac, detail
Michelangelo Merisi,
called Caravaggio (1571–1610)
Ca. 1603
Oil on canvas, 41 x 53 in
Florence, Uffizi Gallery

In Caravaggio's painting, the angel stops Abraham's infanticidal deed by firmly grasping his forearm. The raised knife reinforces the horror of the scene. And Isaac, far from being submissive and trusting as in Gentileschi's picture, cries out in anguish and must be held down forcibly by his father. The ram's head on the right reinforces the impression that the viewer is witnessing the slaughter of a sheep.

who throughout sacred history will reveal himself as *a gracious and merciful God* (Ps 145:8), abhors the monstrous custom of Abraham's time, the practice of sacrificing firstborn sons to the tutelary deity. Later, at the time of the liberation of the Hebrews from slavery in Egypt, Moses will explain that to offer firstborn sons to God means not to sacrifice them to gain the good graces of the gods, but rather to consecrate them so that they and their people may be saved by God.

On the second level, that of the new and eternal covenant inaugurated by Jesus, Gentileschi—unlike Caravaggio or Rembrandt—depicts an Isaac who seems neither constrained nor terrified. The son, who bore the wood of his sacrifice by himself, is depicted as the figure of Christ Jesus, who will bear the cross on which he will agree to be sacrificed. However, Jesus himself will testify that God, his Father, does not want to sacrifice his Son any more than he wanted Abraham to sacrifice Isaac. *No one takes my life; I give it,* he says (Jn 10:18). Why? Because, as Jesus will say again: *There is no greater proof of love than to give one's life for those whom one loves* (Jn 15:13).

The perspective opened by this last statement offers Gentileschi a third level of interpretation, in reference to the fulfillment of the Promise, in accordance with the epilogue of the biblical account. *Isaac said to his father Abraham, "My father! Here is the fire and the wood; but where is the lamb for a burnt offering?" Abraham said, "God will provide himself the lamb for a burnt offering, my son." ... Abraham looked up and saw a ram held by its horns in a bush. He took the ram and offered it as a burnt offering instead of his son* (cf. Gn 22:7-13). Isaac then is a figure of humanity bent under the weight of its disastrous fate, but he will be saved from eternal death by God who, in the person of Jesus, comes to take his place and to offer himself as a sacrifice. ■

Søren Kierkegaard (1813–1855), a great Danish philosopher, the founder of Christian existentialism, was obsessed with the ideas of despair and anxiety, and also with the vertigo of human freedom capable of choosing, acting, and leaping into the unknown. In *Fear and Trembling* (1843), from which this passage is taken, Kierkegaard considers the heroism of faith in God in terms of the figure of Abraham, "father of believers," whom he praises.

Søren Kierkegaard, *Fear and Trembling* (1843), translated from the Danish by Walter Lowrie (Princeton: Princeton University Press, 1941).

The eternal youth of faith

SØREN KIERKEGAARD

Who gave strength to Abraham's arm? Who held his right hand up so that it did not fall limp at his side? He who gazes at this becomes paralyzed. Who gave strength to Abraham's soul, so that his eyes did not grow dim, so that he saw neither Isaac nor the ram? He who gazes at this becomes blind....

Venerable Father Abraham! In marching home from Mount Moriah thou hadst no need of a panegyric which might console thee for thy loss; for thou didst gain all and didst retain Isaac. Was it not so? Never again did the Lord take him from thee, but thou didst sit at table joyfully with him in thy tent, as thou dost in the beyond to all eternity. Venerable Father Abraham! Thousands of years have run their course since those days, but thou hast need of no tardy lover to snatch the memorial of thee from the power of oblivion, for every language calls thee to remembrance—and yet thou dost reward thy lover more gloriously than does any other; hereafter thou dost make him blessed in thy bosom; here thou dost enthral his eyes and his heart by the marvel of thy deed. Venerable Father Abraham! Second Father of mankind!

Jacob was the elder son of Isaac. In his turn, he embodied the fulfillment of the divine promise, in view of the coming of a savior of the world. Joseph was one of the last sons of Jacob, his favorite. The scenario in which he was sold can be dated about seventeen centuries before the Christian era, in the land of the patriarchs Abraham, Isaac his son, and Jacob his grandson, in the land of Canaan, in present-day Israel, between Hebron—where Jacob and his family resided—and Shechem (now Nablus). This was the Promised Land. Jacob was also known in the Bible as Israel; the twelve tribes of Israel were founded by his twelve sons and bear their names.

The beloved son sold as a slave

Constantine Flavitski (1830–1866), a very promising representative of the Russian academic school in the mid-nineteenth century, died young at the age of thirty-six before being able to assert all his talent and establish a body of work. The painting *Joseph Sold by His Brothers,* which he executed in 1855 at the age of twenty-five, earned him the gold medal awarded by the Saint Petersburg Academy of Fine Arts, along with a scholarship for a study trip to Italy.

Flavitski depicts a despicable transaction. A son of Jacob and Rachel, Joseph was his father's favorite child. Jealous, his brothers planned to eliminate him by throwing him into a cistern. He was taken out of it by Midianites and sold as a slave to Ishmaelites, who would carry him off to Egypt. Finally, Joseph would be sold to Potiphar, Pharaoh's chief steward. Now the caravan of the Ishmaelites has arrived; *their camels were loaded with spices, balm, and myrrh that they were going to deliver to Egypt* (Gn 37:25). The negotiation takes place in the left part of the picture, near the cistern from which Joseph has just been drawn out. His fate is sealed: while a Midianite eagerly stretches out his hand to receive *the twenty pieces of silver*, his face marked by greed, the imposing figure of a member of the caravan—in the center—directs the placement of the young man on the camel that will carry him towards his prophetic destiny.

Since the second century, the interpretation of this scene as a prefiguration of Christ has dominated exegetical literature and homilies. Joseph is betrayed by his brothers and he is sold for money, as Jesus was by Judas. He is taken to Egypt, like the Child Jesus on the flight to Egypt. Joseph's success with Pharaoh also prefigures Christ as the Savior of the world. In keeping with these interpretations, Constantin Flavitski depicts a Joseph clutched by the merchants, like a Christ with his arms outstretched, taken down from the cross. A tragic figure in this scene with oriental accents, in which physiognomies and costumes immerse the spectator in a world a thousand leagues from his everyday life, this Joseph emerging from the cistern seems to foretell Jesus, who will emerge victorious from the tomb. ■

THE BIBLE – GN 37:26-28

Then Judah said to his brothers, "What profit is it if we slay our brother and conceal his blood? Come, let us sell him to the Ishmaelites, and let not our hand be upon him, for he is our brother, our own flesh." And his brothers heeded him. Then Midianite traders passed by; and they drew Joseph up and lifted him out of the pit, and sold him to the Ishmaelites for twenty shekels of silver; and they took Joseph to Egypt.

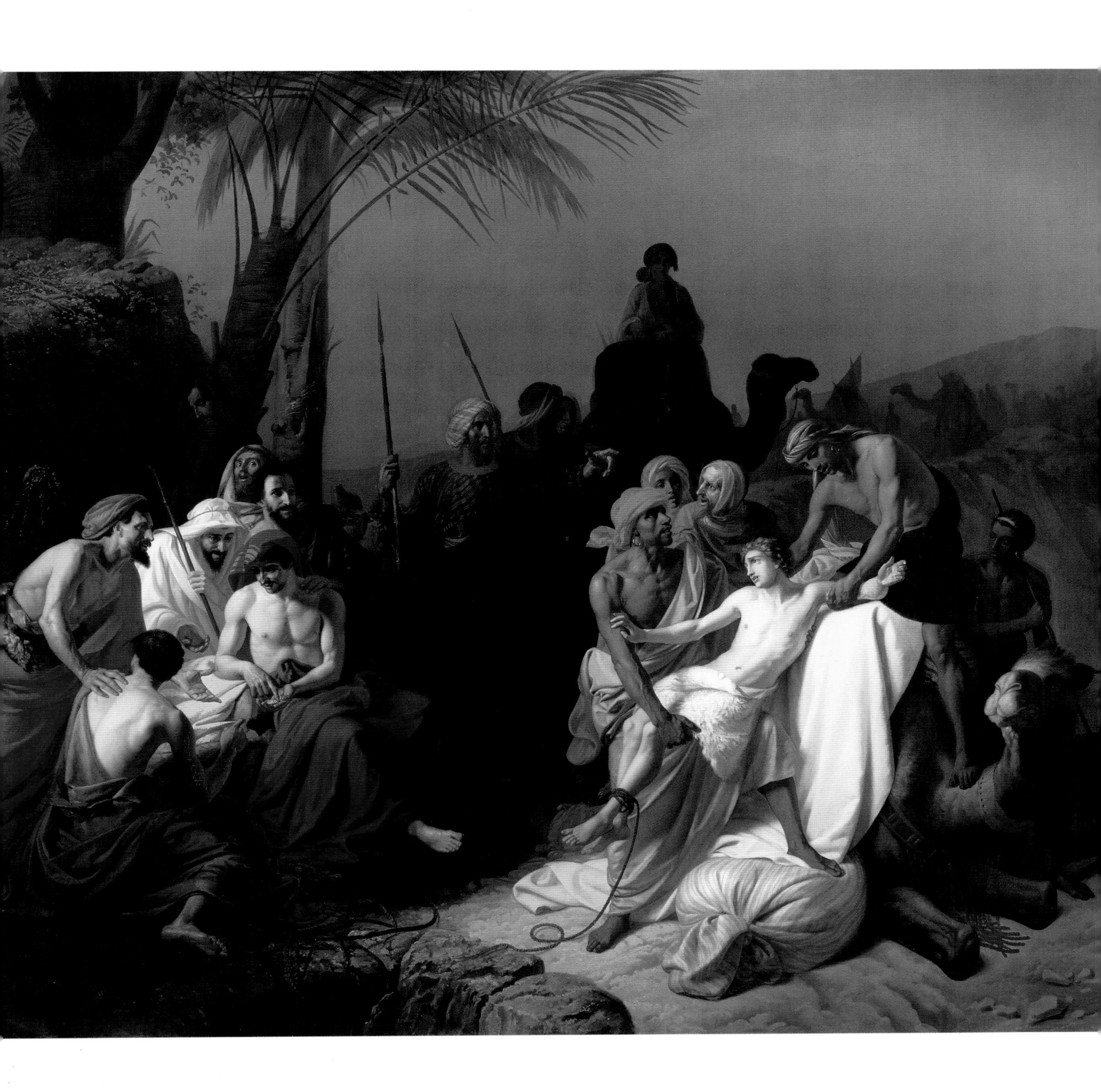

Joseph Sold by His Brothers
Constantin Flavitski (1830–1866)
1855
Oil on canvas, 23 x 30 in
Saint Petersburg, Museum of the Academy of Fine Arts

Moses was born in Egypt of Hebrew parents, but was raised in Pharaoh's court after being "saved from the waters" (the very meaning of the name Moses, according to the popular Hebrew etymology). When he became a shepherd, God manifested himself to him in the burning bush (which burns without being consumed), and entrusted to him the mission of liberating his people who were enslaved in Egypt. In the Bible, the Book of Exodus is the account of the liberation of the Hebrews and then of their crossing the desert for forty years on the way to the Promised Land (Palestine). This epic could have taken place at the time of Ramses II, in the 14th century B.C.

The crossing of the Red Sea

In the foreground, the Egyptian army, red with spilled blood, in disarray and about to be swallowed up by the waves, evokes the violent disorder of sin which brings humanity to its ruin. In the center, Pharaoh crowned, on his chariot, represents power over others, as he is by nature the sovereignty of darkness. With his arms raised, expressing his fury, he hurls insults at Moses.

In a Christian reading, Moses, the first servant of the servants of God, prefigures Jesus who, by becoming a servant of humanity, will make the spirit of service the irresistible weapon of the victory of Good over evil. He is clothed with the gold of divine light and holds up the staff that splits the sea, while the Hebrew people joyfully advance in an orderly fashion towards the other shore. Between the saved and the doomed, as a criterion of discernment, an angel shows the Law, the Ten Commandments that Moses will soon receive on Sinai. From now on, the Hebrews will be the people of God, the people who, until the end of time, will bring divine values to the world, those values of liberation from all slavery, external or internal, which are inscribed in the depths of the human conscience.

THE BIBLE – EX 14:13A, 14-16

And Moses said to the people, "Fear not, stand firm, and see the salvation of the LORD, which he will work for you today. The LORD will fight for you, and you have only to be still." The LORD said to Moses, "Why do you cry to me? Tell the people of Israel to go forward. Lift up your rod and stretch out your hand over the sea and divide it, that the sons of Israel may go on dry ground through the sea."

Marc Chagall (1887–1985) decided to depict at the head of the chosen people—but already a little on the margin—the figure of the wandering Jew, always ready to resume his exodus, bent under his bundle and leaning on his pilgrim's staff. This iconographic and literary motif became, over the years, one of the painter's identifying marks: "The man 'in the air' in my works is me.... Before, I was that way only partially. Now I am completely like that. I am not anchored anywhere. I have no place anywhere" (quoted by Ziva Amishai-Maisels). By following this "man in the air," the viewer of Chagall's works can follow the human, spiritual, and mystical journey of their author.

When he comes out of the sea, the wandering Jew—followed by all the chosen people—enters a dark zone, a fog where the events are not yet perfectly

The Crossing of the Red Sea
Marc Chagall (1887–1985)
1955
Oil on canvas, 85.2 x 57.5 in
Nice, Marc Chagall National Museum
Depository of the National Museum of Modern Art – Pompidou Center

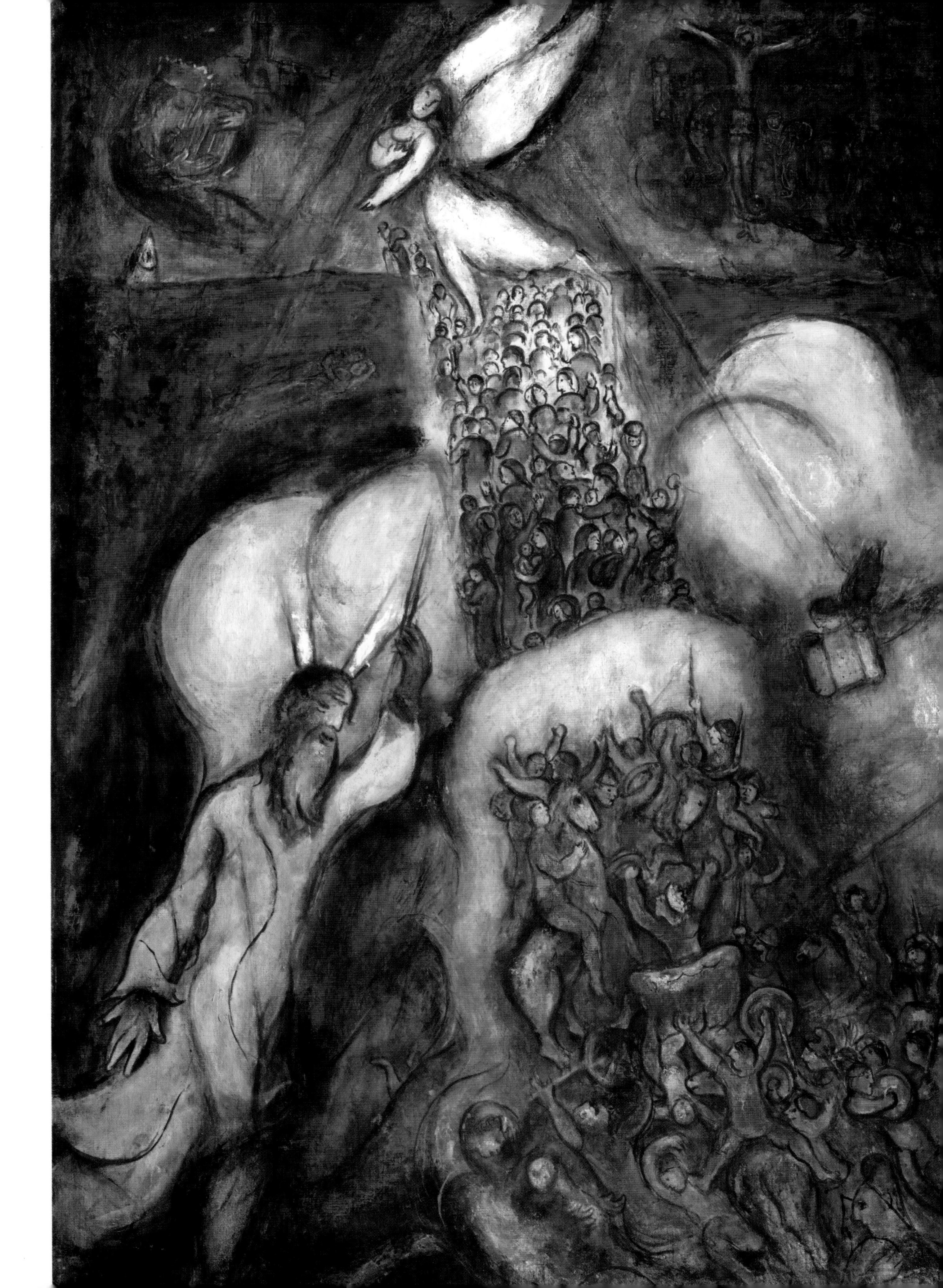

legible: this is the future, in which the fulfillment of history as sacred history will take place. This is shown by the angel on the right (from the viewer's perspective) who holds a scroll of the Torah that can hardly be distinguished.

As they journey through their future, the people of God will follow a path that passes through King David. We recognize him, on the top left, because he plays the lyre to accompany the singing of the psalms, of which he is the author. David recalls in particular the founder of the Kingdom of Israel. He will receive and sing the promise of the coming to Israel of a Messiah sent from God, who will be his descendant. Specifically, after a long pilgrimage through the dark cloud of history, we find in the upper right of the picture the Jew still wandering at the head of the Jewish people: he reaches the foot of the cross, where Jesus is lifted up over the world. For Chagall, the figure of the Crucified One was first that of the Jew, whose suffering is prophetic. This is again the case here, where, in the background of the Cross, he depicted a village in flames at the foot of a synagogue: Vitebsk, in Belarus. There, the painter had come into the world on the same day a gigantic fire destroyed part of the city. This symbolic Vitebsk is said to represent the Jewish community burned and bloodied by anti-Semitic hatred, which was taken to the abominable extremes of the "final solution."

But the more Chagall developed his work, the more central the figure of the Crucified was in it and the richer its significance became—to the point that he "gratuitously included a Christ on the cross in his gift of the Hammarskjöld Window at the United Nations headquarters at New York, despite the fact that UN Policy is to avoid the inclusion of any obvious religious symbols." Many authors have asked whether it is possible to say that Chagall somehow or other depicted "the Crucified" as the Messiah who fulfilled Scripture, or even as the Christ of Christians, in other words, the Risen One, the only mediator and Savior of the world, true God and true man. Geneviève Schmitt-Rehlinger devoted her doctoral thesis to the study of this question. To answer it she examines what she calls "the motif of the Crucified One" in Chagall's work. After thoroughly examining his paintings, she reaches a nuanced conclusion: "Chagall therefore does not explicitly acknowledge Jesus the crucified as Christ, the Messiah, and the Son of God. The Messiah is yet to come."

And yet, in this *Crossing of the Red Sea,* executed primarily for a Catholic place of worship (Calvary Chapel in Vence, France), Chagall, it seems to us, undeniably wanted to represent, at the same time as the symbol of Jewish prophecy, the crucified Jesus of the Gospel, if not the Christ of Christianity. Witness to this is the presence of Mary, the Mother of Jesus, and of John, his disciple, standing at the foot of the cross. We can also make out Mary Magdalene who, having thrown herself on the ground, encircles with her arms the feet of the tortured man and covers them with kisses.

Towards the end of his life, it does seem that Chagall's vision of Jesus took a decisive step towards that which nourishes Christian hope. However, as far as we can tell, he never explicitly professed this hope, even when his works made it clear to see. "The work is always in a prophetic situation," said Roland Barthes. Should we see proof of this maxim in the fact that Marc Chagall was buried in the Catholic cemetery of Saint-Paul-de-Vence?

Be that as it may, as he said himself, from his young years, immersed in Hasidic mysticism, to his intimate acquaintance with the Christian Bible, from the Ten Commandments given to Moses to the New Commandment of the Crucified One: the one commandment by which the Law and the Prophets attain their full significance, Chagall never stopped trying to demonstrate in his work that humanity's reason for existing is love: "Despite the difficulties of our world, I have never renounced in my heart the love in which I was raised, nor man's hope in love. As on the palette of a painter, there is only one color in our life that gives meaning to life and art: the color of love."

Four hundred years earlier, Michelangelo had put it another way: "Love is the wing that God gave to man so as to rise up to him." ■

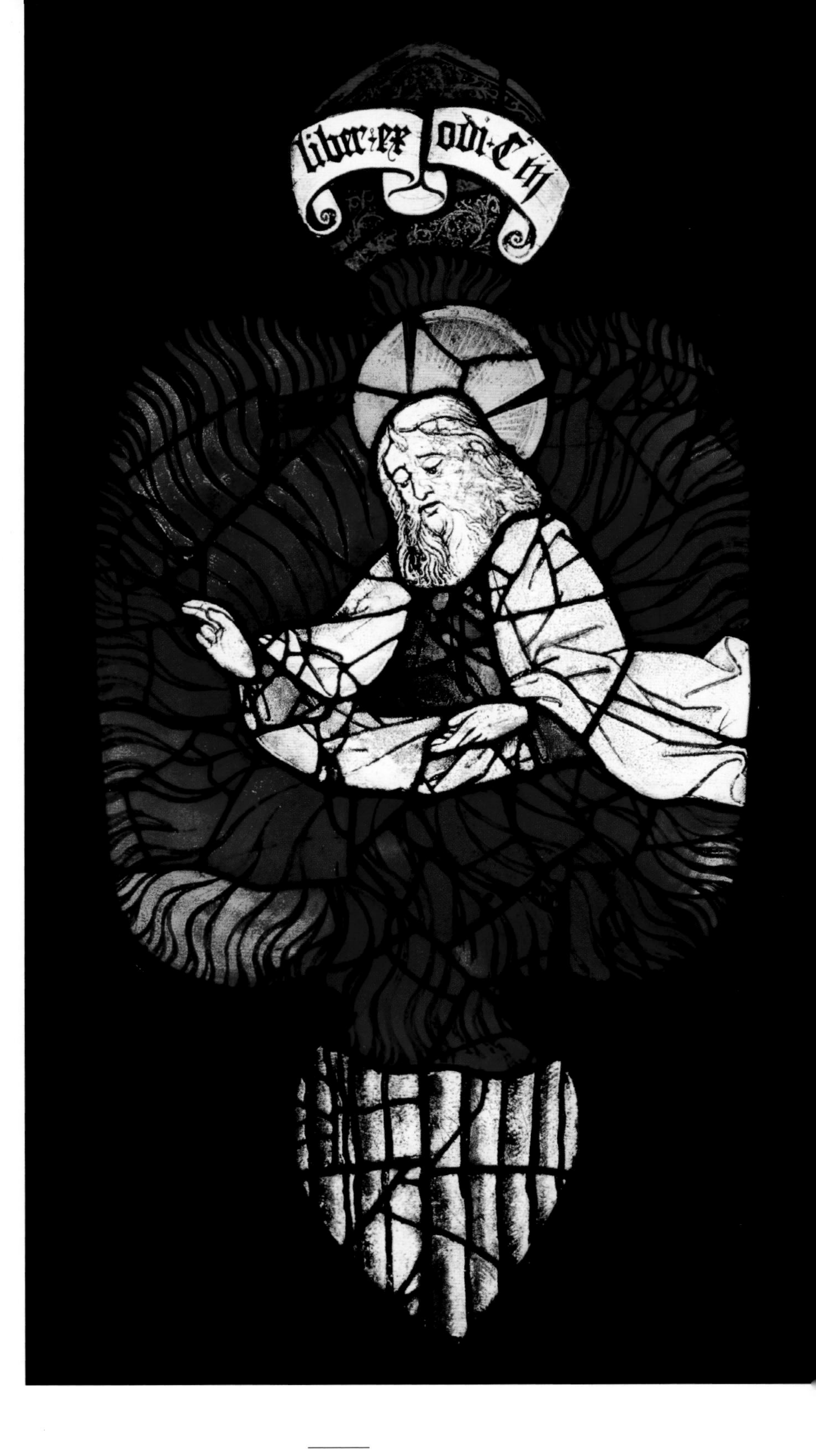

God and the Burning Bush,
1479
Stained glass,
Nuremberg, Lorentzkirche

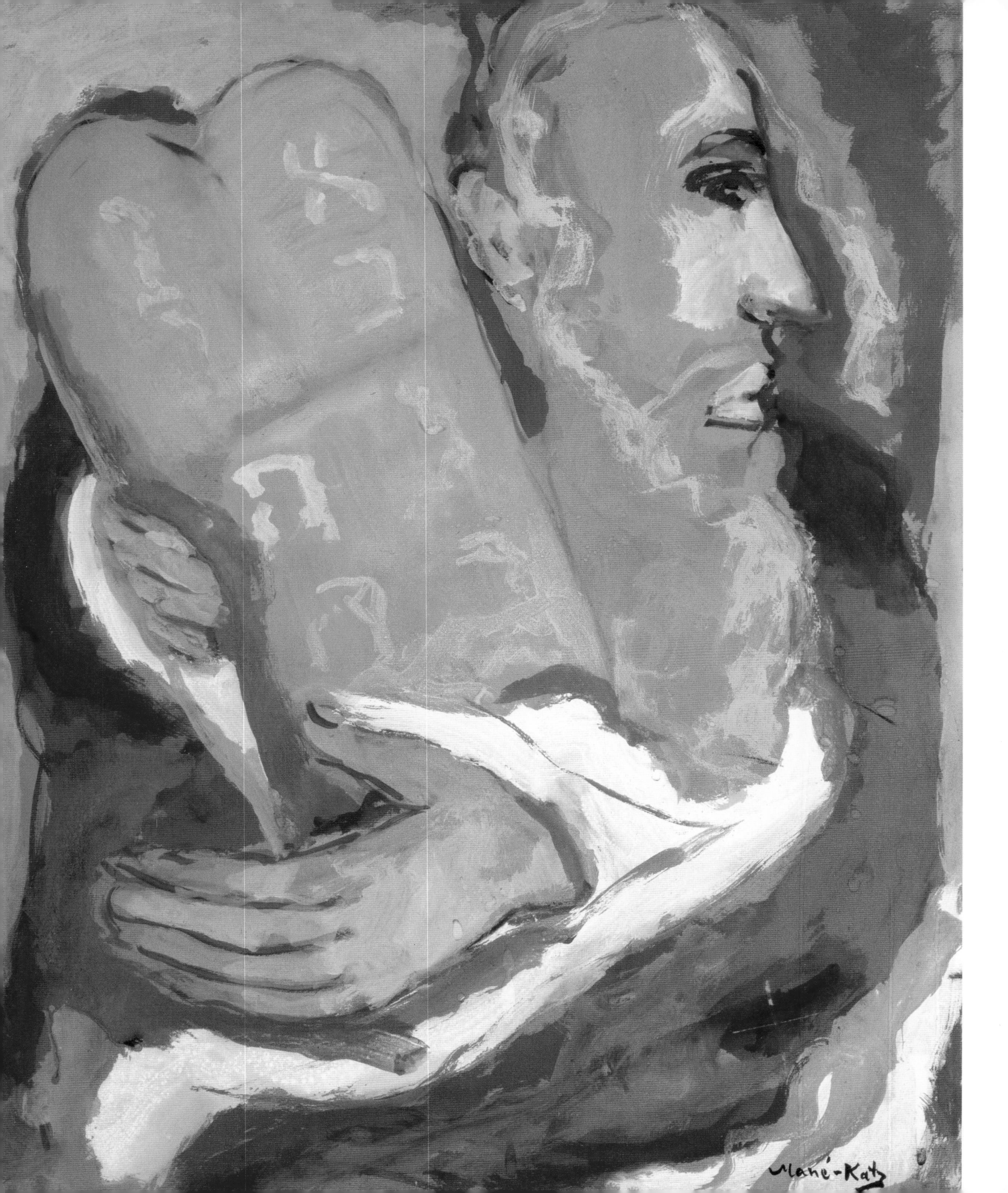
Mané-Katz

The Ten Commandments

We are around the year 1300 B.C., at Mount Sinai, not far from the Red Sea, in present-day Egypt. The Bible relates that the Ten Commandments engraved on the Tables of the Law were received by Moses in a dialogue on the summit with God. They are the backbone of the First Covenant between God and his people. This Decalogue ("Ten Words") is considered the first institutionalized reference to a moral law for humanity. Jesus' teaching will be based largely on this Law, claiming to reveal its full meaning, which is love. In this sense, Jesus will declare that he came not to abolish the Law or the Prophets, but to fulfill them (cf. Mt 5:17).

The father of Emmanuel Katz, known as Ohel Mané-Katz (1894–1962), was in charge of the synagogue of the ghetto in Kremenchuk, Ukraine. He wanted his son to become a rabbi. But from an early age, he had an irrepressible passion for drawing and painting. Transgressing the interpretation of the Mosaic Law by pious Jews, which forbids making images, *a fortiori* for an artistic purpose, the boy secretly learned to draw portraits. As a teenager, he enrolled in the School of Fine Arts in Vilnius, Lithuania, and then in Myrhorod, Ukraine. At the age of nineteen, he landed in Paris, then the world capital of the arts, and went to the school of André Derain and the Fauves. Soon, starting in 1922, he exhibited in many salons and galleries, together with two famous painters of the Jewish soul, Amadeo Modigliani and Chaïm Soutine. He became a naturalized French citizen in 1928.

In this work painted in 1960, two years before his death, Mané-Katz meditated on "the silence of God" at the time when his people were experiencing incomprehensible annihilation—and to what extent!—in his native Ukraine. As we know, between 1942 and 1944, more than one million of the two million Ukrainian Jews were exterminated by the Nazis in appalling conditions, most of them piled alive—men, women, and children—in huge mass graves that they had been forced to dig themselves, before they were executed with a bullet in the back of the head.

With a powerful hand, on the same scale as his faith in God, which in the midst of horror becomes hope against all hope, the Jewish man, draped in the river of blood that mysteriously engulfs him, clings to the luminous Tables of the Covenant. And behold, testimony springs up to the eternal love proclaimed before the world: the Torah, manifested here as a superabundance from the heart of the man of sorrow.

The evangelists, especially Matthew, endeavored to emphasize that Jesus of Nazareth is indeed the new Moses whose coming was announced in the Old Testament. Speaking to the people of Israel, had Moses himself not prophesied, *Yahweh your God will raise up a prophet like me from among you, from among your brethren, and you will listen to him.* (Dt 18:15)? The points of convergence between Moses and Jesus

THE BIBLE – EX 34:28-30

And he was there with the LORD forty days and forty nights; he neither ate bread nor drank water. And he wrote upon the tables the words of the covenant, the ten commandments. When Moses came down from Mount Sinai, with the two tables of the covenant in his hand as he came down from the mountain, Moses did not know that the skin of his face shone because he had been talking with God. And when Aaron and all the sons of Israel saw Moses, behold, the skin of his face shone, and they were afraid to come near him.

Moses and the Tables of the Law
Ohel Mané-Katz (1894–1962)
1960
Gouache on paper, 25.4 x 19.8 in
Private collection

attest, according to the Gospels, that Jesus is indeed the "prophet like me" predicted by Moses: each one is born during the reign of an iniquitous monarch; both escape an ordered slaughter of newborns; they fast forty days in the desert before undertaking their mission; Moses changes water into blood, Jesus changes water into wine, a sign of his blood soon to be shed; Moses enthrones twelve leaders of the people of Israel and seventy elders, Jesus chooses twelve apostles and seventy disciples; Moses receives the Law on a mountain, Jesus proclaims the new and eternal Law on a mountain; Moses feeds his people with manna, Jesus multiplies the loaves; Moses liberates the Hebrews from slavery, Jesus liberates humanity from sin; Moses victoriously crosses the Red Sea with all his people, Jesus victoriously crosses death with all humanity.

However, between these two immense Jewish prophets, one essential difference is revealed: during the theophany on Sinai, Moses only sees the back of God, for *his face cannot be seen* (Ex 33:23). Now although the prologue of the Gospel according to Saint John also states that no one has ever seen God, it does not stop there: *No one has ever seen God: the only-begotten Son, who is in the bosom of the Father, he has made him known* (Jn 1:18). According to the Evangelists, Moses himself attests to this good news on the day of Jesus' Transfiguration (*cf.* page 154). ■

IN ART HISTORY

THE SCHOOL OF PARIS

The name "School of Paris" was born in 1925 from the pen of art critics Roger Allard (1885-1961) and André Warnod (1885-1960) in the magazine *Comoedia*.

It became firmly established in 1931 with the opening of a room dedicated to this new school at the Museum of Foreign Schools, at the Jeu de Paume. Indeed, the Spaniard Pablo Picasso, the Dutchman Kees Van Dongen, the Italian Amedeo Modigliani, the Japanese Tsuguharu Fujita, and or the Ukrainian Mané-Katz, having been drawn by Paris, made the City of Light a veritable international republic of arts and letters. Since the last quarter of the nineteenth century, France has seen the development of the boldest new ideas in the field of the arts: impressionism, fauvism, cubism.

Mané-Katz (1894-1962) should be classified as part of this movement, especially since the so-called "school of Paris" goes far beyond cultural contingencies: the expression quite simply designates the foreign artists present in Paris, which was then the crucible of modern art. These artists gathered around studios that have remained famous, such as those of Montparnasse, the Bateau-Lavoir in Montmartre, or the Ruche studio in the southern part of the capital.

Alongside Mané-Katz, there were numerous Jewish artists from Eastern Europe, including Chaïm Soutine—who likewise arrived in Paris in 1913—and Marc Chagall and Ossip Zadkine. A revival of Yiddish culture started there, notably by means of the magazine *Machmadim*. This first newspaper devoted to Jewish art was created in Paris. The question whether there was one Jewish school of art was debated all the more since the formal paths taken were distinctive. Mané-Katz, for example, did not yield to the sirens of cubism or abstraction. Chagall rejected these debates: for him, art is universal. Mané-Katz is more circumspect.

On the other hand, the anti-Semitic and chauvinistic press denounced the presence of foreign painters as a symptom of degradation that would betray the French tradition. The powerful critic Camille Mauclair, in his book *Les Métèques contre l'art français: La Farce de l'art vivant* published in 1930, thus argues that "among the whites of the Paris school we find about 80% Semites and about as many failures."

Infinitely more refined is the critique offered by Waldemar-George, for whom, if there was indeed a Jewish school within the Paris school, it was the alliance of an anti-formalism and a spiritualism. He wrote: "The painters Chagall and Chaïm Soutine and the sculptor Jacques Lipchitz are the most authorized representatives of Jewish plastic arts of the twentieth century, the world as they evoke it is a formless chaos, a field of carnage and a valley of tears." According to him, the world is breaking down, and Jewish artists are among the most lucid illustrators of this, if not the most talented.

Nothing marks Mané-Katz's membership in the Paris school better than the portrait that Pablo Picasso made of him in 1932.

M. C.

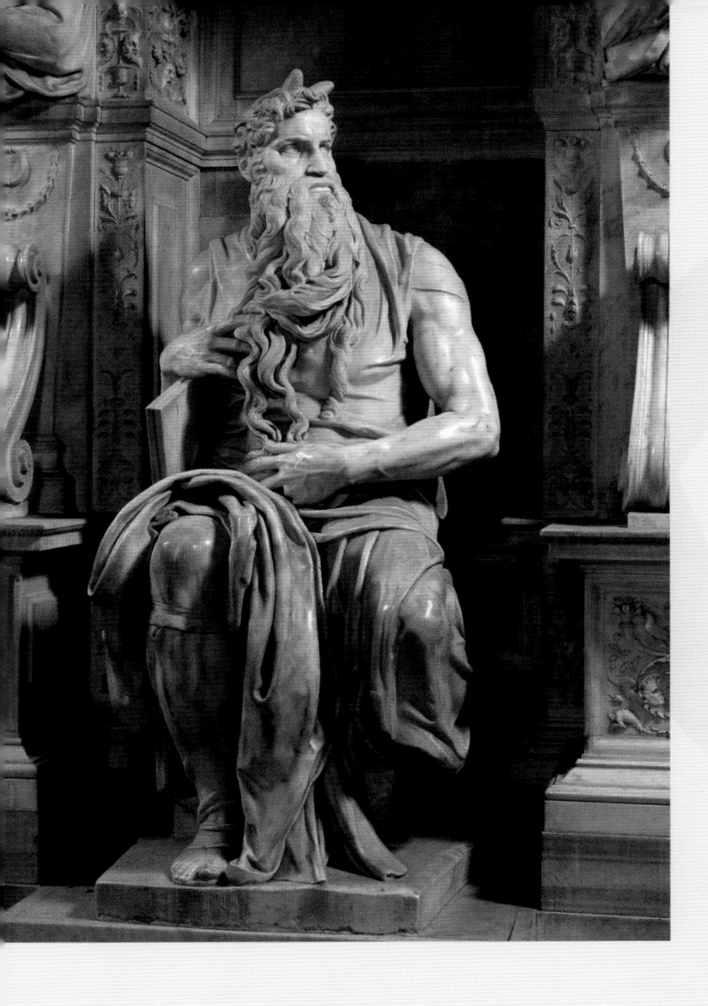

Moses
Michelangelo (1475–1564)
1513–1515
Marble, h.: 92.5 in
Rome, Basilica of Saint Peter in Chains,
Tomb of Julius II

For the Evangelist Matthew,
Jesus is the New Moses.

The eternal light of God and the face of Moses

HONORÉ DE BALZAC

Honoré de Balzac (1799–1850), the prodigiously creative author of *La Comédie humaine* and patron of the realist novel, made an important place for Christianity in his work (*The Parish Priest of Tours, The Mass of the Atheist, The Search for the Absolute*, etc.). In this passage from *Seraphita* (1835) recalling Moses' face, radiant after his encounter with God, which the author links to the Transfiguration of Jesus, Balzac shows not only his finesse in theological matters, but also his great biblical learning.

Love is the light of [the Angels'] world. The eternal rapture of Angels comes from the faculty that God communicates to them to render back to Him the joy they feel through Him. This reciprocity of infinitude forms their life. They become infinite by participating of the essence of God, who generates Himself by Himself.
The immensity of the Heavens where the Angels dwell is such that if man were endowed with sight as rapid as the darting of light from the sun to the earth, and if he gazed throughout eternity, his eyes could not reach the horizon, nor find an end. Light alone can give an idea of the joys of heaven. "It is," says Swedenborg (*Angelic Wisdom*, 7, 25, 26, 27), "a vapor of the virtue of God, a pure emanation of His splendor," beside which our greatest brilliance is obscurity. It can compass all; it can renew all and is never absorbed: it environs the Angel and unites him to God by infinite joys which multiply infinitely of themselves. This Light destroys whosoever is not prepared to receive it. No one here below, nor yet in Heaven can see God and live (Ex 19:12, 21-23). This is the meaning of the saying *Take heed to yourselves that ye go not up into the mount—lest ye break through unto the Lord to gaze, and many perish* (Ex 34:29-35). And again, *When Moses came down from Mount Sinai with the two Tables of testimony in his hand, his face shone, so that he put a veil upon it when he spake with the people, lest any of them die.* The Transfiguration of Jesus Christ likewise revealed the light surrounding the Messengers from on high and the ineffable joys of the Angels who are forever imbued with it. *His face,* says Saint Matthew (17:2-5), *did shine as the sun and his raiment was white as the light—and a bright cloud overshadowed them.*

Balzac, *Séraphita*, translated by Katharine Prescott Wormeley, EBook #1432, Project Gutenberg, 2010, 2016.

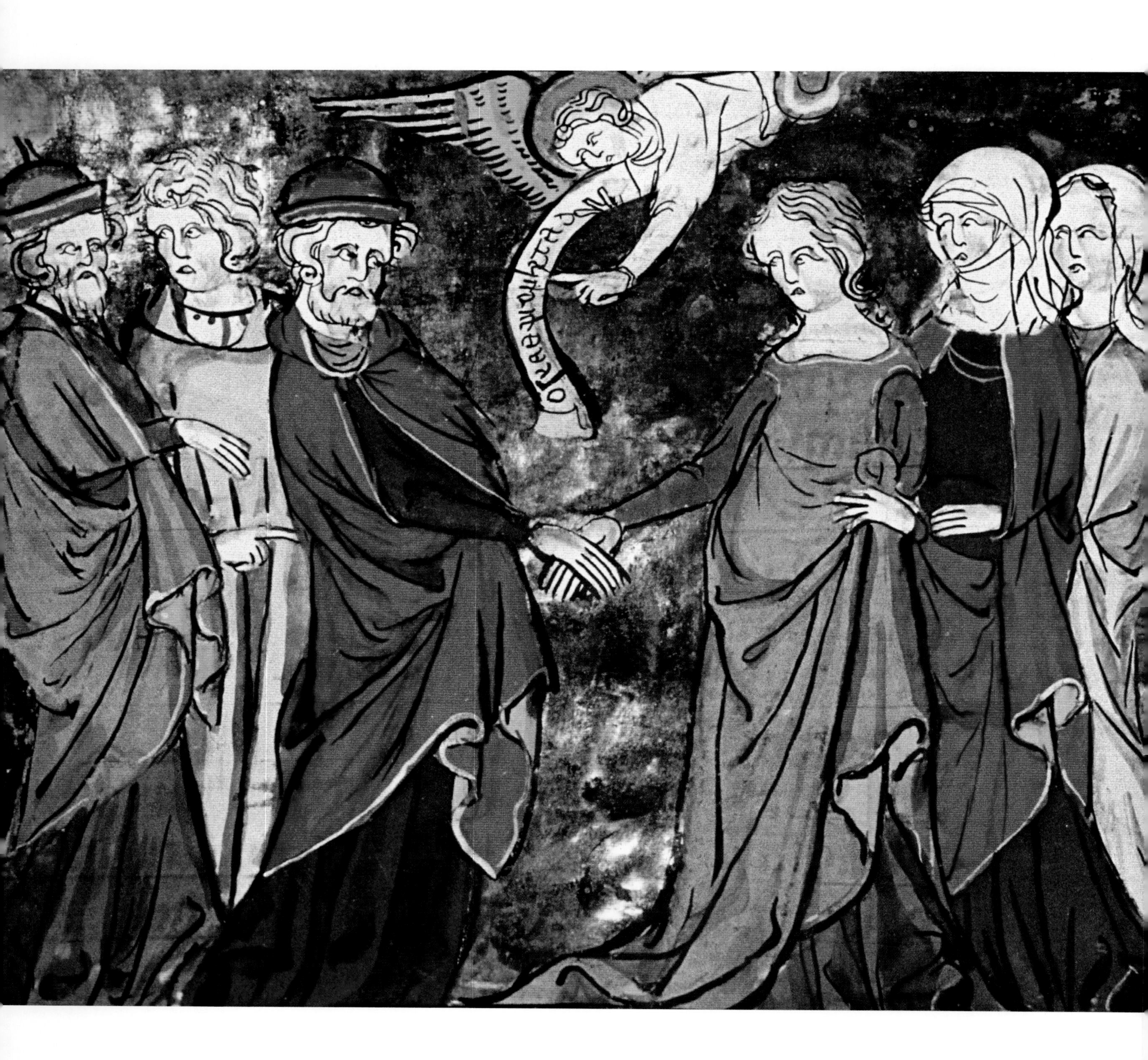

The Marriage of Hosea and Gomer
1320–1337
Illumination, 1.7 x 1.3 in
Paris, Sainte-Geneviève Library
Bible historiale, ms. 21, f° 102

The prophet and the prostitute

The book of Hosea, composed in the 8th century before Jesus Christ, tells the story of a prophet who marries and does not stop loving Gomer, a woman who not only is unfaithful to him but also prostitutes herself. Clearly, this love story is a figure of God's relationship with his chosen people, who never cease to betray their alliance. For Christians, it is a parable of the story of the Son of God and his promised bride, humanity. In the human person of Jesus, God will come to redeem her and save her from her downfall, as Hosea did for Gomer.

Marc Chagall used to include an embracing couple (*cf.* page 43) in his great biblical scenes, thus attesting that the whole of God's history with humanity can be read as the unfolding of a dramatic love story. At the beginning of Scripture, *the human being is created man and woman, in the image of God* (Gn 1:27), so that they may unite (Gn 2:24) through love. But Adam and Eve commit original sin and are expelled from the Garden of Eden. Thus, throughout its history, the people of God never cease to call for the coming of their "Beloved" so as to be lifted up from this fall and to celebrate with him the new and eternal wedding feast. Now when Jesus comes, he inaugurates his mission during a wedding feast in Cana of Galilee, where, by changing the water into wine, he produces the archetype of signs that he will then perform for the glory of God and the salvation of the world: his own sacrifice. Finally, the New Testament ends with the Book of Revelation, the final statement of which is: *The Spirit and the Bride say, "Come!" Whoever hears, may he say: "Come!"* (Rv 22:17).

The work presented here is an illumination of the 14th-century *Bible historiale*, illustrating a text drawn up in the 12th century by Petrus Comestor (Peter the Eater), so called because he had "devoured" an incalculable number of books.

This illumination depicts the episode in which the prophet Hosea marries Gomer, a prostitute (cf. Hos 1:2-3). Gomer, very soon unfaithful, decides to trade her charms again and leaves the conjugal home; her courtesan business is so brisk that she becomes richer than her husband. However, he spares no effort to bring his lost wife back to the fold. Even in the depths of the worst betrayals, he is not discouraged, always forgiving, tirelessly sharing again the fullness of his love and goods. The years pass and with them the market value of Gomer's attractions; she finally falls under the thumb of a pimp. Hosea has never stopped looking for her. He finds her, aged, disfigured by the marks of her depravity. His heart is deeply moved with compassion. He sells everything he owns and redeems his beloved wife from the one who is exploiting her in a brothel. The spouses live happily together for the rest of their days.

This human story is told in the Bible to illustrate the betrayals of the chosen people and the fundamental goodness of their God, *slow to anger and abounding in mercy* (Ps 145:8). In the Christian tradition, Hosea becomes the prophetic figure of Jesus, the Son of God, who will lay down his life for his beloved bride, humanity. ■

THE BIBLE – HOS 2:9

She shall pursue her lovers, but not overtake them; and she shall seek them, but shall not find them. Then she shall say, "I will go and return to my first husband, for it was better with me then than now."

None of the four so-called canonical Gospels, recognized by the Church as authentic, credible, and inspired, mentions the ancestry of Mary, Mother of Jesus. The gospels that are called "apocryphal"—because they are considered inauthentic, late, and often not credible—name Anne and Joachim as Mary's parents, and therefore Jesus' grandparents. Their cult spread widely in the Christian world, and artists enjoyed depicting them.

The grandparents of God

Anne and Joachim, a barren and already elderly couple, are warned separately by an angel that God has blessed their union and that their desire to bring a child into the world will be granted (their child to be born will be the mother of the Savior). Each one hurries to announce the good news to the other, and the spouses fall into each other's arms in front of the Golden Gate in Jerusalem. The story of this meeting, taken up and embellished by Fulbert (*ca.* 960–1028), Bishop of Chartres, is depicted here by Vittore Carpaccio (*ca.* 1460–1526).

Believing that what he had to transmit from his interior spiritual wealth required great delicacy in expression, Carpaccio took care here, as in most of his works, to maintain modesty in his pictorial expression. In this regard, we note the sobriety of treatment and the freshness of the colors, which give the rendering of the scene an almost enameled aspect under the effect of light, in contrast to the naturalism advocated around the same time by Michelangelo.

Anne stood at the gate of Jerusalem and saw Joachim with his flock coming. Immediately she ran to him and threw her arms around his neck saying, "Now I know that the Lord God has blessed me and that I have conceived in my womb." About six months were completed for her and in the seventh month she gave birth. Anne gave birth to her child and called her by the name of Mary.

CF. THE PROTOEVANGELIUM OF JAMES 4:4, 5:2

The Golden Gate symbolizes the Gate of Paradise, and in their embrace Anne and Joachim testify to God's perseverance in his merciful plan: the fundamental covenant of the human couple is founded by the account of Genesis in the Bible: *God created man in his image, in the image of God he created him, man and woman he created them* (Gn 1:27). *God is love,* the First Letter of John professes (1 Jn 4:8), the human being was created out of love to be love and become a "procreator." Far from being abolished through the sin committed by Adam and Eve, this original covenant remains a perpetual foundation at the heart of God's successive covenants with humanity. Thus, from covenant to covenant and from couple to couple, from Adam and Eve, Abraham and Sarah, Jacob and Rachel, Anne and Joachim, Mary and Joseph, the marriage covenant will be fulfilled definitively and perfectly in the New and Eternal Covenant, when Christ Jesus will be *everything to everyone* (1 Cor 15:28). By showing this realistic and chaste embrace of love between a man and a woman, the artist admirably sheds light on this great biblical mystery whereby, in the fulfillment of God's benevolent plan, spouses are called to form one heart, one spirit, and one soul, for the sake of the gift of a new life. ■

Meeting of Joachim and Anne, with Saints Louis and Livrade, detail
Vittore Carpaccio (*ca.* 1460–1526)
1515
Oil on wood, 73.4 x 66.7 in
Venice, Gallerie dell'Accademia

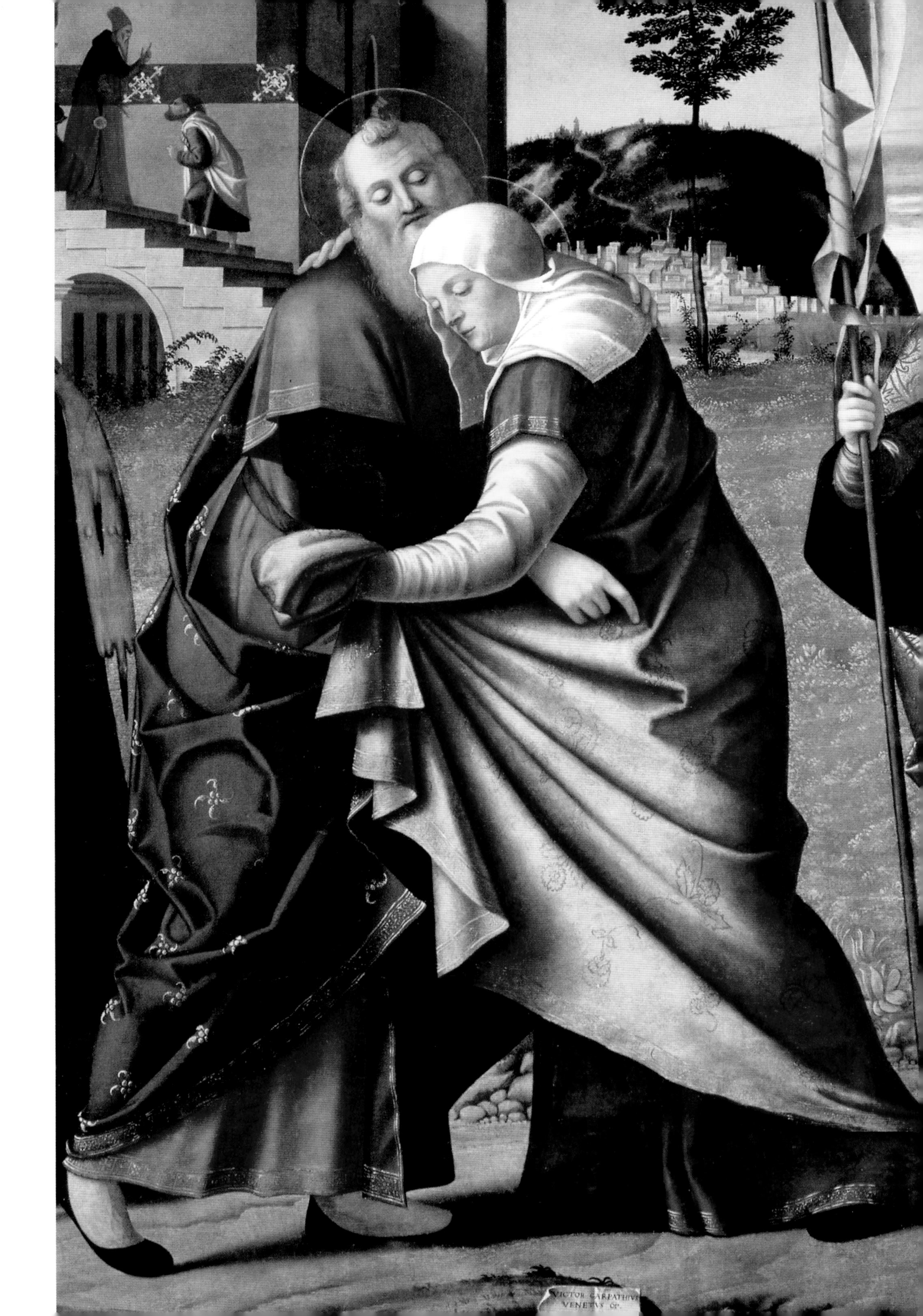
VICTOR CARPATHIVS
VENETVS OP.

John the Baptist, Jesus' cousin, was six months older than he. Perhaps a member of a community of pious Jews who awaited the advent of the Messiah of Israel, he is nevertheless presented in the Gospel as a solitary man and an ascetic, clothed in camel hair and eating locusts and wild honey. On the eastern bank of the Jordan he baptized, announcing the imminent coming of the Messiah and urging everyone to change their lives and to convert, in order *to prepare his way*.

The final prophet

Anton Raphaël Mengs (1728–1779) was a German painter and writer who theorized and embodied the neoclassical reaction to the exuberant Baroque style of the Rococo era.

In 1748, at the age of twenty, Mengs trained in Rome at the Academy of Painting. While he worked there on a *Holy Family*, a lovely peasant woman aged eighteen, Margarita Guazzi, served as his model, lending her features to the figure of the Virgin Mary. Anton fell madly in love with her and proposed. The girl accepted, on the condition that he give up Protestantism to embrace Catholicism. The young suitor consented to the demand of his beloved, and their marriage was soon celebrated. Margarita would be his muse, and it is well known that they lived a wonderful love story together. Twenty children were born of their thirty-year union. Margarita left this world in 1778, followed by Anton less than a year later.

This *Saint John the Baptist in the Desert*, painted in 1774, is a work of his full maturity. Painted on a large scale, the picture does not fail to impress the visitor who discovers it in the corner of a room at the Hermitage Museum. Suddenly, a life-sized and colorful prophet appears to burst out of the canvas to challenge the passerby vehemently. Mengs's genius suggests the resounding voice of the prophet who cries out in the wilderness: *Prepare the way of the Lord, make His paths straight!* (Mk 1:3). This call is embodied here in a prophet with a burning gaze, whose strong body is tense, ready to leap. Impetuousness and conviction are visible in his facial expression and in those open hands which receive the reflections of a golden light.

The work seems like a snapshot. The forerunner of Jesus—whom Christians refer to also as the "last of the prophets"—has just placed his cross-shaped staff against a dried-up trunk that recalls his ascetic life. The flowing folds of a large scarlet fabric partially mask his traditional camel-skin garment. Every detail foretells the blood that will soon be shed, at the tragic moment of his martyrdom, when his head will be offered on a platter to Salome by Herod Antipas, at the instigation of her mother, Herodias. A man of the desert, a man of the absolute, the John the Baptist portrayed by Mengs is as described by the Gospels and, in the same era, by the historiographer Flavius Josephus: uncompromising. ■

THE BIBLE – JN 1:6-9, 15

There was a man sent from God, whose name was John. He came for testimony, to bear witness to the light, that all might believe through him. He was not the light, but came to bear witness to the light. The true light that enlightens every man was coming into the world. John bore witness to him, and cried, "This was he of whom I said, 'He who comes after me ranks before me, for he was before me.'"

Saint John the Baptist in the desert
Anton Raphaël Mengs (1728–1779)
Ca. 1774
Oil on canvas, 82 x 60 in
Saint Petersburg, Hermitage Museum

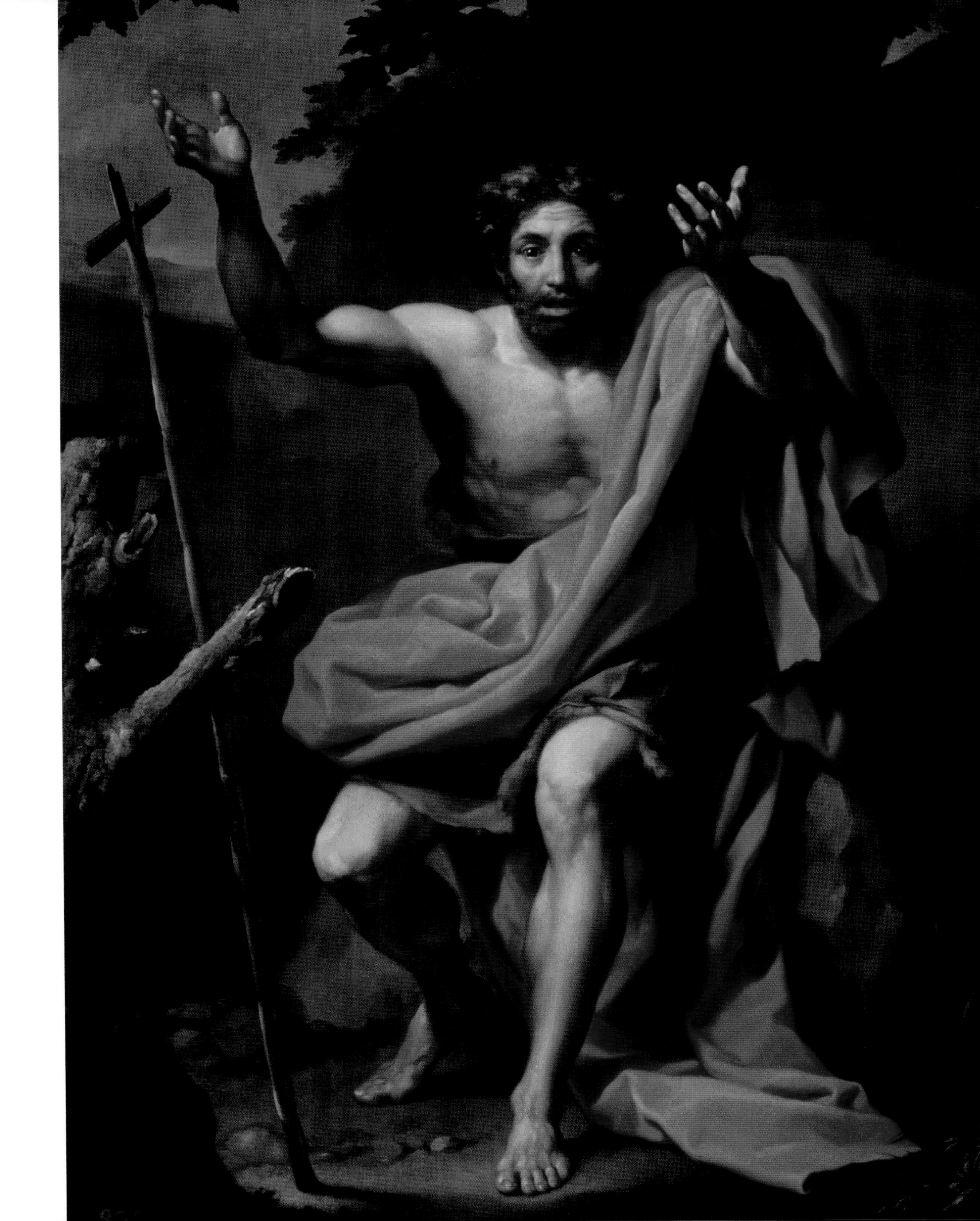

“Seek to understand the final word of what the great artists, the serious masters say in their masterpieces; God will be in it.”

Vincent Van Gogh

Presentation of Christ in the Temple, detail
Fra Angelico (*ca.* 1400–1455)
Ca. 1440
Fresco, 67 x 46 in
Florence, Museum-Convent of San Marco, cell 10

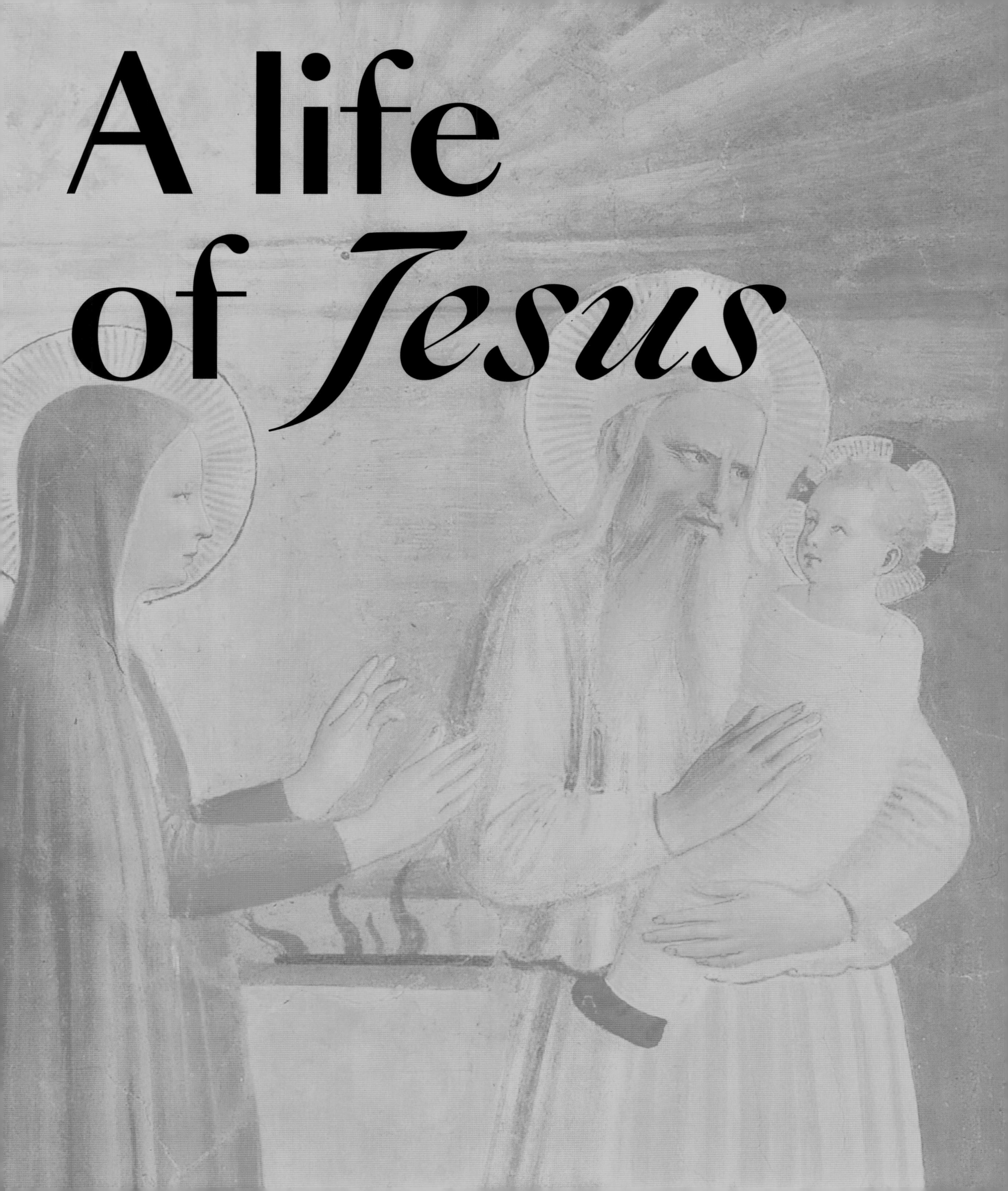

A life of *Jesus*

The scene is recorded only by the evangelist Luke. It takes place in Nazareth, in Galilee, in northern Palestine, a week's walk from Jerusalem. Christian tradition maintains that before writing his Gospel, Luke obtained the testimony from the Virgin Mary herself. At the moment of the Annunciation, Mary was a very young girl—maybe fourteen or fifteen years old. If we correlate this account with the Gospel according to Saint Matthew, she was already married to Joseph, but the spouses were not yet living together, according to the historically attested custom that foresaw that after the marriage ceremony the married woman remained for a time with her family.

The Annunciation

Painted in Novgorod, in Russia, in the 12th century, the *Ustyug Annunciation* is an example of the symbolic language of icons. Mary is standing. Over her sky-blue robe she wears the *maphorion*, a long veil of royal purple that covers her head and shoulders. Like her, the angel stands upright; his hair, the feathers of his wings, and the folds of his garment have been highlighted with gilded brushstrokes according to the so-called "chrysographic" technique, and the precious metal that adorns his body indicates the divinity of the One who sent him. The angel's gesture of blessing is a sign of peace and mercy at the moment when he announces to Mary that she has been chosen by God to bear his Son, whom he will make a king with a never-ending reign. Mary consents: this is the instant of the Incarnation, God becomes man. The first Old Slavonic letters of "Christ"—meaning Anointed One—are represented by the arrangement of the archangel's fingers.

Above them, God the Father, human in appearance but identified by the inscription "Thrice Holy," is framed in a heavenly mandorla. He is clothed in white, seated on a throne of intensely glowing Cherubim, and surrounded by fiery Seraphim. However, he is depicted with the features of the Son. This iconographic choice is based on the words of Jesus Christ himself: *He who sees me, sees the One who sent me* (Jn 12:45). Thus enthroned at the center of the sphere, God the Father contemplates from on high the fulfillment of his will to humble himself and to put on humanity in the Person of his Son.

Mary's hands are busy with a ball of purple yarn; her right hand points to the silhouette of the Child on her heart: Jesus is in his mother's womb, he is fully man. At the same time, it is advisable to show that he is conceived by the Holy Spirit and is fully God. This explains his serious, dignified adult posture, seated on a throne, resembling the Father who shines at the top of the composition. ■

THE BIBLE – LK 1:26-33

In the sixth month the angel Gabriel was sent from God to a city of Galilee named Nazareth, to a virgin betrothed to a man whose name was Joseph, of the house of David; and the virgin's name was Mary.
And he came to her and said, "Hail, full of grace, the Lord is with you! Blessed are you among women." But she was greatly troubled at the saying, and considered in her mind what sort of greeting this might be.
And the angel said to her, "Do not be afraid, Mary, for you have found favor with God. And behold, you will conceive in your womb and bear a son, and you shall call his name Jesus. He will be great, and will be called the Son of the Most High; and the Lord God will give to him the throne of his father David, and he will reign over the house of Jacob for ever; and of his kingdom there will be no end."

Ustyug Annunciation
Novgorod School
1120–1130
Tempera on wood, 94 x 66 in
Moscow, Tretyakov Gallery

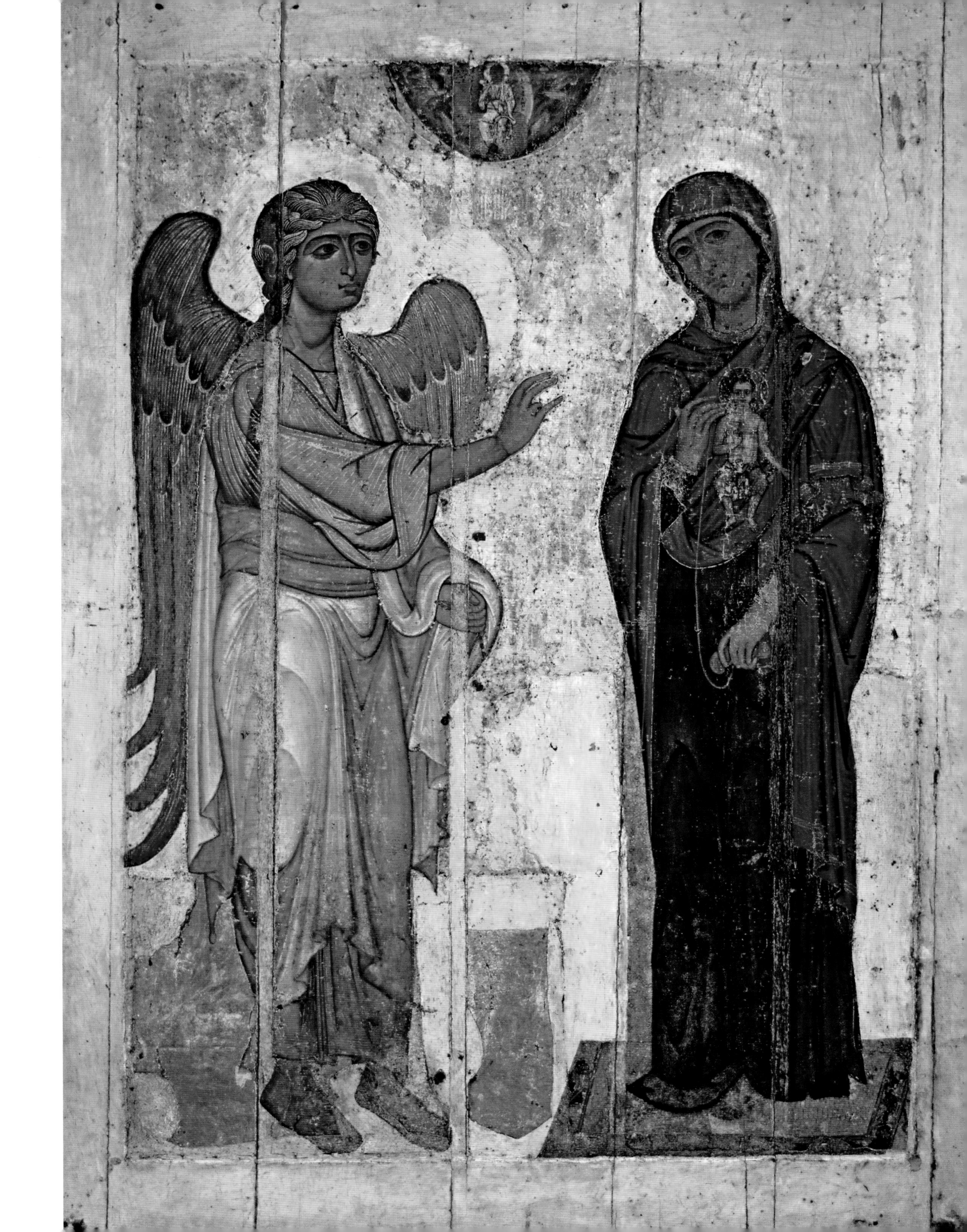

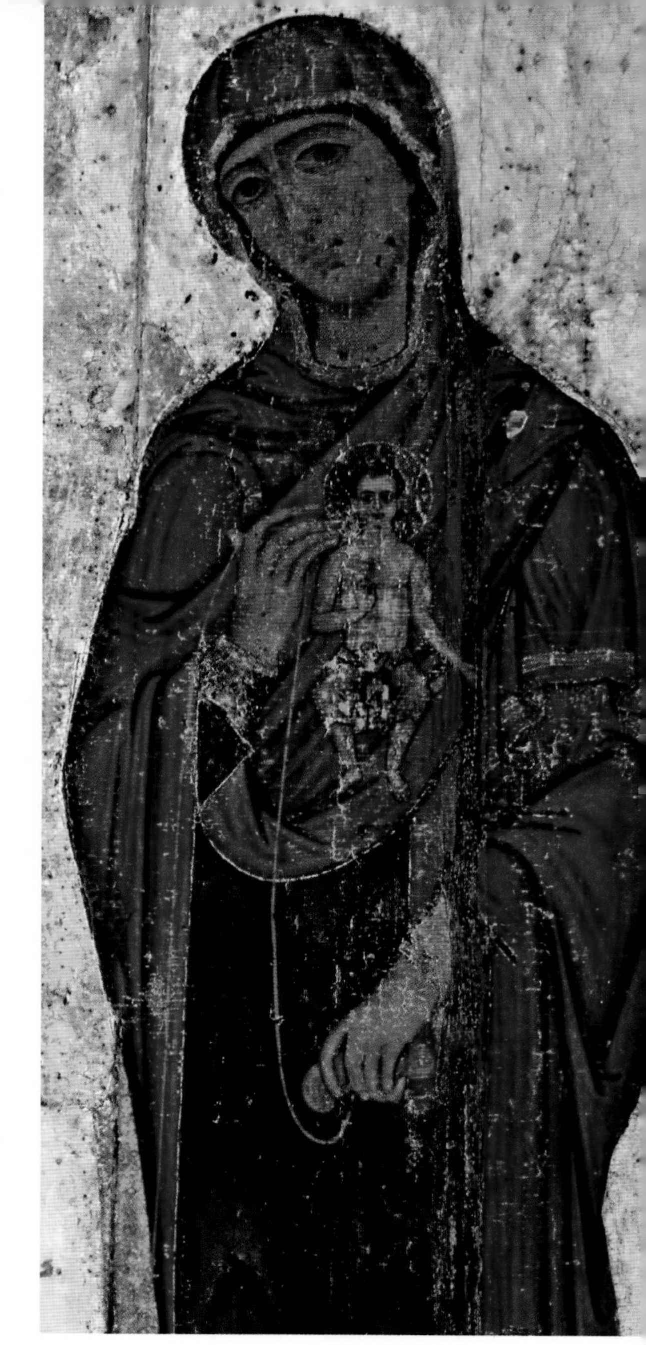

Ustyug Annunciation, detail
Novgorod School
1120–1130
Tempera on wood, 94 x 66 in
Moscow, Tretyakov Gallery

IN ART HISTORY

THE ART OF THE ICON IN RUSSIA

Russia became Christian rather late, following the conversion to Byzantine Christianity of Vladimir I, who renounced paganism at the end of the 10th century. This conversion was decisive in the construction of churches and of the first cathedrals in Rus' in the 11th century: Saint Sophia in Kyiv (present-day Ukraine), and Saint Sophia in Novgorod (now in Russia). A vast iconographic program accompanied this outburst, with paintings that were sometimes monumental, in the form of frescos, or reduced in size and portable, on wood: the art of the icon, which is unique and so variegated in Russia, was born. It has its origins in Byzantine art, since "icon" is derived from the Greek *eikōn*, which means "image" or "representation."

In Orthodox practice, an icon is much more than a work of religious art. An icon, which is blessed once it is completed, literally displays the divine presence. This image is sacred, just like the relics of the saints.

This cult of the icon flourished in the first centuries of Kievan-Russian Christianity and reached its apogee in the 14th and 15th centuries. In the 17th century the custom arose of covering icons with silver-plated metal except for the hands and the faces. This art then fell into a relative decline in the 18th and 19th centuries under the influence of Western religious and secular painting.

In the 20th century, with the help of scientific research, the metallic shields, the multiple coats of varnish, and the repainted portions were removed, restoring these icons to their former glory. Once these somber images are cleaned, they appear luminous. The museums that serve today as their showcases are the Tretyakov Gallery in Moscow (which preserves this *Annunciation*), the Russian Museum in Saint Petersburg, and the museums of painting in Novgorod, Yaroslavl, and Suzdal.

The *Ustyug Annunciation* belongs to a particular stylistic school, the Novgorod School. In the late 13th century, Mongol invasions subjugated Kievan Rus' but left intact Novgorod, one of the oldest cities in European Russia, which then became its artistic capital. The *Ustyug Annunciation* predates the Mongol invasions but already manifests the intense shades, the yellow, the gilding, and the very beautiful color red that will characterize the works of this school.

Other regional stylistic schools made their appearance after the explosive development of one part of Russia: Vladimir, Vologda, Suzdal, Pskov. These different schools were distinguished by the uniqueness of their forms and colors.

In the 14th and 15th centuries, it would be Moscow's turn, in the center of a new state, Muscovite Russia, to become the political and religious center, radiating its influence to all the Russian territories. The Moscow School then succeeded the Novgorod School.

M. C.

Robert Southwell (1561-1596) was among the Jesuit martyrs of Elizabethan England. He came from a well-to-do family and had to travel to the continent for a Catholic education in Douai (Flanders), in Paris, and then as a Jesuit scholastic in Rome. From 1586 to 1592 he ministered in and around London, directed the publication of Catholic catechisms and devotional books, and wrote original prose and poetry. Southwell composed a sequence of poems on the Virgin Mary and Christ, each one in three or four stanzas with six lines each.

The Poetical Works of Rev. Robert Southwell, edited by William B. Turnbull (London: John Russell Smith, 1856), pages 108-118.

Joyful Mysteries

ROBERT SOUTHWELL

Annunciation

With haughty mind to Godhead man aspired,
And was by pride from place of pleasure chased;
With loving mind our manhood God desired,
And as by love in greater pleasure placed;
Man labouring to ascend procured our fall,
God yielding to descend cut off our thrall[1].

Visitation

Eternal lights enclosèd in her breast
Shot out such piercing beams of burning love,
That when her voice her cousin's ear possess'd,
The force thereof did force her babe to move:
With secret signs the children greet each other,
But open praise each leaveth to his mother.

Nativity[2]

Man alter'd was by sin from man to beast;
Beast's food is hay, hay is all mortal flesh [Is 40:6-8];
Now God is flesh, and lives in manger press'd,
As hay the brutest sinner to refresh:
O happy fields wherein this fodder grew,
Whose taste doth us from beasts to men renew!

Presentation

O Virgin pure! thou dost these doves present
As due to law, not as an equal price;[3]
To buy such ware thou wouldst thyself have spent;
The world to reach His worth could not suffice;
If God were to be bought, not worldly pelf*,[4]
But thou wert fittest price next God Himself.

Finding in the Temple[5]

In springing locks lay crouchèd hoary wit*,[6]
In semblance young, a grave and ancient port*;[7]
In lowly looks high majesty did sit,
In tender tongue sound sense of sagest sort:
Nature imparted all that she could teach,
And God supplied where nature could not reach.

1 Slavery

2 Note: the poet alludes to 1 Cor 2:14-16, where Saint Paul contrasts the "spiritual" man with the "animal" or "carnal" man.

3 Lv 12:2-8.

4 Riches.

5 From the poem "Christ's Childhood."

6 White-haired wisdom.

7 Demeanor.

In the Scriptures, the mysterious pregnancy of a young girl—or of a virgin, which is the same word in Hebrew—who was to give birth to the "liberator of Israel" had been announced centuries before by the prophet Isaiah, whose oracle about "Emmanuel" is dedicated to the Messiah who is to come into the world. The prophet proclaims that this liberator will also be the "light of nations," in other words, beyond the Jewish people, the liberator of all humanity.

Behold, a virgin shall conceive

This "portrait" of the Virgin Mary was long considered to be a fragment salvaged from a lost work by Andrea del Sarto (1486–1530) entitled *Madonna with Jesus and Saint John the Baptist*, the existence of which is attested by an engraving by Cornelis Bloemaert (1603–1692). However, in 1999, it was thought that the entire original work, consistent with the engraving, had been discovered in the collections of the national Museum of Fine Arts in Perm, Russia (see below, left), in which the face of the Virgin is similar to the "portrait" presented here. However, as in the engraving, the model seems older, and her face appears much less moving in its expression. The work—a superb one, all things considered—does not come up to the level of Andrea del Sarto's genius, so that, finally, the picture in Perm was attributed to another great Florentine artist, Franciabigio (1484–1525), who shared his studio from 1506 to 1509. Oddly enough, the "fragment," although of superior quality and with a very different technique, received the same attribution. Finally, the picture in Perm was attributed again to Andrea del Sarto.

> The Lord himself will give you a sign. Behold, a virgin shall conceive and bear a son, and shall call his name Immanuel, that is, God-with-us.
>
> THE BIBLE – IS 7:14

We cannot assume that this portrait of the Virgin Mary is a fragment of a lost work by Andrea del Sarto, or a work by Franciabigio imitating the latter. More probably it is a preparatory study, by the hand of Andrea del Sarto himself, for an original work that is lost today, of which Franciabigio made a copy and then Cornelis Bloemart an engraving. This study would therefore be an early work, completed around 1509 by the one whom the Byzantinist Robert Browning considered as "the perfect painter."

This face is a masterpiece, which succeeds in revealing all the complexity of a human soul in a discreet smile. Here, in the humbly lowered eyes, opening onto the invisible, the painter fathoms the interior life of the woman whom *all generations will call blessed* and who treasured *in her heart* and contemplated the wonders that God did for her and through her (cf. Lk 1:48-49; 2:19, 51). The admirable recollection of the young girl's expression suggests the glory of God bearing its fruit of salvation in the womb of the humblest, most delicate femininity.

Andrea del Sarto remains with Raphael, Michelangelo, and Leonardo da Vinci one of the four geniuses who brought the Italian Renaissance to its summit. Of these four, Andrea is the least well known. And yet, what artist ever succeeded in coming so close to the mystery of this woman who became, for Christians, nothing less than the Mother of God? ■

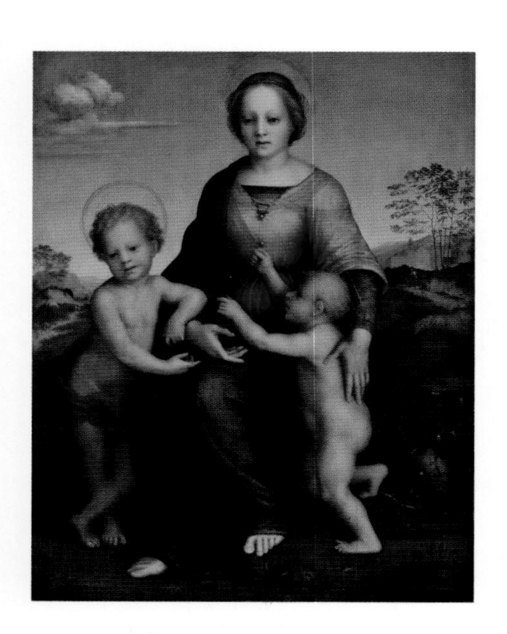

Madonna with Jesus and Saint John the Baptist
Attributed to Andrea del Sarto (1486–1530)
1513
Oil on canvas, 44.7 x 34.7 in
Perm (Russia)
National Museum of Fine Arts

Face of the Virgin
Franciabigio (1484–1525)
Ca. 1509
Oil on wood, 15 x 11.5 in
New York, The Metropolitan Museum of Art

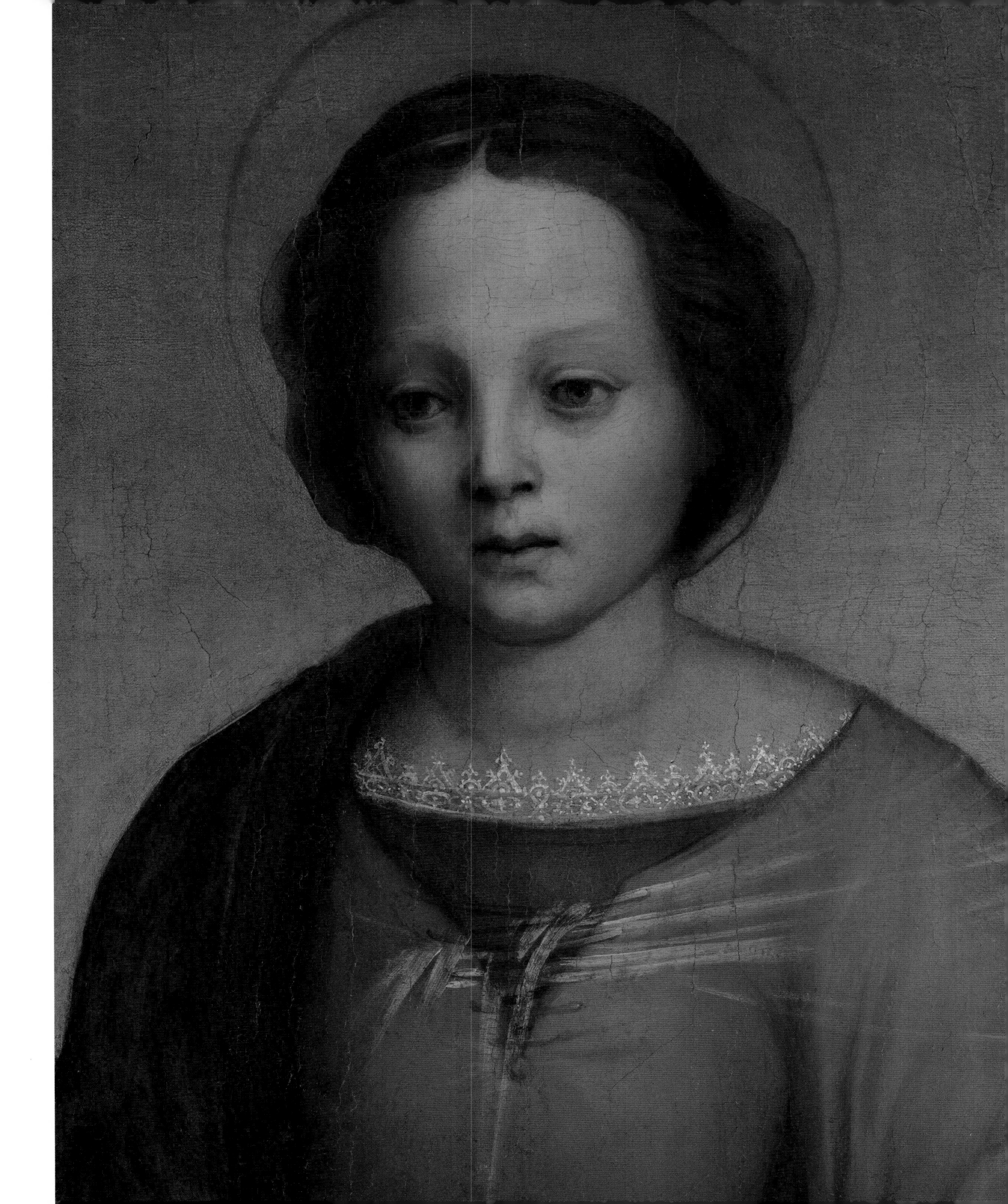

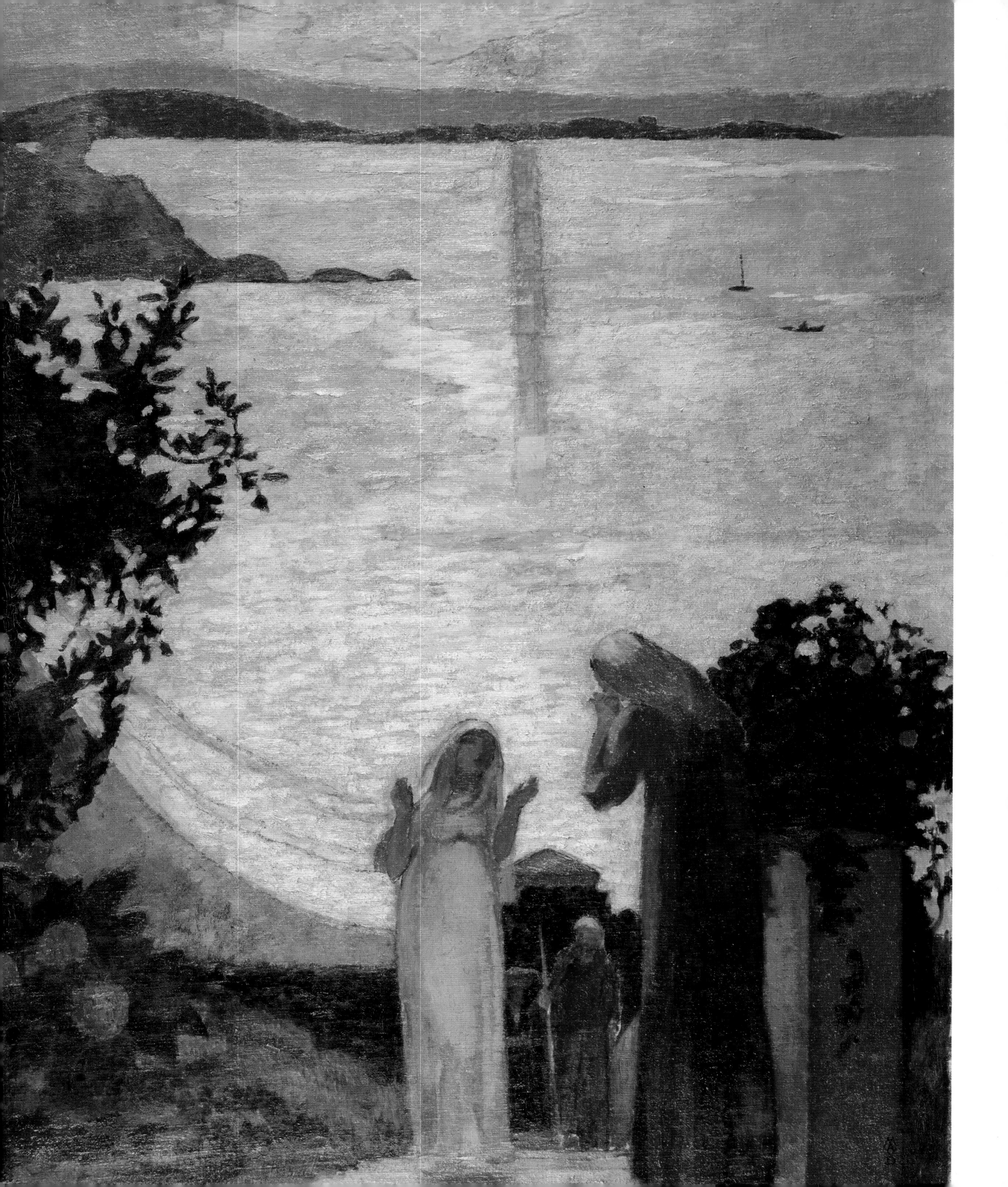

Visitation at sunset

Elizabeth was Mary's cousin. Married to the priest Zechariah, she lived near Jerusalem, in the little town of Ain Karem where the Temple priests stayed. Since Nazareth was located more than one hundred kilometers [62 miles] north of Jerusalem, Mary had to walk for almost a week to pay a visit to her relative. The two women were pregnant: Elizabeth with John the Baptist; Mary with Jesus.

Maurice Denis (1870–1943), a Symbolist painter, was one of the founders of the group of Nabis ("the enlightened" in Hebrew) influenced by Paul Gauguin. He summed up his pictorial choices as follows: "I ban academism because it sacrifices emotion to convention and artifice, because it is theatrical or insipid. I ban Jansenism because it is the death of art, cold, and boring. I ban realism because it is prose and more than anything else I want music and poetry. Finally, I will preach Beauty. Beauty is an attribute of the Divinity."

During his lifetime, Maurice Denis was considered one of the greatest artists of his time and enjoyed worldwide renown. With this *Visitation at sunset* he invites the viewer to discover, in silhouettes that are all the more evocative because they are not completely detailed, as though seen through his clear eye, something of his closeness to the Gospel in heart and spirit. He wanted the mystery of God to become incarnate beneath his paintbrushes, without tambourines or trumpets, but with a keenness and a revelatory ability "that make you want to kneel down and pray, with the simplicity of children."

Against a background of a golden sea, a sweet young woman clothed in blue simultaneously climbs the joyful path to announce her pregnancy to her beloved cousin, Elizabeth, mother of John the Baptist, and already in a prefiguration, follows the way of tears and blood that leads to Golgotha, where the child that she is bearing will be sacrificed.

For Maurice Denis, every life has been taken up fully by the life of the Savior who was *handed over for us.* Therefore he took his inspiration here from a scene in his own life. The view is the one that he enjoyed from his house in Perros-Guirec, to which he gave the beautiful name of *Silencio.* This young pregnant woman, in that summer of 1911, was Marthe, his wife. She would experience the sorrow of losing the child whom she was carrying, before the term of her pregnancy. And in the background, the red silhouette suggesting the reserved humility of Saint Joseph in the presence of the mystery that he guards, is Maurice Denis himself, holding the staff of his mission. Claiming that he is a righteous and devout man (cf. Lk 2:25), he depicts himself climbing the path of his earthly pilgrimage, as husband, father, and painter. ■

THE BIBLE – LK 1:39-42

In those days Mary arose and went with haste into the hill country, to a city of Judah, and she entered the house of Zechariah and greeted Elizabeth. And when Elizabeth heard the greeting of Mary, the child leaped in her womb; and Elizabeth was filled with the Holy Spirit and she exclaimed with a loud cry, "Blessed are you among women, and blessed is the fruit of your womb."

Visitation at sunset
Maurice Denis (1870–1943)
1911
Oil on canvas, 32 x 24 in
Private collection

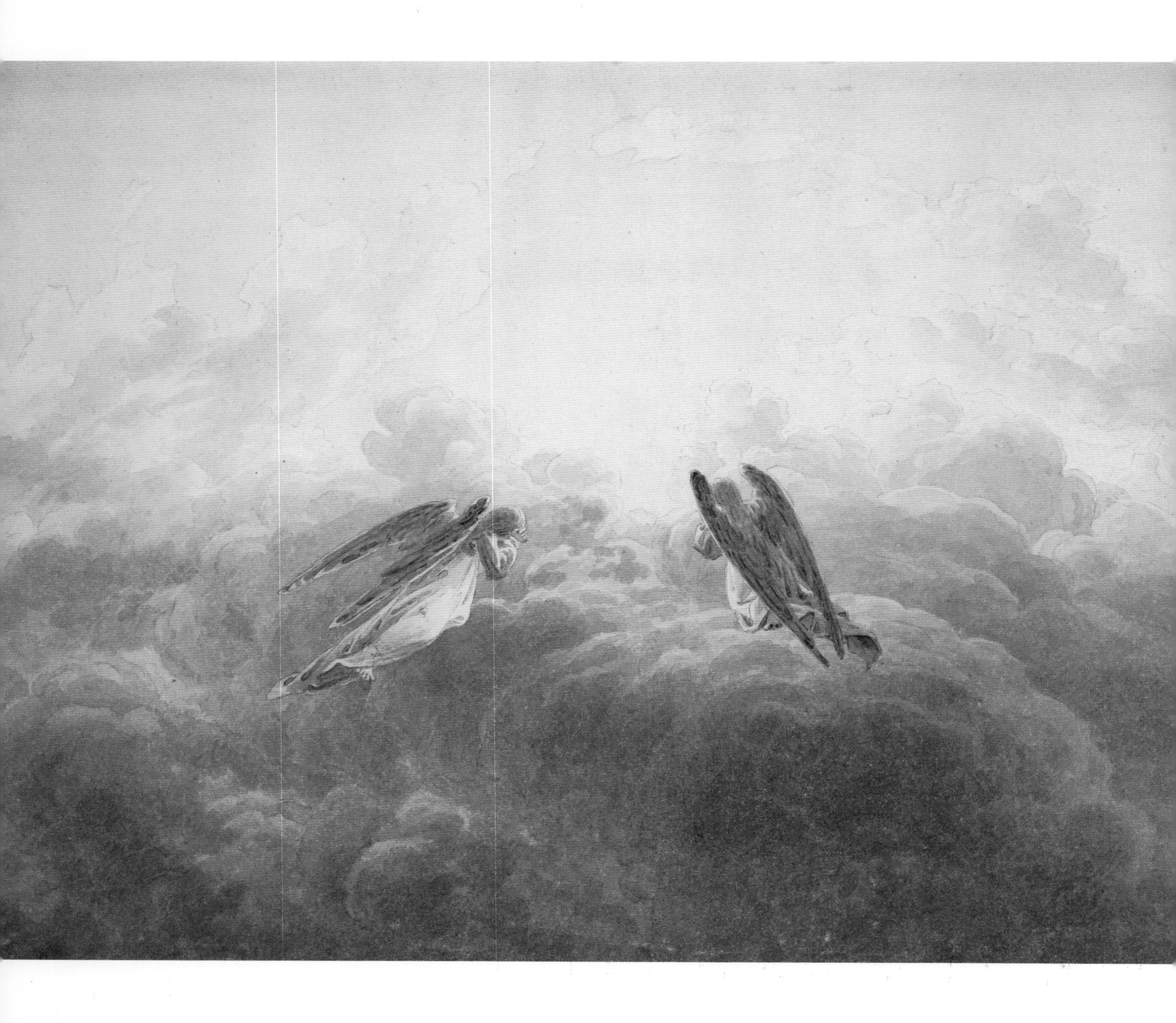

The ages of life
Caspar David Friedrich (1774–1840)
Ca. 1826
Pencil drawing, sepia, 7.3 x 10.5 in
Hamburg, Kunsthalle

Angels we have heard on high

The angels on Christmas night announced the birth of Jesus, in which they rejoiced by singing the glory of God. Ever since Genesis, the angels, in other words the "envoys," have been in fact signs of God's presence. Some of them—like the angel Gabriel at the Annunciation, or the one who announced to the shepherds the birth of Jesus—receive the mission to bring messages to men.

Like François René de Chateaubriand in literature, Caspar David Friedrich (1774–1840) embodied Romanticism in painting. In reaction against the dehumanizing rationalism of the so-called Enlightenment, he thought of life as a novel and his states of soul as one of the criteria for understanding reality. Thus, when he makes the painting of a landscape, he seeks to depict what he feels in seeing it.

However, beyond his Romanticism, Friedrich can be considered the father of symbolism. For him, nature is only the visible part of the divine creation, and the artist's sacred mission is to reveal this true, hidden reality, and to do so by means of symbols. And in fact, Friedrich gave a symbolic significance to all the elements that shape his works. Thus, for example, in a landscape, the mountains are allegories of faith; the rays of the setting sun symbolize the end of the barbarian world.

For Friedrich, in the presence of what the impressionists would call the "motif," the artist's first attitude must be profound recollection. This contemplative approach to nature was expressed perfectly by his close friend, the poet Friedrich Hölderlin, when he has Hyperion say:

"All my being is silent so as to listen to the gentle breezes playing around my body. Lost in the immense blue, often I lift my eyes towards the Ether or I lower them to the sacred sea, and it seems to me that a fraternal spirit opens his arms to me, that the suffering of solitude dissolves into divine life."

In Greek, the name Hyperion, one of the mythological Titans, means "he who sees beyond," and also "he who sees the great Beyond." This fits Friedrich ideally.

THE BIBLE – LK 2:8-14

And in that region there were shepherds out in the field, keeping watch over their flock by night. And an angel of the Lord appeared to them, and the glory of the Lord shone around them, and they were filled with fear. And the angel said to them, "Be not afraid; for behold, I bring you good news of a great joy which will come to all the people; for to you is born this day in the city of David a Savior, who is Christ the Lord. And this will be a sign for you: you will find a babe wrapped in swaddling cloths and lying in a manger." And suddenly there was with the angel a multitude of the heavenly host praising God and saying, "Glory to God in the highest, and on earth peace among men with whom he is pleased!"

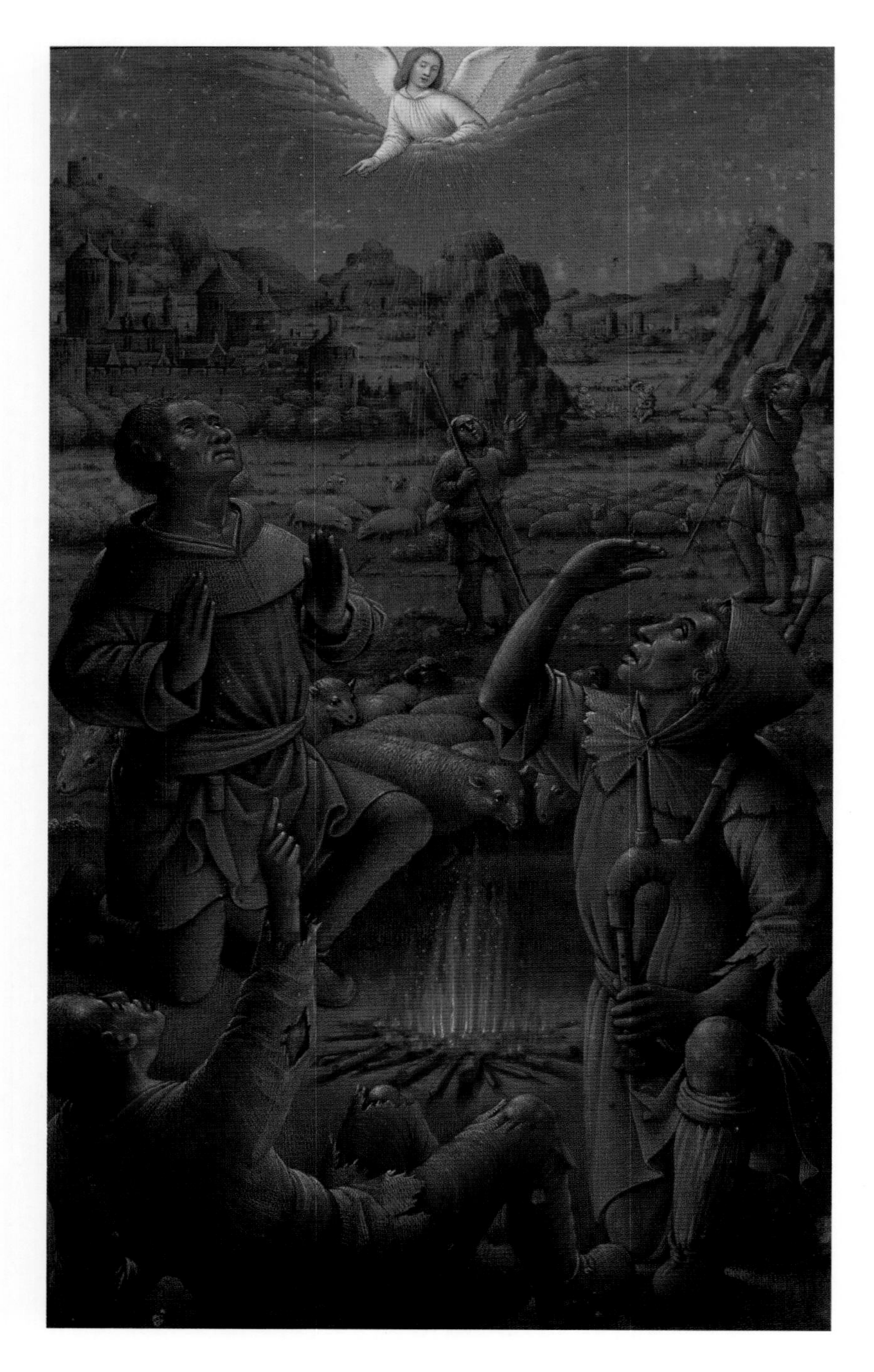

Announcement to the shepherds
Jean Bourdichon
Miniature, 12 x 7.5 in
Paris, National Library of France

Friedrich depicts the angels who contemplate the earth. As for Bourdichon, he depicts the shepherds who contemplate the night sky in which an angel appears to announce: "A Savior is born to you."

But here, conversely, this drawing shows two angels who from the great beyond look down on earth, a reality that the artist does not let us see. The angels live close to God, and the Bible even calls them *you gods* (Ps 29:1). The divine light is exactly what envelops them, leaving a supernatural brilliance on their silhouette and their folded hands. But what earthly reality could be motivating their recollected contemplation? *A swaddled newborn in a manger*, sleeping between an ass and an ox? But then, what transcendent event can this moving but prosaic earthly reality represent, to make angels prostrate themselves before it?

Friedrich's genius succeeds completely in sharing his faith in the divine nature of this newborn, without even needing to show his human reality, simply by the quality of those who adore him and by the place from which they contemplate him. ■

CASPAR DAVID FRIEDRICH: THE TRAGEDY OF THE LANDSCAPE

The art of Caspar David Friedrich, like that of his friend Philipp Otto Runge (1777–1810), is the most mature manifestation of German Romanticism. It is to German painting what his contemporary Ludwig van Beethoven is to music, in a country that, when all is said and done, was quite diverse and broken up.

The painter grew up in the shadow of a church, in a pastor's residence in Greifswald, in a family of modest means. His early youth was marked by the deaths of his mother and several siblings. He confided: "In order to enter into eternity, it is necessary to submit several times to death."

The introduction of religious signs into his works, first and foremost the cross that rises from rocks, forests, mountaintops, or the shores of the sea, authorizes an interpretation in which Protestantism leaves its imprint.

Although the painter develops a magical concept of nature which is dear to the German masters—in his works there are accents of an old pagan Germanic deism, as well as a taste for Nordic mythology—he is nonetheless profoundly Christian. For him, every aspect of nature bears part of the splendor of Revelation.

The sculptor Pierre-Jean David d'Angers (1788–1856) was the first to promote the work of Caspar David Friedrich in France. He writes, "in his pencil there is something of the laconic style of the grand orators," and formulated a statement that has remained famous: "Here is a man who discovered the tragedy of the landscape."

Nothing is more opposed to the sensibility of Caspar David Friedrich than that of his German contemporaries in the movement of the Nazarenes. The latter sought their models in the crowded scenes of the Italian Renaissance, while he affirmed that "God is everywhere, even in a grain of sand." He would never feel the need to prostrate himself before the Italian genius and would never make the trip to Rome.

The first picture that he showed in public, in 1808, caused a scandal. The Countess Maria Theresia von Thun had commissioned a picture meant for the altar of the chapel of the Castle of Teschen, in Bohemia, and the artist, overcoming his reluctance to paint on commission, achieved the unprecedented tour de force of delivering a landscape instead of a devotional image. The work is entitled *The altar of Teschen*, although sometimes it is called *The cross in the mountain*.

The Chamberlain von Ramdohr led the critique and, taking up a paradoxical position, tried to warn the public about the fascination exercised by Caspar David Friedrich's obvious talent. According to him, the picture introduced a dangerous upheaval in the aesthetic domain, and the subversion in painting caused by the painter's talent was dangerous.

A relatively small number of works by Caspar David Friedrich have come down to us: little more than a hundred. Their chronology, however, is less important than for other artists, all the more so since Friedrich neither signed nor dated his works, as though he had situated them outside of time.

His painting anticipates by a century the "magical realism" dear to Franz Roh. He announces the expressionists. Kandinsky, who drew from the same source as Friedrich—the *Treatise on Colors* by Goethe (1810)—saw in him a founding father of abstraction, as others would give that title to William Turner.

One of his last pictures, unfinished, depicts the interior of a church in ruins in which pine trees have sprung up amid the vestiges—mutilated statues, broken altars, demolished holy water fonts.

Painting is said to have been for Caspar David Friedrich a sort of divine service.

M. C.

The name Bethlehem, King David's city, means "house of bread." The "manger" that served as the first cradle of the newborn Jesus was a feeding trough for sheep. The Gospel according to Saint Luke insists on this word "manger": God-made-man lies in a place where food is stored—which prefigures the Eucharist. The visit of the shepherds is not surprising in that region, where David himself had pastured his sheep a thousand years earlier. The tradition of depicting the Crèche as we know it goes back to Saint Francis of Assisi, who instituted it in Greccio, in Central Italy, during the 13th century.

For Christ is born of Mary

Here is a work by Philippe de Champaigne (1602–1674), the most French of all painters, one might be tempted to say, in the sense that he was simultaneously one of the inspirations and one of the interpreters of the "great century of souls," the 17th century, which was for religious historian Daniel-Rops "the unequaled hour of eternal France." It is true that when we contemplate this central motif of his *Adoration of the shepherds*, we cannot help thinking that they were joined in this adoration by, among others, Saint Vincent de Paul, Bérulle, Monsieur Olier, Condren, Saint John Eudes, Saint Louis-Marie de Montfort, Racine, Corneille, Pascal, Bossuet, and so many other great souls. We are in good company.

Let us then be drawn by their "devout" manner—a term that they received as the most exquisite of compliments—to contemplate such a work of art. Let us agree to enter into their sense of transcendence by allowing ourselves to be enveloped, like the Baby Jesus here, by the altogether supernatural blue of the Virgin Mary's cloak. Let us come back to earth quickly, because that is where the divine event is happening! Let us be guided by the hand of Saint Joseph, the gnarled hand of a laborer, a carpenter, a hand that always makes the right gesture and here points out to the shepherds the *true Light that enlightens every man by coming into the world* (Jn 1:9). And indeed, the light of the Child pierces the darkness; it lights up Mary and Joseph. The face of Mary, the Mother of Jesus, is perfectly illumined, without a shadow; it is no longer the face of a young girl but already that of a beautiful lady, of Our Lady. Her hand, placed on her heart, in other words close to God, dedicates to him the events belonging to human life, such as the childlike joy here at Christmas. The color of Joseph's cloak too incites us to meditate on the human condition: the yellowish brown signifies original sin, the weakness of humanity; it is the color of the dust from which man comes and to which he will return, according to the biblical prophecy (Gn 3:19). But look: here, all of a sudden, this earthen yellow shines like gold, as though human nature, thanks to the newborn in the manger, was going to be transfigured by a resplendent light, a divine light. ■

THE BIBLE – LK 2:15-16

When the angels went away from them into heaven, the shepherds said to one another, "Let us go over to Bethlehem and see this thing that has happened, which the Lord has made known to us." And they went with haste, and found Mary and Joseph, and the baby lying in a manger.

Adoration of the shepherds
Philippe de Champaigne (1602–1674)
Ca. 1645
Oil on canvas, 92.7 x 63.6 in
London, Wallace Collection

Lying on the ground is a lamb prefiguring *the Lamb of God* who will take away the sin of the world by giving the greatest proof of love: his life (*cf.* page 200).

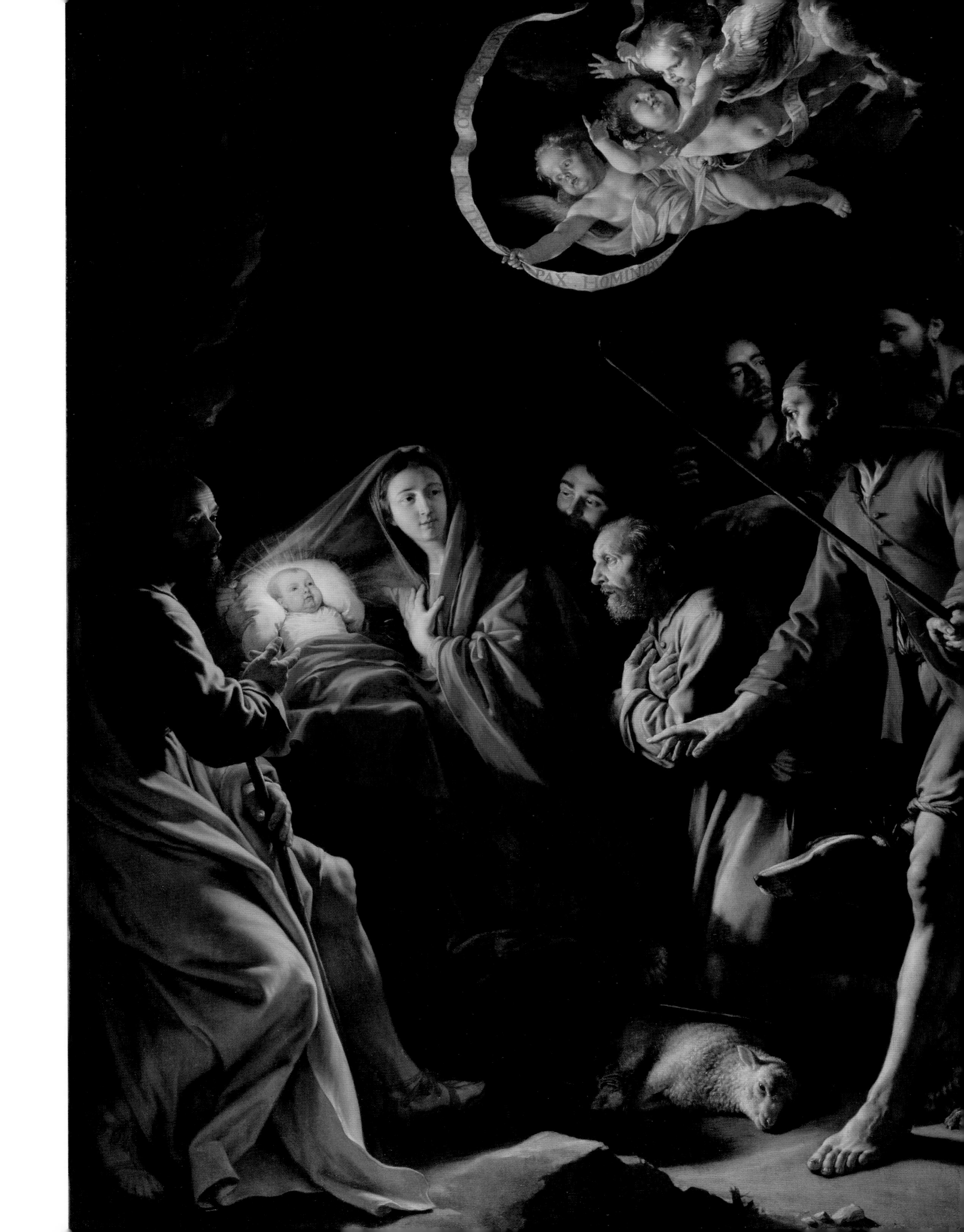
PAX

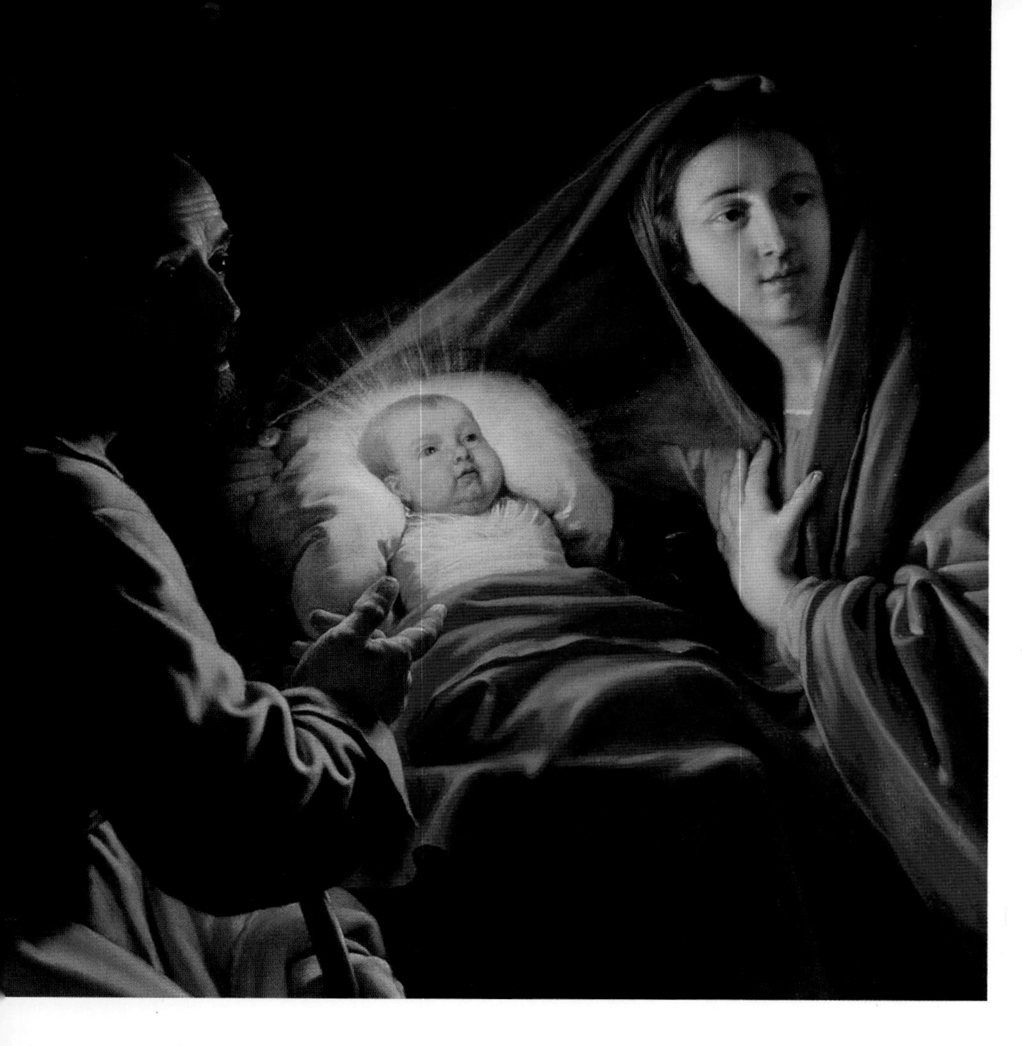

Adoration of the Shepherds, detail
Philippe de Champaigne (1602–1674)
Ca. 1645
Oil on canvas, 92.7 x 63.6 in
London, Wallace Collection

PHILIPPE DE CHAMPAIGNE: A JANSENIST PAINTER

Seventeenth-century French painting, overwhelmed by the tutelary figure of Nicolas Poussin (1594–1665), who spent most of his career in Rome, is nonetheless instantiated most characteristically by the figures of Simon Vouet (1590–1649) and Philippe de Champaigne (1602–1674). After a stay in Rome, the first returned to Paris in 1627. As for the second, originally from Brussels, he settled in Paris in 1621.

The beginnings of de Champaigne's career were crowned with success. He worked for Marie de Medici on decorating the Luxembourg Palace and for Armand Jean du Plessis, Cardinal Richelieu (1585–1642), whom he depicted in cardinalatial garb no less than eleven times.

After Richelieu's death in 1642, which for the painter coincided with a period of personal mourning after the death of his wife (1638) and that of his son (1642), Philippe de Champaigne drew closer to the Jansenist circles and diligently attended the Abbey of Port-Royal des Champs, where his own daughter, Catherine de Sainte-Suzanne (1636–1686) in religion, would pronounce her vows.

From then on the artist's works pictorially reflect austerity and Jansenist rigor. This is expressed by extremely bare compositions, staging a few figures against a neutral background, and a very restricted spectrum of colors.

The present picture, *Adoration of the Shepherds*, dating from around 1645, is unique. Indeed, the artist adapts here a composition already tried around 1630 in the picture on the same subject preserved today in the Museum of Fine Arts in Lyon.

The changes in the composition tend toward greater clarity. In particular we should emphasize a formal simplification and a marked accentuation of the Infant Jesus, the only door and source of salvation.

The colorist talents of Philippe de Champaigne, a classical painter, are expressed forcibly here. The three patches of primary colors on the cloaks of Mary, Joseph, and the shepherd on the right indeed help to structure the scene and to simplify a teeming composition for the spectator's eye. The painter reduces the scene to the main figures and introduces into it the motif of the sacrificed lamb, prefiguring the Passion, in the foreground, a sign of this new attention to the themes of salvation and the Christic sacrifice.

The earliest mention of this work occurs in a catalogue of sale dated 1766. It indicates that this monumental oil painting on canvas was commissioned around 1645 for the Cistercian Abbey of Notre-Dame de Quincy, located in Tanlay, in the departement of l'Yonne. The patron is said to have been Cardinal Richelieu or, more probably, the Abbot of Notre-Dame de Quincy, Mathieu de Mesgrigny. Like most of the work preserved today in the Wallace Collection, the picture became part of the collection of the Francophile Richard Seymour-Conway (1800–1870) in the mid-19th century.

M. C.

Richard Crashaw (1613–1649) was raised a staunch Anglican and became a cleric after studying at Cambridge. The High Church sensibility he acquired at Cambridge led him deeper into the Catholic devotional tradition, and after discovering the works of Saint Teresa of Ávila he became Catholic himself, not long before his death. As a poet, he belonged to the Metaphysical school most famously represented by John Donne.

Richard Crashaw, "On the Blessed Virgin's Bashfulness." Public domain.

A tiny God

RICHARD CRASHAW

That on her lap she casts her humble eye
'Tis the sweet pride of her humility.
The fair star is well fixed, for where, O where
Could she have fixed it on a fairer Sphere?
'Tis Heaven, 'tis Heaven she sees, Heaven's God there lies
She can see Heaven and ne'er lift up her eyes.
This new Guest to her eyes new laws hath given:
'Twas once look up, 'tis now look down to Heaven.

The Magi came from the East, probably from Mesopotamia. The fact that they watched the stars could mean that they were astronomers. Christian tradition interprets this "epiphany," which means "manifestation" in Greek, as the fact that God manifested himself in Jesus not only to the Jews but also to all the peoples on earth. This is why the Magi were associated with the continents that were known at that time: Europe, Africa, and Asia. The three "Christmas gifts" that they offered to Jesus have a very strong symbolic significance: gold is the hallmark of kings, incense is a sign of God, and myrrh is a spice with which the dead were embalmed.

The three kings

The Baroque style arose in the mid-16th century. Like a sun, it illumined the arts, until in 18th century it died the way stars die, in an explosion of masterpieces. Some critics have derisively used the name "Rococo" for this final, sublime manifestation of an art that had taken as its mission the task of inspiring people here on earth with a taste of Paradise. Giambattista Tiepolo (1696–1770) was a major player in this movement, and his work constitutes one of the highest achievements in the art of painting. Giving free rein to his bold imagination, he raised his art to such a degree of perfection that he got people to believe that the impossible is possible for men, while his refined taste made him transcend with the utmost elegance what in anyone else's work would be nothing but affectation and excess.

Mary is seated under the protection of the high stature of Joseph, slightly to the right of a very crowded arrangement of the heads of the visiting dignitaries. She has on her lap the Child who turns to look at the old wise man bowing in veneration, with his hands folded. This creates an encounter involving an intense exchange of glances. In this composition, Tiepolo's great originality is to show the other kings in the background, huddled behind their companion. Turning their backs on the spectator and framing the scene are a beautifully dressed servant whose right elbow sticks out, accentuating the third dimension, and a page from the royal suite, augmenting the scale of the figures and the effect of closeness.

Behold, Wise Men from the East came to Jerusalem.... When they saw the star, they rejoiced exceedingly with great joy; and going into the house they saw the child with Mary his mother, and they fell down and worshiped him. Then, opening their treasures, they offered him gifts, gold and frankincense and myrrh.

THE BIBLE – MT 2:1, 10-11

For once, the presents that were brought from afar are set aside, because the hand carrying a precious vase is anonymous. The ox's presence is only suggested by one of its horns. The main figures are staged in a scene far removed from a simple narration. The stone wall serves as a loggia or gallery, accentuating the separation between what might remain of familial intimacy and the group of witnesses. Applied in large swaths, the colors have a freshness that underscores the typical light of the Venetian style, of which Tiepolo is the greatest genius in the 18th century.

The depiction of the three kings in paintings developed considerably over the course of time. The paleo-Christian era showed travelers and insisted on the

Adoration of the Magi
Giambattista Tiepolo (1696–1770)
1753
Oil on canvas, 160.6 x 82.9 in
Munich, Alte Pinakothek

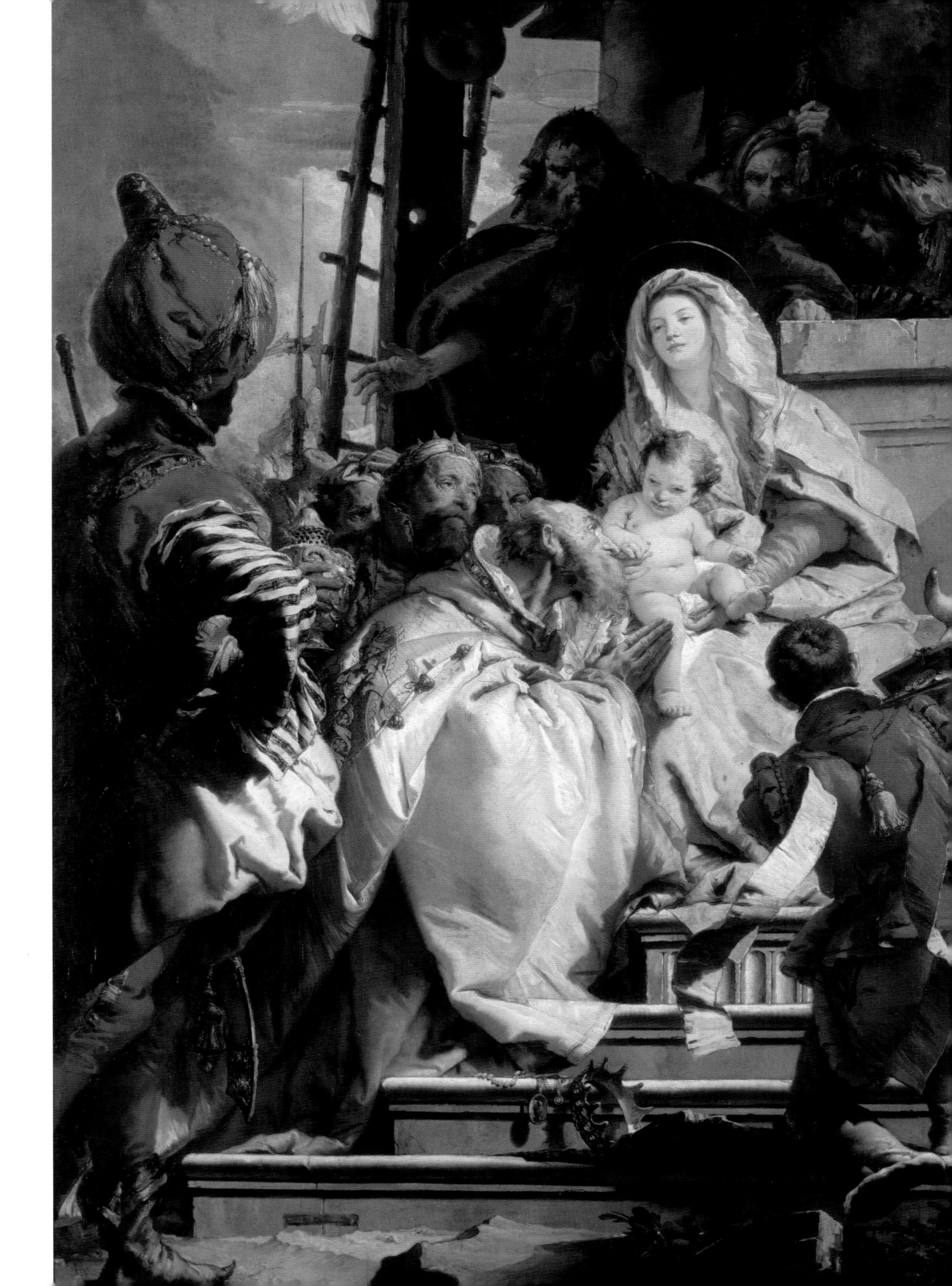

star. In the 5th century, Byzantine art took its inspiration both from the canonical Gospels and from the apocrypha, particularly, it seems, *The Arabic Gospel of the Infancy*. The number of three Magi is fixed. Painters started to differentiate their ages: the first becomes an old man with a long, white beard; the second, a mature man with a brown beard; the third, a young man without facial hair.

As early as the 2nd century, Tertullian had given the Magi the title of kings, alluding to Psalm 72 (verse 10):

May the kings of Tarshish and of the isles render him tribute.
May the kings of Sheba and Seba bring gifts;

and to Isaiah 60:1-3:

Arise, Jerusalem, and shine!
For your light has come, and the glory of the LORD has risen upon you.
For behold, darkness shall cover the earth, and thick darkness the peoples;
but the LORD will arise upon you, and his glory will be seen upon you.
And nations shall walk by your light, and kings in the brightness of your rising.

IN ART HISTORY

TIEPOLO IN WÜRZBURG

The Venetian painter Giambattista Tiepolo (1696–1770) produced this *Adoration of the Magi* in 1753. The picture kept today in Munich (the Metropolitan Museum of Art in New York owns another version of it) was originally supposed to decorate the main altar of the monastery church in Schwarzach. In a dense composition, the painter shows the full extent of Venetian splendor. We should emphasize the profusion of precious fabrics, which is much more than a virtuoso exercise of brushwork. It is also a display of much more literal wealth, and a direct allusion to a Venetian society in love with luxury.

The Abbey of Münsterschwarzach, one of the most important ones in the Benedictine Order, is located in Bavaria, not far from the city of Würzburg, a capital city for Tiepolo.

Indeed, in 1750, Giambattista Tiepolo responded to the invitation by the Prince-Bishop of Franconia, Karl Philipp von Greiffenclau, to decorate the sumptuous episcopal residence in Würzburg. Tiepolo then left Venice, where he nevertheless was pursuing a very brilliant career. Accompanied by his sons Giandomenico (1727–1804) and Lorenzo (1736–1776), he traveled to Germany, where he would stay for three years.

The Venetian painter produced first of all the frescos of the *Kaisersaal*, between 1750 and 1752. The patron, extremely satisfied, kept the Tiepolos (father and sons) and asked them in July 1752 to paint a monumental decor, that of the vault over the stairway of honor designed by the German architect Johann Balthasar Neumann (1687–1753). At the time this was the largest fresco in the world and the masterpiece of the painter's career.

The Tiepolos took advantage of their presence in Würzburg to accept commissions from the nearby convents, particularly one from the Abbey of Münsterschwarzach; the architect of its Baroque basilica dated 1743 is likewise Neumann. The abbey church was then endowed moreover with an altarpiece depicting *The Stoning of Saint Stephen* painted by Giandomenico, and also with works by their Venetian compatriot Giovanni Battista Piazzetta (1682–1754).

Having completed the commission, Tiepolo and his sons returned to Venice in 1753. They would remain there for another ten years before being called to the royal palace in Madrid by Carlos III.

M. C.

Not until these passages were adopted as readings in the liturgy, around the year 1000, did the Magi start to be depicted as kings in iconography. In the early 11th century, the names of the Magi—Caspar (or Gaspard), Melchior, and Balthazar—appear beside pictures of them (they were added at around that period on the mosaics in Ravenna). From the 15th century on, in Italy, Melchior is represented bareheaded, having placed his crown at Jesus' feet; Balthazar wears a royal crown, and Caspar—a caliph's turban. The symbolic color of their clothing was set then: sky blue for Melchior, an earthen brown for Balthazar, rose or orange of the earth mystically united to heaven for Caspar. Hans Memling and Andrea Mantegna, from 1470 on, popularized Melchior as an ambassador of Europe, Balthasar—of Asia, and Caspar—of black Africa. In the 16th century and until the late 17th, Portuguese and Spaniards tried, with no lasting success, to introduce a fourth, Amerindian king into the iconography. ■

The Three Kings
6th century
Mosaic
Ravenna, Basilica of Sant'Apollinare Nuovo

Above the figures, the names of the three kings were added in the 11th century.

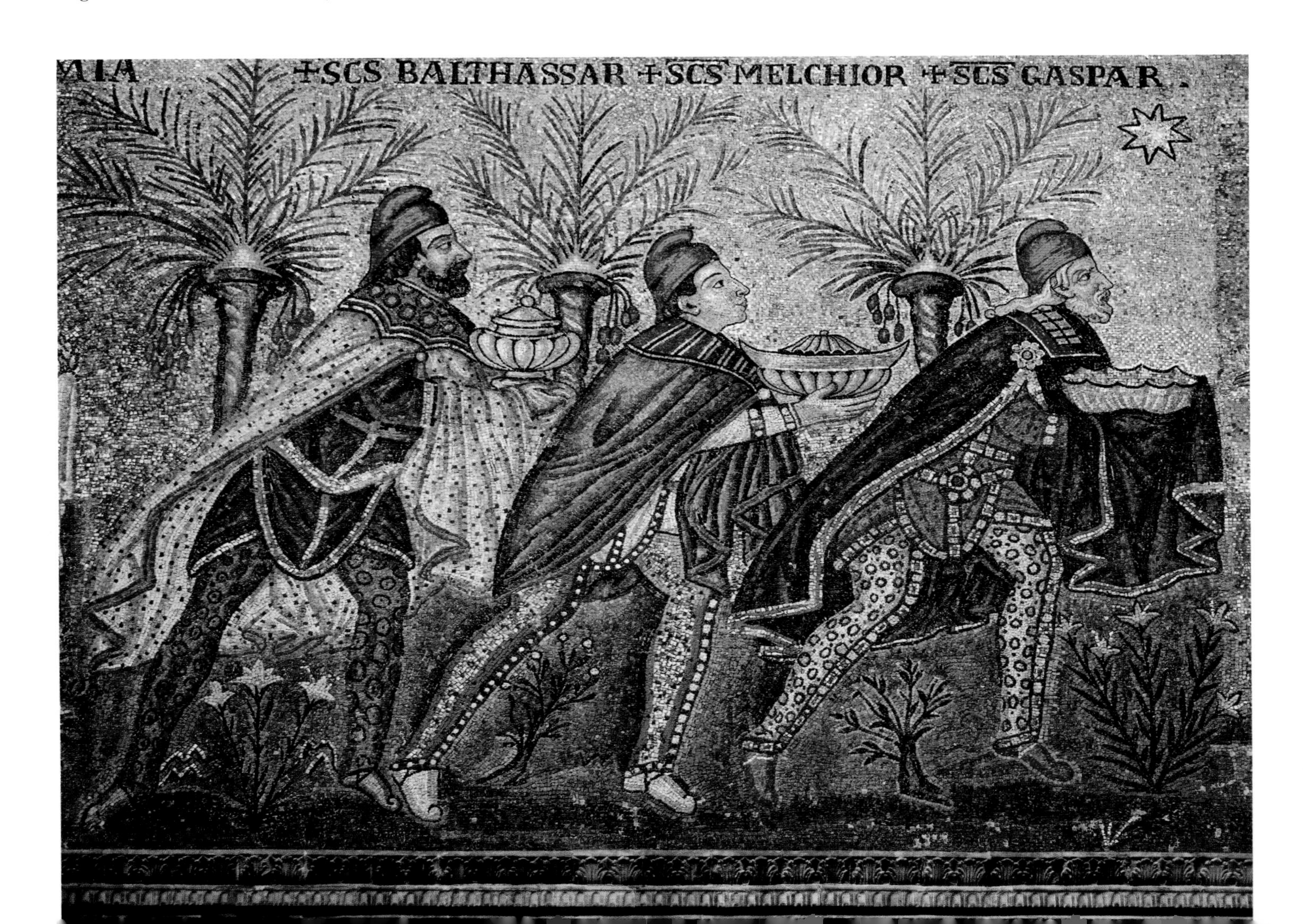

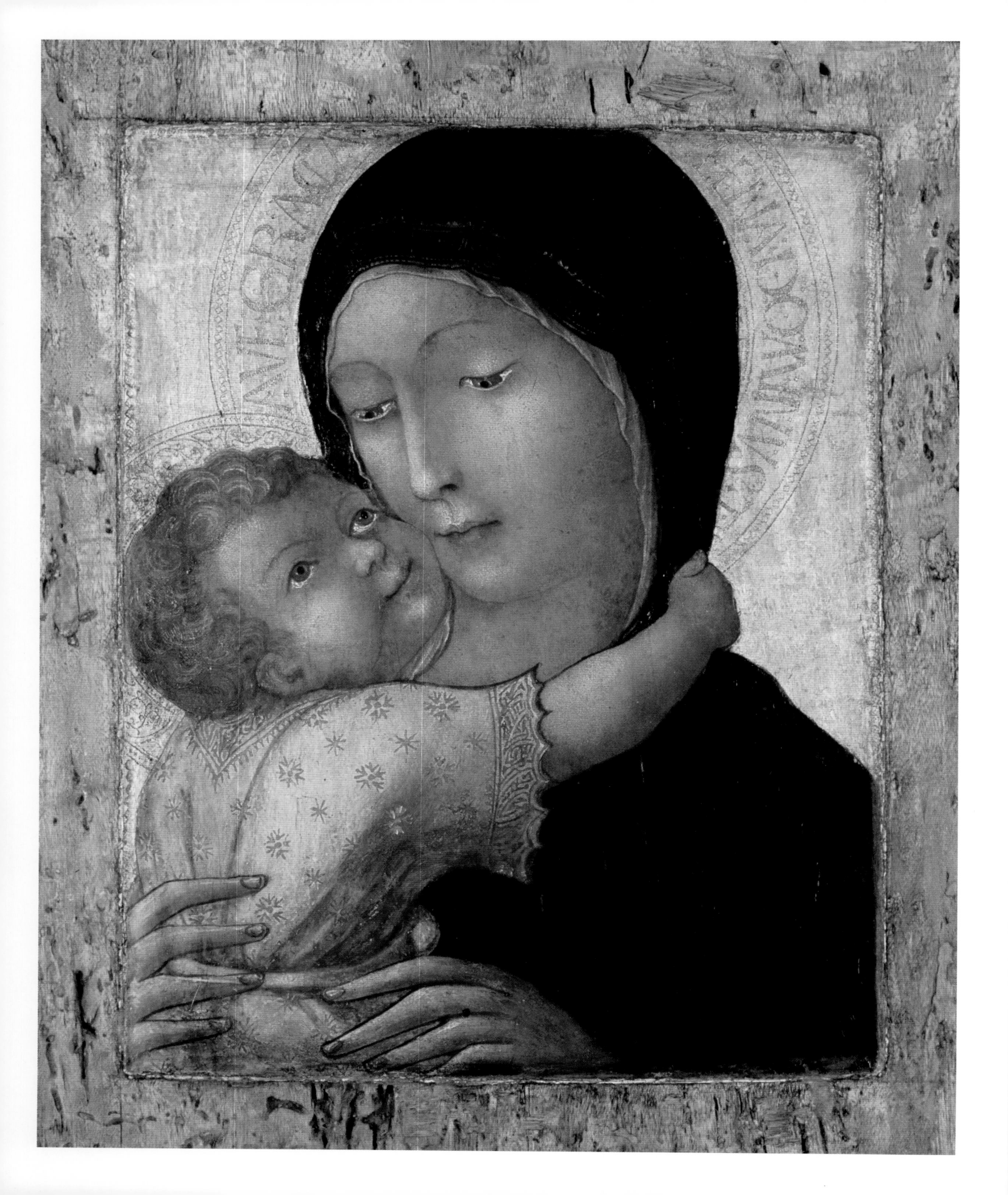

Mary, the Mother of Jesus

In 431, the Emperor Theodosius II assembled the bishops for an Ecumenical Council in Ephesus (in present-day Turkey), under the authority of Pope Celestine I. The Council decreed, among other things, that it is legitimate to call Mary "the Mother of God" (*Theotokos*), to show that Jesus is both "true God and true man" at the same time. This would have considerable influence on the depictions of Mary down through the ages.

This *Virgin with Child* from 1470 is a mystery. An expression of the Sienese style, it is the work of an artist from Verona, Liberale da Verona (*ca.* 1445–1527/1529). While resembling the archaic Byzantine Virgins, it has the grace of the Gothic Virgins and already many of the naturalist innovations of the Renaissance—which was starting in Italy when it was painted. Although very traditional in its technique, it is nonetheless charming for its fanciful, poetic imagination.

A renowned painter and illuminator, Liberale illumined many works of the monastery of Monte Oliveto Maggiore and the Piccolomini Library in Siena and produced several paintings, including this Virgin painted on wood. The work is preserved today in the collection of Baron Lindenau, a well-informed collector of Italian primitives, which in his time were largely unknown, who in the early 19th century created a museum to make his treasures accessible and to make the art that he loved better known.

This Virgin is the heir of the Byzantine icons depicting Our Lady of Tenderness, the *Eleusa*, which dramatize a deep mystical union between Mary and the Child Jesus. Indeed, here the Mother's eyes are completely on the Child who embraces her. Mary retains the sacred character and the elongated eyes of the Byzantine tradition, but the Child is quite modern in the liveliness of his features. The viewer sees what the tenderness that unites them expresses about these two persons. Their attitudes are delicate, their movements gracious and spontaneous. The Child's smile borders on a masterpiece, it succeeds so well in being both natural and delightfully childlike. ■

THE BIBLE – LK 1:46-53

And Mary said, "My soul magnifies the Lord, and my spirit rejoices in God my Savior, for he has regarded the low estate of his handmaiden. For behold, henceforth all generations will call me blessed; for he who is mighty has done great things for me, and holy is his name. And his mercy is on those who fear him from generation to generation. He has shown strength with his arm, he has scattered the proud in the imagination of their hearts, he has put down the mighty from their thrones, and exalted those of low degree; he has filled the hungry with good things, and the rich he has sent empty away."

Virgin with Child
Liberale da Verona (*ca.* 1445–1527/1529)
Ca. 1470
Tempera on wood, 18.5 x 15 in
Altenburg, Lindenau Museum

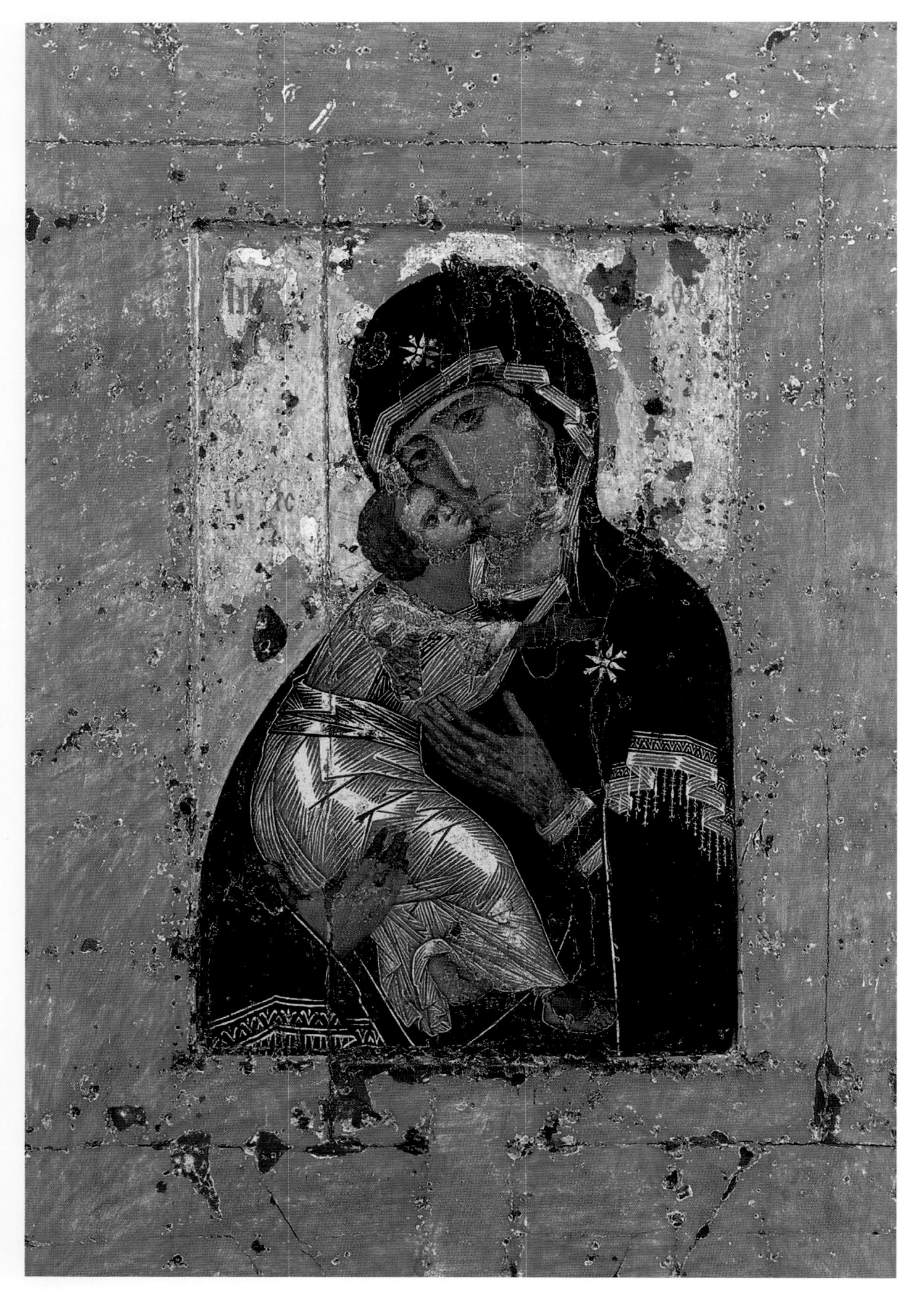

Our Lady of Vladimir,
called *The Virgin Eleusa,*
Early 12th century
Tempera on wood, 41 x 27 in
Moscow, Tretyakov Gallery,
Church of Saint Nicholas in Tomachi

Charles Dickens (1812–1870) was an English author, and remains widely regarded as one of the greatest writers in the English language. Among his many famous works are *A Christmas Carol, Great Expectations*, and *A Tale of Two Cities*.

The Life of Our Lord, written for his children between the years 1846 and 1849 was first published in 1934 by Simon & Schuster. It is a simple retelling of the life of Jesus, based on the Gospel of Luke.

Noel

CHARLES DICKENS

Now the great place of all that country was Jerusalem—just as London is the great place in England—and at Jerusalem the king lived, whose name was King Herod. Some wise men came one day, from a country a long way off in the East, and said to the king, "We have seen a star in the sky, which teaches us to know that a child is born in Bethlehem who will live to be a man whom all people will love." When King Herod heard this, he was jealous, for he was a wicked man. But he pretended not to be, and said to the wise men, "Whereabouts is this child?" And the wise men said "We don't know. But we think the star will show us; for the star has been moving on before us, all the way here, and is now standing still in the sky." Then Herod asked them to see if the star would shew them where the child lived, and ordered them, if they found the child, to come back to him. So they went out, and the star went on, over their heads a little way before them, until it stopped over the house where the child was. This was very wonderful, but God ordered it to be so.

When the star stopped, the wise men went in, and saw the child with Mary his Mother. They loved him very much, and gave him some presents. Then they went away. But they did not go back to King Herod; for they thought he was jealous, though he had not said so. So they went away, by night, back into their own country. And an Angel came, and told Joseph and Mary to take the child into a country called Egypt, or Herod would kill him. So they escaped too, in the night—the father, the mother, and the child—and arrived there, safely.

Forty days after childbirth, Jewish mothers traditionally traveled to the Temple in Jerusalem for a purification rite. On this occasion the parents offered an animal in sacrifice. Mary and Joseph offered a pair of turtledoves, which was the offering prescribed for the poor. At the same time, the parents of Jesus performed the rite of "presentation": in memory of the Passover (liberation from slavery in Egypt), firstborn sons had to be symbolically "redeemed" or "ransomed." In fact they were considered as belonging to God since he had spared the firstborn of the Hebrews when he inflicted the ten plagues on the Egyptians (Ex 7–12).

Presentation of Jesus in the Temple

On the detail of this fresco, Simeon has just received the Infant Jesus from the hands of the Virgin Mary and has taken him in his arms. The old man was *righteous and devout* (Lk 2:25); according to the Gospel, God had revealed to him that he would not die before seeing the Messiah. His encounter with Jesus brings to a close the expectation that had been voiced by a long line of prophets, starting from the election of Israel. And just look: on the side on which the Infant is situated, the green of his robe is as though transfigured into a golden light; thus the hope that had been handed down and reinforced from generation to generation until Simeon dissolves into the reality whose coming had been so longingly desired.

Then the elderly holy man intoned the canticle that would become the famous *Nunc dimittis*, which is traditionally sung at Night Prayer.

In seeing Jesus, Simeon claims that he has seen the salvation that God prepared during the long and tortuous advance of all the sacred history recorded in the Bible. To mark this clearly, Fra Angelico tilts Simeon's head so that he can gaze better at the dear little face of him whom the Bible calls *the fairest of the children of men* (Ps 45:3).

My eyes have seen, Simeon testifies. What have they seen? *The salvation,* he declares. But what does Fra Angelico show? An infant, ultimately and in all respects similar to the children of men, wrapped up in such a way, moreover, that he is unable to make the slightest gesture. What does this mean? Is salvation from God nothing but the love of an inoffensive little child? Certainly, his name is Jesus, which means "God saves." But how will the promised salvation be accomplished through him, with him, and in him?

Fra Angelico gives the answer in another work, entitled *The Descent from the Cross*, which is also located in the Convent of San Marco in Florence. In it we see a man who, the Gospel says, was *a good and righteous man,* like Simeon, who also *was looking for the kingdom of God* (Lk 23:50-51), and we see this man, again like Simeon, receiving Jesus into his arms, from the hands of the Virgin Mary. The man in question is Joseph of Arimathea who, in carrying the body of the dead Jesus, shows that *it is accomplished* (Jn 19:30). ■

THE BIBLE – LK 2:25-32

Now there was a man in Jerusalem, whose name was Simeon, and this man was righteous and devout, looking for the consolation of Israel, and the Holy Spirit was upon him. And it had been revealed to him by the Holy Spirit that he should not see death before he had seen the Lord's Christ. Guided by the Spirit, Simeon came into the temple; and when the parents brought in the child Jesus, to do for him what was customary under the law, Simeon took him in his arms and praised God, saying, "Master, now you are dismissing your servant in peace, according to your word; for my eyes have seen your salvation, which you have prepared in the presence of all peoples, a light for revelation to the Gentiles and for glory to your people Israel."

Presentation of Christ in the Temple, detail
Fra Angelico (*ca.* 1400–1455)
Ca. 1440
Fresco, 67 x 46 in
Florence, Museum-Convent of San Marco, cell 10

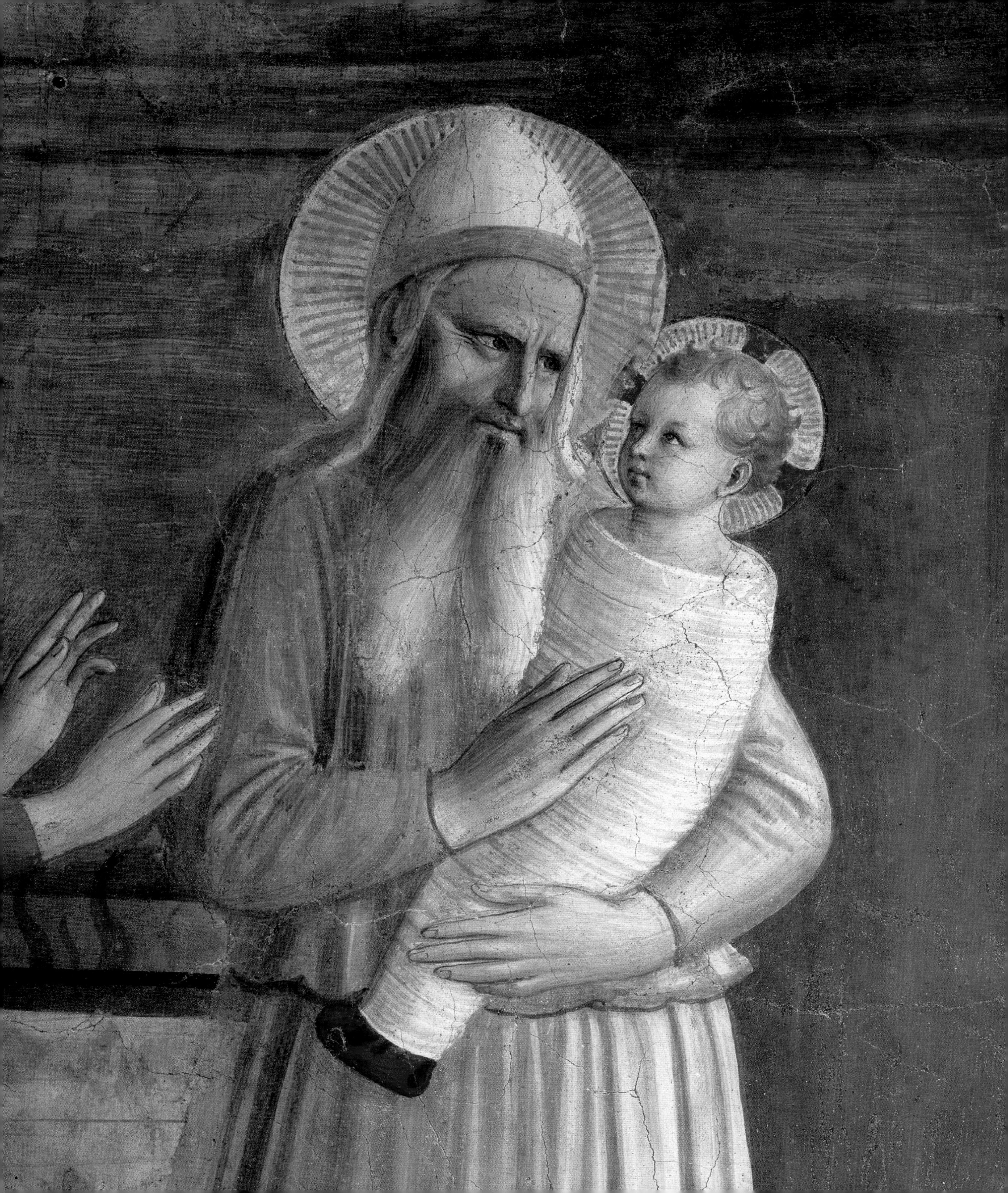

Herod the Great reigned over Judea for more than forty years, until his death in A.D. 4. Although he has rightly gone down in history as a violent, paranoid despot, he was also a great builder, a friend of Rome, and the last "great" Jewish king, who undertook the enlargement and embellishment of the second Temple in Jerusalem (five hundred years after the Babylonians destroyed the first Temple erected by Solomon around 970 B.C.). The canonical Gospels do not report the circumstances of the flight into Egypt, but the Apocrypha offer miraculous accounts of it. Most artists have not failed to take their inspiration from the latter in order to depict this episode.

The flight into Egypt

Odilon Redon (1840–1916), who was active at the same time as the Impressionists, never joined them, although he felt great sympathy toward them: he preferred to remain within the Symbolist movement, which ultimately was closer to his ideas about life and art. This *Flight into Egypt* testifies to the mysterious, dreamlike character of his creations.

In the foreground, a sun shines in the night. Within this sun, the Infant Jesus is enthroned in the arms of Mary, who is mounted on a donkey. The source of the sunlight, with his little hand outstretched, shows to his father Joseph the road to follow. And see how the light engenders the color that clothes the figures. Colors, in Redon's paintings, are a primordial, original reality, something of the earthly paradise that has been maintained. They are, so to speak, the fossil testimony to Creation in which, as God himself testified, *everything... was very good* (Gn 1:31). The coming into this world of the *Light born from Light* (Nicene Creed) revives the original colors and projects them onto the tree of life—which will furnish the wood of the cross. On it leans the dead tree of prostrate humanity, although it too is already bathed in the colors projected by the light. The sap of the tree of life will restore its paradisiacal colors. In the distance, even the walls of the town of Bethlehem are starting to break out of the darkness.

THE BIBLE - MT 2:13-15

Now when they had departed, behold, an angel of the Lord appeared to Joseph in a dream and said, "Rise, take the child and his mother, and flee to Egypt, and remain there till I tell you; for Herod is about to search for the child, to destroy him." And he rose and took the child and his mother by night, and departed to Egypt, and remained there until the death of Herod. This was to fulfil what the Lord had spoken by the prophet, "Out of Egypt have I called my son."

While inviting the viewer to meditate on his work, Odilon Redon wishes to say that everyone has to flee the menacing shadows that Herod's pitch-black soul has created. If we can put it this way, he would like to initiate us into the art of recapturing colors. Nevertheless, this *Flight into Egypt* must not be read as a mystical work. Redon refused to let critics describe him as a spiritualist painter. He protested that the spiritual element in a work of art does not come from the artist but is a constitutive dimension of nature. Of this nature which is depicted by the painter, the spiritual element is the part of reality that we do not know how to see. Thus, for the artist, all art consists of depicting the visible in such a way that the invisible dimension is revealed thereby. ■

Flight into Egypt
Odilon Redon (1840–1916)
Ca. 1903
Oil on canvas, 17.9 x 15 in
Paris, Orsay Museum

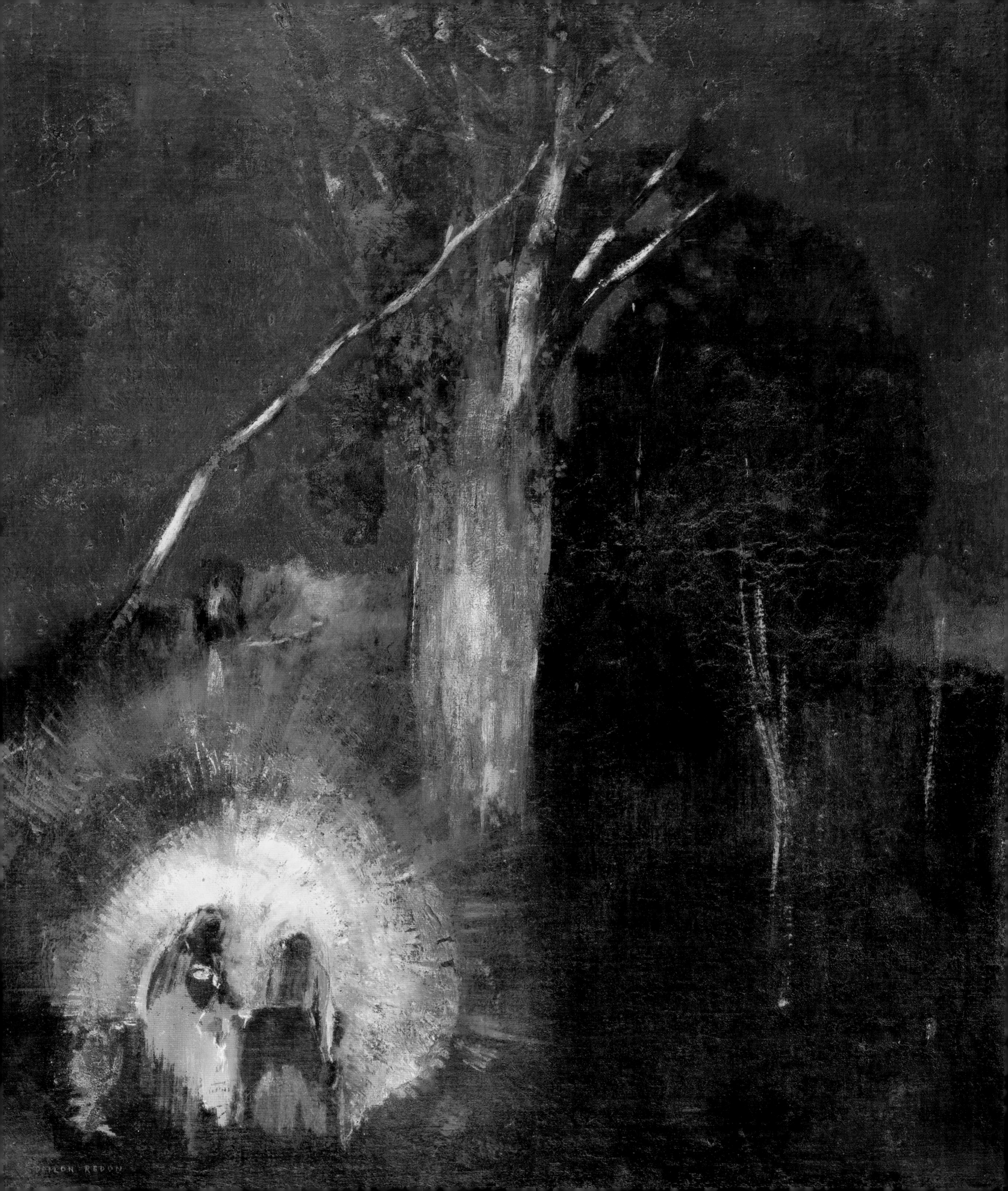
REDON

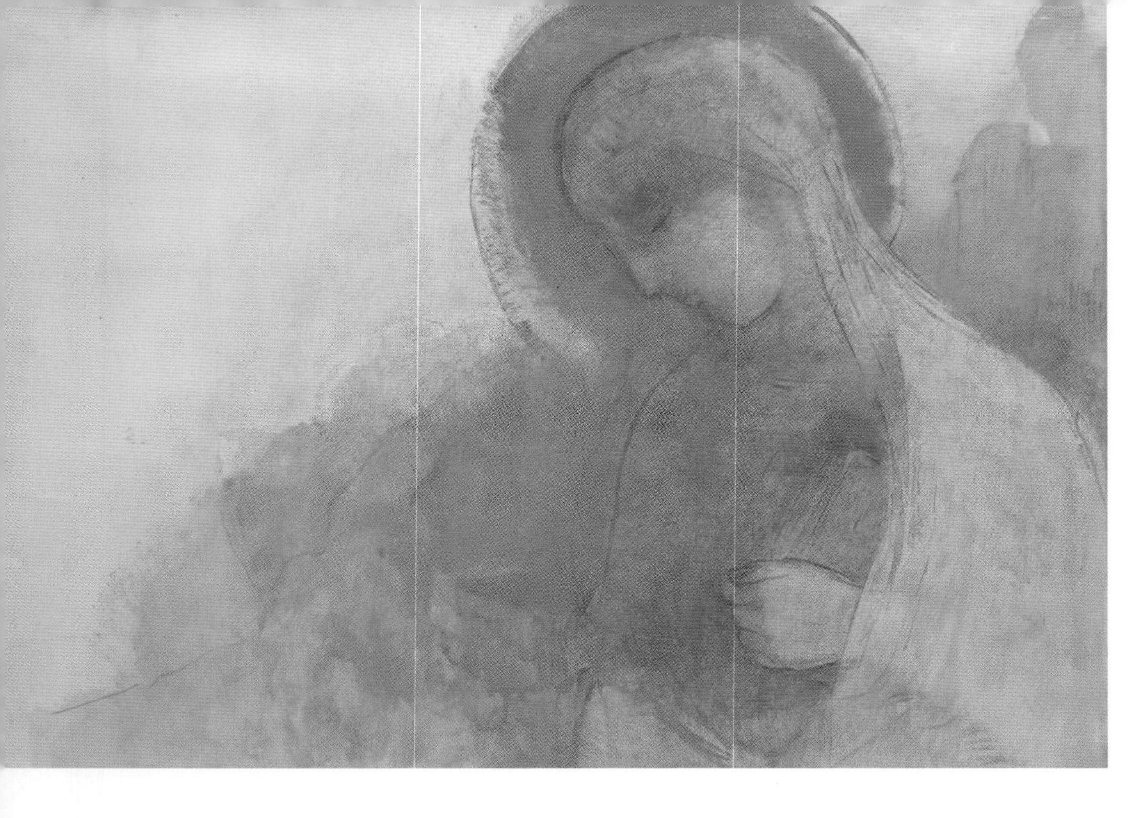

Blessed Virgin
Odilon Redon
1916
Oil on canvas, 19.8 x 27.2 in
Bordeaux, Museum of Fine Arts

When Odilon Redon died on July 6, 1916, this canvas was left uncompleted on his easel.

REDON: BETWEEN SYMBOLIST CLAIMS AND CATHOLIC TENETS

If Odilon Redon is associated with the Symbolist movement, it is because, being a foreigner to the realism of Gustave Courbet or of Édouard Manet (whom he admired, however), he was inspired by the works of Gustave Moreau.

Redon is the most literary of French painters, and his career took off at the same moment as the rise of Symbolism, a movement promoted mainly by writers.

In 1886, in a "Literary Manifesto" published in *Le Figaro*, the poet Jean Moréas defined symbolist poetry as follows: "An enemy of instruction, declamation, false sensibility, and objective description, symbolic poetry seeks to clothe the idea in a sensible form."

Gabriel-Albert Aurier in turn gave a definition of Symbolism in 1891 in the magazine *Mercure de France*: "The work of art must be first of all ideist, since its sole ideal will be the expression of the idea; secondly symbolist, since it will express this idea in a form; thirdly synthetic, since it will write its forms or signs according to a general way of understanding; fourthly subjective, since the object in it will never be considered as an object, but as a sign perceived by the subject; fifthly the work of art must be decorative."

Redon's connection with Catholicism was rather tangential. It was based primarily on friendships: "My art has given me only good friendships among Catholics. They must have something going for them," he wrote to Gabriel Frizeau on September 17, 1909.

These ardent Catholic friendships sometimes ended badly, for instance with Joris-Karl Huysmans or Francis Jammes. On questions concerning faith and spirituality, Redon would always be quite reticent; in this respect he is opposed to the commitment of a painter like Maurice Denis.

The fact remains that the paintings of Redon, who was not a Christian in the strict sense, are bathed in a mystical, Christian universe and repeatedly address evangelical and biblical themes, as had been the case with Gustave Moreau before him.

We can even say that the figure of Christ occupied a central place in Redon's searches during the years 1895–1910: many depictions of the crucifixion, some of them heterodox, several versions of *Christ and the Samaritan woman*, a personal copy of the Christ by Matthias Grünewald, a walking Christ, a *Deposition from the Cross*, and other religious scenes in all genres, including several *Flights into Egypt*.

A hypothesis has been proposed to explain the repeated presence of *The flight into Egypt* in Redon's work, connected with the scene's similar appeal to one of his mentors, the painter and engraver Rodolphe Bresdin, who is partly at the origin of his spiritual development.

Here is what Redon wrote about Rodolphe Bresdin: "What we find everywhere, almost from one end of his work to the other, is man in love with solitude, fleeing the world, fleeing passionately beneath a sky with no fatherland, in the anguish of an exile without hope and without end. This dream, this constant anxiety appears in a great many variations. Sometimes it is in the form of the Divine Infant in the *flight into Egypt* reproduced so often by the artist. Sometimes it is a whole family, a legion, an army, a whole tribe fleeing, always fleeing civilized humanity."

M. C.

V. The flight into Egypt

HENRY WADSWORTH LONGFELLOW

Henry Wadsworth Longfellow (1807–1882) was an American educator, translator, and poet who spent most of his life in New England. Although best remembered for his stirring patriotic ballad "Paul Revere's Ride" and shorter poems about domestic life, he also published well-researched, book-length poems on historical and legendary subjects (*Evangeline, Hiawatha*). Because of his extensive travels and wide reading in the poetry of many nations, his writings transcend "American literature" and enter the mainstream of Western European culture.

The excerpt is from Longfellow's "The Nativity: A Miracle Play," written in the simple, didactic style of the medieval "mystery plays," pageants which told biblical stories in rhymed verse. The encounter between the Holy Family and robbers is not the poet's invention; the legend goes back to the apocrypha and is mentioned by the 4th-century Church historian Eusebius.

Henry Wadsworth Longfellow, "The Nativity: A Miracle Play," in *The Golden Legend* (Boston: Ticknor, Reed, and Fields, 1852), 142-145.

Here shall JOSEPH *come in, leading an ass, on which are seated* MARY *and the* CHILD.

Mary. Here will we rest us, under these
Underhanging branches of the trees,
Where robins chant their Litanies,
And canticles of joy.

Joseph. My saddle-girths have given way
With trudging through the heat to-day
To you I think it is but play
To ride and hold the boy.

Mary. Hark! how the robins shout and sing,
As if to hail their infant King!
I will alight at yonder spring
To wash his little coat.

Joseph. And I will hobble well the ass,
Lest, being loose upon the grass,
He should escape; for, by the mass,
He is nimble as a goat.

(*Here* MARY *shall alight and go to the spring.*)

Mary. O Joseph! I am much afraid,
For men are sleeping in the shade;
I fear that we shall be waylaid,
And robbed and beaten sore!

(*Here a band of robbers shall be seen sleeping, two of whom shall rise and come forward.*)

Dumachus. Cock's soul! deliver up your gold!

Joseph. I pray you, Sirs, let go your hold!
Of wealth I have no store.

Dumachus. Give up your money!

Titus. Prithee cease!
Let these good people go in peace!

Dumachus. First let them pay for their release,
And then go on their way.

Titus. These forty groats I give in fee,
If thou wilt only silent be.

Mary. May God be merciful to thee
Upon the Judgment Day!

Jesus. When thirty years shall have gone by,
I at Jerusalem shall die,
By Jewish hands exalted high
On the accursèd tree.
Then on my right and my left side,
These thieves shall both be crucified
And Titus thenceforth shall abide
In paradise with me.

The plausibility of the massacre of the Innocents has been questioned by certain historians. Yet Herod's pathological jealousy is attested, and several sources note a massacre of newborns that he commanded. Thus, for example, the Roman writer Macrobius, in his *Saturnalia* (III, 4, 11), repeats in the 4th century the following anecdote: "When the Emperor Augustus learned that among the children of Syria [the Roman province of Judea, renamed Syria-Palestine in 135] below the age of two years killed on the orders of Herod, King of the Jews, was his own son, he said that it was better to be Herod's pig than his son."

The massacre of the Innocents

Here is a look that cannot be forgotten. A look in which terror vies with incomprehension and a cry for help. This woman is not alone in expressing the throes of fear, and in the eyes of her child we can also read the intensity of the nightmare that the population of Bethlehem is experiencing. With an economy of means for the setting—which in no way detracts from the novel framing of the scene or from the intensity of the almost photographic rendering of it—Léon Cogniet (1794–1880), a contemporary of Théodore Géricault and Eugène Delacroix, plunges the spectator into the indescribable chaos caused by Herod's search-and-destroy mission. He seems to make us hear the cry of horror and despair of the prophet Jeremiah, repeated by the evangelist Matthew:

> *A voice was heard in Ramah, wailing and loud lamentation,*
> *Rachel weeping for her children;*
> *she refused to be consoled,*
> *because they were no more.* (Mt 2:18)

The sweet peacefulness of Christmas night is long gone! This mother draws the viewer with her into the night of anguish in this remote corner where the footsteps of that other mother who is dashing down the stairs resound, combined with the cries of pursuit and of the confrontations that can be made out in the background. The spectator, too, is attacked by the jagged edge of this section of a ruined wall which assaults the eye and, surprisingly foreshortened, gives a depth and a poignant realism to the composition. So much so that we wonder whether this mother's hand firmly silencing her dear child will enable her to escape the murderous madness. ■

THE BIBLE – MT 2:16

Then Herod, when he saw that he had been tricked by the Wise Men, was in a furious rage, and he sent and killed all the male children in Bethlehem and in all that region who were two years old or under, according to the time which he had ascertained from the Wise Men.

Massacre of the Innocents
Léon Cogniet (1794–1880)
1824
Oil on canvas, 102.9 x 89.9 in
Rennes, Museum of Fine Arts

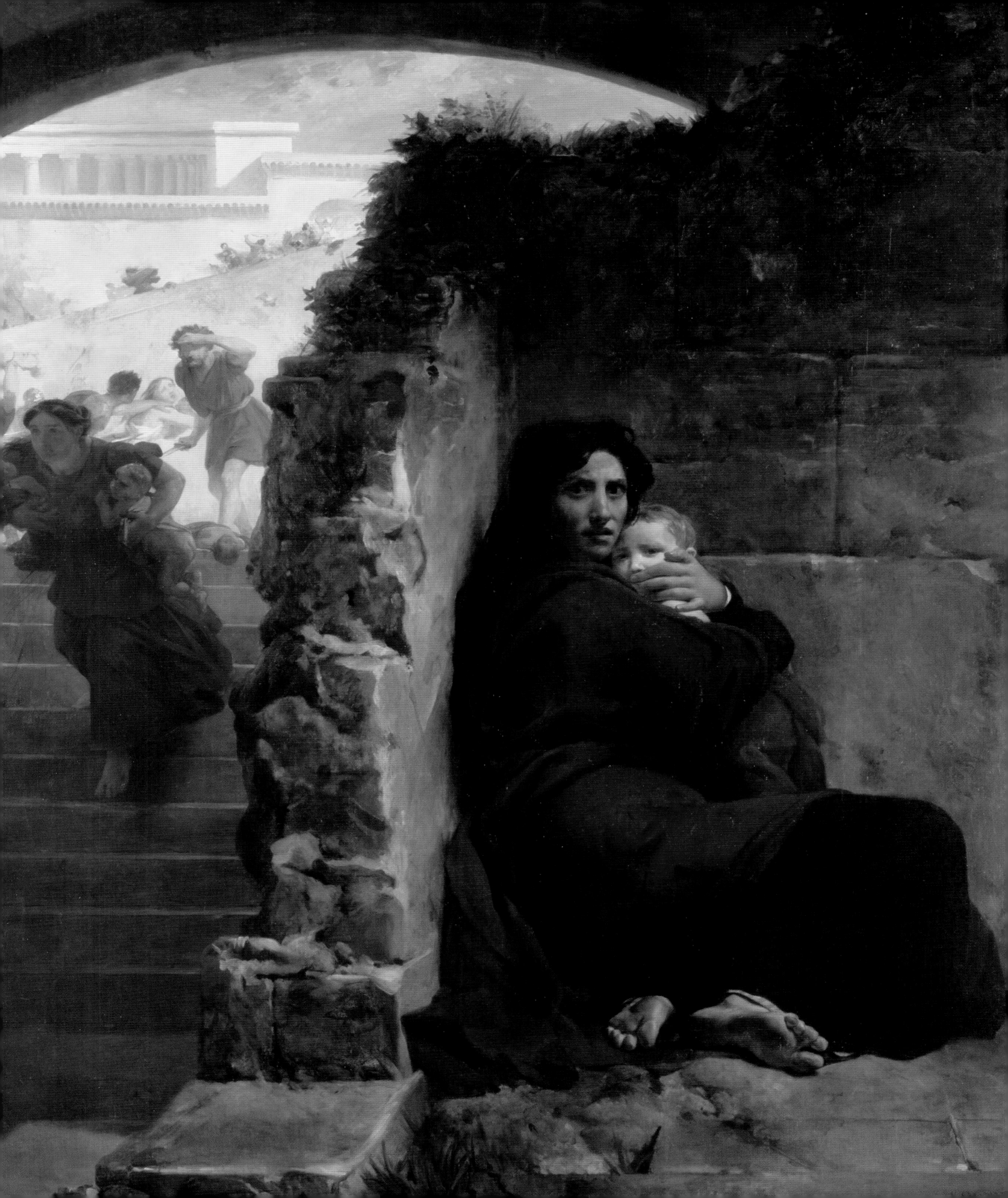

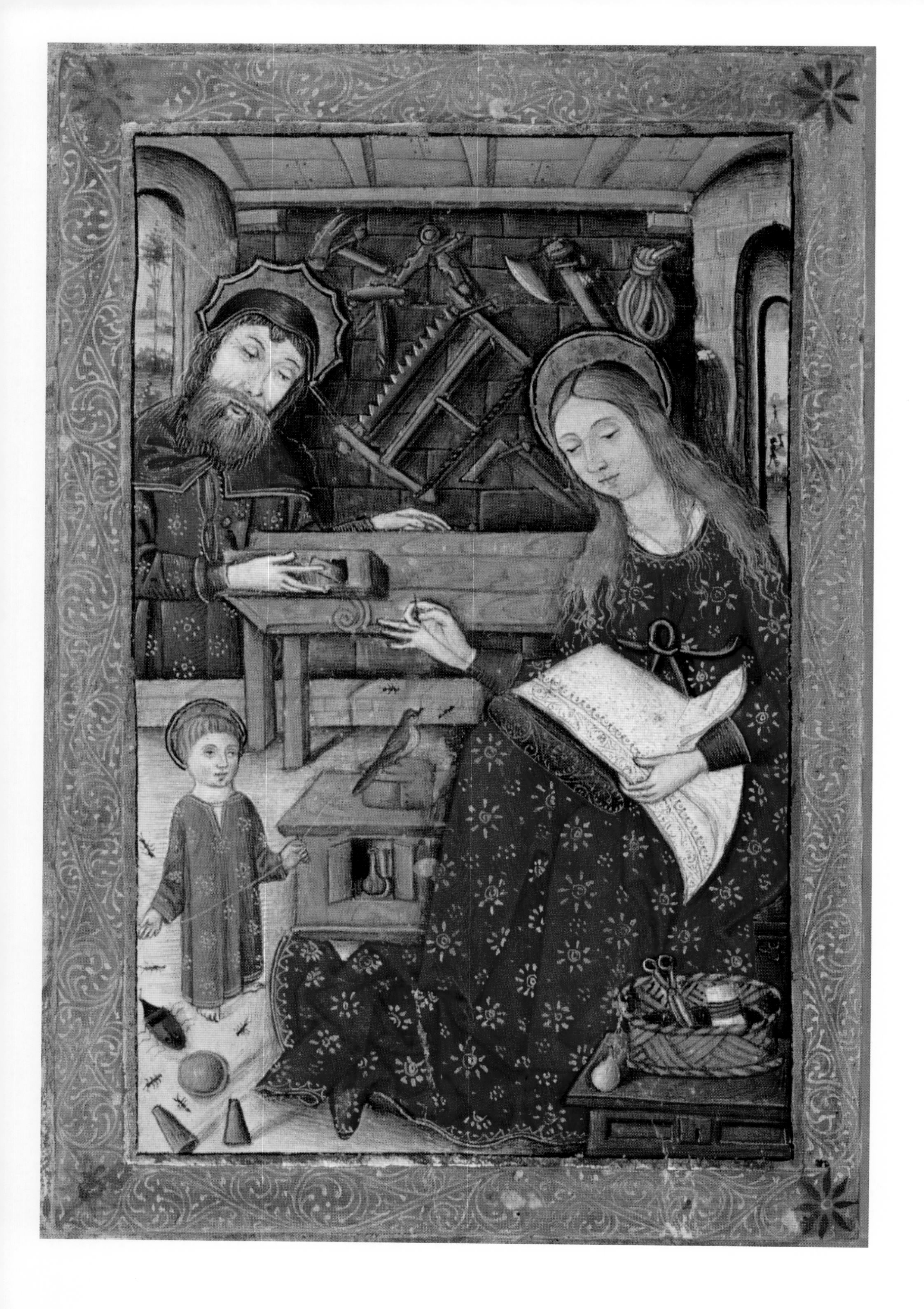

The Holy Family

Between the return to Nazareth and the beginning of Jesus' public life, around thirty years later, the four Gospels relate almost nothing about what is conventionally called "the hidden life" of Jesus, with the noteworthy exception of the episode of the Finding in the Temple (*cf.* page 107). In contrast, the Apocrypha are quite long-winded about this "hidden life" and adorn it with fanciful episodes, each one more miraculous than the rest. Some artists did not fail to draw on them, particularly to provide images of the Holy Family which were greatly appreciated by the faithful.

In the house in Nazareth, the family of Jesus offers a pleasant picture of domestic happiness. This happiness is a blessing. Painted in a coded language, the miniature teaches the story of Jesus who, after passing through suffering and death, will save humanity and will open for it the gates to a blessed eternal life.

Therefore we have to interpret the signs that are offered behind the appearances. Mary, the Mother of Jesus, is neatly hemming a white cloth that foretells the shroud with which they will cover her Son's remains after his execution. A door on the side of a little chest opens to show a flask. This precious receptacle, through which light passes without changing it, is a metaphor for the virginal womb that bore Jesus for nine months: it was penetrated by *the Light from Light*, which nevertheless did not affect her virginity. And there, on the table, is a pear. It symbolizes the sweetness and smoothness of the feelings of the woman to whom Christians will give the title of *Theotokos*, a Greek word meaning "Mother of God." For his part, Joseph, her spouse, planes a joist that suggests the wood of the cross.

On the floor, some ants, working humbly in obscurity, present a model of the good, frugal Christian, who is honest, virtuous, and sociable. There are seven of them. This sacred number signifies the evangelical perfection to which imitation of the Holy Family's humility leads.

As for Jesus, he wears the face of childhood, an allegory for each human person who is called to be reborn to a new life so as to enter into the kingdom of God. However, this little human being reveals his divinity by holding a domesticated songbird, the olive-tree warbler, by a string attached to its foot. This tame sparrow, which surpasses even the nightingale by the virtuosity of its vocalises, symbolizes the Word of God come down from heaven to dwell among us, in the condition of captives of the flesh. At the feet of the God-Child we see a firebug. Its "fiery body" testifies to the love with which the Son of God burns for humanity. And, when we look at it closely, we discover drawn on its back the stylized face of Christ.

THE BIBLE – LK 2:33, 51

And [the Child's] father and his mother marveled at what was said about him.... And he went down with them and came to Nazareth, and was obedient to them; and his mother kept all these things in her heart.

This charmingly naive image is an invitation to rediscover the rich symbolism that enabled 15th-century Christians, who were often illiterate, to read the life of Jesus and to take part in its teaching, even in the contemplation of the humblest objects in their everyday life. ■

The Holy Family
After 1461
Illumination on parchment, 7.7 x 5.1 in
London, The British Library, Catalan Book of Hours
ms. Add. 18193, f° 48 v°

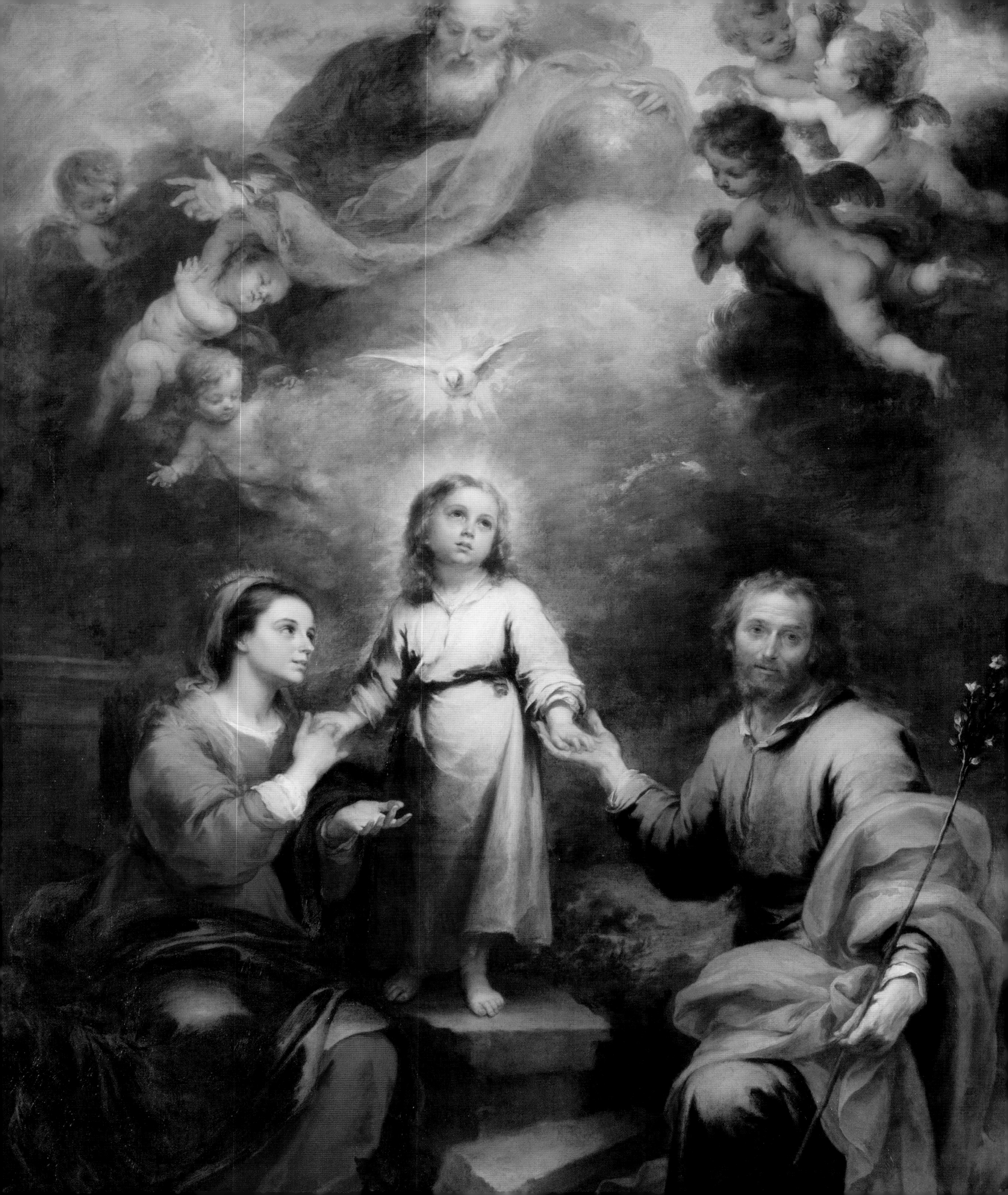

Edgar Allan Poe (1809–1849) is best known for his macabre short stories and poetry, and to some extent as a pioneer of crime fiction. Yet this towering figure of 19th-century American Romanticism was strikingly versatile, as this tender meditation on the Angelus attests.

The Two Trinities
Bartolomé Esteban Murillo (1617–1682)
Ca. 1681
Oil on canvas, 115 x 81.5 in
London, National Gallery

Murillo shares here his meditation on the figure of the Child Jesus. He depicts him at the center of the painting, perched on a ruined earthly pedestal, tenderly offering his hands to Joseph and Mary, so as to form, joined with them, a horizontal trinity which is Humanity. At the same time, the Holy Spirit and God the Father hover over him and encircle him with their glory, constituting a vertical Trinity which is God. Thus, in this Child, the earthly and the heavenly, the visible universe and the invisible universe, the human and the divine converge into one.

Hymn

EDGAR ALLAN POE

At morn—at noon—at twilight dim—
Maria! thou hast heard my hymn!
In joy and woe—in good and ill—
Mother of God, be with me still!
When the Hours flew brightly by,
And not a cloud obscured the sky,
My soul, lest it should truant be,
Thy grace did guide to thine and thee.
Now, when storms of Fate o'ercast
Darkly my Present and my Past,
Let my future radiant shine
With sweet hopes of thee and thine.

After the Council of Trent (1545–1563), the ecclesiastical authorities became less tolerant of the circulation of legendary accounts cobbled together by the apocryphal gospels. In order to treat the childhood of Jesus, then, artists took their inspiration from the meditations of the great spiritual writers of their era, particularly Teresa of Avila in Spain. Then, based on facts attested by the canonical Gospels, it was a matter of creating a scene from the childhood of Jesus that symbolically prefigured the work that he would perform later on, during his public life.

Jesus and his father

When Bartolomé Esteban Murillo was the master in Seville, Sebastián Martínez (1615–1667) was the great painter in Jaén, the gateway to Andalusia on the edge of La Mancha. Both artists received most of their commissions from Church organizations concerned with evangelizing the people through culture. Now, during that period in Spain, the Church had been invited by the monarchy to strike a new balance between her promotion of the vocation of marriage and her support for religious and priestly vocations. Thus, through their works, Martínez and Murillo sang the praises of the Christian virtues of familial life. They liked painting scenes of the Holy Family and the Child Jesus to remind the faithful that they could "follow Jesus" by founding a family, so as *to give thanks for the miracles that God unceasingly works in it*, just as well as by entering a monastery. Besides, wasn't this the invitation that Jesus himself had extended to the paralyzed man after healing him (LK 5:24-25)?

THE BIBLE - MT 13:54-56

And coming to his own country he taught them in their synagogue, so that they were astonished, and said, "Where did this man get this wisdom and these mighty works? Is not this the carpenter's son? Is not his mother called Mary? And are not his brethren James and Joseph and Simon and Judas? And are not all his sisters with us? Where then did this man get all this?"

This painting by Martínez admirably reproduces the expression that all parents in the world have seen—with surprise and emotion—drawn on the face of their child from a tender age, when with a smile and a look he is able to testify to both the fervency of his love and the strength of his own will.

The Child Jesus was about to take some fruit, but Joseph his father firmly holds his arm and prevents him. Here, the basket of fruit symbolizes the mission of Jesus, the business of God, his Heavenly Father, to which he must dedicate himself until it is finally accomplished in his Passion. The purple grapes symbolize divinity; the white—humanity. Between the two the red grapes represent Christ, "true God and true man." It is also the color of the tunic of the Child Jesus and that of the blood mixed with water that would gush from the heart of the Crucified Lord, pierced by the Roman soldier's lance. The pomegranate, containing a myriad of seeds, represents the body of his Church, made up of myriad members. The apple, which recalls the forbidden fruit picked by Eve, symbolizes the ransom of sinful humanity by Christ's sacrifice. Allegorically, the Child seems in a hurry to start his mission, but Joseph, with the light of God the Father around him like an aura, corrects him: "Your hour has not yet come." ■

Saint Joseph and the Child Jesus
Sebastián Martínez (1615–1667)
Ca. 1650
Oil on canvas, 56 x 38 in
Madrid, Prado Museum

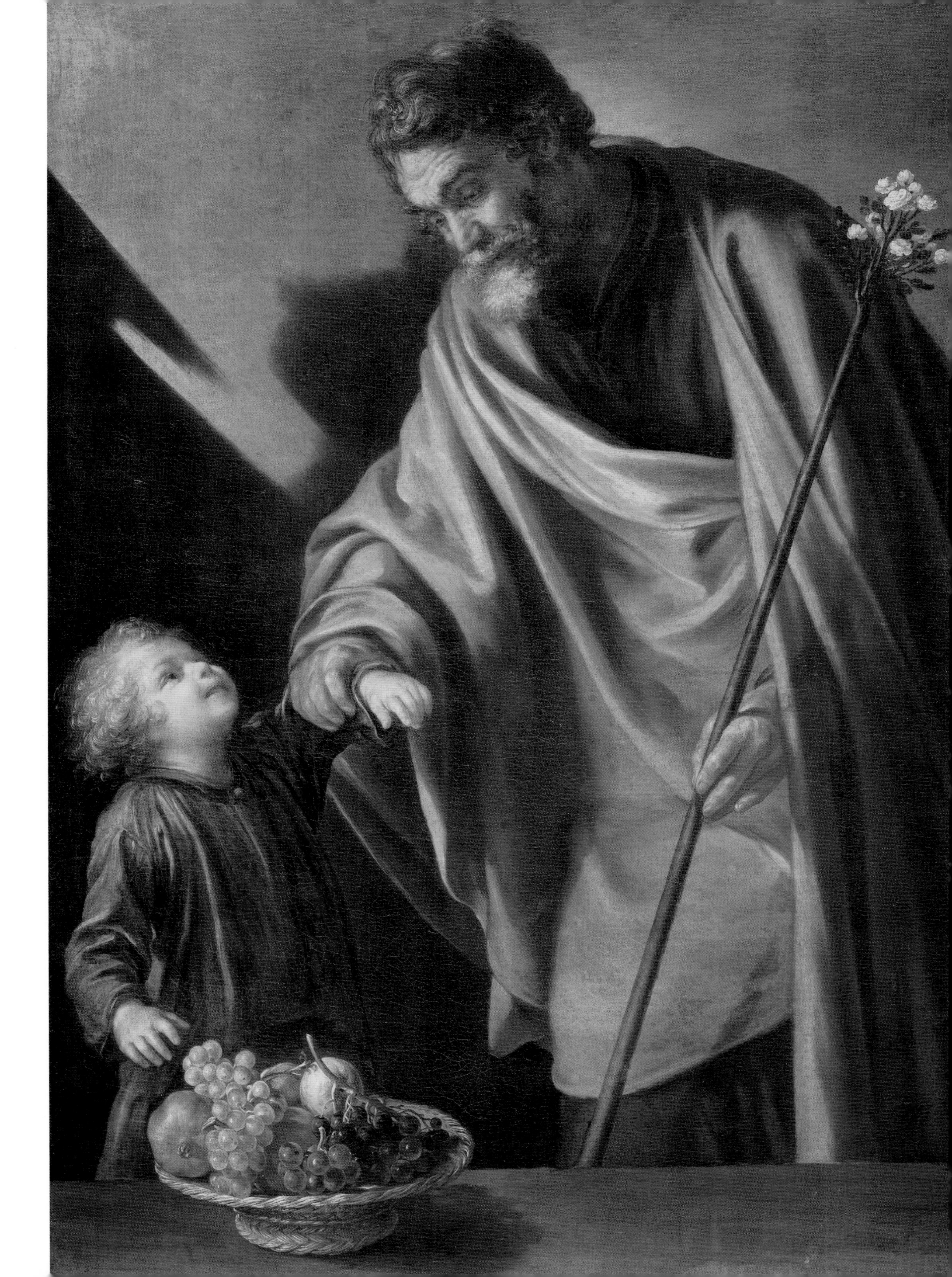

"The fairest of the sons of men"

A disciple of William Bouguereau, Émile Munier (1840–1895) is classified as a member of the artistic current of academism, an heir of Jean Auguste Dominique Ingres and Camille Corot. This movement advocated a return to classical values and techniques. It must be acknowledged that, however charming and moving they may appear to be, some of Munier's works are on the verge of sentimentality, or even mawkishness. Nonetheless the fact remains that most of his portraits of children and adolescents reach great heights in the art of capturing and rendering on canvas a posture, a facial expression, and a depth in the eyes that reveal the soul in a very moving expression of its childhood. Munier had the gift of revealing the beauty of childlike souls, which his contemporary Thérèse de Lisieux, the "Little Flower," was to embody with such delicate splendor in the sanctorale.

In 1885, for the First Holy Communion of his only daughter Marie-Louise, Munier painted this Child Jesus. Later his daughter would say about it: "My father had a special gift for amusing the children whom he liked. I once heard him say that sometimes he was bored in the society of grownups but never with children, no matter which ones. He knew how to bring them out, both in painting and in everyday life. Didn't Jesus say that the kingdom of God belongs to those who resemble them?"

THE BIBLE – PS 45:2-3

My heart overflows with a goodly theme; I address my verses to the king; my tongue is like the pen of a ready scribe. You are the fairest of the sons of men; grace is poured upon your lips; therefore God has blessed you for ever.

According to Munier, this image of the Child Jesus invites us to meditate on the fact that Jesus, the Son of God, spent thirty years of his life on earth living humbly in a family, and only three years "on the road" teaching his disciples so as to send them on their mission. Now, it must be noted, the thirty years spent in Nazareth—ninety percent of his earthly existence—are quite legitimately part of his saving work. So much so that through contemplation of this haloed child, the painter asks us to consider that the world was saved just as much by the hidden life of Jesus as by the public life of Jesus as an adult: thus Jesus offered his entire human life, from the womb of Mary his Mother until his death on the cross, for the salvation of mankind. The moral that the artist intends to give to this little catechism in painting is clear: when the devil tempts us to disdain ordinary life, we are all encouraged to contemplate God as a child and to acknowledge personally that God will perform miracles right where we are, in our human condition. ■

Jesus
Émile Munier (1840–1895)
1893
Oil on canvas, 16.5 x 13.4 in
Private collection

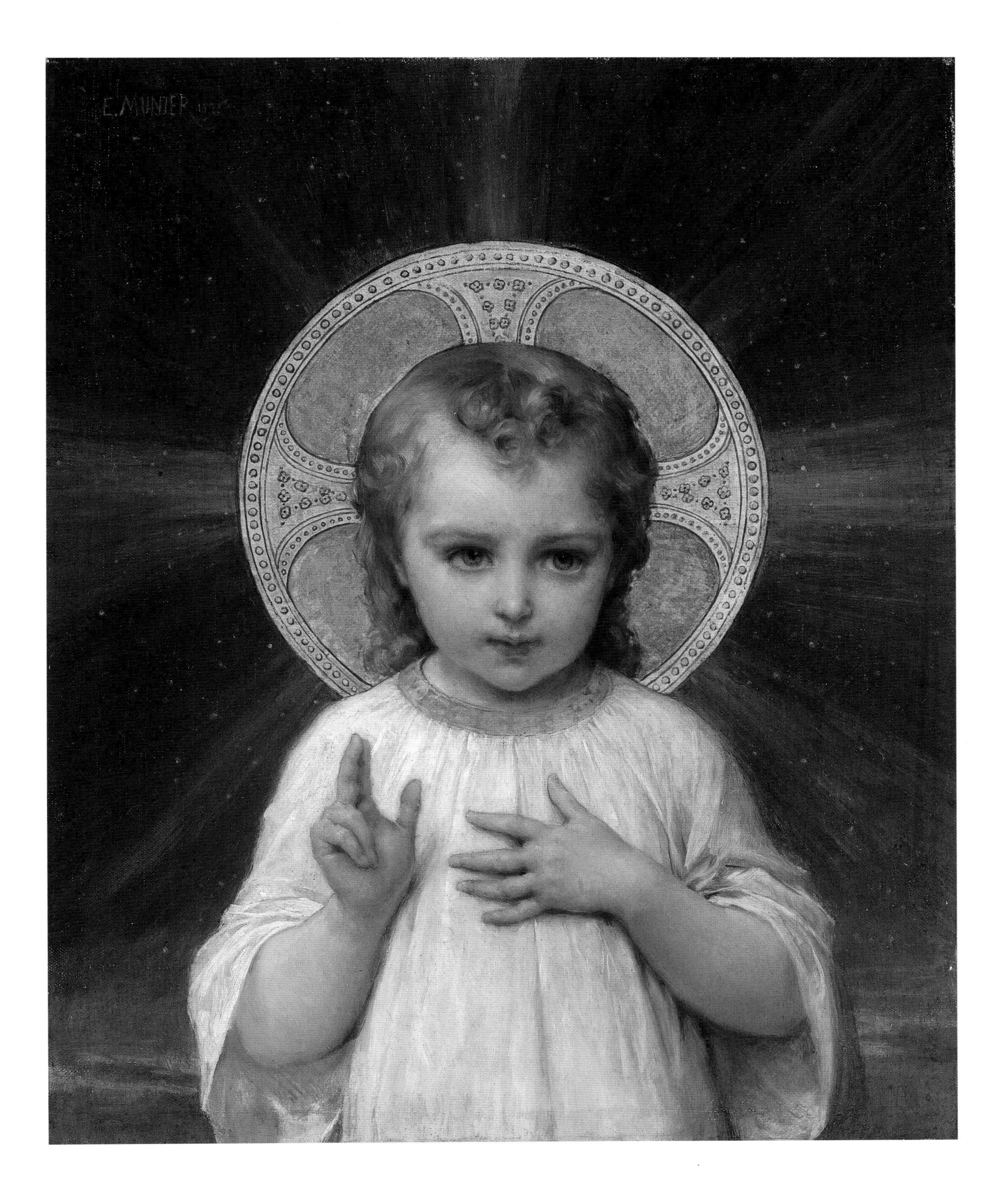
E. MUNIER

IN ART HISTORY

ACADEMISM AND ANTI-ACADEMISM IN FRANCE

The Royal Academy of Painting and Sculpture was instituted in 1648. In the 19th century, its successor, the Academy of Fine Arts, still played a lively role. Academism is marked partly by an affirmation of the hierarchy of genres proposed by the teaching of the School of Fine Arts. The subjects considered noble remain historical subjects above all, and then religious and mythological subjects; primacy is given to the study of the nude, and mastery in drawing is of capital importance. Antiquity, the Renaissance, and French neo-Classicism in the style of Jacques Louis David serve as models.

Artists would present a *morceau d'agrément*, a "piece for approval" to the Academy in order to be admitted to it. During the annual competition, the best students would win the Rome Prize, giving them the opportunity to study in Italy.

The official Salon, directed by the Academy of Fine arts, would exhibit the production of painters who satisfied the criteria of academism, and the others were rejected. Alexandre Cabanel (1823–1889), Jean Léon Gérôme (1824–1904), and William Bouguereau (1825–1905), teacher of Émile Munier (1840–1895), had glorious official careers and were strongly opposed to the nascent Impressionist movement, which they perceived as a disgrace to French painting.

This official taste, however, was vehemently criticized by those who supported a new, modern approach. Charles Baudelaire (1821–1867) praised the transgressions introduced by Eugène Delacroix (1798-1863). Gustave Courbet (1819–1877) attacked the official authorities and strayed from the conventional themes of large- and small-format painting. Soon it would be Émile Zola's turn to sound the charge against *The Birth of Venus* by Cabanel: "The goddess, drowned in a river of milk, has the appearance of a delicious *lorette* [woman of easy virtue], not made of flesh and bone—that would seem indecent—but of a sort of white and pink marzipan" (Émile Zola, *Nos peintres au Champ-de-Mars*, 1867).

In the second half of the 19th century, Édouard Manet (1832–1883) was next in line to embody modernity by his themes, his brushstroke, and his openness to foreign schools. In reality, the birth of the avant-gardes can be dated to the 1863 *Salon des refusés* [Exhibition of the rejects], even before Claude Monet (1840–1926) and Auguste Renoir (1841–1919) invented the Impressionist technique during the summer of 1869.

With Impressionism, art speaks for itself and dispenses with external referents such as mythological and biblical texts. Impressionism would ultimately find patriotic French supporters within the republican trend, which hastened its adoption by the major merchants and their clients who had come from the great liberal bourgeoisie. In the last decade of the 19th century it conquered the salons with a new genre.

In 1890, the National Society of Fine Arts "seceded" by having its own Show, marking the need to oppose the official *Salon* sponsored by the French artists who were heirs to the Academy of Fine Arts. From then on the art world has been international, and modern art in turn has shown its elitist character. This model would spread throughout Europe, as attested by the editions published by the foundation *Biennale di Venezia* [Venice Biennale] since 1895.

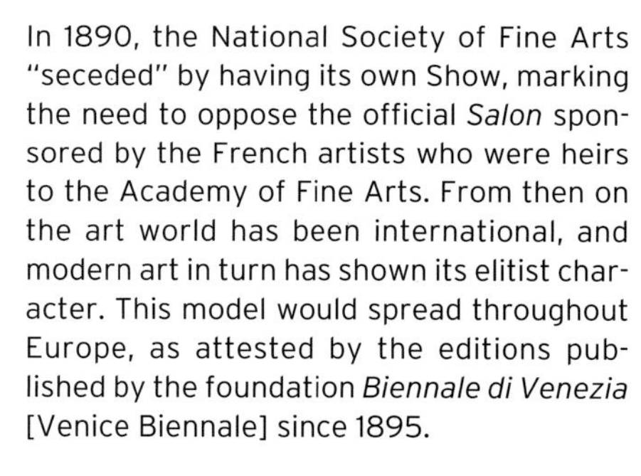

M. C.

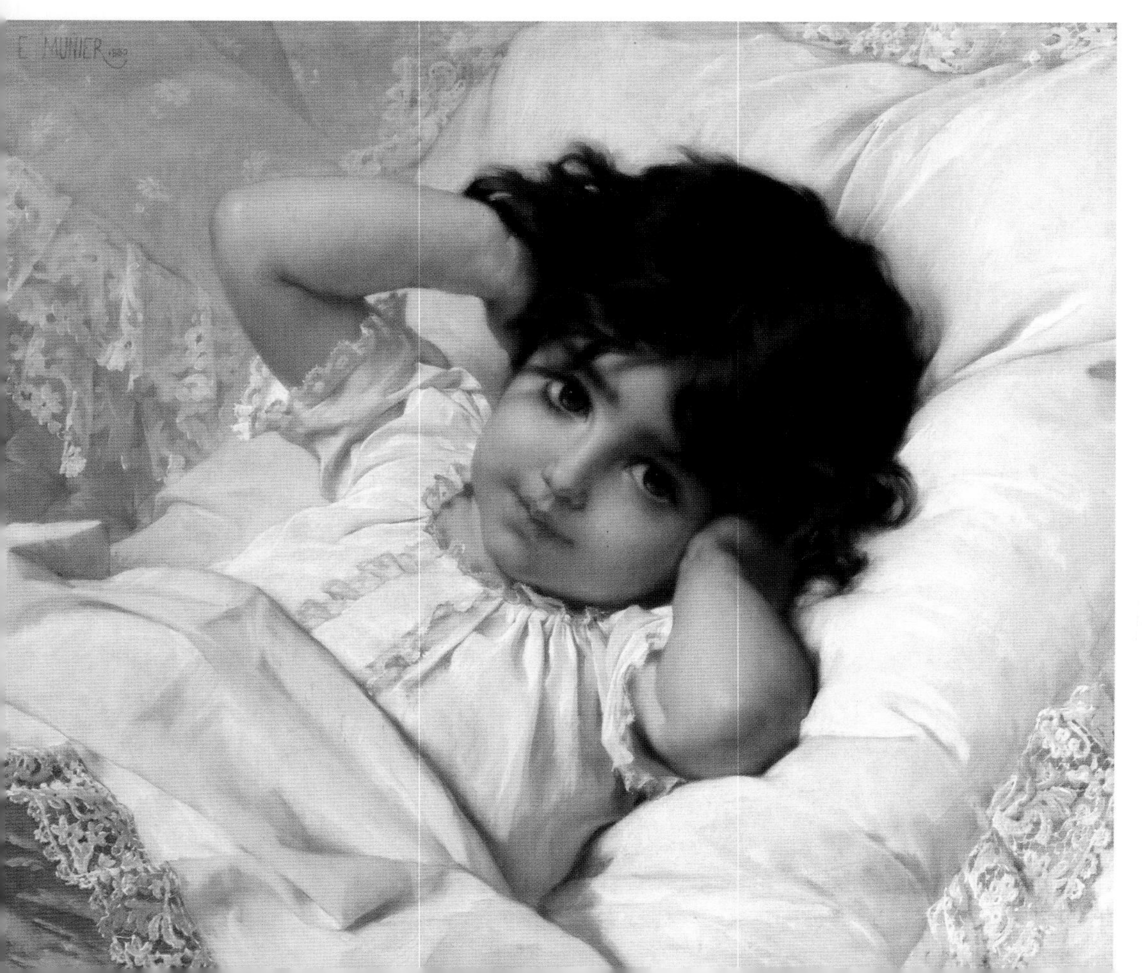

Portrait of Marie-Louise
Émile Munier (1840–1895)
1880
Oil on canvas, 17.7 x 21 in
Private collection

On the occasion of the First Holy Communion of his daughter Marie-Louise, Émile Munier painted the image of the Child Jesus.

Oscar Wilde (1854–1900), an Irish novelist, dramatist, and poet who was heavily influenced by *fin-de-siècle* aestheticism and decadence, was thrown into jail because of his homosexual behavior. His imprisonment was the occasion for a very strong spiritual experience and a conversion to Christ, as he testifies in his "Ballad of Reading Gaol" (1898). But in this passage from "The Selfish Giant," one of the stories in *The Happy Prince and Other Tales* (1888), the figure of Jesus already plays a central role: it is the very figure of love.

The wounds of love

OSCAR WILDE

Every afternoon, when school was over, the children came and played with the Giant. But the little boy whom the Giant loved was never seen again. The Giant was very kind to all the children, yet he longed for his first little friend, and often spoke of him. "How I would like to see him!" he used to say.

Years went over, and the Giant grew very old and feeble. He could not play about any more, so he sat in a huge armchair, and watched the children at their games, and admired his garden. "I have many beautiful flowers," he said; "but the children are the most beautiful flowers of all."

One winter morning he looked out of his window as he was dressing. He did not hate the Winter now, for he knew that it was merely the Spring asleep, and that the flowers were resting.

Suddenly he rubbed his eyes in wonder, and looked and looked. It certainly was a marvelous sight. In the farthest corner of the garden was a tree quite covered with lovely white blossoms. Its branches were all golden, and silver fruit hung down from them, and underneath it stood the little boy he had loved.

Downstairs ran the Giant in great joy, and out into the garden. He hastened across the grass, and came near to the child. And when he came quite close his face grew red with anger, and he said, "Who hath dared to wound thee?" For on the palms of the child's hands were the prints of two nails, and the prints of two nails were on the little feet.

"Who hath dared to wound thee?" cried the Giant; "tell me, that I may take my big sword and slay him."

"Nay!" answered the child; "but these are the wounds of Love."

"Who art thou?" said the Giant, and a strange awe fell on him, and he knelt before the little child.

And the child smiled on the Giant, and said to him, "You let me play once in your garden, to-day you shall come with me to my garden, which is Paradise."

And when the children ran in that afternoon, they found the Giant lying dead under the tree, all covered with white blossoms.

A little boy and his mother

Originally from Andalusia, Pablo Picasso (1881–1973) inaugurated the 20th century by making his debuts in Paris when scarcely twenty years old. There, no doubt, he was the most gifted painter of his generation, and his genius already burst forth in his works, but nonetheless he lived in the deepest poverty. He had to burn all his drawings in order to warm himself a bit during a harsh winter in late 1902 and early 1903.

The scene is January 1901. Picasso is traveling in Spain, particularly in Toledo, where he is fascinated by the pictures of El Greco. Upon returning to Paris in February, he is terribly scarred by the suicide of his longtime friend, the Spanish painter Carlos Casagemas. He then enters into his blue period, which will last until 1904. All his work will be dominated by blue, the color of the melancholy that hangs over his desperate soul. From now on he will emphasize the themes of sickness, misery, and death. During that same year, 1901, he paints this *Mother and Child*, which appears happy but is basically tragic, inspired by the theme of the Virgin with Child that he has just studied during his trip to Spain. We find clearly the influence of El Greco in the long, slender hands of the mother and in the elongated body of the child. This delicate evocation of maternal love, marked by an infinite tenderness, is all the more moving because Picasso used as his model a very sick prostitute who was being treated at the Hôpital Saint-Lazare in Paris. All the love in the world has taken refuge in the embrace between these two persons, on the one hand this mother who will pass away in secret and on the other hand her son who gazes at her as the most precious being that has ever walked the earth.

How can we avoid interpreting this picture as an allegory of the dramatic figure of Our Lady of Sorrows and of the Child Jesus, communing about the tragic destiny that awaits them? Jean Clair, who was the director of the Picasso Museum in Paris, invites us to do so when he writes: "All [Picasso's work] is placed under the banner of the exasperated Catholicism of Southern Spain in which he grew up. We can even say that he is the last great religious painter of the 20th century.... His portraits of mothers with their newborn are pictures of the Madonna; his acrobats with husband, wife, and child recall the Holy Family.

Mother with child
Pablo Picasso (1881-1973)
1901
Oil on canvas, 35.2 x 25 in
Private collection

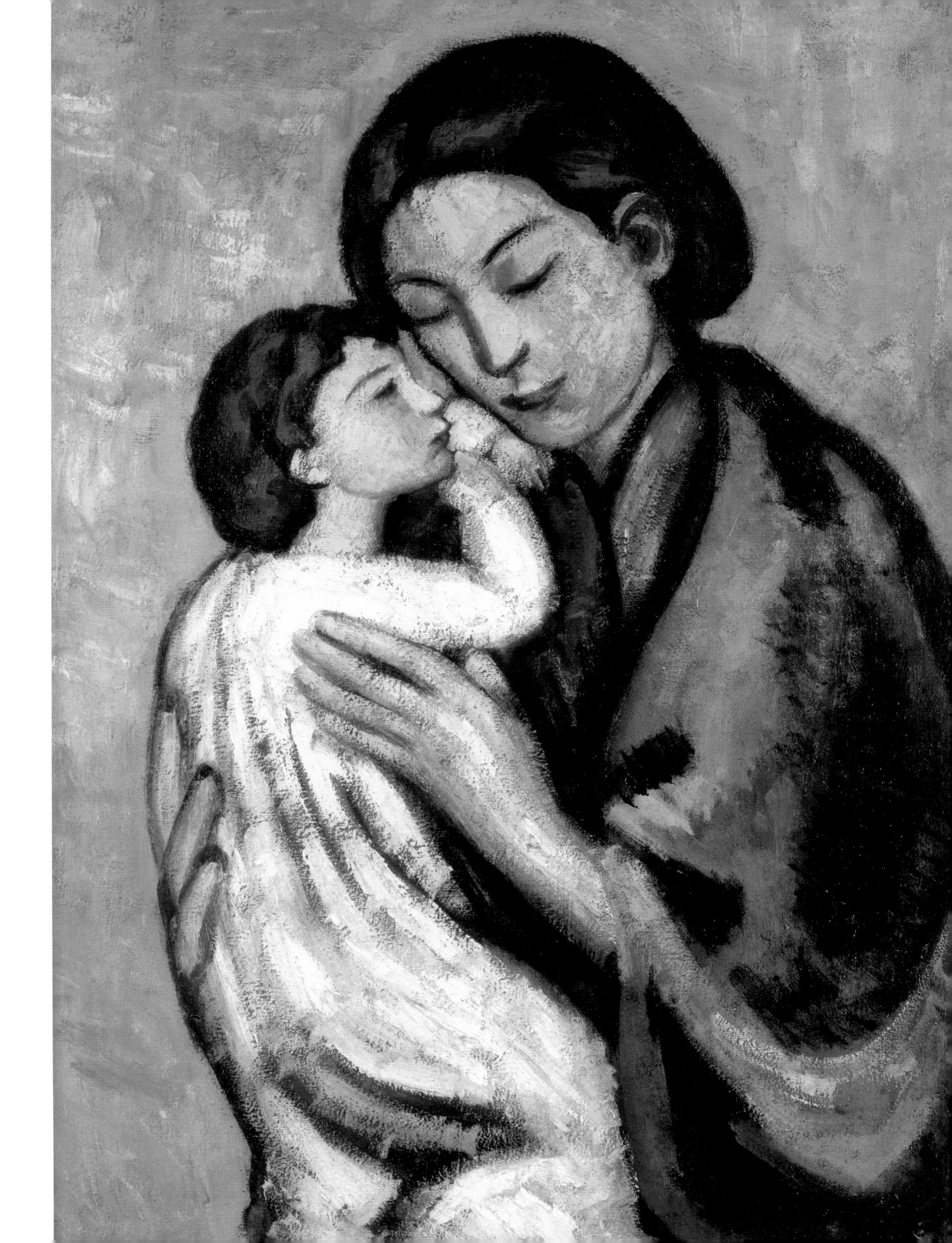

This goes even for *Guernica*, one whole panel of which depicts a Nativity, though certainly a tragic one."

In April 1950, when Picasso told Henri Matisse, a professed atheist, that he was surprised to see him spending the last years of his life exclusively on decorating the Rosary Chapel of the Dominican nuns in Vence, the latter replied: "Yes, I say my prayers, and so do you, as you know very well. When everything goes badly, we plunge into prayer to rediscover the atmosphere of our First Communion. And you do this, too. Basically, Picasso, we must not be show-offs. You are like me: what we all seek to rediscover in art is the climate of our First Communion" (Henri Matisse, quoted by Sister Jacques-Marie). ■

IN ART HISTORY

THE PRE-CUBIST PICASSO

All the beginnings of modernity are found channeled in the works of Pablo Picasso, and all the avant-gardes of the 20th century owe something to him. Many times the Spanish master gave the art of painting new fields to explore; he said everything and in every possible way. He nevertheless took up the weight of tradition and the heritage of the past.

The important thing here is to shed light on his first itinerary, his academic formation leading to the threshold of cubism, via his blue period (among others); this 1901 *Mother with child* dates from the start of it.

Picasso was born in Málaga, where his father taught drawing. As an adolescent, he lived in Barcelona, and soon the academic teaching that he received in the School of Fine Arts no longer satisfied him. During the winter of 1897-1898 he was sent to study in Madrid; there he copied the masters of the Prado Museum. Aware of the gaps in his instruction, though, he put an end to his studies. He sought to complete his training by flying with his own wings, already at the age of seventeen, to follow a more personal path.

The region of Barcelona, where he hobnobbed with Catalan modernists in the bohemian café Els Quatre Gats, was his main field of action and would remain such until 1904, when he settled definitively in Paris, the global epicenter of art.

Picasso had already been sojourning there regularly since the autumn of 1900: one of his paintings had been selected for the Universal Exposition. His Parisian debuts were facilitated by his Catalan friends and by three successive dealers, Pedro Mañach, Berthe Weil, then Ambroise Vollard, who sponsored a show for him in 1901.

Picasso, who took into account the atmosphere of the times, adopted its forms and motifs and kept an eye on the works of Eugène Delacroix, Édouard Manet, Claude Monet, Camille Pissarro, Henri de Toulouse-Lautrec, and Edgar Degas. He combined the techniques of the pointillists, assimilated Vincent Van Gogh, Paul Gauguin, and the Nabis, and ended up integrating into his precocious genius the most modernist pictorial language.

As of 1901, at the age of twenty, he was capable of offering an unprecedented style: he started his blue period.

This *Mother with child* shows exceptional boldness; it is the work of an artist who knows where he is going. It should be noted that in renouncing lively colors, he momentarily turns his back on success and goes against the general trend of those years, which would culminate in the fauvism of Henri Matisse.

The melancholy and the themes of the pictures of this blue period are not explained by Picasso's poverty; on the contrary, his poverty was the direct result of his pictures. During those years 1901-1904 the artist repeated widespread motifs such as the embrace, the kiss, and, here, the mother and child. His groups of figures are regularly redrawn and reintroduced into new works, as with Auguste Rodin.

Soon after he settled in Paris, the rose period would follow, until 1906, then above all the invention of cubism. Indeed, as early as 1907 with *Les Demoiselles d'Avignon*, Picasso succeeded in the tour de force—nothing more, nothing less—of imperiling the Renaissance heritage and perspective illusionism.

But that is another epic.

M. C.

Georges Bernanos (1888–1948), a novelist, essayist, and polemicist, is numbered among the greatest French writers of the first half of the 20th century. His work, which explores the dark regions of the human soul as well as the misfortune that strikes purity, is inhabited by a faith that is impossible to uproot, despite all the doubts and the temptation to despair. In this excerpt from *Diary of a Country Priest* (1936), an old parish priest talks about the Virgin Mary to the narrator, a priest several decades his junior.

Georges Bernanos, *Journal d'un curé de campagne* (Paris: Plon, 1936). This excerpt was translated by Michael J. Miller.

Mother of grace, youngest daughter of the human race

GEORGES BERNANOS

"She is our mother; everyone understands that. She is the mother of the human race, the New Eve. But she is also its daughter. The ancient world—the sorrowful world, the world as it was before Grace—rocked her for a long time on its desolate heart, for centuries and centuries, in the obscure, incomprehensible expectation of a *virgo genitrix* [virgin-mother].... For centuries and centuries, with its old hands, its heavy, crime-laden hands, it protected the wonderful little girl, although it did not even know her name. A little girl, this Queen of the Angels. And so she is still, don't forget it!... The Blessed Virgin had neither a triumph nor miracles. Her Son did not allow human glory to brush against her, not even with the finest tip of its great, wild wing. No one ever lived, or suffered, or died as simply and in such profound ignorance of her own dignity, a dignity that nevertheless sets her above the angels. After all, she was born without sin: what astonishing uniqueness! Such a pure and limpid spring, so limpid and so pure that she could not even see her own image reflected in it, because it was made to be enjoyed by the Father alone—O sacred solitude! The ancient demons, man's familiar spirits, masters and slaves all together, the terrible patriarchs who guided the first steps of Adam at the threshold of the accursed world—Cunning and Pride—you see them looking from afar at this miraculous creature set beyond their reach, invulnerable and disarmed. Certainly our poor species is worth little, but infancy always stirs its heart, the ignorance of the little one makes it lower its eyes—its eyes which know good and evil, its eyes which have seen so many things! But it is only ignorance after all. The Virgin was Innocence. Do you realize what we are for her, we others, the human race? Oh, naturally, she detests sin, but she has no experience of it anyway, whereas the greatest saints, even the Saint of Assisi himself, seraphic as he may be, had that experience. The Virgin's glance is the only truly childlike glance, the only true glance of a child that has ever been directed toward our shame and our misfortune. Yes, my lad, in order to pray to her correctly, you have to feel upon you that glance which is not quite a glance of indulgence—because there is no indulgence without some bitter experience—but rather of tender compassion, of sorrowful surprise, of who knows what other inconceivable, inexpressible sentiment that makes her younger than sin, younger than the race from which she stemmed, and although she is our Mother through grace, the Mother of all grace, she is the youngest daughter of the human race."

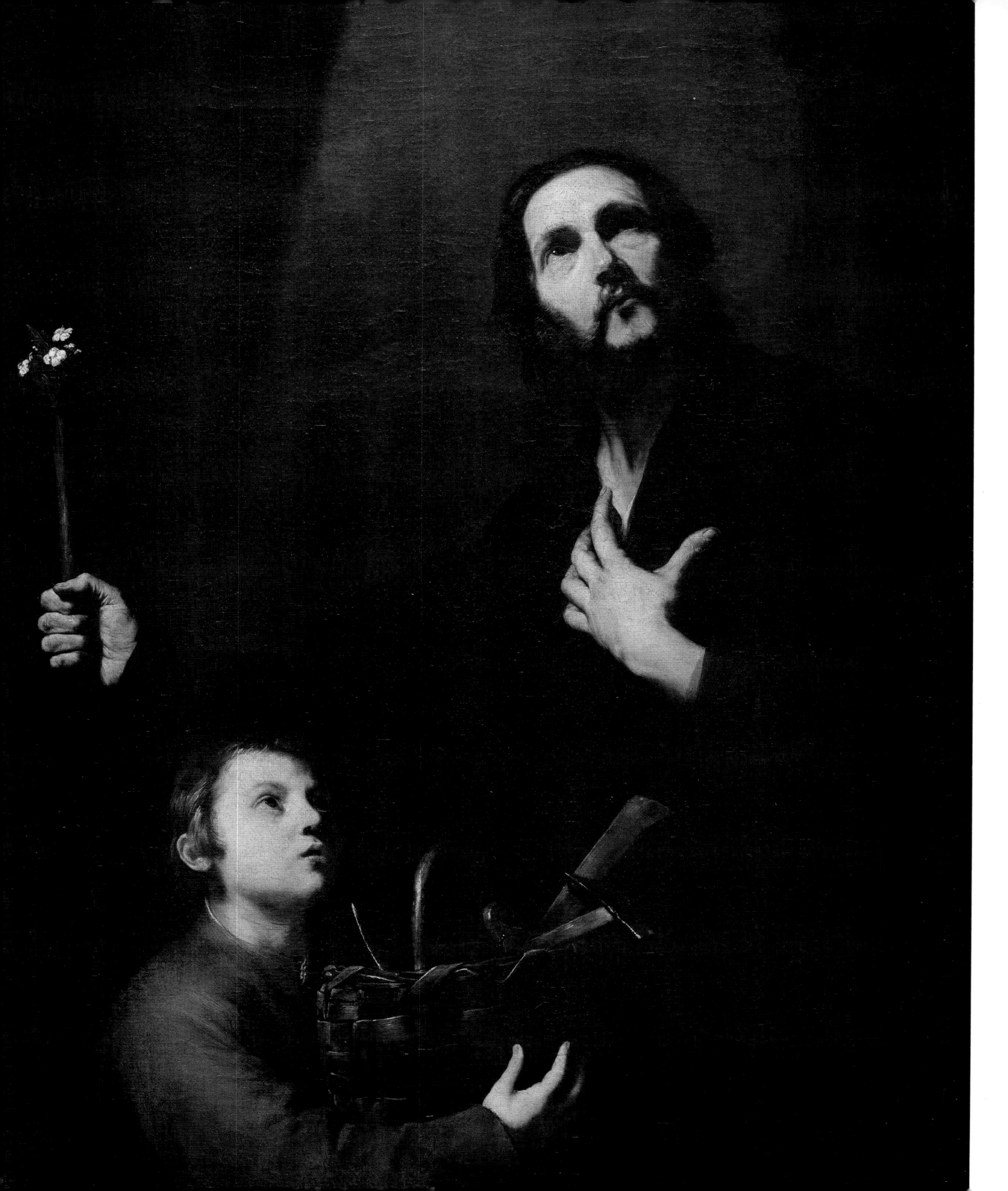

Jesus at work with his father

Nazareth is a very unassuming village; its inhabitants live in the shadow of the "jewel of Galilee": the powerful Sepphoris nearby, with its thousands of citizens and merchants, its Roman villas, its hot baths and theater... One can imagine that it was primarily to fill orders from the big city that Joseph worked on wood, from which he drew beams and planks. Jesus is often depicted by artists as "the carpenter's son" (Mt 13:55), to whom his father teaches the trade so that he might succeed him someday.

José de Ribera (1591–1652) launches here into a meditation on the great mystery of the human fatherhood which, in Joseph of Nazareth, his patron saint, reveals the divine fatherhood. A young, noble, handsome man, Joseph firmly grasps the rod from the almond tree which, according to the apocryphal gospels, flowered on the day he was chosen by the immaculate heart of Mary. Like the rod of Moses and that of Aaron, this rod also recalls the authority conferred by God on Joseph and his vocation. It symbolizes also the pastor's rod, noting that Joseph is a descendant of the shepherd David and indicating that the holy man is responsible for protecting and guiding to maturity the one whom John the Baptist would point out as the "Lamb of God" (Jn 1:29).

Jesus, for his part, carries the carpenter's tools in a basket. Though a child, he already works with his father; most often, probably on the immense construction site of the new city of Sepphoris, three miles from Nazareth. With Joseph, perched on the high ridge beams, he would share at midday the basket-lunch that Mary had prepared for them. From him he would learn everything, not only about the carpentry trade, but also about becoming a man.

Having experienced the human depth of such a community of love and work between a father and his son, Jesus would be able to say later on: *"The son can do nothing by himself unless he sees the father do it"* (cf. Jn 5:19). The maxim is true now about God, his heavenly Father, and he explains: *"My Father is still at work, and I, too, am at work"* (Jn 5:17). Already, when at the age of twelve Jesus had been "lost" in the Temple and his mother had reproached him: *"Your father and I were worried sick about you!"*—he had replied, *"I must be about my Father's business"* (cf. Lk 2:48-49).

But Jesus answered them, "My Father is working still, and I am working." ... "Truly, truly, I say to you, the Son can do nothing of his own accord, but only what he sees the Father doing; for whatever he does, that the Son does likewise. For the Father loves the Son, and shows him all that he himself is doing; and greater works than these will he show him, that you may marvel."

THE BIBLE – JN 5:17, 19-20

This is why Ribera depicts Jesus lifting his eyes toward his father, and his father turning his toward heaven: Joseph accompanies Jesus as he looks toward the heavenly Father. And the young boy's offering of his carpentry tools also ascends to God, his Father: Jesus will offer his life for the salvation of the world on a work fashioned by a carpenter; he will be fastened to the cross with a hammer and nails, the tools of a carpenter. Ribera clearly suggests that the cross of Jesus was mystically constructed largely by Joseph the carpenter, with the help of his apprentice son. ■

Saint Joseph and the Child Jesus
José de Ribera (1591–1652)
1630–1635
Oil on canvas, 50 x 39 in
Madrid, Prado Museum

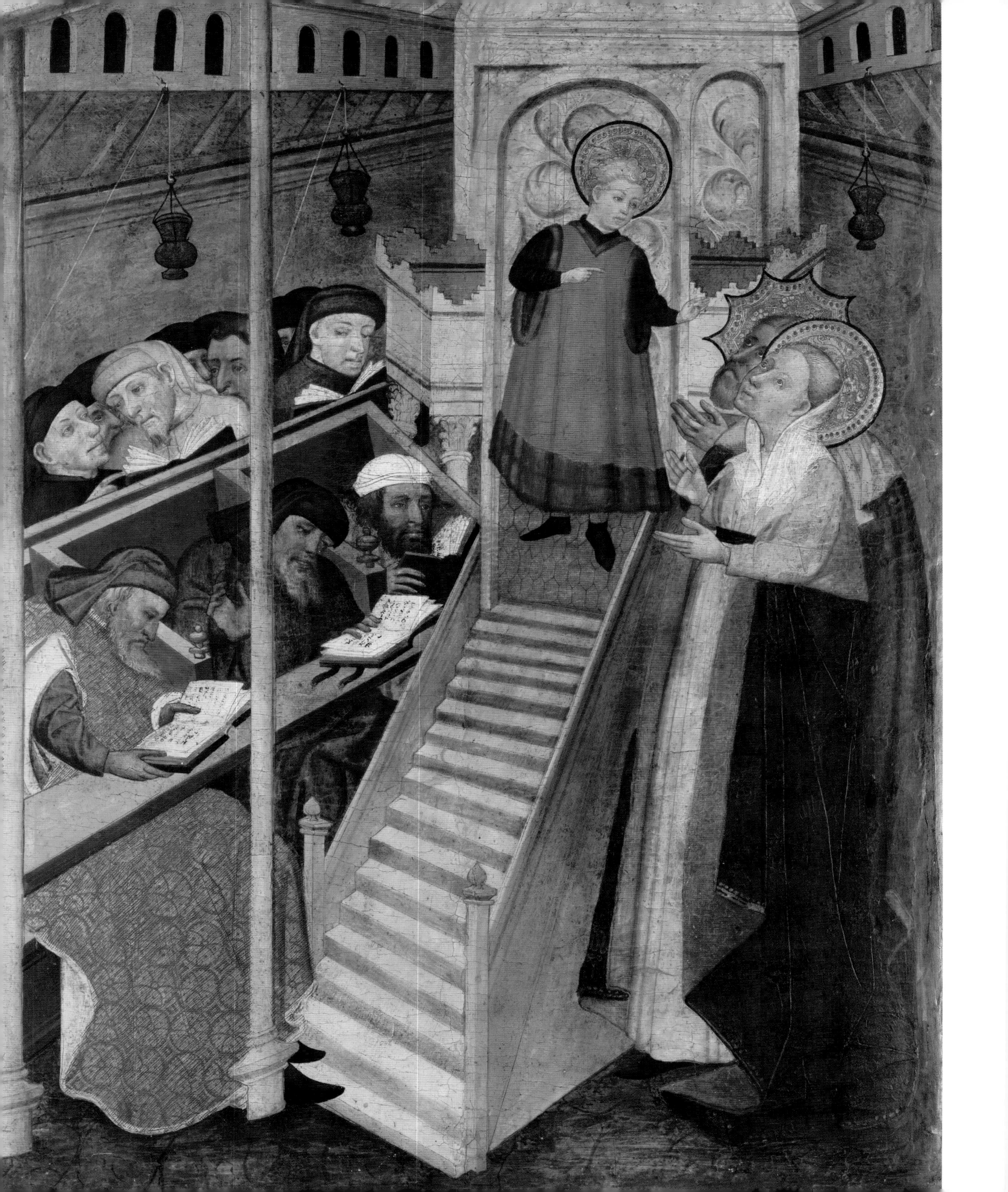

The pious Jews of Jesus' time, even if they lived far from Jerusalem, traveled once a year on pilgrimage to the Temple, the place par excellence of the worship given to the God of Israel. The feast of the Passover begins on the evening of the 14th of the month of Nisan, in other words, the day of the first full moon after the spring equinox. During this episode Jesus was only twelve years old, and therefore had not yet attained religious majority as understood by the Law (thirteen). His intelligence in speaking with the doctors of the Law was therefore quite remarkable.

The twelve-year-old Jesus, found in the Temple

This panel from the altarpiece made of painted wood was probably executed by a disciple of the Catalan master Bernat Martorell. The painter, who remained anonymous, chose to illustrate the moment when Mary and Joseph find Jesus in the Temple after searching for him for three days. The decor is that of a medieval university classroom, and the boy Jesus, wearing the garb of masters in theology, stands in the magisterial "chair." Turned toward his parents, he just heard his Mother say to him: *"Son, why have you treated us so? Behold, your father and I have been looking for you anxiously."* With his right index finger pointed toward them as though he were giving them a lesson, he replies, *"How is it that you sought me? Did you not know that I must be about my Father's business?"* (Lk 2:48-49). Mary and Joseph do not understand the explanation provided by their child (cf. Lk 2:50). And so their hands express a firm demand, and their faces show that they are still waiting for a word that will enlighten them in their confusion. The painter suggests that it is not always easy to be the parents of God.

Mary and Joseph will receive no other response. In a gesture that recalls that of the *Noli me tangere* (*cf.* page 228), the Child-God opposes his open left hand to their request, to signify that a deep mystery is taking place here that many prophets would have wished to see, but that they themselves will not be able to "grasp," at least for the moment. On the other side of the chair, in their stalls, the experts in the Law are immersed in Scripture, so as to reread it from the perspective opened up by the lessons that the Divine Child has given them. Ultimately, the wise and learned men of Israel will not recognize him, and the Gospel emphasizes that a pagan, a centurion of the Roman army, will be the one to exclaim at the foot of the Cross: *"Truly, this man was the Son of God!"* (Mk 15:39). ■

THE BIBLE – LK 2:41-43, 46-47

Now his parents went to Jerusalem every year at the feast of the Passover. And when he was twelve years old, they went up according to custom; and when the feast was ended, as they were returning, the boy Jesus stayed behind in Jerusalem. His parents did not know it. After three days they found him in the temple, sitting among the teachers, listening to them and asking them questions; and all who heard him were amazed at his understanding and his answers.

Christ among the doctors
Catalan school
Early 15th century
Tempera on wood, 44 x 30 in
New York, Metropolitan Museum of Art

Baptism, from a Greek word that means "dipping," is a rite that accompanied a conversion, a change of life. In the first century, it was practiced particularly by the Essenes, followers of a current of Judaism who practiced a demanding asceticism—desert spirituality, combating sin—while they awaited the coming of a Messiah who would liberate Israel. The baptism administered by John, called the Baptist, on the east bank of the Jordan was related to the spirituality of that group. The baptism of Jesus marked the beginning of his public life. He was thirty years old.

Jesus is baptized

This 16th-century stained-glass window in the shape of a heart depicts the manifestation of the Triune God on the occasion of the baptism of Jesus in the Jordan, the river that has its source in the mountains of Lebanon and runs through all of Palestine from north to south, to the Lake of Tiberias, emptying into the Dead Sea, the lowest emerged point in the world.

Above, the crimson cloud (the color of Charity) testifies to the presence of God the Father at this event. From his light proceeds the Holy Spirit, who descends in the form of a dove upon Jesus, the Beloved Son. On one bank, John the Baptist holds in his hand a cross-shaped staff, which bears as a standard his prophetic words: *Ecce Agnus Dei, behold the Lamb of God who takes away the sin of the world* (Jn 1:29). On the other bank, an angel presents the tunic of the Passion that Christ will put on to confront the last baptism: the baptism of death.

Baptism was a rite to which sinners submitted in order to be purified and to attest that they were converting and renouncing their dissolute life. Why, then, did Jesus, who is well known to be sinless, demand that John baptize him?

In Hebrew Jordan is pronounced *Yarden*, which means "the lowest." Indeed, the bed of the Jordan River is situated well below sea level. Jesus insisted on immersing himself in its waters to indicate that he had come down from heaven to raise the human condition from the lowest place where it could be, by taking upon himself the weight of the world's sins. So this stained-glass window shows the Triune God who is manifested on this occasion in three Persons: the baptism of Jesus is literally an "epiphany" ("manifestation" in Greek), since in the communion of the Holy Spirit the Most High testifies to his Beloved Son, who for love of humanity agreed to make himself the "Most Low."

The heart shape of the carved stone frame of the picture window also suggests to the spectators that the stained glass image lets us "see" the word that the Father made audible at the moment when Jesus was baptized: *"This is my Son, my beloved. In him I have placed all my love"* (Mt 3:17). ■

THE BIBLE – MT 3:13-17

Then Jesus came from Galilee to the Jordan to John, to be baptized by him. John would have prevented him, saying, "I need to be baptized by you, and do you come to me?" But Jesus answered him, "Let it be so now; for thus it is fitting for us to fulfil all righteousness." Then he consented. And when Jesus was baptized, he went up immediately from the water, and behold, the heavens were opened and he saw the Spirit of God descending like a dove, and alighting on him; and behold, a voice from heaven, saying, "This is my beloved Son, with whom I am well pleased."

The Baptism of Christ
Early 16th century
Stained glass window
Joigny, Church of Saint John,
Soufflet of the tympanum of picture window 11

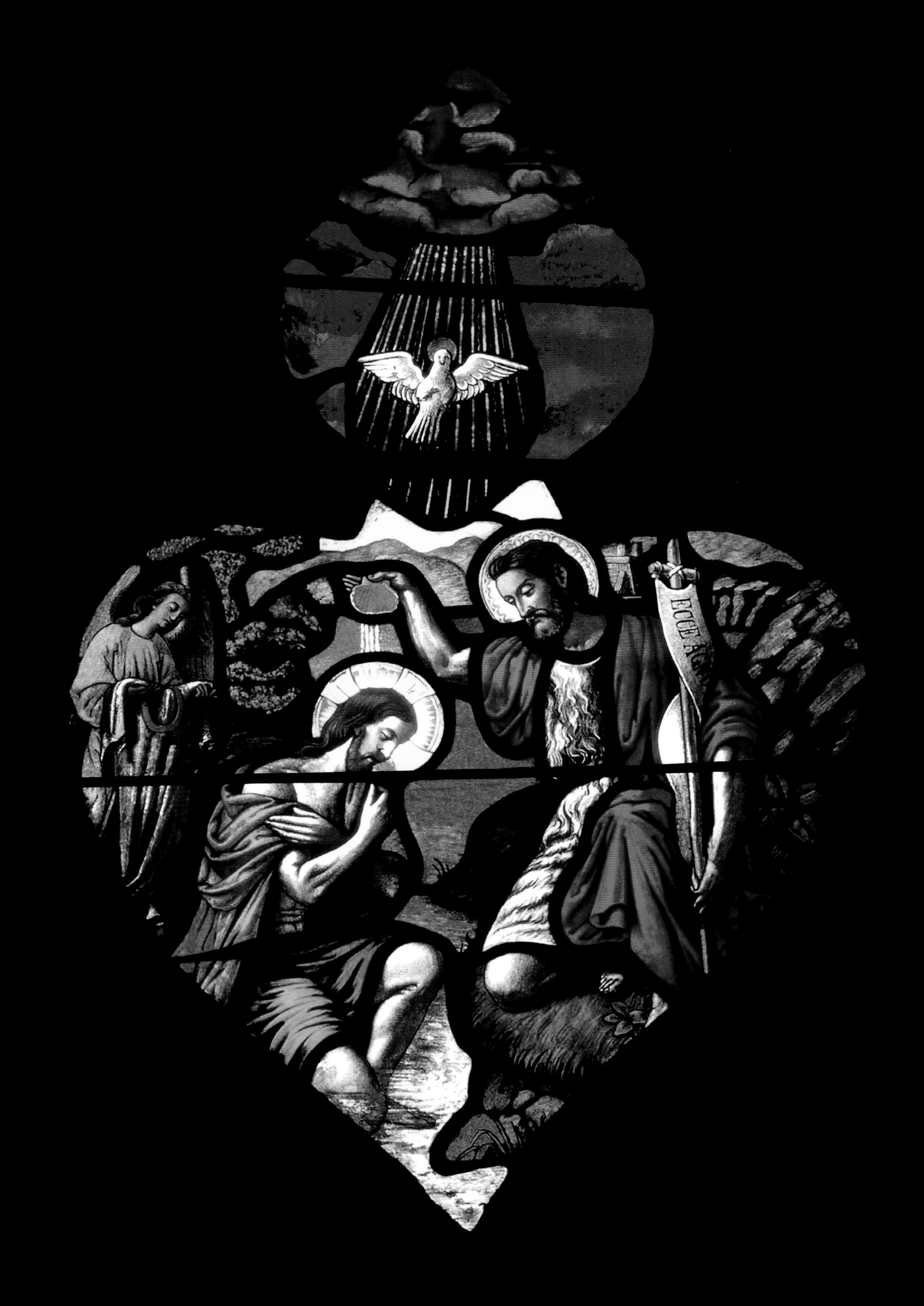
ECCE

Jesus' retreat in the desert took place immediately after his baptism. The geographical location was the desert of Judea, between the Dead Sea to the east, into which the Jordan River empties, and Jerusalem to the west. There, Jesus confirmed his vocation, which was put to the test by temptations. Earlier artists liked to depict the temptations of Jesus with an explicit representation of the devil mentioned in the Gospels. But from the 19th century on, they have preferred to suggest an altogether interior spiritual combat.

Jesus makes a retreat in the desert

In the middle of a desert terrain roughened by outcroppings of rock, Jesus, alone, stays seated, on a retreat. Behind him, the light is winning and starts to dominate the darkness. Here the colors of dusk mingle with those of the dawn: the old Mosaic Law melts away into the new and eternal Law, to reveal the Son of God who comes.

At age thirty he prepares, through spiritual combat, to engage in the final act of his earthly mission. Before beginning his public life—in other words, before fully accomplishing his own vocation as Messiah—the Son of Man had to confront his human freedom in the refining fire of privations and temptations. For this freedom was going to be put to the test sorely for three years, to the point of a supreme sacrifice, to the point of being faced with the choice to say, in an ineffable groan during his agony in Gethsemane: *Father, may your will be done, not mine* (LK 22:42).

According to the late-19th-century Victorian morality that characterized the Christianity of Briton Rivière, it was necessary for Jesus to go through trials in the desert, at least to give a good example, in relation to the laws of love

THE BIBLE – LK 4:1-2, 9

Jesus, full of the Holy Spirit, returned from the Jordan, and was led by the Spirit for forty days in the wilderness, tempted by the devil. And he ate nothing in those days; and when they were ended, he was hungry.... And the devil took him to Jerusalem, and set him on the pinnacle of the temple, and said to him, "If you are the Son of God, throw yourself down from here."

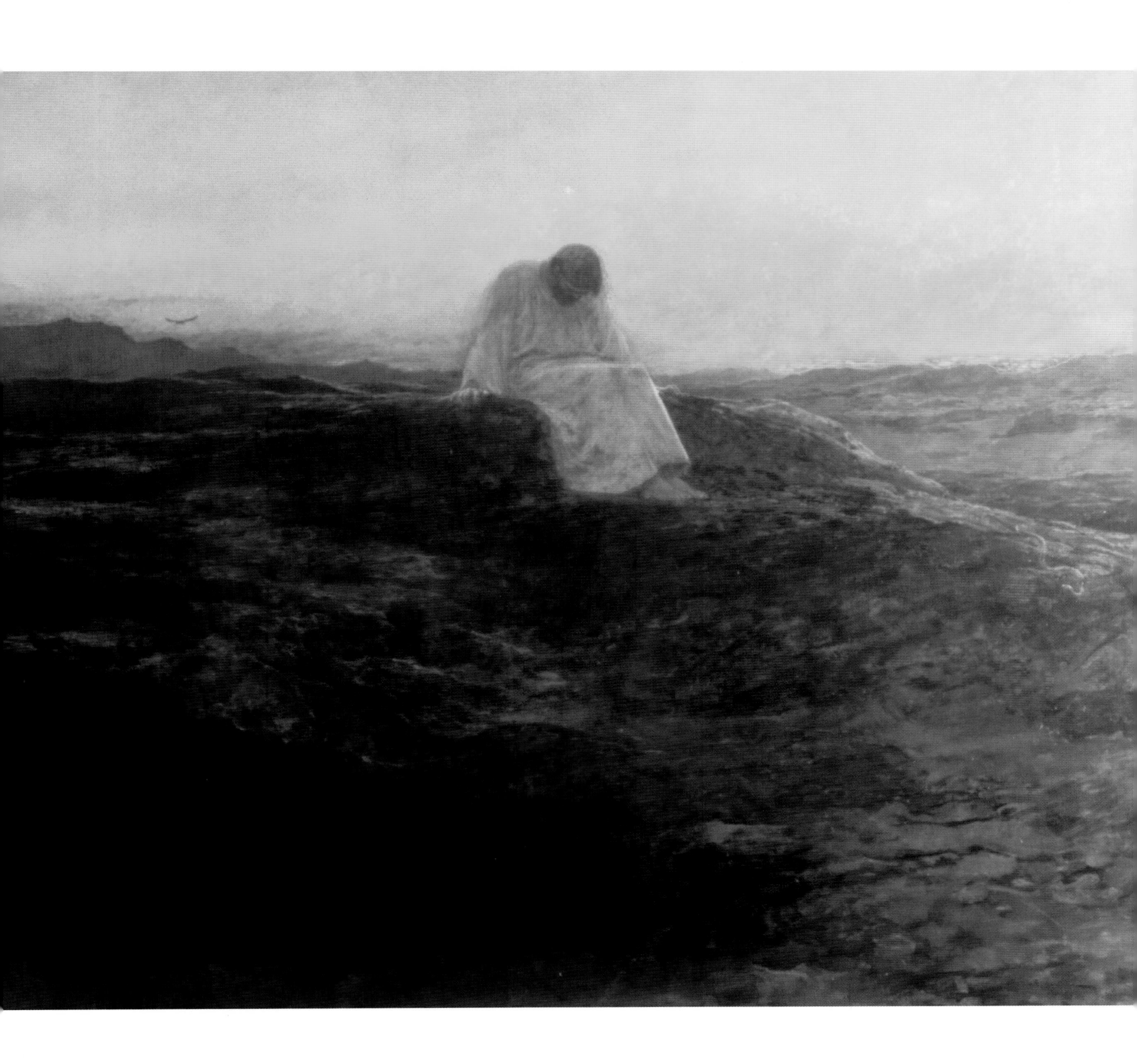

Christ in the desert
Briton Rivière (1840–1920)
1898
Oil on canvas, 46 x 74.5 in
London, Guildhall Art Gallery

and freedom that govern one who wants to dedicate his life to promoting the kingdom of God.

These laws are imposed in the form of questions. The law of love demands: Is what I am doing conducive to accomplishing the all-loving will of God? And the law of freedom: Does what I am doing make me dependent, a slave, preventing me from being totally free so as to let my life be guided by the law of love? In other words, in order to carry out his vocation fully, the man Jesus had to show himself master of whatever might hamper the sovereignty of his freedom. This is why the artist shows Jesus making a retreat in the desert so as to wage a spiritual combat. The Evangelist Luke relates that the devil, *the ruler of this world* (Jn 14:30), appeared repeatedly as the tempter and, given the failure of his attempts, bade farewell to Jesus *until an opportune time* (Lk 4:13) for one last temptation in Gethsemane. ■

IN ART HISTORY

THE HUMANISM BEHIND ANIMAL PAINTINGS

The French-sounding name of Briton Rivière (1840–1920) reveals the origins of a Protestant family that had fled the kingdom of France following religious persecutions. Descended from a line of artists who were members of the Royal Academy for four generations, Briton Rivière, educated in Cheltenham and then at Oxford, began his career as an illustrator and genre painter.

After being influenced for a while by the pre-Raphaelites, Briton Rivière finally gave in to a style from his childhood: he became affiliated with the prestigious English school of animal painting that stretches from George Stubbs (1724–1806) to Edwin Lanseer (1802–1873). Incidentally he is often compared with Lanseer, to whom his debt is both visible and certain.

Throughout his life, Briton Rivière fled the city and human interactions whenever possible. He chose to live far from London, and when spending time there was unavoidable, he would stay in the immediate vicinity of Regent's Park, close to the zoological garden.

The wide diffusion of his engravings and illustrations quickly solidified his status as an animal artist. We should emphasize, however, the radical uniqueness of Rivière's works: the recurring but rarely emphasized presence of the human figure in his compositions, alongside the animal figure.

This dialogue between man and animal is easy to explain when the subject requires it, for instance in his *Saint George and the dragon* (1908–1909) or *Zeus and Ganymede*. Nevertheless, Briton Rivière went farther by choosing to depict in his more ambitious works scenes in which the human and animal worlds are inseparably linked. Thus, among Rivière's masterpieces is a depiction of the mythological episode in which the sorceress Circe transforms men into beasts (*Circe and the companions of Ulysses*, 1871). The same goes for his *Daniel in the lions' den* (1872), one of his most magisterial works, preserved in the Walker Art Gallery in Liverpool.

Briton Rivière exalts each time a human body dominating animal ferocity. From these masterpieces, it seems obvious to us that Rivière's art far surpasses the framework of animal studies.

We must note that Briton Rivière's position as a great animal painter has obscured much of his work. The admirable *Christ in the desert* presented here has the virtue of revealing a new aspect of the evocative power of Rivière, who this time treats the ultimate human figure: that of God made man.

M. C.

Under Satan's Sun takes the reader through the dark night of the life of a priest from northern France, whose spiritual combat is marked particularly by the death of a young girl whom he was unable to protect from suicide. Bernanos shows in this passage that just as the devil in the desert tempted the all-holy Jesus, so too he continues to attack holy men and women throughout human history.

Georges Bernanos, *Under Satan's Sun,* translated by J. C. Whitehouse (Lincoln: University of Nebraska Press, 2001), 96-97.

His hatred is reserved for the saints

GEORGES BERNANOS

Oh, you have never known anything of the world but colors and sounds with no substance, you sensitive souls and sentimental mouths where the harsh Truth would melt like a piece of choice confectionery—tiny souls, tiny mouths—this is not for you. Your flirtations with sin are in keeping with your delicate nerves and precious brains, and the Satan of your strange litanies is nothing but your own distorted image, for he who worships the carnal world is Satan unto himself. The monster watches you and laughs but has not yet speared you on his claws. He is not to be found in your dreary, drivelling books, your blasphemies or ridiculous curses, nor in your greedy eyes, your treacherous hands, or in the roaring in your ears. In vain you will seek him in the most secret flesh your still unslaked lust will pierce, and the blood on the lips you bite will be sickly and pale... But he *is* to be found in the personal prayer of the solitary, in his fasting and penitence, in the depths of the most profound ecstasy, and the silence of the heart. He poisons the purifying water, burns in the consecrated wax, breathes in the breath of virgins, torments the flesh with the hair shirt and the scourge, and corrupts every path. He has been known to utter lies on lips half-open to pronounce the words of Truth, to pursue the just man through the thunder and lightning of beatific rapture, right to the very arms of God... Why then should he trouble to wrest so many from the earth who crawl upon it like beasts, when he knows that the same earth will soon cover them? They are a dismal herd who will go to meet their fate alone. His hatred is reserved for the saints.

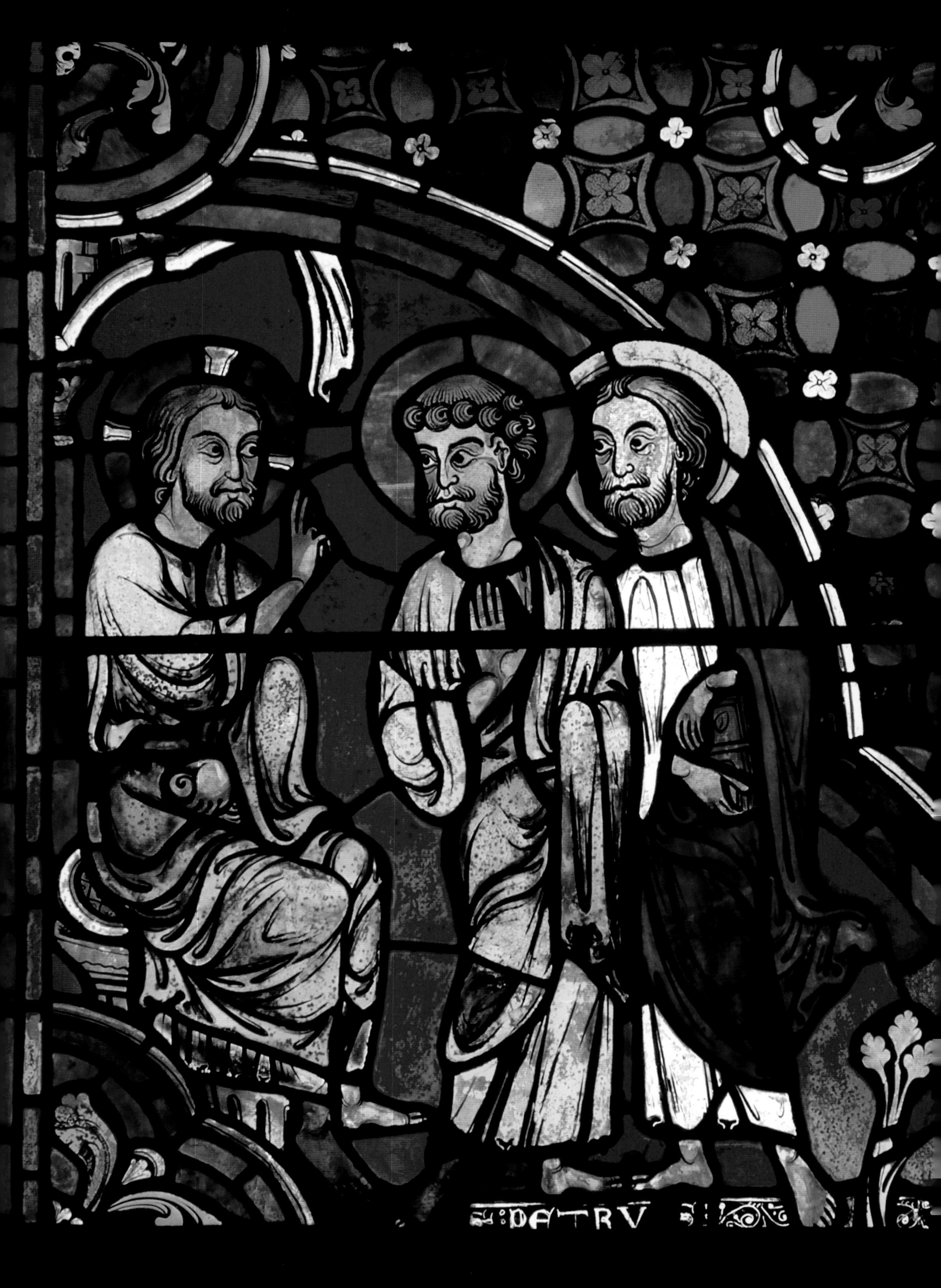
PATRV

Jesus calls the apostles

The public life of Jesus began when he returned to Galilee, after his retreat in the desert of Judea. To accompany him on his mission and then to perpetuate it, he calls twelve men to follow him, who will be his apostles (from the Greek *apostolos*, "sent on a mission").

In the Christian Creed (profession of faith), Jesus receives the title "Light from Light" (Nicene Creed). In keeping with this theological concept of light, architects who built churches in the 12th century invented the broken arch and crossed ogives, which make it possible to balance forces on pillars: the walls therefore no longer have to support the weight of the structure and can be made up of large sets of windows letting in the light that will flood the choir and the nave. Thus "French" art (because it first appeared and developed around Paris, in a province called Île-de-France) was born, described later as "Gothic." This original art, both luminous and refined, would conquer all of Western Christendom.

Since the "Light from Light" is forever the *Logos*, the Word of God, it was absolutely necessary for the light that bathed the sanctuary not to be silent but to express itself. This "miracle" is performed by changing the walls of windows into grandiose, illustrated "books" that are both translucent and brightly colored. Thus the teaching Church, in raising up the cathedrals, had found a new way to edify her faithful.

Here then is a detail from the stained-glass window of the Apostles, produced between 1210 and 1225, that happens to be the central window (347 x 82 in) of the axial chapel of the Cathedral of Our Lady of Chartres. This panel depicts Jesus sending on mission the two brothers and apostles Peter and Andrew. The analogy of the light that illumines the stained-glass windows plays into this theme completely. Didn't Saint Peter himself write that the mission of evangelization consists in calling all men and all women of good will to come *out of darkness into the marvelous light that is Jesus himself* (1 Pt 2:9)?

Jesus is presented in a pose that is still heavily influenced by the rules of Byzantine art, repeated by the Latin Church in Romanesque art. He is seated on the throne of Wisdom. In his left hand he holds the scroll of the Scriptures, the very same ones that he came to fulfill. With his right hand he blesses the apostles who are getting ready to leave on a mission. The draping of his clothing is still marked by the Roman style. The pink of his cloak suggests the union in him of two natures: human (white) and divine (red). The green of his tunic proclaims that he is the only hope of humanity. ■

THE BIBLE – MT 4:17-19

From that time Jesus began to preach, saying, "Repent, for the kingdom of heaven is at hand." As he walked by the Sea of Galilee, he saw two brothers, Simon who is called Peter and Andrew his brother, casting a net into the sea; for they were fishermen. And he said to them, "Follow me, and I will make you fishers of men."

Christ sending Saint Peter and Saint Andrew on a mission
Around 1210–1225
Stained-glass window
Chartres, Cathedral of Our Lady, axial chapel, detail of the Apostles' window

Cana, in Galilee, is located a little more than an hour's walk north of Nazareth. *On the third day there was a marriage at Cana in Galilee, and the mother of Jesus was there. Jesus also was invited to the marriage, with his disciples* (Jn 2:1-2). Therefore this was very probably a marriage within Jesus' family. The fact that Mary is there without Joseph suggests that at that time her husband was already dead. The Gospel according to Saint John reports that the changing of water into wine by Jesus is the *first of the signs* that he performed (Jn 2:11): it is the archetype of all the other miracles that he would work throughout his "ministry."

Jesus changes water into wine

Around 1233, the stained-glass windows were installed in Chartres Cathedral, which had just been rebuilt in the "French" style (today we would say "French Gothic"). It is probably at that same time the Romanesque stained-glass window of the Virgin enthroned in majesty, *Notre-Dame de la Belle Verrière*, miraculous preserved after the fire in 1194, was admirably showcased again, set amid twenty new panels, in an ogival window (294 x 94 in).

The two ranks of this wall of windows dedicated to the wedding in Cana are among the new pieces of this magnificent set. They repeat an episode from the account of the Gospel according to Saint John in which Jesus, Mary his Mother, and his disciples are invited to a marriage in Cana in Galilee. Noticing that the newlyweds have no more wine to offer to delight their guests, Mary turns to the servants, points out Jesus to them, and tells them: *"Do whatever he tells you"* (Jn 2:5).

In this medallion, we see that Mary is made prominent by her imposing stature. She gives her instructions to the servants, who are carrying hopelessly empty wine jugs. Her big eyes illumine her face. Her halo is red, the color of the Charity that she shows in her concern for the good of all. Her veil bears a cross on the front as a reminder that her Son would give her at the foot of the cross as a mother for the whole human race. She holds in her hand the book of the Gospel, the Word of God par excellence.

The first message that the master glass-makers are responsible for transmitting is clear and very direct: to do what Jesus tells them to do, as the miracle at Cana depicted in Our Lady of Chartres insistently encourages us, is to do what is written in the Gospel. The second message assures us that when something essential is lacking, anyone can turn confidently to Mary, who is prompt at interceding with her son with a mother's authority. Thus, above and beyond their artistic function and character, the great narrative windows are conceived as catechisms in images.

Finally, the Gospel says, Jesus, at his Mother's instigation, manifests his "glory" by transforming water into wine, some of the best wine, for the greater joy of everyone. Thus the "sign" given at Cana contains potentially the whole meaning of the work of God-made-man: the consummation of the wedding of the Son of God with humanity, so that, with human love (water) raised to the rank of divine love (wine), humanity might be united forever in God. ■

THE BIBLE: JN 2:3-8AB, 9B-10

When the wine failed, the mother of Jesus said to him, "They have no wine." And Jesus said to her, "O woman, what have you to do with me? My hour has not yet come." His mother said to the servants, "Do what ever he tells you." Now six stone jars were standing there, for the Jewish rites of purification, each holding twenty or thirty gallons. Jesus said to them, "Fill the jars with water." And they filled them up to the brim. He said to them, "Now draw some out, and take it to the steward of the feast." The steward of the feast called the bridegroom and said to him, "Every man serves the good wine first; and when men have drunk freely, then the poor wine; but you have kept the good wine until now."

The Wedding at Cana
Early 13th century
Stained-glass window
Chartres, Cathedral of Our Lady, south deambulatory, detail of *La Belle Verrière*

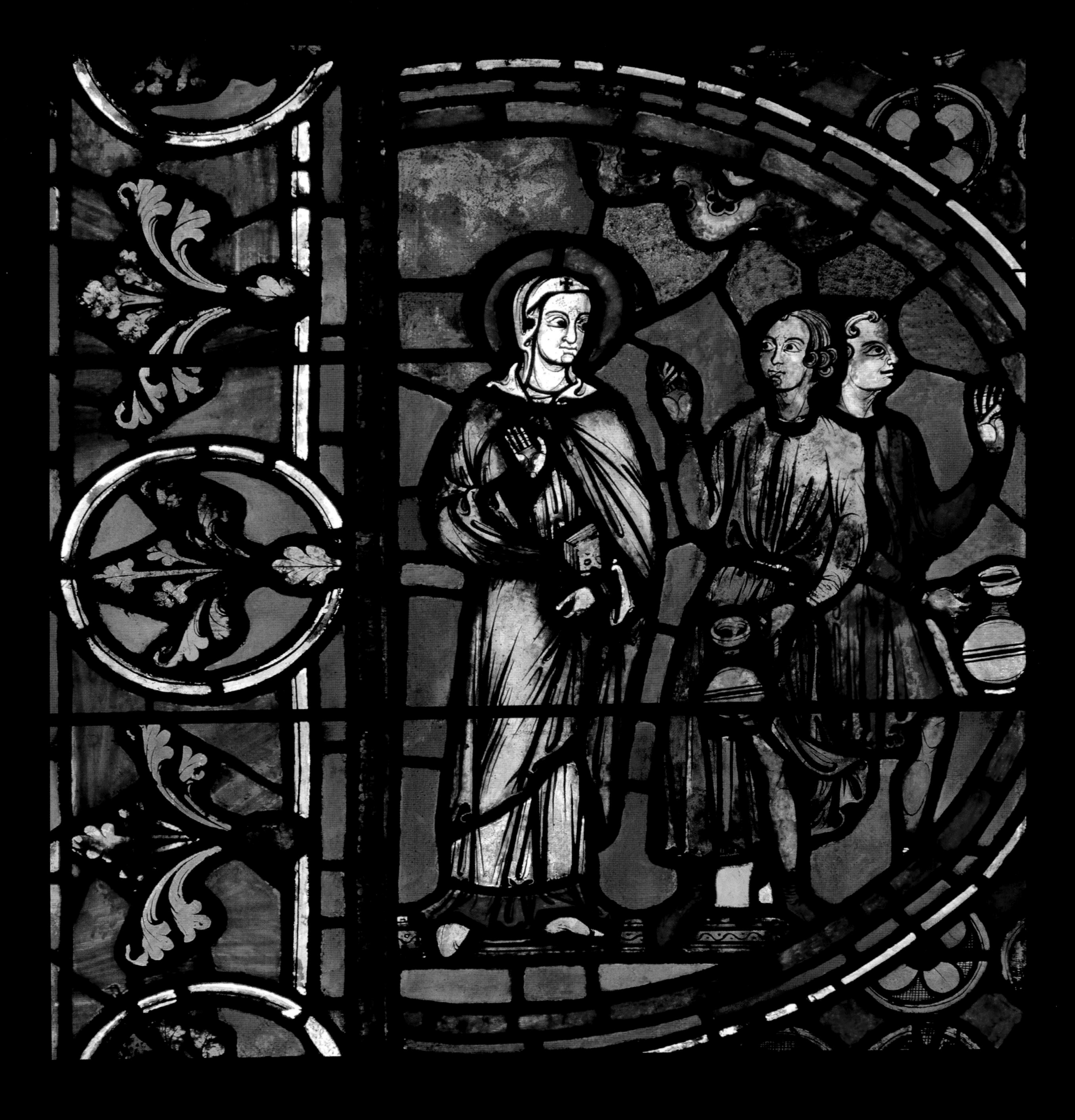

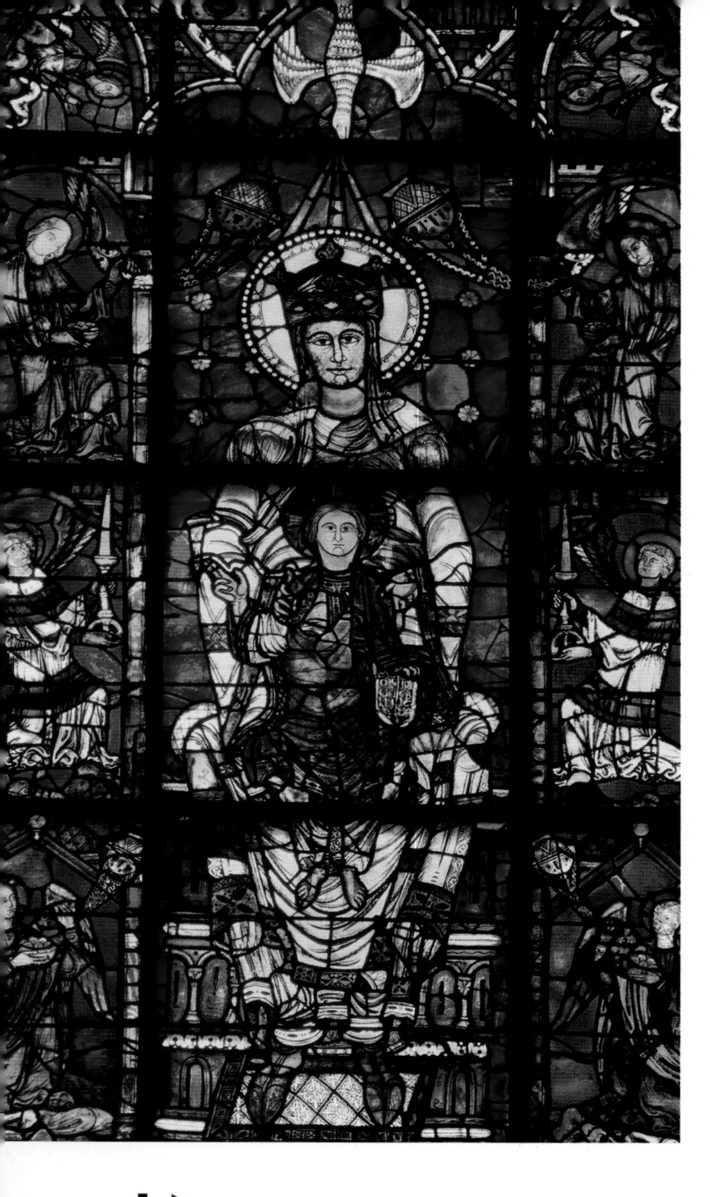

Virgin in majesty, called
Notre-Dame de la Belle Verrière
1180
Stained-glass window
Cathedral of Our Lady of Chartres,
south deambulatory,
detail of *La Belle Verrière*

The *Virgin in majesty*, rescued from the Romanesque period of the Cathedral of Our Lady of Chartres, dominates, in "the Beautiful Wall of Windows," the panels depicting the wedding at Cana, which for their part are representative of the beginnings of "Gothic" art. The set of windows allows us to observe resurgences of the old style, developments, and the original features of the new style.

GOTHIC STAINED-GLASS WINDOWS:
AN ARCHITECTURE OF LIGHT AT THE SERVICE OF A THEOLOGY OF LIGHT

The emergence of the Gothic style accompanies a period of prosperity in 12th-century Europe. It originated on the Île-de-France, in the Abbey Church of Saint Denis, at the instigation of Abbot Suger (*ca.* 1081–1151), and soon extended to the cathedrals in Paris, Laon, and Chartres, then, outside of France, in Germany and England.

Historians mark four phases in the development of Gothic architecture: primitive (12th century, in Saint-Denis), classical (late 12th century to around 1230, in Chartres, Paris, Bourges...), radiant (around 1230 to the second half of the 14th century, choir in Amiens, the Sainte-Chapelle in Paris...), and flamboyant (15th c.–early 16th c., Sainte-Chapelle in Vincennes, abbey church of the Trinity in Vendôme...). As for the term "Gothic," it dates from the Renaissance and was originally pejorative.

In Gothic architecture, pressures are exerted outside the building, the walls no longer have a weight-bearing function, and consequently the constructions become increasingly vertical, aerial, and much more luminous because large bay windows can be carved out.

The surfaces to be filled with glass thus assume considerable dimensions. By way of example, the Romanesque stained glass window of the Abbey Church of the Trinity in Vendôme, dating from around 1130, occupies only 12.4 square feet. Around fifteen years later in Saint-Denis, every bay includes 86 square feet of glass. In 1150, the western bay alone in Chartres has 861 square feet of glass. The whole set of stained-glass windows of Chartres Cathedral unfolds over more than 26,900 square feet, and that of the high chapel alone of the Sainte-Chapelle in Paris unfolds over 6,600 square feet.

The stained-glass window fulfilled three main functions. A practical function, since it allows light to penetrate into buildings in an unprecedented way. A symbolic function, conveyed by the colors of the glass, which can be likened to precious stones and the heavenly Jerusalem. Finally, the stained-glass windows perform a function that is both iconographic and pedagogical, since they present many scenes taken from the Bible or the lives of the saints.

The art of stained glass is especially costly. Thus Suger mentions that to install the stained-glass windows throughout the Abbey Church of Saint Denis, he spent more than 700 pounds, a sum equivalent to half the total cost of the construction of the choir and twice the annual budget of the abbey.

As for Chartres Cathedral, its older stained-glass windows date from the 12th century and the first half of the 13th. The window *Notre-Dame de la Belle Verrière*, famous for its blue, is one of the most ancient medieval stained-glass windows that has come down to our day. Contemporary with those of Saint-Denis, it was spared by the fire in 1194 and escaped destruction and wars, while most of the windows in Saint-Denis that can be observed today date from the 19th century.

M. C.

Caryll Houselander (1901–1954) was a British convert and popular Catholic author. Her spirituality and reflections on lay Christian life anticipate the teachings of Vatican Council II. The excerpt is from her book-length meditation on the Mary, the Mother of Jesus.

Caryll Houselander, *The Reed of God* (New York: Sheed & Ward, 1944), xii-xiii.

Natural love made supernatural

CARYLL HOUSELANDER

Each saint has his special work: one person's work. But Our Lady had to include in her vocation, in her life's work, the essential thing that was to be hidden in every other vocation, in every life.

The one thing that she did and does is the one thing that we all have to do, namely to bear Christ into the world.

Christ must be born from every soul, formed in every life. If we had a picture of Our Lady's personality, we might be dazzled into thinking that only one sort of person could form Christ in himself, and we should miss the meaning of our own being.

Nothing but things essential *for us* are revealed to us about the Mother of God: the fact that she was wed to the Holy Spirit and bore Christ into the world.

Our crowning joy is that she did this as a lay person and through the ordinary daily life that we all live; through natural love made supernatural, as the water at Cana was, at her request, turned into wine.

Chapters 5, 6, and 7 of the Gospel according to Saint Matthew collect various teachings that Jesus proclaimed in Galilee at the beginning of his public life. Ever since the translation from Greek to Latin undertaken by Saint Jerome in the late 4th century, this discourse has customarily been called "the Sermon on the Mount." In it Jesus announces the coming of the kingdom of God (or "of heaven"), sets forth the "Beatitudes," and teaches his disciples the prayer Our Father.

Jesus reveals the secret of happiness

Ever since it was built in the 11th and 12th centuries in a majestic, Romanesque style, the collegial Church of Saint Vincent in Soignies, Belgium, has been spared by the wars, fires, vandalism, and other attacks which history dispenses so prodigally. It therefore offers to the visitor today a rather faithful vision of what its original beauty was. The groin vault overhanging the choir is a sheer miracle in this regard. However, the decoration and the furnishings today represent all styles, mainly Baroque but also academism tinged with Romanticism and even Orientalism, as attested by the painting *The Sermon on the Mount* commissioned from Romain Eugène van Maldeghem (1813–1867).

This drawing is a preparatory study, executed the same year van Maldeghem won the Belgian *Prix de Rome*, in 1838. Jesus is seated at the top of a mountain—where, according to Saint Matthew, he proclaimed the Beatitudes—which one tradition situates not far from Capernaum and the Lake of Tiberias: we can discern the town in the distance, and behind Jesus the artist makes the waters of the lake gleam with a horizontal application of white gouache. Beyond it, closing off the horizon, we see snowy Mount Hermon, in Lebanon. A large crowd has converged on the scene to listen to Jesus' teaching. Closest to him are his apostles, headed by Saint Peter, who makes a sign of his allegiance to him. To the right of Jesus (from the spectator's viewpoint) is Saint John on his knees, sitting on his heels. Following Peter, many disciples listen to the Master.

THE BIBLE – MT 5:1-10

Seeing the crowds, Jesus went up on the mountain,
and when he sat down his disciples came to him.
And he opened his mouth and taught them, saying:
"Blessed are the poor in spirit, for theirs is the kingdom of heaven.
"Blessed are those who mourn, for they shall be comforted.
"Blessed are the meek, for they shall inherit the earth.
"Blessed are those who hunger and thirst for righteousness, for they shall be satisfied.
"Blessed are the merciful, for they shall obtain mercy.
"Blessed are the pure in heart, for they shall see God.
"Blessed are the peacemakers, for they shall be called sons of God.
"Blessed are those who are persecuted for righteousness' sake, for theirs is the kingdom of heaven."

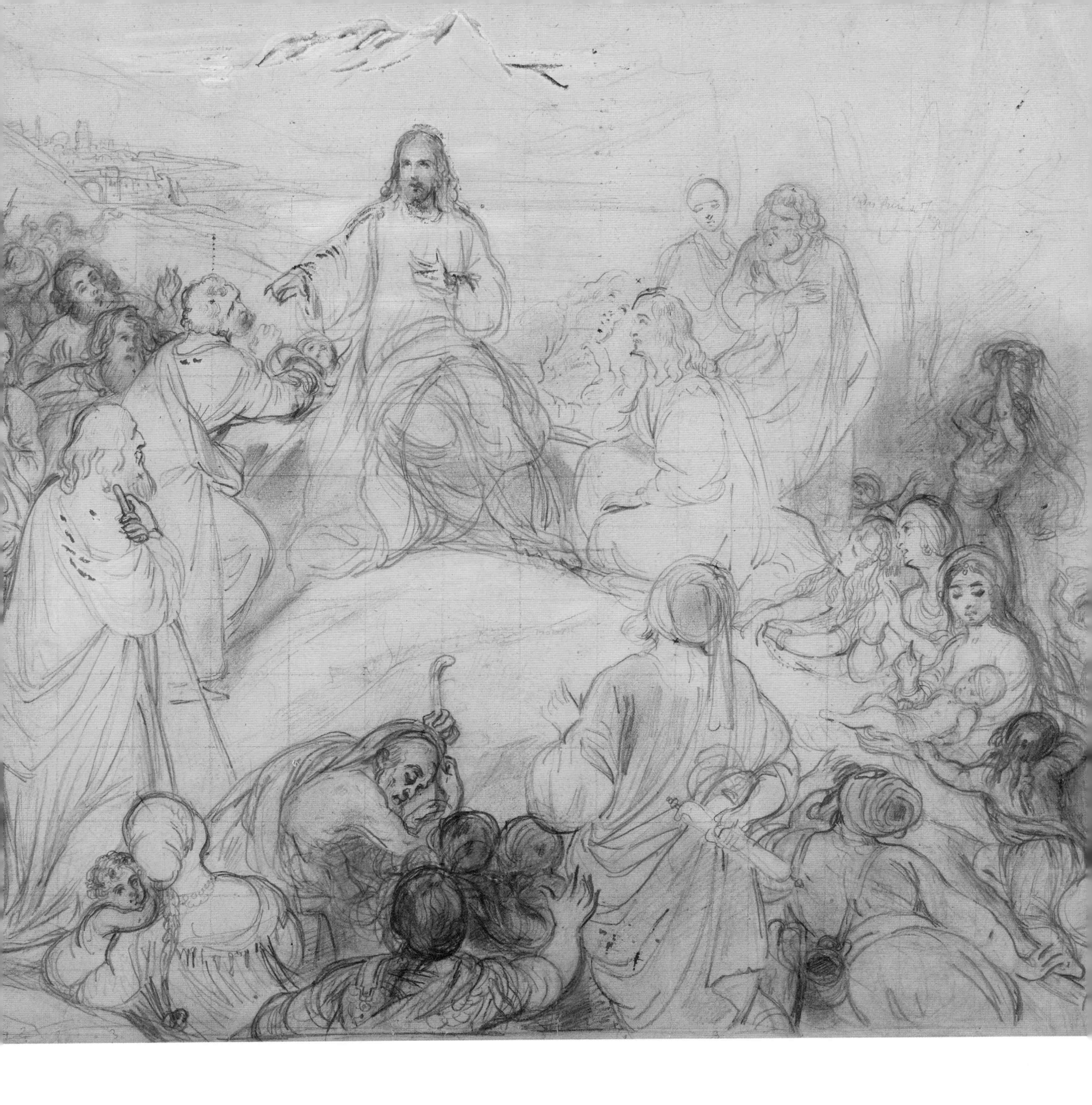

The Sermon on the Mount
Romain Eugène van Maldeghem (1813–1867)
Ca. 1838
Pencil, red chalk, and highlights of white gouache, 16.1 x 18.7 in
Paris, Louvre Museum, department of graphic arts

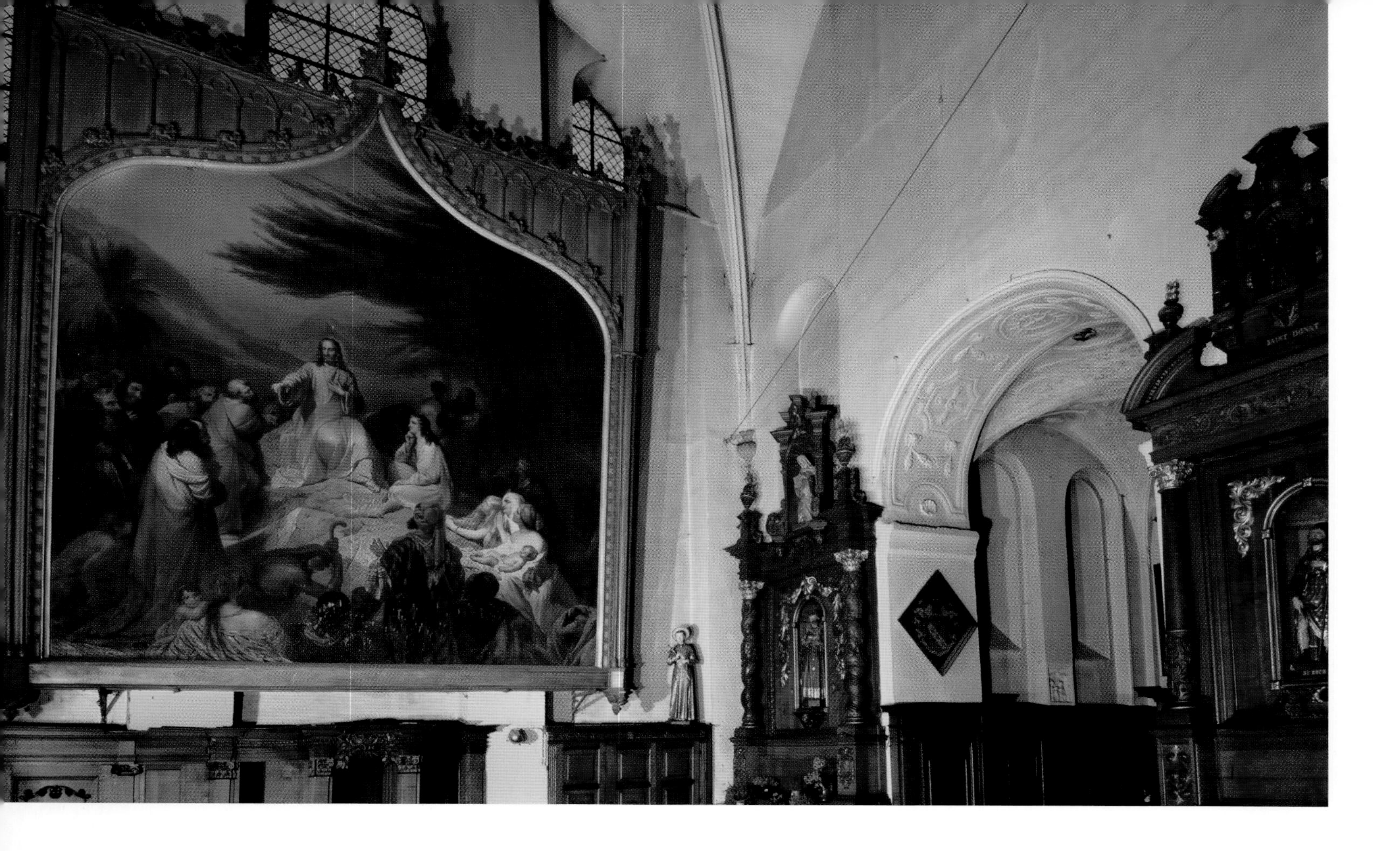

The Sermon on the Mount
Romain Eugène van Maldeghem
1851
Oil on canvas, 236 x 295 in
Soignies (Belgium),
Collegial Church of Saint Vincent

In comparing the preparatory drawing and the monumental canvas in the choir of the Collegial Church of Saint Vincent in Soignies, we can observe the degree to which academism could stultify the best talents: the moving sketch is a living, spiritual work of art, yet the grand painting seems apathetic and soulless.

In front of him the poor and humble of heart circle around: women with children, adolescents, the elderly, the crippled, beggars; a Samaritan woman carrying a jug on her head stands out to the right of the composition; in front of her, in the first row, her hair braided and adorned, is a young courtesan, maybe Mary Magdalene. All the "blesseds" so dear to Jesus' heart are gathered here. But in the midst of them, a little further back from the first row, stands the hieratic silhouette of a religious leader, recognizable by the scroll of the Law that he hides behind his back; he raises his hand as though to make an objection. Most of the figures are depicted with charming naturalness and touching simplicity, and only the figure of the doctor of the Law repeats a cliché of the Orientalist painters.

Jesus, for his part, teaches as a master who has authority, both by his position—on the summit, dominating the audience—and by his gestures: indicative with his right hand which speaks to the intellect, and suggestive with his left hand which speaks to the heart. However, such benevolence emanates from him that obviously he himself is perfectly *meek and humble of heart* (Mt 11:29). Jesus, "the divine pedagogue," is drawn here, the one whom Clement of Alexandria described as "teaching the souls of children and of the humble of heart, who asks us to advance in wisdom and holiness, rather than in knowledge." In this spirit of spiritual childhood, van Maldeghem has sketched here the first draft of what was to become the work of a lifetime. ■

The philosopher Henri Bergson (1859–1941) was not only one of the greatest thinkers of his time but also a remarkable writer, the recipient of the Nobel Prize for Literature in 1927. His thought investigates particularly the enigma of the living thing and that which, in man, exceeds the rational intellect alone. In *The Two Sources of Morality and Religion* (1932), one of his major works, he explores the mystery of love, which transcends mere human morality to give itself to the other. Although he was not Christian, the supreme example of love for him is the Gospel, and Christian holiness.

Henri Bergson,
The Two Sources of Morality and Religion (1932)
Translated by R. Ashley Audra *et al.* (Notre Dame, IN: University of Notre Dame Press, 1977), 59-60.

A morality of the open soul

HENRI BERGSON

The morality of the Gospels is essentially that of the open soul: are we not justified in pointing out that it borders upon paradox, and even upon contradiction, in its more definite admonitions? If riches are an evil, should we not be injuring the poor in giving them what we possess? If he who has been smitten on the one cheek is to offer the other also, what becomes of justice, without which, after all, there can be no "charity"? But the paradox disappears, the contradiction vanishes, if we consider the intent of these maxims, which is to create a certain disposition of the soul. It is not for the sake of the poor, but for his own sake, that the rich man should give up his riches: blessed are the poor "in spirit"! The beauty lies, not in being deprived, not even in depriving oneself, but in not feeling the deprivation. The act by which the soul opens out broadens and raises to pure spirituality a morality enclosed and materialized in ready-made rules: the latter then becomes, in comparison with the other, something like a snapshot view of movement. Such is the inner meaning of the antitheses that occur one after the other in the Sermon on the Mount: "Ye have heard that it was said... I say unto you..." On the one hand the closed, on the other the open. Current morality is not abolished; but it appears like a virtual stop in the course of actual progression. The old method is not given up; but it is fitted into a more general method, as is the case when the dynamic reabsorbs the static, the latter then becoming a mere particular instance of the former. We should need then, strictly speaking, a means of expressing directly the movement and the tendency; but if we still want—and we cannot avoid it—to translate them into the language of the static and motionless, we shall be confronted with formulae that border on contradiction. So we might compare what is impracticable in certain precepts of the Gospels to what was illogical in the first explanations of the differential calculus. Indeed, between the morality of the ancients and Christianity we should find much the same relation as that between the mathematics of antiquity and our own.

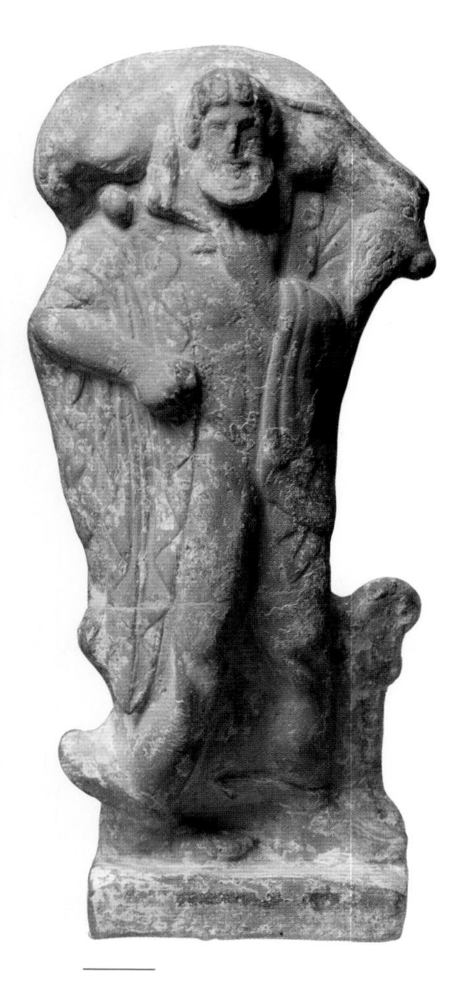

Hermes criophore
First quarter of the 5th century B.C.
Terracotta
Height: 7.2 in
Paris, Louvre Museum

Jesus the Good Shepherd

The Fathers of the Church liked to emphasize that, in order to dispose minds to receive the Good News of salvation, God inspired not only the Old Testament, but also pagan culture, certainly to a lesser degree. The fresco of the *Good Shepherd* in the catacomb of Priscilla, one of the most ancient known depictions of Christ, exemplifies what the Church has always considered the testimony of an anticipatory action of the Holy Spirit among the "Gentiles," the "pagans," in other words, those who did not receive the biblical revelation of God.

A masterpiece of paleo-Christian art (*i.e.* before the year 300 A.D.), this decoration of the "sky" (ceiling) of a Christian burial place repeats the theme of Hermes *criophore* ("carrying a ram") which, in Greco-Roman antiquity, adorned pagan burial places. Mythology attributes to Hermes the role of leading the souls of the departed to the abode of the dead, as well as the "miracle" of having delivered the city of Tanagra from the plague after walking around it while carrying on his shoulders a ram destined to be sacrificed to the gods. The first Christians saw in this image the figure of Jesus, even more readily because it irresistibly evokes the parable of the Good Shepherd who brings the lost sheep back on his shoulders. Moreover, the bucolic decor of the scene, which is quite Virgilian, with green trees and enchanting birds, also evokes the paradisiacal reality toward which the Good Shepherd leads his flock.

The first Christians therefore did not hesitate to repeat this pagan funerary image in decorating their own burial places. However, they made two essential modifications to it: on the one hand, two sheep are added at the feet of the Good Shepherd, symbolizing the flock of the elect that the lost sheep is rejoining; on the other hand, the sheep being carried does not have his head bowed down like the ram destined for sacrifice, but holds its head high triumphantly, knowing that it is loved and has the promise of a blessed life. ■

THE BIBLE – JN 10:11-15

I am the good shepherd. The good shepherd lays down his life for the sheep. He who is a hireling and not a shepherd, whose own the sheep are not, sees the wolf coming and leaves the sheep and flees; and the wolf snatches them and scatters them. He flees because he is a hireling and cares nothing for the sheep. I am the good shepherd; I know my own and my own know me, as the Father knows me and I know the Father; and I lay down my life for the sheep.

The Good Shepherd
250 A.D.
Fresco
Rome, Catacomb of Priscilla

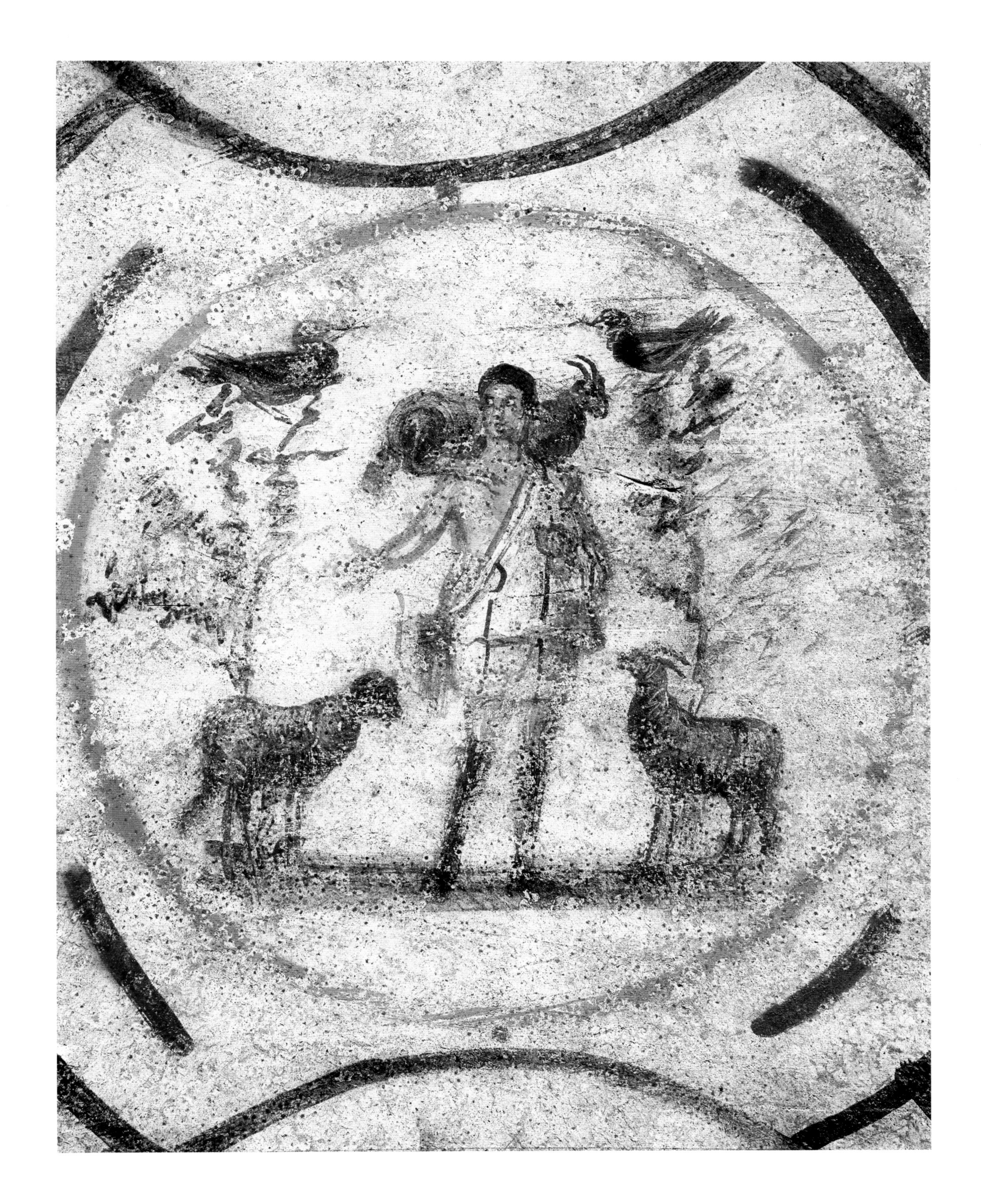

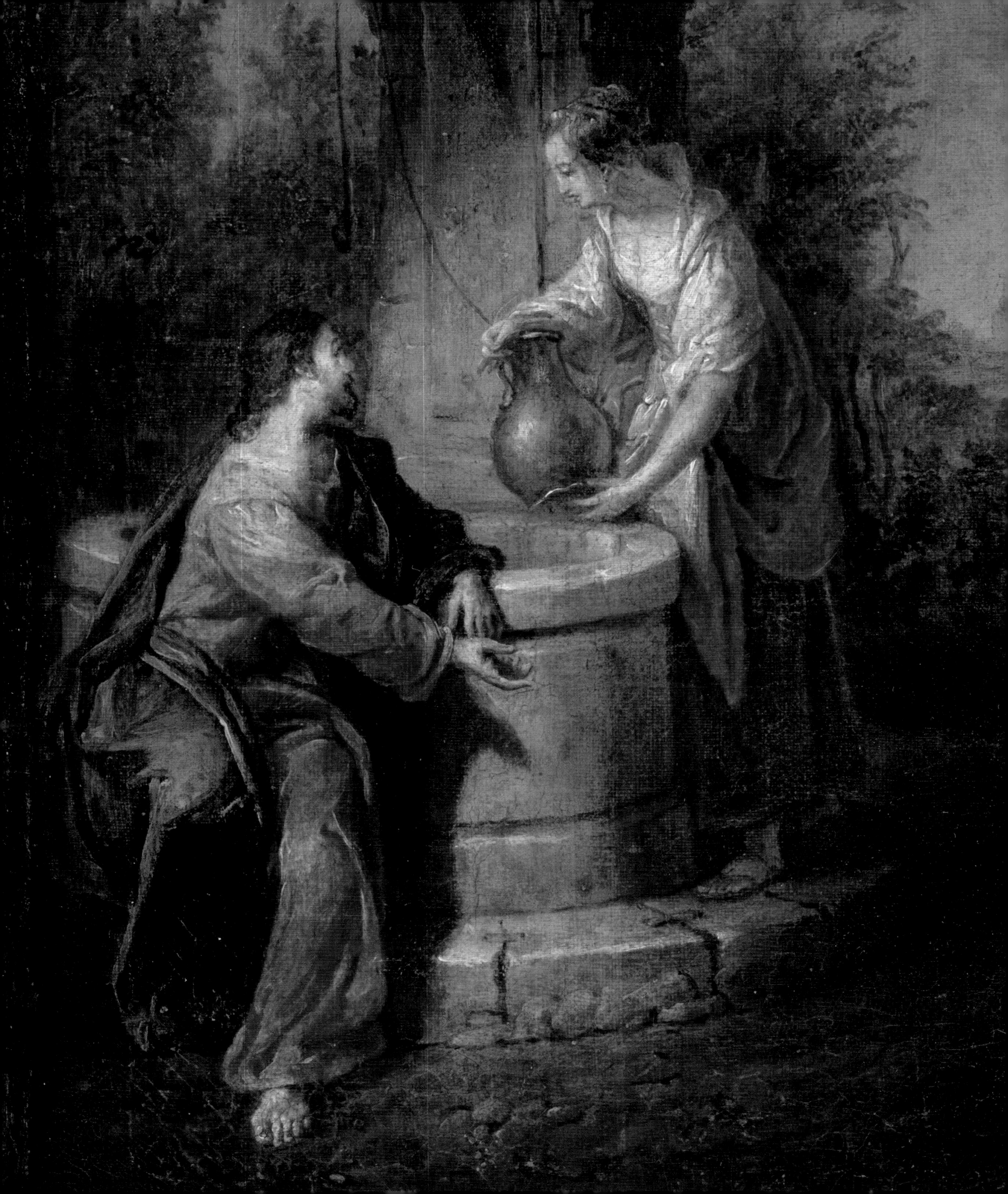

Jesus and the Samaritan woman

The encounter takes place in the heart of Samaria, a region situated between Galilee, where Jesus comes from, and Jerusalem, where he will die. Jesus is sitting beside Jacob's well, in Sychar—present-day Shechem, in Hebrew, or Nāblus, in Arabic. In Jesus' time, Samaritans did not sacrifice at the Temple in Jerusalem but at the temple located on the summit of Mount Gerizim. Religious Jews therefore considered them heretics, members of a dissident sect, almost as non-Jews.

This little picture is a sketch made in view of a larger work. The brush strokes on it, made incisively, without retouching or redoing, are like snapshots of genius. The painter sets up the composition of the work around his principal theme, here the glance that Jesus and the Samaritan woman exchange.

Whereas the disciples will be surprised by the fact that Jesus was speaking to a woman, one on one (Jn 4:27), here the artist dares to offer for our meditation the image of Jesus and this woman conversing eye to eye, which prompts us to ask ourselves about the quality of our own glance.

If, in looking at a woman, you desire her, you have already committed adultery with her in your heart, Jesus had declared (Mt 5:28). In reference to this maxim, the artist's message intends to make clear the fact that Jesus came to save the relations between man and woman, not by liberating them from love, but by liberating them from sin. And, in doing so, he does not cure one alienation by another. In the Christian way of life, curing evil desires does not mean shutting women away and hiding their face under a veil; it means that everyone sanctifies the act of looking at another person. This liberation, obviously, can work only if it goes hand in hand with the restoration of the sanctity of marriage, as it had been instituted by God at the beginning of the world. Indeed, according to Jesus' teaching, intimate relations between a man and a woman, which are very good in themselves (cf. Gn 1:31), presuppose that, through love, the spouses have given themselves to one another irrevocably, to the point of making themselves eunuchs with regard to any person other than their spouse (Mt 19:12). In reality *they are no longer two but one* (Mt 19:6).

Thus—and this is the moment captured in this picture—at the Samaritan woman's request: *"Lord, give me this water, that I might no longer thirst,"* Jesus replies first: *"Go call your husband and come back with him!"* (Jn 4:15-16), echoing one of the last words of the Bible: *The Spirit and the Bride say: Come!... And let him who is thirsty come, let him who desires take the living water, through grace* (Rv 22:17). ■

THE BIBLE – JN 4:7-10

There came a woman of Samaria to draw water. Jesus said to her, "Give me a drink." For his disciples had gone away into the city to buy food. The Samaritan woman said to him, "How is it that you, a Jew, ask a drink of me, a woman of Samaria?" For Jews have no dealings with Samaritans. Jesus answered her, "If you knew the gift of God, and who it is that is saying to you, 'Give me a drink,' you would have asked him, and he would have given you living water."

Christ and the Samaritan woman
Vinzenz Fischer (1729–1810)
1763
Oil on canvas, 18.3 x 13.6 in
Budapest, Museum of the Fine Arts

Although the Mosaic Law prescribed it, in Jesus' day adulterous women were very rarely stoned. The trap set for Jesus is nonetheless effective: if Jesus answers in favor of applying the Law, he contradicts his own teaching about God's mercy; if he answers that it should not be applied, he could be disqualified as someone guilty of despising the commandments given by God to Moses.

The adulterous woman

Rembrandt depicts here the moment when the leading men asked Jesus to take a position on what the sinful woman's fate should be. The protagonists are at the entrance to the Temple in Jerusalem, plunged into darkness. The only light seems to come from outside the picture to illumine the scene, and it diminishes as soon as one moves away from it. We distinguish, in the background, an assembly that is performing an expiatory rite on a platform. Rembrandt illumines the subject in front of a scene that is plunged in blackness. Into the night of the world the light of salvation starts to pierce, while the veiled light of the Old Covenant will go out.

With his left hand, an expert in the Law holds the adulterous woman by her veil, and with his right hand he points her out to Jesus. With his head turned toward him, he orders him to answer his question: "And you, what do you say?" In the front row of the circle that has formed around the unfortunate woman, leading men in oriental costumes insistently await the answer. The woman is on bended knee, with her head lowered in an attitude of a contrite penitent. She is dressed like a woman married that same day, in a white robe, veil, and train. Her face is uncovered, and with her right hand she uses the veil to wipe her tears. Her train could be held by a matron of honor, but an armed guard does that job. She is young and pretty, without the artist lapsing into indulgence, quite modest where others like to reveal the charms permitted by the credible depiction of a seductress.

Finally, here is Jesus. As always in Rembrandt's work, he is of a taller stature than the other figures. He is God. But nothing else is remarkable in the depiction of him. The light does not emanate from him. His garments are sober, simple, rustic. They are dull-colored—unlike, for example, the celestial blue of the French classics in the same period. Rembrandt communicates his vision of Jesus more realistically than symbolically: whereas many Catholic painters seek to suggest with a whole language of symbols the divinity under the human appearance of Jesus, Rembrandt tends to suggest without flourishes his humanity in a divine stature.

THE BIBLE – JN 8:3-7

The scribes and the Pharisees brought a woman who had been caught in adultery, and placing her in the midst they said to him, "Teacher, this woman has been caught in the act of adultery. Now in the law Moses commanded us to stone such. What do you say about her?" This they said to test him, that they might have some charge to bring against him. Jesus bent down and wrote with his finger on the ground. And as they continued to ask him, he stood up and said to them, "Let him who is without sin among you be the first to throw a stone at her."

The Adulterous Woman
Rembrandt (1606–1669)
1644
Oil on wood, 33 x 25.8 in
London, National Gallery

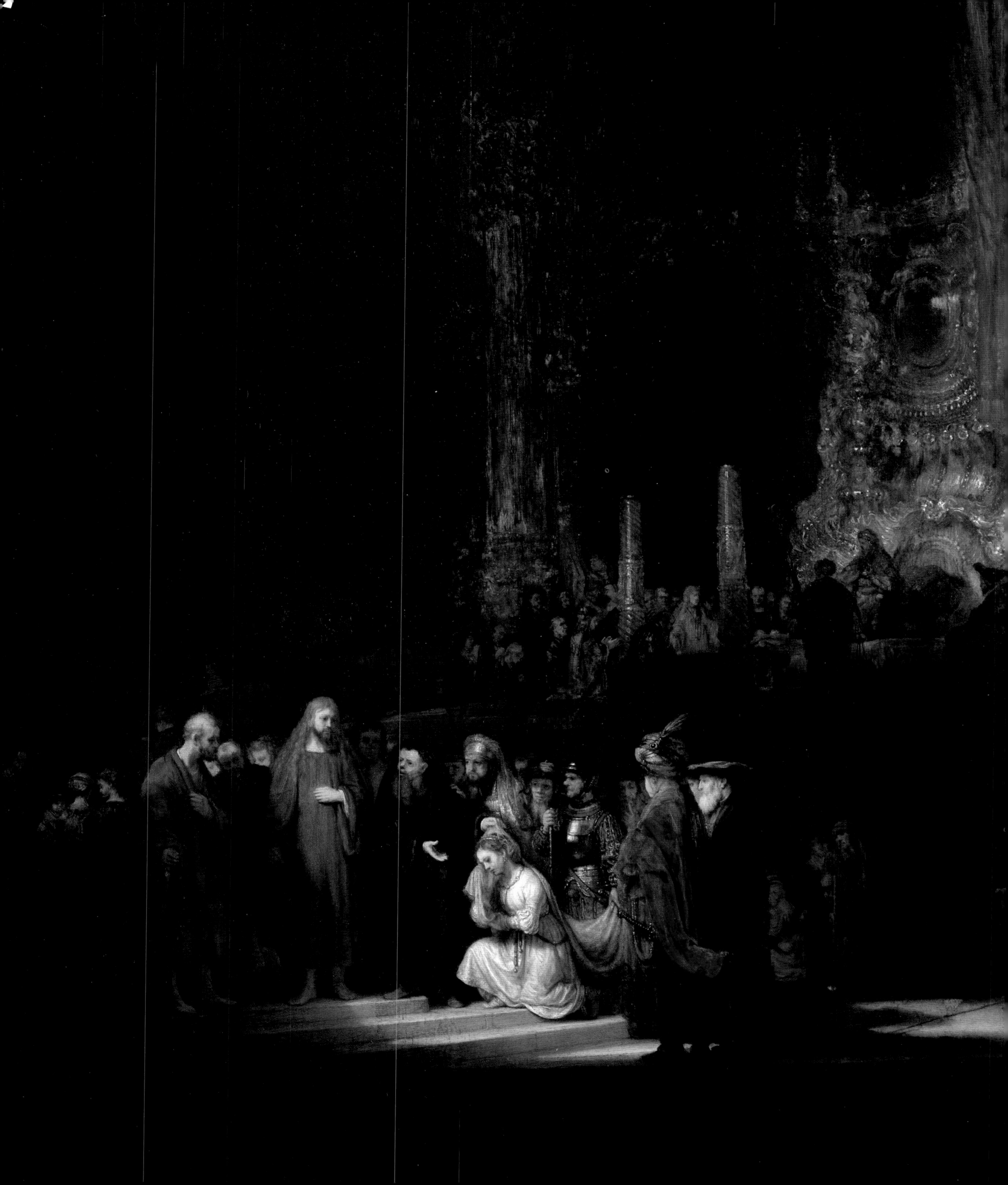

His face is handsome, in a humble way—he is no Apollo. He has long, red, slightly wavy hair. His expression reveals a profound interior life. He looks at the woman with compassion, as though he was seeking to meet her gaze. A diagonal, emphasized by the hand of the accuser, is thus drawn: around it the whole composition of the picture is organized.

Rembrandt grew up in the most demanding Calvinist Protestantism. We sense in this picture the tension created in him by the doctrine of salvation given by divine grace alone and in no way acquired through works of charity. Here, it is indeed grace (Jesus' intervention) that saves the sinful woman, but her attitude expresses contrition, therefore the value of deeds. It is significant that Rembrandt treats this subject and does so in this manner. When Calvin reigned as theocratic dictator over the Republic of Geneva, adultery committed by a woman was punished by death, often by drowning. If the scandal was public, the sentences were executed preferably after sessions of horrible torture. And Rembrandt, of all people, dares to depict the adulterous woman *surprised in the very act* in a wedding gown, so as to underscore the unforgivable gravity of her betrayal, yet repentant and, better than forgiven, benefiting so to speak from a dismissal of her case for lack of evidence: *"Where did your judges go? Did they not condemn you? Neither do I condemn you: go, but from now on sin no more"* (Jn 8:10-11).

However, the more deeply Rembrandt read the Gospels, the more he tended toward an ecumenical understanding of his Christian life. He considered as brothers both the members of the other Protestant churches and the Catholics. Living in a Jewish district in Amsterdam, he kept up many friendships with the Israelites there. He drew closer to the Mennonites, members of an evangelical church that branched off from the Anabaptists, who advocated complete non-violence, even in cases of legitimate defense. We can see therefore in this picture the testimony of an important stage in the development of his faith.

Thus, Rembrandt navigated from rigorist Calvinism to charitable evangelical Christianity, following the inclinations of his soul, as Baudelaire said about him (in the poem "The Beacons"), in admiration despite the appearances which are worth the trouble getting beyond through contemplation of this painting:

Rembrandt, sad hospital of murmurs, where
[*i.e.* Christ's charity, completely filled with human afflictions]
Adorned alone by one great crucifix,
[Jesus, gigantic and scrutinized]
From offal-heaps exhales the weeping prayer
[the sinful woman in tears]
That winter shoots a sunbeam to transfix.
[the chiaroscuro in which the light wells up
along the diagonal Jesus/sinful woman]. ■

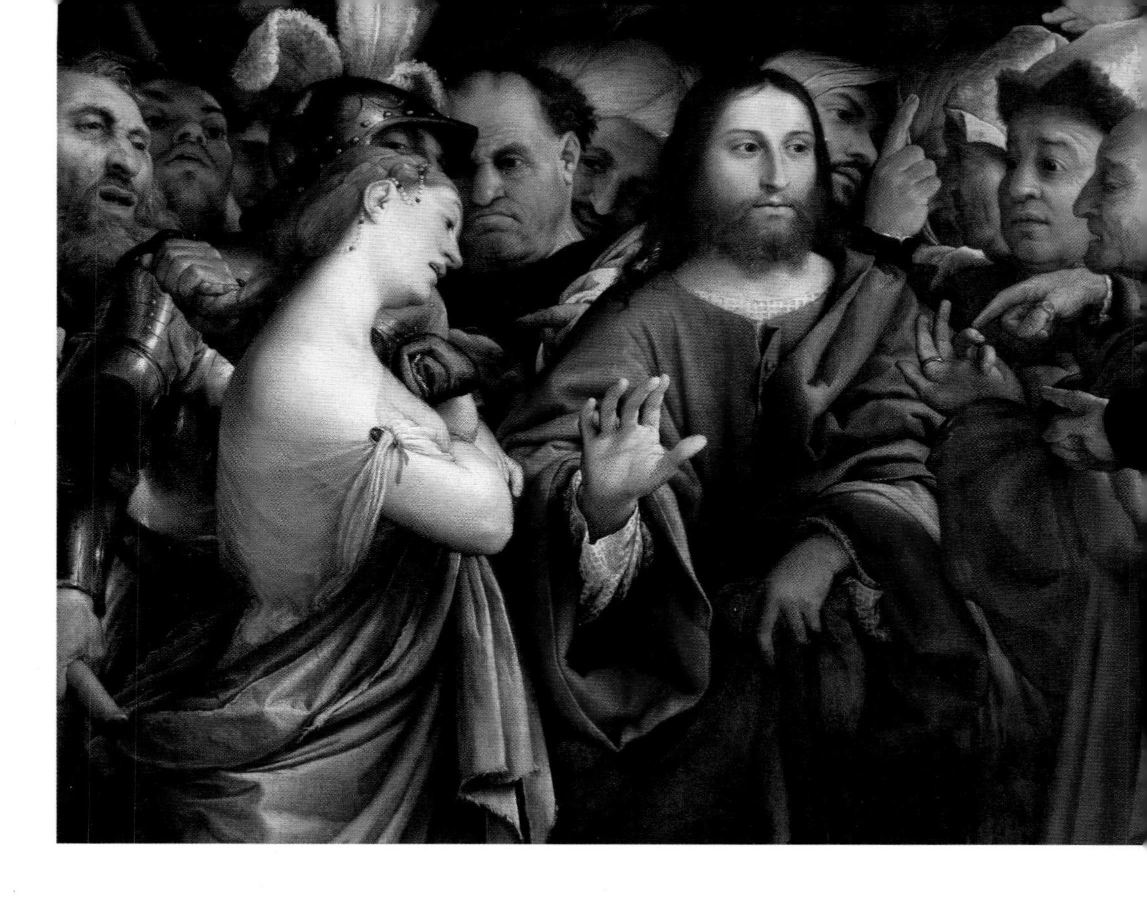

The Adulterous Woman, detail
Lorenzo Lotto (1480–1557)
1527–1529
Oil on canvas, 49 x 61 in
Paris, Louvre Museum

Many artists, especially Italians and Frenchmen, liked to depict the adulterous woman as a seductive courtesan, if not in the scanty clothing in which she was surprised.

BETWEEN CLOSENESS AND DISTANCE: THE FOCAL POINT IN REMBRANDT'S WORKS

To illustrate closeness and the intimate point of view in the works of Rembrandt Harmenszoon van Rijn (1606–1669), we must consider in the first place his self-portraits. The Dutch artist, a genius of the Golden Age, thus depicted himself almost one hundred times in various paintings but also in engravings and drawings. In these genuine "portraits of the soul" from his beginnings in Leyden in 1629 until his death in 1669, the artist depicts himself at all ages, sometimes in costume, sometimes staged with accessories. Against a neutral background in anything from grey to ochre, the painter depicts himself from the torso up, his face turned toward the spectator, on whom he fixes his gaze. With a gripping psychological authenticity, this set of self-portraits marks the originality of his work and distinguishes him from contemporaries, such as Jacob van Ruisdael (1628/1629–1682) and Johannes Vermeer (1632–1675), who were distinguished for their landscapes or genre paintings.

Biblical subjects shed a different light on Rembrandt's pictorial talents and his distancing of the subject matter and the characters. While keeping his taste for ochre colors and choice of a rough, almost unrefined pictorial matter, Rembrandt develops in them unique compositional schemes.

In *The Adulterous Woman*, the perspective chosen is particularly distant from the main scene, which as a result occupies less than the lower third of the canvas. Once again the scenery, by the neutrality of its motive and colors, plays an essential role in bringing out the scene. Whereas in portraits and self-portraits of the artist the decor has the function of projecting the model toward the spectator, thus creating an intimate closeness through the absence of depth, its purpose is the opposite in this picture.

The group of figures takes its place in a majestic, almost unreal setting. Rembrandt signifies thereby the majesty of the scene more than its richness. The crowd is thus crushed by the solemnity of the place. Only Christ and the adulterous woman, through exceptional lighting, are distinguished nobly in this massive staging.

The same technique would be used by Rembrandt in engraving in a marvelous etching that is considered one of the most accomplished by the artist (who was an excellent engraver), known as *The Hundred Guilder Print*. Christ is prominent at first glance because of his stature but also because of a prodigious play of chiaroscuro, emerging from the magma of a crowd gathered in a neutral space that seems excessively high, with no upper limit. Dated 1648–1649, five years after *The Adulterous Woman*, it is classified, like the latter, as being fully in the late style of the artist.

M. C.

Today the Lake of Tiberias (696 feet below sea level), or the Sea of Galilee, is still prey to violent storms, in particular because of the extreme differences in temperature between the surface of the water and the surrounding areas, which are characterized by steep changes in elevation.

The storm calmed

The so-called "Ottonian" art flourished within the Germanic Holy Roman Empire (present-day Germany) between 950 and 1050. An heir of Carolingian art and precursor of Romanesque art, it bears witness to the religious and cultural golden age which, in Europe, marked the definitive emergence from "barbarian" times. With its ingeniously free interpretation, this miniature is typical of this art. We know that "miniature" does not mean "small-sized illustration" but "painting with *minium* [red lead]," more exactly with white lead that served as a primer and a pigment. This miniature, therefore, is part of the illumination of a Gospel book on vellum (lambskin or kidskin), probably produced in Cologne, around 1020, by the archdiocesan scriptorium (workshop of copyists). Its editor was probably Hitda, the abbess of the Convent of Saint Mary of the Capitol in Cologne. Hitda's bold cultural activity testifies to the eminent role that women played in the Ottonian renaissance, particularly as sponsors and patronesses but also as master artists.

Depicted here very suggestively is the (humanly speaking) inevitable shipwreck of the Church during her crossing through history *to the other shore* (Mk 4:35). Peter has let go of the sheets and allows the mainsail to flap; the other apostles cling to each other, terrified; they abandon their oars. Even the figurehead of the frail skiff seems to fear the worst! Meanwhile, Jesus is sleeping peacefully.

On this illustration, painted a thousand years ago, one apostle grabs Jesus' shoulder with his hand and shakes him vigorously to awaken him. In the mind of the miniaturist painter, maybe a monk who thought of his art as a religious mission, this hand is supposed to be a wake-up call to the Christians who will meditate on his work. It should shake them, too, and invite them not only to join the clamor of their prayers to his action but also to oppose the unleashing of the forces of evil with the holiness of their lives. ■

THE BIBLE – MK 4:37-40

And a great storm of wind arose, and the waves beat into the boat, so that the boat was already filling. But he was in the stern, asleep on the cushion; and they woke him and said to him, "Teacher, do you not care if we perish?" And he awoke and rebuked the wind, and said to the sea, "Peace! Be still!" And the wind ceased, and there was a great calm. He said to them, "Why are you afraid? Have you no faith?"

Christ calming the storm
Ca. 1020
Illumination on vellum
Darmstadt, Universitäts- und Landesbibliothek,
Codex Hitda, Gospel book of Abbess Hitda of Meschede,
Codex 1640, folio 117 r°

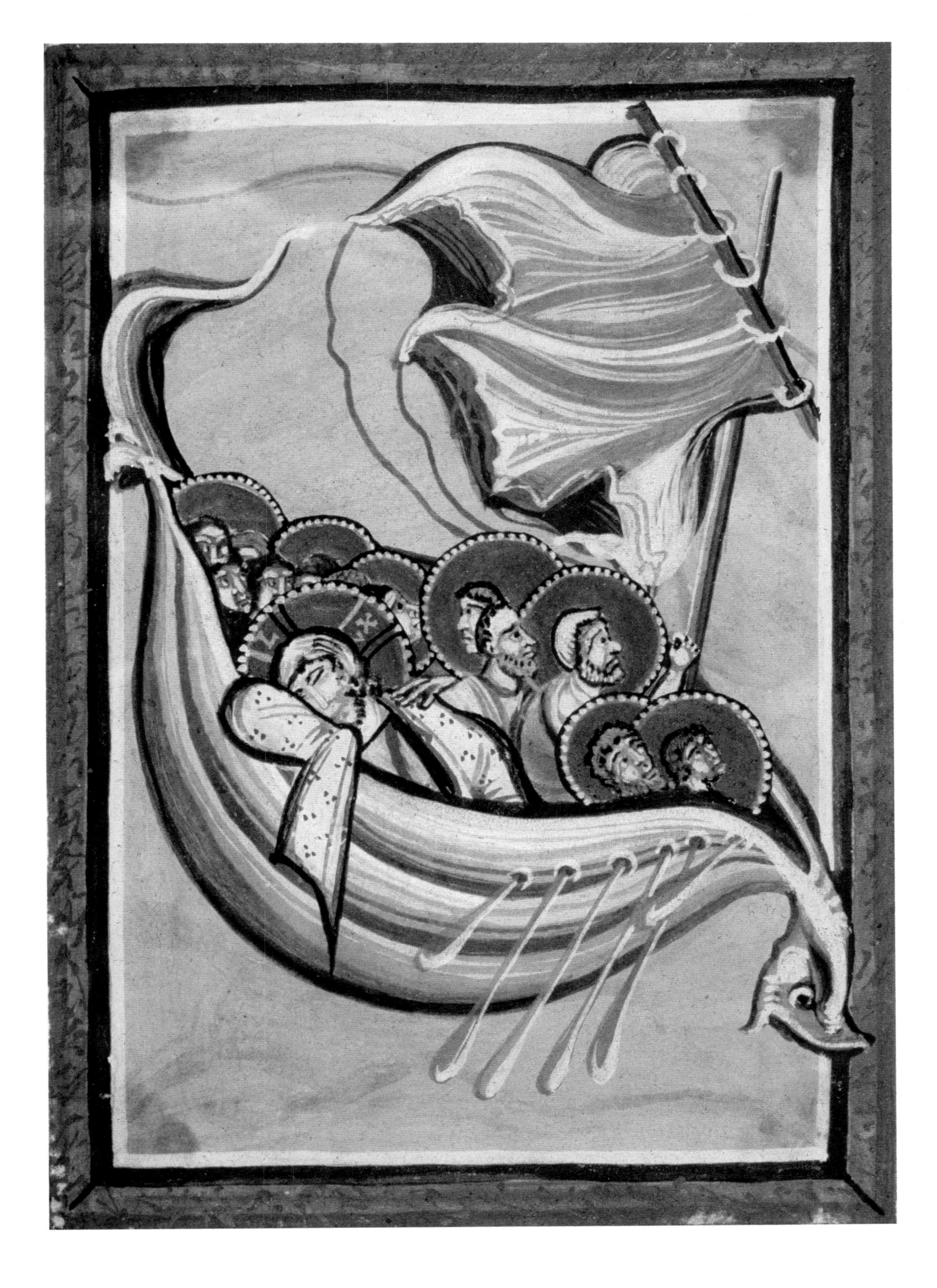

Gregory of Nazianz (*ca.* 329–390 A.D.), like Augustine of Hippo, was born of Christian parents but put off receiving baptism until adulthood. Before that, he completed his studies in rhetoric in Athens. As his ship sailed back home to Achaia, it ran into a great storm that lasted twenty days. He described the experience twice in later autobiographical poems.

Gregory Nazianzen, *De Rebus Suis*, verses 314-319, and *De Vita Sua*, verses 139-142, 167-174. As cited in John Anthony McGuckin, *St. Gregory of Nazianzus: An Intellectual Biography* (Yonkers, NY: St. Vladimir's Seminary Press, 2001), 49-50.

Faith in the midst of a storm at sea

SAINT GREGORY NAZIANZEN

The waves foamed all around the ship
Towering up like mountainous crags on every side.
Water flooded in on us.
All the rigging shook and whistled
In the lashing blasts of wind.
The heavens grew black with storm clouds
Lit up by cracks of lightning
And great thunder crashes on all sides.

A confused and heartrending cry rose up:
Sailors, helmsmen, officers and passengers alike,
All called out as one to Christ,
Even they who had not formerly acknowledged God.

I could not stop sending up great shouts,
Stretching out my hands to God.
My shouts were even louder than the pounding of the waves.
I lay prostrate and prone, my garments torn,
And though it seems beyond belief,
Every word is true,
For they all forgot their private fears,
And these righteous sailors on a sea of woes
Then joined their prayers to mine,
To give me solace in my grief.

THE MANUSCRIPT IN THE OTTONIAN PERIOD

An evangeliary is a liturgical book used for the proclamation of the Gospel during Mass. It does not necessarily contain the entire text of the four Gospels, but may be a collection of pericopes, *i.e.*, excerpts from these canonical Gospels. Besides the evangeliary, the list of Catholic liturgical books is long: lectionary, psalter, Book of the Hours, breviary, missal, sacramentary, etc. They all arrange texts so as to provide the readings necessary for certain prayers or religious ceremonies.

The evangeliary, like other liturgical books, was produced laboriously in the Middle Ages in scriptoriums—workshops of monastic copyists, where the inventiveness of Christian artists was revealed very early: these early publishing houses saw the flourishing of the arts of the miniature, illumination, gilt decoration, and bookbinding—the covers could even be adorned with ivory or gold and precious stones.

The National Library of France preserves many of these early evangeliaries; one of the most ancient is Carolingian: the Godescalc Evangeliary, intended for Charlemagne and his wife Hildegarde. Dating from the years 781–783, it contains a half-dozen miniatures depicting the four evangelists separately, as well as a *Christ in Glory* and a *Fountain of Life*. Copied and decorated for use in the Palatine Chapel in Aix-la-Chapelle/Aachen, it is the most famous of the Carolingian books.

The evangeliary of Hitda, dating from the Ottonian period (10th c.–early 11th c.), continues the tradition of the Carolingian evangeliary. It was produced shortly after the year 1000 and contains more than twenty sumptuous miniatures, including this *Christ calming the storm*.

Ottonian art developed in the Germanic Holy Roman Empire over a relatively short period, between the coronation of Otto in 967 and the extinction of the Ottonian dynasty with the death of Henry II in 1024. Production continued nonetheless for several decades.

The sacramentary of Henry II preserved in the Bayerische Staatsbibliothek in Munich is one of the greatest expressions of this imperial art: the Emperor depicted in the center is larger than everyone else, including Christ. He holds in his left hand the imperial sword (*Reichsschwert*) and in his right hand the Holy Lance. Once again, this is an almost literal copy of the Carolingian models, with a distinct taste for the density and richness of the decoration.

The page by the master of the *Registrum Gregorii* (collection of letters by Pope Gregory the Great), preserved today in the Condé Museum in Chantilly, is another Ottonian masterpiece. On it, Otto is depicted enthroned, receiving honors from the four allegories of the provinces of Germany, France, Italy, and Allemania. Here the Emperor is again exalted in an antiquary and refined style.

Ottonian art continues elements of the Carolingian style not only in its manuscripts, but also in the goldsmith's art or, on another scale, in architecture.

M. C.

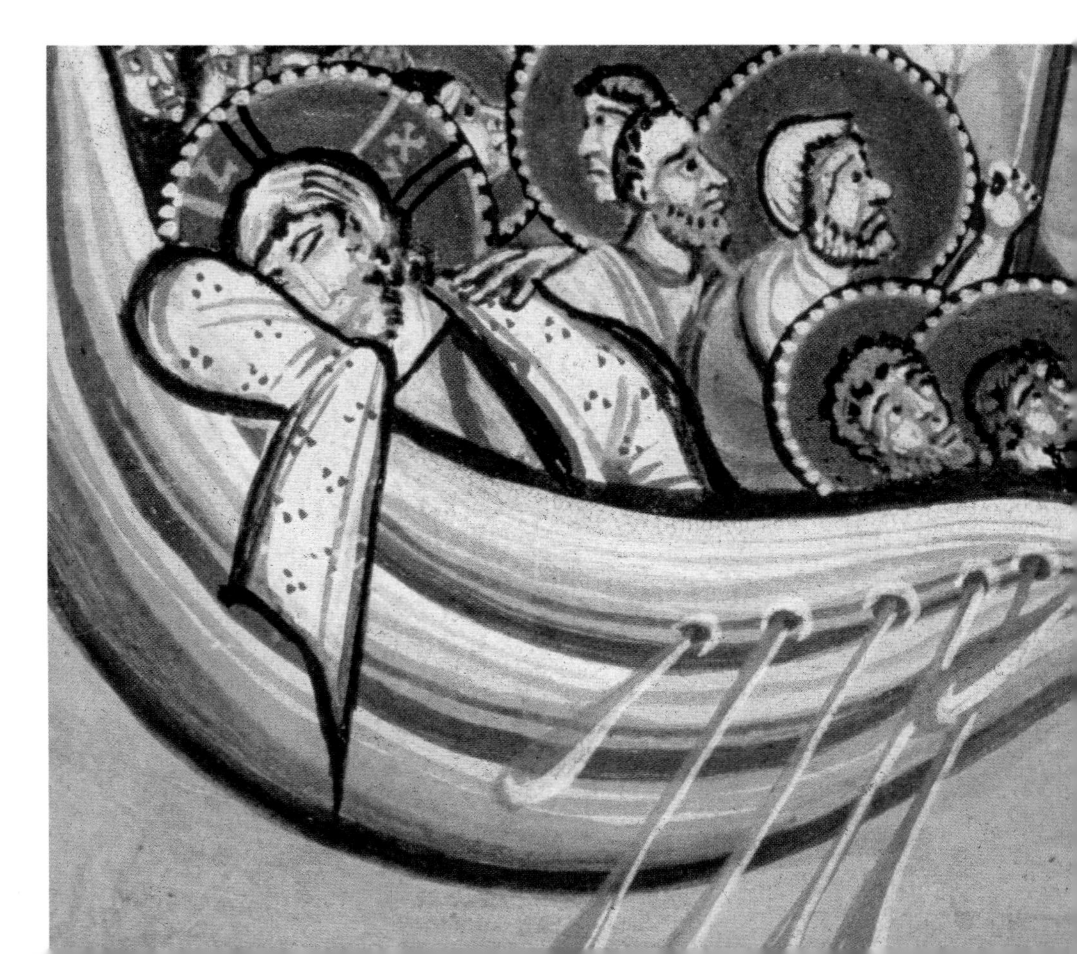

Christ calming the storm, detail
Ca. 1020
Illumination on vellum
Darmstadt, Universitäts- und Landesbibliothek, *Codex Hitda*, Gospel book of Abbess Hitda of Meschede,
Codex 1640, folio 117 r°

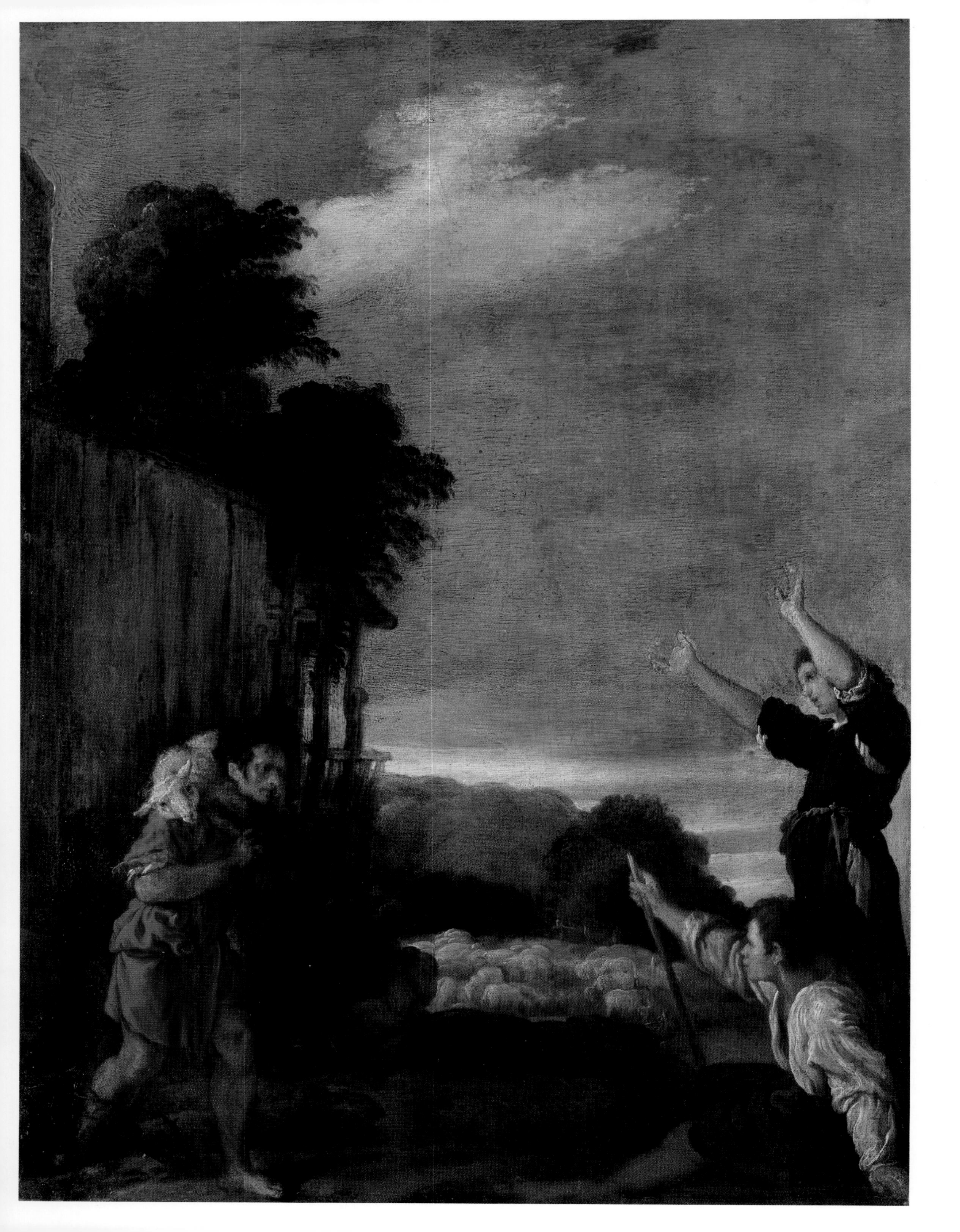

The lost sheep

It stands to reason that a good shepherd does not run the risk of leaving ninety-nine sheep so as to go to the trouble of retrieving one that is lost. However, what is important in Jesus' parables is not the anecdotal staging of everyday life, but the teaching that is to be drawn from it, namely here, that for God every human being has an inestimable value. And this is what artists have endeavored to show.

Domenico Fetti (1589–1623) developed an original pictorial style with a wealth of color. At the end of his life he dedicated himself to achieving a series of small-format works on religious themes, particularly the parables. This type of production, quite new at the time, prefigures popular imagery, in the sense that all the parables, like the one here about the lost sheep, are depicted by Fetti as an illustration of the Gospel suited to catechizing the lowly.

The parables recounted by Jesus are simple stories that everyone can understand. Fetti advocates keeping only their main, obvious lesson, without running the risk of blunting their point by giving elaborate meanings to the incidental circumstances of the narration. Here, Jesus responds to the Pharisees who exasperate him by claiming to be just, and even the only just men; at the same time, he addresses above all those who are conscious of their unworthiness and suffer because they are not numbered among God's blessed by the religious authorities. And, for them, he confirms in a graphic way what Scripture already affirms: Even if your mother were to abandon you, your God and Father will never abandon you, however long you may be entangled in sin (cf. esp. Is 49:15).

Domenico Fetti repeats in an image the meaning given by Jesus himself to the parable: the Father sent into this world the one whom he designated as his "beloved Son" on the day of the baptism in the Jordan (Mt 3:17), with the mission of going to seek sinners one by one and bringing them back to the sheepfold on his shoulders: *"For the Son of man came to seek and to save what was lost,"* he insists (Lk 19:10). So therefore, the moral of this charming little picture is clear: however far men may have strayed, God seeks them, God finds them, God saves them. We can understand the Pharisees' consternation: it is insane, this justice of God according to Jesus, which expects us to search for the guilty, not to condemn them, but for the sole purpose of helping them to escape the chastisement which, according to the Law, this justice ought to inflict on them! ■

THE BIBLE – LK 15:3-6

So he told them this parable: "What man of you, having a hundred sheep, if he has lost one of them, does not leave the ninety-nine in the wilderness, and go after the one which is lost, until he finds it? And when he has found it, he lays it on his shoulders, rejoicing. And when he comes home, he calls together his friends and his neighbors, saying to them, 'Rejoice with me, for I have found my sheep which was lost.'"

The Parable of the Lost Sheep
Domenico Fetti (1589–1623)
Ca. 1619–1920
Oil on wood, 23.6 x 17.5 in
Dresden, Gemäldegalerie Alte Meister

Jesus traveled ceaselessly for three years. During the days preceding this scene he was in Capernaum, north of the Lake of Tiberias. Here, he was in Judea, nearly a hundred miles further south, to the west of the Jordan and of the Dead Sea. The word "children" is central in Jesus' teaching. It occurs around fifty times in the Gospel.

Jesus and the children

In his day, Noël Hallé (1711–1781) was at least as famous as his contemporary Jean Honoré Fragonard. At first glance, his work *Let the little children come to me* resorts to the most successful expressive devices of French classicism: his composition adopts all its rules. The figures make hand gestures that speak more eloquently than words. The exchanges of glances are like real conversations, while their sight lines structure the space of the picture along the diagonal earth-heaven drawn by the position of Jesus' body. And here color comes to life in the movement of this transcendence and, particularly, manifests the supernatural by the prodigious blue of Jesus' cloak, a blue "invented" for this purpose by Philippe de Champaigne a century earlier. The color became an explicit metaphor for the ineffable, so as to lead the viewer contemplating the enjoyment of earthly realities to consider the heavenly realities. Classic too is the color of the shawl covering Saint Peter's shoulders, a sienna that makes this piece of cloth the stole of Christ's representative on earth.

The three children whom Peter with a firm hand tries to prevent from approaching Jesus are dressed as the three theological virtues: in red, Charity; in white and blue, Faith; and in green, Hope. These colors show that from now on the head of the apostles must make no mistake on this point: *"Let the little children come to me,"* Jesus will exclaim, *"the kingdom of God belongs to those like them."*

Although Hallé adopts the composition and the chromatic palette of the classics, unlike them he does not seek to raise the spectator to a spiritual and moral ideal: he tends to communicate emotions, in an approach that will soon found Romanticism. The great classical artists rejected all expressions of feelings and all dramatization so as to highlight reflection and interiority. Hallé addresses the sentiments. For him, "the great [17th] century of souls" is already in the distant past. He dares to make the faces speak in a way that touches the heart, bordering on sentimentalism. Jesus shows that he is almost exasperated by Saint Peter's lack of comprehension for the things of the kingdom of heaven. The mother and the little children, on the contrary, reveal that they have understood everything. The children seek to capture the sympathy of the man to whom they lift their eyes: praying, trusting, loving, adoring, they do not seem to doubt for an instant that the kingdom of heaven is made for them and that God who is Love can only open his arms to welcome them. ■

THE BIBLE – MK 10:13-16

And they were bringing children to him, that he might touch them; and the disciples rebuked them. But when Jesus saw it he was indignant, and said to them, "Let the children come to me, do not hinder them; for to such belongs the kingdom of God. Truly, I say to you, whoever does not receive the kingdom of God like a child shall not enter it." And he took them in his arms and blessed them, laying his hands upon them.

Let the little children come to me
Noël Hallé (1711–1781)
1751
Oil on canvas, 122 x 74.8 in
Paris, Church of Saint Sulpice

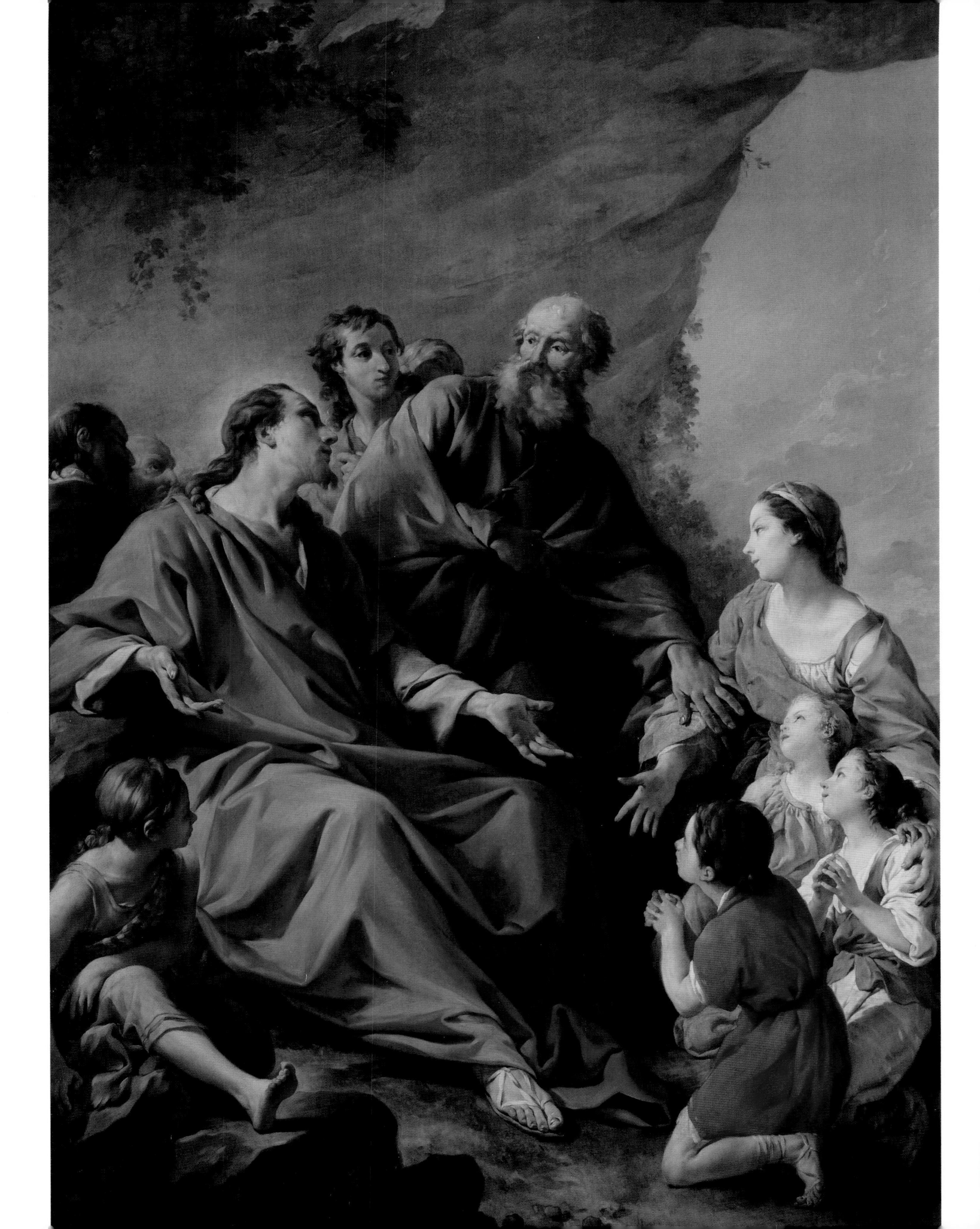

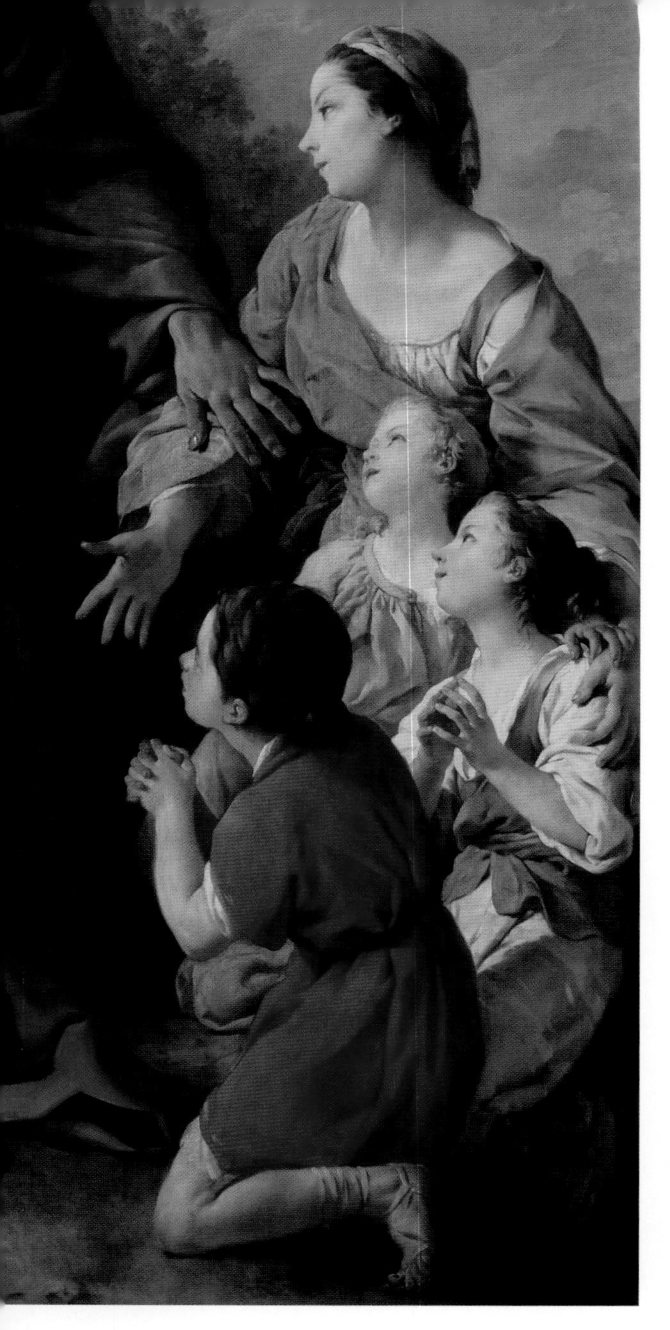

Let the little children come to me,
detail
Noël Hallé (1711–1781)
1751
Oil on canvas, 122 x 74.8 in
Paris, Church of Saint Sulpice

SAINT SULPICE IN THE 18TH CENTURY

Reconstruction work on the Church of Saint Sulpice began as early as the mid-17th century but, after an interruption of almost forty years, during the 18th century the building truly took on its present character, little by little.

Starting in 1719, renovations in the nave and the transept began under the direction of Gilles-Marie Oppenord (1672-1742), the Regent's architect. Oddly enough, they were financed by a royally approved lottery organized by the curate, Jean-Baptiste Languet de Gergy. However, the bell tower, erected in 1726, had to be destroyed in 1731 because of a design error that made its weight excessive and dangerous. Gilles-Marie Oppenord was then dismissed as director of the construction site.

To design the façade, a competition was organized with 6,000 pounds as the prize. It was won in 1732 by the Italian Giovanni Niccolo Servandoni (1695-1766), who was already at Saint Sulpice and had just completed part of the decoration of the Blessed Virgin's chapel. The architect planned furthermore to arrange a vast semicircular pavement surrounded by buildings, one of which would ultimately be raised to the status of 6 Place Saint-Sulpice. Although that ambitious project was abandoned, Servandoni nevertheless did complete the two levels of the façade with rows of columns, and then, under the direction of Oudot de Maclaurin and finally of Jean-François Chalgrin, the construction of the upper floor and the two towers was started in 1765.

As for the interior furnishings, the church, consecrated in 1745, was endowed in the second half of the 18th century with a great organ, built by François Henri Clicquot between 1776 and 1781 (enlarged by Aristide Cavaillé-Coll in 1862). The greatest Parisian artists were enlisted to execute an especially meticulous decorative program. Among those working on it were the painters François Lemoyne and Carle Van Loo, and the sculptors Edme Bouchardon and Jean-Baptiste Pigalle. Noël Hallé took part in this period of creative effervescence with his picture *Let the little children come to me*.

The decoration of the Church of Saint Sulpice would be extensively enriched over the course of the 19th century. The visitor can still admire two frescos by Michel-Martin Drolling in the Saint Paul Chapel, as well as the famous paintings by Eugène Delacroix that adorn the walls and the vault of the Holy Angels Chapel.

M. C.

Leo Tolstoy (1828–1910), a genius of 19th-century Russian literature, created monumental works of fiction, anchored in realism. He explores the collective and individual stories with an interpretive prism that is in the first place strongly psychological. Although very Christian, he gradually broke with the Orthodox Church to which he belonged, and developed a personal theology bound up with radical non-violence. In this passage from *Anna Karenina* (1877), the character Levin, inspired by the author himself, muses about the purity of his wife, starting from a famous saying by Jesus about spiritual childhood.

Leo Tolstoy, *Anna Karenina* (1877), translated from Russian by Constance Garnett
Part Five, Chapter 19.

The children and those who are like them

LEO TOLSTOY

"Thou hast hid these things from the wise and prudent, and hast revealed them unto babes." So Levin thought about his wife as he talked to her that evening. Levin thought of the text, not because he considered himself "wise and prudent." He did not so consider himself, but he could not help knowing that he had more intellect than his wife and Agafea Mihalovna, and he could not help knowing that when he thought of death, he thought with all the force of his intellect. He knew too that the brains of many great men, whose thoughts he had read, had brooded over death and yet knew not a hundredth part of what his wife and [her old maidservant] knew about it. Different as those two women were, Agafea Mihalovna and Katya, as his brother Nikolay had called her, and as Levin particularly liked to call her now, they were quite alike in this. Both knew, without a shade of doubt, what sort of thing life was and what was death, and though neither of them could have answered, and would even not have understood the questions that presented themselves to Levin, both had no doubt of the significance of this event, and were precisely alike in their way of looking at it, which they shared with millions of people. The proof that they knew for a certainty the nature of death lay in the fact that they knew without a second of hesitation how to deal with the dying, and were not frightened of them. Levin and other men like him, though they could have said a great deal about death, obviously did not know this since they were afraid of death, and were absolutely at a loss what to do when people were dying. If Levin had been alone now with his brother Nikolay, he would have looked at him with terror, and with still greater terror waited, and would not have known what else to do.

Jesus was in Judea, in Jericho this time. The city, established in the Jordan Valley, not far from the northern shore of the Dead Sea, is the lowest in the world, over 780 feet below sea level.

Jesus restores sight to the blind men

Jesus holds in his left hand a scroll of Scripture, as a reference to the Letter to the Hebrews: *When Christ came into the world, he said* [to his Father], *"Sacrifices and offerings you have not desired, but a body have you prepared for me. Then I said: Behold, I have come to do your will, O God"* (Heb 10:5, 7). The "roll of the book" is therefore the Old Testament which, under the shadows and figures of the Law and the Prophets, reveals the life and work of the future Messiah. Jesus stretches out his right hand to touch the eyes of the blind men. We see benevolence on his face, and compassion in his look.

Behind Jesus stand his disciples, and in the first row we recognize Peter and John. The two blind men have their eyes closed. Nevertheless, with uplifted head they "look" insistently and shrewdly in the direction of Jesus. With the eyes of faith they see clearly that he can save them by bringing them healing. With open hands they show their complete trust and their full readiness to receive the gift from God. In the background looms a high mountain covered at the top with a cloud. From Sinai to Tabor, the "high mountain" represents the dwelling place of God, the cloud suggesting the omnipotence of the Father, inasmuch as he is at work in the earthly activity of his beloved Son, Jesus.

And behold, from the side of the mountain a tree has sprouted. It suggests the tree of life that was planted at the origin of the world (Gn 3:24) and will flourish at the end of it (Rv 22:2). It bears seven branches, like the sacred candelabra that God prescribed that Moses should make. Metaphorically, from the wood of this tree the cross of Jesus will be fashioned. In the art of icons, the tree on the side of a mountain symbolizes the mission of the Son, both in the work of creation and in the work of redemption. The tree leans toward the left, as though by the force of a slight breeze. This is the Holy Spirit, who manifests himself as communication between the Father and the Son. Thus this mosaic admirably emphasizes the investment of the whole Divine Trinity in the earthly work of Jesus, the Incarnate Son. ■

THE BIBLE – MT 20:29-34

And as they went out of Jericho, a great crowd followed him. And behold, two blind men sitting by the roadside, when they heard that Jesus was passing by, cried out, "Have mercy on us, Son of David!" The crowd rebuked them, telling them to be silent; but they cried out the more, "Lord, have mercy on us, Son of David!" And Jesus stopped and called them, saying, "What do you want me to do for you?" They said to him, "Lord, let our eyes be opened." And Jesus in pity touched their eyes, and immediately they received their sight and followed him.

Christ heals two blind men at the gates of Jericho
12th century
Mosaic
Monreale (Sicily), Cathedral of Santa Maria Nuova

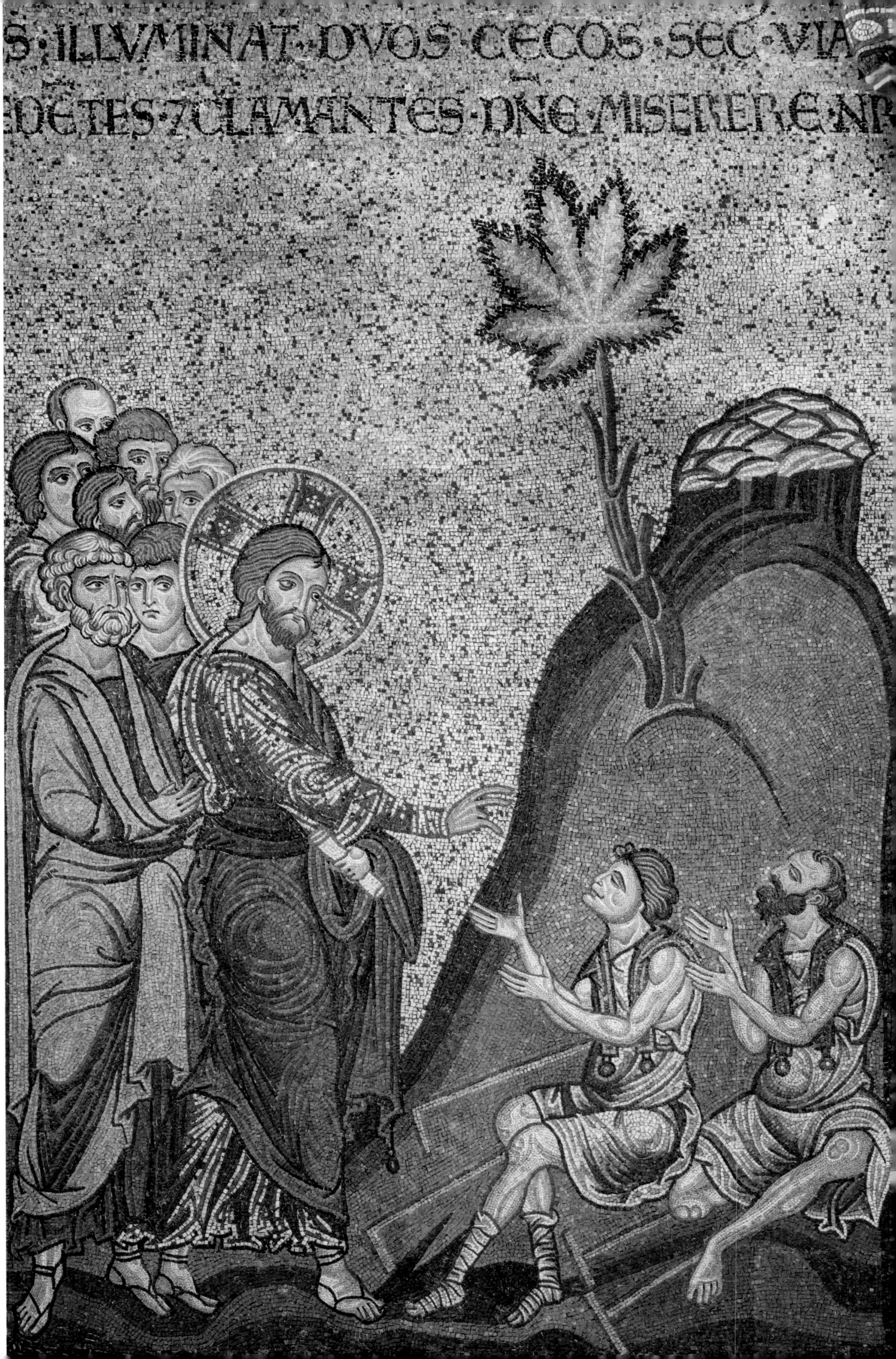

S·ILLVMINAT·DVOS·CECOS·SEC·VIA
EDETES·7CLAMANTES·DNE·MISERERE·NR

Jesus teaches about the commandment of the Mosaic Law: "Love your neighbor as yourself." A Pharisee interrupts him and asks him this question: "But in fact, whom should I consider my neighbor?"

The Good Samaritan

A legend has been created about the painter Gustave Moreau (1826–1898), born of the irreconcilable contradictions between the man, as he was according to his relatives and friends, and the idea of the artist that one gets by contemplating his work. The first was a distinguished, very cultivated man, a tireless worker and admirable instructor, who was at the same time spiritual and passionate, thoughtful and moderate, cheerful, generous, and tender-hearted. The personality of the second could be summed up by this witticism by Paul de Saint-Victor: "The author of the works of Gustave Moreau is an opium smoker who has at his service the hands of a goldsmith with which to set and mount his dreams." Certainly, the work of Gustave Moreau speaks only "the language of symbol, myth, and sign" and does so in a way that is at least singular, creating a world that is mysterious, fascinating, but a tad distressing for rational minds.

Gustave Moreau paints not what he sees but what he thinks. And when he wants to share the vision of his thoughts, he lacks neither the resources of a highly cultured artist nor those of an exuberant imagination. Hence the profusion of details in his works, unabashedly including anachronisms and unlikely fantasies, making ornate Arabesques from *The Thousand and One Nights* spring up on his canvas in sumptuous landscapes. Along with—even if it means bordering on delirium—fantastic architecture in which are set mythic scenes, abstruse as they are strange. We should add finally the immoderate, prodigious character of the painter's love for "color... the product of thought, imagination, and reverie" that can be shocking when, for the first time, the viewer finds himself facing one of these gigantic bravura pieces that Gustave Moreau enjoyed painting for the official salons.

His watercolors are less luxuriant. Not that they are simply sketches, furtive witnesses of the spontaneous outpouring of a vision: there is an idea elaborated at length and a lot of work behind a watercolor by Gustave Moreau. Witness *The Good Samaritan*, which illustrates the parable invented by Jesus to shed light for his listeners on love of

THE BIBLE – LK 10:30-36

Jesus replied, "A man was going down from Jerusalem to Jericho, and he fell among robbers, who stripped him and beat him, and departed, leaving him half dead. Now by chance a priest was going down that road; and when he saw him he passed by on the other side. So likewise a Levite, when he came to the place and saw him, passed by on the other side. But a Samaritan, as he journeyed, came to where he was; and when he saw him, he had compassion, and went to him and bound up his wounds, pouring on oil and wine; then he set him on his own beast and brought him to an inn, and took care of him. And the next day he took out two denarii and gave them to the innkeeper, saying, 'Take care of him; and whatever more you spend, I will repay you when I come back.' Which of these three, do you think, proved neighbor to the man who fell among the robbers?"

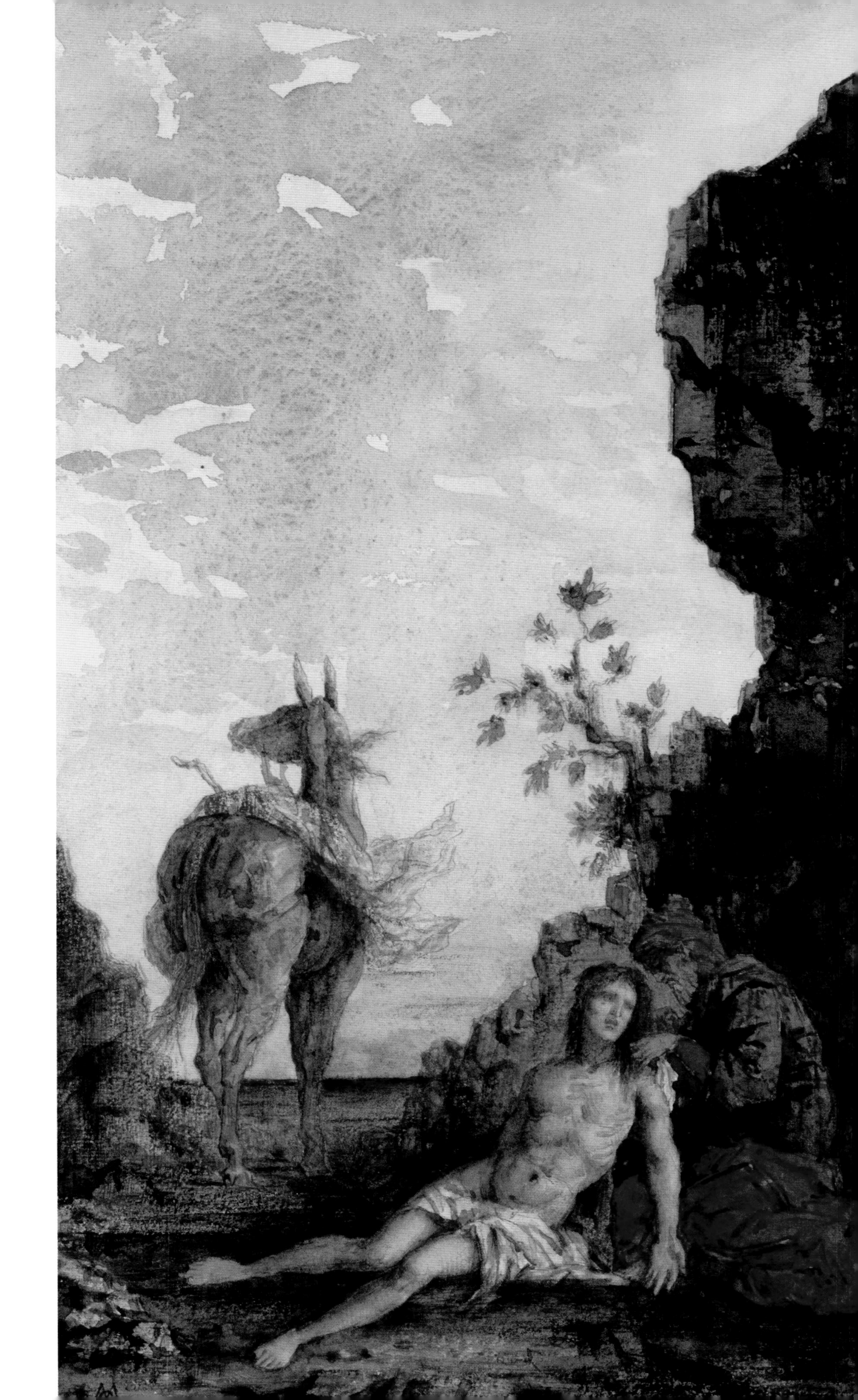

The Good Samaritan
Gustave Moreau (1826–1898)
Watercolor, 10.6 x 5.9 in
Paris, Gustave Moreau Museum

neighbor and therefore on the person of the "neighbor"; and consequently on the nature of this love, this time obeying the new commandment that he himself would soon enact: *Love one another as I have loved you* (Jn 13:34)—a fundamental commandment for Christians, who see Jesus as the model for putting it into practice.

This story—short, but rich in significance—testifies in part to what Cardinal de Lubac liked to call "the anticlericalism of the saints," a form of "anticlericalism" often present in the Gospel: indeed, a priest and then a Levite, both of them with duties at the Temple, are the ones who go on their way while noticing a man left for dead, possibly because they had to arrive punctually in Jerusalem to celebrate a worship service there. A Samaritan (the Samaritans were often despised by the Jews) comes along, and not only does he care for the unfortunate man, but he also pays for his long convalescence in a reputable inn. Gustave Moreau invites us to set out with him to discover the deep meaning of this parable.

The composition of the work is highly refined. It is inspired by the early Italians, who took Byzantine icons as their inspiration. The scene is set within the V formed by a narrow pass that symbolizes the precariousness of human existence and all the threats weighing on it. As a reference to Sinai, where Moses received the Law of God, and to Tabor, where Jesus gave the New Law of the Beatitudes, the mountain on the right represents the place where God reveals himself to human beings. The path that must be taken in order to reach it is a narrow, rough, steep road with plenty of trials. Standing out at mid-height, overhanging the figures, is the tree of the earthly paradise, the one from which, at the origin of humanity, Eve took the fruit of the knowledge of good and evil, giving in to the temptation of the serpent and *ipso facto* causing suffering and evil to enter into human destiny: since then, all human existence plays out in an incomprehensible tragedy, which is rendered visible here in the exact balance of this tree.

What perverts the human heart, in this case the desire for riches, drove robbers to spread suffering. The naked, bruised body of their victim crudely testifies to the scandalous treatment undergone by the innocent man, who is stripped and fatally wounded. But the solicitude of the Good Samaritan reveals, at the same time, that the only truly human response—one that is also truly divine, as we will understand later—lies in love for others, a love that acts through compassion and service.

Together with Christian tradition, Gustave Moreau liked to see the figure of the Good Samaritan as a type or symbol of Jesus, the Son of God who came to earth to save humanity, giving the example to follow by making himself, out of love, the neighbor on the paths of the life of all human beings, bringing the cure for their misfortunes, and offering to those who follow him a new life beyond the reach of the powers of evil and death. The painter clearly adopts this symbolism, but ingeniously he also represents the victim as a Christ figure: so that there will be no possible doubt, he derives from the traditional iconography of Christ the inert posture and the *perizonium* (loincloth) of the *Pietà* scenes, or more precisely, of the *Deploratio* [*Lamenting*] (*cf.* page 149).

When he undertakes the major subjects from the life of Jesus, Gustave Moreau refuses to give in to his immoderate taste for symbolic and coloristic richness, guided in this by the fact that a watercolor allows no second chances. He forces himself into an almost classic moderation. These works are poignant, unlike his grandiose oil paintings, because of the intensity of the drama that plays out in them and the depth of the emotion that they convey. The viewer admires here the mystery of the landscape in the light that falls at dusk, the two persons composing something like a tragic medieval *Pietà*, hope taking despair into its arms, suffering delivered into the hands of compassion, and all this in a basically emotional style yet forcing itself into a strict, classical form for fear of illegitimately expressing what is inexpressible.

This is because Gustave Moreau conveys in his painting all his personal spiritual questions. He once said, "Man is a tool that has value only when he is able to place himself at the service of the hand that must guide him. That hand is the hand of God. If this condition is not satisfied, he can do nothing." The scenes from the life of Jesus, of the prophets, or of the saints represent more than one quarter of his production. Joris-Karl Huysmans wrote: "Moreau could have been a great Christian painter, a modern Fra Angelico, if he had flourished along that line exclusively." And the artist himself concluded: "God is immensity and I feel him in myself.... I believe only in him alone. I do not believe in what I touch or in what I see. I believe only in what I do not see and exclusively in what I feel. My brain, my reason, seems ephemeral to me and dubiously real; my interior feeling alone seems to me eternal and indisputably certain."

Gustave Moreau's intention in this watercolor is to invite the spectator to meditate on the two figures of Jesus with which he can identify. On the one hand, the figure of the Good Samaritan whose virtue of Charity illustrates the necessary, qualifying final clause, *"as I have loved you,"* of the new commandment: *"Love one another...."* On the other hand, the victim of the robbers, whose agony illustrates the passion of Jesus, the Christ who endorsed the human condition and loved humanity to the end; and its corollary, the criterion that he gives for the Last Judgment, which will irrevocably decide the eternal lot of each one: *"Whatever you did to the least of my human brothers and sisters, you did to me"* (cf. Mt 25:40). ■

IN ART HISTORY

THE FAITH OF GUSTAVE MOREAU

The coexistence of pagan mythology and biblical subjects in the paintings of Gustave Moreau indicates not only the uniqueness of his work and his symbolism, but also his connection with the artists of the Renaissance. Although the presence of mythological figures is preponderant in the oeuvre of Moreau (Hercules, Leda, Galatea, Oedipus, Prometheus...), it by no means eclipses the importance of the figures from the Old and the New Testament or his depiction of the lives of the saints.

This cohabitation is sometimes taken to the point of syncretism, as in the polyptych [many-paneled work] that he executed in 1886, *The Life of Humanity*.

Baptized but not a practicing Christian, Moreau was still profoundly moved by the faith and became a tireless advocate of the supernatural.

For Moreau, Catholicism remained a moral point of reference, as demonstrated for example by the fact that, while he was working on his famous *Oedipus and the Sphinx*, he produced in 1863, a few years after his return from Rome and Italy, a Way of the Cross for an obscure little church in Aveyron, Notre-Dame de Decazeville, a relaxing spiritual change of pace for which Moreau had wished to remain anonymous—although that anonymity would be lifted more than a century later.

The Gustave Moreau Museum in Paris preserves his most important religious works. One year before his death, which occurred in 1898, Moreau had decided to bequeath to the state the mansion at 14 rue de La Rochefoucauld, which served as his residence and studio, with all its contents: paintings, drawings, portfolios.

The large movable showcases of the museum, arranged facing away from the daylight so as to ensure the optimal conditions for conservation, allow us to gauge the importance of draftsmanship in the genesis of a picture by Moreau. The watercolor *The Good Samaritan*, preserved today as part of this collection, had been offered, along with its counterpart, *The Wicked Rich Man*, to his muse and best friend Alexandrine Dureux. This is a subject that Moreau treated several times, as he did *The Prodigal Son*.

Not until the 1961 retrospective requested by André Malraux and organized by Jean Cassou in the galleries of the Louvre did Gustave Moreau finally occupy the place that he deserves. His students Henri Matisse and Georges Rouault had died a few years before. André Breton had just published a tribute in *L'Art fantastique de Gustave Moreau*, and it was left to Georges Bataille to publish in advance in the periodical *Arts*, on the occasion of the exposition, the article "The 'outdated' Gustave Moreau, precursor of surrealism."

M. C.

Pietà
Gustave Moreau (1826–1898)
Ca. 1876
Oil on wood, 9 x 6.3 in
Tokyo, National Museum of Western Art

In order to depict the unfortunate wounded man, Gustave Moreau repeated the classic image of the dead Christ taken down from the Cross.

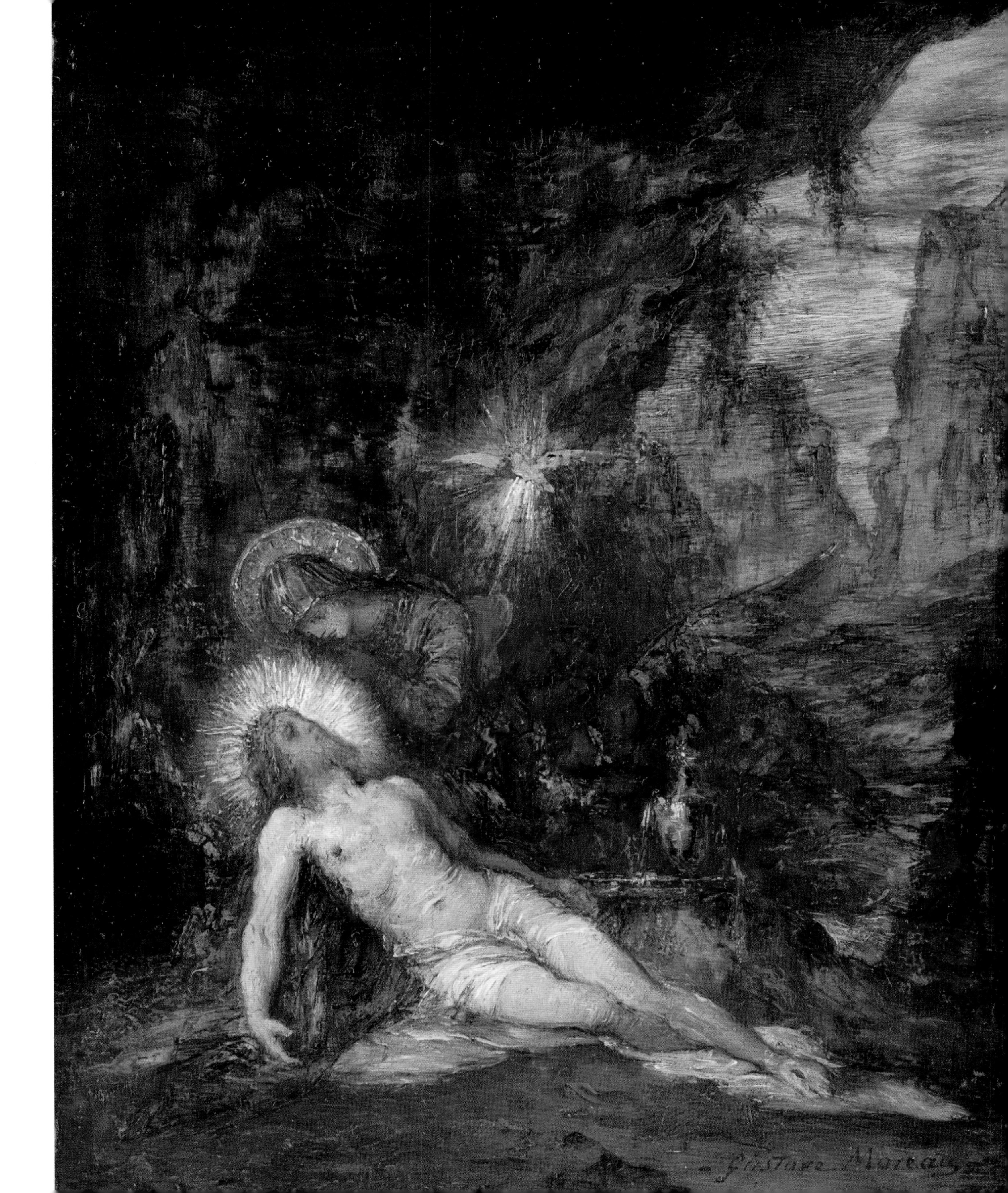
Gustave Moreau

The long parable called "The Prodigal Son" runs more than twenty verses in Chapter 15 of the Gospel according to Saint Luke, after two short parables about the gold coin that is lost, then found again, and about the lost sheep that is brought back to the fold. This set of "parables of mercy" is Jesus' answer to his accusers, who complained about him in these terms: *This man welcomes sinners and eats with them!* (Lk 15:2).

The Prodigal Son

The parable called "The Prodigal Son" is often read as referring to the destiny of Israel (the older son who is faithful) and that of the pagan nations (the prodigal son who is pardoned). This theme was one of the favorite subjects of Guercino (1591–1666). In this version, seeking to convey the teachings of the recent Council of Trent (1545–1563) on the sacrament of penance (confession), the painter shows a son in rags, half-naked, certainly a sinner but sincerely contrite, shedding hot tears in the arms of the Divine Mercy, represented by an obviously powerful father who is nonetheless deeply compassionate. The tears of the young penitent here, as in the confessional, are those of remorse. Soon they will be tears of joy at being reconciled with his Father (God) and taking his place again within his family (the Catholic Church).

This parable, as related in the Gospel according to Saint Luke, proposes instead the figure of a hardened sinner, even in his motives for going back home. The "prodigal son" does not return because he finally renounces his dissolute life, but because he no longer has the means of indulging in it. Be that as it may, not only does his father run to meet him and embrace him tenderly, not only does he restore his dignity as son, but he also mobilizes his estate for a banquet in his honor and again gives him the right to an inheritance, although he had squandered it the first time!

On a preparatory sketch for this commission (see page 152), Guercino depicts the father helping his son up from a fall, exactly as if he were God the Father hastening to support Jesus bending under the weight of the cross on his ascent to Calvary. In his initial insight, before adopting the vision of his patron, the artist grasped perfectly the point of the parable: the Son of God became man to take up and represent all human beings of all times in the sight of God the Father, so that, when they returned to him, he might love in each one of them for all eternity what he has loved in him, the Son, from all eternity. ■

THE BIBLE – LK 15:12-14, 17, 20-24

The younger son said to his father, "Father, give me the share of property that falls to me." And he divided his living between them. Not many days later, the younger son gathered all he had and took his journey into a far country, and there he squandered his property in loose living. And when he had spent everything, a great famine arose in that country, and he began to be in want. But when he came to himself he said, "How many of my father's hired servants have bread enough and to spare, but I perish here with hunger!" And he arose and came to his father. But while he was yet at a distance, his father saw him and had compassion, and ran and embraced him and kissed him. And the son said to him, "Father, I have sinned against heaven and before you; I am no longer worthy to be called your son." But the father said to his servants, "Bring quickly the best robe, and put it on him; and put a ring on his hand, and shoes on his feet; and bring the fatted calf and kill it, and let us eat and make merry; for this my son was dead, and is alive again; he was lost, and is found." And they began to make merry.

The return of the Prodigal Son, detail
Giovanni Francesco Barbieri, called Il Guercino (1591–1666)
1651
Oil on canvas, 53.9 x 43.7 in
Włocławek (Poland), diocesan museum

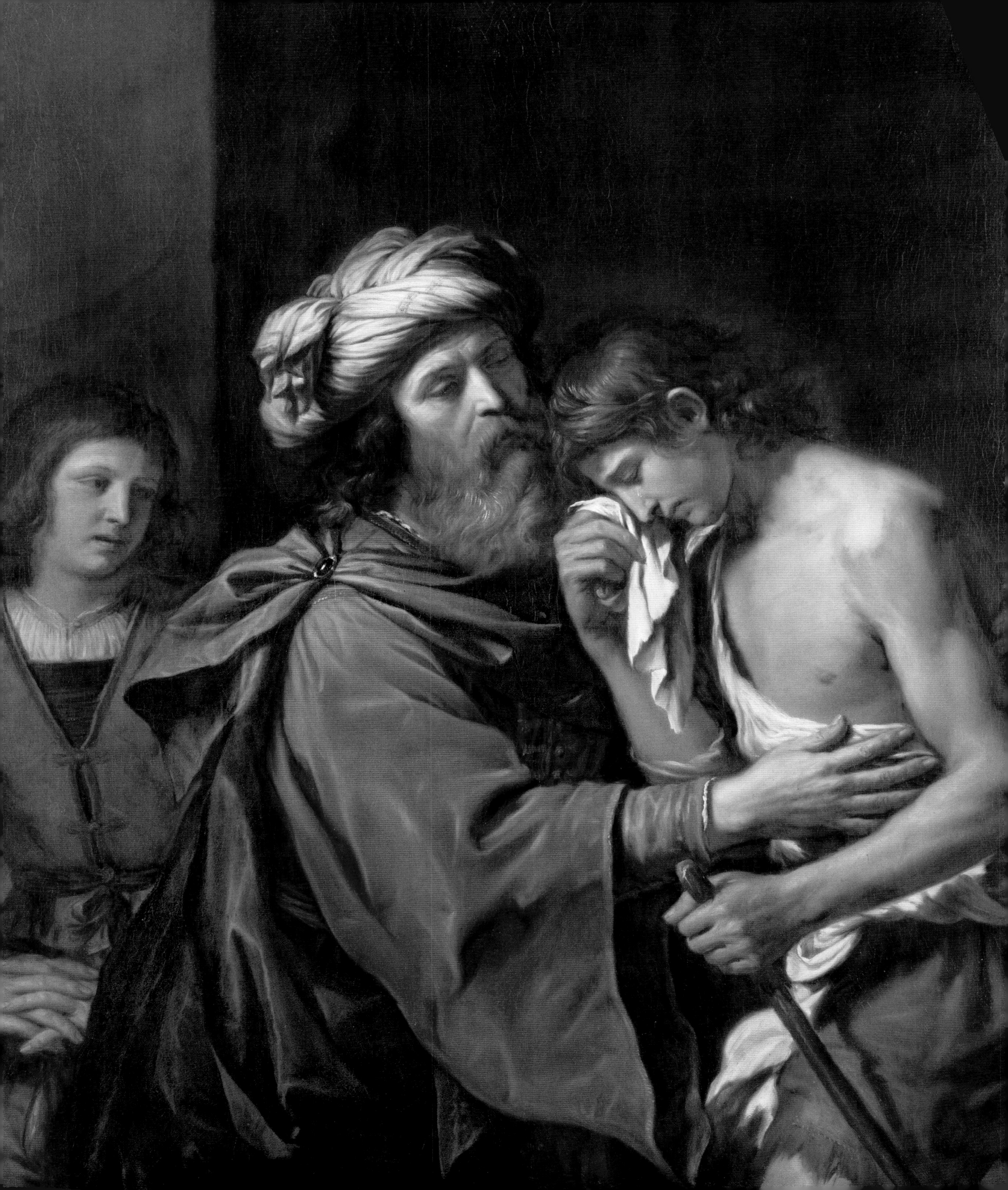

IN ART HISTORY

THE RETURN OF THE PRODIGAL SON, A RECURRING SUBJECT IN THE WORK OF GUERCINO

Giovanni Francesco Barbieri (1591–1666), called "Il Guercino" (the little one-eyed man) because of his squint, was an artist originally from Cento, in the Province of Ferrara. The painter and draftsman worked there until his departure for Rome in 1621. He spent the final years of his life in Bologna, a city in which he was an artist of the first rank, particularly after the death of the painter Guido Reni in 1642, who became a strong influence on him after he had already fully integrated the lessons of Caravaggism. The present picture can be dated to this final Bolognese period.

Among the many biblical themes that populate the artist's canvases throughout his works, the Return of the Prodigal Son is a subject that particularly inspired Guercino. Indeed, several pictures by his hand are known which, from the start of his career, develop the parable through different compositions. Let us take as one example the marvelous painting, dated 1619, preserved today in the Kunsthistorisches Museum in Vienna.

In the 1651 painting, the intensity of the colors red and blue with which the father's clothing is depicted is reinforced by the monochrome ochre of the background that structures this composition with virtuosic simplicity, and guides the spectator's view toward the focal point, the faces of the father and of his son. The beard of the former merges into the hair of the latter, and the crossing of their forearms further accentuates this physical overlapping. The jealous brother, for his part, is relegated to an observation post in the background and, by a subtle play of shadow, the artist detaches him symbolically from the central group by distinguishing the background color, a lighter tone of ochre.

The date 1651 is attested by a payment of 72 *ungari*. This was a commission paid to the artist by the Venetian collector Giovanni Nani. From the end of the 18th century on, we can trace the movements of the picture in England, where it passed through the hands of several collectors until it was acquired in 1943 by a Polish bishop. Auctioned at Christie's, it was in fact purchased by Cardinal Karol Mieczysław Radoński, Bishop of Włocławek, who was residing in London with the Polish government then in exile, which explains its presence today in the collections of the diocesan museum in Włocławek, of which it is one of the masterpieces.

M. C.

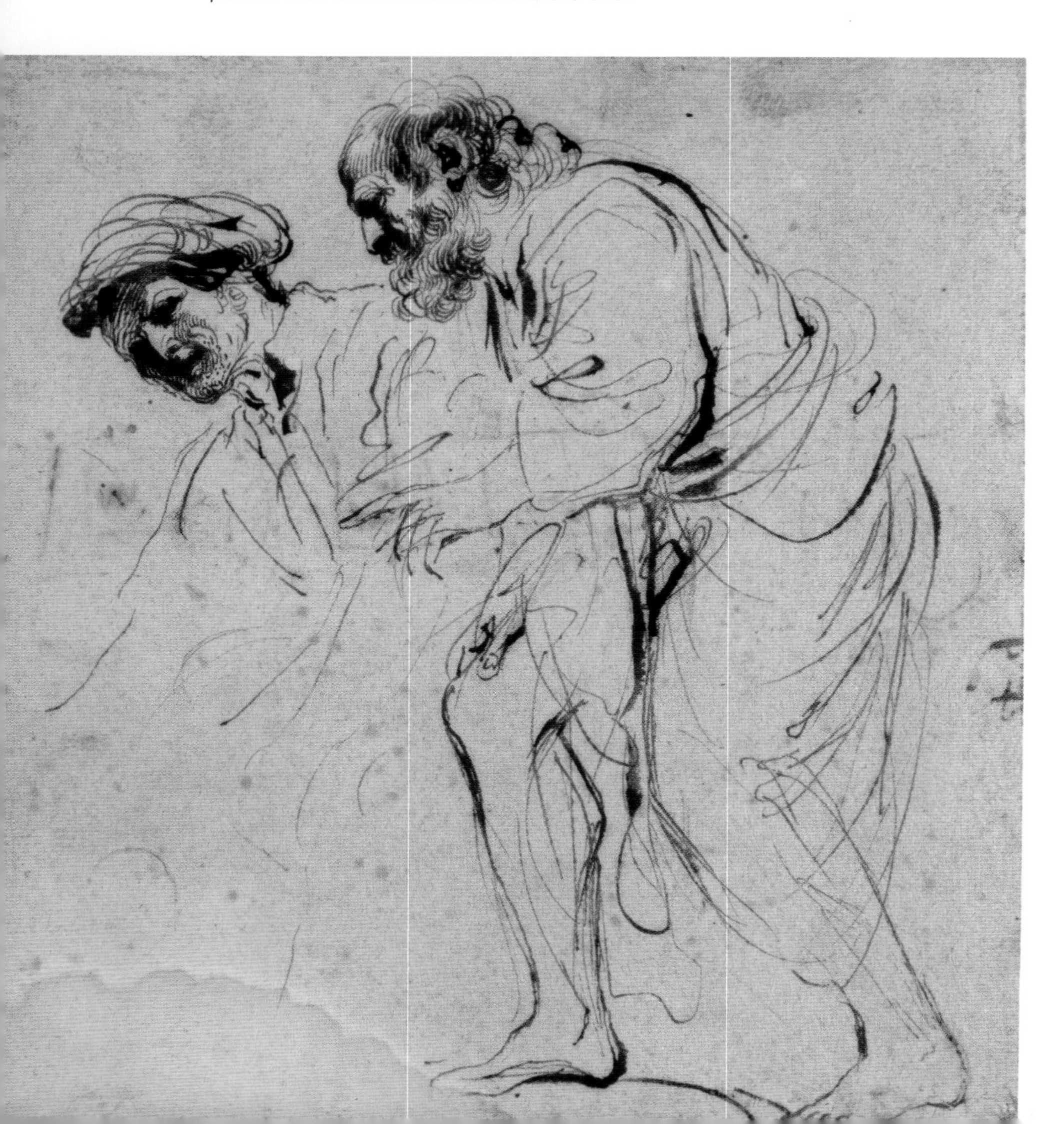

Study for *The return of the Prodigal Son*
Giovanni Francesco Barbieri,
called Il Guercino (1591-1666)
Around 1607
Brown ink, wash, 15.7 x 10.6 cm
Bucharest, National Museum of Art

Love (III)

GEORGE HERBERT

George Herbert (1593–1633) was the fifth son of an aristocratic family in Montgomery (Wales). He studied at Trinity College, Cambridge, where he was later appointed a Reader in Rhetoric and then Public Orator. He was a Member of Parliament for two years. In 1629 he married Jane Danvers, and in 1630 he was ordained a priest in the Church of England. Herbert died of consumption just short of his fortieth birthday. Almost all his surviving English poems were collected in one volume, *The Temple*, and published posthumously in 1633.

Love bade me welcome: yet my soul drew back,
  Guiltie of dust and sinne.
But quick-ey'd Love, observing me grow slack
  From my first entrance in,
Drew nearer to me, sweetly questioning,
  If I lack'd any thing.

"A guest," I answer'd, "worthy to be here."
  Love said, "You shall be he."
"I, the unkinde, ungrateful? Ah, my deare,
  I cannot look on thee."
Love took my hand, and smiling did reply,
  "Who made the eyes but I?"

"Truth, Lord, but I have marr'd them; let my shame
  Go where it doth deserve."
"And know you not," sayes Love, "who bore the blame?"
  "My deare, then I will serve."
"You must sit down," sayes Love, "and taste my meat."
  So I did sit and eat.

George Herbert, "Love (III)" in *The Temple* (1633), Part II, *The Church*. Reprinted in *The English Poems of George Herbert*, edited by C.A. Patrides (London: J. M. Dent & Sons, Ltd., 1974, 1991[8]), 192. Quotation marks added.

Christian tradition situates the scene of the Transfiguration on Mount Tabor, a small, isolated mountain dominating a region of plains between Nazareth and the Lake of Tiberias, or Sea of Galilee. Mount Tabor welcomed during the first centuries A.D. many monks and hermits. It has remained to this day an important place of pilgrimage. The current Basilica of the Transfiguration there is staffed by the Franciscans, who built it in the early 20th century.

Jesus transfigured

When the teachings of the Council of Trent (1545–1563) began to bear fruit within the context of what would be called the Catholic Reformation, the Church gave art a privileged place as a means of social communication, and so she was worried about the vagaries of the Mannerists, which were launched in an exaggerated display of intellectual subtlety. In the late 16th century, Mannerism had a tendency to become an artistic game of borrowing motifs and using increasingly obscure codes and symbols, which could be understood only by a small, highly literate elite. The artists concerned were in particular Tintoretto and Veronese, whose genius however was well recognized.

The Church therefore encouraged artists to produce religious works that would be more immediately comprehensible for the faithful. In response to these words of encouragement, which were ringing but often clumsy, Ludovico Carracci (1555–1619) created in 1585 an academy of painting called the *Incamminati* [roughly, "Innovators"], with two of his cousins, Agostino and Annibale. Innovators of the Baroque style and also of Classicism, the Carraccis are the fathers of 17th-century European painting and more broadly of all academic art to this day.

THE BIBLE – MK 9:3-5

His garments became glistening, intensely white, as no fuller on earth could bleach them. And there appeared to them Elijah with Moses; and they were talking to Jesus. And Peter said to Jesus, "Master, it is well that we are here; let us make three booths, one for you and one for Moses and one for Elijah."

In this *Transfiguration of Christ* on a monumental scale, Ludovico Carracci makes use of a grandiose art that seeks to impress the believer before inviting him to contemplation. The beauty and the variety of the splendid lights, the freshness and contrasts of the colors, the loose-fitting draperies that envelop the figures majestically, everything contributes to the construction of a lyrical and luxurious composition in which the characters in the scene pose in studied attitudes that are as explicit as possible. In heaven, the prophets Moses (on the left), the founder of the people of God, and Elijah (on the right), its restorer, are conspicuously turned toward the transfigured Jesus, to show clearly that the way prepared by the Old Covenant leads to him. On earth, facing the blinding mystery of light, Saint John (on the right) is immersed in contemplative prayer, while Saint James covers himself in his cloak—blood red, because he will be the first apostle to be martyred—to manifest the fear that seizes him. As for Saint Peter, his cloak assumes an earthy color as a sign of his impending denial; he stands to speak in a loud voice to Jesus, without really knowing what he is saying. In response, with his right hand, Jesus signals to him to listen to the voice that makes itself heard from the cloud, testifying: *"This is my beloved Son; listen to him!"* (Mk 9:7). ■

The Transfiguration of Christ
Ludovico Carracci (1555–1619)
1595–1596
Oil on canvas, 172 x 105 in
Bologna, Pinacoteca nazionale

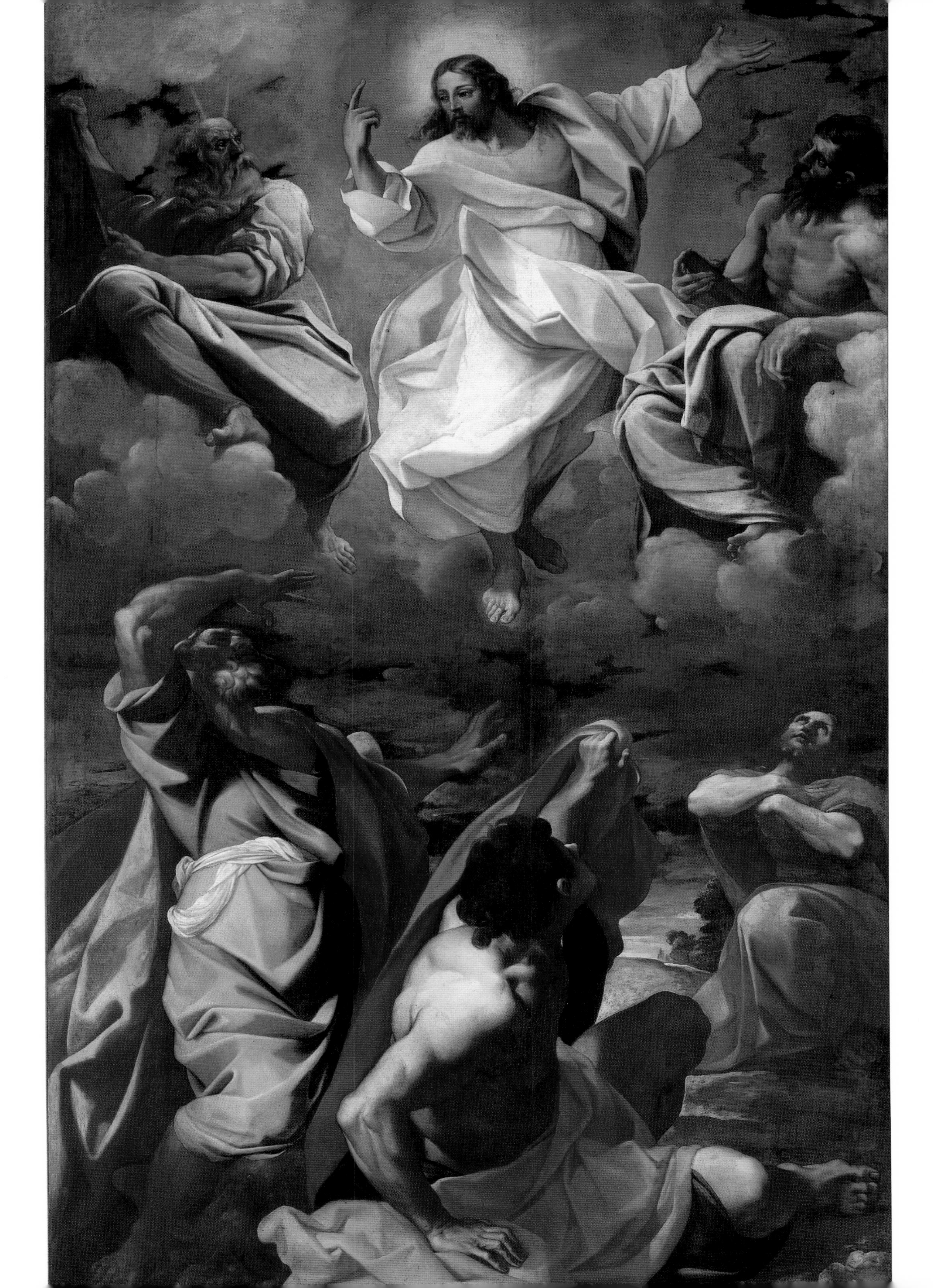

Reverend James M. Hayes, born in 1875, was a priest, poet, and professor of literature in the early 20th century. He was for many years dean of the Sisters' College at the Catholic University of America.

This poem, "Transfiguration," is from Hayes' collection *The Grave of Dreams, and Other Verses* (New York: Encyclopedia Press, 1917), pp. 7-8. It was also included, with two others by Hayes, in Joyce Kilmer's classic *Anthology of Catholic Poets*.

The Transfiguration

JAMES M. HAYES

He seeks the mountains where the olives grow,
    The Lord of Glory, veiled in humble guise;
His soul is shadowed with a coming woe,
    The grief of all the world is in His eyes:
His spirit struggles in the dark caress
Of anguish, pain and utter loneliness.

He always loved the mountain tops, for there
    Away from earth, He treads the mystic ways,
And sees the vision of the Fairest Fair,
    As Heaven dawns upon His raptured gaze;
The loneliness, the pain, the grief depart;
Surpassing gladness fills His Sacred Heart.

That day He stood upon the olive hill,
    And Peter, James and John in wonder saw
The burning glories of the God-head fill
    His soul with grandeur, and in holy awe
They fell upon the ground and cried for grace,
Lest they should die beholding God's own Face.

As minor chords that sob from strings of gold
    The Master speaks in accents sweet and sad:
The vision past, the chosen three behold
    No one but Jesus and their souls are glad.
The awe, the splendor and the glory gone,
How sweet the face of Christ to look upon!

Raphael's last work, produced in the year of his death (1520) and left partly unfinished, this *Transfiguration* opens the way to Mannerism which, exacerbated by Pontormo, Bronzino, Tintoretto, and Veronese, among others, was to dominate art until the classical reaction of the Carracci, which manifested itself from 1582 onwards with the creation of the Accademia delle Incarmminati in Bologna.

The Transfiguration of Christ (1516-1520), Raffaello Sanzio, called Raphael (1483-1520), oil on wood, 161.4 x 109 in., Vatican Museums, Vatican City.

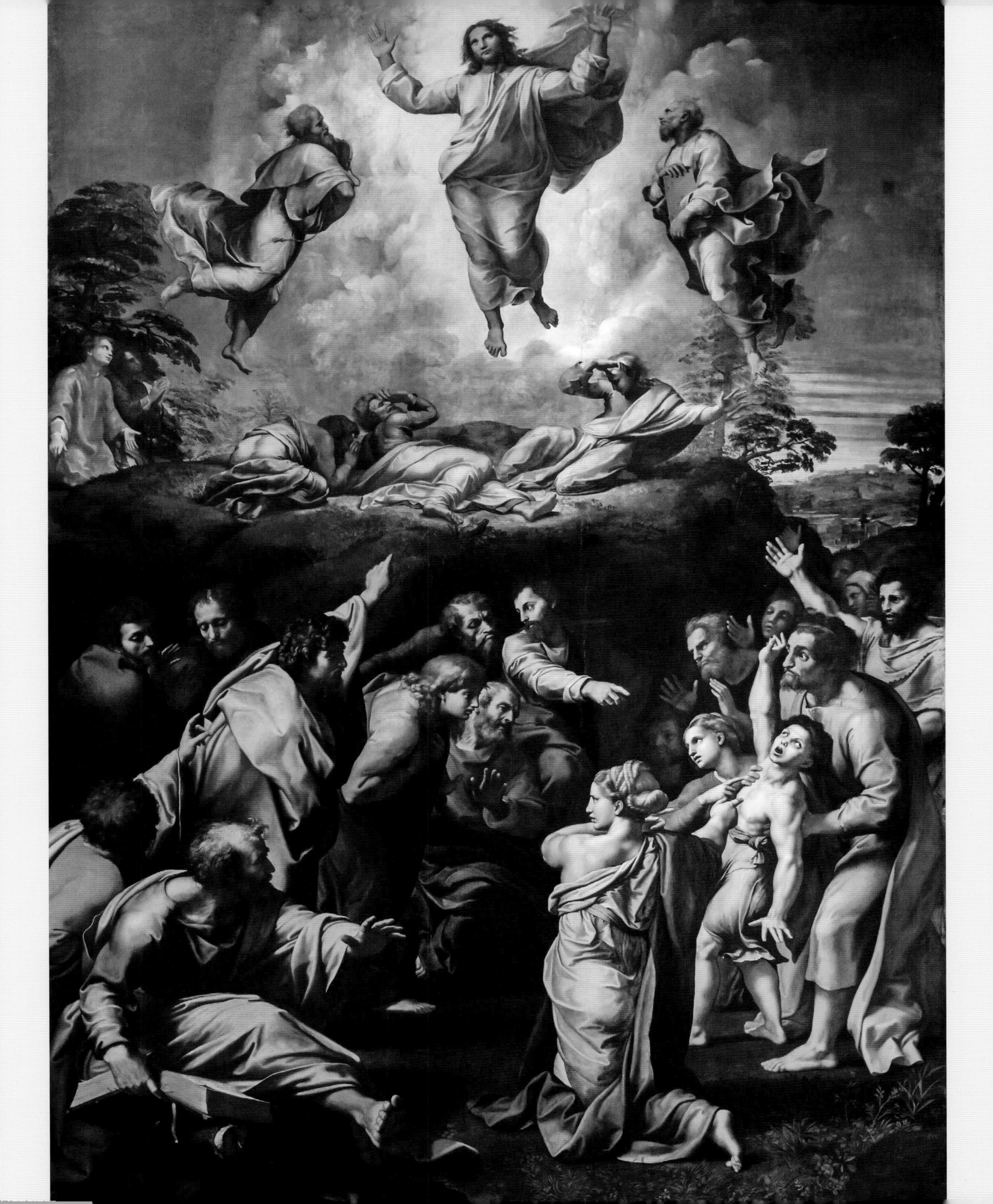

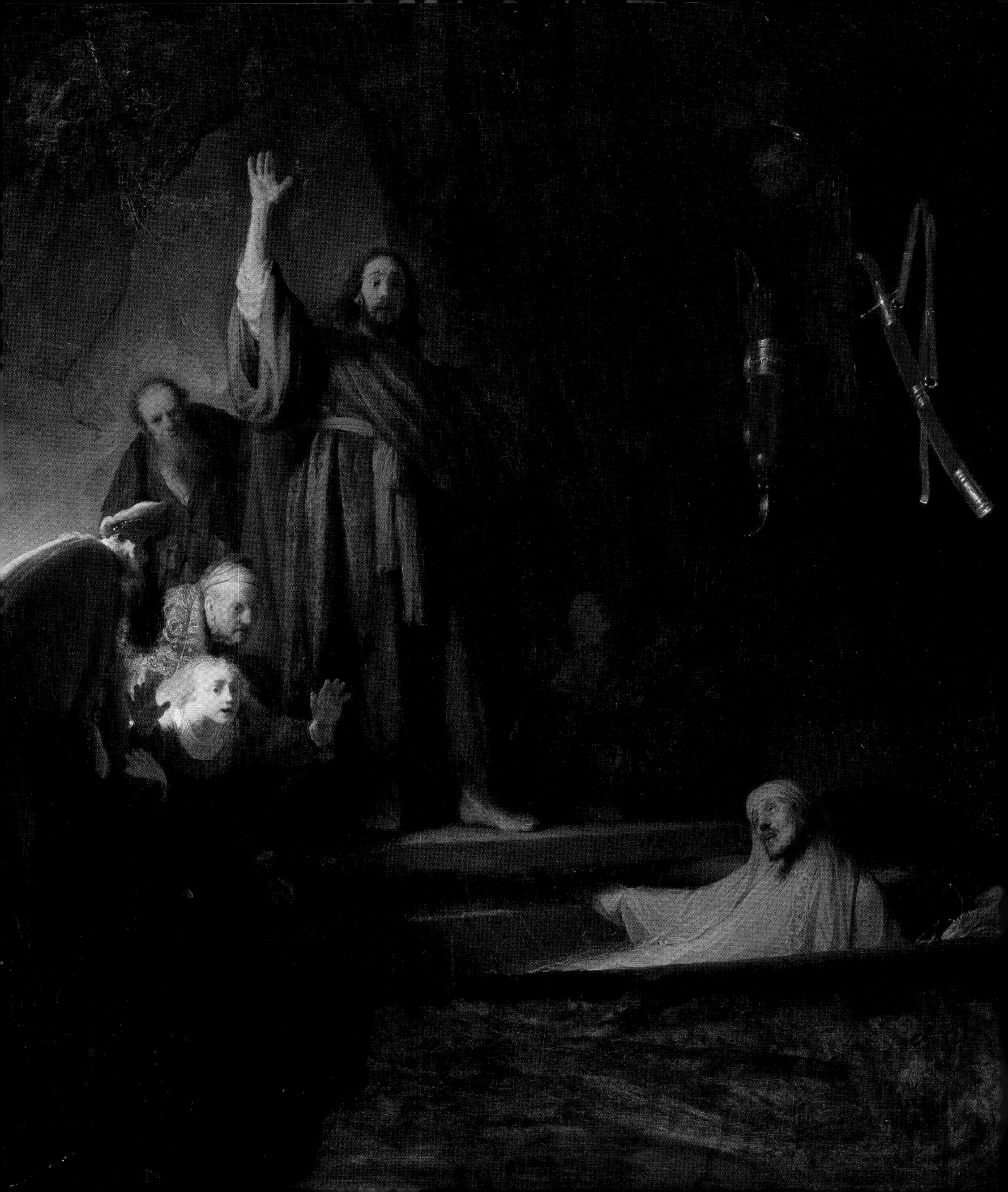

Jesus raises his friend Lazarus

The village of Bethany (probably present-day Al-Eizariya [Lazarus in Arabic]) is described by the Evangelist John as a small town in Judea situated around "fifteen stadia" (a Greek measurement of distance) from Jerusalem—in other words less than a half hour's walk—below the Mount of Olives. That was where three close friends of Jesus resided: Lazarus and his two sisters, Martha and Mary.

For a long time Rembrandt (1606–1669) kept this early work; deep in debt, he had to part with it in 1656, a quarter-century after painting it. The reason is that what he had depicted in it was the salvation that he hoped for at the end of desperate human situations that too often he had had to face: the incomprehensible, revolting death of one dear friend, and then of another...

Rembrandt had the gift of compassion. In his case this was not a form of sentimentality, but rather a desire to imitate Jesus Christ by giving the greatest proof of love. He was convinced of the truth that the ultimate motive of the powers of evil is to put love to death. And that they have the means to do so. For in their malevolent plan, they triumph surely and tragically over every ridiculous wish to make love live and survive on the cross of human existence. Except for one man, a man whom the Gospel according to Saint John describes as the most human of men, the close friend of Lazarus, Martha, and Mary, a man who mourned his friend with tears—*See how he loved him!* the witnesses exclaimed—a man so human that he melts while confronting the suffering of those whom he loves; and Rembrandt suffered greatly to be the one left when his mother, his father, his children, his wife, his friends were horribly crushed by sickness and then snatched away by death; yes, the powers of evil always triumph, except that that man, in tears, who was human, so human, suddenly said: *"I am the resurrection and the life. Whoever believes in me, though he die, yet shall he live"* (Jn 11:25). And Rembrandt, who had lost so many dear ones, believed in him.

The most significant feature of his picture is the chiaroscuro effects: the light that rips through the shadows, the love that shines more powerfully on evil than suffering invades the flesh, the life that finally triumphs over death. An intense ray of light surges at the middle of the left side, obliquely illumines the middle of

THE BIBLE – JN 11:17, 32-36, 38-39A, 41, 43-44

Now when Jesus came, he found that Lazarus had already been in the tomb four days. When Mary came where Jesus was and saw him, she fell at his feet, saying to him, "Lord, if you had been here, my brother would not have died." When Jesus saw her weeping, and the Jews who came with her also weeping, he was deeply moved in spirit and troubled; and he said, "Where have you laid him?" They said to him, "Lord, come and see." Jesus wept. So the Jews said, "See how he loved him!" Then Jesus, deeply moved again, came to the tomb; it was a cave, and a stone lay upon it. Jesus said, "Take away the stone." So they took away the stone. And Jesus lifted up his eyes and said, "Father, I thank thee that thou hast heard me." When he had said this, he cried with a loud voice, "Lazarus, come out." The dead man came out, his hands and feet bound with bandages, and his face wrapped with a cloth. Jesus said to them, "Unbind him, and let him go."

The Raising of Lazarus
Rembrandt (1606–1669)
Ca. 1630–1632
Oil on wood, 38 x 32 in
Los Angeles County Museum of Art (LACMA)

the scene, and strikes the tomb of Lazarus. The persons present at the miracle, Martha in silhouette, Mary in the full light, and the Jewish dignitaries, are captivated. Along the vertical axis which subdivides the composition appears the figure of Jesus, a Jesus with a human face, still quite upset, but a Christ of superhuman stature: twice as tall as the other figures, his right hand raised masterfully: with the power of God he orders his friend to get up.

As background music to accompany the silent contemplation of this picture, we offer the following poem by the young Thomas Merton, "For My Brother: Reported Missing in Action, 1943."

Sweet brother, if I do not sleep,
My eyes are flowers for your tomb;
And if I cannot eat my bread,
My fasts shall live like willows where you died.
If in the heat I find no water for my thirst,
My thirst shall turn to springs for you, poor traveler.
Where, in what desolate and smoky country,
Lies your poor body, lost and dead?
And in what landscape of disaster
Has your unhappy spirit lost its road?
Come, in my labor find a resting place
And in my sorrow lay your head,
Or rather take my life and blood
And buy yourself a better bed—
Or take my breath and take my death
And buy yourself a better rest.
When all the men of war are shot
And flags have fallen into dust,
Your cross and mine shall tell men still
Christ died on each, for both of us.
For in the wreckage of your April Christ lies slain,
And Christ weeps in the ruins of my spring.
The money of Whose tears shall fall
Into your weak and friendless hand,
And buy you back to your own land:
The silence of Whose tears shall fall
Like bells upon your alien tomb.
Hear them and come: they call you home. ■

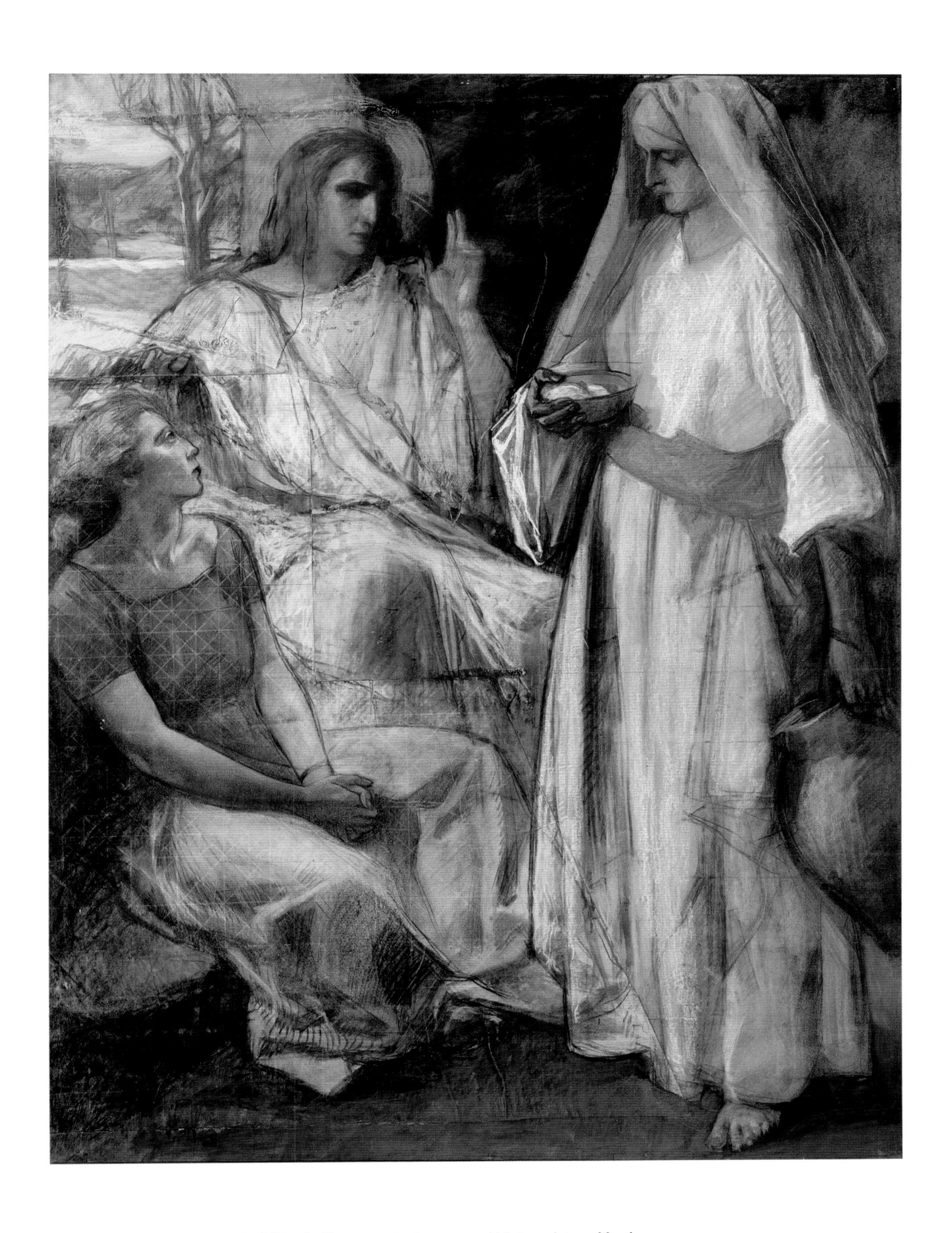

Jesus at the home of Martha and Mary
René Marie Castaing (1896–1943)
1924
Pastel, preparatory study, 58 x 45 in
Pau, Musée des Beaux-Arts

Jesus had friends. For example, Lazarus and his two sisters, Martha and Mary, at whose house he used to stay whenever he went up to Jerusalem. One day, Martha was busy preparing a meal while Mary listened to Jesus. Finally Martha said to Jesus: "You could tell my sister to come help me!" Jesus replied: "Martha, Martha, you are worried about many things, but only one thing matters. Mary has chosen the better part, and it will not be taken from her."

Fyodor Dostoevsky (1821–1881), with Leo Tolstoy, dominated the 19th-century Russian novel. The Christian question runs throughout his oeuvre. In this passage from *Crime and Punishment* (1866), Sonia, a young woman forced into prostitution, gives a reading from the Gospel about the raising of Lazarus to the assassin Raskolnikov in the hope of converting him. This scene can be considered as the pivotal point of the novel, inasmuch as the reminiscence of it forms the denouement of the book in the final pages.

Fyodor Dostoevsky,
Crime and Punishment (1866),
translated from Russian by Constance Garnett
Part II, Chapter 4.

Four days in the tomb

FYODOR DOSTOEVSKY

Sonia opened the book and found the place. Her hands were shaking, her voice failed her. Twice she tried to begin and could not bring out the first syllable. "Now a certain man was sick named Lazarus of Bethany..." she forced herself at last to read, but at the third word her voice broke like an overstrained string. There was a catch in her breath.

Raskolnikov saw in part why Sonia could not bring herself to read to him and the more he saw this, the more roughly and irritably he insisted on her doing so. He understood only too well how painful it was for her to betray and unveil all that was her *own*. He understood that these feelings really were her *secret treasure*, which she had kept perhaps for years, perhaps from childhood, while she lived with an unhappy father and a distracted stepmother crazed by grief, in the midst of starving children and unseemly abuse and reproaches. But at the same time he knew now and knew for certain that, although it filled her with dread and suffering, yet she had a tormenting desire to read and to read to *him* that he might hear it, and to read *now* whatever might come of it!... He read this in her eyes, he could see it in her intense emotion. She mastered herself, controlled the spasm in her throat and went on reading the eleventh chapter of St. John. She went on to the nineteenth verse: "And many of the Jews came to Martha and Mary to comfort them concerning their brother. Then Martha as soon as she heard that Jesus was coming went and met Him: but Mary sat still in the house. Then said Martha unto Jesus, Lord, if Thou hadst been here, my brother had not died. But I know that even now whatsoever Thou wilt ask of God, God will give it Thee...." Then she stopped again with a shamefaced feeling that her voice would quiver and break again.

"Jesus said unto her, thy brother shall rise again. Martha saith unto Him, I know that he shall rise again in the resurrection, at the last day. Jesus said unto her, I am the resurrection and the life: he that believeth in Me though he were dead, yet shall he live. And whosoever liveth and believeth in Me shall never die. Believest thou this? She saith unto Him," (And drawing a painful breath, Sonia read distinctly and forcibly as though she were making a public confession of faith.) "Yea, Lord: I believe that Thou art the Christ, the Son of God Which should come into the world."

She stopped and looked up quickly at him, but controlling herself went on reading. Raskolnikov sat without moving, his elbows on the table and his eyes turned away. She read to the thirty-second verse.

"Then when Mary was come where Jesus was and saw Him, she fell down at His feet, saying unto Him, Lord if Thou hadst been here, my brother had not died. When Jesus therefore saw her weeping, and the Jews also weeping which came with her, He groaned in the spirit and was troubled, and said, Where have ye laid him? They said unto Him, Lord, come and see. Jesus wept. Then said the Jews, behold how He loved him! And some of them said, could not this Man which opened the eyes of the blind, have caused that even this man should not have died?"

Raskolnikov turned and looked at her with emotion. Yes, he had known it! She was trembling in a real physical fever. He had expected it. She was getting near the story of the greatest miracle and a feeling of immense triumph came over her. Her voice rang out like a bell; triumph and joy gave it power. The lines danced before her eyes, but she knew what she was reading by heart. At the last verse "Could not this Man which opened the eyes of the blind..." dropping her voice she passionately reproduced the doubt, the reproach and censure of the blind disbelieving Jews, who in another moment would fall at His feet as though struck by thunder, sobbing and believing.... "And *he, he*—too, is blinded and unbelieving, he, too, will hear, he, too, will believe, yes, yes! At once, now," was what she was dreaming, and she was quivering with happy anticipation.

"Jesus therefore again groaning in Himself cometh to the grave. It was a cave, and a stone lay upon it. Jesus said, Take ye away the stone. Martha, the sister of him that was dead, saith unto Him, Lord by this time he stinketh: for he hath been dead four days." She laid emphasis on the word *four*.

"Jesus saith unto her, Said I not unto thee that if thou wouldest believe, thou shouldest see the glory of God? Then they took away the stone from the place where the dead was laid. And Jesus lifted up His eyes and said, Father, I thank Thee that Thou hast heard Me. And I knew that Thou hearest Me always; but because of the people which stand by I said it, that they may believe that Thou hast sent Me. And when He thus had spoken, He cried with a loud voice, Lazarus, come forth. And he that was dead came forth." (She read loudly, cold and trembling with ecstasy, as though she were seeing it before her eyes.) "Bound hand and foot with graveclothes; and his face was bound about with a napkin. Jesus saith unto them, Loose him and let him go. Then many of the Jews which came to Mary and had seen the things which Jesus did believed on Him."

She could read no more, closed the book and got up from her chair quickly.

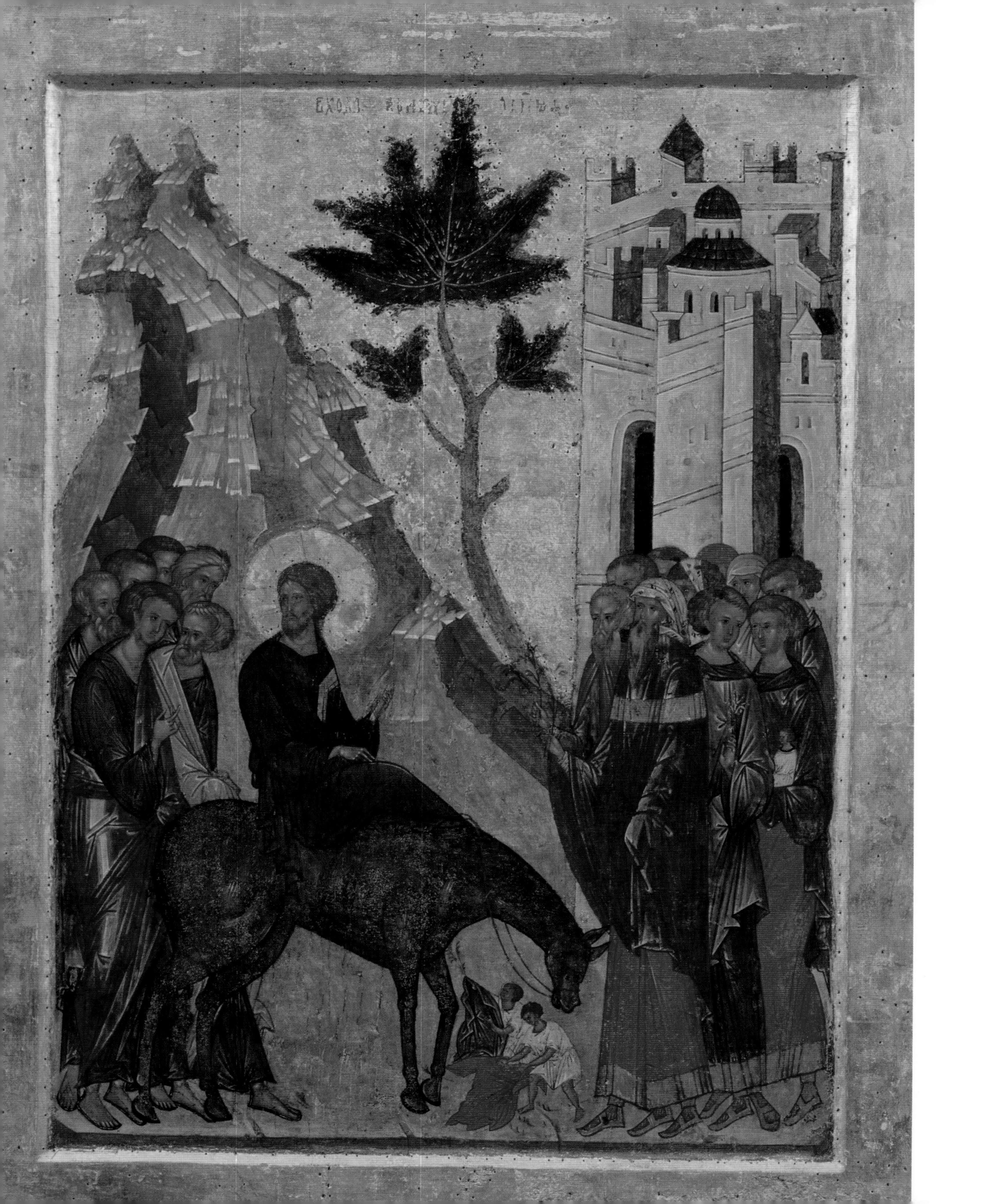

Jesus enters Jerusalem in triumph

This scene of popular jubilation, during which the crowd in Jerusalem greets Jesus as him *who comes in the name of the Lord* (Mt 21:9), takes place several days before the great yearly feast of the Jewish Passover. The cloaks and the palm branches strewn to make a path for the one who advances on a donkey are signs of great deference. A few days later, Jesus will be crucified amid the shouting of the crowd.

This icon painted in 1497 is preserved in the museum of Saint Cyril-Belozersk monastery, located in northern Russia. It depicts the triumphal entry of Jesus into Jerusalem according to a scenario inspired by the Gospel accounts. When news of the resurrection of Lazarus had spread, the inhabitants of Jerusalem learned that Jesus was approaching the Holy City: they went out in a crowd to meet him and to give him a triumphal welcome (cf. Jn 12:12-13). In the shadow of the Mount of Olives, symbol of the divine presence, Jesus advances. The prophecies (cf. Zec 9:9) and the Gospels (cf. Mk 11:2) describe him seated on a donkey. However, in the late 15th century, this animal was unknown in the northern regions of Russia, and so hagiography replaced it here with a horse. Jesus is followed by his apostles, with Peter and John in the lead, as it would happen again soon at the tomb on Easter morning. He turns his head toward them, and with his right hand points out to them entrance into the city, referring to the episode in which they begged him not to return to Jerusalem (cf. Jn 11:7-16).

The tree of life that is rooted on the holy mountain is placed at the center of the icon, as it was in the center of the earthly paradise. This is the tree that will furnish its palm branches to exalt the "New Adam" (cf. 1 Cor 15:45-49), as well as the wood of the cross on which he will die. The tree of life divides the icon in two, distinguishing between the Old and the New Covenant. On the right, leaving the Holy City and coming before Jesus, the crowd of the just men of the Old Testament appears, branches in hand. They prefigured the Savior and desired his coming so much that they form a triumphal procession for him. At the head of the crowd, Elijah and Moses point to Jesus as truly being the Messiah. And with them come many Jews, contemporaries of Jesus who believed in him. Finally, in the avant-garde of this crowd are *children of the promise* (Gal 4:28), carpeting Jesus' path with their coats, fulfilling the prophecy of Psalm 8:1-3:

O Lord, our Lord, how majestic is your name in all the earth!
You whose glory above the heavens is chanted by the mouth of babies and infants,
you have founded a bulwark because of your foes, to still the enemy and the avenger.

After entering the city, Jesus will go to the Temple. There, the priests and the scribes will be scandalized by the fact that the children acclaim him, shouting: *Hosanna to the Son of David!* Jesus will silence them by citing this same Psalm 8 (cf. Mt 21:15-16). ■

THE BIBLE – MT 21:7-11

They brought the donkey and the colt, and put their garments on them, and he sat on them. Most of the crowd spread their garments on the road, and others cut branches from the trees and spread them on the road. And the crowds that went before him and that followed him shouted, "Hosanna to the Son of David! Blessed is he who comes in the name of the Lord! Hosanna in the highest!" And when he entered Jerusalem, all the city was stirred, saying, "Who is this?" And the crowds said, "This is the prophet Jesus from Nazareth of Galilee."

Christ's entry into Jerusalem
1497
Tempera on wood, 33 x 24.8 in
Kirillov (Russia), monastery, Museum of Saint Cyril-Belozersk

The Last Supper of Jesus with his apostles in the Cenacle before his arrest was probably held on the eve of the Jewish Passover. The event is attested by the four evangelists, and Saint Paul notes it in one of his letters.

Jesus shares his last meal

This *Last Supper*, painted for an altarpiece, is attributed to the Master of the Housebook (Hausbuch), who was active in Frankfurt in the late 15th century. This artist was the first to use the technique for so-called drypoint engraving, which consists of scratching the design with a sharp stylus into a soft medium, usually a copperplate. He was also an admirable painter on glass, to whom a number of exceptionally fine stained-glass windows are attributed.

The last supper that Jesus took with his close disciples before being put to death coincided with the Passover meal that was celebrated each year by the Jews in memory of the liberation of their ancestors from slavery in Egypt. During this supper Jesus instituted the Eucharist (from the Greek word for "thanksgiving") which has been celebrated since then by Christians as a memorial. This is the "Mass" (from the Latin, "dismissal") for Catholics, the "Mass" or the "Last Supper" for Protestants, and the "Divine Liturgy" for the Orthodox and Eastern-rite Catholics.

In the center, Jesus presides, with the head of young John resting on his chest. To his right, lost in wonder, is Saint Peter, the head of the apostles. Going around the table, the viewer can admire how the artist was able to depict each apostle with particular features and his own personality, as though in a circle of family members or friends. And this is indeed a circle, since he was able to make quite visible the fact that the guests at the Last Supper form an ensemble, a unique entity at the moment when the Eucharist is instituted. They are the members of a communal body—unfortunately with the possibility that some may deny their membership or even betray it.

The tragic episode at the Last Supper in which Jesus points out the traitor who will betray him is depicted precisely (Jn 13:21-30): he dips a morsel of bread into the dish with the Paschal lamb, and then offers it to Judas. At the bottom of the picture, Judas is the only one without a halo. Whereas his neighbor on the left asks him about his intentions, he is getting ready to go off to his destiny, but not without taking the common purse with him. ■

THE BIBLE – MT 26:26-28

Now as they were eating, Jesus took bread, and blessed, and broke it, and gave it to the disciples and said, "Take, eat; this is my body." And he took a chalice, and when he had given thanks he gave it to them, saying, "Drink of it, all of you; for this is my blood of the covenant, which is poured out for many for the forgiveness of sins."

The Last Supper, a panel from the Speyer altarpiece
Master of the Housebook (Hausbuch) (active 1470–1500)
Tempera on pine wood, 51 x 29.5 in
Berlin, Gemäldegalerie

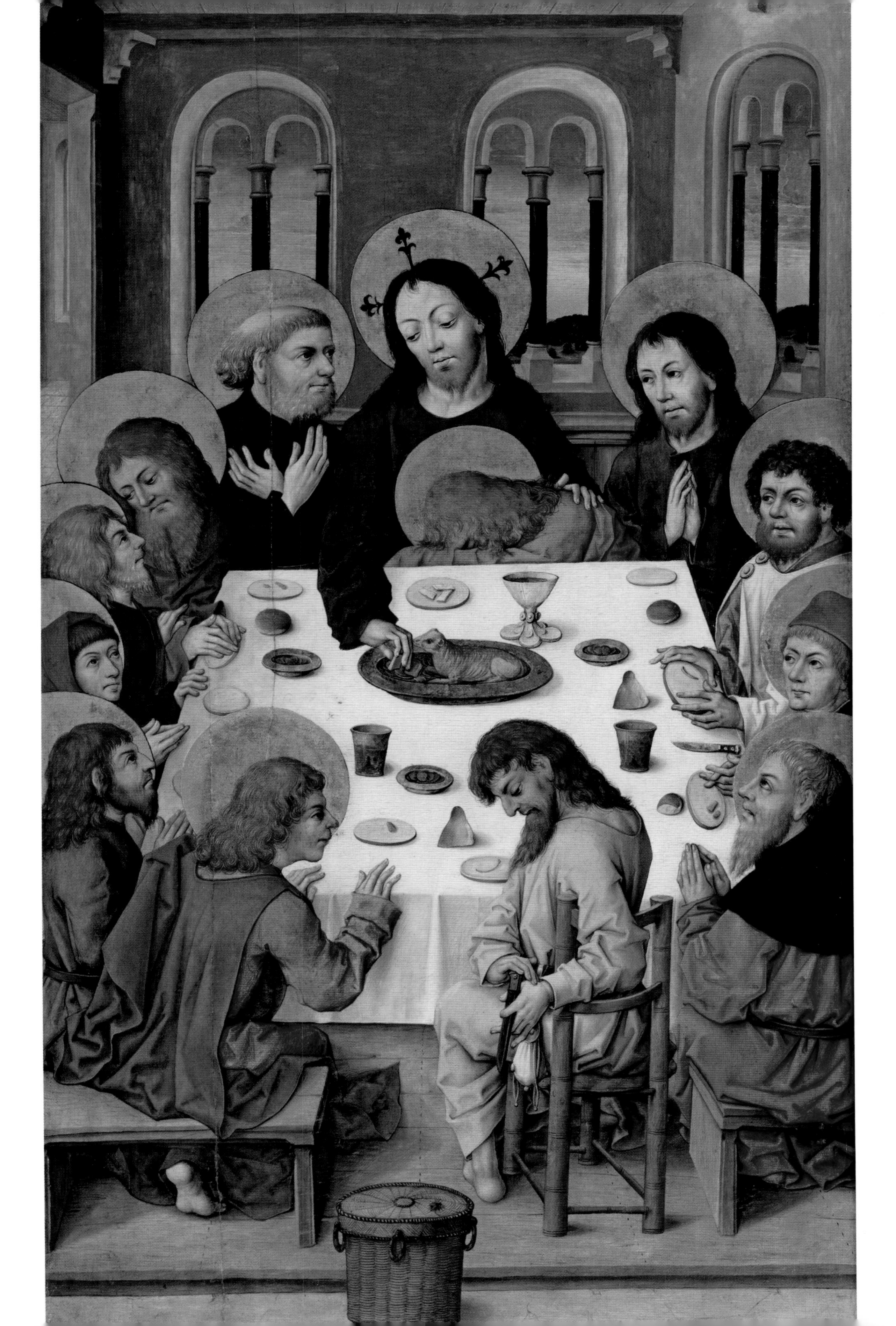

Jesus and his disciples are gathered in a place that is conventionally called the "Cenacle"—an "upper room"—to partake in the Passover meal. Foot-washing was a customary gesture for the benefit of all the persons who arrived at a house, often after long walks in sandals in the dust. This gesture was the task of slaves, since free servants balked at performing it.

Jesus washes the feet of his companions at table

Born in Tuscany, near Florence, around the year 1266, Giotto is considered one of the greatest artistic geniuses of all time. On the brink of the 14th century, he launched the renewal of Western painting and started the process which, a century later, would lead to the artistic revolution of the Renaissance in Italy. Hence Giotto's work gains such magnitude that the story of his life has been embroidered with legends... except that we are not sure they are all legendary. Thus Giorgio Vasari related in the 16th century that as a child Giotto was a shepherd, and that at the age of twelve, while guarding a flock of goats, the famous Cimabue caught him, near a river, drawing on a rock with a coal. Amazed by the genius evident in the work, the renowned Cimabue is said to have recruited him immediately for his studio.

In the late 13th century, particularly in Italy, so-called "Gothic" art preserved many features of Byzantine art, but in another style. Its depictions resort to abstract and symbolic conventions, setting hieratic, coded figures on a stage. Giotto himself moved gradually from this style to the realism of natural representation and, instead of painting stationary tableaus, tells stories by making the characters interact. He also opened up the space to a third dimension, which invented perspective.

In order to keep sending messages without detracting from the realism he intended to establish, Giotto represents human emotions and makes his figures speak through their posture, and thus through their gestures, and above all through their face. Here, the gesture of Jesus' right hand and his exchange of glances with Saint Peter are eloquent, and we do hear the dialogue given to them by the Gospel account: *"You will never wash my feet!"* Peter protests; and Jesus replies: *"If I do not wash you, you will have no part in me"* (Jn 13:8).

Saint Peter does not protest against the service itself, which was a blessing, but against the fact that Jesus is the one who renders it, because this service was allotted to slaves. That Christ should lower himself to a servile duty was inconceivable. We see, standing behind Jesus, Saint John, the youngest of the apostles

THE BIBLE – JN 13:3-5, 12-14

Jesus, knowing that the Father had given all things into his hands, and that he had come from God and was going to God, rose from supper, laid aside his garments, and tied a towel around himself. Then he poured water into a basin, and began to wash the disciples' feet, and to wipe them with the towel that was tied around him. When he had washed their feet, and taken his garments, and resumed his place, he said to them, "Do you know what I have done to you? You call me Teacher and Lord; and you are right, for so I am. If I then, your Lord and Teacher, have washed your feet, you also ought to wash one another's feet."

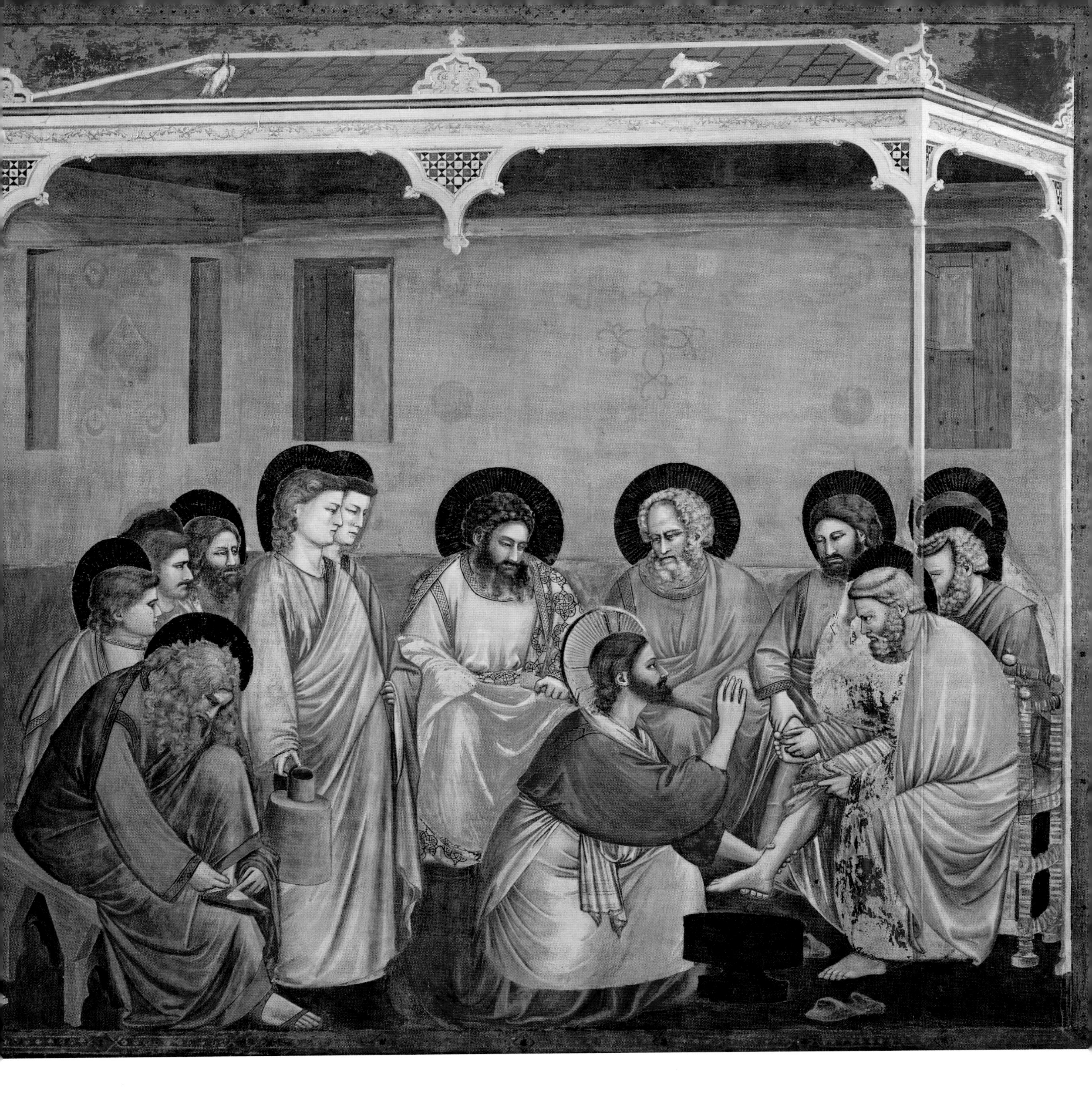

The Washing of the Feet
Giotto di Bondone (*ca.* 1266–1337)
1303–1305
Fresco, 79 x 73 in
Padua, Chapel of the Scrovegni

(it is conjectured that he was scarcely twenty years old). He asks no questions: he carries the jug filled with water and stands ready to serve; another apostle, close to Saint Peter (most certainly his brother Andrew), has already removed his sandals; the other apostles are still wearing them, it seems.

The halo of Jesus is made of gold: as incredible as it may seem, the Master himself is indeed the one who has put on a smock, knelt at his disciples' feet, and made himself their slave! But in the light of this moment, something is obscuring, of which the somberness of the washing basin bears the trace. The apostles' halos darken, like an entry into the imminent night of Gethsemane where death reigns. Do they not already bear, however, in spite of the wear of time, rays of gold, rays of grace announcing the Easter morning, when the light will tear apart this darkness? Only one halo, deformed by a deterioration of the fresco, is lacking gold. It is Judas', yet one of the twelve. The expression on his face and the yellow of his robe complete his designation as the traitor.

The chapel of the Scrovegni family is entirely covered with frescos, arranged in cycles. Giotto, at the start of the Passion cycle, insisted on depicting first *The Last Supper*, then *The Washing of the Feet*—reversing the traditional order—in the same vein, within the same framework of the cenacle in Jerusalem. We can see this as a plea. And more than a plea: a manifesto.

Giotto had a way of receiving the Gospel message that was inspired by the Beatitudes, just like Saint Francis of Assisi. Deep down he was in stark disagreement with the image of the Gospel given by the institutional Church of his time, even though he himself was not as radical as the "little poor man of Assisi," much less anti-establishment. He recognized the legitimacy of the ecclesiastical system, especially since he was intent on keeping his good image and lucrative social position. He was nevertheless sincere when he was upset by the image of Jesus and by the concept of Christian perfection that were conveyed by the drift of this theocratic system. He manifested this internal tension in his painting. This is probably the case here, when he sheds light on the mystery of faith celebrated at the Last Supper by the washing of the feet. Doesn't he intend to teach a lesson this way? A lesson with two considerations. On the one hand, in order to live authentically according to the Gospel, it is not enough to proclaim oneself a "servant" as the pope and all the clerics do; on the other hand, the Eucharist of Jesus is inseparable from the new commandment of the same Jesus: *Love one another as I have loved you.* In doing so, he gives a pictorial answer to the question that many readers familiar with the Gospel wonder about: why in the Gospel according to Saint John does *the disciple whom Jesus loved* (cf. Jn 13:23), certainly a privileged witness, not relate the institution of the Eucharist during the Last Supper?

The answer lies precisely in meditation on chapter 13 of this Gospel. And this is what Giotto invites the viewer to do. This chapter starts by recalling the profound meaning of the Eucharist: *Jesus, having loved his own who were in the world, loved them until the end* (Jn 13:1). Then, he recounts the washing of the feet (Jn 13:2-10), making it quite clear that this took place during the meal and that it therefore constitutes an integral part of the celebration of the Last Supper. Then, the disciple whom Jesus loved reports the words of Jesus explaining his gesture of washing feet: *Do you understand what I have just done for you?* (Jn 13:12); *I have given you an example so that you, too, might do as I have done for you* (Jn 13:15); *Blessed are you if you do these things* (Jn 13:17). Immediately afterward, Jesus points out the traitor, who leaves the Cenacle. Jesus then gives the new commandment: *Love one another as I have loved you* (Jn 13:34).

The message that Giotto conveys, inspired by the evangelist who witnessed the Last Supper and the Crucifixion, is clear: to remove or minimize in the celebration of the Eucharist the dimensions given to it by the washing of the feet and the proclamation of the new commandment is to deny the work of Jesus. In what sense? Well, in acting as though Jesus' saying: *Do this in memory of me* (Lk 22:19) concerned only the celebration of the memorial of the sharing of the bread and wine. Now Giotto wants to show that, after having celebrated the Eucharist of the Lord and partaken of his Body and Blood, it is still up to his disciples to do *this* fully in memory of him: to make themselves truly servants as Jesus made himself a servant and to love one another as he loved us. The Jesus depicted in this *Washing of the Feet* seems to exclaim to Christians: *Blessed are you if you do these things!* (Jn 13:17), with his hand raised in solemn testimony. Dante, his contemporary and friend, writes that "now Giotto has the cry" (*Purgatorio*, XI, 94*).

In a French translation, Lamennais translates "public acclaim," in other words, fame and reputation. French writer Philippe Sollers adds an entirely different dimension: "It is necessary to take it in this sense, without however attenuating the heartrending implication that this can have. It can rend the deafness, the opacity, the wall of silence.... It is a cry that has to have a note of the utmost distress, with no one to turn to. It is therefore a responsibility. It is a cry of beauty, however horrible the subject may be." And Sollers obviously is thinking about the ineffable cry of Jesus on the cross. But in Giotto's mind, wouldn't it be necessary instead to understand it as an authentically Franciscan cry that the Christians would address to themselves: "What have we done with Jesus?"

This cry resounds beneath the vault of the centuries:

For if thine utterance shall offensive be
At the first taste, a vital nutriment
'Twill leave thereafter, when it is digested.
This cry of thine shall do as doth the wind,
Which smiteth most the most exalted summits,
And that is no slight argument of honour (Paradiso, XVII, 130-133). ■

During a Jewish meal, the host of the meal himself distributed mouthfuls to the various guests. The Gospel according to Saint John indicates that Jesus did the same during his "Last Supper" for his twelve apostles, even for Judas who would hand him over to those who wanted to kill him. What Christian believers call "Communion" is the performance of this gesture at each Mass. Only about fifteen years after the death of Jesus, the Apostle Paul testified that this usage had already taken firm root in the first Christian communities.

Jesus gives communion to the disciple whom he loves

Every February 18, the day of his death, the Roman Martyrology commemorates the Dominican friar Fra Angelico as follows: "In Rome, in 1455, Blessed John of Fiesole, nicknamed Angelico, a priest in the Order of Preachers, who was constantly devoted to Christ and expressed in his painting what he contemplated interiorly, in order to raise the minds of men to the realities above." The painter from Florence was beatified and made patron of artists, along with Saint Luke, by Pope John Paul II in 1982.

What Fra Angelico paints here on the walls of San Marco Convent is not a depiction of the last supper of Jesus, but rather a meditation on the actualization of the "mystery" of the Eucharist: communion with the body of Christ is the source and summit of the communal religious life of the friars (and also of the faithful), the food and the goal of all prayer life. The scene is not situated in the upper room but rather in the refectory of the friary. In this detail, we see *the disciple whom Jesus loved* (cf. Jn 13:23), his hands crossed on his chest as a sign of adoration, and Saint Peter, his hands folded in thanksgiving. Fra Angelico has totally stripped down the decor of this Communion given by Jesus himself: nothing can distract in the least from contemplation of the main subject. The ground and the back wall are bare, painted in earth colors that magnify the simplicity of the life of the religious. The light that envelops the whole scene comes from nowhere; it makes no shadows except those absolutely indispensable for the design. This immanent light makes the colors and the figures that it bathes translucent. The figures are idealized; they are as if already clothed with their glorified bodies. Didn't Michelangelo say about Fra Angelico: "This good friar visited Paradise and it was granted to him to choose his models there"? ■

THE BIBLE – 1 COR 11:23-29

For I received from the Lord what I also delivered to you, that the Lord Jesus on the night when he was betrayed took bread, and when he had given thanks, he broke it, and said, "This is my body which is for you. Do this in remembrance of me." In the same way also the chalice, after supper, saying, "This chalice is the new covenant in my blood. Do this, as often as you drink it, in remembrance of me." For as often as you eat this bread and drink the chalice, you proclaim the Lord's death until he comes. Whoever, therefore, eats the bread or drinks the chalice of the Lord in an unworthy manner will be guilty of profaning the body and blood of the Lord. Let a man examine himself, and so eat of the bread and drink of the cup. For any one who eats and drinks without discerning the body, eats and drinks judgment upon himself.

The Communion of the Apostles, detail
Fra Angelico (*ca.* 1400–1455)
Ca. 1440
Fresco, 73 x 98 in
Florence, Museum-Convent of San Marco, cell 35

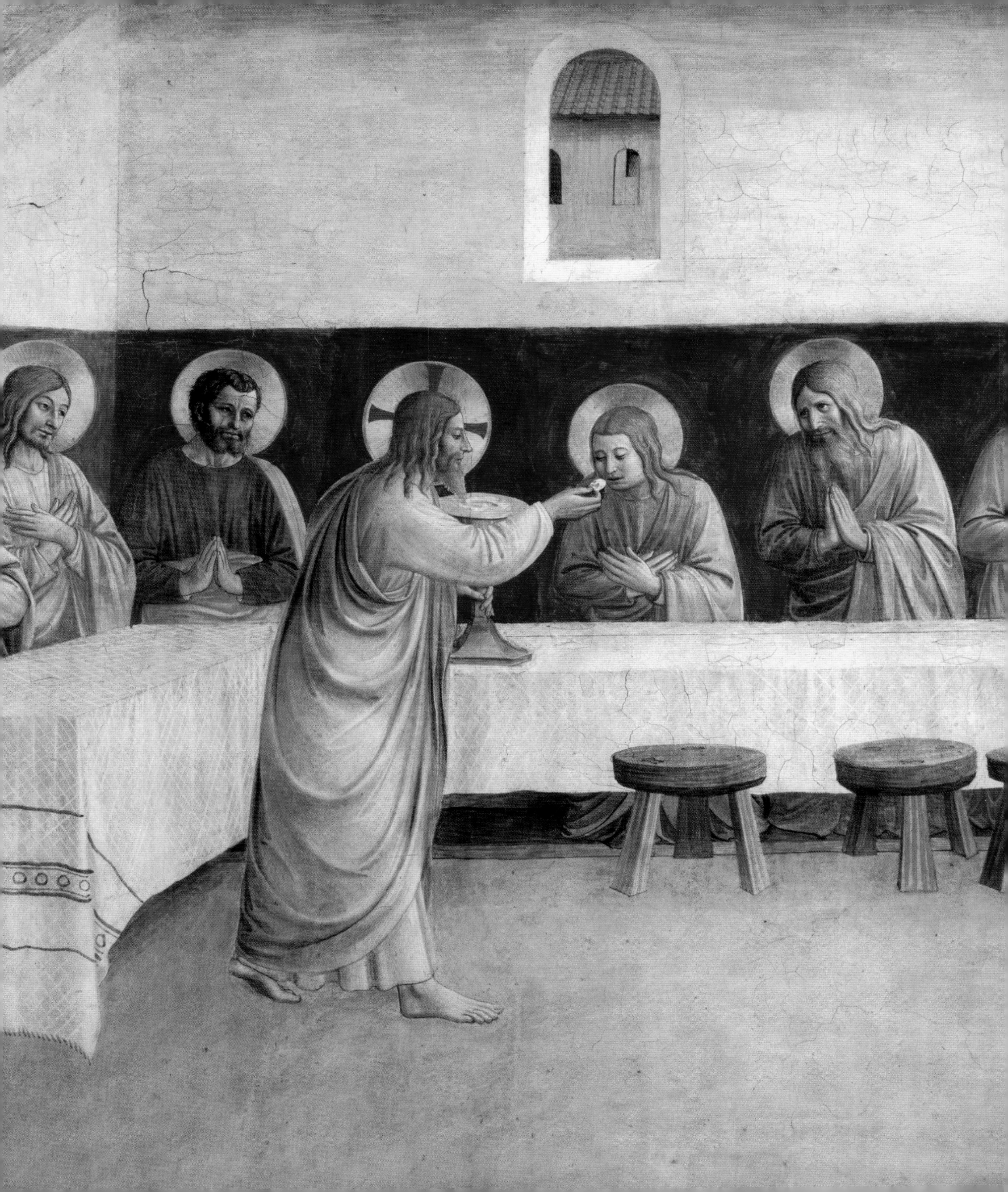

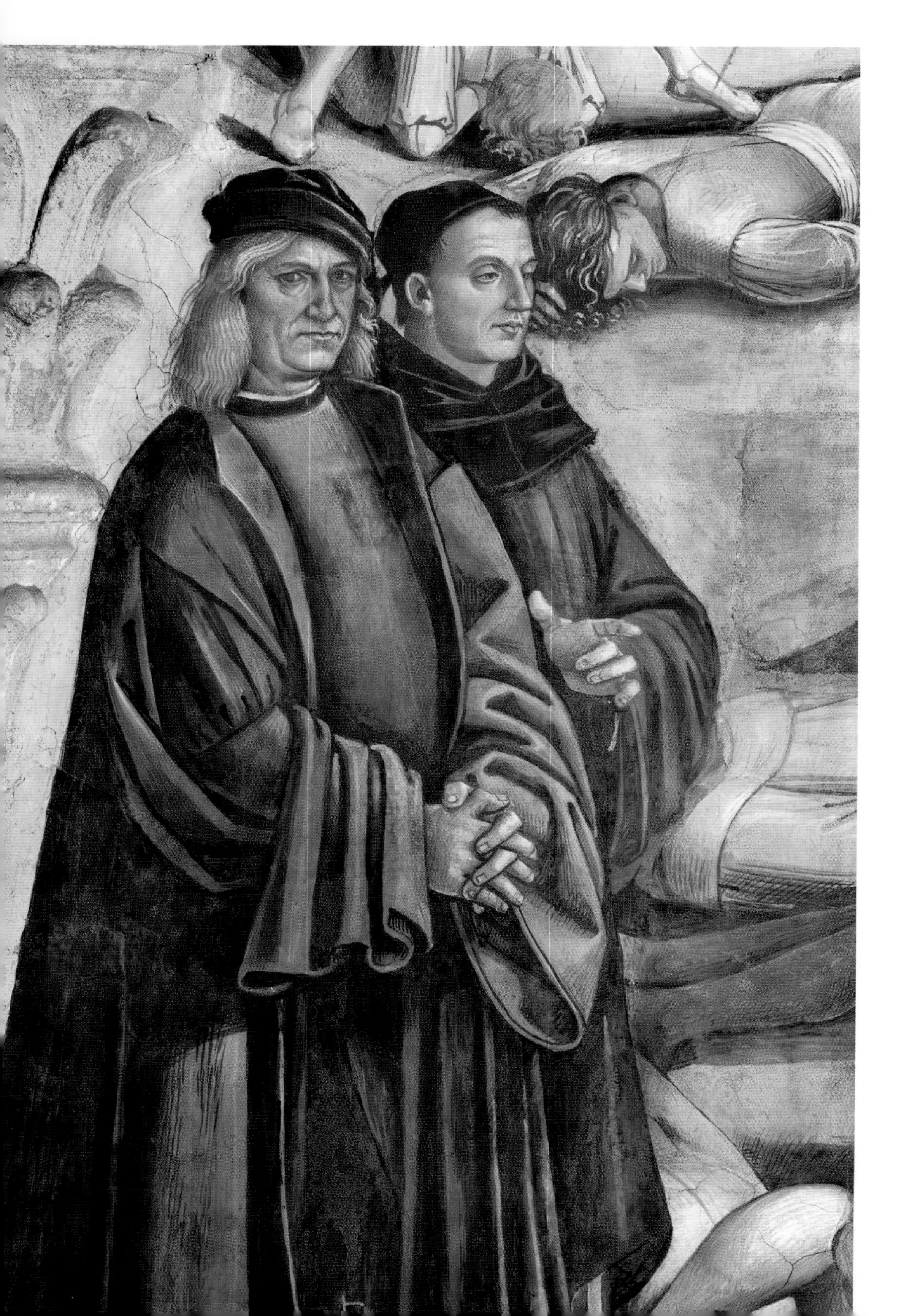

Self-portrait of Luca Signorelli
with Fra Angelico, detail from
The Preaching and the acts
of the Antichrist
Luca Signorelli (*ca.* 1445–*ca.* 1523)
Ca. 1499–1502
Fresco, 275 in wide
Cathedral of Orvieto, San Brizio Chapel

In this detail from his absolute masterpiece, the cycle of frescos on the Apocalypse, Luca Signorelli depicted himself (in the foreground) beside Fra Angelico in a Dominican habit. The portrait of Angelico is posthumous: this is homage to the one whose works Signorelli completed after his death.

In his fictional panorama *La Comédie Humaine* [The Human Comedy], Balzac assigns an important place to the Catholic religion. "The Red Inn" dramatizes the dilemma of Prosper Magnan, a surgeon who is horribly tempted by the idea of assassinating the extremely wealthy industrialist who is sharing his room: he imagines robbing him and fleeing into the night. In this passage, at the end of his interior struggle, he chooses to do what is right. And then the memory of his First Communion resurfaces.

Honoré de Balzac, "The Red Inn" (1831), in *La Comédie Humaine*, translated by Katharine Prescott Wormley, v. 28, (Boston: Little, Brown, and Company, 1899) pp. 175-222, at 195-196.

The memory of his First Communion

HONORÉ DE BALZAC

"When I stood by the bed," he said to me, "I commended myself mechanically to God." At the moment when he raised his arm collecting all his strength, he heard a voice as it were within him; he thought he saw a light. He flung the [surgical] instrument on his own bed and fled into the next room, and stood before the window. There, he conceived the utmost horror of himself. Feeling his virtue weak, fearing still to succumb to the spell that was upon him he sprang out upon the road and walked along the bank of the Rhine, pacing up and down like a sentinel before the inn. Sometimes he went as far as Andernach in his hurried tramp; often his feet led him up the slope he had descended on his way to the inn; and sometimes he lost sight of the inn and the window he had left open behind him. His object, he said, was to weary himself and so find sleep.

But, as he walked beneath the cloudless skies, beholding the stars, affected perhaps by the purer air of night and the melancholy lapping of the water, he fell into a revery which brought him back by degrees to sane moral thoughts. Reason at last dispersed completely his momentary frenzy. The teachings of his education, its religious precepts, but above all, so he told me, the remembrance of his simple life beneath the parental roof drove out his wicked thoughts. When he returned to the inn after a long meditation to which he abandoned himself on the bank of the Rhine, resting his elbow on a rock, he could, he said to me, not have slept, but have watched untempted beside millions of gold. At the moment when his virtue rose proudly and vigorously from the struggle, he knelt down, with a feeling of ecstasy and happiness, and thanked God. He felt happy, light-hearted, content, as on the day of his first communion, when he thought himself worthy of the angels because he had passed one day without sinning in thought, or word, or deed.

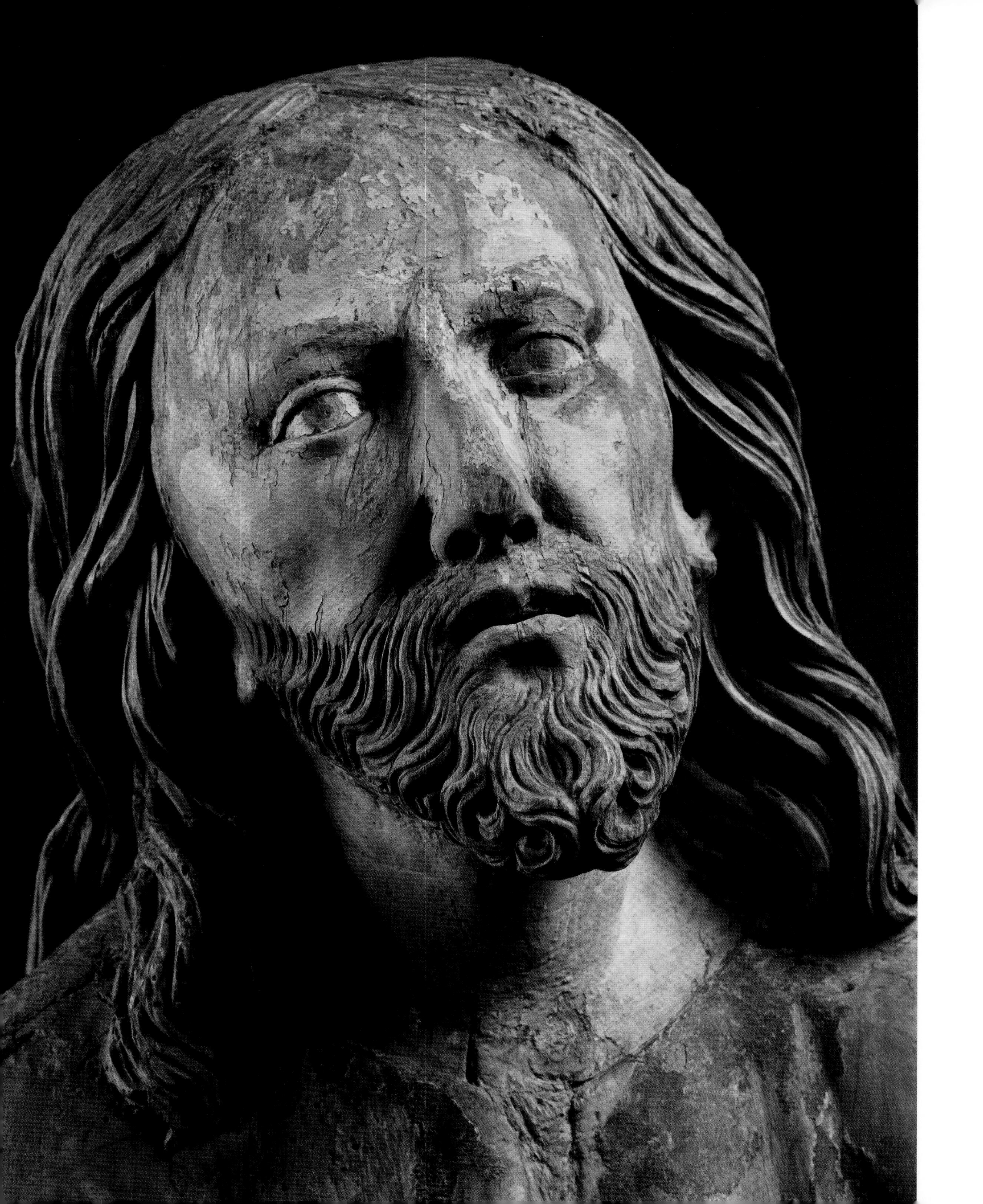

Jesus enters into his agony

After his "last supper" with his twelve apostles in the Cenacle, Jesus walks to the garden on the Mount of Olives, where he customarily goes to pray alone or with his disciples. This extensive garden is situated on the hill directly facing the Temple of Jerusalem, on the other side of the torrent of Kidron. The evangelists Matthew and Mark mention a place named Gethsemane, which means "olive press," because that is the place where olives gathered in the garden were pressed.

When Michelangelo in Rome was chiseling his *Pietà* in marble, Niklaus Weckmann (active 1481–1526) in Ulm (South Germany) was carving in lime wood a statue of Jesus kneeling in the Garden of Gethsemane. Here then is the face of this Christ, one of the most beautiful and most admirably expressive that the artist ever created. The look on this poignant face is like a window opening onto Christ's soul, just after he had confided to Peter, James, and John: *"My soul is sorrowful unto death."* Sad but not dejected, anguished but not tormented, imploring but not desperate, this is the look of the interior man who, in the midst of the trial, dialogues with God, who is closer to him than he is to himself. But it is also the look of a man who in the night already glimpses the shadow of death that is coming. It is also the look of a man who questions God's silence. When all is said and done, it is the look of humanity as a whole which, as one man, scrutinizes his destiny so as to try to read in it the fulfillment of an intelligent, benevolent, loving plan.

If the ravages of time do not destroy a sculpted work of art, they often embellish it. This statement holds truly preeminently in the case of bronzes, to which the patina of the centuries gives an incomparable sheen. It is true too, in another way, of polychrome wood statues. This face testifies to it: its colors are in shreds, the wood of which it is made is uneven, damaged, worm-eaten. And yet, having been mistreated this way, it seems even more beautiful, even truer than when it was just produced by the sculptor's hands. How is this possible? Because the ravages of time have made this face a truthful icon of wounded human nature which will be restored gloriously, yet keeping the marks of its passion. This face, being pockmarked, more authentically represents the face of Jesus, true man in agony and true God the savior. ■

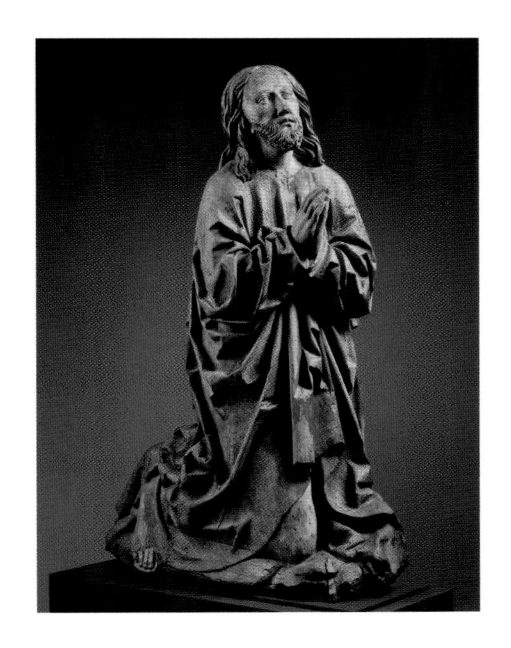

THE BIBLE – MT 26:36-38

Then Jesus went with them to a place called Gethsemane, and he said to his disciples, "Sit here, while I go over there and pray." And taking with him Peter and the two sons of Zebedee, he began to be sorrowful and troubled. Then he said to them, "My soul is very sorrowful, even to death; remain here, and watch with me."

Christ in prayer
Studio of Niklaus Weckmann
Ca. 1500–1520
Lime wood, traces of polychrome, 45 x 37 x 17 in
Paris, Louvre Museum

Jesus' agony, his fear, his sadness, and his anguish, with their physical and moral expressions, are described explicitly by the evangelists Matthew, Mark, and Luke.

Jesus is comforted by an angel

In comparison to an initial version now preserved in the Louvre Museum (*cf.* page 180), which had been executed a dozen years earlier, blackness has completely invaded the little picture of *Christ in the Garden of Olives* dated 1819. Now the hour of abominable night has come, now the all-engulfing hour of death has come. It has chosen its prey, it draws closer, it already spies it. Confronting this bloodthirsty monster, man finds himself alone, infinitely alone, in fear of being crushed and destroyed forever, annihilated, abolished.

His arms outstretched in the form of a cross, his face crying out to heaven the tragedy of the human condition, *behold the man...* He implores from on high a ray of hope. This is the hope in which he has lived. This is the hope in which now, against all hope, he wants to die. This is why he has put on the white robe that an angel presented to him at his baptism (*cf.* page 109). The robe that will become the garment of the elect whom the divine light makes radiant with brightness—without this light dispelling the advancing darkness, however: true man, Jesus would, willingly, not escape from the crossing of the final baptism—death.

But lo, the angel presents to him not only the chalice in his left hand but also a ciborium in his right hand. This interpretation by Goya is in keeping with the accounts of the evangelists, who relate first the chalice of the Passion presented to Christ, then the comfort that is brought to him by an angel. Goya likens this comfort to the viaticum, the Holy Communion that the Church gives to the dying who are entering into their agony and which the artist himself, critically ill, has just received. But what is then this food capable of comforting a man crushed by fear of suffering and dread of death? Jesus himself says it: *My food is to do the will of my Father* (Jn 4:34). In this picture, by making the viewer enter into the heart of his own agony, during which he received in the viaticum the grace to commune with the Father's will, Goya exalts the Eucharistic mystery. ■

THE BIBLE – LK 22:40-45

And when he came to the place he said to them, "Pray that you may not enter into temptation." And he withdrew from them about a stone's throw, and knelt down and prayed, "Father, if you are willing, remove this chalice from me; nevertheless not my will, but yours, be done." And there appeared to him an angel from heaven, strengthening him. And being in an agony he prayed more earnestly; and his sweat became like great drops of blood falling down upon the ground. And when he rose from prayer, he came to the disciples and found them sleeping for sorrow.

Christ in the Garden of Olives
Francisco de Goya (1746–1828)
1819
Oil on canvas, 18.5 x 14 in
Madrid, Calasancio Museum of the Piarist Fathers

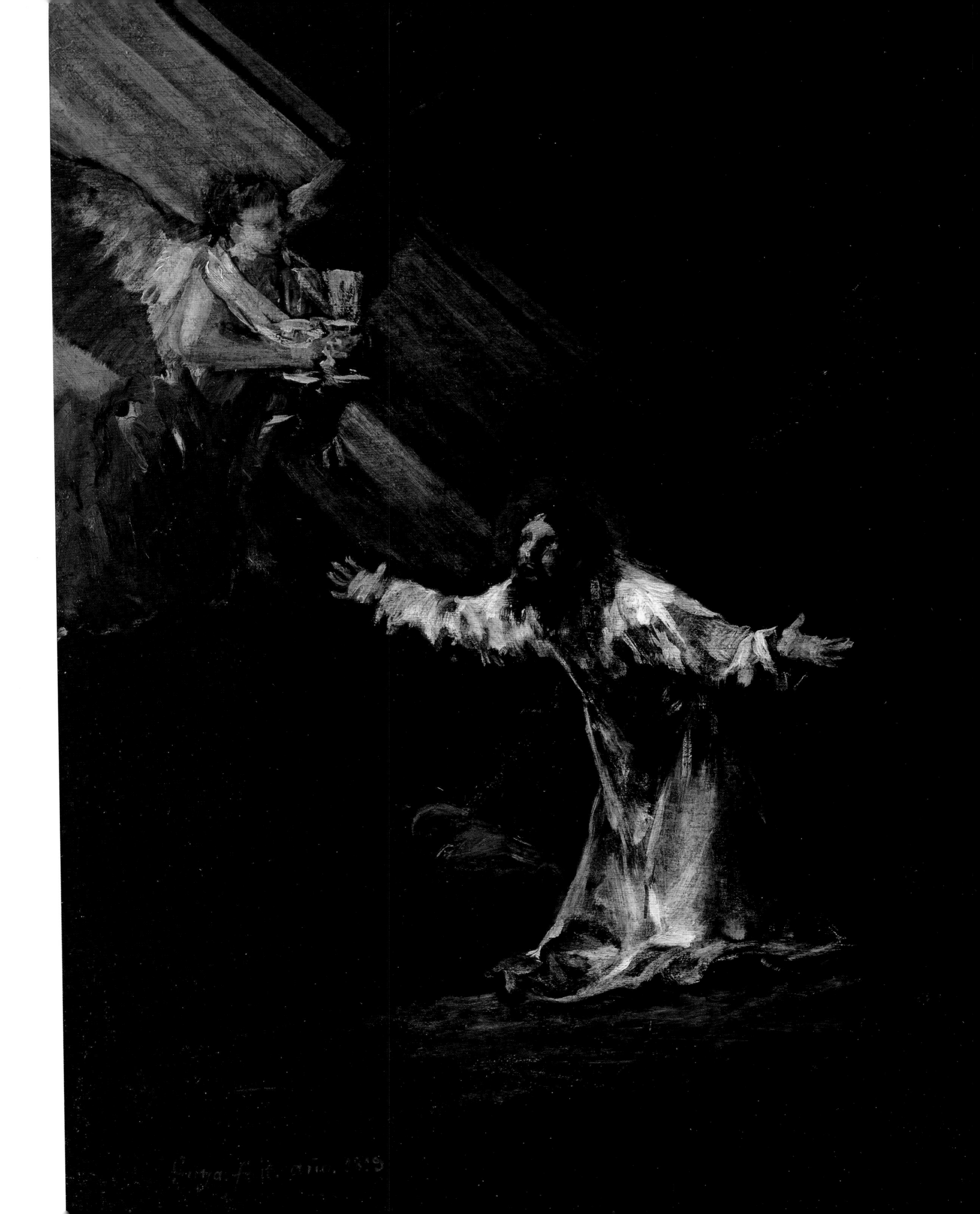

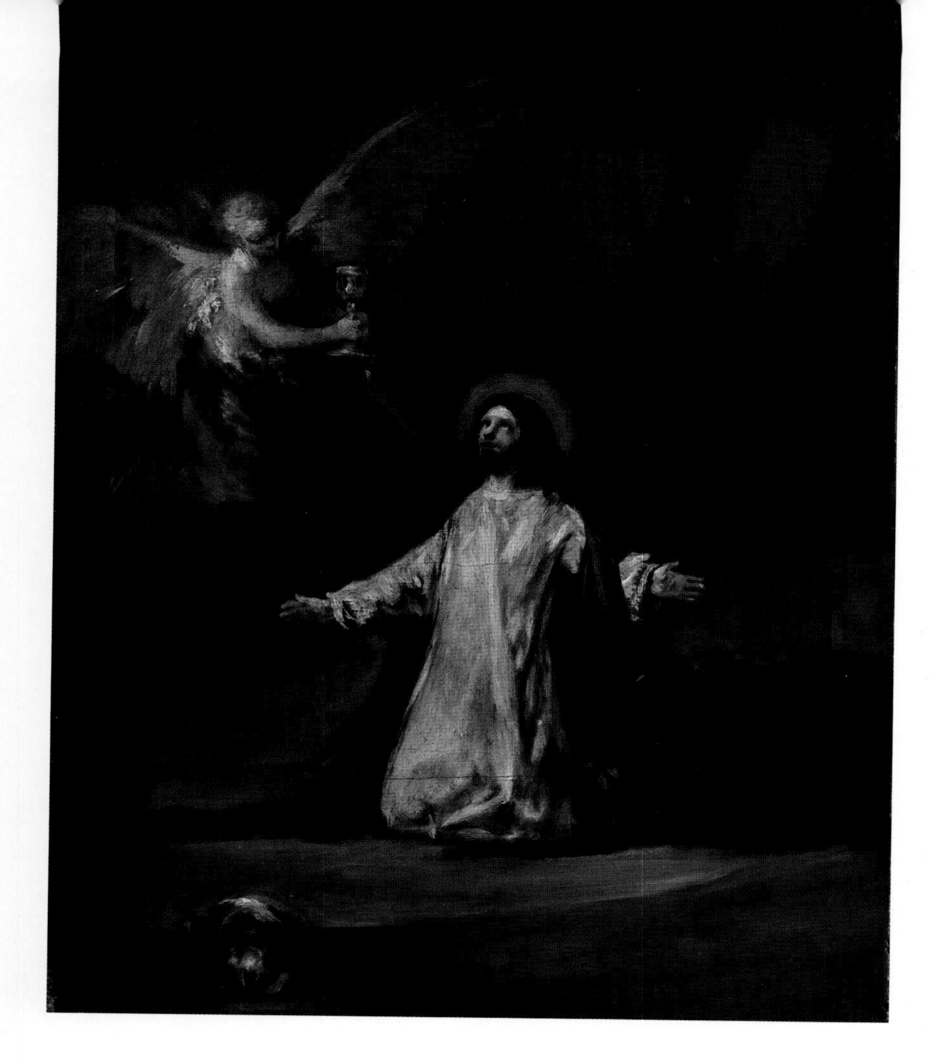

Christ in the Garden of Olives
Francisco de Goya (1746–1828)
Ca. 1810
Oil on canvas, 18.5 x 14 in
Paris, Louvre Museum

This first version is especially moving, embellished as it is (in the foreground) with the dog who by his faithfulness honored Goya in his trials: it was not fitting that Jesus in agony should be utterly abandoned. However, the second version (see preceding page), painted when the artist thought that he was doomed, is poignant in a different way, crying out with the voice of a man who is really tried by the anguish of death.

THE RELIGIOUS PAINTINGS OF THE BOISTEROUS GOYA

The public seems to picture Francisco Goya as an artist who gained recognition late in life and paradoxically, a frivolous but mordant and irreverent portraitist and engraver at the court, who in the latter part of his career became a painter haunted by death, poignantly denouncing the bloody disasters of war and the wickedness of the human soul, whose genius culminated in his terrifying cycle of black paintings. In short: a pre-Romantic artist seduced by the Enlightenment who nevertheless cannot be categorized, whose unique heritage is claimed by the most modernist artists of the 20th century.

The religious works by Goya, although numerous, are rarely the subject of commentary. The painter from Aragon, a cruel righter of wrongs by the clergy, is accused of having no religious sense, and since he had only a little faith, he supposedly could not express it. This does not take into account the contradictions in the painter's complex personality.

Never mind; the chroniclers of his time reproached him, not only for painting too fast and being careless, but also for injecting into his religious painting a whiff of the profane and a touch of his legendary eccentricity. He scorns the conventions of sacred art by painting figures with gestures and postures that are not very godly.

Thus the frescos adorning the cupola of the chapel of the hermitage of San Antonio de la Florida in Madrid, a masterpiece 20 feet in diameter painted in 1798 and dedicated to Saint Anthony of Padua, had aroused vehement criticism by his contemporaries because of brushwork that was judged too rapid and the somewhat vulgar tone set at the bottom of the composition by the very realistic presence of the people of Madrid.

Twenty years before, in the early 1770, Goya had decorated the cupola and the choir vault of the Basilica of Our Lady of the Pillar in Zaragoza, and designed the ambitious iconographic program for the walls of the palace chapel in Sobradiel, as well as the scenes from the *Life of the Virgin and of Christ* at the Carthusian monastery of Aula Dei. His admirable *Christ crucified* came in 1780.

In reality, since his youth Goya had painted admirable little devotional pictures, first in a late Baroque and Rococo style, but also a sequence depicting four Church Fathers—Saint Ambrose, Saint Augustine, Saint Gregory, and Saint Jerome—for the pendentives of the provincial church of Nuestra Señora del Pilar (later San Juan) in Calatayud (1766–1767), a program repeated three times for other buildings, in 1772 and then in 1796–1799, mainly in Aragon.

Although some of the artist's works have been lost or destroyed, such as the decoration of the reliquary in Fuendetodos (his native town), the altarpieces of the Church of San Fernando de Monte Torrero in Saragossa, and the paintings of the college of Calatrava in Salamanca, a great many Gospel and biblical scene have been preserved.

In the evening of his life, Goya produced most certainly his most mystical works at the Cathedral in Seville, with *Saints Justina and Rufina* (1817–1818), and in the chapel of the college of San Antonio Abad in Madrid, with the *Last Communion of Saint Joseph Calasanz* (1819).

Although he used to draw a little cross at the beginning of his letters, the painter certainly did not lead a life in keeping with Christian morality, contrary to what is implied by Martín Zapater (1747–1803), his best friend and first biographer. Nevertheless, the significance of his religious work, if it must be sought, lies in its intrinsic qualities and not in supposedly lacking virtues. This is why we can conjecture that Goya, until his last days in Bordeaux, continued to have nostalgia for the Christ of his childhood, whom he did finally serve well.

M. C.

Blaise Pascal (1623–1662), a mathematician, philosopher, and writer, was one of the most powerful French minds of the 17th century. After a profound conversion, he dedicated his genius and the eight remaining years of his life to the defense of the Christian religion as the only possible path of happiness and truth. In the *Pensées* [Thoughts], a posthumous collection of his preparatory notes for an *Apology* for Christianity, he anchors his reflection in human philosophy and Sacred Scripture. This passage entitled "The Mystery of Jesus" is a meditation on the agony of Jesus in the Garden of Olives.

Blaise Pascal, "The Mystery of Jesus," *Pensées* (1669–1670), translated by W. F. Trotter, selection 553 [749 in the French edition].

Agony and abandonment

BLAISE PASCAL

Jesus seeks some comfort at least in His three dearest friends, and they are asleep. He prays them to bear with Him for a little, and they leave Him with entire indifference, having so little compassion that it could not prevent their sleeping even for a moment....

Jesus is alone on the earth, without any one not only to feel and share His sufferings, but even to know of it; He and Heaven were alone in that knowledge.

Jesus is in a garden, not of delight as the first Adam, where he lost himself and the whole human race, but in one of agony, where He saved Himself and the whole human race.

He suffers this affliction and this desertion in the horror of night.

I believe that Jesus never complained but on this single occasion; but then He complained as if He could no longer bear His extreme suffering. "My soul is sorrowful, even unto death."

Jesus seeks companionship and comfort from men.

This is the sole occasion in all His life, as it seems to me. But He receives it not, for His disciples are asleep.

Jesus will be in agony even to the end of the world. We must not sleep during that time.

Jesus, in the midst of this universal desertion, including that of His own friends chosen to watch with Him, finding them asleep, is vexed because of the danger to which they expose, not Him, but themselves; He cautions them for their own safety and their own good, with a sincere tenderness for them during their ingratitude, and warns them that the spirit is willing and the flesh weak.

Jesus, finding them still asleep, without being restrained by any consideration for themselves or for Him, has the kindness not to waken them, and leaves them in repose.

Jesus prays, uncertain of the will of His Father, and fears death; but, when He knows it, He goes forward to offer Himself to death.

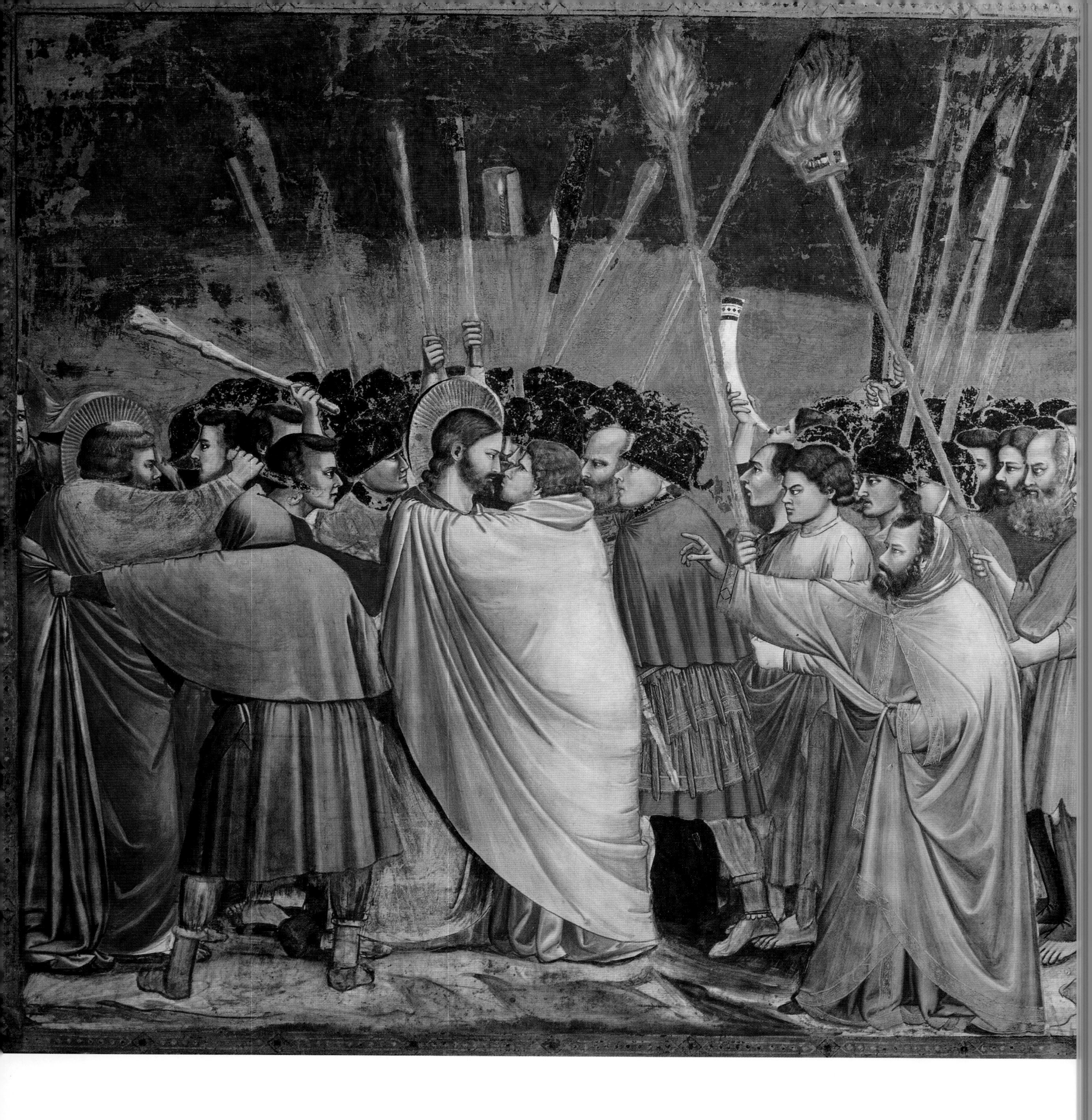

The Kiss of Judas
Giotto di Bondone (*ca.* 1266–1337)
1303–1305
Fresco, 79 x 73 in
Padua, chapel of the Scrovegni family

Jesus receives the kiss of Judas

From 1303 to 1305, assisted by his whole studio, Giotto (*ca.* 1266–1337) painted in fresco the fifty-three "pictures" in the chapel of the Scrovegni family, in Padua, Italy, magnificently illustrating scenes from the life of the Virgin Mary and from the life of Jesus and the major themes of the Vices and the Virtues. This enormous project was commissioned by Enrico Scrovegni, heir of a brilliant dynasty of rich merchants and bankers.

One of these pictures is the scene *The kiss of Judas*, all the more striking here because Judas' reputation is one of a man ready to do anything to earn money, while the Scrovegni had built their fortune on the practice of lending at interest, which was then forbidden by the Church. According to the Gospel account, the Apostle Judas led the troop dispatched by the priests so as to arrest Jesus at night. They agreed that, in the darkness, the traitor would identify Jesus by giving him a kiss.

Giotto immortalized the scene at the moment when the faces come close to each other and the kiss is about to be given. The whole composition is centered on the exchange of looks between Christ and the apostle who is betraying him. Giotto intended to record for all posterity the depth and intensity of this exchange, inviting the spectator to feel what Jesus himself experienced, along the lines of a meditation on Psalm 55:

If an enemy had taunted me, then I could bear it;
if an adversary had risen up against me, then I could hide from him.
But it is you, my chosen one, my companion, my familiar friend!
My apostle, my trusted associate!
How well we understood each other,
when we walked in fellowship within God's house!
Traitor! You stretch out your hand against me and violate our covenant.
Your speech is smooth and inviting, but war is in your heart;
your kiss is softer than perfume, but it is a dagger. (Cf. Ps 55:13-15, 21-22)

THE BIBLE – MK 14:43-46

And immediately, while he was still speaking, Judas came, one of the Twelve, and with him a crowd with swords and clubs, from the chief priests and the scribes and the elders. Now the betrayer had given them a sign, saying, "The one I shall kiss is the man; seize him and lead him away safely." And when he came, he went up to him at once, and said, "Master!" And he kissed him. And they laid hands on him and seized him.

The betrayer is not an adversary, an enemy; it is Judas, his chosen disciple, called from among a thousand, his beloved apostle. We see Giotto's Jesus pleading with his eyes and giving the traitor one last chance. Let anyone who cannot get over having been unfaithful, having ruined what was most beautiful in his life, contemplate this look of Jesus and read in it what is written there for him: "My friend, it is never too late: yes, give me this kiss and let me give it back to you; my friend, let yourself be loved."

Despite the fury of the soldiers and his friend's perseverance in betrayal, the face of Jesus shows impressive strength that is both determined and serene. The face of Judas is more of a caricature, swollen with malevolence. Above the face of Jesus, like outgrowths of his halo, are two anonymous, menacing hands, brandishing clubs ready to strike, thus manifesting the hidden side of the kiss. Fra Angelico, in his extraordinary fresco of *The mocking of Christ* in San Marco Convent in Florence, adopted and generalized this process to signify that, although God's love did indeed take upon himself all the sins of the world, his justice refuses to recognize the perpetrators: *Who is it that struck you?* (Mt 26:68).

Without a halo, Judas is stoop-shouldered, as though the burden of remorse already weighed on him. He places his hand on Jesus' shoulder and takes him into his arms. In doing so, he wraps him entirely in his own cloak. Whereas they will seal their radical separation by a kiss, Jesus and Judas now seem to be one, being covered with the same cloak. This cloak is yellow, the color of gold, whose glorious beauty is made infernal by the greed of venal persons. Thus, since the 13th century and the return of the Crusades (in which there was no lack of traitors) to Christendom, yellow has symbolized disloyalty, treachery, perfidy. Doesn't the fact that Jesus and Judas share a cloak of ignominy signify that they are mysteriously in solidarity in fulfilling the Scripture? *Friend, do that for which you have come,* Jesus says (Mt 26:50). J.R.R. Tolkien noted that a traitor can betray himself and do something good that he had not had intended.

When Giotto was producing this fresco, Pope Boniface VIII had just died: after having his predecessor imprisoned, he brought the theocratic absolutism of the papacy to its extreme. In the *Divine Comedy*, Dante puts him in hell, in the pit of simoniacs. Giotto, along the same lines as his friend Dante, indicates here that in his Church, even more than outside of it, Jesus is destined until the end of time to be clothed in the mantle of Judas:

Surely he has borne our griefs and carried our sorrows;
Yet we esteemed him stricken, struck down by God, and afflicted.
And they made his grave with the wicked and with a rich man his death. (Is 53:4, 9)

Not only did Judas betray him, but all his disciples fled. In his Passion, Jesus was desperately tested by the certainty, stirred up by Satan, that he had witnessed the irreversible collapse of his Church, founded on the columns that the apostles were supposed to be. The kiss of Judas thus marks Jesus' entry into the final trial that Satan had promised him in the desert for *the favorable moment*:

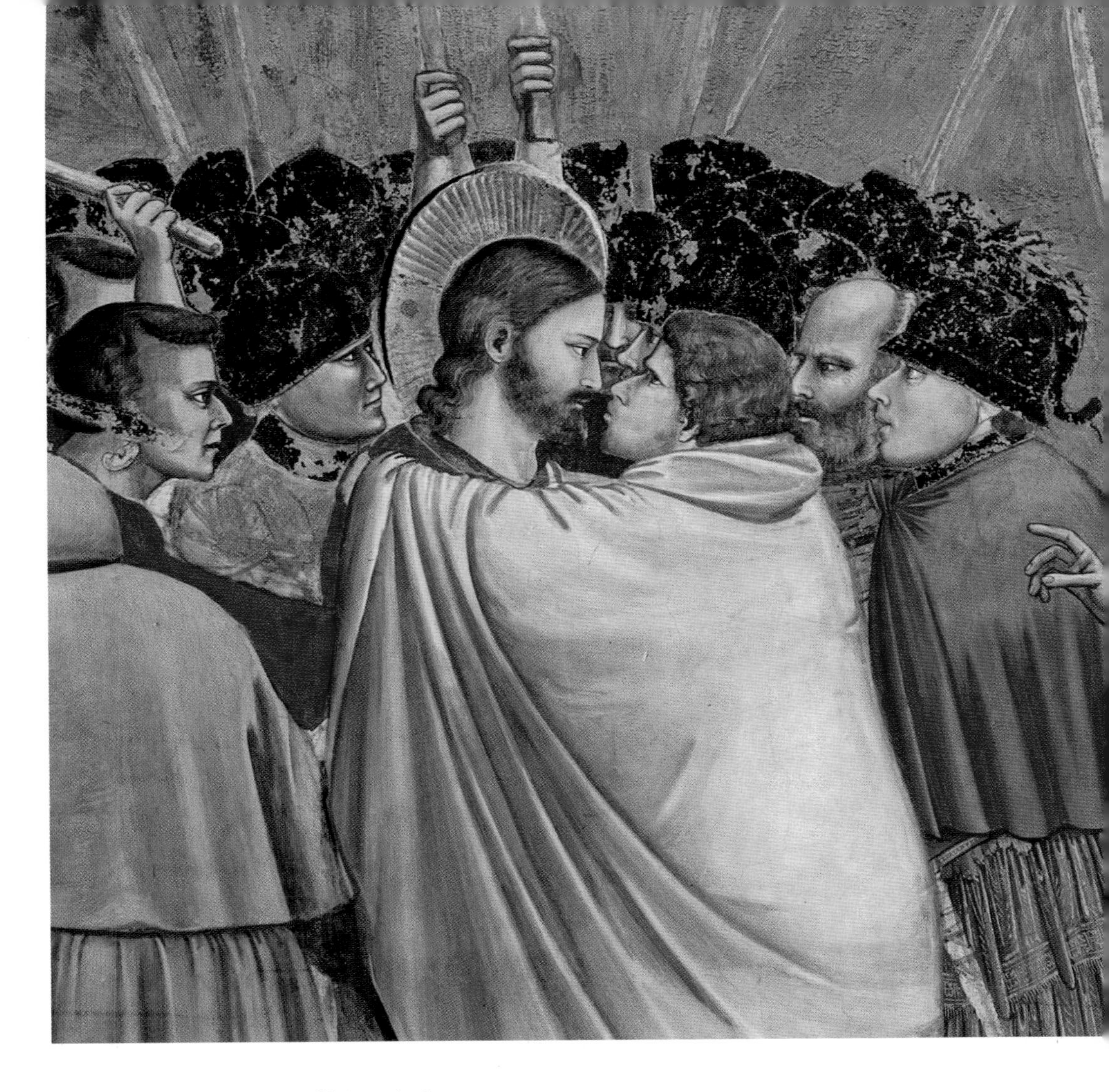

The Kiss of Judas, detail
Giotto di Bondone (*ca.* 1266–1337)
1303–1305
Fresco, 79 x 73 in
Padua, chapel of the Scrovegni family

the temptation to despair when faced with the obvious failure of his mission, a failure confirmed by the silence of God his Father. This temptation would end in that cry that was lost in the emptiness of the skies: *My God, my God, why have you abandoned me?* This is the cry of the "suffering servant" of Psalm 22 (Ps 22:2). It echoes another desolate lament in Scripture:

> *My heart is in anguish within me, the terrors of death have fallen upon me.*
> *Fear and trembling come upon me, and horror overwhelms me* (Ps 55:5-6).

The Kiss of Judas by Giotto should be compared with his *Noli me tangere* [*Touch me not*], painted on the opposite wall in the chapel of the Scrovegni family. The two works, both of them frescos, are constructed around protagonists who look each other in the eye: Jesus and Judas in the one, Jesus and Mary Magdalene in the other. And these looks, as though in suspense until the end of time, are also quite eloquent. The distance between the two figures is much greater in the *Noli me tangere*: thus, proximity signifies rupture, and distance signifies the union of love. At the meal hosted by Simon the Pharisee, Mary Magdalene had covered Jesus' feet with kisses. Not for an instant had she hidden the fact that she did so out of love, which did not fail to scandalize the Pharisee. At that same meal, Judas had become indignant because Mary Magdalene had poured a very costly perfume on Jesus. But he had masked his real motivation, money, behind his concern to not let it go to waste so as to offer alms to the poor. In Gethsemane, he masks his treachery behind a gesture of love. And yet Jesus does not push him away when he is about to embrace him. And he does. Three days later, in the first light of dawn on Easter, Mary Magdalene, overwhelmed that she has recognized Jesus alive, wants to prove to him her love with her habitual ardor, without any mask. She throws herself down at his feet. And Jesus pushes her away: *Noli me tangere*: "Do not touch me!" (Jn 20:17).

Two lessons emerge from these two frescoes which curiously mirror one another. First, Jesus is the true *sign of contradiction* prophesied by the aged Simeon, *who reveals the thoughts of many hearts* (Lk 2:34-35). More generally, the artist intends to express by his work the profession of faith that the Catholic Church has the priest chant during the Mass after the elevation: *The mystery of faith*. Certainly. ■

IN ART HISTORY

PERSPECTIVE IN GIOTTO'S PAINTINGS

Classified as one of the Italian primitives, Giotto di Bondone (*ca.* 1266–1337) follows shortly after the precursor of the Florentine Renaissance, Cimabue (*ca.* 1240–1302), of whom he was a student, according to Giorgio Vasari. In the 13th and 14th centuries, the ancient models were known in sculpture, in architecture, and in literature, but none in painting except through descriptions, particularly those of Pliny the Elder. Hence Giotto could take his inspiration only from nature in order to enter into this movement advocating a return to antiquity.

In doing so, he broke definitively with medieval painting and anticipated in some respects the first *quattrocento* (in other words, the 15th century, the first period of the Italian Renaissance) of Fra Angelico (*ca.* 1400–1455) and Masaccio (1401–1428), and the second *quattrocento*—or classical Renaissance—of Sandro Botticelli (1445–1510), Leonardo da Vinci (1452–1519), Michelangelo (1475–1564), and Raphael (1483-1520).

The frescos by Giotto in the chapel of the Scrovegni family in Padua fit into the architecture and divide the narrative space into cells.

Although Giotto still resorts to archaic systems of composition that lack a single vanishing point, he nevertheless develops a decor that is treated three-dimensionally in an intuitive perspective, and skillfully elaborated.

Pretend architecture, frontal or oblique, often circumscribes and designates a place, a spatial identification that serves the narrative, even though in Giotto's works the figures start to become liberated from their frame. In this *Kiss of Judas*, it is not architectural elements but rather the soldiers' lances that animate the space by crossing it in depth, and the effect is accentuated by the ranking of heads, suggesting a crowd. Finally, the circulation of looks from side to side within the frame reinforces the new dimension thus created.

The strong diagonals (here, the lances and the garments) that are characteristic of Giotto place the figure of Christ at the center of their point of intersection, in Padua or elsewhere, as in the frescos of the life of Saint Francis of Assisi, or those of the cycles of Saint John the Evangelist and of Saint John the Baptist in Florence.

The treatment of the figures is sculptural, and the sober draperies reveal monumental bodies, giving a strong impression of the sculpture practiced at that time.

This dramatization is combined with a humanization of the figures, particularly through their faces, which corresponds to the humanization of the faith advocated then by the Franciscan message.

Note that before Giotto, it was unthinkable to depict the apostles from the back, which he does here with the apostle who stands in front of Peter, who is cutting off the Roman soldier's ear.

The blue backgrounds that aim to be naturalistic mark in themselves a crucial stage in the history of representation.

Giotto's new space was immediately noticed by his more attentive contemporaries. Dante (1265–1321) already understood him as a reviver of painting in his day, just as Bocaccio would soon after (1313–1375). Later, Cennino Cennini (*ca.* 1360–*ca.* 1440), in his *Il libro dell'arte*, declares that "Giotto changed the art of painting; he made it pass from the Greek style to the modern Latin style." In the 16th century, Giorgio Vasari (1511–1574), in his *Lives of the most excellent painters, sculptors, and architects*, insists on it: Giotto "completely drove out the ridiculous Greek style. He revived the art of beautiful painting."

M. C.

After the publication of his first novel, *Under the Sun of Satan*, in 1926, Georges Bernanos set to work on a diptych made up of *The Imposture* (1927) and *Joy* (1929). In them he denounces a Christianity based on ambition, and explores the tragedy of the human soul shut up in pride and hypocrisy, taking in counterpoint the figures of a holy priest and a young woman, Chantal, a mystic who is concerned with the truth and the salvation of souls. In this passage from *Joy*, Chantal is rapt by the Passion of Jesus and shares his anguish at the thought that the betrayal by Judas could ruin him eternally.

Georges Bernanos, *Joy*, translated by Louise Varèse (New York: Pantheon Books, 1946), 236-237.

Jesus hands himself over to Judas

GEORGES BERNANOS

It is over the betrayal that he is weeping, it is the execrable idea of betrayal that he vainly tries to cast out of him with the sweat of his blood, drop by drop.... He has loved like a man, humanly, man's humble heritage, his poor fireside, his table, his bread, his wine—the gray roads golden in the shower, the villages with their smoke, the little houses hidden in the thorn hedges, the peace of the falling evening and the children playing on the doorstep. He has loved all that humanly, after the manner of men, but as no man has ever loved it before, would ever love it again. So purely, so intimately with the heart he himself has made, just for that, with his own hands. And the night before, while the disciples were discussing among themselves plans for the following day, where they would sleep, what food they would take with them, like soldiers before starting out on a night's march—but still a little ashamed to have let the Rabbi go up there, almost alone, and for that reason talking loudly in their strong peasant voices, clapping each other on the back after the manner of neatherds and horse-dealers. He, having blessed the first fruits of his coming Agony—just as he had blessed earlier that day the wine and the bread, consecrating for his people, for suffering mankind, his work, the holy Body—he gave it as an offering to all men, lifted it toward them with his holy, venerable hands, over the large sleeping earth whose seasons he had so loved. He offered it once, once and for all, while he was still in all the splendor and force of his youth, before delivering it up to fear, before leaving it face to face with hideous Fear, during that interminable night, until the remission of the dawn. And although he had, indeed, offered it to all men, he was thinking of only one. The only one to whom that Body really belonged, humanly belonged, as a slave belongs to his masters, he having possessed himself of it by ruse, having already disposed of it as a legitimate possession, by virtue of a deed of sale in due order, faultless. The only one thus who could defy pity, walk straight into despair, make it his home, cover himself with despair as the first murderer covered himself with the night. The only man among men who really possessed something, was provided for, having nothing more to receive from now on from anyone, eternally.

In Jerusalem, around A.D. 30, the procurator of Judea, Pontius Pilate, interrogated Jesus, specifically in the praetorium—the place where Roman justice was administered and where the Antonia Fortress is traditionally situated, north of the Temple. Jesus had just been sentenced to death by the religious leaders of the Jews. But the Roman occupier had to confirm the sentence and he alone had the power to have it executed.

Jesus is condemned to death

Tintoretto (1518–1594) is probably the greatest painter of the trinity that reigned over the Venetian arts in the 16th century, outshining even Titian, his master, and the Veronese, his rival, although both are reputed to be unsurpassable. He dedicated twenty-five years to the project of decorating the Scuola Grande di San Rocco in Venice, fifty-five impressive paintings, "with dizzying, dynamic spaces." There is the chapel of the Scrovegni in Padua, there is San Brizio Chapel or Cappella Nuovo in Orvieto, there is the Sistine Chapel in Rome, and... there is San Rocco in Venice. This *Christ before Pilate* is one of the jewels.

Tintoretto's perspective for this scene is *di sotto in sù* (from below to above), from the orchestra pit, we might say. And indeed, a grandiose, tragic opera is playing onstage. Viewed from this low angle, on a canvas more than 16 feet tall, the architectural elements in the background—which suggest the majestically towering palaces of *La Serenissima* [the sovereign state of Venice]—become colossal, unsettling, crushing. They symbolize the blind machinery of human justice when it grinds down the innocent. The man condemned to death, Jesus, his hands bound, appears elongated to the point where he acquires a fascinating dimension of mystical majesty, even in his humiliation. El Greco, a student of Tintoretto, would remember the lesson and make it a method. The principal figure in the picture (to tell the truth, the only one), Jesus, stands like a white flame that would not fully shine yet but already denounces the surrounding darkness. The painter has clothed him in an ample, white, silky toga that is admirably draped. It is a luxurious, refined robe that suits a God whose baptism in death is about to be celebrated. A diabolically invented baptism in which we see water poured not on the head of the candidate but rather on the hands of the unjust judge. Cézanne saw it all when he said about Tintoretto's work: "Everything is there, from still life to God." Here, the still life is the silver pitcher and the copper basin that form the center around which the whole picture is composed; God is the ineffable character manifested by the sublime figure of the condemned man.

Tintoretto insisted on giving witness that he was a true disciple of Jesus and sought through his art to make him better known in all his dimensions. When he took up his palette to illustrate the Bible, he considered himself sent on a mission. He applied himself first to showing the continuity between the Old and the New Testament. But he recapitulated the "before the historical Jesus" as well as the "after,"

THE BIBLE – MT 27:22-26

They all said, "Let him be crucified." And he said, "Why, what evil has he done?" But they shouted all the more, "Let him be crucified." So when Pilate saw that he was gaining nothing, but rather that a riot was beginning, he took water and washed his hands before the crowd, saying, "I am innocent of this righteous man's blood; see to it yourselves." And all the people answered, "His blood be on us and on our children!" Then he released for them Barabbas, and having scourged Jesus, delivered him to be crucified.

Christ before Pilate
Jacopo Robusti, called Tintoretto (1518–1594)
1566–1567
Oil on canvas, 203 x 150 in
Venice, Scuola Grande di San Rocco

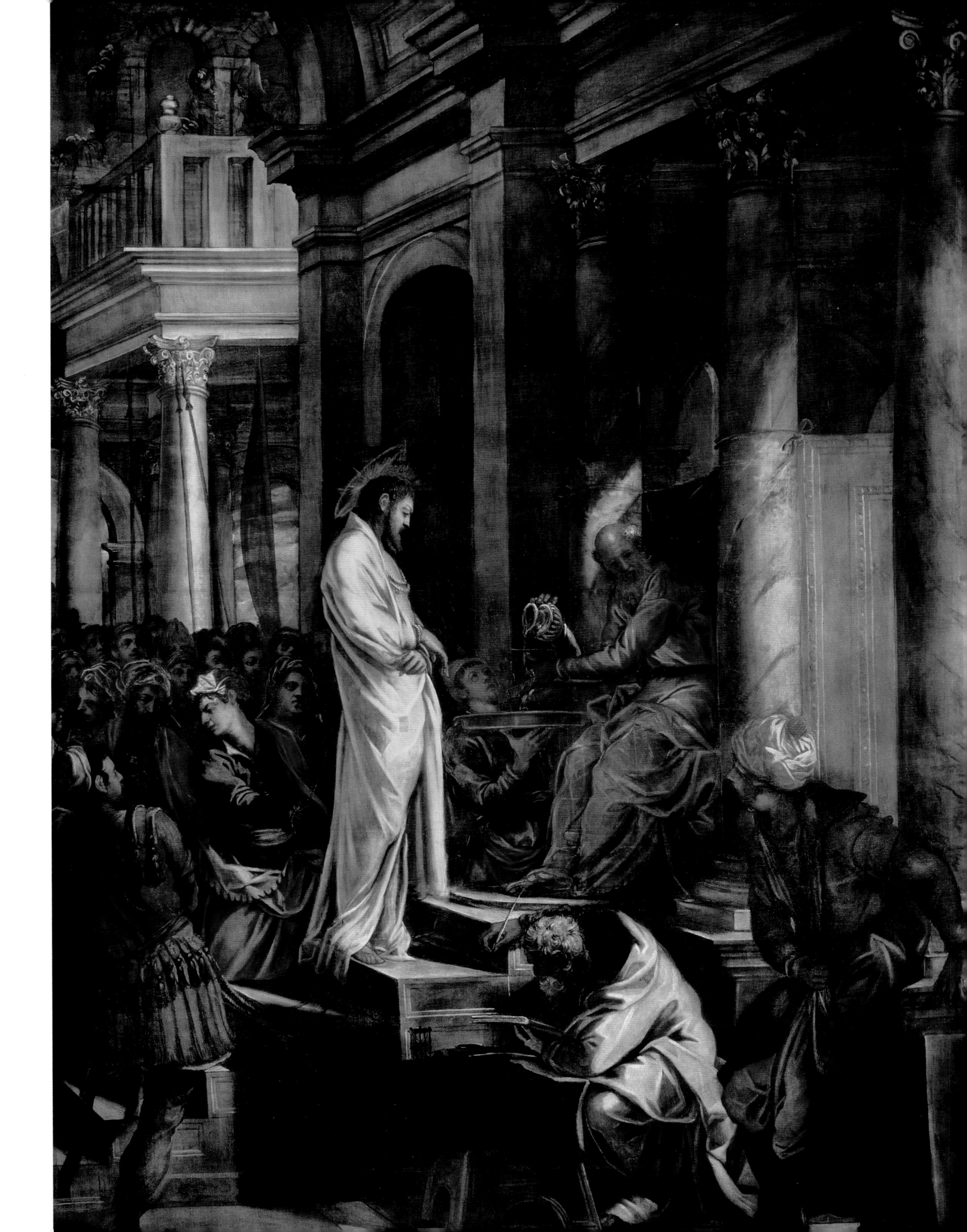

from the Creation to the end of time, using the most elaborate codes to signify figures from the past and the future fulfillments of the episodes that he depicted. Here, for example, the baptismal robe of Jesus signifies his passage through death, of course, and also prefigures his glorious Resurrection, the decisive moment when this white flame that illumines only itself would shine on the world, and furthermore his ascension to God's right hand so as to represent humanity there forever.

Still more profoundly, with this absolutely innocent figure—so much so that throughout the picture, from Pilate to the scribe, via the High Priest's guard who dragged Jesus to Pilate with the halter he still holds in his hand, everyone turns his head away, unable to bear looking at him as a criminal sentenced to death and to risk meeting his glance—with this innocent man, then, about whom Pilate says prophetically: *"Here is the man!"* (Jn 19:5), Tintoretto is not content to question the justice—or rather the injustice—of men, but he also questions the idea the men make for themselves of God's justice. He makes visibly untenable a blasphemous focus on death and the corruption of creation as punishments from an angry God, rather than the mysterious consequences of sin. *The Prince of this world* (Jn 16:11) is Satan. He is on the side of Pilate and the hate-filled crowd. As for God, he is on the side of the victim, so much so that he *is* the victim here. Whatever happens, he is in solidarity with humanity from its genesis until its divine fulfillment. Now, it is for the worst, so that finally it might be for the better. ■

IN ART HISTORY

SAINT ROCCO AND THE PLAGUE IN VENICE

The Scuola di San Rocco was instituted in Venice in 1478. As a confraternity placed under the patronage of San Rocco (sometimes called Saint Roch), its purpose was to perform works of charity. *La Scuola* is also the name of the place where the confraternity met. The sumptuous decor of the Scuola di San Rocco is a brilliant testimony to the art of Jacopo Robusti, called Tintoretto (1518–1594). Besides a Passion cycle, to which *Christ before Pilate* belongs, Tintoretto painted there a *Saint Rocco in glory*, which adorns the ceiling of the Salla dell'Albergo, a work that won him the commission to decorate the hall of the Scuola. We can admire also other works by his hand in the nearby Church of San Rocco, *Saint Rocco curing the plague victims, Saint Rocco struck by the plague*, and *Saint Rocco in prison comforted by an angel*.

Saint Rocco, protector and healer from the plague, is the object of particular devotion in Venice. Indeed, *La Serenissima*, a strategically sensitive commercial city and a point of contact between East and West, had to face very early the epidemics spread by the merchant ships that it welcomed, and particularly the terrible plague. From 1348 on, the year that marks the arrival of the Black Plague in Venice, until the last major epidemic in 1630–1631, the sickness was a constant worry for the Venetian authorities.

The special magistracy which in 1258 was put in charge of safeguarding what we call today "public health" in times of epidemic was instituted perpetually in 1485. Under the guidance of three magistrates, it controlled the foodstuffs imported into Venice, the water tanks, the sanitation of the city, and the cemeteries. The Island of Saint Mary of Nazareth (Lazzaretto Vecchio) served from 1420 on to isolate the sick so as to slow the spread of the scourge.

Finally, the relics of the body of Saint Rocco were moved from Montpellier, the saint's native town, to Venice in that same year 1485. The translation was the occasion for the confraternity to build with great pomp a church housing his relics as well as a *scuola* in the immediate vicinity, both dedicated to the Saint.

Alas, despite all these precautions, *La Serenissima* was once again devastated in 1575–1577 by this terrible plague, and the painter Tintoretto may have been one of the victims. These epidemics remain anchored in the memory of Venice. Every year, Saint Roch is worthily celebrated at the Church of San Rocco, and above all, because of a vow made in 1576 , the grand feast of the Redeemer is celebrated in thanksgiving for the end of the plague that raged at that time, just as the feast of *La Salute* commemorates the end of the plague in 1630-1631. Moreover, one of the most popular carnival masks, white with a long nose, is a direct imitation of the masks worn by the "plague doctors" of former times, which were filled with herbal medicines.

M. C.

The wife of Pilate

GERTRUD VON LE FORT

Gertrud von Le Fort (1876–1971) was the daughter of a Prussian colonel and a mother whose family belonged to the lesser nobility. Her father encouraged her to start reading history at a young age. A trip to Rome in 1907 and her subsequent decision in 1908 to study in Heidelberg were of decisive importance for her life's work as an author of poetry and historical fiction. Her most famous work in English translation is *The Song of the Scaffold*, about the Carmelite martyrs of the French Revolution.

The excerpt quoted here is from another work, *The Wife of Pilate*, one of her later novellas. The story is narrated by Praxedis—a freedwoman and servant of the title character, Claudia Procula—who has just told the Procurator about the dream that her mistress had during the night.

Gertrud von Le Fort, *The Wife of Pilate* (1955), in *The Wife of Pilate and other stories*, translated by Michael J. Miller (San Francisco: Ignatius Press, 2015), pages 7–48, at 14–15.

Now I hurried back to my mistress and notified her that the Procurator had listened to me benevolently. That seemed to calm her somewhat. She allowed me to dress her and also applied extensively the many cosmetics and ointments by which she set great store, notwithstanding her youthful freshness. Then we went over to the *triclinium*, the dining room, where we could not hear the ongoing uproar of the people. I read several Greek love poems aloud to her, which she was especially fond of hearing because they reflected the feelings she was accustomed to demanding of her husband.

Suddenly the slave girl whom I had questioned previously on account of the riot burst in. "O my lady, your husband is allowing the prisoner to be crucified after all," she cried, "and his friends firmly believed that God's angels would come to his aid." My mistress jumped up and literally fled the room. I followed her but could not catch up with her. Then we two were standing on the flat roof above the low porch of the palace, from which one has a view of the whole square at the foot of the courthouse. We leaned over the wall.

The Procurator now sat on the judge's bench, glaring ominously; evidently he had already pronounced the sentence, for the legionaries were laying hands on the prisoner who stood before him. He was clothed in a ragged red military cloak and wore a crown of thorns around his bleeding head. But the truly distressing thing about his appearance was that this pitiful being looked as though he had pity on the whole world, even on the Procurator, his judge—yes, even on him! This pity engulfed the entire face of the condemned man—and if my life depended on it, I could not say the slightest thing about it except that it wore this expression of an unbounded, perfectly incomprehensible pity, at the sight of which I was seized by a peculiar vertigo. It seemed to me as though this pity would necessarily engulf the whole known world, just as it had engulfed the prisoner's face to the point where he was unrecognizable. Indeed, the impression that the whole world as I knew it had somehow begun to totter was so overwhelming that, despite its all-powerful influence, it aroused my opposition. I felt a hopeless resistance abruptly rise up within me; I clung to my condemned world and persisted in this attitude, motionless, albeit helpless. All this took place in an instant, and in the next the legionaries were already roughly dragging the condemned man away so as to lead him to his crucifixion. The Procurator stood up from the tribunal and went back into the palace with the same ominous expression.

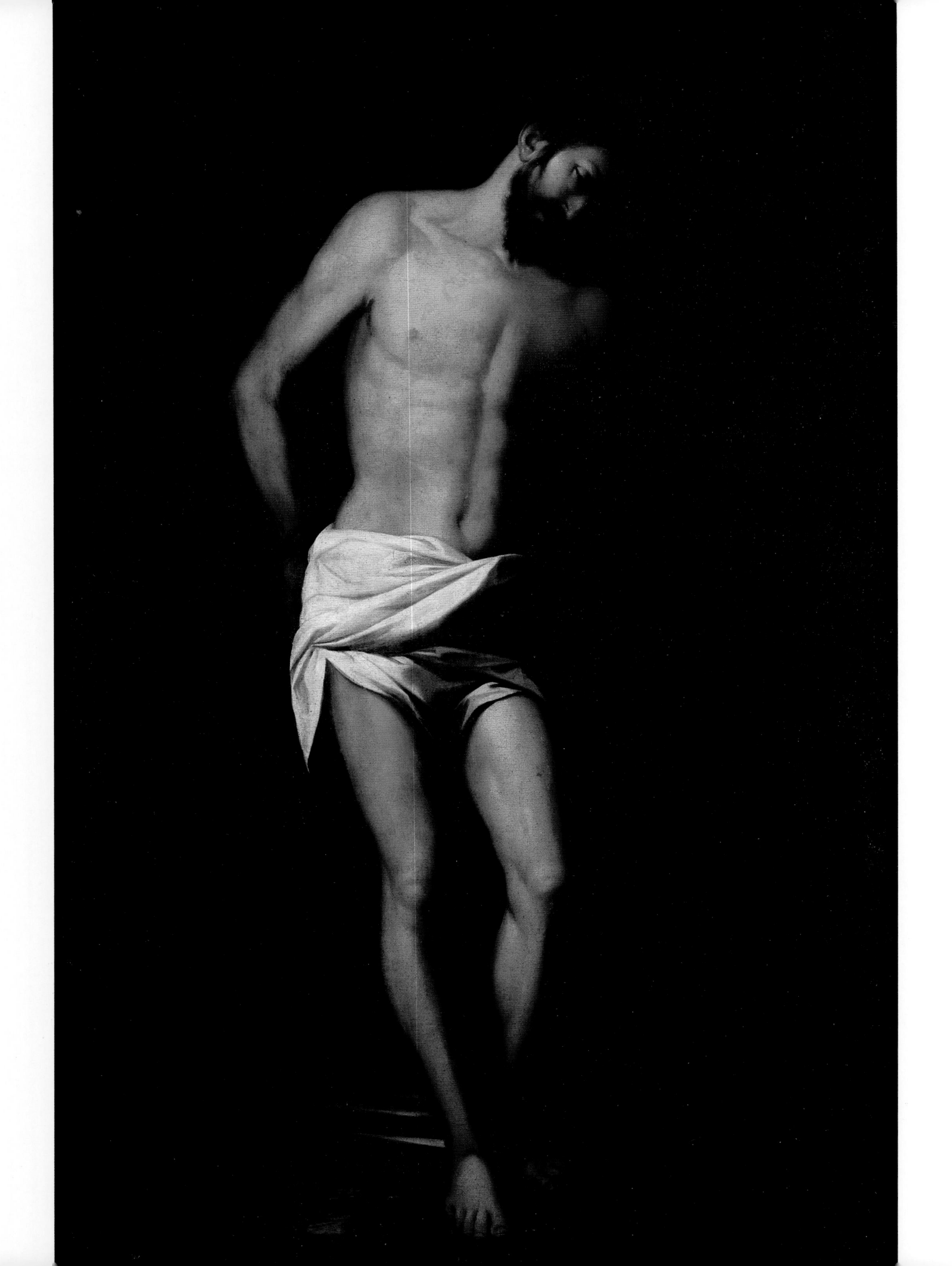

According to the accounts set down by the evangelists Matthew, Mark, and John, Pilate had Jesus scourged before crucifying him.

Christ at the pillar

An ingenious painter, an extraordinary sculptor, and an architect, Alonso Cano (1601–1667) was nicknamed "The Spanish Michelangelo." Except for the anachronism, he deserves it.

Then he released for them Barabbas, and having scourged Jesus, delivered him to be crucified.

THE BIBLE – MT 27:26

As Goya would do (*cf.* page 178), Alonso Cano invites the viewer to interpret the Passion as an unfolding of the Eucharistic mystery. He shows Jesus bound to his pillar before he was subjected to scourging and insults. His friends have fled; his executioners have gone to get the instruments of torture. Once again, he is alone, surrounded by darkness. A light from elsewhere causes him to emerge from the night. His body is exposed by it, as though on a stage. Or rather, as though on an altar, in an elevation. But there is nothing glorious about his posture: painfully wrenched to the left, with his head leaning on his shoulder, he seems to contemplate within himself the Scripture that is being fulfilled.

Alonso Cano lets the viewer see the body of Jesus before it was disfigured by torture. This body is human, perfectly human, to be sure, but beautiful as the body of Adam when it was fashioned and came from the hands of God at the dawn of the world. It is not a matter of entering into the picture, then, but rather of reading in it the mystery of the faith: here is the mortal body of the Son of Man, as Jesus calls himself, of the New Adam. It will be crushed by suffering and destroyed by death. It will be disfigured, because of the sin of the world, by the powers of evil and by death. However, Alonso Cano's genius manages to suggest that the invisible is manifested in this visible body, the incommensurable within its limits, holiness in its disgrace, eternity in its imminent end. And that this is indeed the body about which Jesus said: *This is my body which is given for you* (Lk 22:19). ■

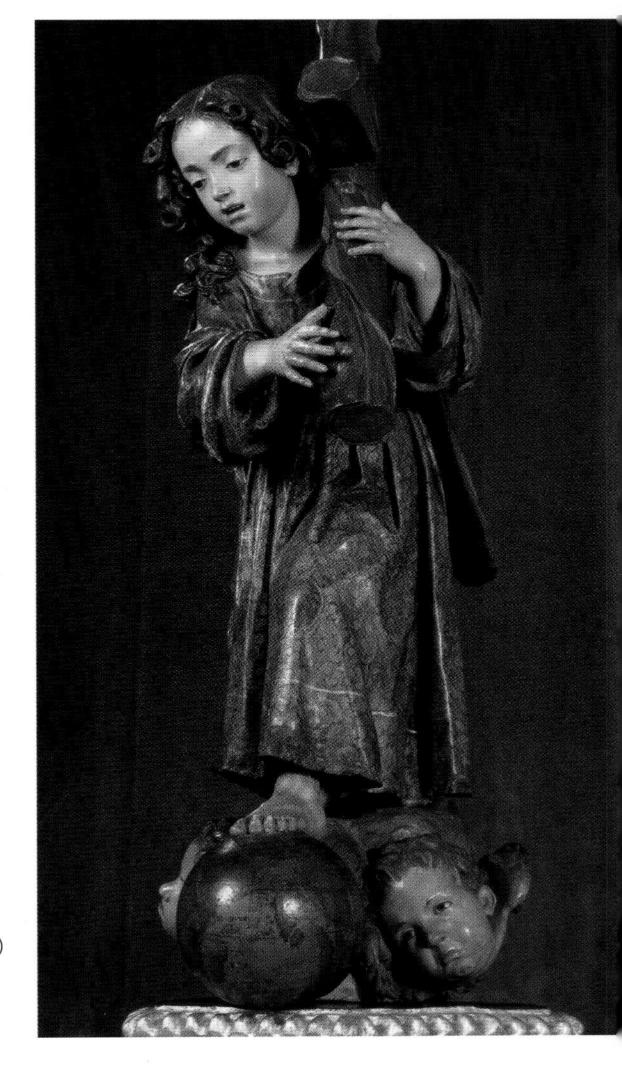

Child of Sorrows
Attributed to Alonso Cano (1601–1667)
1657–1660
Chestnut wood, polychrome
22 in tall
Madrid, Real Congregación San Fermin de los Navarros

Alonso Cano was also a gifted sculptor.

Christ at the pillar
Alonso Cano (1601–1667)
Oil on canvas, 63.7 x 40 in
Pau, Museum of Fine Arts

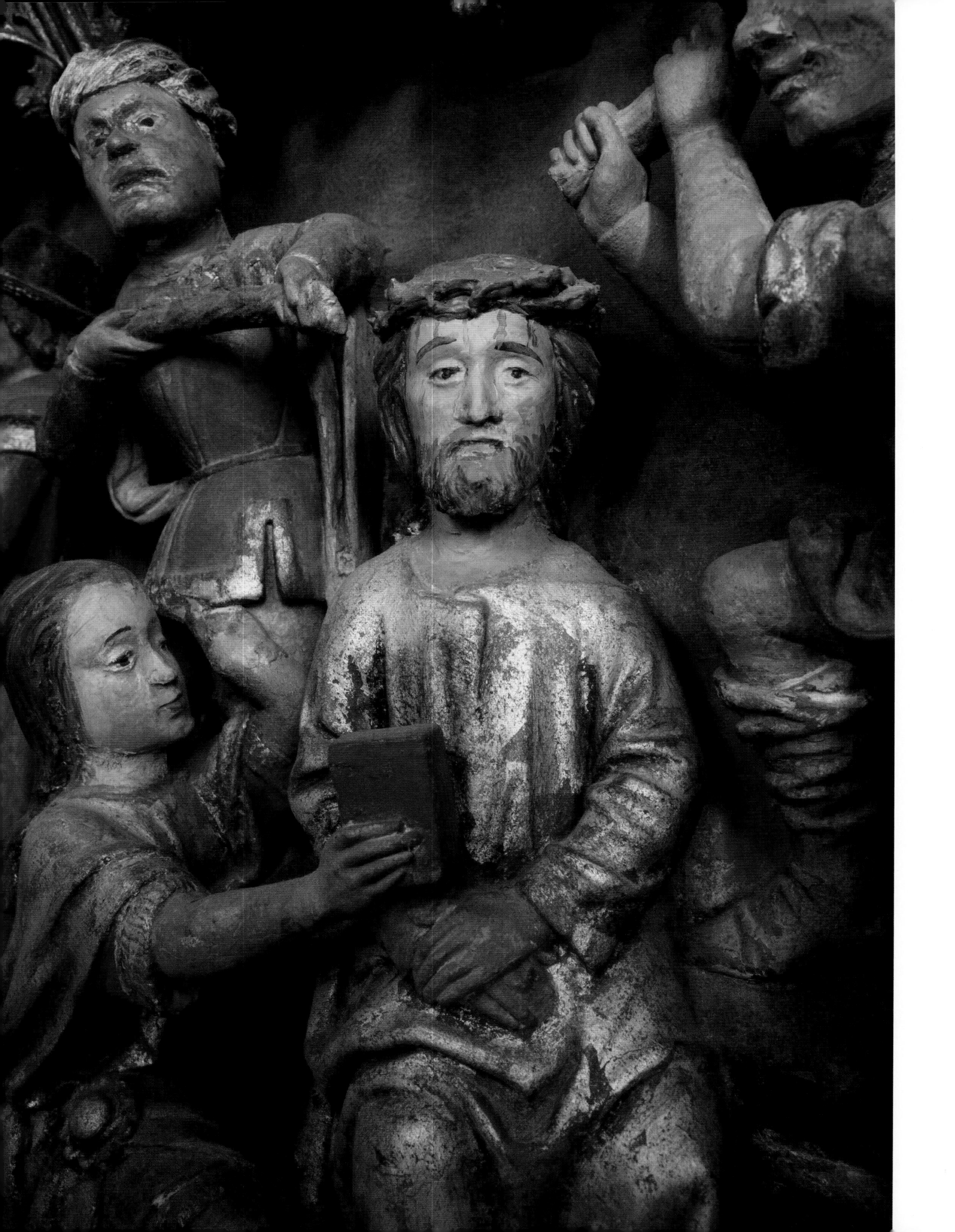

Jesus is crowned with thorns

The Gospels describe a Jesus who is hated from his birth by the powerful, who quite wrongly feared the rise of a king who would call their authority into question (*cf. The flight into Egypt*, page 84, and *The massacre of the Innocents*, page 88). Thirty years later, the first question that Pilate asked him during his trial was: "Are you the king of the Jews?" When the death sentence was pronounced, the balance of power was reversed: such an obviously powerless royalty became the object of mockery, derision, and insults.

In the hamlet of Houssaye, in Britanny, a chapel houses one of those treasures in which the faith of the people and art are joined intimately to produce masterpieces which, although anonymous, are nonetheless precious. On an expanse more than four meters long, multiple figures sculpted in stone in very high relief reenact the vivid account of the Passion and then of Easter morning. In the "late Gothic" style in its composition, the postures, and the draperies, but already showing the marks of naturalism and Renaissance expressivity in the faces, this admirable ensemble is placed behind the altar. The function of this altarpiece is to show the faithful what happened in the time of Jesus and what is made present on the altar at every Mass.

On this panel, Jesus is enthroned as a mock king. His only courtiers are executioners—their faces deformed by wickedness, each armed with a rod—who pay him the homage of their mockery and spitting.

This majestic, insulted Jesus speaks eloquently with his eyes to the viewer. According to the tradition of *The Imitation of Christ*, a devotional book that was very popular in the early 16th century, he invites the faithful to behave like children of God when they themselves are humiliated by violence and their dignity is trampled on by injustice.

THE BIBLE – JN 19:2-3

And the soldiers plaited a crown of thorns, and put it on his head, and clothed him in a purple robe; they came up to him, saying, "Hail, King of the Jews!" and struck him with their hands.

Jesus endures these insults with an impressive supernatural dignity: this is indeed the Lord, the King of kings, the sculptor insistently testifies. But the artist shows also that Jesus was seized with fear in the Garden of Gethsemane, that he would collapse under the weight of the Cross, and that he would howl in his physical and moral suffering when they crucified him. However, always, in anguish or in serenity, facing torture or exhaustion, when in command or abandoned, Jesus would always retain the expression that the sculptor gives him here, without rebellion, without violence, without hatred, and without judging his tormentors.

In a rather rare interpretation of the Gospel episode, here is an angel, his hand lifted as a sign of public testimony, giving Jesus a little book. This is the angel who proclaims on the last day that *the mystery of God, as he announced to his servants the prophets, should be fulfilled* (Rv 10:7). And the book is the one that will be opened at the sound of the seventh trumpet of the Apocalypse. ■

The Crowning with Thorns
Picard workshop
Ca. 1510
Limestone polychrome and gilded
Pontivy, Notre-Dame chapel in La Houssaye,
detail from the *Altarpiece of the Passion and the Resurrection*

Ecce homo in Latin, *Idoù ho ánthrōpos* in the original Greek of the Gospel according to Saint John, means, "Here is the man!" Christians attribute a prophetic dimension to this phrase in which Pilate points out Jesus. Indeed, Jesus suffering, Jesus tortured, Jesus ridiculed, Jesus condemned to death recapitulates in himself the destiny of every human being who comes into the world... here for the worse, but ultimately, the Gospels promises us, for the best. The *Ecce homo* has been one of the favorite motifs of artists.

Here is the man!

Painted for the Abbey of Port-Royal des Champs, this *Ecce Homo* translates into pictorial language the Jansenist vision, which is that of the *Pensées* by Blaise Pascal and also of the theatrical works by Jean Racine, and later, fifty years after Philippe de Champaigne (1602–1674) produced it, that of the theology of Jacques-Bénigne Bossuet at the end of his life. A tragic vision of a world to come in which God becomes a "hidden God," who ceases to appear in the rational and economic structures that come to replace those of the world in which he manifested himself a little while ago. A frightened prophetic vision, which uncovers the foundations of a religious crisis in which, gradually, the evidence of God vanishes for man, who is left to his own devices. A tragic vision that offers no alternative but to leave God absolutely for the world or to leave the world absolutely for God. The tragedy of Jansenism was to let itself be locked into this dilemma.

THE BIBLE – JN 19:4-5

Pilate went out again, and said to them, "Behold, I am bringing him out to you, that you may know that I find no crime in him." So Jesus came out, wearing the crown of thorns and the purple robe. Pilate said to them, "Here is the man!"

Here, then, is this *Ecce homo* thrown onto the canvas like a challenge to the new world that was germinating in the 17th century, a world that will claim to be man's only chance and only perspective, under the names of "Enlightenment" and "Progress." In this composition, marked by a refined and austere classicism, in which the face of Christ is impressive for its interiority, Philippe de Champaigne, suddenly hit by a Baroque inspiration, throws into the spectator's face, as though shouting a profession of faith, this admirably draped tunic of Roman purple which gives the picture an almost supernaturally three-dimensional effect. Confronted by the same tragic vision, whereas Pascal and Racine had chosen to refuse to live, whereas Bossuet would choose to wage a final battle that was lost in advance, a mystical painter testified in a blood-red mandorla that, until the end of times, the "hidden God" would not cease to manifest his glory in every human being who gives the greatest proof of love: to lay down one's life for those whom one loves (cf. Jn 15:13).

This king subjected to ridicule is anything but ridiculous. He has his hands tied; one of them holds with difficulty a reed scepter. His head is encircled by a crown of plaited thorns, the wood of which is still green. His purple toga—imperial down to its admirable folds and its gold brooch—should scoff at the spectator as a supreme mockery. It makes us see Jesus as though clothed with the blood he has shed. The frame within which the king—yes, definitely, the king—is seated is so austere that it vies in magnifying the sublime dignity of

Ecce homo
Philippe de Champaigne (1602–1674)
Ca. 1655
Oil on canvas, 73 x 50 in
Magny-les-Hameaux, National Museum of Port-Royal des Champs

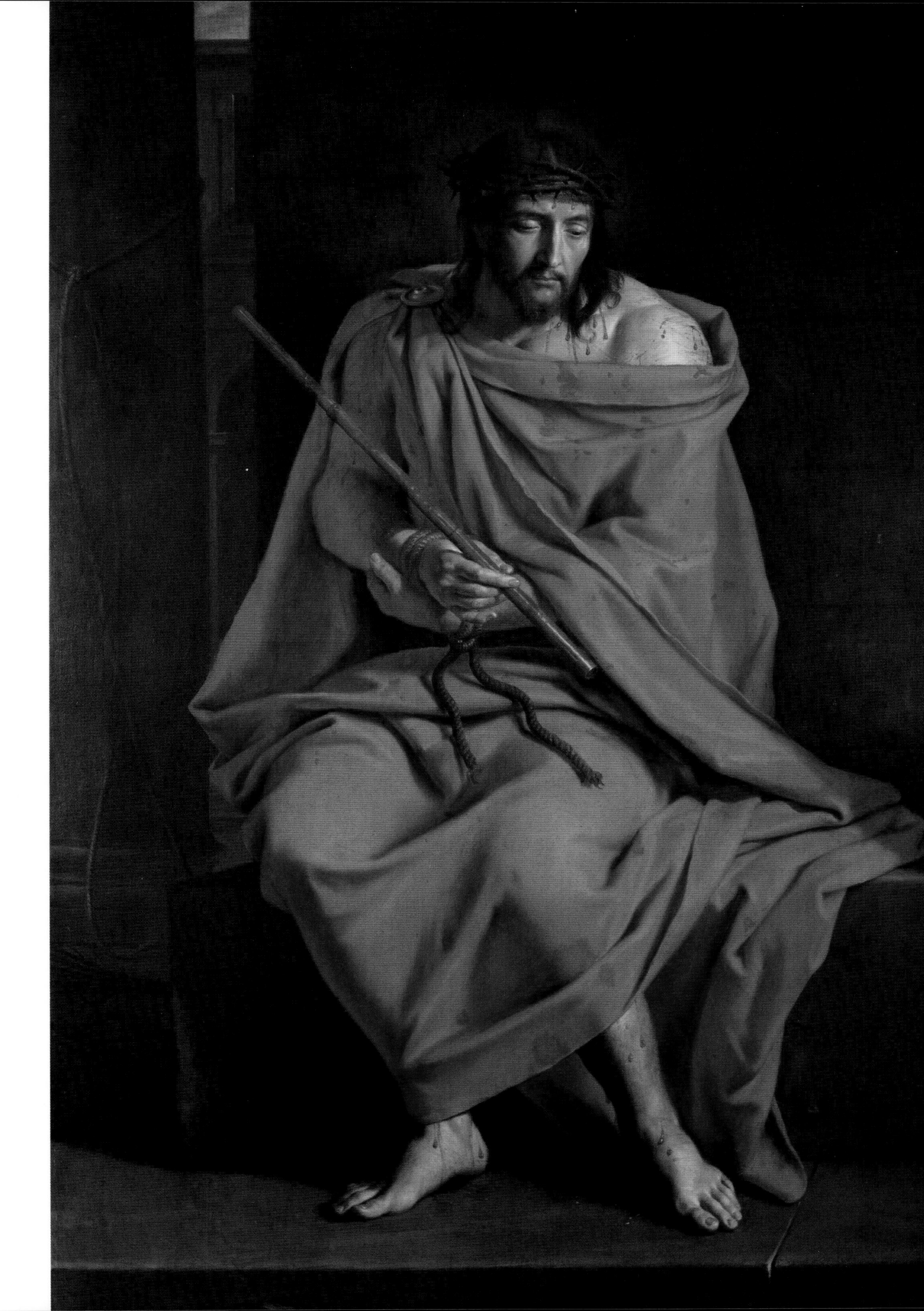

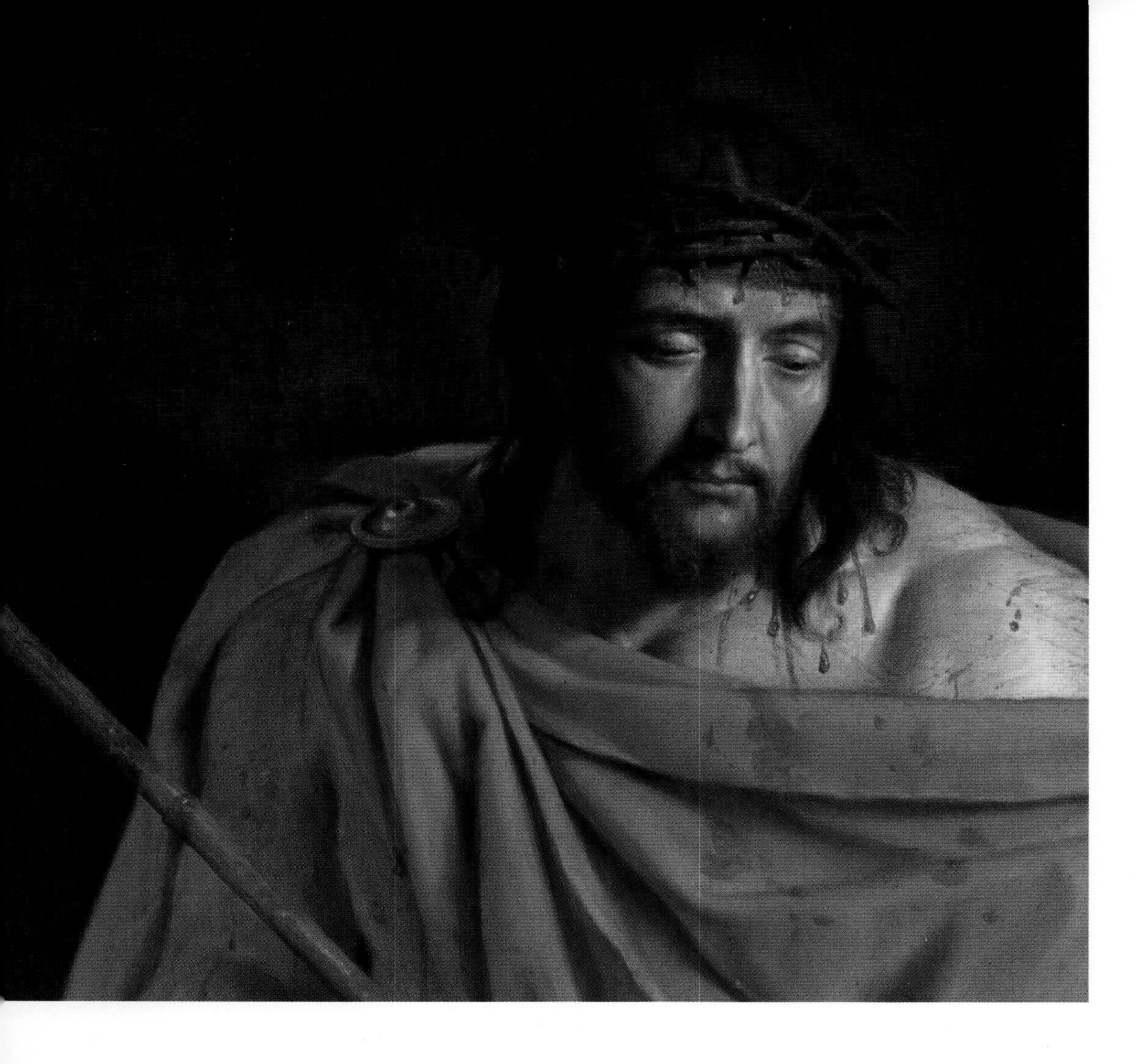

Ecce homo, detail
Philippe de Champaigne (1602–1674)
Ca. 1655
Oil on canvas, 73 x 50 in
Magny-les-Hameaux, National Museum
of Port-Royal des Champs

the supposed laughingstock. And what can we say about the profound mystery that marks his expression? In the shadow, to the right of Jesus, the column to which he was bound, with the base of the whip used to torture him. Yes, here is the man! A man being mocked, yet Philippe de Champaigne manages to make him emanate a superior sovereignty. Yes, this is indeed a king, this man crushed by torture and doomed to an ignominious death! And it is indeed a prophecy that Pilate pronounced: "Here is the man," because in this man every human person who suffers and will die acquires a royal dimension forever. At this point, this picture presents itself no longer as an object of admiration but as a subject of meditation, if you like, while we savor two strophes of the spiritual canticle composed by a friend of the painter, Jean Racine:

The Word, the image of the Father,
Left his eternal throne,
And willed to be born a man, a mortal,
From a mortal Mother.
Since pride was the crime
Of which he was born the Victim,
He put aside his splendor,
And came poor and miserable,
So as to teach guilty man
His true greatness. ■

In this fragment from the *Pensées*, Blaise Pascal (1623–1662) illustrates his famous theory of the three orders (of bodies, of minds, and of charity), which distinguishes beings and their relation to the world depending on whether they obey the flesh, reason, or the heart. Since the orders are incommensurable, there is an infinite distance from the body to the mind, as well as from the rational mind to the heart's charity ("the heart has its reasons which reason knows not at all"). The heart's knowledge rises higher than all worldly or merely rational knowledge, and it allows us to detect the true grandeur of Jesus. For his *kingship is not of this world* (Jn 18:36).

Blaise Pascal, "Proofs of Jesus Christ," 11, from *Pensées* (1669–1670), translated by W. F. Trotter, selection 793 [339 in the French edition].

Jesus came with the splendor of his kingdom

BLAISE PASCAL

The saints have their power, their glory, their victory, their lustre, and need no worldly or intellectual greatness, with which they have no affinity; for these neither add anything to them, nor take away anything from them. They are seen of God and the angels, and not of the body, nor of the curious mind. God is enough for them....

Jesus Christ, without riches, and without any external exhibition of knowledge, is in His own order of holiness. He did not invent; He did not reign. But He was humble, patient, holy, holy to God, terrible to devils, without any sin. Oh! in what great pomp, and in what wonderful splendor, He is come to the eyes of the heart, which perceive wisdom!...

It would have been useless for our Lord Jesus Christ to come like a king, in order to shine forth in His kingdom of holiness. But He came there appropriately in the glory of His own order.

It is most absurd to take offence at the lowliness of Jesus Christ, as if His lowliness were in the same order as the greatness which He came to manifest. If we consider this greatness in His life, in His passion, in His obscurity, in His death, in the choice of His disciples, in their desertion, in His secret resurrection, and the rest, we shall see it to be so immense, that we shall have no reason for being offended at a lowliness which is not of that order.

Seeing Jesus coming toward him, John the Baptist had pointed him out to the disciples in these terms: *Behold the Lamb of God, behold him who takes away the sin of the world* (Jn 1:29). Now, in his Passion, when as an innocent victim Jesus offers his life in sacrifice for his friends and also for his executioners, this title of "Lamb" reveals its profound meaning.

The Lamb of God

The motif of this picture is found at the merging of the biblical types with their fulfillment. We find here the ram (Gn 22:13) that was substituted for Isaac to be sacrificed as an offering to the Most High (*cf.* page 38), and *the lamb without blemish, a male* (Ex 12:5) immolated for the Passover, and also *the lamb that is led to slaughter* prophesied by Isaiah, all recapitulated in Jesus, *the Lamb of God that takes away the sin of the world* proclaimed by John the Baptist.

Francisco de Zurbarán (1598–1664) was together with Diego Velázquez (1599–1660), Alonzo Cano (1601–1667), and Bartolomé Esteban Murillo (1617-1682) one of the four major stars in the galaxy of artists from Seville who magnified the Spanish Golden Age. Although Velázquez was the greatest, Cano the most eclectic, Murillo the most moving, Zurbarán was the most spiritual and the best painter of still lifes. In this respect some compare him to Cézanne: under his brush, which is always controlled and reserved, the humblest object acquires a mystical significance. This *Agnus Dei* is a fascinating example of his art.

Although the "Lamb" is still alive in it, it is not treated as a portrait but rather as a still life. Everything in the picture is artificial, the motif has been isolated, placed into a fictive space with a size and a matter that are created *ad hoc*, and staged in a composition that is as minimalist as possible yet grippingly bold. It could have appeared like a scene in a butcher's shop if too much had been made of it (*cf.* Picasso, next page), or a morgue, if too little had been done. As it is, the scene is gentle, serene, peaceful, moving, and endowed with a limitless mystical dimension. In fact, it is a "human" scene, if we can say that about a ram depicted in still life. It doesn't matter, that is indeed the word: the scene is so right that it is touching in its humanity and perhaps, at the end of our contemplation, it even causes an unexpected dimension to appear. Did you say "divine"?

Zurbarán attempted—successfully!—this mad wager of turning a still life into one of the most humanly overwhelming pictorial works that have ever existed. ■

IN THE BIBLE – IS 53:7-8

He was oppressed, and he was afflicted, yet he opened not his mouth; like a lamb that is led to the slaughter, and like a sheep that before its shearers is silent, so he opened not his mouth. By oppression and judgment he was taken away; and as for his generation, who considered that he was cut off out of the land of the living, stricken for the transgression of my people?

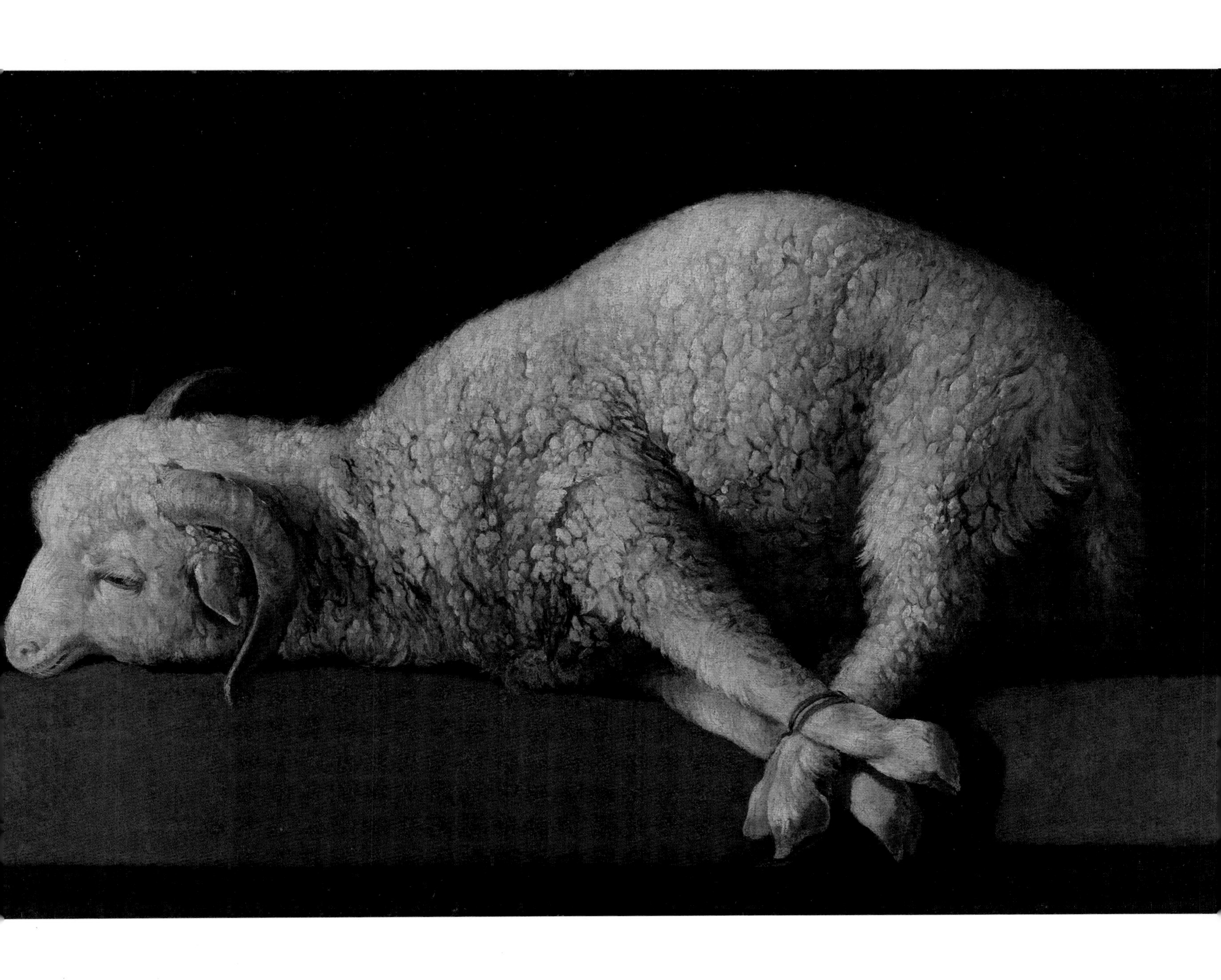

Agnus Dei
Francisco de Zurbarán (1598–1664)
1635–1640
Oil on canvas, 14.7 x 24.4 in
Madrid, Prado Museum

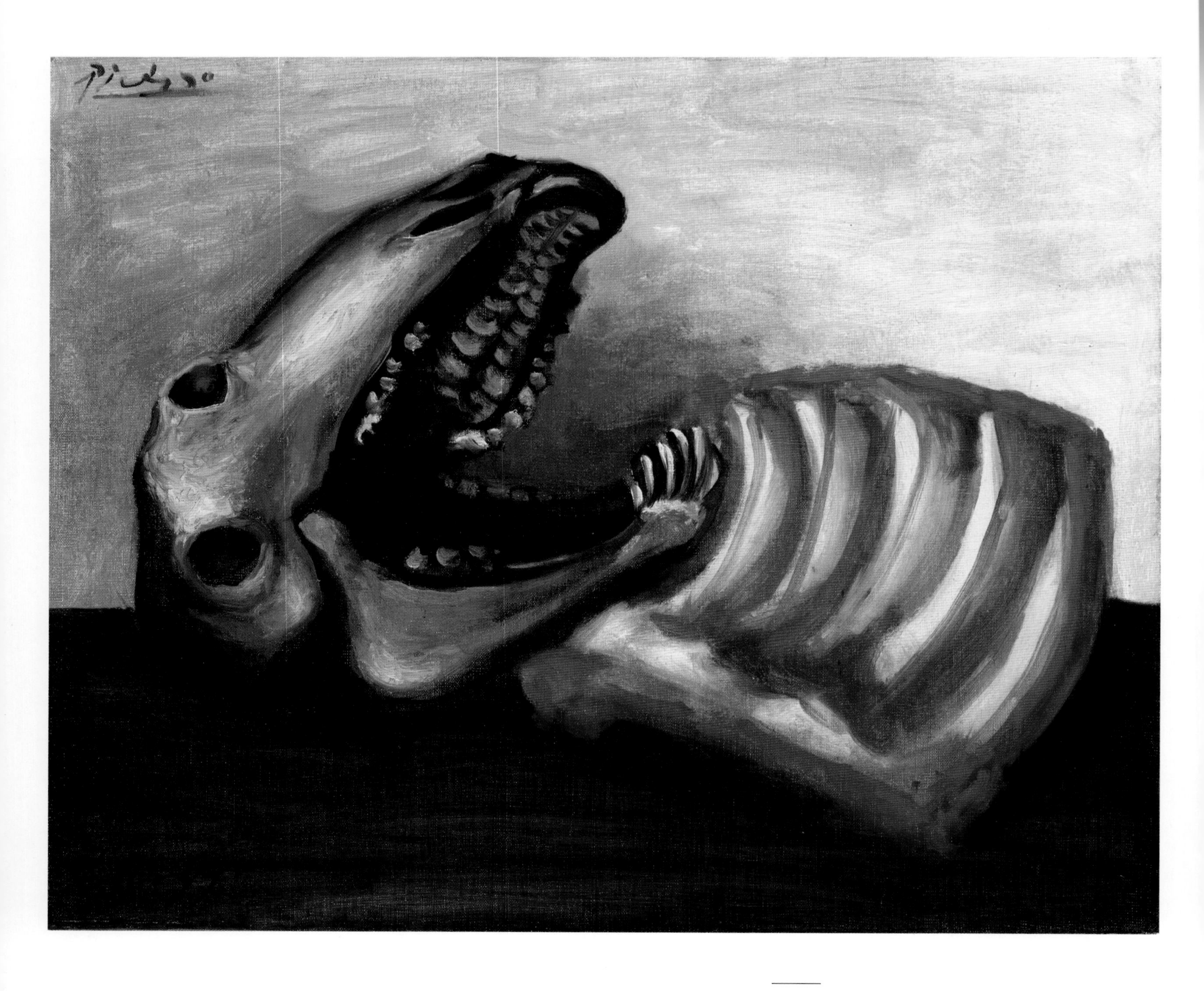

Still life with a lamb's head
Pablo Picasso (1881–1973)
1939
Oil on canvas, 20 x 24 in
Private collection

We know that Picasso painted this still life with reference to the *Agnus Dei* of Zurbarán. The atheist "cry" to heaven in it is unbearably powerful.

Paul Verlaine (1844–1896), one of the greatest French poets, was for years troubled by the question of God. He had a strong religious experience in 1874, when he was imprisoned for firing at Rimbaud. In the following decades, he published several explicitly Christian collections (*Sagesse* in 1881, *Amour* in 1888, *Bonheur* in 1891). In his *Liturgies intimes* (1892), dedicated to Baudelaire, the poet meditates on the Christian mysteries, including this *"Agnus Dei."*

Paul Verlaine, *"Agnus Dei,"* in *Liturgies intimes*, Paris, Léon Vanier, 1893, translated by John Gray in *Spiritual Poems*, 1896.

Agnus Dei

PAUL VERLAINE

The lamb seeks bitter heath to eat;
The salt it is he loves and not the sweet;
Like falling rain upon the dust his rustling feet.

To reach his end, by nothing stayed,
He butts and thrusts with great strokes of his head;
Then, clamouring for his dam, is anxiously obeyed.

God's Lamb, thou Saviour of us men;
God's Lamb, who tell'st us passing to our pen;
God's Lamb, have pity of us that we are but men.

Give us thy peace; O Lamb, abate
For us the terror of thy dread just hate;
O God, the only son of God the Uncreate.

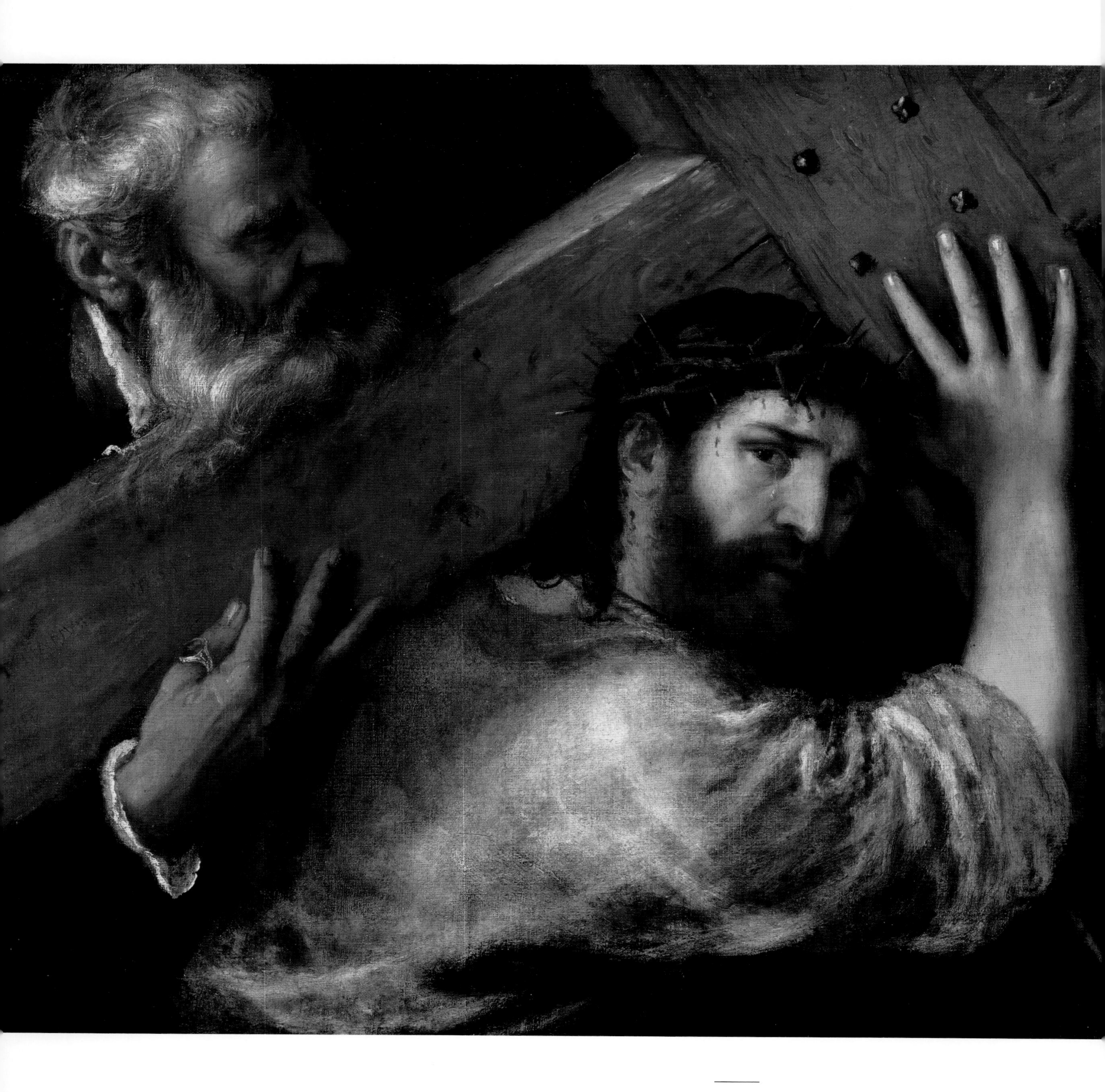

The Carrying of the Cross
Tiziano Vecellio, called Titian (1488/1489–1576)
Ca. 1565
Oil on canvas, 26 x 30 in
Madrid, Prado Museum

Simon of Cyrene is forced to help Jesus

Those condemned to the ignominious death of crucifixion—which was reserved for slaves, parricides, and traitors—were led on foot from the place of their sentencing to the place of their execution. This is the "way of the cross." To humiliate and exhaust the condemned man even more, he himself had to carry the *patibulum*, or transverse beam of the cross, to the place of torment. However, as here, most artists have depicted Jesus carrying his entire cross.

Titian (1488/1489–1576) was born in the late 15th century and died, brush in hand, toward the end of the 16th century, at the age of almost ninety. He was more than seventy-five years old—a ripe old age in his day—when he painted *The carrying of the cross*. This picture is small, at 26 inches tall (as compared with the more than 16 feet of Tintoretto's painting, page 189), and was designed for private devotion.

In those days, when the faith was starting to be experienced as a more individual, less communal practice, many individuals commissioned works to adorn their residence. In addition, the work of art was now sought for its formal beauty by an ever increasing number of enlightened amateurs. It was a fortuitous mixture of religious sentiment and a taste for collecting art. Moreover, the ecclesiastical teaching authorities had less direct influence on these works, which were not meant to be visible to the public in sacred places. The artist could therefore express his sensibility and his vision more freely in them.

Titian made several versions of this picture. The first commission, involving the dimensions and the description of the theme, is said to have been made by Philip II, King of Spain, who specified that the work was to be hung in his private chapel in the Escorial Palace. A second version, presented here, is said to have been painted for Francesco Zuccato, a famous maker of mosaics and a friend of Titian. In it the Cyrene assumed the features of the patron, who allegedly insisted on indicating this fact by wearing his seal on the thumb of his right hand, the one that supports the cross.

This picture is truly composed, within the four corners of a space marked out by a cross made of two magnificent, heavy joists skillfully assembled by a master carpenter. Above and to the left, Simon of Cyrene gives the impression that he is hanging on to it as a life preserver rather than helping to carry it, so that as his load Jesus carries both Simon and the cross. His neck is encircled by the cord with which they pull him and force him to keep walking, and he is still wearing the white baptismal robe that he wore in the presence of Pilate when he was sentenced to death; now it is soiled by his falls, as humanity's original innocence was soiled by sin. With his mighty arm, and with the splayed fingers of his hand, which produce a sublime effect of omnipotence within

THE BIBLE – LK 23:25C-26

He delivered Jesus up to their will. And as they led him away, they seized one Simon of Cyrene, who was coming in from the country, and laid on him the cross, to carry it behind Jesus.

this most conspicuous weakness, Jesus blocks the cross, just in case it decides to burst out of the picture, so that it does not crush sinners by loading down their shoulders.

With his vibrant pictorial touch that dissolves the contours of the forms, Titian manages to make almost physically palpable the drama that is playing out. Jesus has stopped along his way of the cross. He has, so to speak, suspended time, because he plainly has something to say to those at the side of the road who are contemplating him in his Passion. In a close-up (a very uncommon method in Titian's work), he fixes on the spectator his eyes, bloodshot and bathed with tears. This portrait of Jesus is incomparable, because it is sustained by a very subtle analysis of the psychology both of the condemned man/savior and of the spectator/saved person. Here the spectator is attacked by a look from which it is impossible for him to escape, the same look that will stare at Peter after his denial, an imploring look that begs: *Do you love me?* (Jn 21:15). ■

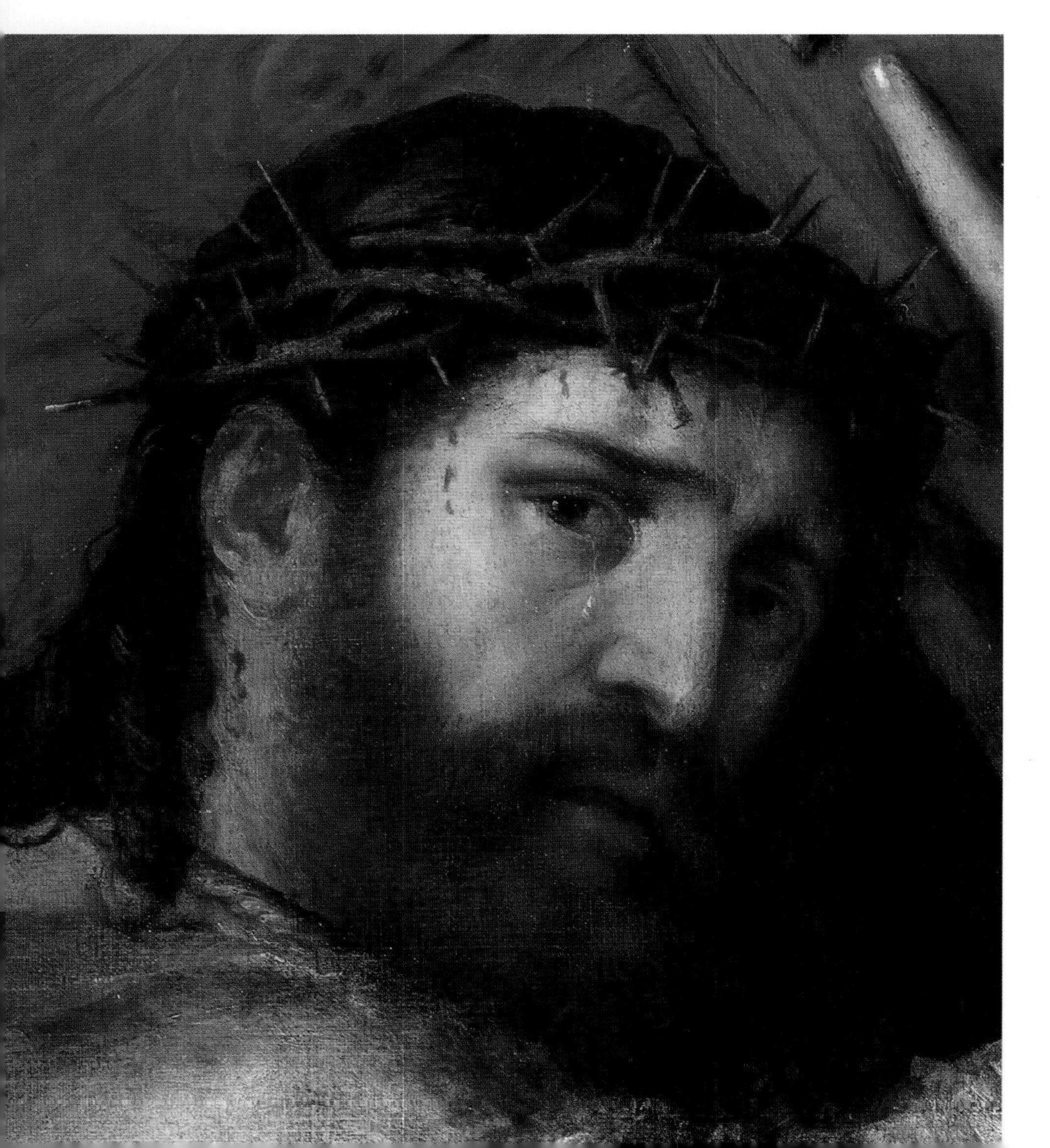

The Carrying of the Cross, detail
Tiziano Vecellio, called Titian (1488/1489-1576)
Ca. 1565
Oil on canvas, 26 x 30 in
Madrid, Prado Museum

Born on May 30, 1903, in New York City, Countee Cullen was one of the most important voices of the Harlem Renaissance. In this poem, written in 1924, he envisions Simon of Cyrene, who hailed from North Africa, as a black man.

Simon the Cyrenian speaks

COUNTEE CULLEN

He never spoke a word to me,
And yet He called my name;
He never gave a sign to me,
And yet I knew and came.

At first I said, "I will not bear
His cross upon my back;
He only seeks to place it there
Because my skin is black."

But He was dying for a dream,
And He was very meek,
And in His eyes there shone a gleam
Men journey far to seek.

It was Himself my pity bought;
I did for Christ alone
What all of Rome could not have wrought
With bruise of lash or stone.

The crowd gathered and followed the condemned man the entire length of his infamous way, from the praetorium, which tradition situates in the Antonia Fortress, north of Jerusalem, to the place of the crucifixion, to the west, just outside the ramparts. Indeed, execution was considered unclean and could not take place within the city precincts. An apocryphal gospel relates that along the way a woman named Veronica wiped the face of Jesus, preserving an image of it imprinted on the cloth.

The Holy Face

This portrait was probably made all at once, *in movimento*, the way one draws a sketch. The tradition associated with this little picture relates that it was painted by Simon Vouet (1590–1649) around 1626, inspired by a *Head of Christ* by Correggio (1489–1534), perhaps the one that is preserved today in the Getty Museum in Los Angeles. This attribution is plausible—in particular we can compare this work with the self-portrait by Simon Vouet found today in the Museum of Fine Arts in Lyon, which dates from exactly the same period. The work, a simple piece of painted paper, is said to have been given then by Simon Vouet to the painter who was his student and collaborator in Rome from 1624 to 1627, Claude Mellan (1598–1688). During their stay in the Eternal City, the two artists quickly struck up a friendship. They lived in the same villa and often worked together; Claude Mellan made the portrait of Simon Vouet's wife, the famous painter Virginia da Vezzo, on the occasion of their marriage in 1626.

The rare paintings by Claude Mellan that have been preserved confirm that he was a talented, first-class portraitist. Therefore we cannot rule out the possibility that he himself painted this *Holy Face*. If that was the case, then the attribution to Simon Vouet would be baseless. Whatever its attribution may be, this little-known work, despite its modesty, ranks as one of the chief masterpieces of the art of painting.

THE BIBLE – LK 23:27-28

And there followed him a great multitude of the people, and of women who bewailed and lamented him. But Jesus turning to them said, "Daughters of Jerusalem, do not weep for me, but weep for yourselves and for your children."

Having gained renown as a painter and engraver, as a protégé of Richelieu who was called to reside at the Louvre, Claude Mellan became a leading figure in the artistic and intellectual life of Paris. He met regularly with Cyrano de Bergerac, Molière, Gabriel Naudé and Father Marin Mersenne. Like most young men of letters and noblemen, he was tempted by the "libertinage" which, at that time, mainly meant disdaining religion. (Not until the 18th century did the sense of "debauchery" appear, one thing leading to another). Claude Mellan came back from it, drawn by the deep spiritual current that washed over the second half of the 17th century. In 1649, he carved what would become the most famous engraving in the world: a prodigious work, *The veil of Saint Veronica*, also called *The Holy Face*, modeled on the sketch painted in oil that was attributed to Simon Vouet. Executed by the method called *taille claire* in French, this engraving consists of one line throughout, turning in a spiral in one uninterrupted pass, which starts out from the point of Jesus'

The Holy Face
Simon Vouet (1590–1649) or Claude Mellan (1598–1688)
Ca. 1626
Oil on paper, mounted on canvas in the 19th century
Private collection

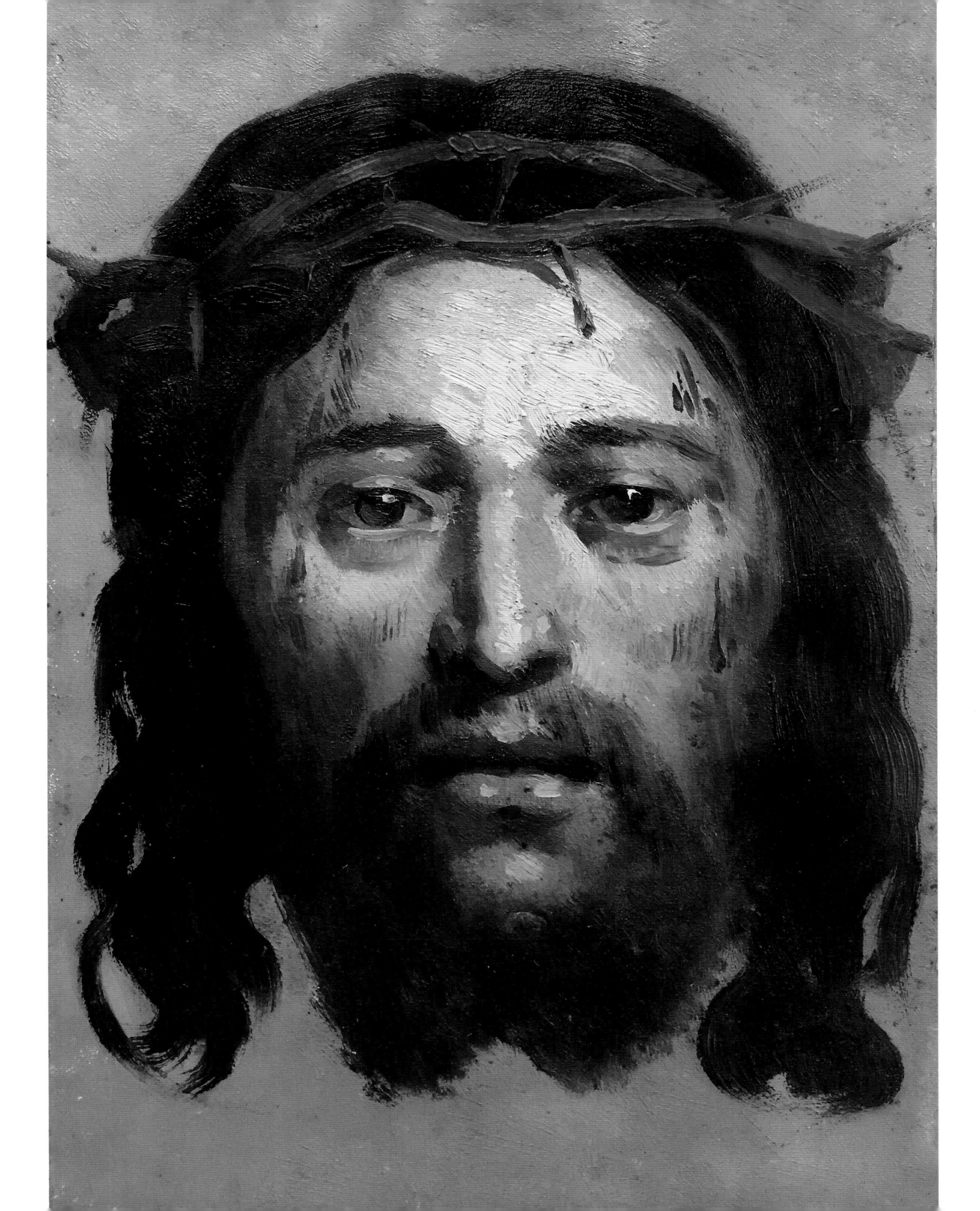

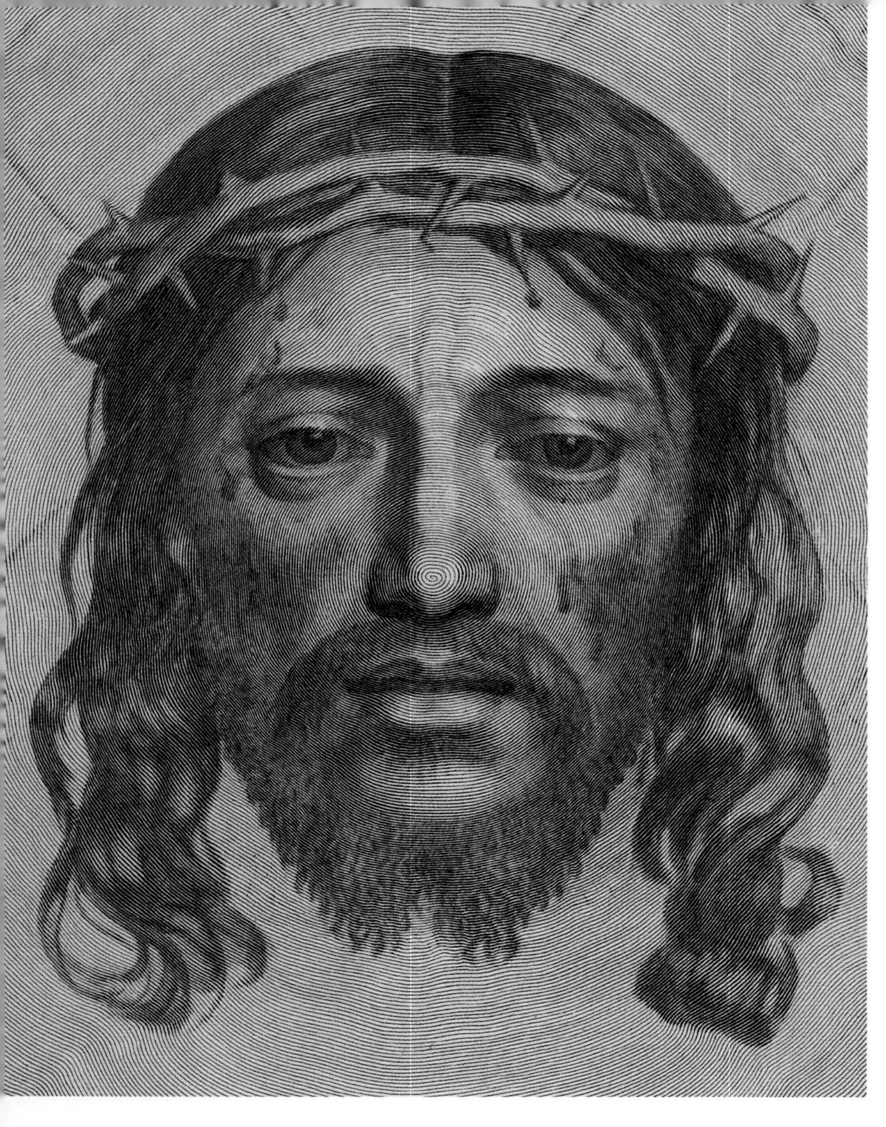

The veil of Saint Veronica
or *The Holy Face*
Claude Mellan (1598–1688)
1649
Engraving, 16.9 x 12.3 in
Amsterdam, Rijksmuseum

nose and, without revisions or additions, creates the image with its swells and tapers alone. Thus the face of Jesus is depicted with one line almost 500 feet long! The original copper plate of this work, often described as an "absolute masterpiece," is preserved at the *Chalcographie* of the Royal Library of Belgium. The motto appearing beneath the image expresses the marvel well: *Formatur unus unica*, "One man is formed by a single line."

The painting entitled *The Holy Face* presented here served as a model for the famous engraving. It is obviously of an even superior quality. The face of Jesus appears in relief, without neck or bust, as though suspended in space, detaching itself from a watery green background that does not repeat the slightest texture or the slightest folds of Veronica's veil. However, it is neither a *trompe-l'oeil* nor a stereotype in the manner of an icon; it is a lively portrait—if we can say that, given the context—of a man whom we can call Jesus because he is crowned with thorns and bruised, in keeping with the account of the Passion that the Gospels give.

The technique utilized, typical of the art of sketching, is extraordinary for its spontaneity and successful improvisation. We do not find therefore in this painting the finish of completed works, but we recognize in it the outburst of genius in its raw manifestation—in the style of Manet, we might say, if we were not afraid to commit an anachronism. But in their sketches and drafts don't the geniuses of all times meet, beyond the periods and schools? The strong light that illumines this face makes the brush strokes perfectly discernible. No retouching and no do-overs; everything seems instinctive without being impulsive, direct without being simplistic, spontaneous without being thoughtless, free without being casual. It recalls an aphorism attributed to Edgar Degas (cited from memory), whereby the master replied to an art critic who asked him how much time he spent to make a particular sketch of a dancer: "I spent twenty years so as to do it in twenty minutes."

When confronted with this so-called "transitive" work, the spectator is invited to enter into a relation with it. This is the will of its creator: the mouth of his Jesus speaks, his ears listen, his eyes plunge into the eyes that contemplate him. His communication with the spectator is the result of a powerfully tragic expression, certainly, but one that is so moving, because it is radically empathetic, benevolent, and friendly.

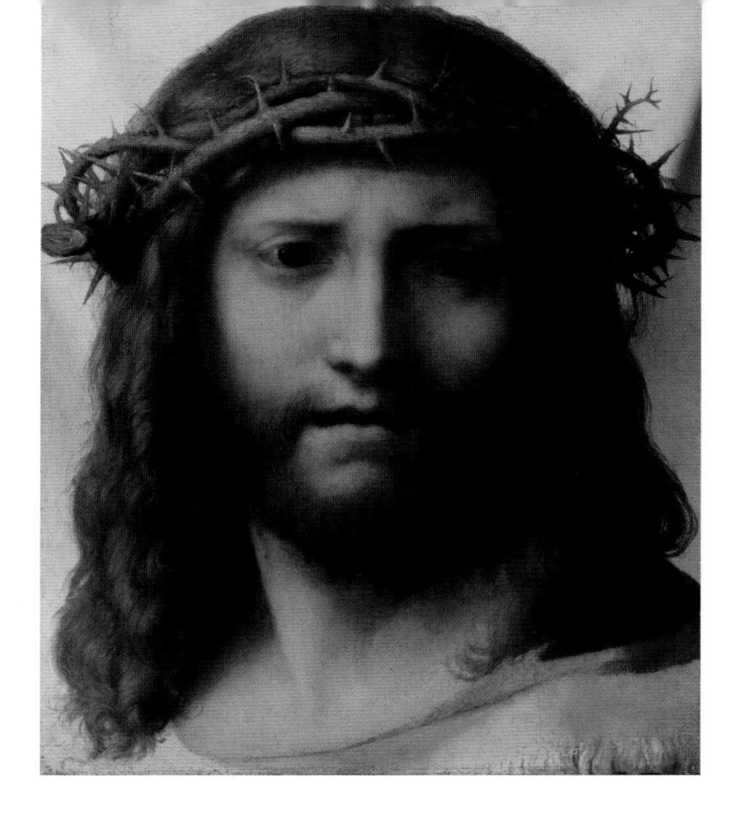

Head of Christ
Antonio Allegri, called Correggio (*ca.* 1489–1534)
1525–1530
Oil on wood, 11.2 x 9.3 in
Los Angeles, Getty Museum

A reproduction cannot express itself as well as an original. Nevertheless we can try to enter into the mystery of this Jesus. What does he see? What does he hear? What does he say? It is advisable to start by standing in front of it and contemplating his face for a long time in silence. Then, you will enter into yourself. And dare to start talking to him, not worrying about what you will say to him: the words will arise by themselves, like evidence uncovered after being buried for too long. Finally, you will be able to listen to him, in other words, you will have gone down to the innermost part of yourself, and you stay there until you hear what this unique Jesus has to say, face to face. ■

SCIENCE AND FAITH: NICOLAS-CLAUDE FABRI DE PEIRESC, PATRON OF CLAUDE MELLAN

Nicolas-Claude Fabri de Peiresc (1580–1637), a councilor at the parliament of Provence, had settled in the city of Aix-en-Provence and, starting from there, set up a network of relations extending throughout all of Europe. All his efforts were aimed at creating ties between erudite representatives of the sciences and also literature and the arts, so as to coordinate their work for the good of humanity.

This man of letters, also a man of science and an eclectic collector, had the benefit of encyclopedic skills like none other. His office, where antiques, paintings, engravings, and drawings mingled with natural objects, was peerless, and his library, like his collections, addressed all possible and imaginable subjects of study.

Deeply religious, this friend of princes of the Church and also of simple country curates did not hesitate to support as a benefactor–solely at his expense when necessary, and with the utmost discretion–enterprises like the restoration of the Abbey of Notre-Dame de Guître, in Guyenne.

Open-minded, he worked with complete independence in search of the truth and was thus among the greatest defenders of his friend Galileo (1564–1642). His tolerance also led him to develop solid friendships in both Protestant and Jewish circles.

Well before Blaise Pascal (1623–1662), he thought that science would never contradict God and that the delights offered by research into the two infinities would lie partly in a truth that would always be revealed to investigation.

When Claude Mellan engraved his famous *Holy Face*, Peiresc was no longer in this world to admire this prodigious work. However, to a great extent Mellan owed his prestigious career to this wealthy man.

Indeed, Peiresc, a friend of established artists like Peter Paul Rubens, enabled the young and relatively unknown Claude Mellan to set out on his decisive trip to Rome by making it easier for him to stay there for a dozen years. Mellan arrived in Rome in mid-August 1624 with letters of recommendation addressed to two of Peiresc's friends, the first to Girolamo Aleandro (1574–1629), the erudite humanist and secretary of Maffeo Barberini (Pope Urban VIII after 1623), and the second to Cardinal Scipione Cobelluzzi (1564–1626), a humanist and friend of Galileo.

In the year of Mellan's arrival in Rome, Simon Vouet (1590–1649), with whom he lodged for a time, was appointed head of the Accademia di San Luca. Once he had been introduced at the papal court, Mellan approached the best engravers: his elders Antonio Tempesta (1555–1630) and Francesco Villamena (*ca.* 1565–1624), who would leave their mark on his style and his career.

During his long stay in Rome, Mellan stayed in close communication with his patron in Aix. Upon his return to France in 1636, he stopped first in Aix-en-Provence to visit his benefactor. The portrait of Peiresc, first drawn and then engraved, which Mellan executed a few months before the death of his protector in 1637, dates from that stay.

If any engraved work by Mellan signals even more clearly his collaboration with Peiresc in scientific and artistic matters, it is certainly the set of plates depicting the faces of the moon. Peiresc and Gassendi (1592–1655), another polymath, had teamed up to produce a detailed map of the moon, a project which unfortunately remained unfinished because of the death of Peiresc. Naturally they turned to Mellan for the work of engraving, because of his technical precision. Besides his erudition, Peiresc's legendary modesty and kindness have been described as the most outstanding features of his character; the man is said to have put his time and his fortune at the service of all. On August 28, 1636, Mellan could thus write to Gassendi, concerning the man who had unceasingly supported him: "He is an angel, the most accommodating and the most affectionate in the world."

M. C.

A crucified man dies slowly by suffocation, in terrible sufferings. The Gospels report however that on the cross Jesus found the strength to pronounce seven last words: for the benefit of his executioners, whom he forgives; for the thieves who are crucified with him; for Mary, his Mother, and his beloved disciple, who are standing at the foot of the cross; finally for God the Father, to whom he cries out. Jesus would die on Friday, the eve of the Jewish Passover, at the same hour when the lambs were being slaughtered for the feast.

Jesus dies, Jesus is dead

They say that Édouard Manet confided to the art critics: "You will be able to claim to understand something about painting when you have grasped why Velázquez is the greatest painter who ever lived."

Indeed, who could be unmoved in the presence of his *Christ crucified*?

Against a background of darkness so impenetrable that it is mute, a white body is projected toward the spectator, like a cadaver from which all life has fled and which, nevertheless, still has something to say. It is the most gripping depiction of a dead man that could ever be. Because Velázquez intended to paint a livid dead man so that no one could doubt that he had shed even the very last drop of his blood for the salvation of mankind. Because Velázquez intended to paint a dead Jesus so authentic that it demonstrates that death will be conquered. His hair hides half of his face, falling like a cascade of blackness on the cold whiteness that signals death. What is there behind this mask, then, that cannot be shown? What is there behind this theatrical curtain which seems to veil the scene of a terrible tragedy? In fact an ineffable or even inconceivable drama is playing out, and the genius of the master of masters can reveal its existence only by concealing it. Behind that hair there is the door of the great mystery of Holy Saturday, the opening to something else, the gate of hell, and, beyond that, the door leading to something still more frightening than death itself; there is the door that opens onto true death, the formidable *second death* (Rv 20:6), the door to the place of the kenosis of all kenoses, the scandal of all scandals, the ultimate test in which the true God, in order to be true man, must go so far as to take up the possibility of the eschatological "no" to the grace of salvation, the definitive "no" that every human being is free to pronounce. There, in this infernal place, the Son of God will really experience the privation of the vision of God: *My God, my God, why have you abandoned me!* And, mysteriously, he will experience and pass through the eternal consequences of that privation.

In making this curtain woven of God's hair fall on the face of the crucified man, Velázquez poses the question that will remain until the end of time: is it possible that, until the end, until the most irremediable refusal, God's judgment on sin could, still and forever, dissolve into his love? ■

THE BIBLE – LK 23:44-47

It was now about the sixth hour [*i.e.* noon], and there was darkness over the whole land until the ninth hour, while the sun's light failed; and the curtain of the temple was torn in two. Then Jesus, crying with a loud voice, said, "Father, into thy hands I commit my spirit!" And having said this he breathed his last. Now when the centurion saw what had taken place, he praised God, and said, "Certainly this man was innocent!"

Christ crucified, detail
Diego de Silva Velázquez (1599–1660)
Ca. 1632
Oil on canvas, 98 x 67 in
Madrid, Prado Museum

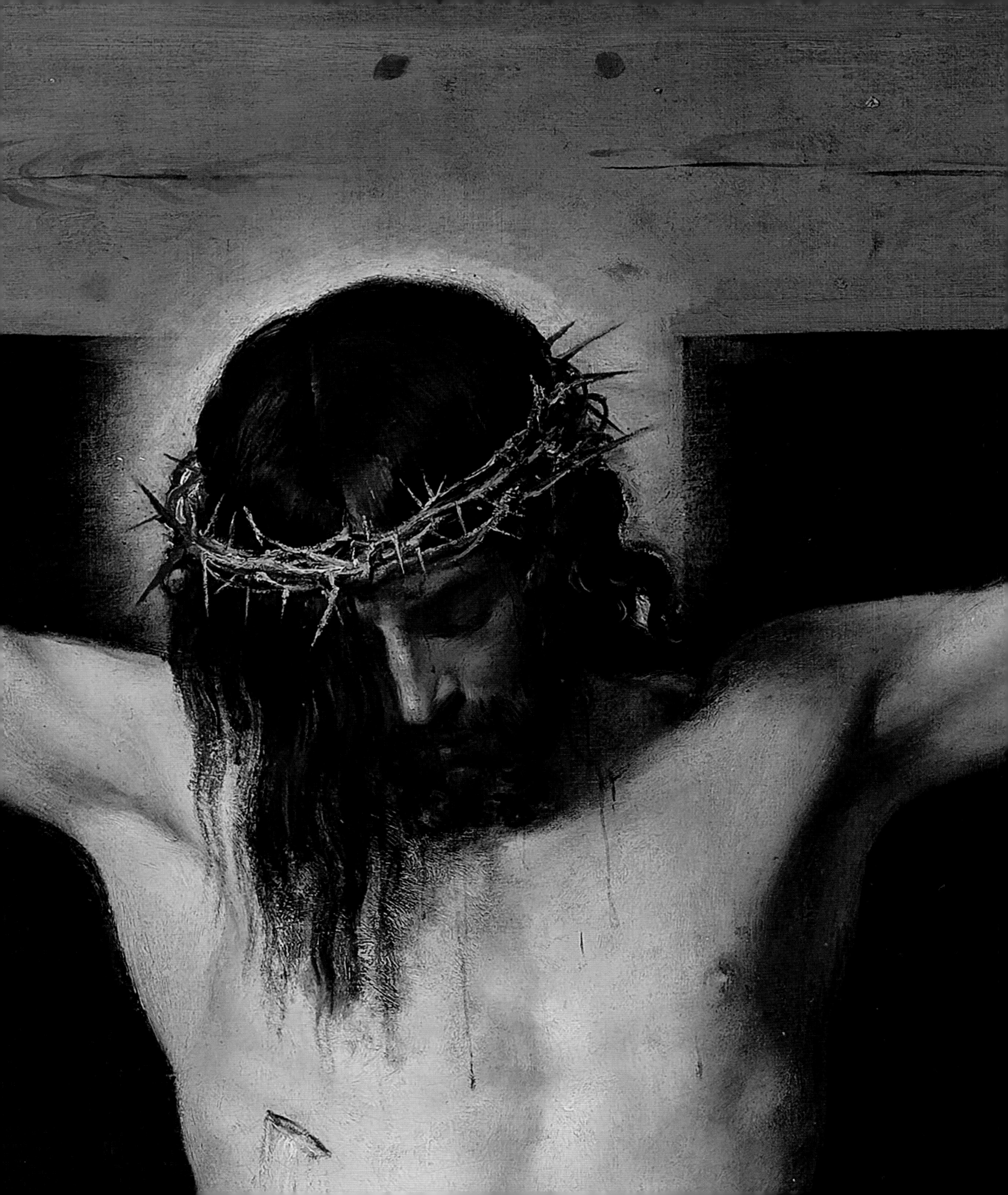

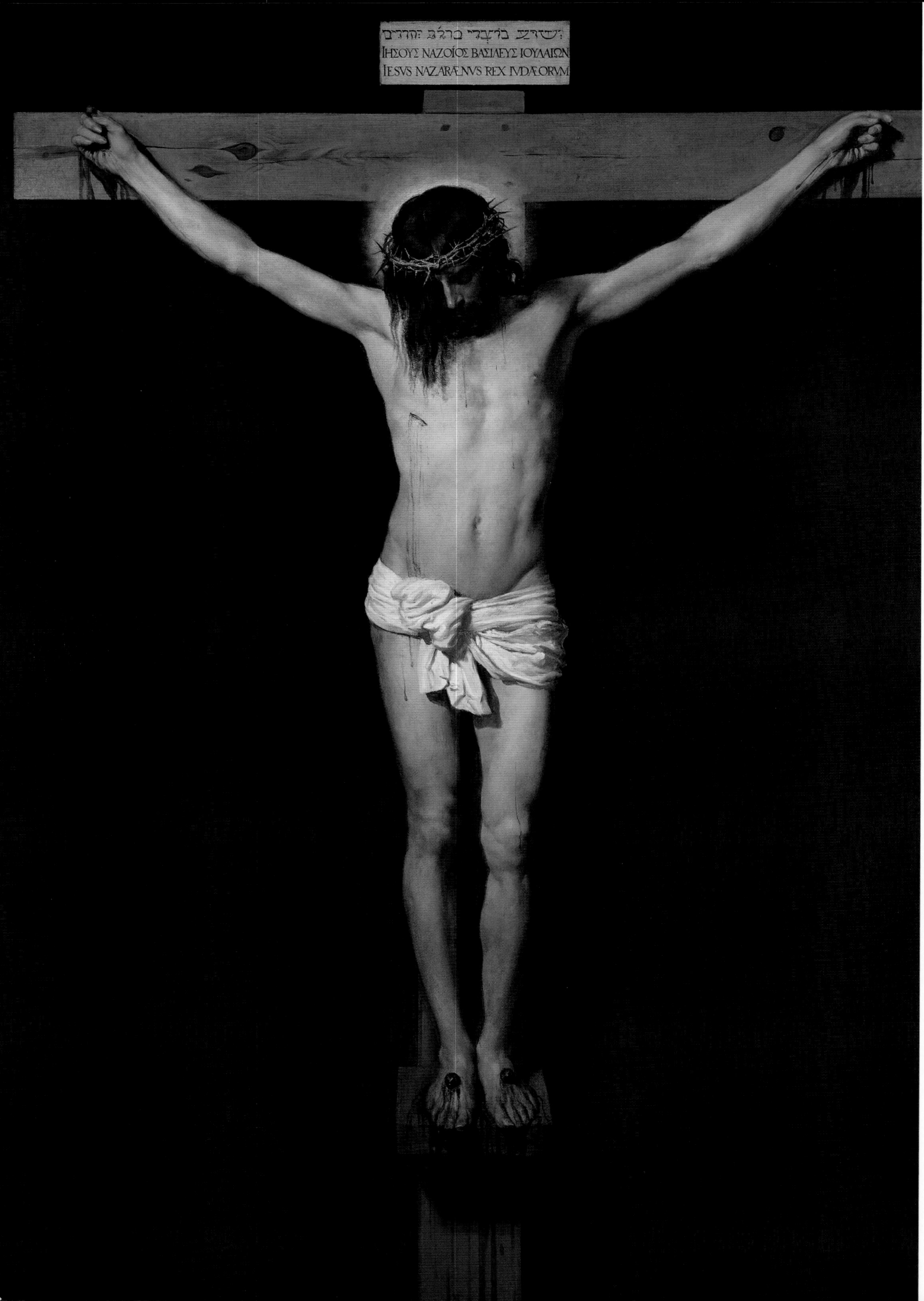

ΙΗΣΟΥΣ ΝΑΖΟΊΟΣ ΒΑΣΙΛΕΥΣ ΙΟΥΛΑΙΩΝ
IESVS NAZARÆNVS REX IVDÆORVM

IN ART HISTORY

THE CHRIST OF VELÁZQUEZ, BETWEEN UNIQUENESS AND TRADITION

Although the dating of Velázquez's famous *Christ crucified* is only approximate, it is certain that the work postdates the artist's first stay in Venice, Rome, and Naples, which enabled him to make a deeper study of the great Italian masters.

This Crucifixion, which has become one of the most widespread devotional images, is unique on more than one count. Here Christ is more incarnate than ever through his pallor and through the harsh light that emanates from it, through the naturalness of the slight *contrapposto* (counterpoise, with shoulders and hips slanted in opposite directions) and the tilt of the head. There is no lack of other details distinguishing the work, such as the unique rendering of the sanded wood and the polish of the cross.

Except for his early works in Seville, Velázquez painted almost no religious subjects at all at the court in Madrid—nothing but mythological or historical subjects: the artist was working for one patron, Philip IV, and produced mainly portraits of the king, his family, and his retinue.

This put Velázquez in a position very different from that of his friend and contemporary Francesco Zurbarán (1598-1664), who, because of his personality and his patrons, mainly treated religious subjects.

However, Juan José Lahuerta, the conservator at the Prado Museum, emphasizes that the one Crucifixion by Velázquez can be compared with the multiple versions by Zurbarán, starting with the *Christ on the cross* painted in 1627 for the Dominicans of San Pablo de Real in Seville (today preserved at the Art Institute in Chicago) and *Christ with a donor* (1640), of comparable dimensions and preserved in the Prado not far from the *Christ crucified* by Velázquez.

These Crucifixions reflect the same sensibility and are to be compared also with those by Alonso Cano (1601-1667), sharing the same naturalism, the same solitude of Christ, the same removal from the narrative context of the Passion.

Somewhat earlier than the master of the Spanish Golden Age, there is Francisco Pacheco (1564-1654), a painter and theoretician, master and father-in-law of Velázquez—and master of Alonso Cano. Pacheco, who supported by the Jesuit circles of Seville and with the help of much study of the Church Fathers as well as the medieval mystics, developed in his treatise *The Art of Painting* the idea of an iconography favoring four nails instead of the three usually reserved for the Crucified. At the conclusion of a long reflection, he hopes to take up again a depiction of Christ that is more respectful of the majesty and the grandeur of the Son of God: the presence of a step and one nail per foot aims to limit the twisting of the body, which is driven to extremes with three nails—one for each hand and one for the two feet—in Gothic works. Pacheco is also the instigator of the inscription in three languages on the sign—Hebrew, Greek, and Latin—which is repeated by Velázquez in his *Christ crucified*.

The austere Crucifixions of the painters of the Spanish Golden Age show that they were more interested in the solitude of Christ on the cross than in the turbulent narrative drama of the Passion, as painted by their contemporaries in the Northern schools, Peter Paul Rubens (1577-1640), Anthony Van Dyck (1599-1641), and Rembrandt (1606-1669).

M. C.

Christ crucified
Diego de Silva Velázquez (1599-1660)
Ca. 1632
Oil on canvas, 98 x 67 in
Madrid, Prado Museum

Jesus is crucified on Calvary, in Hebrew Golgotha, a mound in plain sight along the main access road to Jerusalem. The Gospels report that Jesus was crucified between two other condemned men, whom tradition calls the "thieves." The panel, or *titulus*, composed by Pilate himself to designate Jesus, reads: *Iesus Nazarenus Rex Iudeorum* ("Jesus the Nazarene, King of the Jews"). This is the origin of the acronym INRI placed at the top of the cross on most artistic representations.

Jesus left hanging on the cross

This face of Christ on the cross adorns the great fresco in the chapter house of San Marco Convent in Florence. Unlike the forty-four frescos painted by Fra Angelico in the cells, which were meant to nourish the private meditation of the friars, this one was supposed to inspire the decisions the chapter was called to make in governing the monastery.

In the Dominican order, contemplation of the crucified Lord is the source of faith, real knowledge, and love of neighbor, three criteria that define Christian discernment. More radically, for Saint Dominic, love of the cross alone can form the mystical union between the Master and the disciple. In the paintings of the Dominican Friar Angelico, Jesus always remains *the fairest of the children of men* (Ps 45:3). In contrast to the other figures, whom he depicts in a rather naturalistic manner and whose faces express feelings and emotions, Fra Angelico in all circumstances represents an idealized face of Jesus, which never loses its serenity, sweetness, and gentleness. This is the case particularly here, where the face of the Crucified, depicted just after his death, is nevertheless not tortured by pain, as it might naturally be. Not that the suffering does not affect the one who carried the sins of humanity, but it is veiled by a hint of majestic serenity, which reveals the saving presence of the divinity at the heart of the tragedy of the human condition. The beautiful face of the Crucified appears then as though illumined by its own light, which is a fusion of natural light and supernatural light: this is already the light of the Resurrection living in this flesh tinted with the dawn, an effect obtained by translucent shades blending into earthly ochres. ■

THE BIBLE – JN 19:17B-19

Jesus went out, bearing his own cross, to the place called the place of a skull [Calvary], which is called in Hebrew Golgotha. There they crucified him, and with him two others, one on either side, and Jesus between them. Pilate also wrote a title and put it on the cross; it read, "Jesus of Nazareth, the King of the Jews."

Crucifixion and saints, detail
Fra Angelico (*ca.* 1400–1455)
Ca. 1441–1442
Fresco, 217 x 374 in
Florence, San Marco Museum-Convent, chapter house

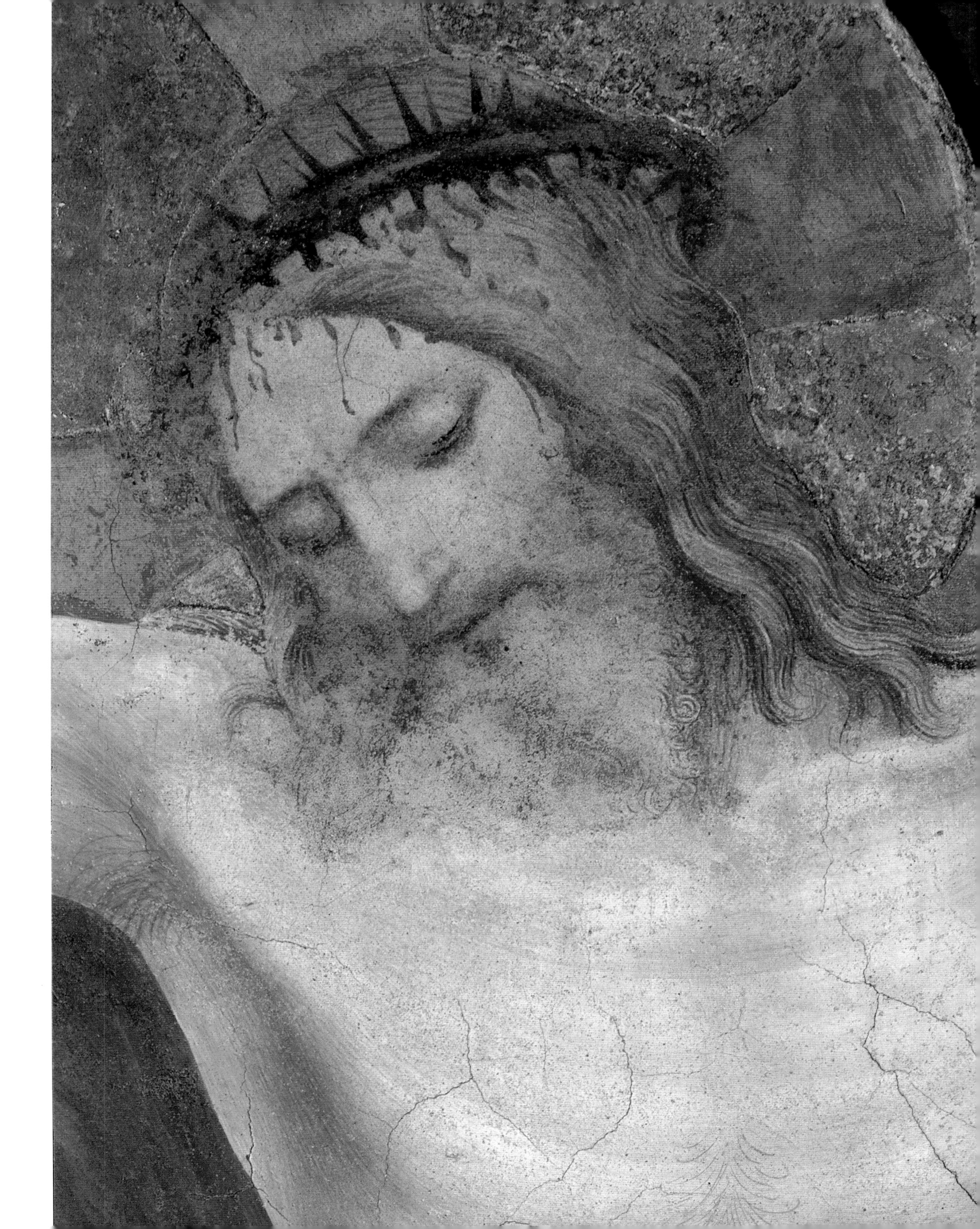

François René de Chateaubriand (1768–1848), an author of considerable importance in French literature and a precursor of Romanticism, is famous today primarily for his *Mémoires d'outre-tombe* ["Memoirs from Beyond the Grave"], published posthumously. In *The Genius of Christianity* (1802), of which *Atala* and *René* are parts, Chateaubriand writes an apologia for the Christian religion, intending to prove that, by its grandeur and "excellence," it is the truth itself. This passage deals with the mystery of the suffering and death of the God of love in the Person of Jesus.

François-René de Chateaubriand, *The Genius of Christianity* (1802), translated by Charles I. White (Baltimore: John Murphey & Company, 1856, 1884), Volume 2, Part 4, Book 3, Chapter 1, pp. 530-531.

A sigh of mercy

FRANÇOIS-RENÉ DE CHATEAUBRIAND

Had the Son of man descended from his celestial abode in all his power, it would certainly have been very easy to practice so many virtues, to endure so many afflictions; but herein lies the glory of the mystery: Christ was the man of sorrows, and acquainted with griefs; his heart melted like that of a merely human creature, and he never manifested any sign of anger except against insensibility and obduracy of soul. *Love one another*, was his incessant exhortation. *Father*, he exclaimed, writhing under the torments inflicted by his executioners, *forgive them; for they know not what they do.* When on the point of quitting his beloved disciples, he was all at once dissolved in tears; he experienced all the terrors of death, all the anguish of the cross; the blood-sweat trickled down his divine cheeks; he complained that his Father had forsaken him. *Father*, said he, *if it be possible, let this chalice pass from me; nevertheless, not as I will, but as thou wilt.* Then it was that that expression, fraught with all the sublimity of grief, fell from his lips: *My soul is sorrowful, even unto death.* Ah! If the purest morality and the most feeling heart—if a life passed in combating error and soothing the sorrows of mankind—be attributes of divinity, who can deny that of Jesus Christ? A pattern of every virtue, Friendship beholds him reclining on the bosom of St. John or bequeathing his mother to his care; Charity admires him in the judgment of the adulteress; Pity everywhere finds him blessing the tears of the unfortunate; his innocence and his tenderness are displayed in his love of children; the energy of his soul shines conspicuous amid the torments of the cross, and his last sigh is a sigh of mercy.

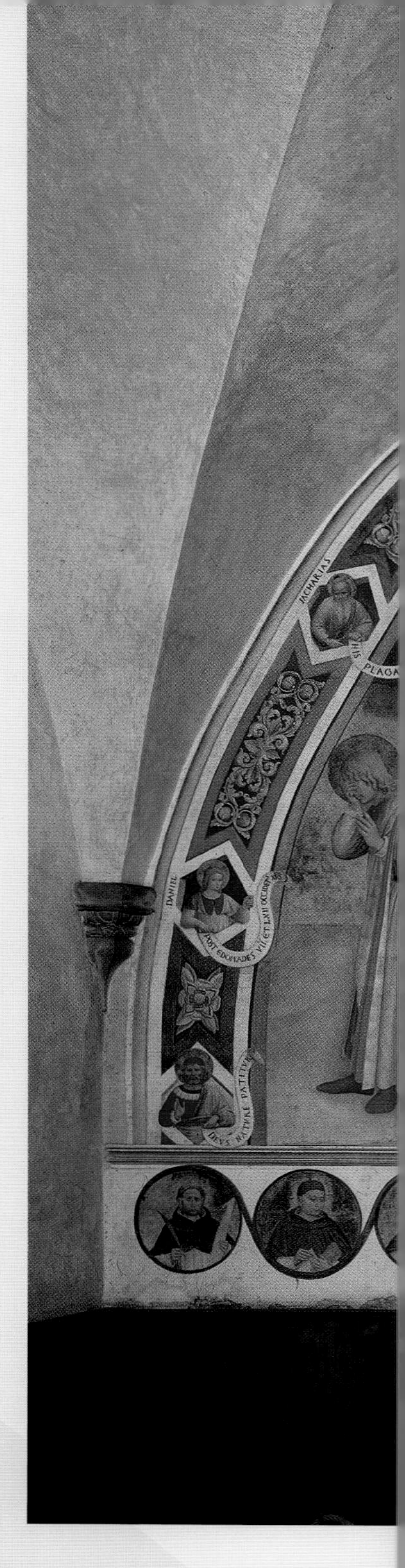

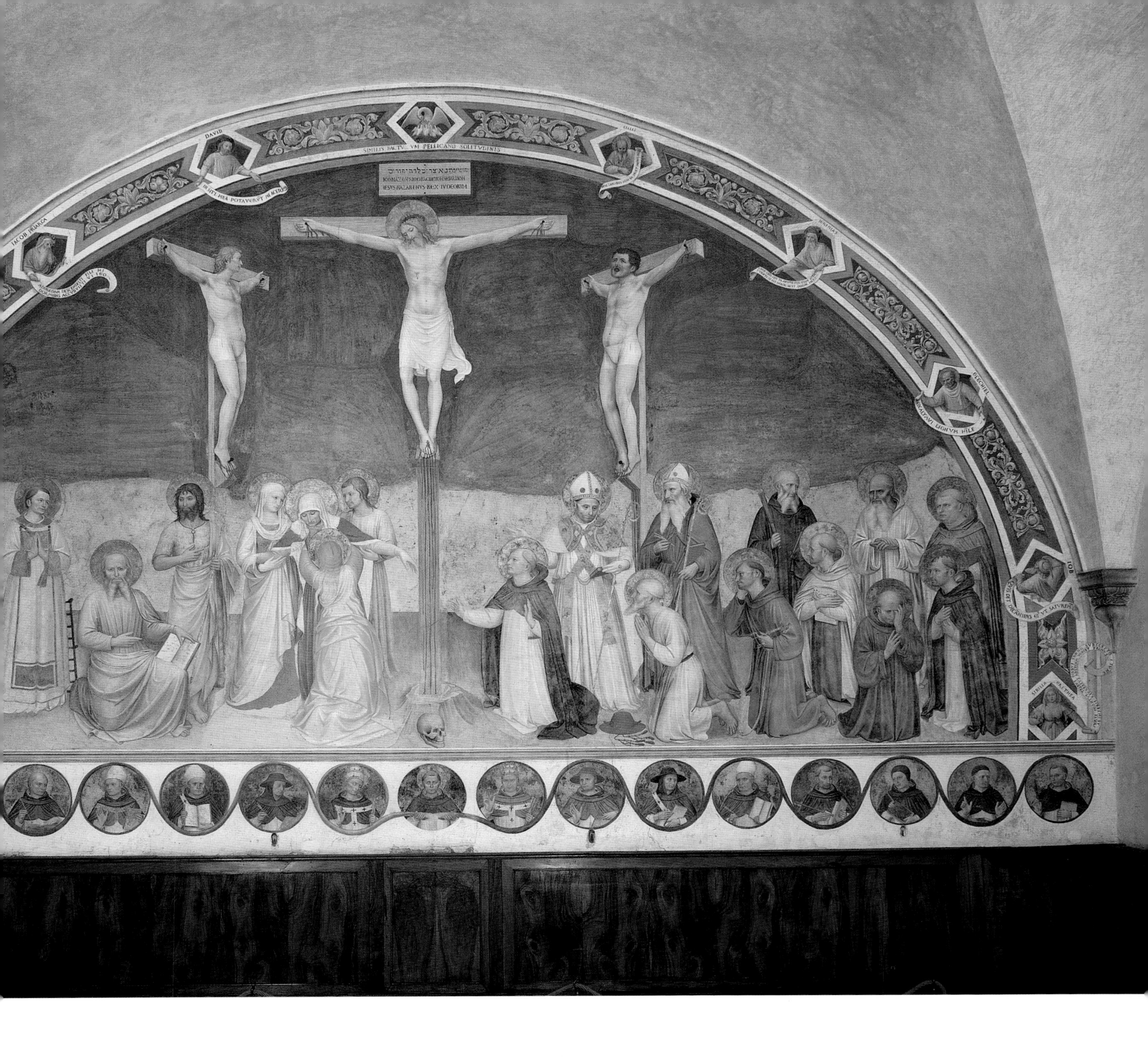

Crucifixion and saints
Fra Angelico (*ca.* 1400–1455)
Ca. 1441–1442
Fresco, 217 x 374 in
Florence, San Marco Museum-Convent, chapter house

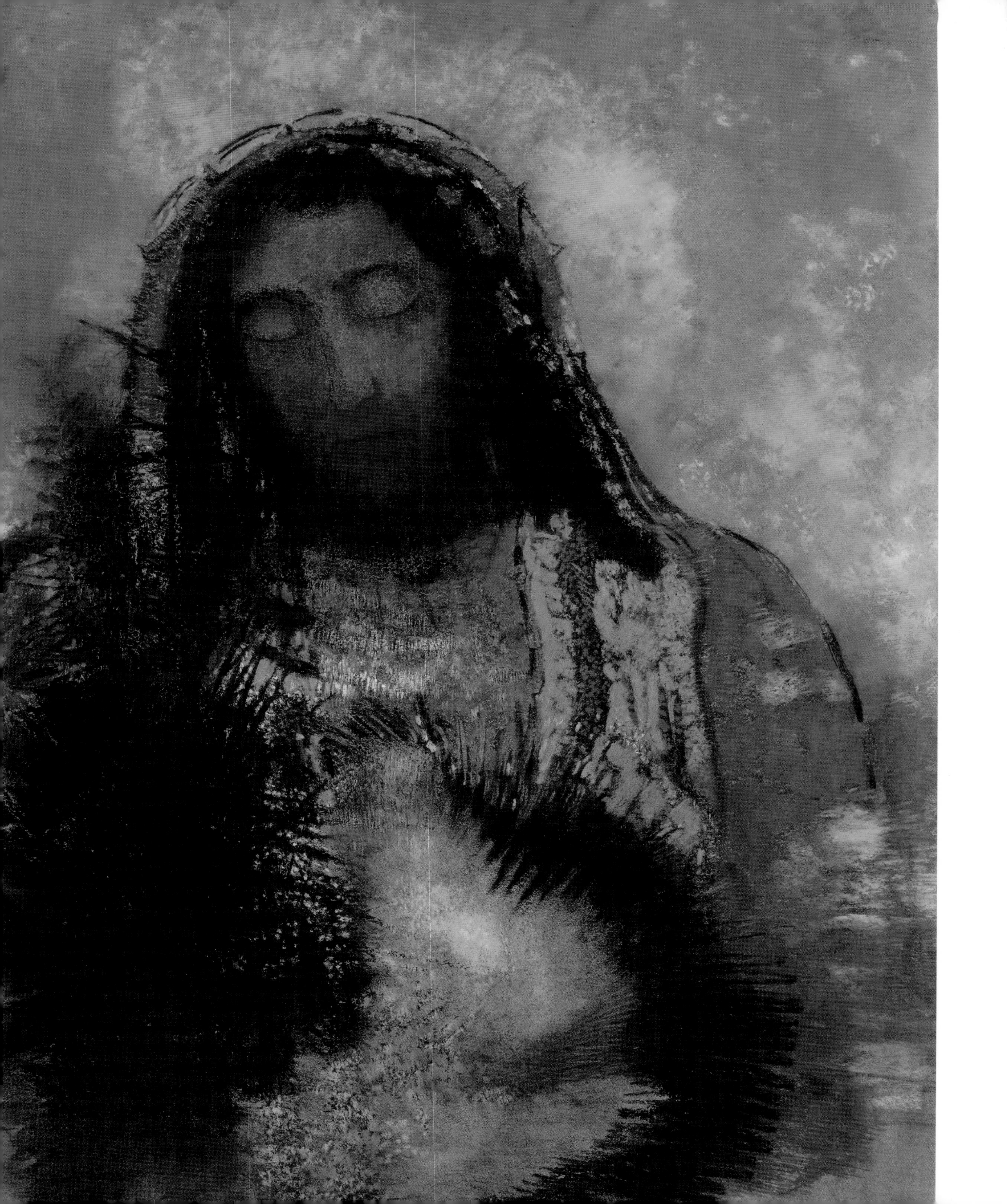

The Sacred Heart of Jesus

If crucified criminals survived too long on the cross, delaying the execution of others who were condemned to death, or hampered the religious authorities as a feast day approached, as was the case with Jesus on the eve of the Jewish Passover, it was the custom to break their legs so that they could no longer support themselves on their feet and breathe.

In the work of Odilon Redon (1840–1916), in the beginning was the black. But not black as the absence of color, but rather black as "the most essential color." The color that best expresses the states of the soul that is plunged into the dark night; the color of darkness that gives its fundamental tonality to the human condition. The black of the *Los caprichos* [*The Caprices*, a set of prints] by Francisco de Goya.

Passionately interested in the works of Charles Darwin and de Lamarck, the father of modern atheism, Odilon Redon was turned away from rationalism by reading Charles Baudelaire, about whom Léon Bloy said: "Baudelaire was indisputably Catholic in the deepest part of his thought. But he was a Catholic the wrong way around." Temperamentally disposed to depression, Redon lived by devoting himself to transfiguring his basically pessimistic temperament with the luminous colors of Christian hope. And death carried him off as he was putting the finishing touch on a portrait of Mary (*cf.* page 86), the woman who brought into the world *the light of the world* (Jn 8:12).

Here, the figure of Jesus is portrayed in an intense black, a black without shadow, if you can say that. But this black explodes at the level of his heart in a mystical big bang that spatters with light the whole palette of the colors of daylight, the colors of life. The side of the Crucified opens up like a crater. In this explosion, it seeds the universe with its incandescent lava. From now on the heart of human nature, which is subject to evil and doomed to death, is a sacred heart. Odilon Redon testifies to the hope that is his: the water of suffering and the blood of death are called to spring up again in life and in eternal colors. ■

THE BIBLE – JN 19:31-34

Since it was the day of Preparation, in order to prevent the bodies from remaining on the cross on the sabbath (for that sabbath was a high day), the Jews asked Pilate that their legs might be broken, and that they might be taken away. So the soldiers came and broke the legs of the first, and of the other who had been crucified with him; but when they came to Jesus and saw that he was already dead, they did not break his legs. But one of the soldiers pierced his side with a spear, and at once there came out blood and water.

The Sacred Heart
Odilon Redon (1840–1916)
1910
Pastel, lead pencil on chamois paper, 23.6 x 18.3 in
Paris, Orsay Museum

On the evening of Jesus' death, his mother and his few close friends who had not fled took part in his burial. Present, besides Mary, were Joseph of Arimathea, the "beloved disciple," and three women, including Mary Magdalene, the prostitute who had poured very costly perfume on the feet of Jesus while kissing them with love. After he was laid in the tomb, Mary Magdalene meditated on the death of her beloved Master.

Mary Magdalene, who loved dearly

Mary Magdalene was a repentant "sinner." After making a living by trading on her charms, she became part of a group of Jesus' closest disciples. In order to make the "portrait" of this convert, Giovanni Bellini (*ca.* 1433–1516) depicts here a young Venetian courtesan, her gaze lost in contemplation beyond all worldly horizons, and her hands crossed over her bosom, protecting a heart that has become the tabernacle of noble love.

Mary Magdalene appears in the Gospel at the end of Jesus' life. She probably had been distressed by his public preaching. Most artists, in keeping with the Latin tradition, recognize Mary Magdalene in the three figures of forgiven sinful women presented in the Gospel. In this tradition, it was permissible to fuse, as we will do presently, the different accounts of the "anointings" in Bethany and in the house of Simon, so as to popularize their teaching. One day, seeing Jesus at table dining at the house of a notable man named Simon, Mary Magdalene rushed toward him to express to him her love, and ardently, sumptuously poured out, together with her tears, a perfume of great price on his feet, while kissing them and wiping them with her luxuriant hair. The perfume, the lips, the tears, the caresses of the hair—everything is carnal in this account, and it all adds up to a magnificent declaration of love. Now, Jesus does not reject this anointing. He receives it as an anticipated embalming of his body in view of his impending death.

The notable man snickers interiorly at this prophet who cannot even discern what sort of woman is publicly paying him the tribute that he accepts (Lk 7:39). He also judges this courtesan, who is mad to believe that a gesture of carnal love can exonerate her from her sins of the flesh. He, who boasts of *loving God*, whom he has never seen, *with all his heart, with all his soul, and with all his mind* (*cf.* Dt 6:5), basically detests Mary Magdalene. He and those like him will end up detesting Jesus and killing him, for the love of God. As for Mary Magdalene, she deeply loved the man Jesus whom she saw. The moral of the story is a question: Which of the two loved God in truth?

The Gospel according to Saint Luke adds that Jesus, having read Simon's thoughts, made this reply, which challenges the conformist

THE BIBLE – MT 27:57-61

When it was evening, there came a rich man from Arimathea, named Joseph, who also was a disciple of Jesus. He went to Pilate and asked for the body of Jesus. Then Pilate ordered it to be given to him. And Joseph took the body, and wrapped it in a clean linen shroud, and laid it in his own new tomb, which he had hewn in the rock; and he rolled a great stone to the door of the tomb, and departed. Mary Magdalene and the other Mary were there, sitting opposite the tomb.

Mary Magdalene, detail of Virgin with Child between Saints Catherine and Mary Magdalene
Giovanni Bellini (*ca.* 1433–1516)
Ca. 1500
Oil on wood, 23 x 42 in
Venice, Gallery of the Accademia

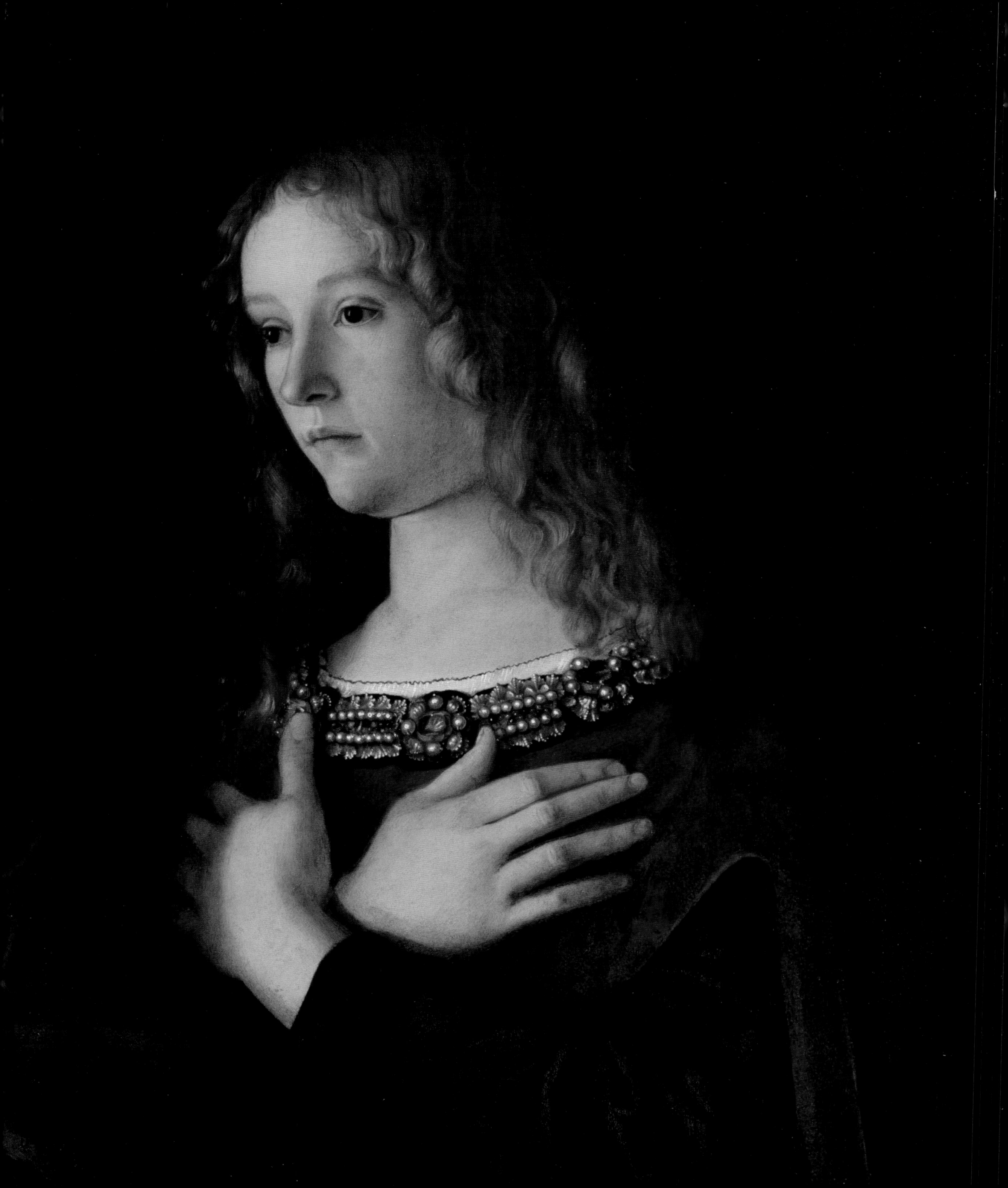

mentality of his host: *Do you see this woman? Well, her sins, her many sins are forgiven because she loved much* (Lk 7:44, 47).

Starting in the 12th century, and then especially in the Renaissance, artists were fond of depicting Mary Magdalene. The personage, who had become mythical in her contradictions—sensuality and asceticism, worldly pleasures and spiritual devotion—was a passionate challenge to the graphic arts. In addition, her character as a seductress did not fail to feed the fantasies that have produced for art some of the most beautiful depictions of feminine charms, in all the ambiguity of their expressions.

The chief patron of artists, the Catholic Church, tolerated some interpretations that were marked with sensuality because she hoped to showcase this attractive and popular personage. Didn't her journey show to hardened sinners the path to their conversion: encounter with Jesus, devotion to his person, following him along the way of the cross, experience of the empty tomb and of the Risen Lord, regular reception of the sacraments, witness of faith? From the 19th century on, the personage of Mary Magdalene was furthermore showcased as a reaction against Victorian prudery. For the Church it illustrated the reminder that Jesus did not come to transform human love into a purely "spiritual" love, but to save and sanctify it, including its carnal dimension, so as to restore to it the full humanity that belonged to it before concupiscence entered into the human heart. ■

IN ART HISTORY

HOLY CONVERSATION

From the 15th century on, the pictorial innovations of the Italian Renaissance, with Florence at its hub, stimulated Italian artistic production as a whole and then spread throughout Europe.

Among the themes explored by artists in decorating churches was that of Holy Conversation or *Sacra Conversazione*.

A Holy Conversation is a picture representing the Virgin and Child in glory, most often placed on high on a throne or a dais and surrounded by saints, prophets, or donors. For patrons this was an ideal pretext to put themselves into the scene, directly or by way of their patron saints, beside the Christ Child. This iconographic formula, which was to be immensely successful, was highlighted in the early 15th century by Fra Angelico (*ca.* 1395/1400–1455), for example in the famous frescos that adorn the wall of the convent of San Marco in Florence.

The marvelous *Mary Magdalene* painted in the final years of the 15th century by Giovanni Bellini (*ca.* 1433–1516) constitutes the right-hand side of a picture representing a Virgin and Child flanked by two female figures, traditionally identified as Saint Mary Magdalene and Saint Catherine of Alexandria. The painter, a pioneer of the Venetian Renaissance, does not set out to show a biblical scene, as might have been the case with an Adoration of the Shepherds or a Crucifixion. The artist chooses a sober, symmetrical composition, set off from a somber background, unlike the pretend architecture in the treatment of the same motif by his brother-in-law Andrea Mantegna (1431–1506), who nonetheless had a very great influence on Bellini.

M. C.

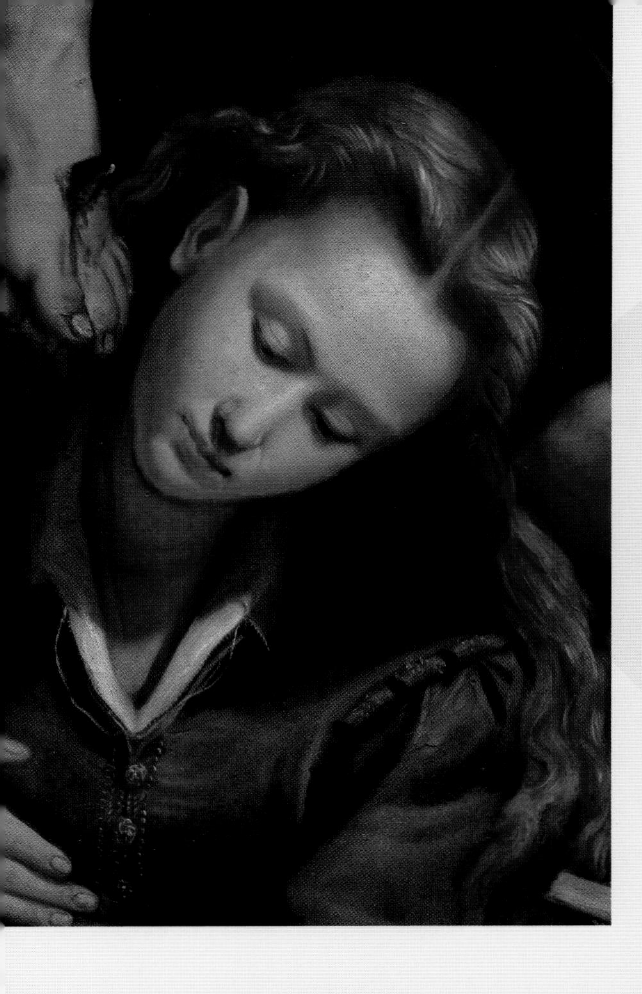

Mary Magdalene, detail from
The vision of Saint Thomas Aquinas
Santi di Tito (1539–1603)
1593
Oil on wood, 143 x 92 in
Florence, Basilica of San Marco

Mary Magdalene embraces the foot of the Cross, her face at the height of Jesus' feet, as when, in a prefiguration, she bathed them with her tears and caressed them with her hair during a meal hosted by the pharisee Simon.

Mary Magdalene, or the offering of human sympathy

CARYLL HOUSELANDER

Caryll Houselander (1901–1954) was a British convert to Catholicism. Her spirituality was based on her reading of the Gospels. She became a prolific writer for Catholic publications. Her first book, *The War Is the Passion,* published in 1941, is a meditation on individual suffering within the Mystical Body of Christ. She had a gift of empathy, and during the War, doctors sent patients to her for counsel and therapy.

The Letters of Caryll Houselander: Her Spiritual Legacy, edited by Maisie Ward (New York: Sheed and Ward, 1965). Reproduced by kind permission of Continuum International Publishing Group, a Bloomsbury Company.

As to your Lent...I can only tell you my own experience. A mass of good resolutions, I think, are apt to end up in disappointment and to make one depressed. Also direct fault-uprooting: it makes one concentrate too much on self, and that can be so depressing. The only resolution I have ever found that works is: "Whenever I want to think of myself, I will think of God." Now, this does not mean, "I will make a long meditation on God," but just some short sharp answer, so to speak, to my thought of self, in God. For example:

"I am lonely, misunderstood, etc."

"The loneliness of Christ at his trial; the misunderstanding even of his closest friends."

Or:

"I have made a fool of myself."

"Christ mocked—he felt it; he put the mocking *first* in foretelling his Passion: 'The Son of Man shall be mocked, etc.,' made a fool of, before all whom he loved."

Or:

"I can't go on, unhelped."

"Christ couldn't. He couldn't carry the cross without help; he was grateful for human sympathy—Mary Magdalene—his words on that occasion [Lk 7:36-50] —other examples as they suggest themselves—just pictures that flash through the mind." This practice becomes a habit, and it is the habit which has saved me from despair!

The rising of Jesus from the dead as such is not related in the Gospels, because there were no witnesses. The empty tomb is highlighted instead: Christian tradition recognizes that the reality of the Resurrection is not self-evident. Nevertheless, the testimony of the empty tomb and of the meetings with the risen Jesus invites us to believe and awaits a response from the personal freedom of each individual. This is why Christian artists were at first hesitant to depict the very moment of the Resurrection.

Jesus rises from the dead

To depict the resurrection of Jesus, Christian artists were content at first to circle the Chi-Rho symbol—Christ's monogram, made up of the Greek letter *X* (chi) and *P* (rho)—with a plaited crown in homage to the conqueror of death. This reserve is understandable: not the slightest account of the Resurrection itself exists, not even mythical or legendary. The space of the Resurrection in the Gospels is empty, furnished only by the tomb that was found unoccupied after the fact, without body, without persons, without speech or action.

From the 5th century on in the East, and from the 6th century in the West, some artists ventured for the first time to illustrate directly the "moment" of the Resurrection with the depiction of Jesus himself, often snatched from the tomb by the hand of God the Father. Not until the 12th century do images appear of Jesus standing in an open sarcophagus, then rising above it.

THE BIBLE – MT 28:2-4

And behold, there was a great earthquake; for an angel of the Lord descended from heaven and came and rolled back the stone, and sat upon it. His appearance was like lightning, and his clothing white as snow. And for fear of him the guards trembled and became like dead men.

Here, Veronese conceives of the Resurrection as a dazzling explosion which, by its blast and its radiation, topples and blinds the soldiers guarding the tomb. It surrounds the crucified Jesus with a *mandorla*, an oval-shaped halo, and propels him victoriously toward heaven. He is quite recognizable by his arms outstretched in the form of a cross, by the marks of the nails on his hands and feet, and by the wound left in his side by the blow of the lance. Wearing a beautiful expression, his eyes uplifted toward the highest heavens (cf. Lk 2:14), he contemplates the glory of his Father who, according to Saint Irenaeus, Bishop of Lyon in the late 2nd century, is pleased with humanity now victorious over evil and death: "The glory of God is man fully alive," he used to say.

Thus Veronese "reconstructed," according to Church teaching, the supreme moment when, without witnesses, like a living flame, the Paschal Victim rose up to God in a perfect offering of thanksgiving (*eucharistia* in Greek). In the background, the vestiges of a proud edifice symbolize the completion of the first Covenant, certified by the ruination of the Temple in Jerusalem. But even more, these vestiges recall the remains of the Tower of Babel; the foolish dream of its builders will come true in a way surpassing all the illusions of human pride. Reunited in one body with the risen Lord through the Eucharist, the "sacrament of unity," humanity now has the promise that it will be raised up to share in the divinity of him who took on our humanity. ■

Resurrection of Christ
Paolo Caliari, called Veronese (1528–1588)
1570–1575
Oil on canvas, 54 x 41 in
Dresden, Gemäldegalerie Alte Meister

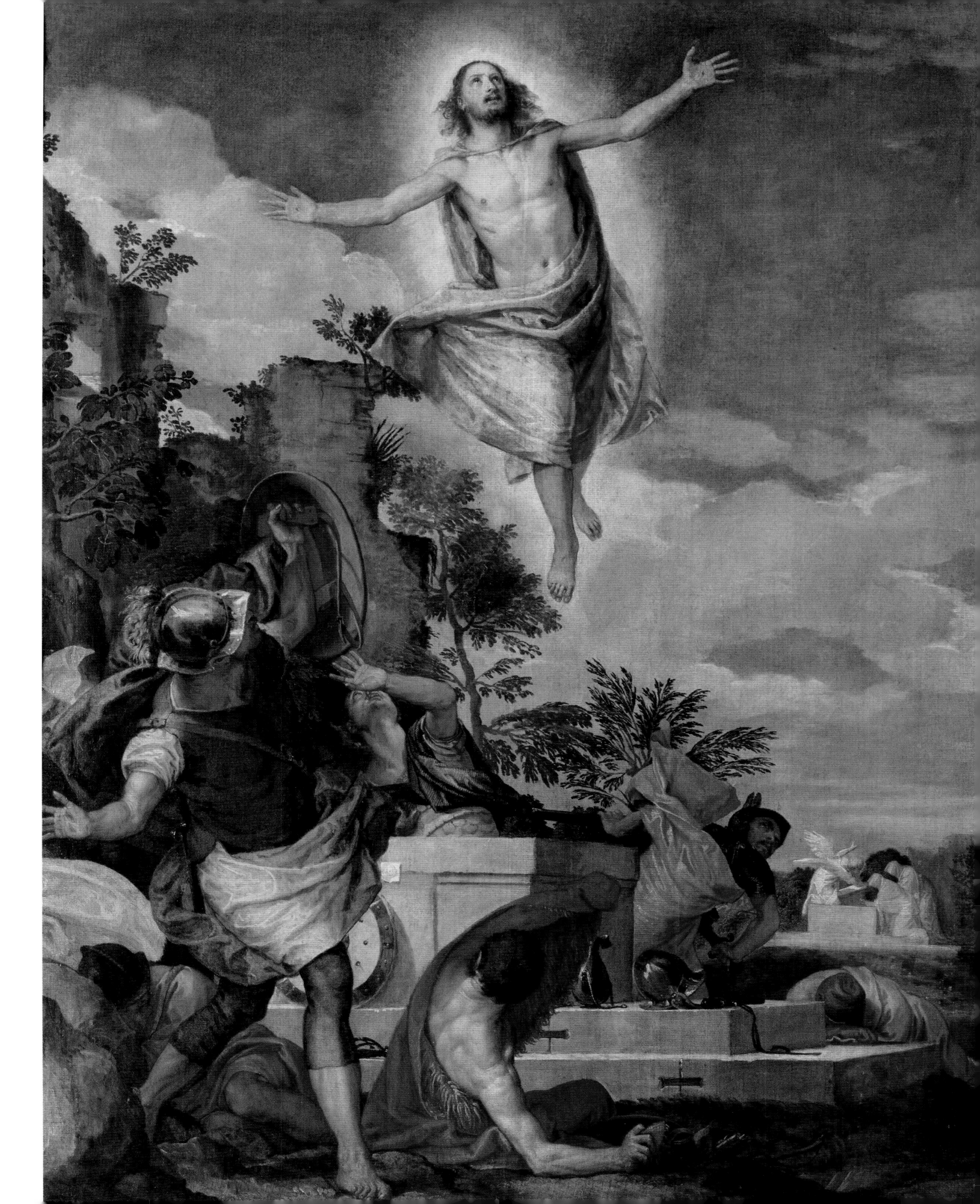

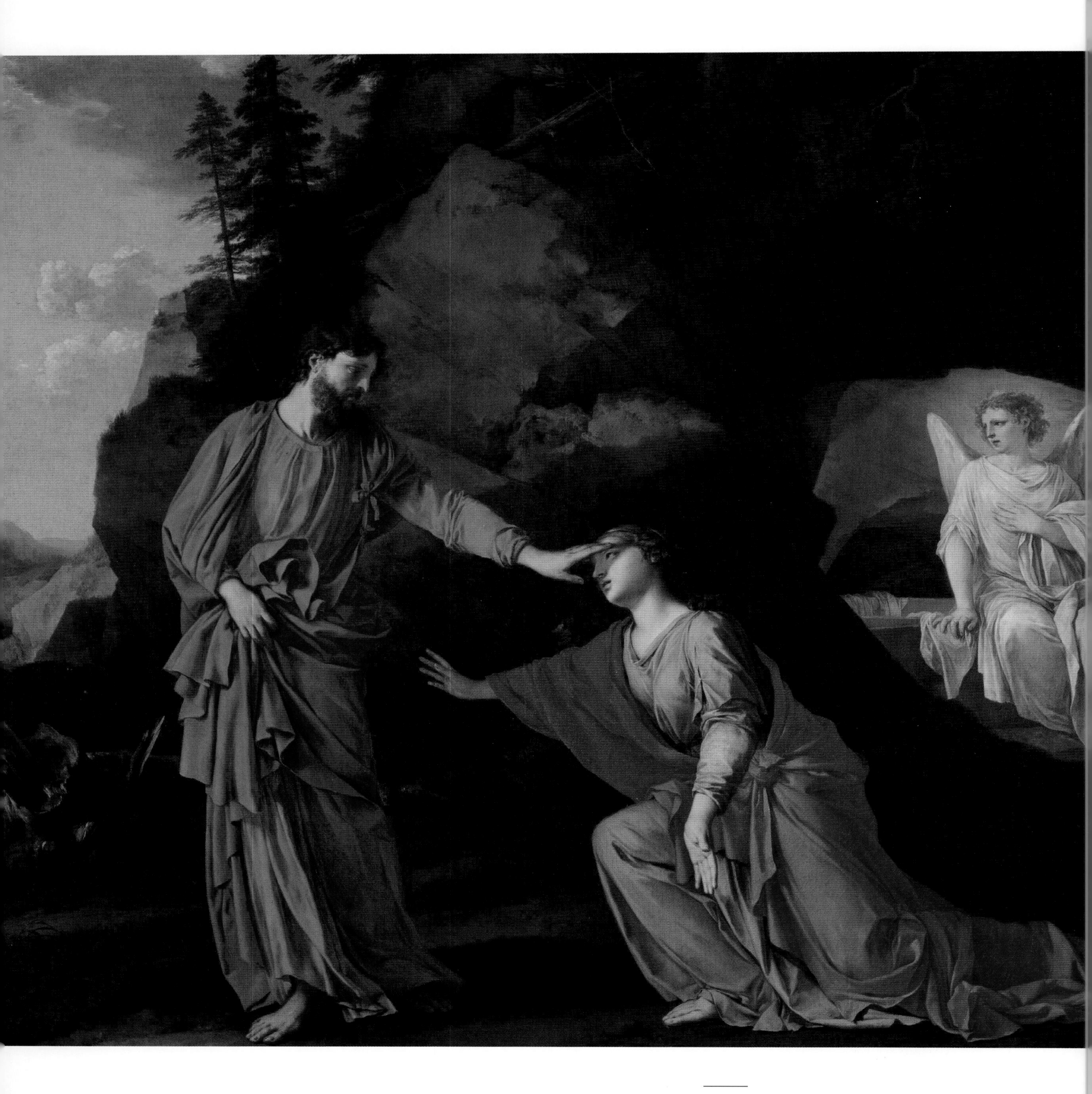

Christ appears to Mary Magdalene
(Noli me tangere)
Laurent de La Hyre (1606–1656)
1656
Oil on canvas, 64 x 71 in
Grenoble, museum

Easter morning at dawn

It is Sunday morning, in other words, the day after the Jewish Passover, "the third day" after the death of Jesus. Actually the biblical way of counting days is not linked to a number of hours but rather considers the alternation of day and night, as at the Creation. Since Jesus died on a Friday afternoon, the "third day" begins two days afterward at sunrise.

A paragon of classicism in the French manner, in reaction to the effusions of the Roman Baroque style, Laurent de La Hyre (1606–1656) rejected all lyricism and all sensuality to adopt a mode of expression that was at the same sober and refined, nourished by ancient poetry and spiritual contemplation.

This work is the artist's last, painted in the same years as his death. It was commissioned by the monastery of the Grande Chartreuse: this is why the landscape in the background does not depict the vicinity of Golgotha; far from it! We see instead a mountainous site that suggests the French Alps, the location of the monastery that commissioned the painting. The subtitle of the work is *Noli me tangere*, "Touch me not," the words which on Easter morning the risen Jesus speaks to Mary Magdalene who, upon recognizing him, throws herself down at his feet to embrace him. The scene is arranged along a diagonal that rises from right to left. Mary Magdalene's back, the left arm of Jesus, and the opening of the tomb describe this oblique line.

La Hyre takes to the highest degree of perfection the symbolic contrast of the colors and the harmony of the forms. Mary Magdalene's sienna robe recalls her sinful, mortal humanity, *dust that shall return to dust* (Gn 3:19). However, her tunic transfigures the earthen color by mixing it with the purple that represents God who is Love. The luminous orange that results symbolizes human love, saved and raised to the rank of divine love, as the water was changed into wine at the wedding feast in Cana. In contrast, a sight as gripping as it is admirable, the risen Jesus is clothed in a celestial blue, a mixture of lapis lazuli and indigo, which has an extraordinary power to evoke the "heavens," the universe to which he will ascend again, the kingdom of his Father, of our Father (cf. Jn 20:17).

Without being Jansenist, strictly speaking, La Hyre socialized with members of the Port-Royal movement, and this had its effect on his theological and spiritual language. At the time when he was painting this picture, the battle of the *Provinciales* was raging. Pascal had experienced his "night of fire" two years earlier; over

THE BIBLE – JN 20:11, 14BC-17

But Mary stood weeping outside the tomb, and as she wept she stooped to look into the tomb. She turned around and saw Jesus standing, but she did not know that it was Jesus. Jesus said to her, "Woman, why are you weeping? Whom do you seek?" Supposing him to be the gardener, she said to him, "Sir, if you have carried him away, tell me where you have laid him, and I will take him away." Jesus said to her, "Mary." She turned and said to him in Hebrew, "Rabboni!" (which means Teacher). Jesus said to her, "Do not hold me, for I have not yet ascended to the Father; but go to my brethren and say to them, I am ascending to my Father and your Father, to my God and your God."

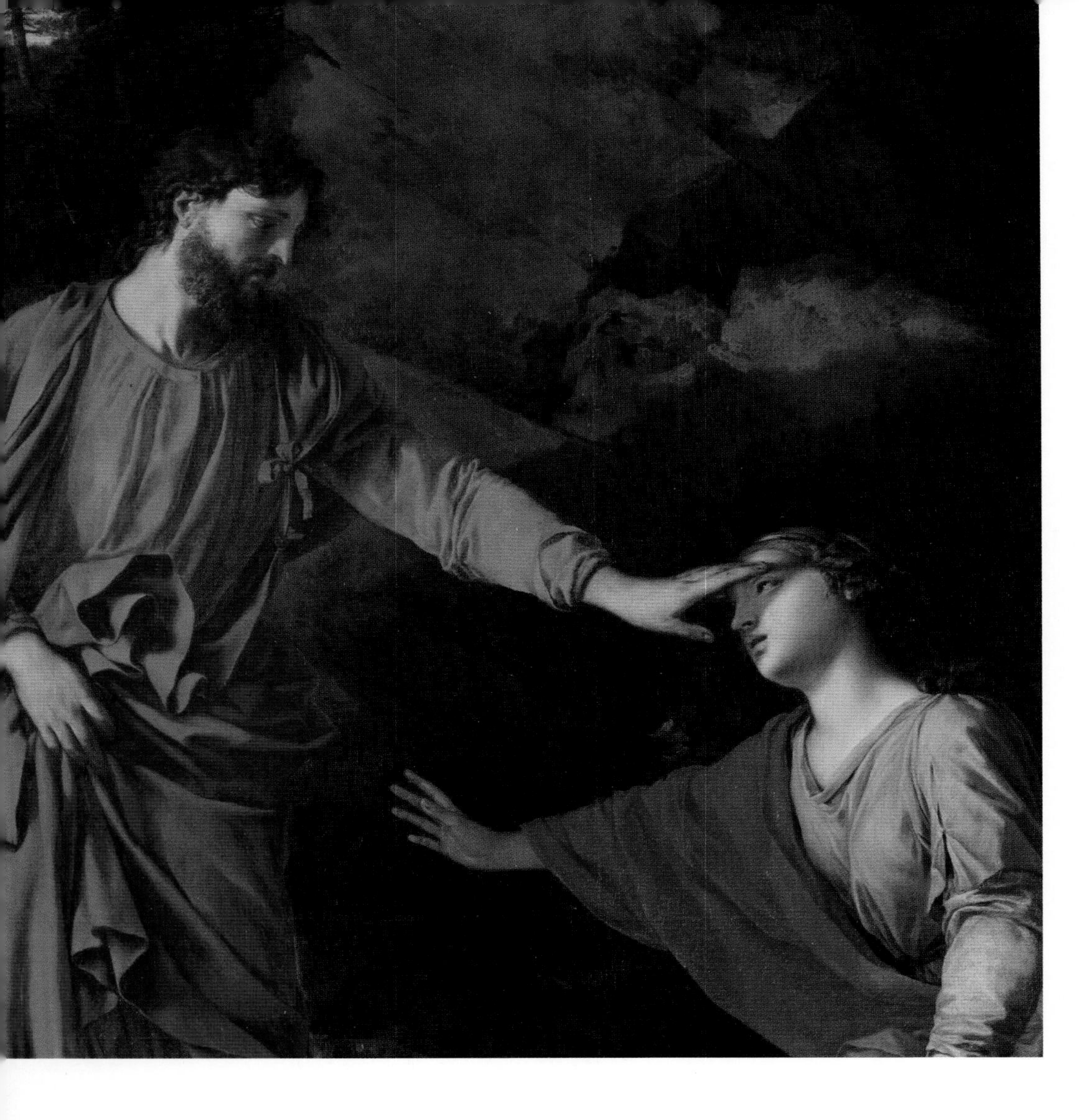

Christ appears to Mary Magdalene (Noli me tangere), detail
Laurent de La Hyre (1606–1656)
1656
Oil on canvas, 64 x 71 in
Grenoble, museum

the course of meetings and discussions, he was already developing the theme of the hidden God, which he would put at the heart of his *Pensées*, according to the revelation of Isaiah: *You are truly the hidden God, the God of Israel, the Savior* (Is 45:15, as translated by Lemaistre de Sacy).

In the spirit of Pascalian mysticism, the Jesus of Laurent de La Hyre is not content to keep Mary Magdalene at a distance; he brushes her forehead with her hand so as to cast a shadow on her eyes. This is because, even after his Incarnation and Resurrection, God must still remain hidden until the end of the world, so as to be found and *loved by us in deed and in truth and not only in word and in thought* (1 Jn 3:18). Even though Jesus decided to fulfill his promise to remain really present among men after his ascension into heaven, until his final coming, Pascal declares, "He chose to remain here in the strangest and most obscure secret of all," in other words in the sacramental species.

And so a Christian is someone who, with his eyes opened by faith, recognizes the Spirit of Jesus in the written Gospels, communes with his Body and Blood under the appearances of the Eucharistic bread and wine, and finally loves the person of Jesus in each one of his human brothers and sisters whom Providence makes his neighbors along his earthly pilgrimage, so that, at the end of time, Christ Jesus will be able to say with good reason to the blessed of his Father: "Whatever you did out of love for the least of my human brothers and sisters, you did it for me in them" (*cf.* Mt 25:40).

Thus, through this masterpiece and testament, it was La Hyre's plan, inspired by Pascal's thought, to show that on the morning of the Resurrection, Christ the Victor wanted to remain the hidden God. But why? So as to start being through everyone, with everyone, and in everyone the God who is *everything to everyone* (1 Cor 15:28). ■

Jesus appears to the three Marys
Laurent de la Hyre (1606–1656)
Ca. 1653
Oil on canvas, 157 x 99 in

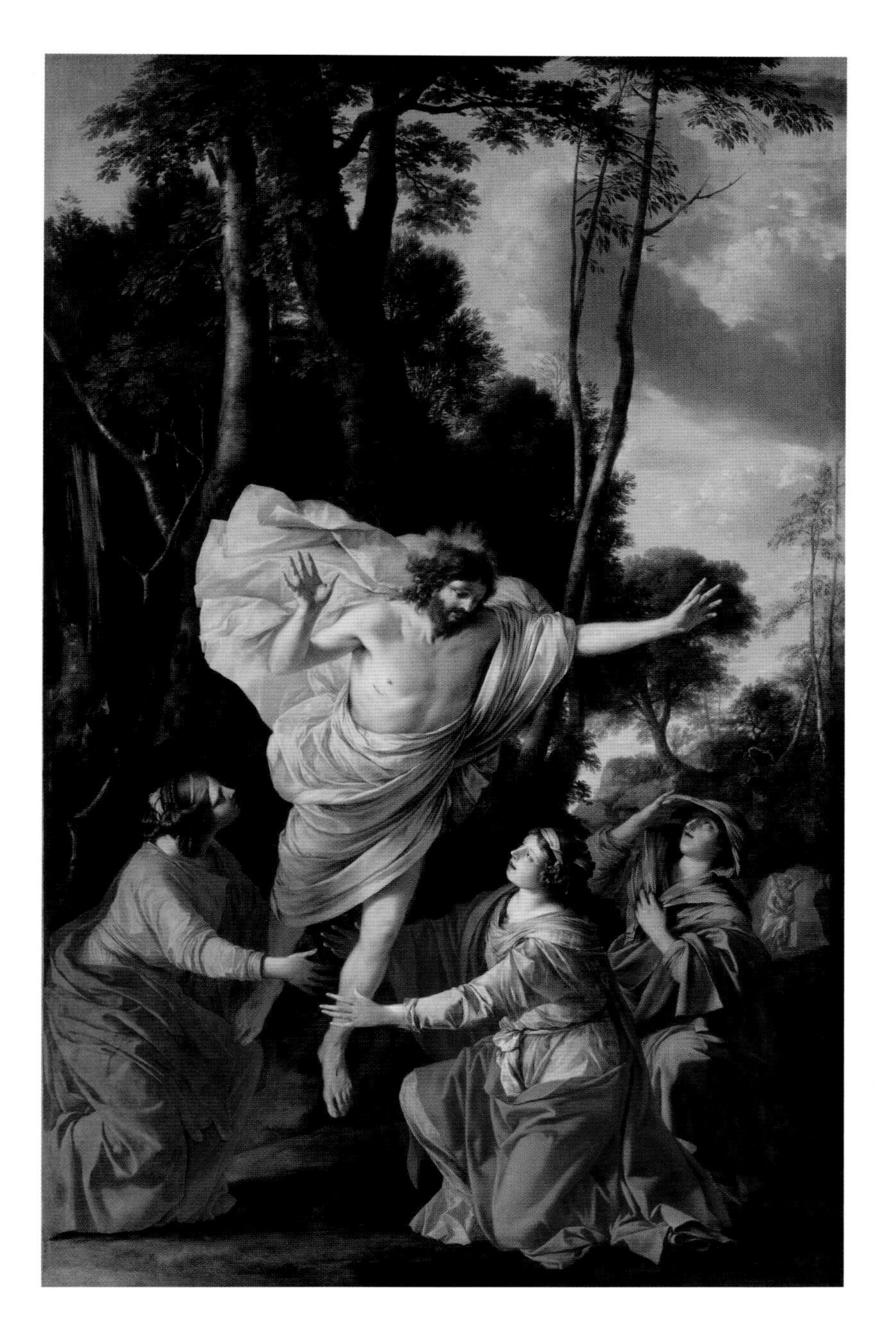

PARISIAN ATTICISM

In the mid-17th century, during the regency of Anne of Austria (1643–1651), a pictorial style derived from classicism developed in the Parisian artistic circle, called "Parisian Atticism"—the expression favored by the French art historian Jacques Thuillier (1928–2011).

Parisian Atticism, of which Laurent de La Hyre (1606–1656) is a perfect representative, is distinguished by a learned method of painting which, in reaction to the Baroque style and its excesses, multiplies references to Antiquity and the Renaissance—which had attempted to reformulate an imagined Antiquity. Led by the painter Eustache Le Sueur (1616–1655), this local movement did not sacrifice everything to the Italian cult. These artists observed or, more exactly, contemplated Italy through the daring works of Rosso Fiorentino (1494–1540) and Francesco Primatice (1503–1570), whose decorations La Hyre admired at Fontainebleau Castle. They were also enthusiastic about the pictorial innovations of the Frenchmen who returned from Rome, such as Simon Vouet (1590–1649) and Nicolas Poussin (1594–1665) during his brief return to Paris between 1640 and 1642. Laurent de La Hyre, for his part, would never travel to Rome.

The rigor of the compositions, as *Christ appears to Mary Magdalene* testifies, corresponds to a demand for clarity. This is also why the painter never multiplies the number of figures and is not at all intent on rendering an illusionist perspective. The reef that Laurent de La Hyre manages to avoid here would be absolutely rejecting all sentiment in painting, even if it meant going to the other extreme of depicting disembodied figures.

Nevertheless, the colors are luminous and the half-tones have an important place on the artist's palette. They are at the service of the liveliest brushstrokes, such as the luminous blue that adorns Christ's cloak here [in the 1656 painting]. This is in deliberate opposition to the violent contrasts of Baroque painting. The desire for austerity, nevertheless, in no way diminishes a great delicacy of brushstrokes, or dancing, supple gestures.

Parisian Atticism favors the themes of Greek and Roman antiquity as well as biblical subjects, choices which of course support the Church's commissions. Nevertheless, within this current there is an emphasis on landscape; Laurent de La Hyre distinguished himself in this regard along with Henri Mauperché (*ca.* 1602–1686) and Pierre Patel (*ca.* 1605–1676): all three developed the landscape as a source of interest, each in his own manner.

M. C.

The village of Emmaus to which two disciples were walking on the Sunday of the Resurrection may have been Emmaus Nicopolis, located seven miles to the west of Jerusalem, near the present-day Cistercian monastery of Latroun. But since the Evangelist Luke's chronology requires a place about two hours' walking distance from Jerusalem, some wonder whether the Benedictine monastery of Abu Gosh, situated in Kiryat-Yearim, might not be more credible.

Along the way, Jesus explains the Bible

Fritz von Uhde (1848–1911) enjoyed great renown in Germany and the United States as one of the chief representatives of impressionist naturalism in the Germanic world.

In a significant part of his work, he devoted himself to showing the presence of Jesus in the world, the contemporary representative and agent of the life of his era, most often in popular milieus. Naturalist religious art was not allowed by most Protestant churches, including the Lutheran church to which the painter belonged, because they deemed it inappropriate for Scriptural figures to be depicted—*a fortiori* in a contemporary, ordinary, or trivial manner.

Here, however, von Uhde paints the Gospel episode of "the road to Emmaus" (cf. Lk 24:13-32). The path that winds through the valleys symbolizes the unfolding of salvation history along humanity's march toward its eternal destination. The pilgrims' place on that path marks the time of the historical manifestation of salvation in the person of Jesus of Nazareth. The way already traveled represents the sacred history of Israel, of which Jesus reveals the ultimate meaning to his two traveling companions: *Starting with Moses and all the Prophets, he interpreted for them, in all the Scriptures, the things concerning himself* (Lk 24:27). The two travelers, each of them turned with his head bent toward Jesus who stands between them, give the impression that they want to slow their pace so as to ask for an explanation. Through all these postures, the painter means to emphasize the crucial importance of the words pronounced by Jesus.

The path ahead of the travelers meanders through the low hills and vanishes where the horizon meets the sky; it represents the time still granted to history before it ends. In Emmaus, at the inn where they will stop to eat, the two disciples will recognize Jesus when he blesses bread, breaks it, and gives it to them. Then he will "vanish out of their sight" (cf. Lk 24:30-31). They will conclude from this that it is up to them from now on to be his visible, acting body, all along the way humanity must still travel on earth. ■

THE BIBLE – LK 24:17-20, 25-27

And he said to them, "What is this conversation which you are holding with each other as you walk?" And they stood still, looking sad.
Then one of them, named Cleopas, answered him, "Are you the only visitor to Jerusalem who does not know the things that have happened there in these days?" And he said to them, "What things?" And they said to him, "Concerning Jesus of Nazareth, who was a prophet mighty in deed and word before God and all the people, and how our chief priests and rulers delivered him up to be condemned to death, and crucified him."
And he said to them, "O foolish men, and slow of heart to believe all that the prophets have spoken! Was it not necessary that the Christ should suffer these things and enter into his glory?"
And beginning with Moses and all the prophets, he interpreted to them in all the scriptures the things concerning himself.

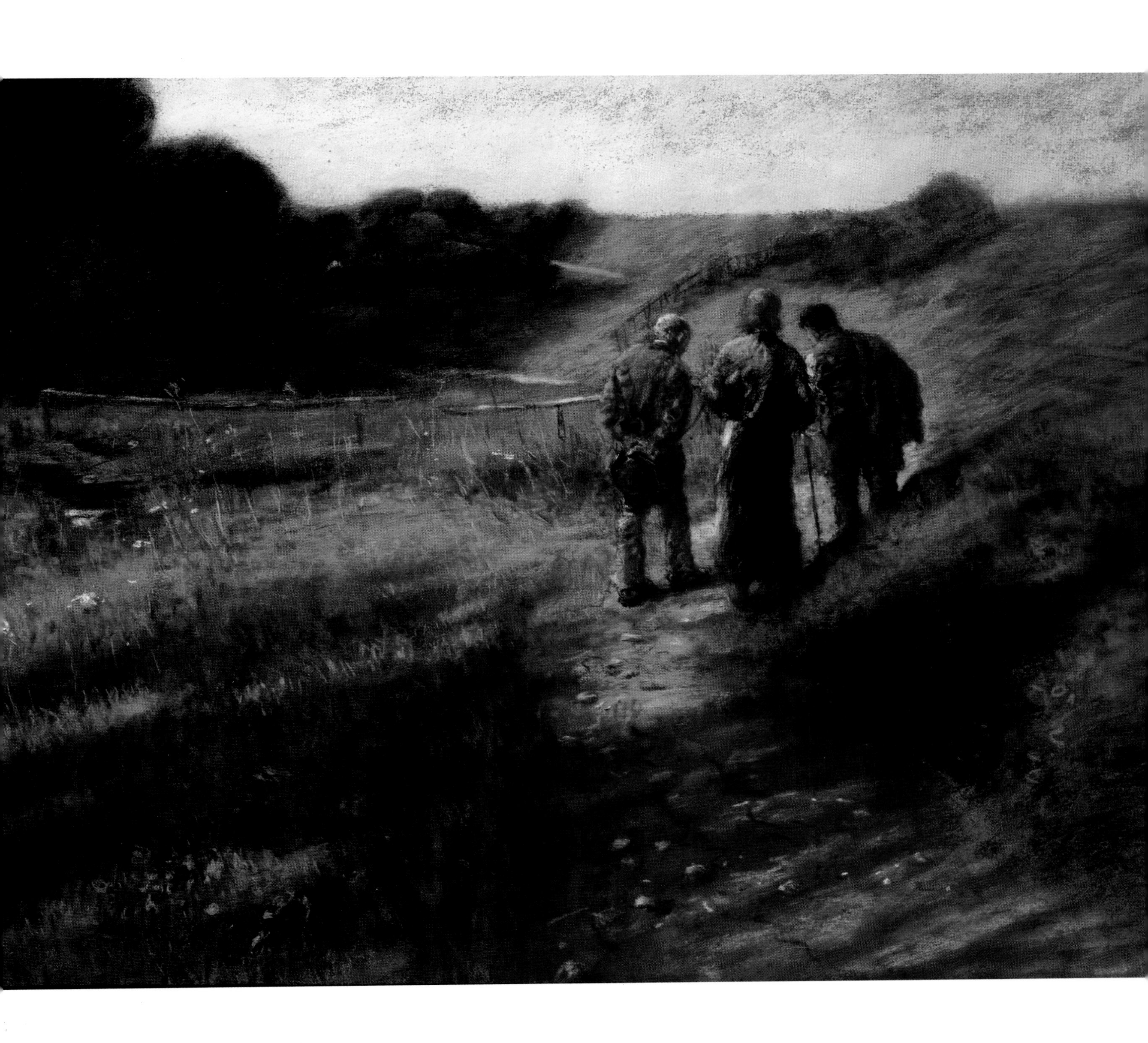

The Road to Emmaus
Fritz von Uhde (1848–1911)
1891
Pastel on paper, 26 x 35 in
Dresden, Galerie Neue Meister

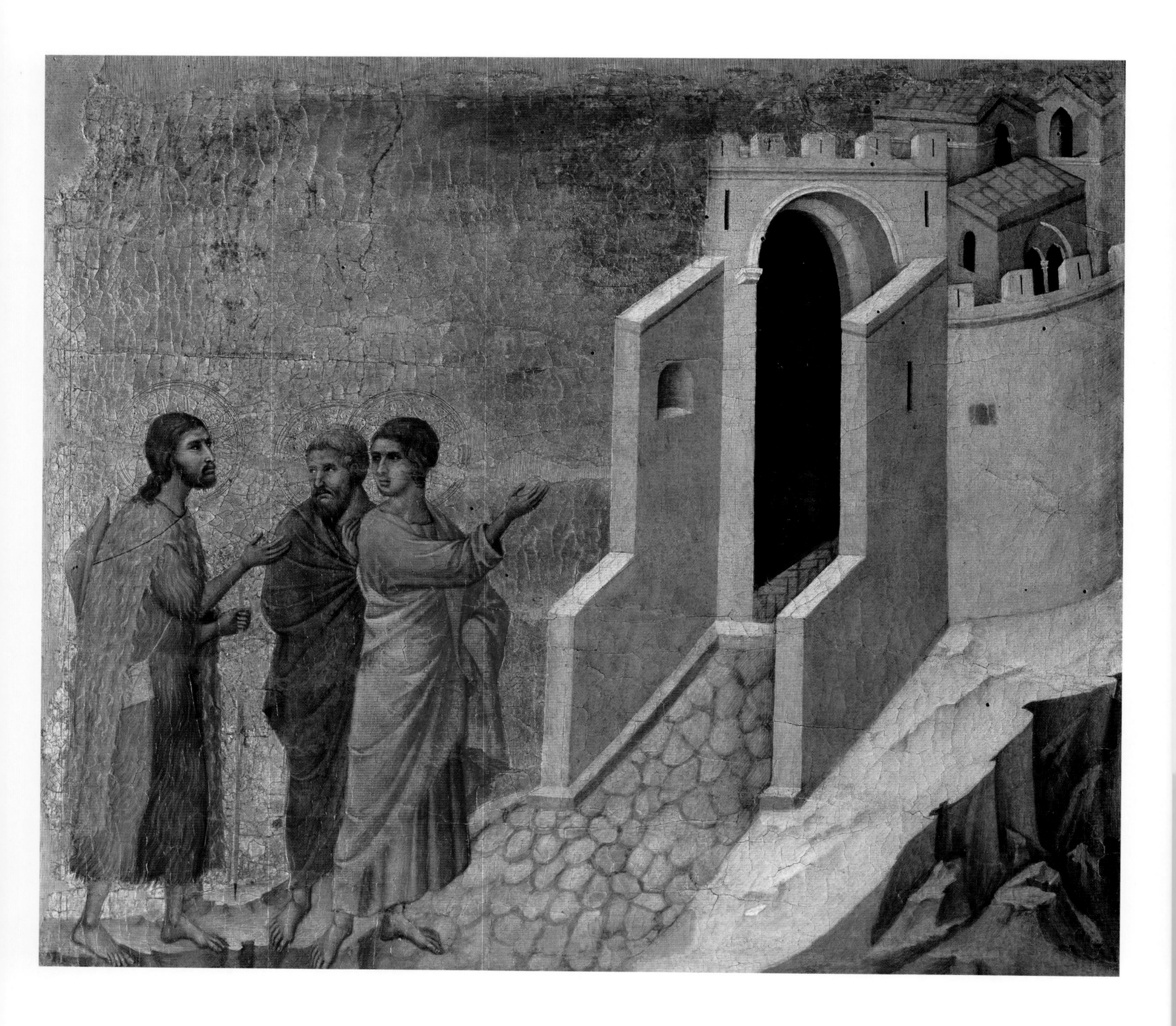

On the road to Emmaus
Duccio di Buoninsegna
(*ca.* 1260–*ca.* 1318/1319)
1308–1311
Tempera and gold on wood, 20 x 22 in
Siena, Museo dell'Opera Metropolitana
Detail of the altarpiece of the *Maestà*

Duccio, like Giotto a student of Cimabue, is a painter emblematic of the 14th century in Siena. He illustrates here the passage from the Gospel according to Saint Luke: *They drew near to the village to which they were going. He appeared to be going further, but they constrained him, saying, "Stay with us, for it is toward evening and the day is now far spent." So he went in to stay with them* **(Lk 24:28-29)**.

In his *Life of Jesus* (1936), Nobel Prize winner François Mauriac offers an account based on the Gospels. He is careful to be faithful not only to the human history that they have transmitted to us, but also to their spiritual meaning and to the divine incarnation of the Son of God: Jesus of Nazareth. In this passage he extends his meditation of the Resurrection of Jesus to his contemporary life as a Christian and a writer. Thus he strives to express how the risen Lord came to meet him personally to open his eyes about his own existence.

François Mauriac, *The Life of Jesus*, translated by Julie Kernan (London: Longmans, Green, 1937), 241, 243.

Who has not walked on this road?

FRANÇOIS MAURIAC

When many Gospel relations [accounts] seem unimaginable to us, there is none closer to our proven experience than that which treats of the risen Christ....

There is no meeting of Christ with one of his followers which does not recall to the Christian some event in his own life....

We, too, have sometimes recognised him. Why not admit it?...

Who among us does not know the inn at Emmaus? Who has not walked on this road one evening when all seemed lost? Christ was dead within us. They had taken Him from us—the world, the philosophers and sages, our passions. There was no Jesus for us on the earth. We followed a road, and Someone walked at our side. We were alone and we were not alone. It was evening. Here was an open door, the obscurity of a room where the flame from the fireplace lighted only the trampled earth and made the shadows move. O bread that was broken! O breaking of the bread, consummated despite so much misery. “Stay with us... the day declineth....” The day declineth, life is finishing. Childhood seems further away than the beginning of the world: and of lost youth we hear only the last groaning of the dead trees in some strange wood.... “And their eyes were opened, and they recognised him; and he vanished from them. And they said one to another, ’Was not our heart burning within us whilst he spoke to us on the way, whilst he laid open to us the scriptures?’”

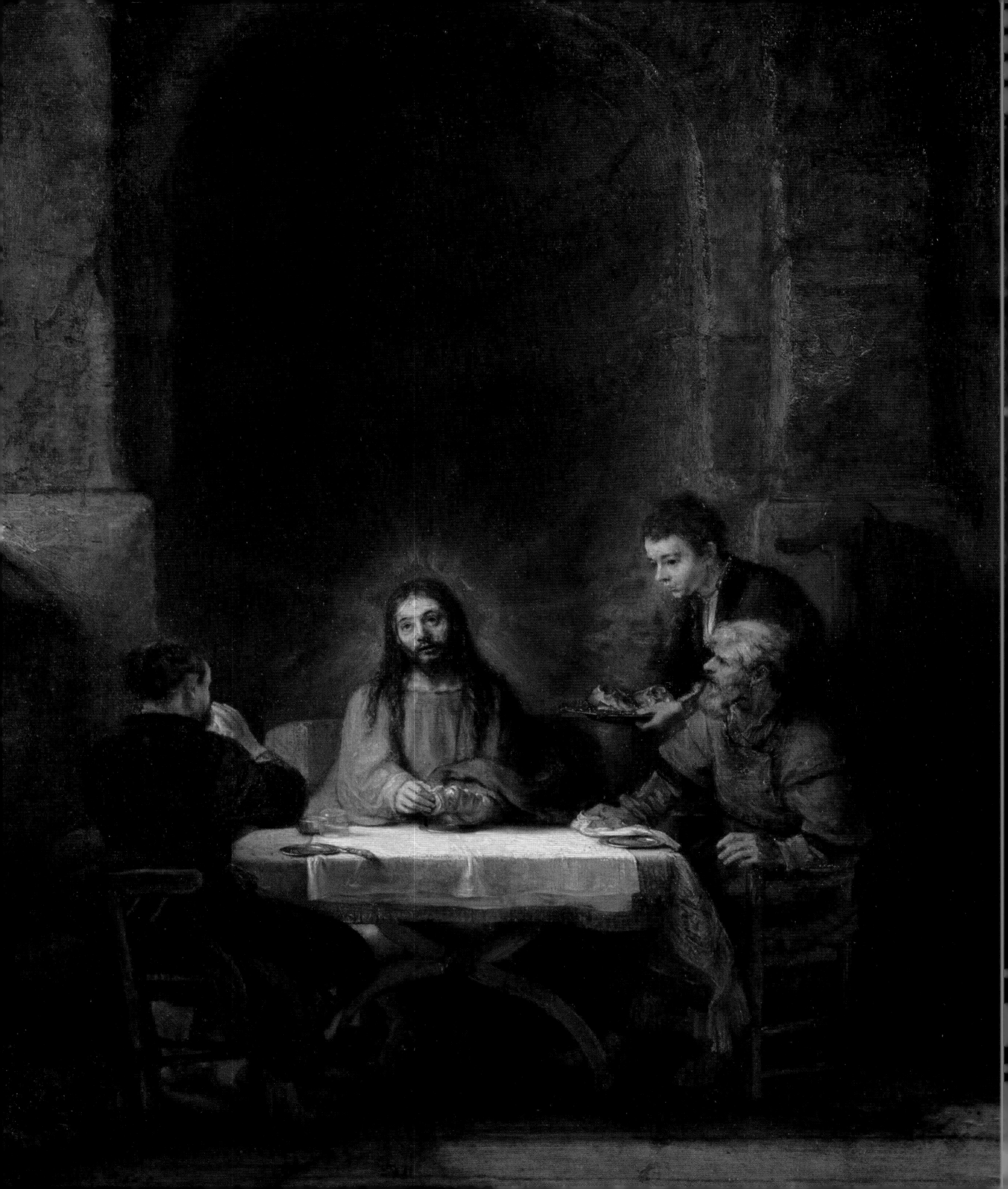

Jesus celebrates the first Mass

According to the Gospels, when Jesus shows that he is alive after Easter, he displays no triumphant or glorious feature. Mary Magdalene mistakes him for the gardener, and the two disciples on the road to Emmaus think that they are dealing with a random traveler. Later, in his boat on the Lake of Tiberias, Peter does not recognize him when he receives fishermen's instructions from him, the very same ones that had enabled him three years earlier, at the start of the epic, to make a miraculous catch of fish.

In depicting him in Emmaus at the inn, Rembrandt (1606–1669) is not afraid to show a human Jesus, too much so to be the Risen Lord. His face is haggard, like a Christ still experiencing his Passion. In this way, the painter of the miracle means to illustrate the doctrine whereby the renewal of the Last Supper—the Eucharist—is "the source and summit of all Christian life," because this rite makes present, actually but "in an unbloody manner," the supreme sacrifice of Jesus that was offered on the cross "for the glory of God and the salvation of the world." Again according to this doctrine, during the Mass, on the altar, the victim is indeed the same as on the cross, and the minister who offers the sacrifice is also the same, because the priest does not consecrate in his own person but *in persona Christi* (in the person of Christ); he does not say "This is the body of Jesus..." but rather *"This is my body...."*

Here, therefore, Rembrandt depicted, in a way, in an almost Catholic way, the first Mass, at any rate the first time in history in which Jesus' offering of his life was renewed. Rembrandt depicts this first time in conformity with the Gospel account: celebrated by Jesus himself, after a powerful "Liturgy of the Word" along the way.

In Emmaus at the inn, Rembrandt captures Jesus at the very moment when he is pronouncing the words and making the gestures of the institution of the Eucharist: "On the eve of his Passion, he took bread into his most sacred hands and, raising his eyes to heaven, to you, God, his almighty Father, and giving thanks, he blessed it, broke it, and gave it to his disciples...." Rembrandt captures this moment in which the real presence of Jesus is revealed, and he gives meaning to it by the light that emanates from it in the chiaroscuro and by the obvious astonishment of the two disciples. Moreover, he even manages to suggest that the moment after this instant of grace, when the two disciples are about to take and eat the bread, the body of Jesus will have been given in Communion down to the last atom, to the point where he vanishes from their sight. ■

IN THE BIBLE – LK 24:28-31

So they drew near to the village to which they were going. He appeared to be going further, but they constrained him, saying, "Stay with us, for it is toward evening and the day is now far spent." So he went in to stay with them. When he was at table with them, he took the bread and blessed, and broke it, and gave it to them. And their eyes were opened and they recognized him; and he vanished out of their sight.

The Pilgrims at Emmaus
Rembrandt (1606–1669)
1648
Oil on wood, 27 x 26 in
Paris, Louvre Museum

The Gospel according to Saint John relates that after the announcement of the Resurrection, the apostles continued to hide, shutting themselves away in the upper room. That is where Jesus appeared to them the first time. But Thomas, one of the Twelve, was not present. The others tried to tell him: *We have seen the Lord!* but he replied: *Unless I see in his hands the print of the nails, and place my finger in the mark of the nails, and place my hand in his side, I will not believe!* (Jn 20:25)

Doubting Thomas

To guide the composition of his picture, Rembrandt (1606–1669) follows the Gospel reading (Jn 20:27-29). News of the Resurrection of Jesus spread among his disciples. In order to believe the unbelievable, the Apostle Thomas demands proof; Jesus presents this proof to him in person, allowing him to observe the stigmata of his Passion. *"Put your finger here, and see my hands; stretch out your hand and put it into my side: stop doubting and believe."* Immediately Thomas, disconcerted, exclaims: *"My Lord and my God!"* And Jesus says to him: *"Because you have seen me you believe."* Then the risen Lord adds, in view of the disciples in future ages: *"Blessed are those who believe without having seen."*

To believe without having seen... At the time of Rembrandt and his contemporary René Descartes (1596–1650), there was a tendency to subject the faith to doubt. Certitudes that had been considered sacred were called into question. Protestantism rejected the doctrinal authority of the pope and of Catholic Tradition; astronomy questioned the biblical view of the universe; miracles were confronted with the laws of physics; even atheism started to make its arguments openly. In this context, the question whether Christ had truly risen was posed. And some dared to answer in the negative. Rembrandt was not unaware of these debates. A citizen of the United Provinces (today the Netherlands), where Descartes spent most of his life, he was a compatriot of Baruch Spinoza (1632–1677), in a sense the precursor of modern atheism—they could have met in Leyden or Amsterdam.

Many critics have seen in the *Doubting Thomas* painted by Caravaggio around 1603 (see next page), with Saint Thomas almost scientifically probing the wound in Christ's side, a strong but dissembling expression of the skepticism that was winning over many minds. Rembrandt was well acquainted with that picture, which had caused quite a sensation; he had seen several copies of it. He adopts here some elements from it, such as the chiaroscuro and the faces of the disciples who are bent over to examine the wounded side. However, there is no trace whatsoever of skepticism in *Doubting Thomas* by Rembrandt. On the contrary, this work can only be interpreted as a strong testimony of his faith in the Resurrection. Confounded, Rembrandt's Thomas does not need to probe

THE BIBLE – JN 20:24-29

Now Thomas, one of the twelve, called the Twin, was not with them when Jesus came. So the other disciples told him, "We have seen the Lord." But he said to them, "Unless I see in his hands the print of the nails, and place my finger in the mark of the nails, and place my hand in his side, I will not believe." Eight days later, his disciples were again in the house, and Thomas was with them. The doors were shut, but Jesus came and stood among them, and said, "Peace be with you." Then he said to Thomas, "Put your finger here, and see my hands; and put out your hand, and place it in my side; do not be faithless, but believing." Thomas answered him, "My Lord and my God!" Jesus said to him, "Have you believed because you have seen me? Blessed are those who have not seen and yet believe."

Doubting Thomas
Rembrandt (1606–1669)
1634
Oil on wood, 20.9 x 19.9 in
Moscow, Pushkin Museum

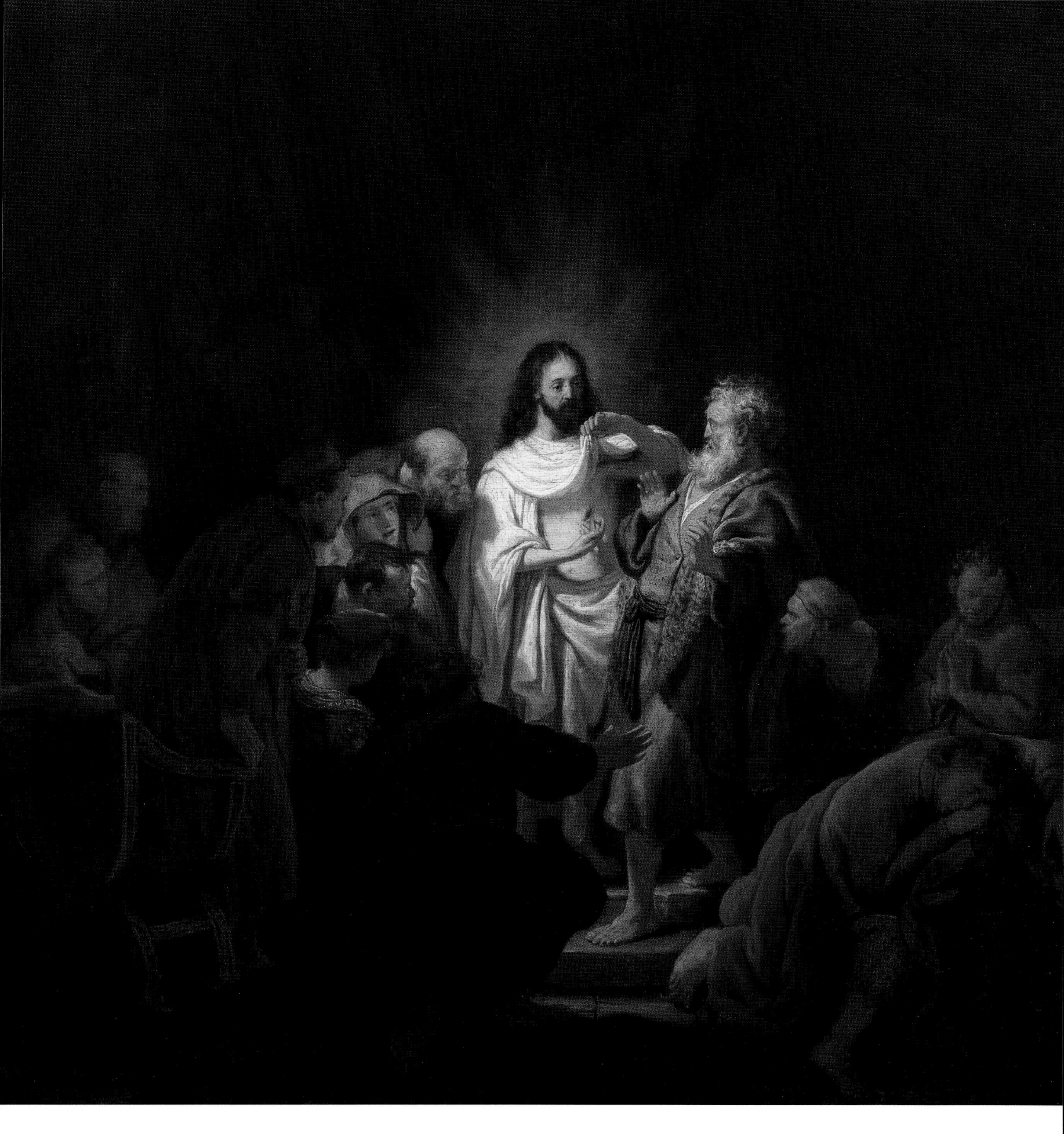

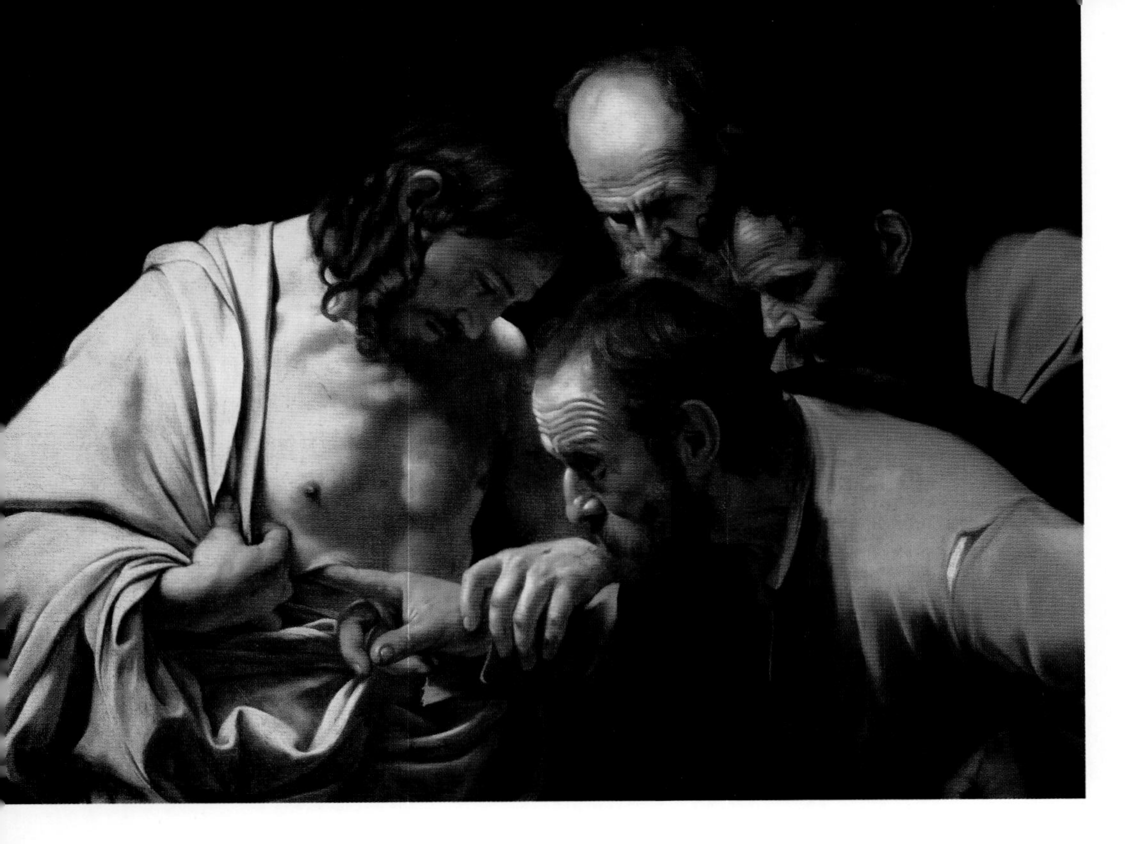

The incredulity of St. Thomas,
Michelangelo Merisi,
called Il Caravaggio (*ca.* 1571–1610)
ca. 1603
Oil on canvas, 42.1 x 57.5 in.
Schloss Sanssouci, Postdam, Germany

in order to believe: the real presence of Jesus and his word suffice.

Some like to think that in Caravaggio's picture the dark background represents the universe of obscurantist ignorance from which the lights of scientific investigations emerge. In Rembrandt's picture, the darkness from which the disciples emerge, each one lit more or less by the presence of the Risen Jesus, are on the contrary the place of rock-solid faith. In fact, Rembrandt adopts here the mystical insight developed by the Spanish poet John of the Cross (1542–1591), whereby the most beautiful faith is one that reaches its perfection in "the dark night." This is why, at the heart of this darkness, Rembrandt depicts, half lying down and asleep, the disciple whom Jesus loved (cf. Jn 13:23), identified by Tradition as the Evangelist John. In that posture, this disciple illustrates the words that Jesus will address to doubting Thomas: "Blessed is he—that one, who believed without having seen!" Indeed, as Saint John attests somewhat humorously in his Gospel, while speaking about his personal experience at the empty tomb, when, in the absence of Jesus' body, there was nothing more to see: *he saw, and he believed* (Jn 20:8). Now, when Thomas wants at all costs to touch, to probe his finger into Christ's wound, the same John is therefore sleeping peacefully:

On a dark night...
In secret, when none saw me,
Nor I beheld aught,
Without light or guide,
Save that which burned in my heart.

(John of the Cross, *Dark Night of the Soul*, composed around 1598, translated by E. Allison Peers.)

"Faith indeed tells what the senses do not tell, but not the contrary of what they see. It is above them, and not contrary to them.... Two extremes: to exclude reason, to admit reason only." The moral of this picture might lie in this *Pensée* by Blaise Pascal, published in 1669, the same years as Rembrandt's death. ■

The poet Denise Levertov (1923–1997) was born in England but spent most of her life in the United States as a professor of literature. Many of her poems focus on religious themes. The volume from which this excerpt is taken was, in her words, meant to "trace my slow movement from agnosticism to Christian faith." She converted to Catholicism towards the end of her life.

Denise Levertov, excerpt from "St. Thomas Didymus," in: *The Stream and the Sapphire: Selected Poems on Religious Themes* (New York, NY: New Directions Books, 1997), 81-82.

I believe

BY DENISE LEVERTOV

And after the empty tomb
when they told me that He lived,
   had spoken to Magdalen,
told me
that though He had passed through
   the door like a ghost
He had breathed on them
the breath of a living man –
even then
when hope tried with a flutter
   of wings
to lift me –
still, alone with myself,
my heavy cry was the same: Lord
I believe,
help thou mine unbelief.

I needed
blood to tell me the truth,
the touch
of blood. Even
my sight of the dark crust of it
round the nailholes
didn't thrust its meaning all the way
   through
to that manifold knot in me
that willed to possess all knowledge,
refusing to loosen
unless that insistence won
the battle I fought with life

But when my hand
led by His hand's firm clasp
entered the unhealed wound,
my fingers encountering
rib-bone and pulsing heat,
what I felt was not
scalding pain, shame for my
obstinate need,
but light, light streaming
into me, over me, filling the room
as I had lived till then
in a cold cave, and now
coming forth for the first time,
the knot that bound me unravelling,
I witnessed
all things quicken to color, to form,
my question
not answered but given
its part
in a vast unfolding design lit
by a risen sun.

The Ascension is the moment when Jesus left the earth to go back to God, his Father, in the other world. The circumstances of this event remain mysterious, as though it took place in a way that surpassed the understanding of the witnesses. The Gospel according to Saint John predicts this "ascent" to the Father (cf. Jn 20:17) but gives no account of it. Matthew reports the farewell discourse that Jesus gives from a mountaintop in Galilee (Mt 28:16-20) but stops there. Mark finishes his narrative by mentioning simply that Jesus *was taken up into heaven.* Luke is the most prolix, recording that Jesus *parted from them, and was carried up into heaven* (Lk 24:51). Most artists have taken this formulation literally so as to depict Jesus leaving this world and going up into heaven.

Jesus passes from this world to his Father

Andrea Mantegna (1431–1506) was the great innovator of the Renaissance in Northern Italy. Called by Ludovico III Gonzaga, Marquis of Mantua, he became his official painter in 1460. He was not yet thirty years old. This *Ascension* is said to date from this period. Christ is carried up to heaven by a cloud of cherubim, holding in his hand the victorious standard of the cross, as the prophet Isaiah says:

On that day, the root of Jesse, the father of David,
shall be set up as a standard for the peoples;
the nations shall seek him,
and his dwelling shall be glorious. (Is 11:10)

It is all accomplished (Jn 19:30) on that day when Jesus, true God who has died and true man who has risen, leaves earth and time so as to return to where he came from, alongside God his Father, outside of time. All is accomplished in his mission to save humanity, but according to his promise, all will be manifested only at his glorious return, at the end of time. Saint John assures us of this in a letter to the very first Christians: *Beloved, we are God's children now, but what we shall be is not yet evident. We know that when he appears we shall be like him for we shall see him as he is* (1 Jn 3:2).

Then the Lord Jesus, after he had spoken to them, was taken up into heaven, and sat down at the right hand of God.

THE BIBLE – MK 16:19

As Jesus goes away, his last glance on earth is directed toward his disciples. His expression seems to convey a final message: "I place my work into your hands until I come again." His right hand, lifted up like a scepter, confirms that he is the Rabbi, the Master of all teaching, being the Word of the Father. *And this is the Father's commandment: that we should have faith in his Son Jesus Christ, and love one another as he taught us*, Saint John concludes (1 Jn 3:23).

Mantegna depicts the glorious Christ mounting the skies as if he were painting a statue from antiquity. Certainly, Jesus will be welcomed in his humanity to rest on the bosom of God the Father. But he is God who is returning to God. His figure is statuesque, powerful, stylized, already sculpted in his eternity, although for one last moment he still has to ascend in order to leave time. ■

The Ascension, detail
Andrea Mantegna (1431–1506)
1460–1464
Tempera on wood, 33.9 x 16.7 in
Florence, Galleria degli Uffizi, panel from the Uffizi triptych

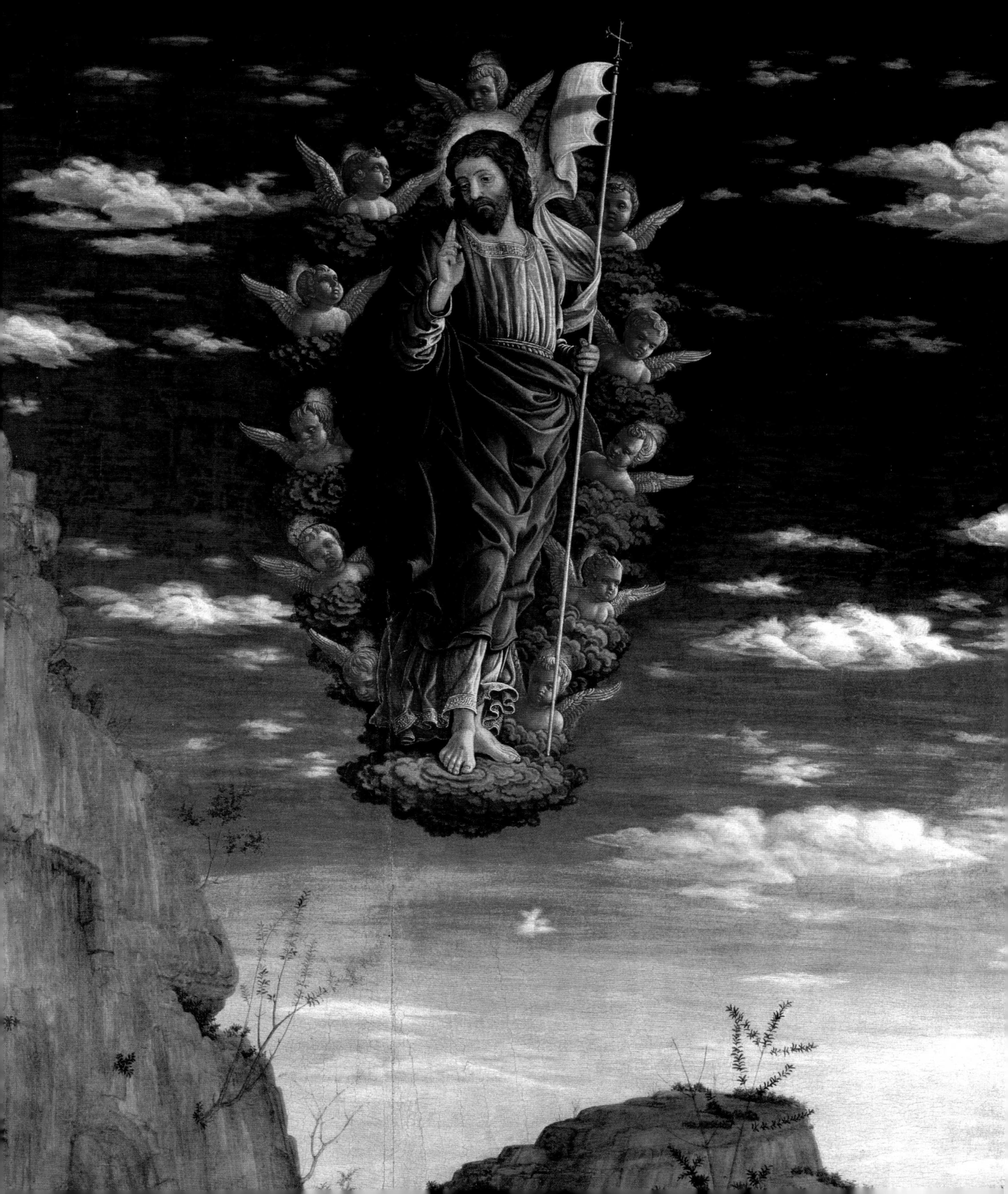

C.S. Lewis (1898–1963) was born in Northern Ireland (Ulster). He taught English literature as a university fellow at both Oxford and Cambridge. He published popular apologetic works such as *Mere Christianity* and *The Screwtape Letters*. His allegorical series of children's books, *The Chronicles of Narnia*, also remains popular. Reprinted here are Lewis' reflections on the mystery of Christ's Ascension.

C.S. Lewis, *Miracles: a preliminary study* (London & Glasgow: Collins/ Fontana, 1947, revised 1960; reprinted New York: HarperOne, 2001), 149, 243-244, 263-266.

Heaven as remaking

C.S. LEWIS

The records represent Christ as passing after death (as no man had ever passed before) neither into a purely, that is negatively, "spiritual" mode of existence nor into a "natural" life such as we now know, but into a life which has its own new Nature. It represents Him as withdrawing six weeks later, into some different mode of existence. It says—He says—that He goes "to prepare a place for us." This presumably means that He is about to create that whole new Nature which will provide the environment or conditions for His glorified humanity and, in Him, for ours. The picture is not what we expected—though whether it is less or more probable and philosophical on that account is another question. It is not the picture of an escape from any and every kind of Nature into some unconditioned and utterly transcendent life. It is the picture of a new human nature, and a new Nature in general, being brought into existence. We must, indeed, believe the risen body to be extremely different from the mortal body: but the existence, in the new state, of anything that could in any sense be described as "body" at all, involves some sort of spatial relations and in the long run a whole new universe. That is the picture—not of unmaking but of remaking. The old field of space, time, matter and the sense is to be weeded, dug and sown for a new crop. We may be tired of that old field: God is not. (*Miracles*, 149)

We can [spiritualize the Ascension] only if we regard the Resurrection appearances as those of a ghost or hallucination. For a phantom can just fade away; but an objective entity must go somewhere—something must happen to it. And if the Risen Body were not objective, then all of us (Christian or not) must invent some explanation for the disappearance of the corpse. And all Christians must explain why God sent or permitted a "vision" or a "ghost," whose behavior seems almost exclusively directed to convincing the disciples that it was not a vision or a ghost but a really corporeal being. If it were a vision then it was the most systematically deceptive and lying on record. But if it were real, then something happened to it after it ceased to appear. You cannot take away the Ascension without putting something else in its place. (*Miracles*, 243-244)

The remark so often made that "Heaven is a state of mind" bears witness to the wintry and deathlike phase of this process in which we are now living. The implication is that if Heaven is a state of mind—or, more correctly, of the spirit—then it must be only a state of the spirit, or at least that anything else, if added to that state of spirit, would be irrelevant. That is what every great religion except Christianity would say. But Christian teaching by saying that God made the world and called it good teaches that Nature or environment cannot be simply irrelevant to spiritual beatitude in general, however far in one particular Nature, during the days of her bondage, they may have drawn apart. By teaching the resurrection of the body it teaches that Heaven is not merely a state of the spirit but a state of the body as well: and therefore a state of Nature as a whole. Christ, it is true, told His hearers that the Kingdom of Heaven was "within" or "among" them. But His hearers were not merely in "a state of mind". The planet He had created was beneath their feet, His sun above their heads; blood and lungs and guts were working in the bodies He had invented, photons and sound waves of His devising were blessing them with the sight of His human face and the sound of His voice.

We are never merely in a state of mind. The prayer and the meditation made in howling wind or quiet sunshine, in morning alacrity or evening resignation, in youth or age, good health or ill, may be equally, but are differently, blessed. Already in this present life we have all seen how God can take up all these seeming irrelevances into the spiritual fact and cause them to bear no small part in making the blessing of that moment to be the particular blessing it was—as fire can burn coal and wood equally but a wood fire is different from a coal one. From this factor of environment Christianity does not teach us to desire a total release. We desire, like St Paul, not to be unclothed but to be re-clothed: to find not the formless Everywhere-and-Nowhere but the promised land, that Nature which will be always and perfectly—as present Nature is partially and intermittently—the instrument for that music which will then arise between Christ and us.

And what, you ask, does it matter? Do not such ideas only excite us and distract us from the more immediate and more certain things, the love of God and our neighbours, the bearing of the daily cross? If you find that they so distract you, think of them no more. I most fully allow that it is of more importance for you or me today to refrain from one sneer or to extend one charitable thought to an enemy than to know all that angels and archangels know about the mysteries of the New Creation. I write of these things not because they are the most important but because this book is about miracles. From the title you cannot have expected a book of devotion or of ascetic theology. Yet I will not admit that the things we have been discussing for the last few pages are of no importance for the practice of the Christian life. For I suspect that our conception of Heaven as merely a state of mind is not unconnected with the fact that the specifically Christian virtue of Hope has in our time grown so languid. Where our fathers, peering into the future, saw gleams of gold, we see only the mist, white, featureless, cold and never moving.

The thought at the back of all this negative spirituality is really one forbidden to Christians. They, of all men, must not conceive spiritual joy and worth as things that need to be rescued or tenderly protected from time and place and matter and the senses. Their God is the God of corn and oil and wine. He is the glad Creator. He has become Himself incarnate. The sacraments have been instituted. Certain spiritual gifts are offered us only on condition that we perform certain bodily acts. After that we cannot really be in doubt of His intention. To shrink back from all that can be called Nature into negative spirituality is as if we ran away from horses instead of learning to ride. There is in our present pilgrim condition plenty of room (more room than most of us like) for abstinence and renunciation and mortifying our natural desires. But behind all asceticism the thought should be, 'Who will trust us with the true wealth if we cannot be trusted even with the wealth that perishes?' Who will trust me with a spiritual body if I cannot control even an earthly body? These small and perishable bodies we now have were given to us as ponies are given to schoolboys. We must learn to manage: not that we may some day be free of horses altogether but that some day we may ride bare-back, confident and rejoicing, those greater mounts, those winged, shining and world-shaking horses which perhaps even now expect us with impatience, pawing and snorting in the King's stables. Not that the gallop would be of any value unless it were a gallop with the King; but how else—since He has retained His own charger—should we accompany Him? (*Miracles*, 263-266)

"Learning to express the hidden voice of things:
this is the path and the purpose of art."

Giorgio De Chirico

Christ in majesty, detail
390–401/417
Mosaic
Rome, Basilica of Santa Pudentiana, apse

The End of History

When Jesus had left this earth, his disciples dedicated themselves to spreading his teaching and worship by declaring that he is the Savior of the world: *We have seen and testify that the Father has sent his Son as the Savior of the world,* Saint John writes (1 Jn 4:14). This was the beginning of Christianity. From the 4th century on, it was no longer persecuted by the Roman Empire and was even set up as the official religion in 392. From then on, Christian iconography flourished, elaborated in such a way as to support the devotion of the faithful. And so the figure of the *Salvator mundi*, the "Savior of the world," would be depicted abundantly throughout the history of the Church.

Jesus, the Savior of the world

This work by a disciple of Quentin Matsys (*ca.* 1466–1530), wrongly entitled *Christ blessing*, is a typical example of a pictorial variation on the theme of the *Salvator mundi*, the "Savior of the world." Jesus is shown in majesty: the front view, the fixed stare, and the purple cloak are characteristic. He raises his right hand like a scepter: the two folded fingers designate his two natures, human and divine; the thumb and the other two joined fingers, forming a heart, signify the Trinity, *for God is love* (1 Jn 4:8). This gesture also signifies that he is the teacher of all truth. His left hand covers a transparent globe surmounted by the cross, illustrating his saying: *All authority has been given to me on earth* (Mt 28:18), since the globe is the symbol of humanity, potentially redeemed, saved, and glorified—and with it the whole cosmos.

The motif of the *Salvator mundi* is a later development of the *Majestas Domini* (Christ in majesty), the first examples of which go back to the late 4th century in Rome, and also of the *Pantocrator* of the Eastern tradition. This theme—which appears for the first time at the heart of the Basilica of Saint Pudentiana (*cf.* page 251)—was elaborated magnificently in the sermons of Saint Gregory the Great (*ca.* 540–604): the Christ of the "eternal glory" is constantly present in the sacrifice that his Church offers to the Father at each Mass. This is why this motif was always adopted for the vault over the semicircular back wall that surrounds and overhangs the altar in early Christian, Byzantine, and then Romanesque churches. During the Renaissance, it became the *Salvator mundi* of small-scale pictures, for the purpose of private devotion. Nowadays, the figure of the *Salvator mundi* is marked by a strong mystagogical and liturgical significance since, in 1925, Pope Pius XI instituted the Feast of Christ the King and, in 1970, the reform resulting from Vatican Council II made it the feast concluding the liturgical year: the accent is on the grandiose vision of Jesus' cosmic triumph at the "end of time" and, in him, the final success of Creation, more than on the personal prayer to Jesus the Savior present in the life of everyone. ■

THE BIBLE – JN 4:42

They said to the woman, "It is no longer because of your words that we believe, for we have heard for ourselves, and we know that this is indeed the Savior of the world."

Christ blessing
Studio of Quentin Matsys (*ca.* 1466–1530)
1510–1525
Oil on wood, 22.9 x 13.1 in
London, National Gallery,
detail of the *Diptych of Christ and the Blessed Virgin*

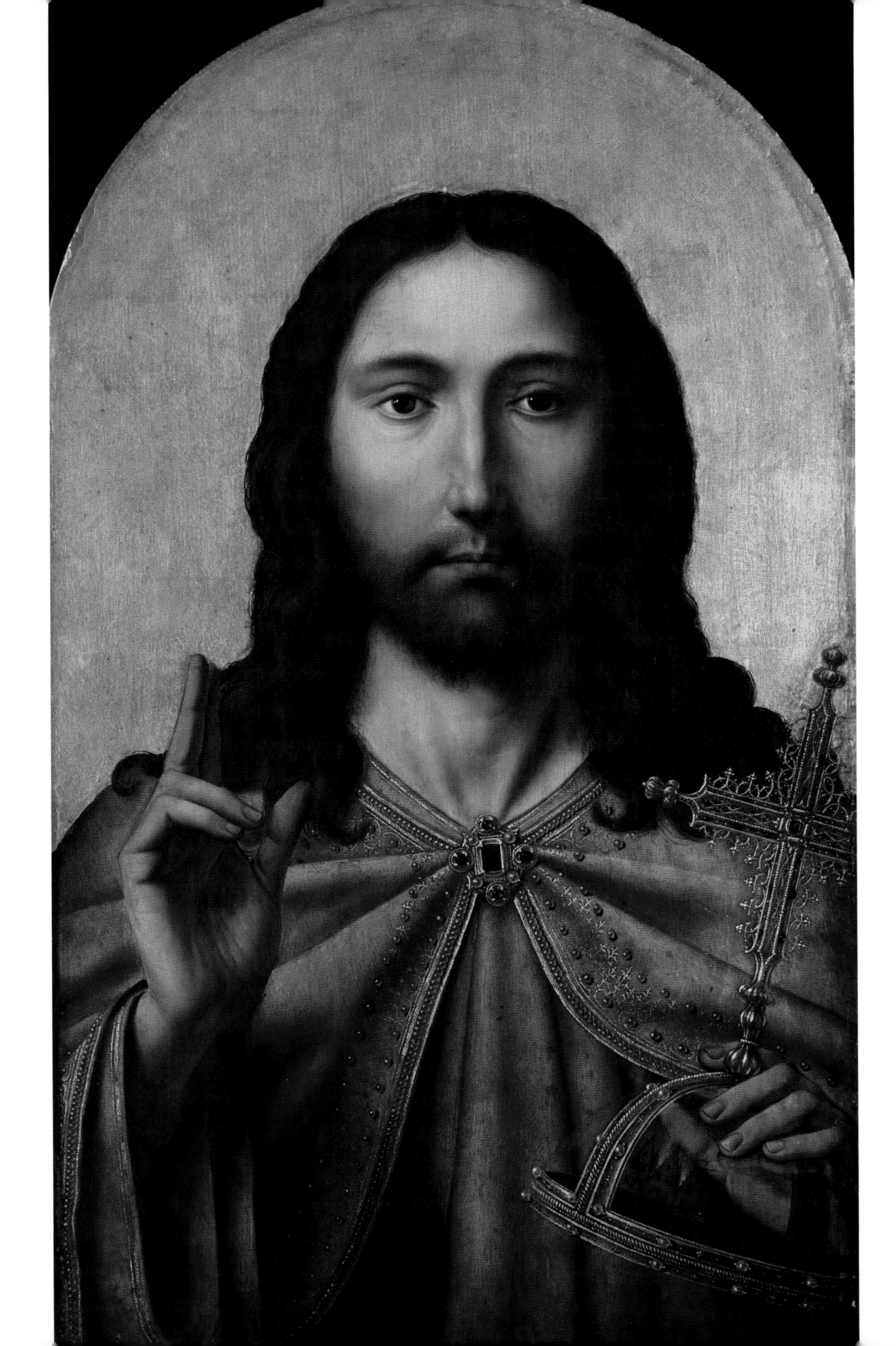

Paul Claudel (1868–1955), French writer and diplomat, is most famous for his poetic and dramatic work, marked from 1886 by his dazzling conversion to Catholicism.

Paul Claudel, *I Believe in God*, Agnès du Sarment, Ed., Helen Weaver, Tr., © 1973 by Holt, Reinhart and Winston, New York – San Francisco, CA: Ignatius Press, 2002. pp. 70, 78, 79

Christ the King

PAUL CLAUDEL

Take it now, miraculous Son! Take the world, says the prophet (Dan 7), take eternity! Ascend the throne of David, ascend the throne of Solomon, the one his Mother prepared for him and whose center is made of a beating heart! Become the center of all our scattered longing! At the intersection of the two diameters, divinity and humanity, verify that instrument which, from all six directions, attracts everything to itself, by which justice has forever bound itself to love and where necessity has consumed death. In the center of all this has been driven a kind of nail to prevent my ever leaving again. It is love which has achieved this. There is a man who holds God fast by means of his Word...

He is come, the One before whom all powers on earth, in heaven, or in hell are obliged to bend the knee, and on whose garment and flank is inscribed this name: *King of kings and Lord of lords* (Rev 19:16).

"I came to cast fire upon the earth; and would that it were already kindled!" (Lk 12:49). The eyes and face of Christ are a silent answer to that universal human longing to do away with the old self, to exhale the substance through the soul, and to illumine our whole estate with the conflagration of that heart on which the Spirit breathes...

It is Christ's eyes on us, and our eyes turned toward him as a servant toward his master, that brings about our participation and our understanding. One look from him at Peter, at John and Andrew at their nets, at Matthew at his ledgers, at Bartholomew under the fig tree, was enough to appoint them apostles, to brand on them indelibly that new name—the name of their Master.

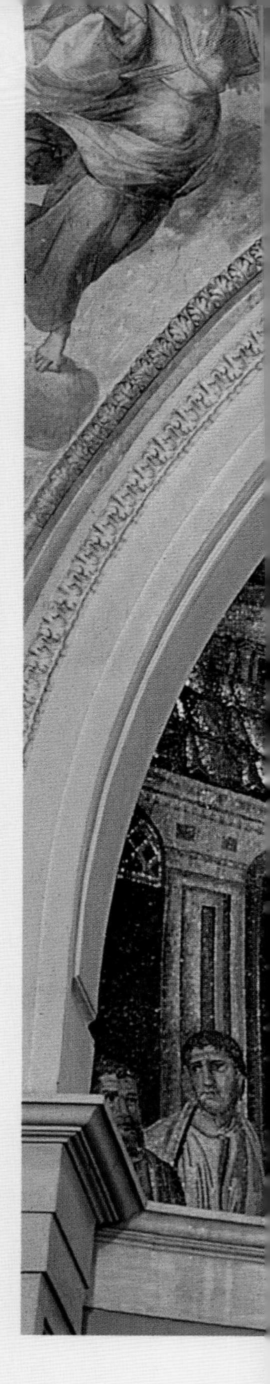

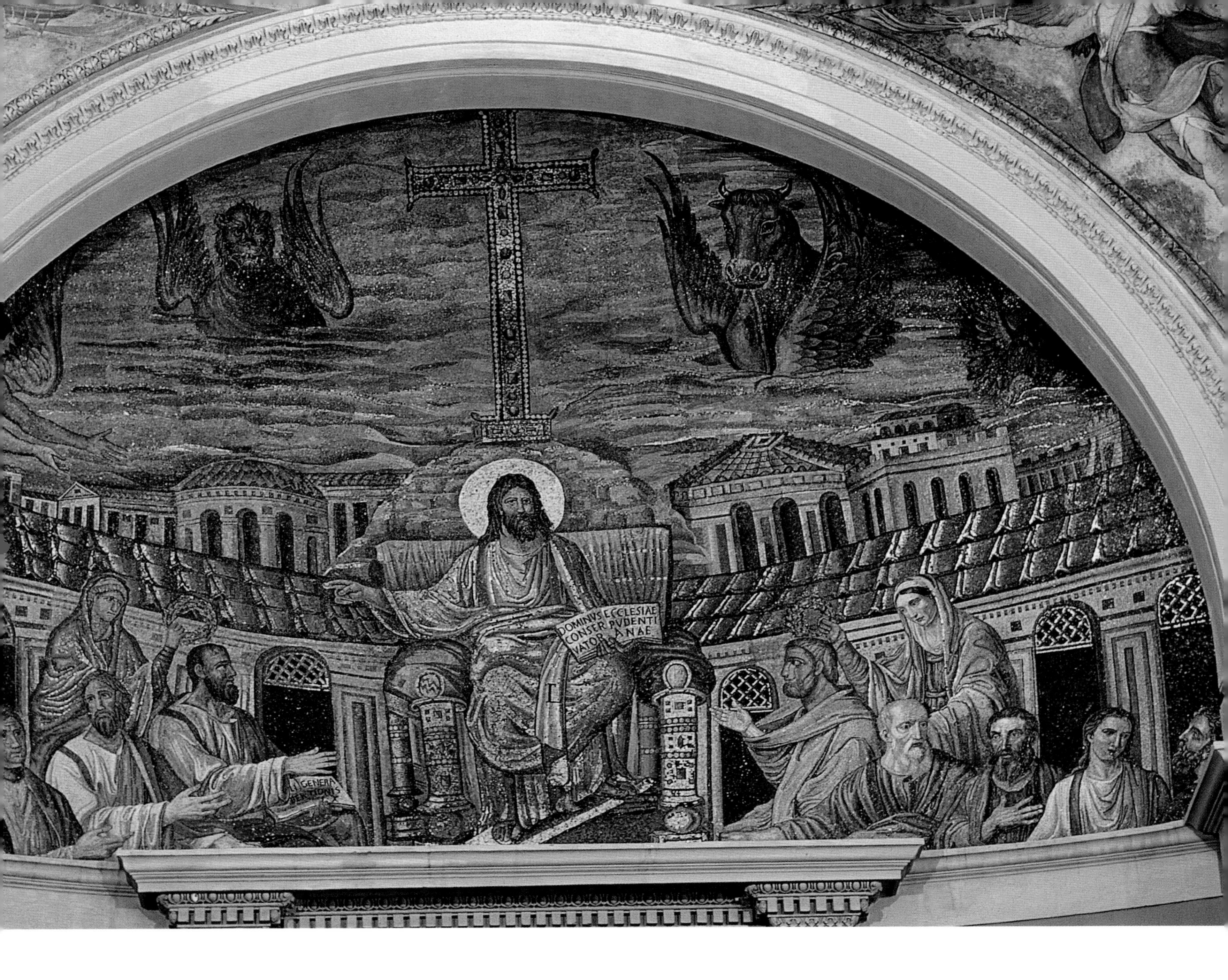

Christ in majesty
390–401/417
Mosaic
Rome, Basilica of Santa Pudentiana, apse

In 381, the divinity of Christ was solemnly reaffirmed at the Council of Constantinople. Iconography shows him as the ruler of the universe, at the place of honor, above the Emperor: he is seated here on a monumental throne of gold set with precious stones. Jesus presents an open book in his left hand, which proclaims: *Dominus Conservator ecclesiae Pudentianae*, "The Lord and Savior of the assembly of Saint Pudentiana." This is a far cry from the kind shepherd, all meek and humble, of earlier depictions.

According to the Acts of the Apostles (which is the continuation of the Gospel according to Saint Luke), fifty days after Easter, the twelve apostles were gathered with Mary, the Mother of Jesus, probably in the Upper Room. An extraordinary event would conquer their fears and inspire them with astonishing zeal to go out on missions. This was in effect the birth of the Church founded by Jesus.

Jesus sends the Paraclete

Simon Marmion (*ca.* 1425–1489) was a painter attached to the court of the Dukes of Bourgogne Philip III the Good (1396–1467) and then Charles the Bold (1433–1477). Famous in his time, he was one of the most eminent representatives of the Flemish primitives. He is known above all for his exceptional talent as a miniaturist, as witnessed by this illustration from a Book of Hours.

The Book of Hours, a sort of breviary for lay people, proposes times for prayer, modeled on the monastic offices, for well-defined hours of the day: usually Lauds in the morning, None at midday, Vespers at 5:00 in the afternoon, and Compline upon retiring. No two medieval books of hours contain exactly the same prayers; they depend on the geographic origin of the copyist's workshop and even more on the local rites, since the Roman liturgy had not been adopted in all dioceses until after the Council of Trent (1545–1563).

To paint this miniature, the workshop of Simon Marmion utilized a technique that photographers would popularize many centuries later, the so-called "close-up": the artist frames the figures on Pentecost from a nearby vantage point, flattening the perspective and the distances between the apostles, who are crowded against each other, thus signifying the unity of the members of the Church in *one body* (Rom 12:5). The procedure tends to associate the spectator with them, and by placing Mary at the center of this unity, the artist confirms that this body made up of baptized persons united in the communion of the Holy Spirit is indeed the body of Jesus that she brought into the world. This is precisely why Mary, unlike the apostles, is not turned toward the Holy Spirit: he already came down on her three decades before, at the moment of the Annunciation. In the foreground we recognize Peter, who is already aged, by his grizzled hair, and John, the young beardless man.

According to the Acts of the Apostles, after this event, which took place fifty days after Easter, during the Jewish feast of Pentecost, the disciples of Jesus, headed by Peter, set out to announce in all Jerusalem, then throughout the Roman Empire, the "Good News" (*evaggelion*, Greek for Gospel) of the Resurrection of Jesus. ■

THE BIBLE – ACTS 2:2-8

And suddenly a sound came from heaven like the rush of a mighty wind, and it filled all the house where they were sitting. And there appeared to them tongues as of fire, distributed and resting on each one of them. And they were all filled with the Holy Spirit and began to speak in other tongues as the Spirit gave them utterance. Now there were dwelling in Jerusalem Jews, devout men from every nation under heaven. And at the sound the multitude came together, and they were bewildered, because each one heard them speaking in his own language. And they were amazed and wondered, saying, "Are not all these who are speaking Galileans? And how is it that we hear, each of us in his own native language?"

Pentecost
Studio of Simon Marmion (*ca.* 1425–1489)
1485–1490
Illumination on parchment, 5.9 x 4.1 in
London, British Library, *Huth Book of Hours*,
ms. add. 38126, f° 45 v°

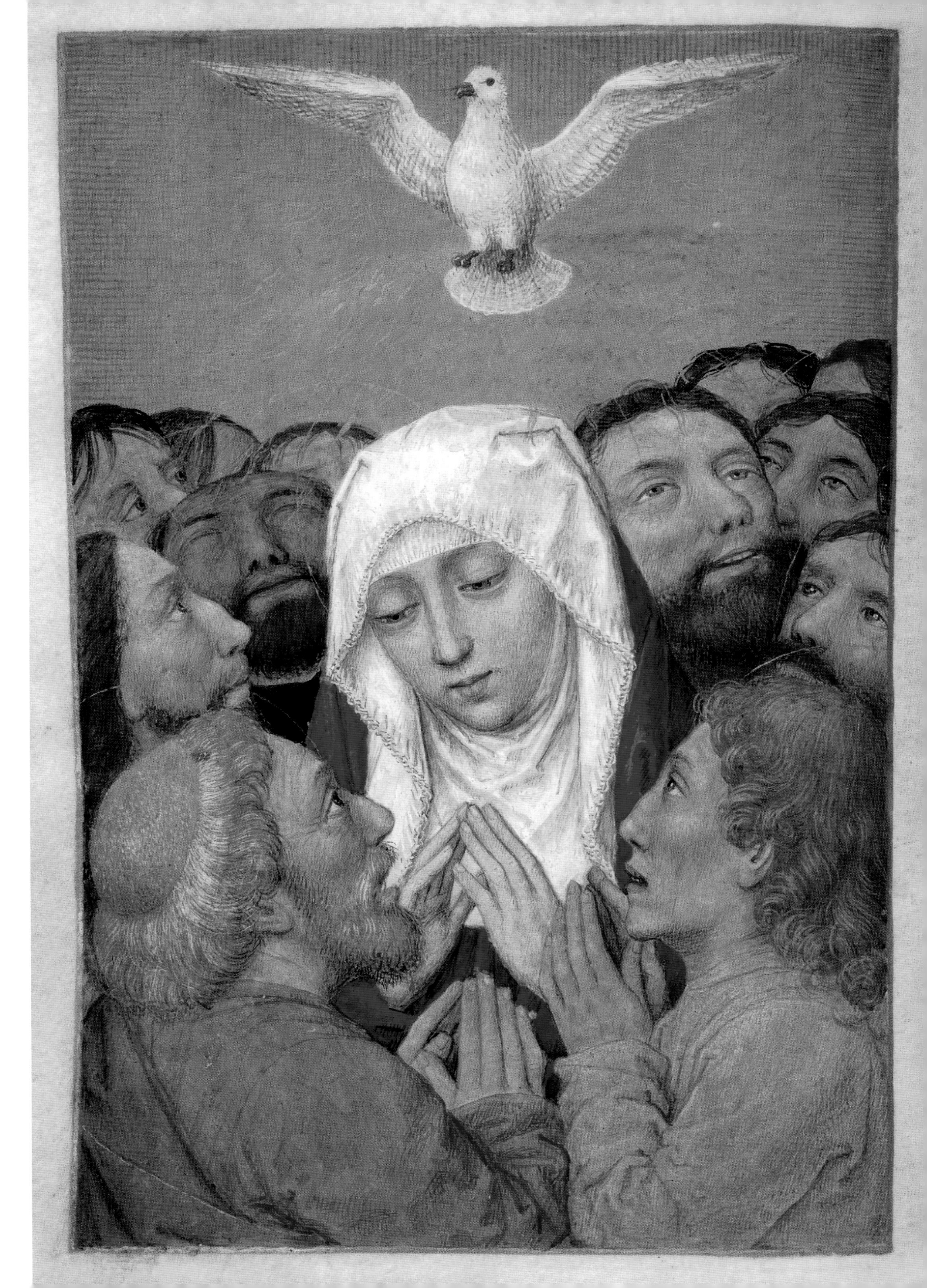

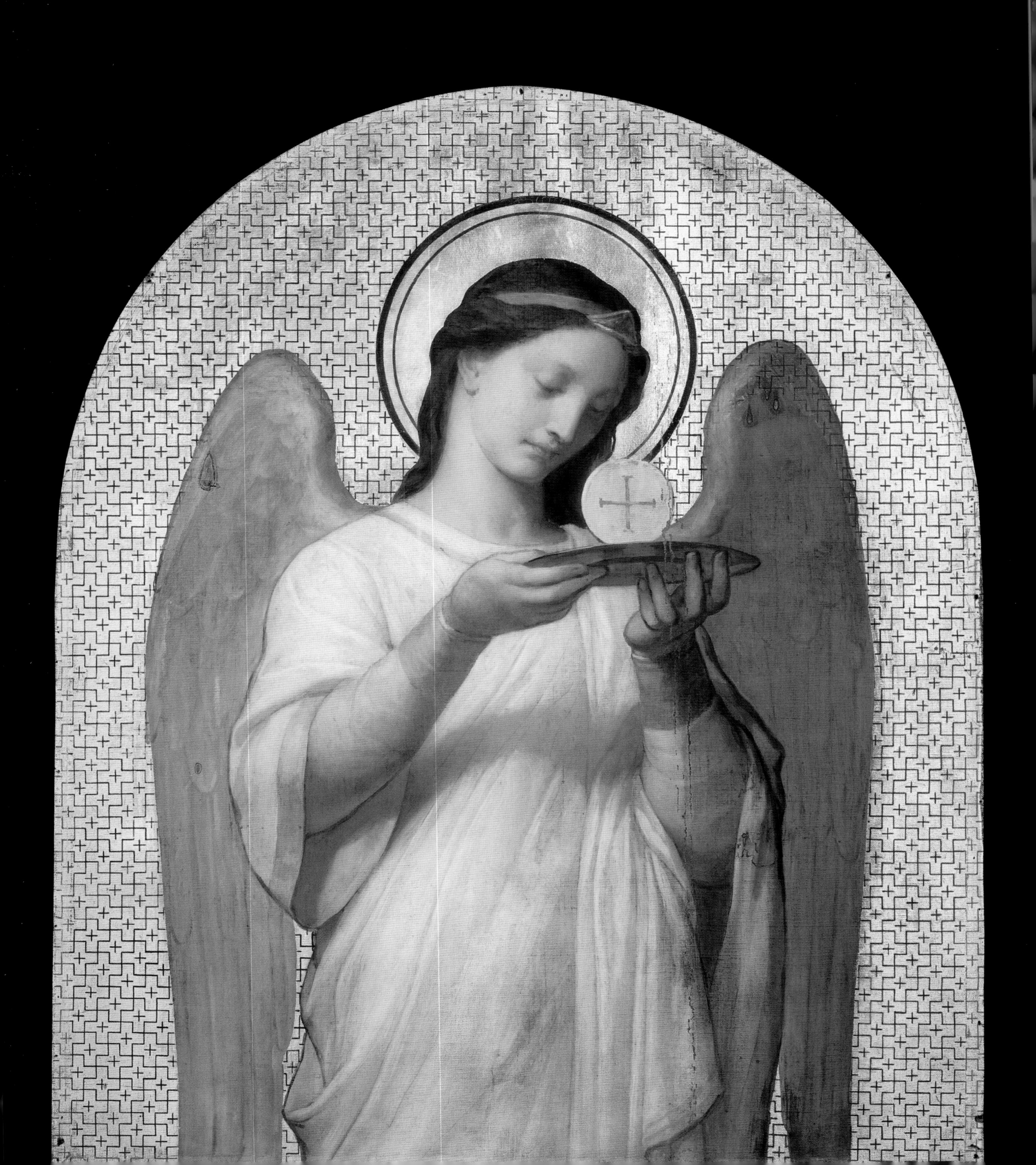

Jesus hidden in a mouthful of bread

The Acts of the Apostles and the letters of Saint Paul attest that the sharing of the Eucharistic bread and wine, which is inseparable from faith in the real presence of Jesus under these appearances, goes back to the very beginning of the Church. It would even seem that these weekly Sunday gatherings around this sharing are what made the Church.

The Élysée Palace became the official residence of the President of the French Republic by a law dated December 12, 1848—a statute that was confirmed with the proclamation of the Third Republic on September 4, 1870. On December 20, 1848, Prince-President Louis-Napoleon, the future Emperor Napoleon III, moved into it. He ordered sumptuous remodeling projects and, in particular, erected in it a richly decorated chapel.

A century later, in 1947, French President Vincent Auriol had this chapel closed so as to replace it with two offices, and the paintings that adorned it were transferred to the Louvre Museum. However, in 1959, when Charles de Gaulle became the 18th President of the French Republic, he reconverted one of those offices into a very simple chapel. A fervent Catholic, the General faithfully came to pray there and to attend Mass, often celebrated by his nephew Father François de Gaulle. Finally, in 2007, President Nicolas Sarkozy definitively closed the chapel so as to convert it into a waiting room for his visitors.

The chapel had been decorated by one of the best students of Jean Auguste Dominique Ingres, Sébastien Melchior Cornu (1804–1870). This *Angel holding a host* was originally placed above one of the two doors. It recalls the *Lauda Sion*, the sequence (chanted poem) written by Thomas Aquinas for the Feast of Corpus Christi in honor of the Blessed Sacrament: "Behold, the bread of angels has become the food of wayfarers." This motif was thus a reminder about the necessary viaticum (food for the journey) for those who after their devotions were returning to their worldly business. Just as during their travels in the Sinai Desert the Hebrews had been fed by manna, the *bread of angels* (Ps 78:25), so too along their earthly pilgrimage those who have become children of God through Baptism are nourished by *the living bread which came down from heaven* (Jn 6:51). But the cross traced on the host underscores an essential difference: although the manna sustained life that remained perishable, the true bread of Christians sustains a life that will spring up again in "eternal life," because it makes them members of the body of the risen Jesus. ■

THE BIBLE – JN 6:53-56

Jesus said to them, "Truly, truly, I say to you, unless you eat the flesh of the Son of man and drink his blood, you have no life in you; he who eats my flesh and drinks my blood has eternal life, and I will raise him up at the last day. For my flesh is food indeed, and my blood is drink indeed. He who eats my flesh and drinks my blood abides in me, and I in him."

Angel holding a host
Sébastien Melchior Cornu (1804–1870)
1864
Oil on canvas, 42.5 x 35 in
Paris, Louvre Museum

In the *Pensées*, according to a Christian theology inherited from the Prophet Isaiah, among others, Blaise Pascal richly develops the theme of the "hidden God," in other words, the humble God of paradoxical power, who does not impose himself on man but allows himself to be discovered by the faithful heart. During his earthly life, Jesus enduring his Passion is the expression par excellence of the hidden God. But Christians believe that in the consecrated bread, which is the body of Jesus, God continues to give himself to human beings in a veiled manner. This is the topic of this passage from a letter to Mademoiselle de Roannez.

Blaise Pascal, *Thoughts, Letters and Minor Works,* The Harvard Classics 48 (New York: P. F. Collier & Son Company, 1938), p. 354.

A God hidden in a piece of bread

BLAISE PASCAL

If God discovered [*i.e.* uncovered, revealed] himself continually to men, there would be no merit in believing him; and, if he never discovered himself, there would be little faith. But he conceals himself ordinarily and discovers himself rarely to those whom he wishes to engage in his service. This strange secrecy, in which God is impenetrably withdrawn from the sight of men, is a great lesson to betake ourselves to solitude far from the sight of men. He remained concealed under the veil of the nature that covers him till the Incarnation; and when it was necessary that he should appear, he concealed himself still the more in covering himself with humanity. He was much more recognizable when he was invisible than when he rendered himself visible. And in fine, when he wished to fulfill the promise that he made to his apostles to remain with men until his final coming, he chose to remain in the strangest and most obscure secret of all, which are the species of the Eucharist. It is this sacrament that St. John calls in the Apocalypse a concealed manner; and I believe that Isaiah saw It in that state, when he said in the spirit of prophecy: *Truly thou art a God concealed.* This is the last secrecy wherein he can be.... All things cover some mystery; all things have veils that cover God. Christians ought to recognize him in every thing. Temporal afflictions cover eternal goods to which they lead. Temporal joys cover eternal ills that they cause. Let us pray God to make us recognize and serve him in every thing; let us give him countless thanks that, having concealed himself in all things for others, he has discovered himself in all things and in so many ways for us.

Angel holding a chalice
Sébastien Melchior Cornu (1804–1870)
1864
Oil on canvas, 41 x 34 in
Paris, Louvre Museum

This picture was the counterpart of the *Angel holding a host* in the decoration of the chapel of the Élysée Palace.

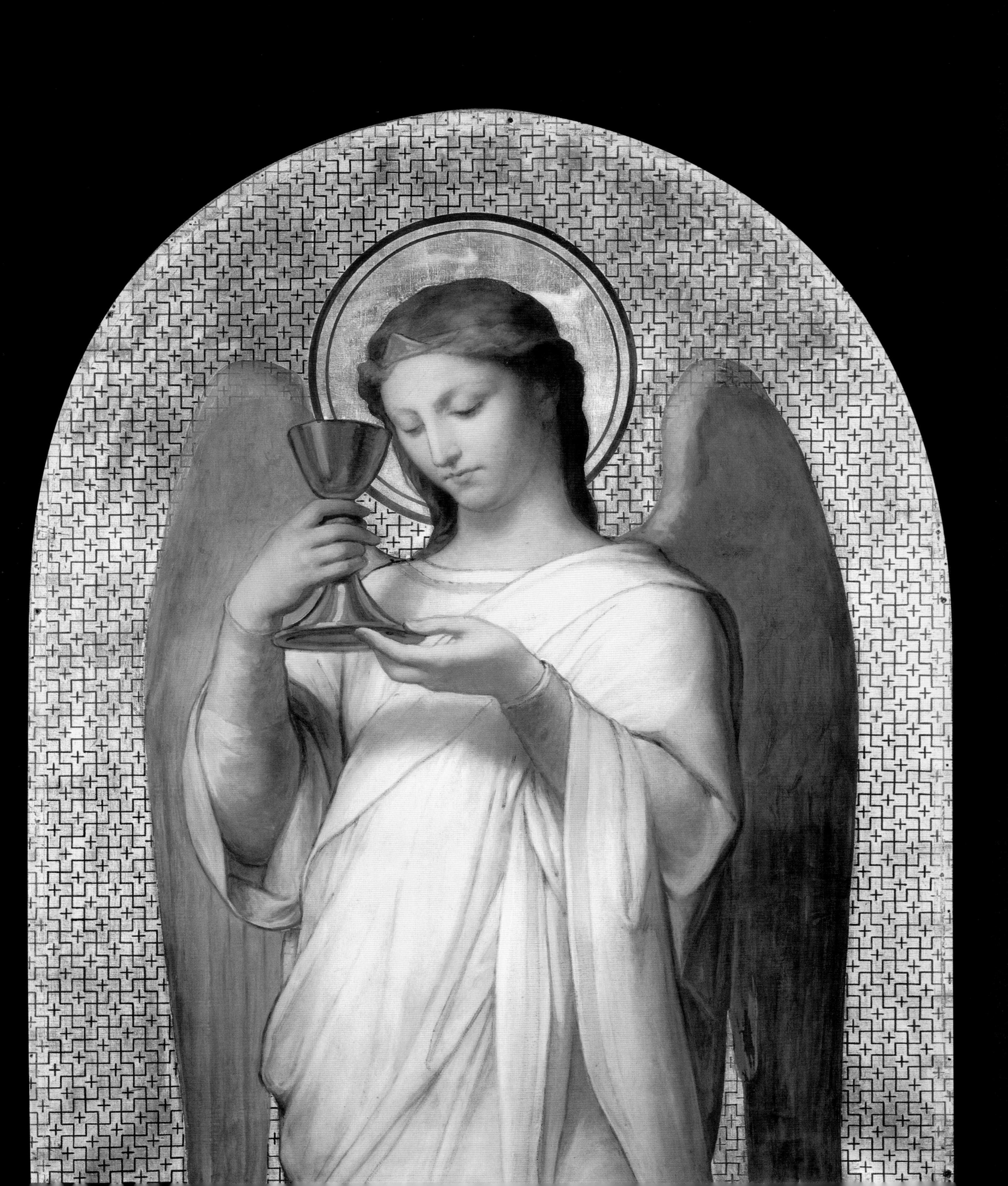

Although the primacy of the Apostle Peter in the service of the Church is explicit in the Gospel, the special vocation of Paul comes in later. To tell the truth, this Jew affiliated with the Pharisees and nevertheless a Roman citizen was not personally acquainted with Jesus and was initially a virulent persecutor of the first Christians. After his sudden conversion on the road to Damascus, though, Paul put so much zeal into his work of evangelizing that he too is considered an apostle, an "envoy."

Jesus hidden in his Church

The iconography of Saint Peter and Saint Paul goes back to early Christian art. Inseparable, they already appear together on the frescos of the Roman catacombs, sarcophagi, and objects used in worship dating from the early fourth century. Peter was called by Jesus himself, and he appears as the "first" of the apostles in the Gospels. Paul, for his part, though not part of the circle of the Twelve, was nonetheless "called" by the risen Jesus during an apparition. And he played a decisive role in the first decades of the Church; he was recognized as the "Apostle to the Gentiles."

Together Peter and Paul founded the Church of Rome, the capital of the Roman Empire, where they died as martyrs around the year 65, during the reign of Nero. Impelled by these two evangelists and organizers, the Church that Jesus had founded was already expanding rapidly only thirty years or so after his death. It had opened its doors to the pagans, and those who were now called "Christians" formed communities that often played an important role in the major urban centers of the Empire. Saint Peter and Saint Paul have an altogether exceptional status in the Church: the Byzantine hymnography for their liturgical feast (June 29) grants them the title of "supreme apostles," and the Latin tradition calls them "the two pillars of the Church."

The origin of the depiction of the two apostles holding a model of a church building goes back to the early post-Byzantine period, in other words after Constantinople, capital of the Byzantine Empire, fell in 1453 under the dominion of Islam. The oldest icons of this type probably come from Crete, at that time a possession of the Republic of Venice. The works of the Cretan masters were in demand both by the Orthodox and by Catholics who followed the so-called "Greek" (*maniera greca*) or Italian (*maniera latina*) Byzantine style. The career of the Spanish painter El Greco (1541–1614), who was born on Crete and trained in Venice then in Rome before pursuing his career in Madrid

THE BIBLE – ACTS 15:1-12

But some men came down from Judea and were teaching the brethren, "Unless you are circumcised according to the custom of Moses, you cannot be saved." And when Paul and Barnabas had no small dissension and debate with them, Paul and Barnabas and some of the others were appointed to go up to Jerusalem to the apostles and the elders about this question.... When they came to Jerusalem, they were welcomed by the Church and the apostles and the elders, and they declared all that God had done with them. But some believers who belonged to the party of the Pharisees rose up, and said, "It is necessary to circumcise them, and to charge them to keep the law of Moses." The apostles and the elders were gathered together to consider this matter. And after there had been much debate, Peter rose and said to them, "Brethren, you know that in the early days God made choice among you, that by my mouth the Gentiles should hear the word of the gospel and believe. And God who knows the heart bore witness to them, giving them the Holy Spirit just as he did to us...." And all the assembly kept silence; and they listened to Barnabas and Paul as they related what signs and wonders God had done through them among the Gentiles.

The Holy Apostles Peter and Paul
Cretan school
Second half of the 16th century
Tempera and golden background on larch wood, 22 x 17 in
Paris, Louvre Museum

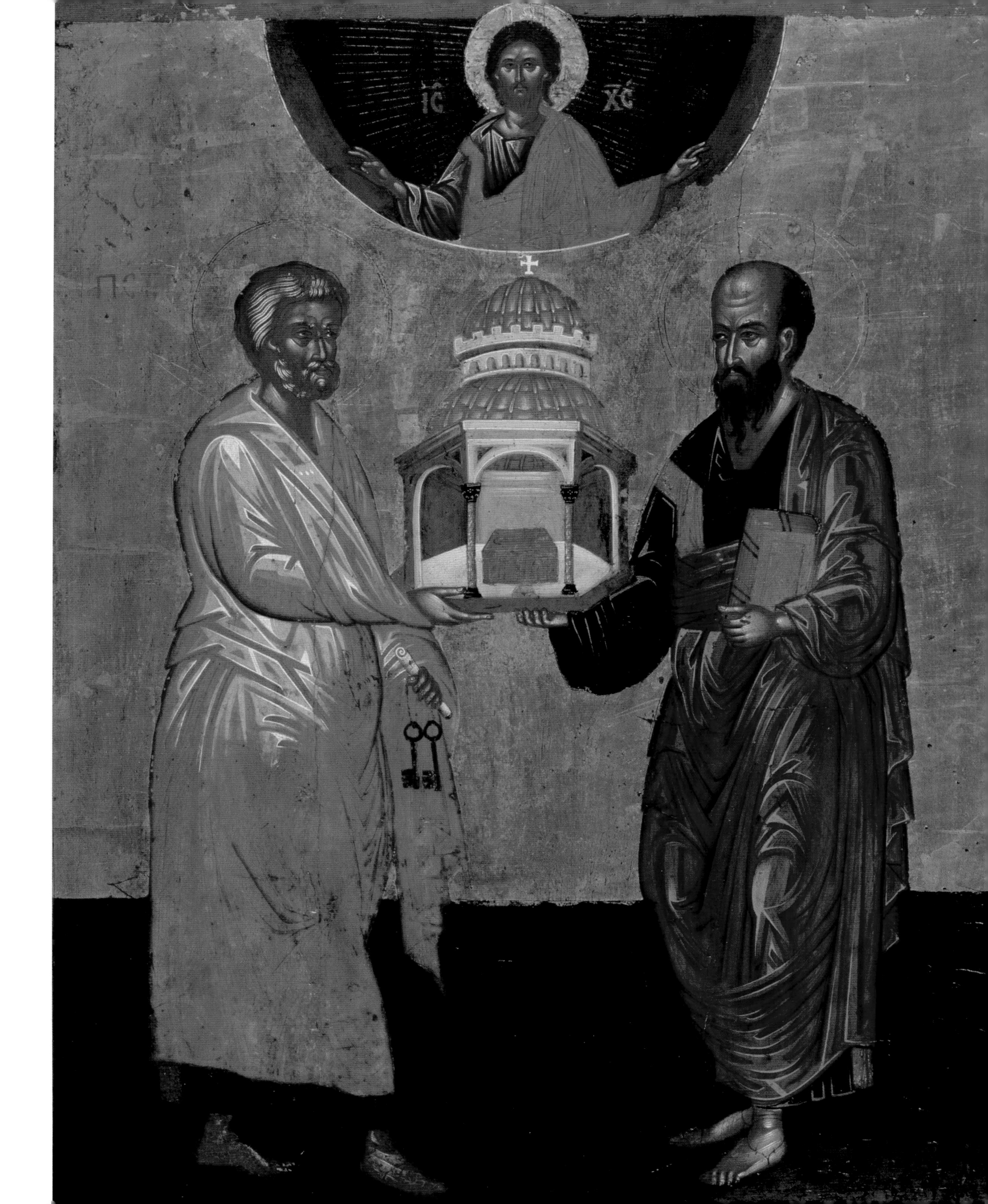
IC
XC

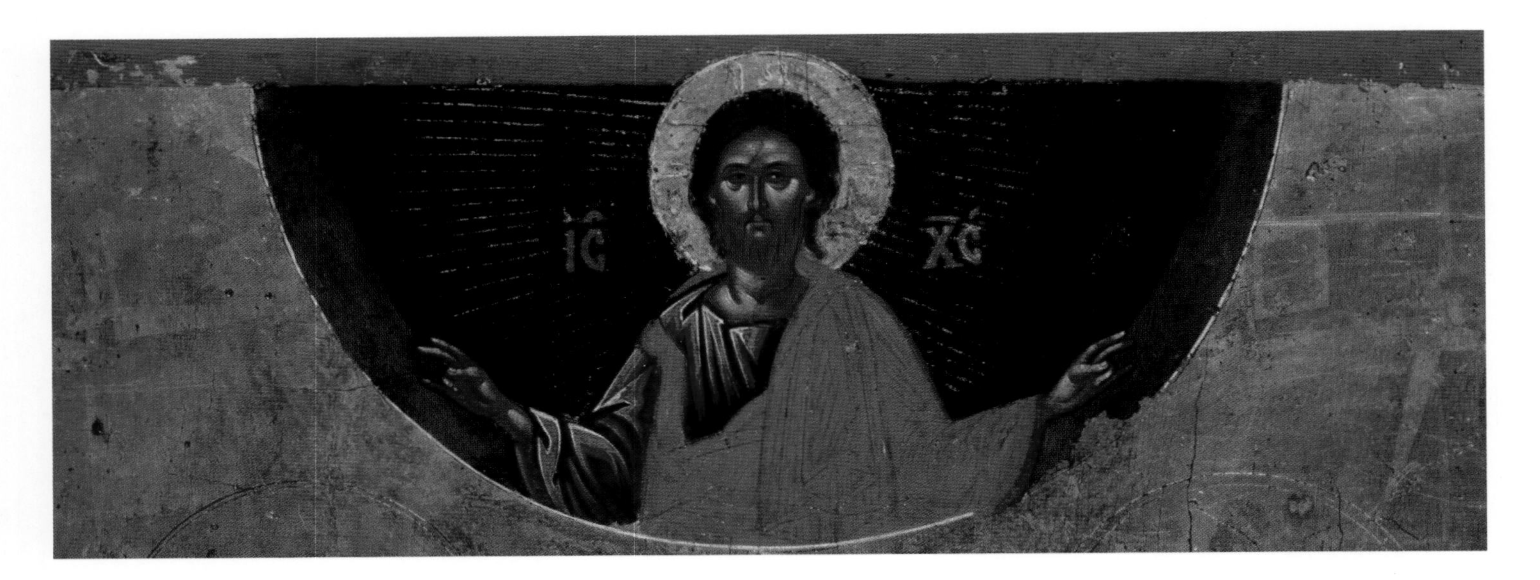

The Holy Apostles Peter and Paul, detail
Cretan school
Second half of the 16th century
Tempera and golden background on larch wood, 22 x 17 in
Paris, Louvre Museum

and Toledo, testifies to the vitality of the cultural exchanges between Crete and the West by way of *La Serenissima* [the Republic of Venice] at that time.

The icon of the Holy Apostles Peter and Paul is clearly an example of the Greek style. Saint Peter holds in his left hand a set of keys, sign of the "keys to the kingdom of heaven" that Jesus entrusted to him (cf. Mt 16:19). He also holds a scroll that symbolizes the two short letters he addressed to Christian communities that were recorded in the New Testament. Beside him, Saint Paul holds a book, which indicates the abundance of his epistolary production (his "Epistles"). The two apostles support a church building that obviously symbolizes the Church founded by Jesus; their responsibility is to build it up. The fact that they carry the building at arm's length indicates that Church history is not destined to flow like a long, tranquil river. Depicted in the style of a Byzantine basilica, it includes a narthex, an open portico where the non-baptized are welcomed, in particular the catechumens being instructed with a view to their baptism and integration into the community. In the early basilicas, that was where the baptistries were set up, since only baptized persons were admitted to the interior of the building. On some icons from the 17th and 18th centuries, variations on the same theme, we can discern, within the church this time, an altar or a chalice: this signifies that the Eucharist and the liturgy in general are the foundation and heart of the Church.

The semi-circle forming heaven at the top of the icon has a "theophanic" dimension; in other words, it illustrates a manifestation of God during a historical event, making visible what is invisible yet quite present in the course of the world. Here, Jesus is shown clothed in a golden cloak (he is in glory) and a purple robe (he is the Lord), extending his arms to indicate that he takes up the historical journey of the Church and that he is united with it by a mysterious communion of destiny, in a way that will be fully accomplished at the end of time, when everything will be manifested and the visible universe will meet the invisible universe to merge into it. ■

In this passage from *The Brothers Karamazov* (1880), Dostoyevsky assigns a speech to one of the most remarkable characters in the novel, the *starets* [elder] Zosima, an old monk whom the author presents as a luminous figure of Christian purity and radical love in the middle of a violent, unjust world. Here, the *starets* recalls the fundamental importance for Christians of being united, in response to the commandment of love given by Jesus, who founded the Church upon the gift of his life for everyone. But human beings often do not believe that this union is possible, not even in little things.

Fyodor Dostoyevsky, *The Brothers Karamazov* (1880), translated by Constance Garnett (New York: The Lowell Press, 1930).

The Church, place of the union of all human beings

FYODOR DOSTOYEVSKY

"And can it be a dream, that in the end man will find his joy only in deeds of light and mercy, and not in cruel pleasures as now, in gluttony, fornication, ostentation, boasting and envious rivalry of one with the other? I firmly believe that it is not and that the time is at hand. People laugh and ask: 'When will that time come and does it look like coming?' I believe that with Christ's help we shall accomplish this great thing. And how many ideas there have been on earth in the history of man which were unthinkable ten years before they appeared! Yet when their destined hour had come, they came forth and spread over the whole earth. So it will be with us, and our people will shine forth in the world, and all men will say: 'The stone which the builders rejected has become the corner stone of the building.'

"And we may ask the scornful themselves: If our hope is a dream, when will you build up your edifice and order things justly by your intellect alone, without Christ? If they declare that it is they who are advancing towards unity, only the most simple-hearted among them believe it, so that one may positively marvel at such simplicity. Of a truth, they have more fantastic dreams than we. They aim at justice, but, denying Christ, they will end by flooding the earth with blood, for blood cries out for blood, and he that taketh up the sword shall perish by the sword. And if it were not for Christ's covenant, they would slaughter one another down to the last two men on earth. And those two last men would not be able to restrain each other in their pride, and the one would slay the other and then himself. And that would come to pass, were it not for the promise of Christ that for the sake of the humble and meek the days shall be shortened.

"While I was still wearing an officer's uniform after my duel, I talked about servants in general society, and I remember everyone was amazed at me. 'What!' they asked, 'are we to make our servants sit down on the sofa and offer them tea?' And I answered them: 'Why not, sometimes at least?' Every one laughed."

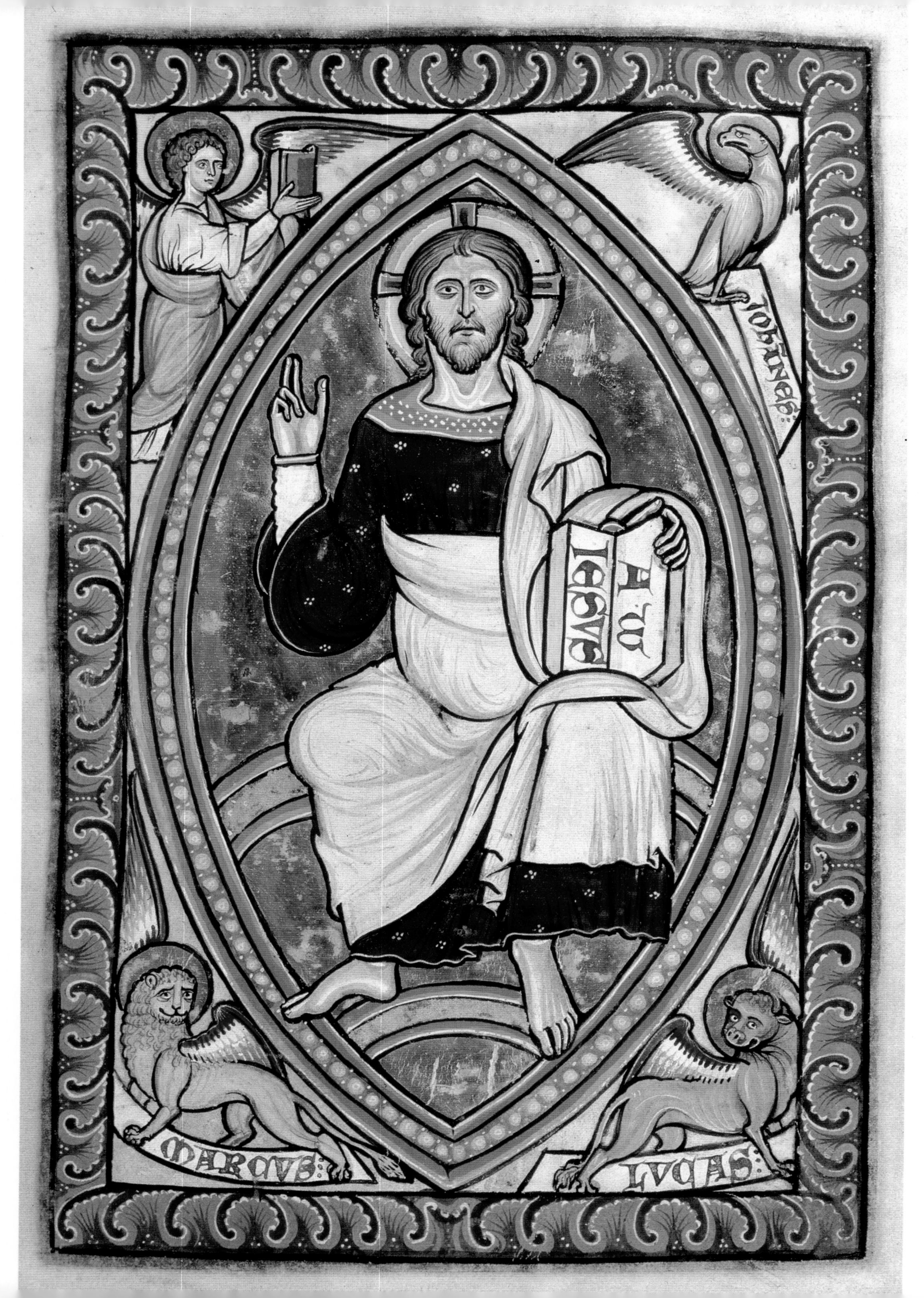
A ω
IESVS
IOHĀNES
MARCVS
LVCAS

Jesus hidden in his Word

In the last book of the Bible—The Apocalypse, which means "revelation"—Saint John bears witness to a "vision" that he received, about the end of time and humanity's definitive entry into God's eternity. This vision describes in particular a throne set up in heaven, around which four winged living creatures stand: a lion, an ox, a man, and an eagle. Christian tradition sees them as symbols of the four evangelists.

Jesus in majesty, the Alpha and the Omega of human history, appears here in a *mandorla*, which reveals the presence of God. At the corners of the image the four evangelists are depicted, those whose testimonies unceasingly nourish the faith of *those who believe without having seen* (Jn 20:29) and, as this illumination shows, make Jesus present through his Word. These *four living creatures* (Rv 4:6) who proclaim the Gospel to the *four winds of the earth* (Rv 7:1), in other words to the cardinal points of the compass, are depicted allegorically by figures taken from the visions of Ezekiel (Ez 1:5-14) in the Old Testament and from John (Rv. 4:7-8) at the end of the New. This *tetramorph* ("fourfold form") is usually explained as follows, referring to the first verses of each of the four Gospels: the man represents Matthew, who gives the human genealogy of Jesus; the lion represents Mark, because the Gospel according to Mark starts in the wilderness; the ox represents Luke, who opens his account with the priest Zechariah offering a sacrifice in the Temple in Jerusalem; finally, the eagle represents John because his prologue reaches dizzying mystical heights.

However, there are multiple interpretations, and each of these four *living creatures* also represents the allegory for a mystery from the life of Jesus, the Living One par excellence: then the man is said to represent the Incarnation; the lion—the temptations in the desert and the beginning of the public life; the ox—the sacrifice on the Cross; the eagle—the Resurrection and Ascension. Finally, each figure supposedly reveals an aspect, one of the dimensions of the person of Jesus: thus the man is said to represent the Messiah, New Moses and "son" (descendent) of David; the lion—Christ the King; the ox—both the priest and the offering; the eagle—the Second Person of the Trinity who descended from heaven and ascends there again when his earthly mission is accomplished. ■

THE BIBLE – RV 4:6-7

Before the throne there is as it were a sea of glass, like crystal. And round the throne, on each side of the throne, are four living creatures, full of eyes in front and behind: the first living creature like a lion, the second living creature like an ox, the third living creature with the face of a man, and the fourth living creature like a flying eagle.

Christ in majesty with the symbols of the four evangelists
Ca. 1200–1250
Illumination on parchment, 9 x 6.1 in
London, British Library, *Westminster Psalter*
Royal ms. 2A XXII, f° 14 r°

The last verse of the Gospel according to Saint Matthew relates that just before leaving this world, Jesus promised: *Behold, I am with you always, to the close of the age* (Mt 28:20). Christians firmly believe that the "hidden" Jesus remains really present in their midst, among them, particularly when they gather to pray, and *a fortiori* to bless a family meal.

Jesus hidden at the heart of our lives

After a stay in Paris to study in 1879, the painter Fritz von Uhde (1848–1911) was more than ever a realist and impressionist. Nevertheless, he claimed to remain an idealist without seeing any contradiction in that. He said: "Many French artists seek the light in nature. I want to find the light in the figure that I present. In the person of Christ, I grasp at the same time the incarnation on the outside [the natural reality] and the interior light [an idea of beauty]." He claimed to be "the first idealist of naturalism." In the art of painting, certainly, he was. In literature, he had been preceded slightly by the mature Dostoyevsky (1821–1881), a realist and even naturalist novelist, if there was such a thing, yet for whom, as for Uhde, the reference point for the Beautiful, the True, and the Good was the figure of Jesus.

Again I say to you, if two of you agree on earth about anything they ask, it will be done for them by my Father in heaven. For where two or three are gathered in my name, there am I in the midst of them.

THE BIBLE - MT 18:19-20

In this idealist spirit, von Uhde liked to paint, in a naturalist framework and with an impressionist technique, a Jesus who is a companion of the poor, of peasants and Christian families, living among them and sharing their activities. Here, he brings the spectator into the simple, dignified dining room of a family of peasants. The scene captures the moment just before the meal, when everyone stands at his place for the blessing of the food and to say grace. In the foreground we see a figure more imposing than the others, with long hair and dressed like a vagabond, whom a discreet halo designates as being Jesus. He extends his right hand over the table and blesses it. The mother of the family and one of the children contemplate this person; their faces are gently illumined by the faint light that emanates from him. The father of the family, the oldest of the children, and the grandmother are recollected. The youngest, his arms crossed, is on his best behavior, but behind his bangs we can see his eyes wide open to observe the guest.

This work testifies to a tradition, very much alive then among the European peasantry, of reserving the place of honor at table at the noon meal every Sunday for a needy person: this was "the poor man's place." And the tradition also prescribed that the guest be asked to bless the meal, whereas that duty usually fell to the father, head of the family. This was because even if the poor person was simple, vulgar, or even frankly repellent, everyone knew that it was Jesus himself who was invited to the meal. ■

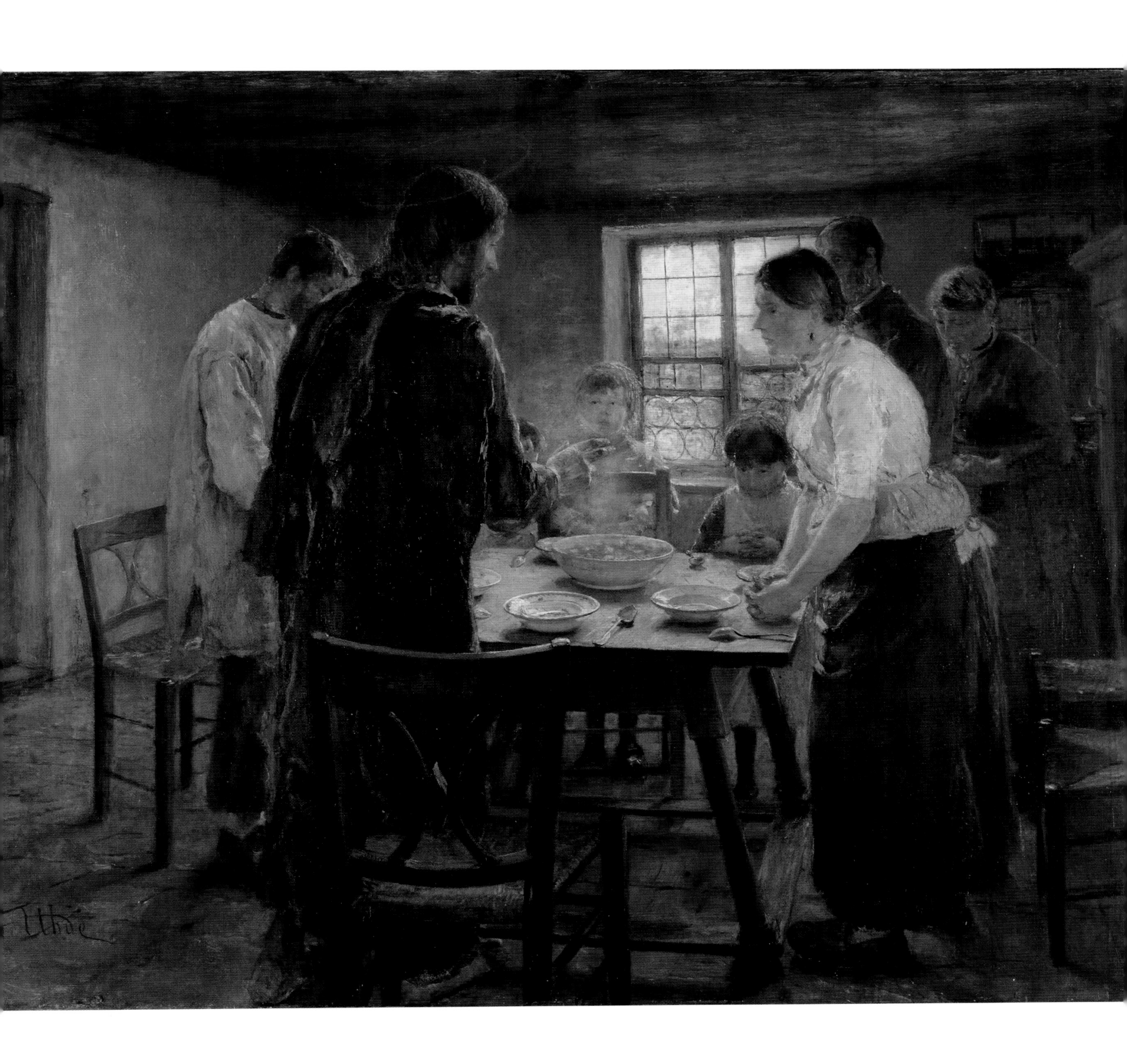

Christ among the peasants
Fritz von Uhde (1848–1911)
1887–1888
Oil on wood, 20 x 24 in
Paris, Orsay Museum

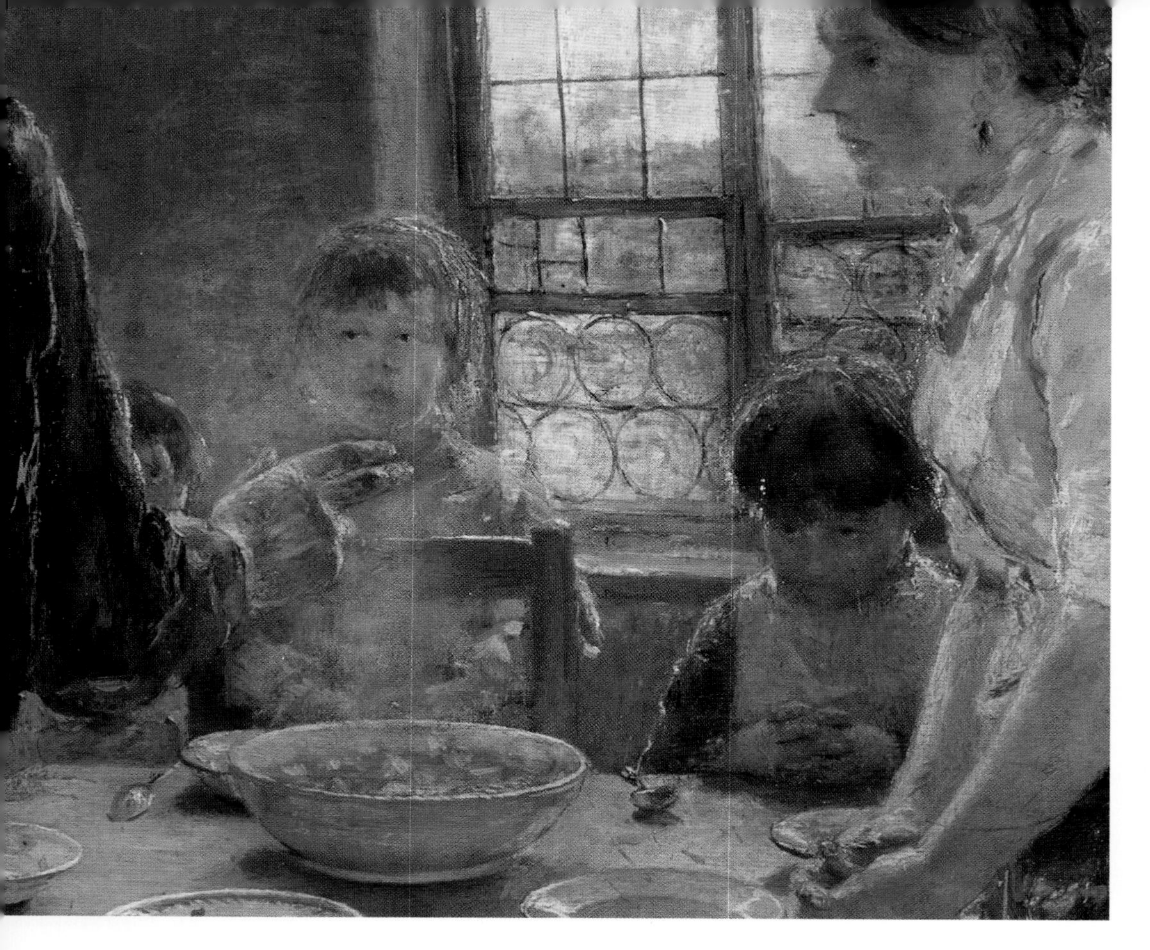

Christ among the peasants, detail
Fritz von Uhde (1848–1911)
1887–1888
Oil on wood, 20 x 24 in
Paris, Orsay Museum

THE CONTEMPORARY CHRIST OF FRITZ VON UHDE

Fritz von Uhde (1848–1911) came from a family that was heavily committed to practicing the Lutheran faith. He studied first in Dresden and Munich, and then undertook a trip to Paris to complete his training. Besides many genre scenes testifying to his fascination with the Northern schools, he was among the first in Germany to introduce open-air painting in the style of the French impressionists. With his friend Max Liebermann he formed the German counterpart of French naturalism and impressionism and participated in the important venture of the German review of art and literature *Pan*, which promoted innovative ideas.

In 1892, Fritz von Uhde was one of the founders of the Munich "Secession" together with Max Slevogt and Lovis Corinth, then a member of the Berlin Secession. Thus, von Uhde and his acolytes followed in the footsteps of the French National Society of Fine Arts, founded in 1861, which immediately became a model in a Europe that had grown weary of all sorts of conservatism.

These secessions everywhere institutionalized a new artistic approach typical of the salons that had emancipated themselves from custom and showed instead works by European painters and amateurs who circulated and advocated these ideas. This international model of free aesthetics promoted by Fritz von Uhde foretold a cosmopolitan tone but was nonetheless part of a movement to build national identities.

As a modernist, Fritz von Uhde was suspected of internationalism, but by reorienting his sensibility, in the same movement he directed his painting toward a socially conscious art with a Christian inspiration. He is particularly well known for transposing scenes from the life of Christ to contemporary peasant and working-class settings.

Like Jean-François Millet before him and like his contemporary Vincent Van Gogh, he painted the simple people, those of modest means, peasants, laborers, fishermen, and in every instance notes their dignity. But von Uhde goes even further than Millet and Van Gogh by literally transposing Christ so as to root him in a contemporary reality. The presence of Christ among the humblest persons expresses a thirst for justice. Whereas Christ proclaimed that his kingdom was not of this world, von Uhde claims the justice of the Kingdom for his own time. This moral aspiration of von Uhde explains why conservative Christian circles kept their distance from his work.

Nevertheless, von Uhde is part of an historical context proper to the 19th century. David Friedrich Strauss in Germany and Ernest Renan in France published in 1835 and 1863 respectively two reinterpretations of the life of Christ emptied of its divine substance. Soon, in the domain of the arts, painters would be able to reevaluate the figure of Christ by "contemporizing" it, at the risk of making Christ appear more immanent than transcendent—unless their art succeeded in transcending banality and everyday life.

Art history ascribes to Fritz von Uhde this new tendency that would spread with the help of the exchanges facilitated by the development of the European secessions. The naturalist Christ transposed to a contemporary setting appears subsequently in France in the work of artists such as Léon Lhermitte and Jacques-Émile Blanche.

M. C.

Jacques-Bénigne Bossuet (1627–1704), bishop, preacher, and writer, was one of the great French orators. Very concerned about proclaiming the truth of the Gospel, even in the presence of powerful men whom he often accused of betraying it, Bossuet declares in his sermon "On the Eminent Dignity of the Poor in the Church" that the latter have first place in the Church, not only in heaven but even here below, since in them especially the crucified Jesus continues to live, and everyone should serve and adore him in them.

Jacques-Bénigne Bossuet, "On the Eminent Dignity of the Poor in the Church" (a sermon preached in 1659), translated by Edward R. Udovic, C.M., in *Vincentian Heritage Journal* 13/1 (1992): 37-58, at 47-49, 56.

The majesty of the kingdom of the poor

JACQUES-BÉNIGNE BOSSUET

This city of the poor [built by Christ] is the holy Church, and if you as Christians ask me why I call it the city of the poor, I will tell you the reason that I have for saying this: the Church has been built by divine plan, from its very beginnings, only for the poor. The poor are the true citizens of this blessed city, which is characterized in Scripture as the city of God....

My brothers, isn't this the reason why this same God humbled himself when he said, "I want my house to be full," and then ordered his servants to search out and invite the poor to his banquet? Note the instructions that he gave to his servants: "Go out quickly into the streets and alleys of the town and bring in the poor and the crippled, the blind, and the lame." These are the people who he wanted to come and fill his house. He didn't want to see anyone there who was not weak, because he did not want to invite anyone who did not carry the same burden as he did, that is to say, the weakness of the cross.... This is the reason that the divine psalmist calls them "the poor of God."...

Wasn't it their prerogative to be the people to whom the Savior was sent? As Jesus told us, "he has sent me to bring glad tidings to the poor." Didn't he speak directly to the poor in the sermon on the mount, while condescending to speak to the rich only in order to strike down their pride? "Blessed are you poor, the reign of God is yours."...

The crown of our monarch is a crown of thorns, the brilliance which shines from it are afflictions and sufferings. It is in the poor, and in those who suffer, that the majesty of this spiritual kingdom resides. Jesus himself was poor and indigent; thus, it is proper that he associates with those who are like him, and that he gives his favors to those who share his lot.

For a believer, the formula *the Word was made flesh* (Jn 1:14) found in the prologue to the Gospel according to Saint John allows for no ambiguity: in Jesus Christ, a Christian acknowledges a fully Divine Person who is also fully man. And this certitude of faith leads him to recognize the face of God in every human being.

The face of every human being, a face of God

Rembrandt (1606–1669) never stopped seeking a way to paint the face of Jesus, not by repeating the stereotypes of a tradition, but by having the firm intention to make the true portrait of a living person whom he had really encountered. Do the many faces of Jesus that he painted come from a contemplative image formed in his innermost self? Probably, in some respect. But the inventory he made of his goods includes a *Head of Christ painted from nature*, and to explain this expression, which is at the very least surprising, some authors do not hesitate to declare that Rembrandt had been the beneficiary of apparitions and that, in his studio, "Jesus himself had come to pose." Or, at least, that the artist had experienced the illusion that that was the case.

More probably, Rembrandt could have taken as his models some young rabbis who lived in the Jewish quarter of Amsterdam where his residence was located. For the humanity of Christ and his mysterious closeness to his "brethren" (Mt 25:40), human beings of all times, is what Rembrandt's mystic quest drove him to depict on canvas. The Jesus of this portrait is consistent with the reality of Jesus as a man present in the midst of men, to which Rembrandt wanted to bear witness. At first glance, we take this Jesus for a "neighbor"—a word that acquires a special meaning in Christian terminology (*cf.* p. 144). Everything in his posture, his apparel, his hair style, his way of posing, makes us think of the young Jewish man next door in 17th-century Amsterdam. For a Christian—all the more so if he is close to the evangelical communities, as Rembrandt came to be—Jesus can be encountered, really present in the course of everyday life, in what theologians call "the sacrament of the brother" or "the sacrament of the neighbor," the word "sacrament" being understood as "a visible sign of a hidden reality"—here, the "neighbor," the other, or at Mass the consecrated host—manifesting the real presence of Jesus.

When the Son of man [Jesus] comes in his glory, and all the angels with him, then he will sit on his glorious throne. Then the King will say to those at his right hand, "Come, O blessed of my Father, inherit the kingdom prepared for you from the foundation of the world; for I was hungry and you gave me food, I was thirsty and you gave me drink, I was a stranger and you welcomed me, I was naked and you clothed me, I was sick and you visited me, I was in prison and you came to me." Then the righteous will answer him, "Lord, when did we see you hungry and feed you, or thirsty and give you drink? And when did we see you a stranger and welcome you, or naked and clothe you? And when did we see you sick or in prison and visit you?" And the King will answer them, "Truly, I say to you, as you did it to one of the least of these my brethren, you did it to me."

THE BIBLE – MT 25:31, 34-40

Head of Christ
Rembrandt (1606–1669)
Ca. 1648–1656
Oil on oak wood, 14.1 x 12.3 in
Philadelphia Museum of Art

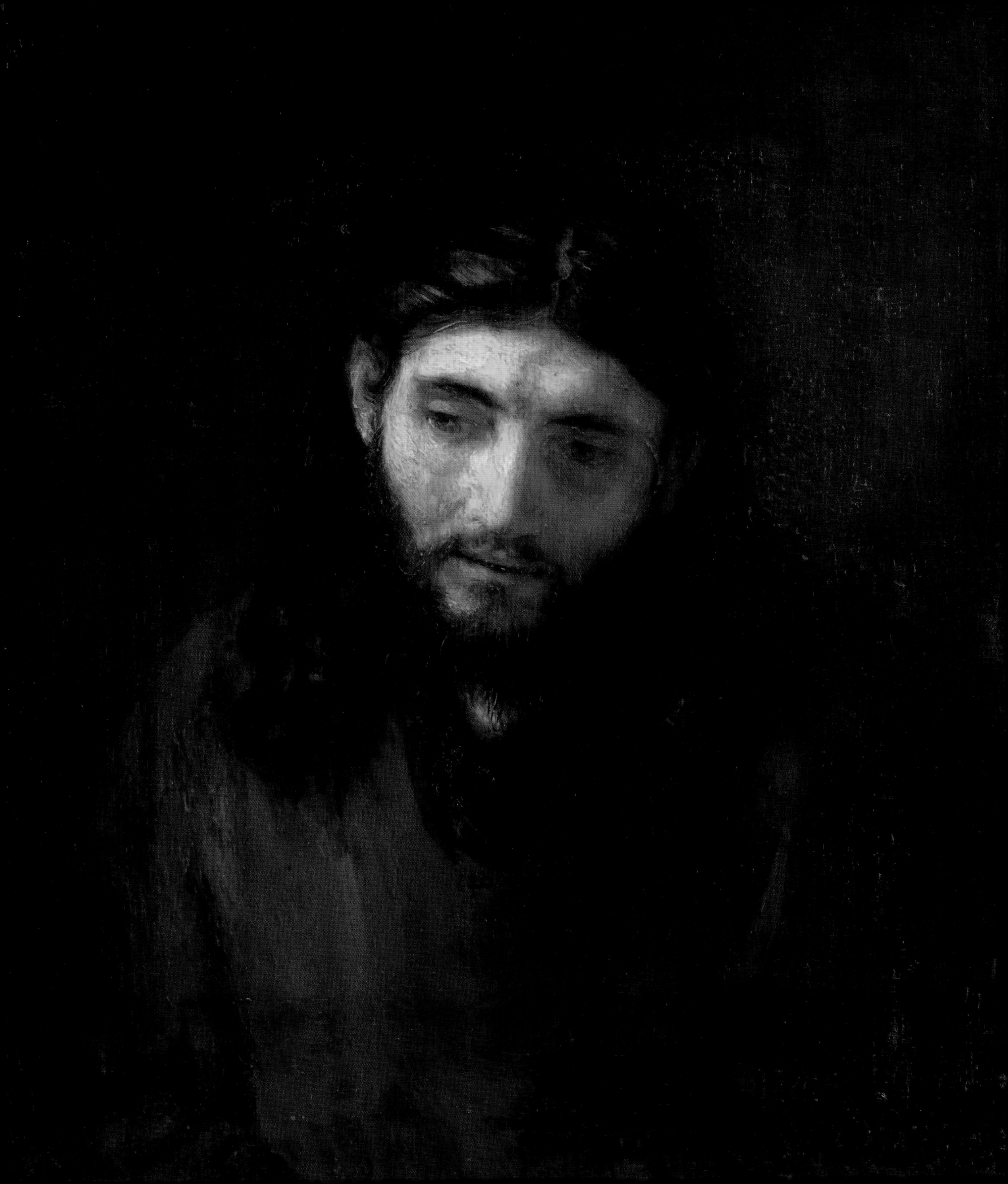

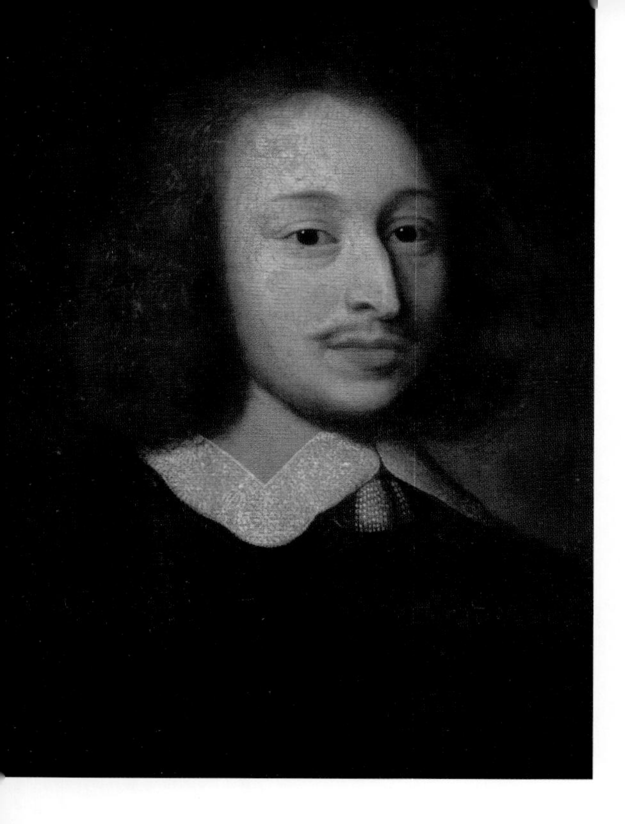

Portrait presumably
of Blaise Pascal
Anonymous
Ca. 1650
Oil on canvas, 23.6 x 19.9 in
Paris, Carnavalet Museum

This "sacramental" consideration is particularly well expressed by another Dutch speaker, Jan Van Ruysbroeck (1293–1381), whose writings were printed during Rembrandt's lifetime. Van Ruysbroeck is the father of *Devotio moderna*, a spiritual approach that puts the emphasis on personal prayer, and a story taken from his hagiography perfectly illustrates this spirituality of the closeness of Jesus. Thus it was reported that one day a monk came to attend the community Mass with a steaming mug of herbal tea, which he did not drink. Van Ruysbroeck, observing this and intrigued, asked him why he had brought it. His answer was: "Because I have to bring this tea to a sick person and take care of him; but 'Milord God is the first to be served,' and so I will go after Mass." Van Ruysbroeck rebuked him, saying: "Go right away to that sick person. The God whom you will find is even more certainly there than the God whom you will leave at Mass."

This certitude that Jesus is present in every human being Providence places along our path is based on Jesus' own words: *"Whatever you do to the least of my human brothers and sisters, you do to me"* (cf. Mt 25:40). This is not a figure of speech but rather a solemn warning, since Jesus made it the sole criterion for the Judgment to which every human being will be subjected at the end of the world. A disciple of Jesus cannot help but believe in it, and Rembrandt was one.

Other great minds of his time testified that they adopted this teaching of the Gospel as their own. Thus, for example, in 1662, a few years after Rembrandt painted this *Head of Christ*, Blaise Pascal, who had entered his agony, asked to receive Viaticum, in other words, to receive Holy Communion, since he believed that the Body of Jesus is really present in the consecrated host. Alas, he was unable to swallow anymore, so the priest did not grant his request. Pascal then found the strength to say: "Go find a poor man in the street and bring him into my room. That way, since I cannot commune with the Head, I will be able to commune with a member of his Body." And so it was done. Likewise, to make this "portrait" of Jesus, Rembrandt most likely went into the street to look for the poor man next door.

Rembrandt lets us contemplate here a face of Jesus that testifies to what he himself experienced of the Lord's presence in his own life. This Jesus is probably the most humanly human that a painter was ever able to render. But in this very quality of his humanity, doesn't Rembrandt succeed in suggesting his faith in his divinity? At the beginning of this work there is the dark brown background that covers the whole canvas. This is the darkness of sin, which submerges all humanity. From the depth of this abyss emerges a gentle light that warms without burning, lights without dazzling, and consoles without condemning. Rembrandt admirably suggests that grace springs up in the midst of sin. Now this divine light that shines in the darkness assumes a face, and what a face! A face that is ours here and now! And also the face of Jesus forever. ■

The Englishman Gilbert Keith Chesterton (1874–1936) studied art as a young man but made his career as a prolific journalist, essayist, novelist, and poet. Through his use of clever wordplay and paradox he offers a fresh perspective on everyday things and startling, profound insights.
The passage is from *The Everlasting Man*, a Christian apologetic which Chesterton wrote in response to H. G. Wells's gloomy *Outline of History*.

G. K. Chesterton, *The Everlasting Man* (London: Hodder & Stoughton, 1925), Part Two, Chapter 6, entitled "The Five Deaths of Faith."

Christianity dying and rising

G.K. CHESTERTON

I have said that Asia and the ancient world had an air of being too old to die. Christendom has had the very opposite fate. Christendom has had a series of revolutions and in each one of them Christianity has died. Christianity has died many times and risen again; for it had a God who knew the way out of the grave. But the first extraordinary fact which marks this history is this: that Europe has been turned upside down over and over again; and that at the end of each of these revolutions the same religion has again been found on top. The Faith is always converting the age, not as an old religion but as a new religion. This truth is hidden from many by a convention that is too little noticed. Curiously enough, it is a convention of the sort which those who ignore it claim especially to detect and denounce. They are always telling us that priests and ceremonies are not religion and that religious organisation can be a hollow sham, but they hardly realise how true it is. It is so true that three or four times at least in the history of Christendom the whole soul seemed to have gone out of Christianity; and almost every man in his heart expected its end. This fact is only masked in medieval and other times by that very official religion which such critics pride themselves on seeing through. Christianity remained the official religion of a Renaissance prince or the official religion of an eighteenth-century bishop, just as an ancient mythology remained the official religion of Julius Caesar or the Arian creed long remained the official religion of Julian the Apostate. But there was a difference between the cases of Julius and of Julian; because the Church had begun its strange career. There was no reason why men like Julius should not worship gods like Jupiter for ever in public and laugh at them for ever in private. But when Julian treated Christianity as dead, he found it had come to life again. He also found, incidentally, that there was not the faintest sign of Jupiter ever coming to life again. This case of Julian and the episode of Arianism is but the first of a series of examples that can only be roughly indicated here. Arianism, as has been said, had every human appearance of being the natural way in which that particular superstition of Constantine might be expected to peter out. All the ordinary stages had been passed through; the creed had become a respectable thing, had become a ritual thing, had then been modified into a rational thing; and the rationalists were ready to dissipate the last remains of it, just as they do to-day. When Christianity rose again suddenly and threw them, it was almost as unexpected as Christ rising from the dead. But there are many other examples of the same thing, even about the same time. The rush of missionaries from Ireland, for instance, has all the air of an unexpected onslaught of young men on an old world, and even on a Church that showed signs of growing old. Some of them were martyred on the coast of Cornwall; and the chief authority on Cornish antiquities told me that he did not believe for a moment that they were martyred by heathens but (as he expressed it with some humour) "by rather slack Christians."

For a long time the prospect of the Last Judgment was expounded in sermons so as to arouse in the faithful a "salutary fear" and to persuade them to lead a life worthy of disciples of Jesus. A number of famous pictures illustrate what was called the "preaching of the Last Things." Thérèse of Lisieux, two years younger than Georges Rouault, who was her devoted admirer, liked to sum up this prospect with a phrase inspired by the poet John of the Cross: "We will be judged on our love."

Jesus hidden in every human being

Rouault was, together with Matisse and Desvallières, one of the most gifted students of Gustave Moreau. In 1936 he produced this print entitled *Christ and Mammon*, plate number 14 of a collection on the Passion. In the Bible, Mammon is the god of money and riches. It is also one of the names of the devilish tempter.

In the middle of the picture, the figure of Jesus dominates. He is situated and designed as an *Ecce homo* [Behold the man]. In contrast to the many Holy Faces that he painted, in which he confers a true personality on the face of Christ, here Rouault gives him generic traits, the features of Mr. or Ms. Everyperson. His colorless garment, with neither drapery nor style, reinforces his anonymity. It could be a child or an old man, a man or a woman. And yet, it is indisputably Jesus himself, an actor in his Passion, that the artist intended to depict right in the center of his print. And we make no mistake in thinking so. He is there, posing as a stranger, in the middle of a group that is unaware of his presence. Or rather, that seems quite determined to ignore him and is perfectly content to do so. Given the obvious statement pronounced by Jesus: *You cannot serve both God and Money* (Mt 6:24), they have clearly made their choice: they have served, are serving, and will serve Money.

The figures in this group are caricatures: the pot-bellied potentate about whom we could prophesy, paraphrasing the fairy tale, that he swelled up so much with his riches that he burst; the haughty blonde woman, radiant with her beauty (which she maintains at such great cost) and with the gleaming of her jewelry and gems; the young wolves of Finance who will manage to earn millions or billions—but at what personal expense?... They do not see Jesus, who is nevertheless quite

THE BIBLE – MT 25:31, 41-46

When the Son of man [I, Jesus] comes in his glory... he will say to those at his left hand, "Depart from me, you cursed, into the eternal fire prepared for the devil and his angels; for I was hungry and you gave me no food, I was thirsty and you gave me no drink, I was a stranger and you did not welcome me, naked and you did not clothe me, sick and in prison and you did not visit me." Then they also will answer, "Lord, when did we see you hungry or thirsty or a stranger or naked or sick or in prison, and did not minister to you?" Then he will answer them, "Truly, I say to you, as you did it not to one of the least of these, you did it not to me." And they will go away into eternal punishment, but the righteous into eternal life."

Christ and Mammon, plate 14 of *Passion*
Georges Rouault (1871-1958)
1936
Aquatint on beige laid paper, 12 x 12 in
Chicago, Art Institute

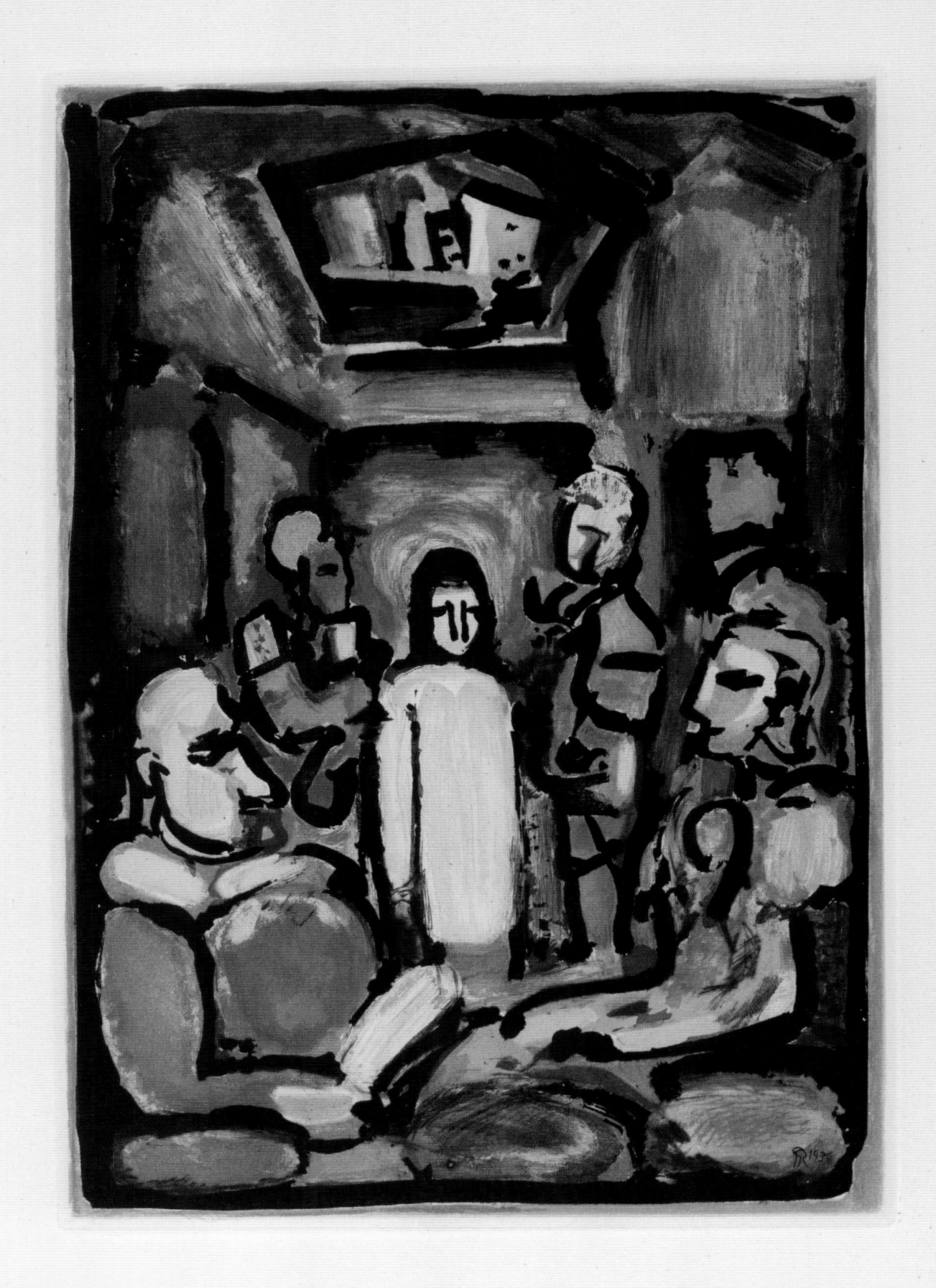

present in the midst of their life. And they and the likes of them will go off to a place of condemnation where this time, obviously, they will not see Jesus *for good*—if we can say that. That will not change them. On the contrary, they will see Mammon as he is. *And they will go to eternal damnation* (Mt 25:46). ■

IN ART HISTORY

ROUAULT, WITNESS TO THE CHRISTIAN SUPERNATURAL

Baptized out of family tradition, Georges Rouault (1871–1958) was raised without the Christian faith. A comrade from Gustave Moreau's studio, Antonin Bourbon, a Benedictine Oblate, would pave the way for him. In that same studio, Rouault was part of a group of young artists who would become the Fauvists, including Henri Matisse. The place occupied by Rouault within his generation was nevertheless one of the loneliest: he was "the man of an individual revolution," as Lionello Venturi described him.

From Moreau he kept the rejection of the realism that was fashionable in academic painting. From Honoré Daumier he learned to scrutinize the interior secrets of his figures. About Paul Cézanne, he said: "We all owe him something," and from Vincent Van Gogh he took his posture as a mystical companion of the suffering working class..

In this *Christ and Mammon*, a plate resulting from a series of original etchings in colors and outlines carved in wood, published by Ambroise Vollard in 1939, Christ appears, as he often does in Rouault's works, surrounded by suffering humanity with, in this case, the terrible figure of Mammon, prince of hell and the embodiment of avarice.

The twenty or so plates illustrate the text *Passion* by André Suarès (1868–1948), unless the creative process was the other way around, since Rouault was the one who requested it from his friend, a poet and writer.

Roualt once said about Suarès, who was of Jewish descent, that he did not know whether he shared his faith in the Resurrection. It makes little difference, since Suarès had written to Rouault: "There is a sphere of feeling, an enclosed universe, a mystical thought in which I have no other companion but you" (quoted by Jean-Pierre Jossua). The title *Passion* appears for the first time in their correspondence in a letter penned by Suarès in 1927, and the book was not completed until 1939. The decade that passed between these two dates was one of the most dramatic for Rouault, who was compelled to deliver a large number of paintings and books in order to satisfy the clauses in the demanding contract binding him to his dealer.

Paradoxically, Rouault's art evolved at the same time toward a style marked by splendor and serenity. His engravings, the fruit of long years of frustrated work, were nonetheless masterful. A refinement and an economy of means are displayed in them; these characteristics are supported by the flat surface of the print which induces a clearness of hues, as opposed to the impasto technique and the superimposed layers of paint that are common in the artist's oil paintings and gouaches.

The black outlines compartmentalize the plate and completely separate the strident colors that make it rhythmic. François Chapon correctly notes that the light that bathes this scene is emitted from a single center in the white silhouette of the Divine Child, who thus becomes "light of light."

Here, the Redeemer humbles himself to be in the midst of human beings and their executioners. Note that Rouault paints not so much characters as suffering souls. Behind the appearance of the work, the only reality that he points toward is that human beings are in God's image. His art, with its fantastic note, is part of the apocalypse and means to testify in favor of the Christian supernatural.

M. C.

In *The Blood of the Poor* (1909), Léon Bloy deploys his theological thought by way of very brief chapters anchored both in the Passion of Jesus, who died on the Cross two thousand years ago, and in the contemporary perpetuation of injustice and violence by the selfishness of the rich, whose money is nothing but the blood of the poor, therefore the blood of the Poor Man par excellence who is Christ. In this passage, his prophetic cry aims in particular to show the horror of the exploitation of children.

Léon Bloy, *The Blood of the Poor*, translated by Richard Robinson (Portland, OR: Sunny Lou Publishing Co., 2021), pages 45, 56, 105.

The cry of a prophet

LÉON BLOY

Man is situated so close to God that the word *poor* is an expression of tenderness. When the heart bursts for compassion or love, when one almost cannot hold back the tears anymore, it is the word that comes to one's lips.... As much as one adores riches, there is, all the same, a tenacious prejudice that militates obstinately for poverty. It is as if the very modest lance that pierced the side of Jesus had pierced every heart. That wound does not heal after twenty centuries now. There are countless lamentations, women, old men, small children; there are the living and the dead. All those people bleed, all that multitude jets blood and water from the middle of the Cross of misery, in the Orient, in the Occident, under every sky, under all executioners, under all scourges, amidst all men and tempests of nature—for so long now! It is poverty, that is the immense poverty of the world, the total and universal poverty of Jesus Christ! It really must be that that counts and that that is recuperated!...

What is even more incomprehensible in the world, it is the patience of the poor, somber and *miraculous* medal of God's Patience in his palaces of light.... The Sweating of Jesus' Blood begins again silently in the night, under the tranquil olive trees in the Garden, the disciples ever sleeping. He must continue that Agony for so many miserable wretches, for a very great number of defenseless beings, men, women, and children above all!

For here is the horror of horrors: the labor of children, the misery of all the little ones exploited by industry in the production of riches! And that in all lands. Jesus said: "Let the children come to me." The rich people say: "Send them to the factory, to the workshop, into the darkest and most mortal places of our hells. The efforts of their feeble arms will add something to our opulence."

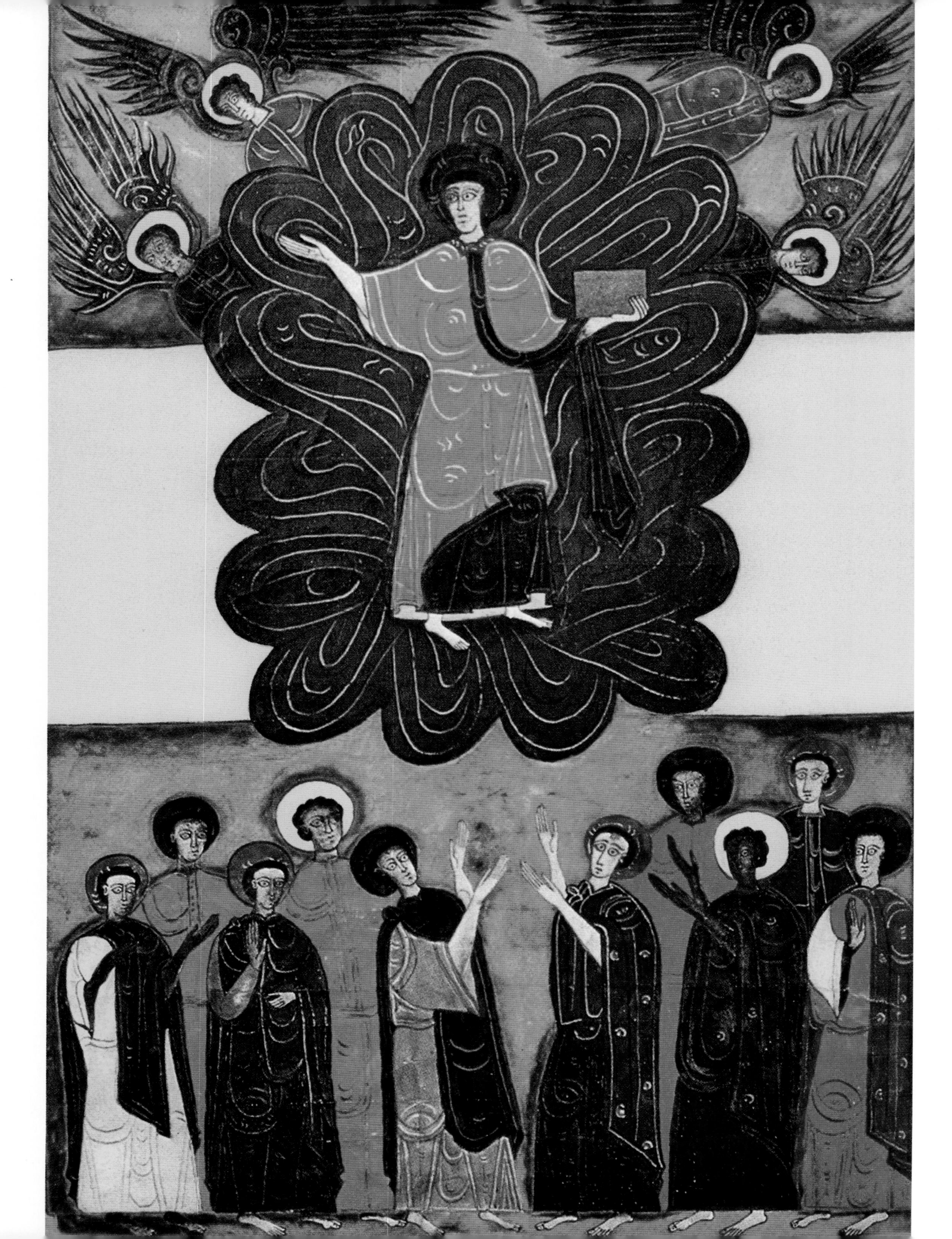

Jesus will come again in glory

The four evangelists mention the return of Jesus *at the end of time*. Matthew, Mark, and Luke do so in imagery and mythical language. They insist on the cosmic dimension of the event: all Creation, of all times, with the heavens and the light and all humanity, will be taken up by the "glory" of God. In the Gospel according to Saint John, Jesus speaks without images to insist on the consequences of his return for mankind: the resurrection of the dead, which is the very meaning of his coming, because *"This is the will of him who sent me, that I should lose nothing of all that he has given me, but raise it up at the last day"* (cf. Jn 6:39).

In the early 8th century, Visigoth Spain, at that time Christian, came under Muslim domination. All of it? No, because in the north of the Iberian Peninsula, entrenched in inaccessible grottos within the mountain peaks of Europe, some Christians refused to submit. And yet the methods of repression utilized by the invaders had until then discouraged any hint of opposition.

In 722 these fierce holdouts took the famous oath of Covadonga: "No Spaniard will take a moment of rest as long as the Moors still hold one bit of the Iberian Peninsula, even if it were the size of an olive pit." And they founded the Kingdom of Asturias, from which the whole Reconquest or *Reconquista* would start. In this context, the Book of Revelation by Saint John became the guarantee of their human and Christian hope. None of them doubted that he was an agent of the divine revelations that are fulfilled in history: wasn't Islam the "Beast" (Rv 13) that rose out of the sea? Weren't the Islamic armies satanic forces that sowed terror and death? For this little remnant of "witnesses of Christ" in the land of Spain, the last book of the Bible gave the assurance that at the end of the combat, Jesus would come again in glory to crown the victory of the forces of Good and to inaugurate on earth a reign of peace for a thousand years.

This work was painted within that Christian enclave, in 1047, to strengthen its spirit of resistance. Its style makes a very original synthesis between the Visigoth and Romanesque influences, but with Arabic and Coptic features also. Picasso would be fascinated by this naively stylized art and was inspired by it, particularly for his grand apocalyptic fresco *Guernica*, which denounces the barbarity of war. Here, against a background of three bands the colors of blood and gold—which we find again in the Spanish flag from the 18th century on—is depicted the parousia (the last coming of Christ at the end of the world): *Behold, he is coming with the clouds, and every eye will see him.... Even so. Amen* (Rv 1:7). In heaven, four angels prepare to gather the elect from the four corners of the earth. Below, on an earth reddened by the blood of martyrs, the elect who have gone through the great trial rejoice while singing:

Blessed be he that comes, the Christ, the King of the universe!
Peace on earth and glory to God in the highest heavens! ■

THE BIBLE – MT 24:27-31

For as the lightning comes from the east and shines as far as the west, so will be the coming of the Son of man. Wherever the body is, there the eagles will be gathered together. Immediately after the tribulation of those days the sun will be darkened, and the moon will not give its light, and the stars will fall from heaven, and the powers of the heavens will be shaken; then will appear the sign of the Son of man in heaven, and then all the tribes of the earth will mourn, and they will see the Son of man coming on the clouds of heaven with power and great glory; and he will send out his angels with a loud trumpet call, and they will gather his elect from the four winds, from one end of heaven to the other.

Christ carrying the book of life
1047
Illumination on parchment, 14 x 11 in
Madrid, National Library of Spain, *Beatus de Facundus*,
Commentary on the Book of Revelation by Beatus of Liébana, Vit. 14-2, f° 43 v°

Christians ardently desire the return of Jesus, which will signify the "end of time"; this is the object of their hope. They are in a hurry to be introduced through him, with him, and in him into what they call "the communion of saints." Then, the prayer of Jesus at the Last Supper will be answered, perfectly and forever: *"That they may all be one, even as you, Father, are in me, and I in you, that they also may be in us.... The glory which you have given me I have given to them, that they may be one even as we are one, I in them and you in me"* (Jn 17:21-23).

Humanity raised to the highest heavens

Trained by Jean Fouquet, Jean Bourdichon (*ca.* 1457–1521) was, from 1481 on, the official painter of four Kings of France: Louis XI, Charles VIII, Louis XII, and Francis I. Since all his paintings have been lost, he is unknown today except as a brilliant miniaturist. Now for three years, from 1516 to 1519, he was the first painter of Francis I, at the same time as Leonardo da Vinci—the latter had settled in Clos Lucé, whereas Bourdichon's studio was located in the Castle of Plessis-lès Tours, about twelve miles away as the crow flies. They produced together the decors for the feasts that Francis I gave in his castles in the Loire Valley.

Collaboration between the two artists did not come about automatically, however, so antagonistic were their concepts of art. Leonardo posed as one of the most radical actors of the Renaissance. He was interested primarily in man and his destiny, in his ability to explain the world to himself by himself. For him, divinity was still an interesting subject, to be sure, but primarily in the perception that man has of it. "The mind of the painter acquires the likeness of the divine," he professed. As for Bourdichon, he was devoted to a "naive" and "enchanted" vision of the world that he had inherited from the Middle Ages. In 1503 he received the commission for the manuscript that remains a supreme masterpiece of illumination: the *Great Book of Hours of Anne of Brittany*. Since it took five years of work, the book was not delivered until 1508 to the woman who was twice Queen of France.

Among the forty-nine large, full-page illuminations that adorn this magnificent Book of Hours, this one depicts Christ in majesty. Seated on a golden throne, wearing the royal and imperial crown, Jesus has the visible universe beneath his feet, while the mandorla (Italian for "almond") situates him in the invisible universe where he receives "all adoration and all glory for ever and ever." With his left hand, he presents

THE BIBLE – RV 21:1-7

Then I saw a new heaven and a new earth; for the first heaven and the first earth had passed away, and the sea was no more. And I saw the holy city, new Jerusalem, coming down out of heaven from God, prepared as a bride adorned for her husband; and I heard a great voice from the throne saying, "Behold, the dwelling of God is with men. He will dwell with them, and they shall be his people, and God himself will be with them; he will wipe away every tear from their eyes, and death shall be no more, neither shall there be mourning nor crying nor pain any more, for the former things have passed away." And he who sat upon the throne said, "Behold, I make all things new." Also he said, "Write this, for these words are trustworthy and true." And he said to me, "It is done! I am the Alpha and the Omega, the beginning and the end. To the thirsty I will give water without price from the fountain of the water of life. He who conquers shall have this heritage, and I will be his God and he shall be my son."

Christ in majesty and saints
Jean Bourdichon (*ca.* 1457–1521)
1503–1508
Illumination on parchment, 12 x 7.5 in
Paris, National Library of France
Grandes Heures d'Anne de Bretagne,
ms. latin 9474, f° 209 v°

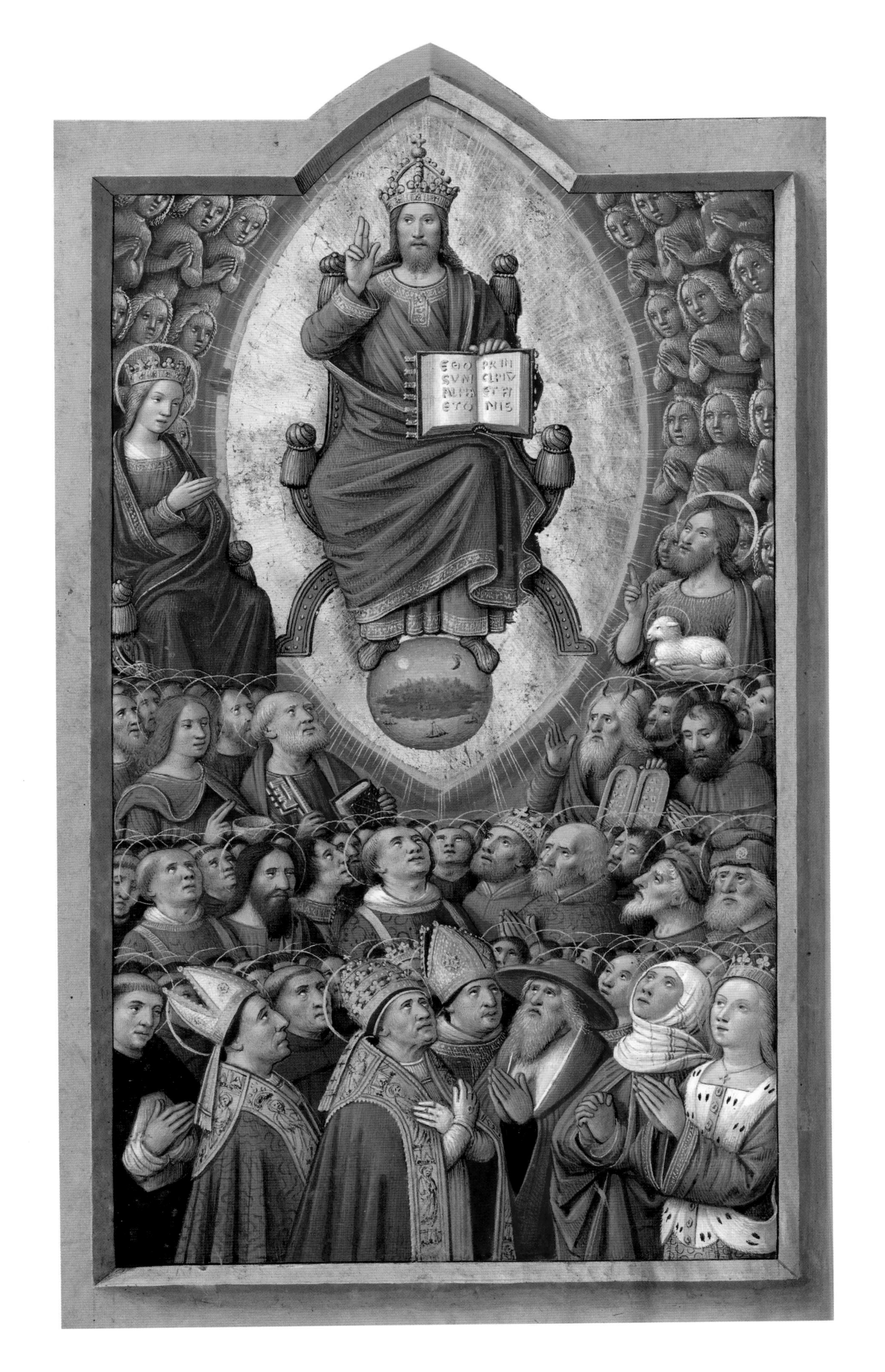
EGO
SVM
ALPHA
ETO
PRIN
CIPIV
ET FI
NIS

the "book of life" described in Revelation, opened to these words: *Ego sum Alpha et Omega, principium et finis ("I am the Alpha and the Omegea, the beginning and the end")* (Rv 1:8). With his right hand, he makes a gesture often interpreted as a blessing, but it is in fact the gesture of the Master who teaches all truth.

Encircled by the divine light with a halo of gold, Christ the King is surrounded by the nine choirs of angels. Taking his place beneath the angels, to Jesus' left and closer to the viewer, is Saint John the Baptist, the greatest of the prophets, carrying the Lamb of God in his arms. Further down come Moses with the Tablets of the Law, Elijah, and all the prophets of Israel. In front of Moses and lower on the image, King David wearing the French royal crown with the *fleur de lys*: and for a good reason, because his features are those of Louis XII, who was just proclaimed "Father of the people" at the States General in 1506. In the lowest row in the right-hand corner we recognize his wife, Queen Anne of Brittany, who commissioned the book, flanked by her patron saint, Anne, the mother of the Virgin Mary, and therefore the grandmother of Jesus. The clothing of Anne of Brittany is lined with ermine, which is an allusion to the legend about her: the story goes that during a hunt Anne noticed a female ermine which, although being tracked by the hounds, refused to cross a mud puddle and preferred to face the pack rather than soil her white robe; Anne saved her from the fierce dogs and adopted her. Her coat of arms, as Duchess of Brittany, was already "party azure with three fleurs de lys of gold and ermine"; and so she also had the motto added: *Potius mori quam foedari,* which can be translated: "Better to die than to be sullied," inasmuch as Anne, being a good Christian, meant primarily the stain of sin. But there was also the chivalrous aspect, since the motto can also be translated: "Better death than dishonor."

To the right of Saint Anne, in the foreground, we recognize the great Western Church Fathers: Saint Jerome robed as a cardinal, then Saint Ambrose as a bishop, Pope Saint Gregory the Great with the tiara, and Saint Augustine as a bishop. They are accompanied by the founders of the two mendicant religious orders: Saint Francis of Assisi in a coarse brown woolen habit, and Saint Dominic, occupying the left corner. Standing out from the crowd of saints, the deacons and martyrs Saint Lawrence and Saint Vincent wearing the dalmatic—green and fuchsia respectively—looking up to heaven; between them, the first Christian martyr, Saint Stephen, considered the very first deacon, who was stoned in Jerusalem. Above, at the level of Moses, we see Saint Peter with the keys and the book containing his letters, and beside him Saint John carrying a cup and tracing over it a sign of the cross—*The Golden Legend* relates that he was forced to drink a cup filled with lethal poison and drank it without being troubled after blessing it. Behind them the other ten apostles line up. Finally, on the uppermost rank, the only person at the level of the angels, is the Queen of Heaven, Mary, crowned and seated on a throne of gold like Jesus, her Divine Son. ■

André Malraux (1901–1976) was a novelist, essayist, art theorist, and politician. Deeply sensitive to transcendence although agnostic, he dedicated an important part of his work to Christian art. In *The Metamorphosis of the Gods* (1957), he scrutinizes, through the mystery of artistic creation, man's relation to the supernatural. In this passage he describes the tympanum of the portal of the Cathedral of Autun, on which is enthroned Christ in majesty, surrounded by the elect.

André Malraux, *The Metamorphosis of the Gods: The Supernatural* (1957), translated by Stuart Gilbert (London: Secker and Warburg, 1960), 204.

Christ gathers mankind in love

ANDRÉ MALRAUX

We are shown a bishop, but also a pilgrim and a crusader; in the medallions, a shepherd, a thresher of wheat, a vinegrower in his vat—all gathered around Christ, giver of flocks, of vines and wheat. Here the Savior's presence reinforces the teaching of the Church, for it reveals the element of the divine present in even the humblest living creature. The labors of the seasons figure in the medallions at Vézelay, between the signs of the Zodiac; for men's works and days are also willed by God. Like the Beaulieu Christ whose outstretched arms, casting the shadow of the Cross, summon towards Him every human joy and grief, this Pantocrator welcomes the bishop with his crozier, the king with his crown, the vinegrower with his vine-shoot, the blind man with his dog, when the king has acknowledged him despite the crown, when the vinegrower has recognized him in the vineyard and the blind man in the dog. His patron saints have brought them to him trade by trade, and he told them: "I shed this drop of blood for the vinegrowers." In the most clement emblem of the Last Day that has ever been sculpted, around the Pantocrator who will disappear, the religion of love finally discovers the expression of love.

The image of the harvest, as a prediction of the end of human history in this temporal world, is common in the Bible. Jesus uses it many times to indicate that everything good will enter into eternity and that humanity will be divinized. Now, the great teaching of Jesus to which Christians adhere is that the eternal destiny of each individual plays out in his everyday life, here and now, with his new commandment as the sole criterion: *Love one another even as I have loved you* (Jn 13:34).

Where do we come from? What are we? Where are we going?

Paul Sérusier (1864–1927) was the "thinker" in a group of artists that initially gathered around Paul Gauguin in Pont-Aven, Brittany, and would take for itself the name of "nabis" (in Hebrew, "the illumined," "prophets"). The nabis were part of the avant-garde of the Symbolist movement. At the dawn of the 20th century, they asserted their new style "to liberate painting from slavery" both to academic realism and to Impressionism.

This harvest landscape is indicative of their profoundly spiritual interpretation of the "motifs" of nature. Inspired by the sonnet "Correspondences" by Charles Baudelaire, "the red-bearded Nabi" (Maurice Denis' nickname for his friend Paul Sérusier) celebrates nature as a temple in which human life travels "through forests of symbols":

Nature's a temple where each living column,
At times, gives forth vague words. There Man advances
Through forest-groves of symbols, strange and solemn,
Who follow him with their familiar glances.

As long-drawn echoes mingle and transfuse
Till in a deep, dark unison they swoon,
Vast as the night or as the vault of noon—
So are commingled perfumes, sounds, and hues.

There can be perfumes cool as children's flesh,
Like fiddles, sweet, like meadows greenly fresh.
Rich, complex, and triumphant, others roll

With the vast range of all non-finite things—
Amber, musk, incense, benjamin, each sings
The transports of the senses and the soul.

Harvest
Paul Sérusier (1864–1927)
First quarter of the 20th century
Oil on canvas, 27 x 18 in
Nantes, Art Museum

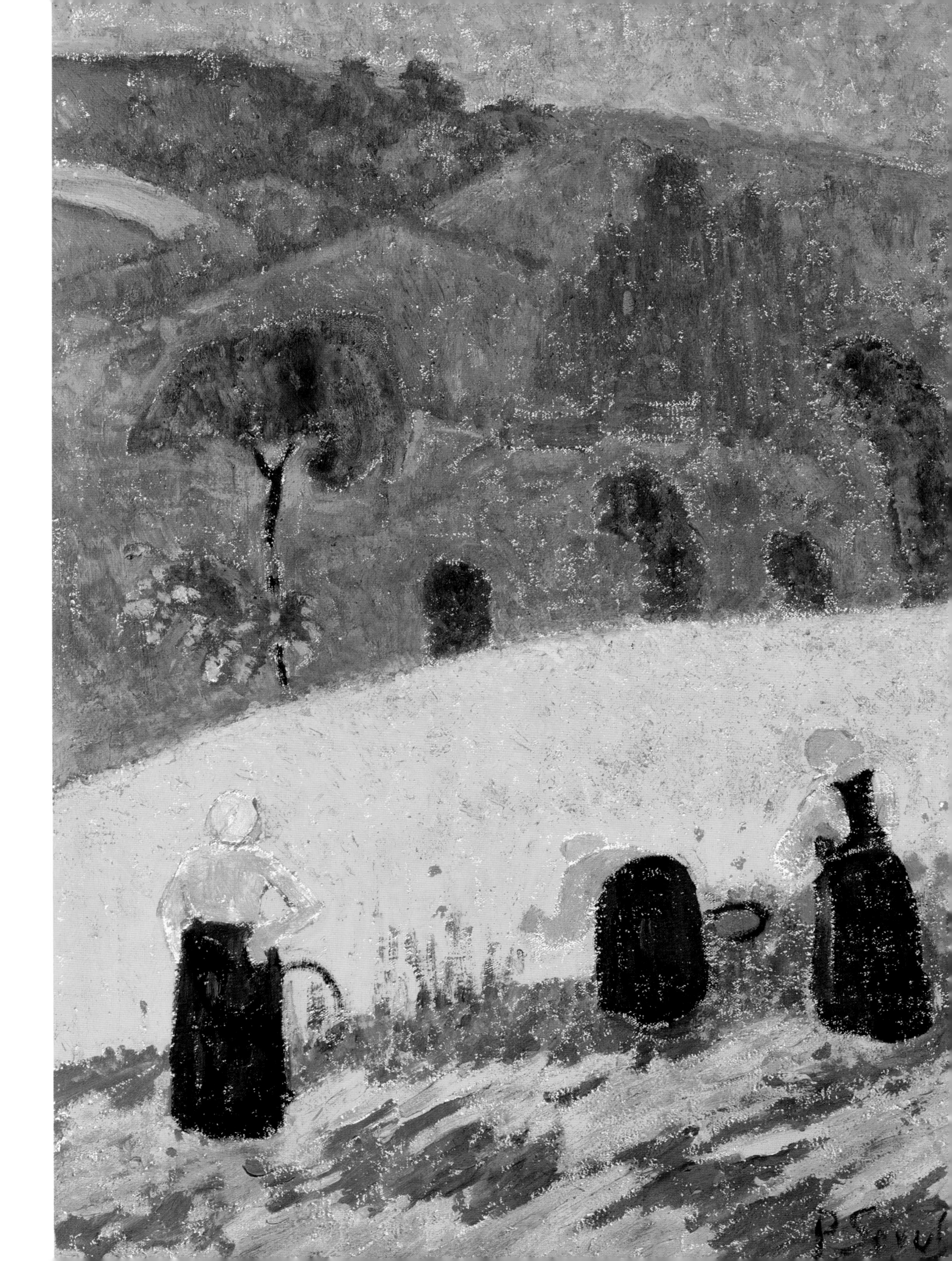

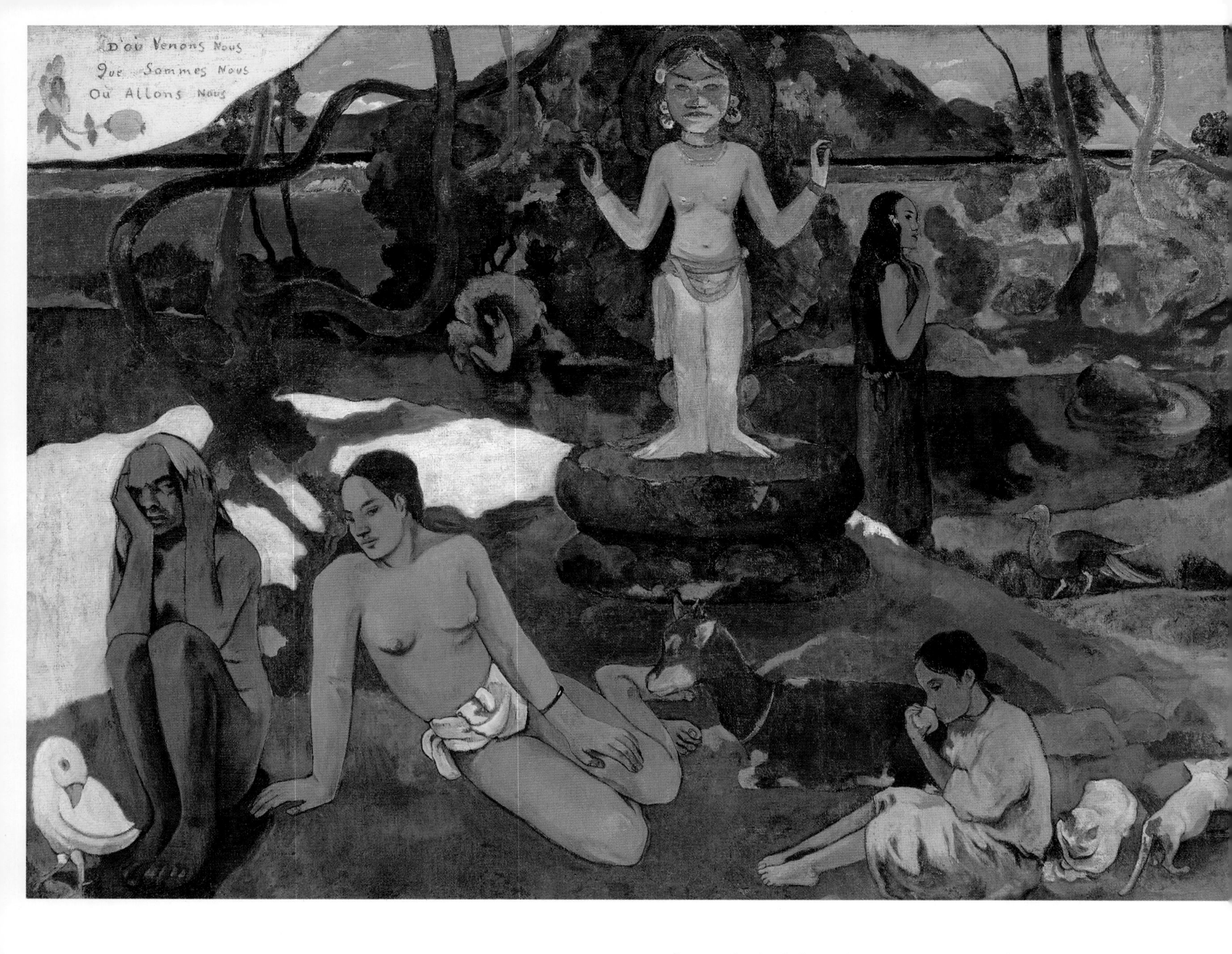

THE BIBLE – JN 4:35

Do you not say, "There are yet four months, then comes the harvest"? I tell you, lift up your eyes, and see how the fields are already white for harvest.

The method of the nabis invites us therefore to contemplate this countryside as we would meditate on the revelation of a higher reality. The conflict of colors and the placement of ranks one above the other perform the function of perspective. Quite metaphorical, the women with Breton headdresses in the foreground embody nothing less than the three most fundamental questions about the human condition, the ones that Paul Gauguin already posed in his famous "mad picture" in the winter of 1897–1898: the first woman, with her hand on her hip, contemplates human destiny and symbolizes the question, "Where do we come from?"; the second, who is cutting wheat—"What are we?"; and the third, who is binding sheaves—"Where are we going?" The verdant background, deliberately rendered

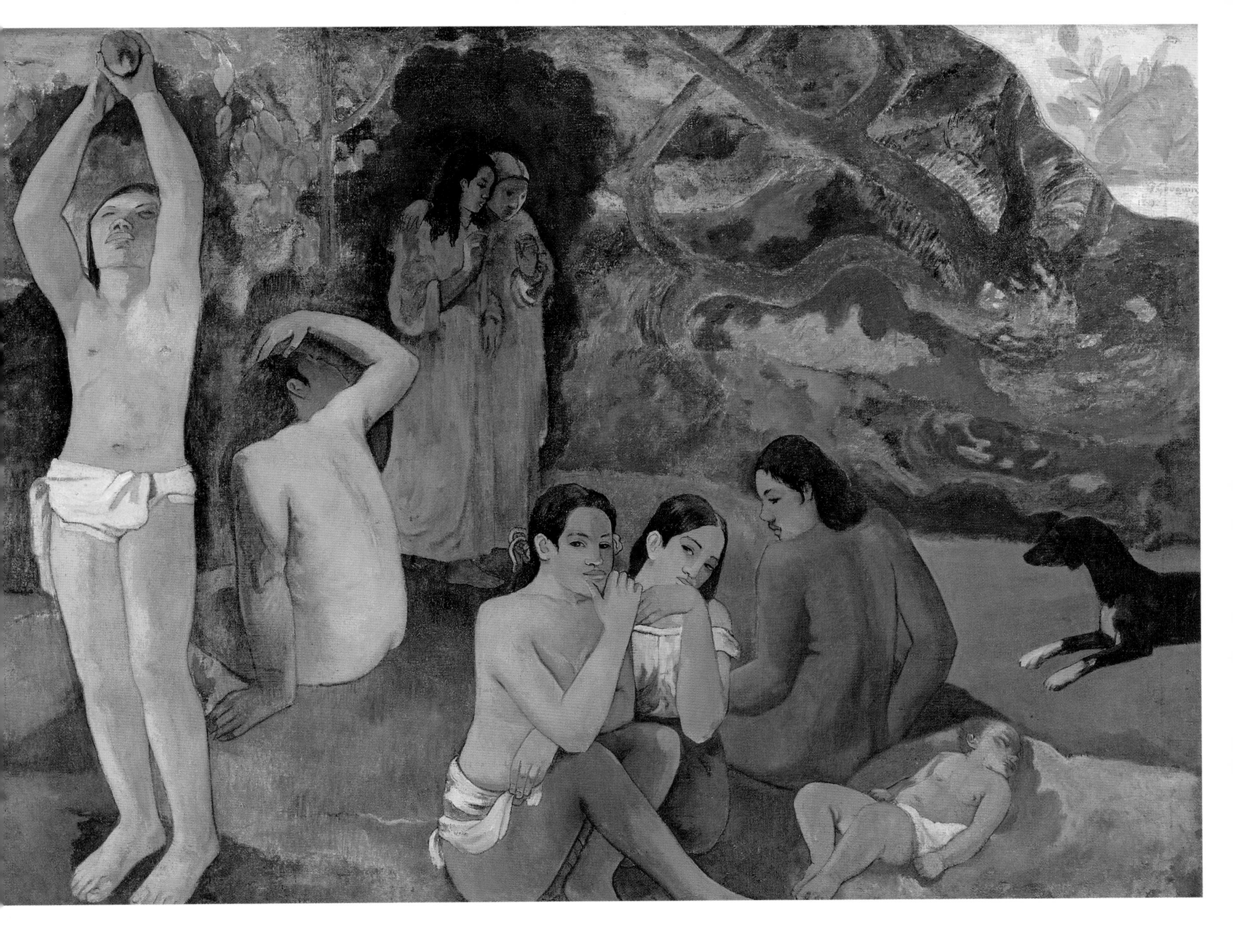

Where do we come from? What are we? Where are we going?
Paul Gauguin (1848–1903)
1897–1898
Oil on canvas, 54.8 x 147.5 in
Boston Museum of Fine Arts

This lengthy work of art runs from the viewer's right to the left. The three main groups illustrate the three metaphysical questions posed in the title. The work opens with a newborn and concludes, in Gauguin's own words, with "a strange white bird holding in its foot a lizard, which represents the futility of words." Behind the bird, "an old woman approaching death appears to be reconciled and resigned to the idea": in the background, the totem statue represents the next life.

with impressionist brushstrokes, perhaps in ridicule, suggests the universe of creation as the non-initiated person sees it at the first step: In order to get from error to the truth, it is necessary to pass through ignorance, Paul Sérusier used to say. But look at the golden wave of the ocean of grain that submerges the picture. It symbolizes the fusion between the divine glory, which is the first and the last word of created things, and humanity's destiny in history, which is to have been sown and to have the promise of being harvested. The stalks of wheat already cut and bound into sheaves are the avant-garde of this immense, luminous, vibrant multitude in the wind of the Holy Spirit, which advances so as to melt into the glory of God. In the midst of the ripe ears that are presented to the sickle of death, some poppies bloom in discreet red patches, recalling that this harvest is glorious because it was saved by the blood of a God who, by being overwhelmed himself, conquered death. ■

Art Credits

Cover: © BPK, Berlin, Dist. RMN-GP / Elke Estel / Hans-Peter Klut. **P. 9:** © Dist. RMN-GP / image du Prado. **P. 21:** © Arthotek / La Collection. **P. 22:** © akg-images / André Held. **P. 25:** © BPK, Berlin, Dist. RMN-GP / Elke Walford. **P. 26:** © akg-images. **P. 29:** © Dist. RMN-GP / image of the MMA. **P. 31:** © akg-images / Eric Vandeville. **P. 33:** © RMN-GP / René-Gabriel Ojéda. **P. 34:** © Iberfoto / Bridgeman Images. **P. 36:** © Mondadori Portfolio / Electa / Bridgeman Images. **P. 38:** © akg-images. **P. 41:** © akg-images / WHA / World History Archive. **P. 43:** © RMN-GP / Gérard Blot. © Adagp, Paris, 2022. **P. 45:** © Interfoto / La Collection. **P. 46:** © Christie's / Artothek / La Collection. © Adagp, Paris, 2022. **P. 49:** © akg-images / Rabatti & Domingie. **P. 50:** © akg-images / Jean-Claude Varga. **P. 53:** © Bridgeman Images. **P. 55:** © akg-images. **P. 59, 60:** © akg-images. **P. 63:** Public domain. CC0 1.0. **P. 62:** © Courtesy Perm State Art Gallery / with the collaboration of the agency La Collection. **P. 64:** © Catalogue raisonné Maurice Denis. **P. 66:** © BPK, Berlin, Dist. RMN-GP / Elke Walford. **P. 67:** © BnF, Dist. RMN-GP / image BnF. **P. 71, 72:** © Dist. RMN-GP / The Trustees of the Wallace Collection. **P. 75:** © akg-images. **P. 77:** © Frank Buffetrille / Bridgeman Images. **P. 78:** © Bildarchiv Foto Marburg / Bridgeman Giraudon. **P. 80:** © Heritage Images / Fine Art Images / akg-images. **P. 83:** © Nicolò Orsi Battaglini / Bridgeman Images. **P. 85:** © RMN-GP / Hervé Lewandowski. **P. 86:** © Mairie de Bordeaux, musée des Beaux-Arts, photo L. Gauthier. **P. 89:** © MBA, Rennes, Dist. RMN-GP / Adélaïde Beaudoin. **P. 90, 92:** © British Library Board. All Rights Reserved / Bridgeman Images. **P. 95:** © Dist. RMN-GP / image du Prado. **P. 97:** © Christie's Images / Bridgeman Images. **P. 98:** © Painters / Alamy Stock Photo. **P. 101:** © Bridgeman Images. © Succession Picasso 2022. **P. 104:** © RMN-GP / image du Prado. **P. 106:** © Dist. RMN-GP / image of the MMA. **P. 109:** © Jean-Paul Dumontier / La Collection. **P. 110, 111:** © Guildhall Art Gallery / Bridgeman Images. **P. 114:** © Jean-Paul Dumontier / La Collection. **P. 117:** © Jean-Paul Dumontier / La Collection. **P. 118:** © Bridgeman Images / photo Josse. **P. 121:** © RMN-GP / Thierry Le Mage. **P. 122:** © Guy Focant. **P. 124:** © Iberfoto / Bridgeman Images. **P. 125:** © RMN-GP / Hervé Lewandowski. **P. 126:** © Museum of Fine Arts, Budapest, 2021 / with the collaboration of the agency La Collection. **P. 129:** © Bridgeman Images. **P. 131:** © RMN-GP / Franck Raux. **P. 133, 135:** © Artothek / La Collection. **P. 136:** © Artothek / La Collection. **P. 139:** © COARC. **P. 143:** © Ghigo Roli / Bridgeman Images. **P. 145:** © RMN-GP / Gérard Blot. **P. 149:** © akg-images. **P. 151:** © Alinari / Bridgeman Images. **P. 152:** © RMN-GP / Gérard Blot. **P. 155, 157:** © Mauro Magliani / RMN-GP. **P. 158:** © akg-images / Album. **P. 161:** © Bridgeman Images. **P. 164:** © Heritage Images / Fine Art Images / akg-images. **P. 167:** © BPK, Berlin, dist. RMN-GP / Jörg P. Anders. **P. 169:** © Mondadori Portfolio / Archivio Antonio Quattrone / Bridgeman Images. **P. 173:** © Domingie & Rabatti / La Collection. **P. 174:** © akg-images / De Agostini Picture Lib. / S. Vannini. **P. 176, 177:** © RMN-GP / Thierry Olivier. **P. 179:** © akg-images / Erich Lessing. **P. 180:** © RMN-GP / Benoît Touchard. **P. 182, 185:** © Mondadori Portfolio / Archivio Antonio Quattrone / Bridgeman Images. **P. 189:** © Raffaello Bencini / Bridgeman Images. **P. 192:** © Bridgeman Images. **P. 193:** © akg-images / Album. **P. 194:** © Clément Guillaume. **P. 197, 198:** © Bridgeman Images. **P. 201:** © Dist. RMN-GP/ image du Prado. **P. 202:** © Christie's Images / Bridgeman Images. © Succession Picasso 2022. **P. 204:** © akg-images / Album. **P. 209:** © Lionel Antoni. **P. 210:** Photo public domain. **P. 211:** Photo Digital image courtesy of the Getty's Open Content Program. **P. 213, 214:** © Dist. RMN-GP / image du Prado. **P. 217, 219:** © Electa / Leemage. **P. 220:** © RMN-GP / Hervé Lewandowski. **P. 223:** © Bridgeman Images. **P. 225:** © La Collection / Domingie & Rabatti. **P. 227:** © Staatliche Kunstsammlungen Dresden / Bridgeman Images. **P. 228, 230:** © akg-images / Erich Lessing. **P. 231:** © RMN-GP / Gérard Blot. **P. 233:** © akg-images. **P. 234:** © Luisa Ricciarini / Bridgeman Images. **P. 236:** © RMN-GP / Gérard Blot. **P. 239:** © AISA / Leemage. **P. 240:** © Bridgeman Images. **P. 243:** © Bridgeman Images. **P. 249:** © The National Gallery, London, dist. RMN-GP / National Gallery Department. **P. 251:** © akg-images / Mondadori Portfolio / Arnaldo Vescovo. **P. 253:** © British Library Board. All Rights Reserved / Bridgeman Images. **P. 254:** © RMN-GP / Hervé Lewandowski. **P. 257:** © RMN-GP / Hervé Lewandowski. **P. 259, 260:** © RMN-GP / Jean-Gilles Berizzi. **P. 262:** © British Library / Robana / Leemage. **P. 265:** © Photo Josse / Bridgeman Images. **P. 269:** © akg-images. © Adagp, Paris, 2021. **P. 273:** © akg-images. **P. 274:** CC0 Paris Musées / Musée Carnavalet. **P. 276:** © Pictures from History / Bridgeman Images. **P 279:** © BnF, Dist. RMN-GP / image BnF. **P. 283:** © Bridgeman Images. **P. 284, 285:** © Museum of Fine Arts, Boston / Tompkins Collection / Bridgeman Images.

Credits and sources of the citations

P. 4: Henri Matisse, cited by Sister Jacques-Marie, *Henri Matisse: La chapelle de Vence* (1992), new edition, coll. "Cahiers et Couleurs" (Paris: Bernard Chauveau Édition, 2014). **P. 10: Georges Braque,** *Le Jour et la Nuit: chaiers 1917-1952* (Paris: Gallimard, 1952) © Éditions Gallimard. **P. 18: Paul Valéry,** "L'infini esthétique," *Oeuvres*, vol. II, coll. "Bibliothèque de la Pléiade" (Paris; Gallimard, 1960). **P. 20: Charles Baudelaire,** "L'Homme et la mer" and "La Vie antérieure," *Les Fleurs du Mal* (1857), English translation by Roy Campbell, "Man and the Sea" and "Former Life," in *Poems of Baudelaire* (New York: Pantheon Books, 1952). **P. 22** ("bitter abyss"): **Charles Baudelaire,** "Man and the Sea," translated by Roy Campbell. **P. 28** (paragraph 1): **Auguste Rodin,** (1st citation) *L'Art, entretiens réunis par Paul Gsell* (Paris: Bernard Grasset, 1911). (2nd citation) "La Tête Warren," *Le Musée: Revue d'art antique* vol. 1, n. 6 (novembre-décembre 1904). **P. 32** (paragraph 1): **Charles Péguy,** "Présentation de la Beauce à Notre-Dame de Chartres," *La Tapisserie de Notre-Dame* (Paris: Cahiers de la Quinzaine, 1913). **P. 39: Søren Kierkegaard,** *Fear and Trembling* (1843), translated from the Danish by Walter Lowrie, (Princeton; Princeton University Press, 1941). **P. 42:** (paragraph 2): **Marc Chagall,** cited by Ziva Amishai-Maisels, "Chagall und der Holocaust," *Chagall und Deutschland: Verehrt, Verfemt*, catalogue of an exposition at the Jewish Museum in Frankfurt-am-Main (Munich: Prestel, 2004). **P. 44** (beginning of paragraph 2): **Sidney Alexander,** *Marc Chagall: A biography* (New York: Putnam, 1978), 422. **P. 44** (end of paragraph 2): **Geneviève Schmitt-Rehlinger,** *Jésus le Christ dans l'oeuvre de Marc Chagall: Le motif du Crucifié* (Metz: Université Paul Verlaine, 2006). **P. 45** (paragraph 2): **Roland Barthes,** *Critique et vérité* (Paris: Éditions du Seuil, 1966). **P. 45** (paragraph 3): **Marc Chagall,** cited in *Chagall et l'avant-garde russe*, catalogue of an exposition in the Musée de Grenoble (Paris: Centre Pompidou, 2011). © Adagp, Paris [2021]. **P. 45** (last paragraph): **Michelangelo,** *Lettres familières, 1497-1509*, translated from Italian into French by Éliane Deschamps-Pria (Caen: L'Échoppe, 1989). **P. 48** (art history commentary, col. 3, top): **Camille Mauclair,** *Les Métèques contre l'art français: La Farce de l'art vivant* (Paris: Nouvelle Revue critique, 1930). **P. 56: Vincent Van Gogh,** Letter dated July 1880 to his brother Théo, in *Lettres à son frère Théo*, translated from Dutch to French by Georges Philippart (Paris: Bernard Grasset, 2002), © Éditions Grasset & Fasquelle, 1972. **P. 65: Maurice Denis,** (paragraph 1), *Nouvelles théories sur l'art moderne, sur l'art sacré: 1914-1921* [New theories on modern art and sacred art] (Paris: L. Rouart et J. Watelin, 1922). **P. 67** (paragraph 4): **Friedrich Hölderlin,** *Hyperion*, translated from German into French by Philippe Jaccottet (Paris: Mercure de France, 1965) © Éditions Gallimard. **P. 69** (art history commentary, col. 2, above): **Pierre-Jean David d'Angers,** cited by Henry Jouin, *David d'Angers, sa vie, son oeuvre*, vol. I (Paris: Plon, 1878). **P. 86** (art history commentary, col. 1): **Jean Moréas,** Manifeste littéraire, *Le Figaro*, Supplément littéraire (18 septembre 1886). **P. 86** (art history commentary, cols. 1-2): **Gabriel-Albert Aurier,** "Le symbolisme en peinture: Paul Gauguin," *Mercure de France* (mars 1891). **P. 86** (art history commentary, col. 3): **Odilon Redon,** *À soi-même: Journal (1867-1915)* (Paris: H. Floury, 1922). **P. 87: Henry Wadsworth Longfellow,** "The Nativity: A Miracle Play," in *The Golden Legend* (Boston: Ticknor, Reed, and Fields, 1852). **P. 96** (paragraph 2): **Marie-Louise Munier,** cited by Éric Divry, great-great-grandson of Émile Munier, on the occasion of the centennial of his death: http://munier.chez.com/sa_vie.ht. **P. 98** (art history commentary, col. 2, below): **Émile Zola,** "Nos peintres au Champ-de-Mars," *La Situation* (1 juillet 1867). **P. 100** (end of last paragraph): **Jean Clair,** cited by Philippe Royer, "Picasso, le religieux," *Le Pèlerin* 6941 (10 décembre 2015). **P. 102: Henri Matisse,** cited by Soeur Jacques-Marie, *Henri Matisse: La chapelle de Vence* (1992), new edition in the collection Cahiers et Couleurs (Paris: Bernard Chauveau Édition, 2014). **P. 119: Caryll Houselander,** *The Reed of God* (New York: Sheed & Ward, 1944). **P. 130** (end of last paragraph): **Charles Baudelaire,** "Les Phares," *Les Fleurs du Mal* (1857); English translation by Roy Campbell, "The Beacons," in *Poems of Baudelaire* (New York: Pantheon Books, 1952). **P. 144** (paragraph 1, first citation): **Paul de Saint-Victor,** "Salon de 1876," *La Liberté* (19 mai 1876). **P. 147** (last paragraph, 3rd citation): **Gustave Moreau,** cited in *Gustave Moreau*, ed. Henry Roujon in the series "Les Peintres illustres" (Paris: P. Laffite, 1914); and by Georges Rouault, *Souvenirs intimes: G. Moreau, Léon Bloy, Cézanne*, 2nd ed. (Paris: E. Frapier, 1926). **P. 156:** "Laetatur hodie Matris Ecclesiae sancta devotio," in *Lyra Messianica: Hymns and Verses on the Life of Christ, Ancient and Modern* (London: Longman, Green, Longman, Roberts, and Green, 1864). **P. 157:** "Phos Hilaron," translated as "O Radiant Light, O Sun Divine" by William George Storey. **P. 160: Thomas Merton,** "For My Brother: Reported Missing in Action, 1943," from *Collected Poems*, copyright 1968 by the Abbey of Gethsemani. Reprinted by permission of New Directions Publishing Corporation. **P. 171** (paragraph 3): **Philippe Sollers,** *La Divine Comédie: Entretiens avec Benoît Chantre* (Paris: Desclée de Brouwer, 2000). **P. 171** (last paragraph): **Dante,** *The Divine Comedy: Paradise*, translated from Italian by Henry Wadsworth Longfellow (1867, public domain), XVII, 130-133; cited in Philippe Sollers, *op. cit.* **P. 172** (end of last paragraph): **remark attributed to Michelangelo,** cited in the article by Georges Didi-Huberman, "Fra Angelico," *Encyclopaedia Universalis.* **P. 186** (art history commentary, col. 3, first citation): **Cennino Cennini,** *Traité de la peinture*, translated from Italian into French by Colette Déroche (Paris: Berger-Levrault, 1991). **P. 186** (art history commentary, col. 3, second citation): **Giorgio Vasari,** *Les Vies des meilleurs peintres, sculpteurs et architectes*, translated from Italian into French edited by A. Chastel (Paris: Berger-Levrault, 1981-1988). **P. 191: Gertrud von Le Fort,** *The Wife of Pilate and other stories* (San Francisco: Ignatius Press, 2015). **P. 198: Jean Racine,** Sur les vaines occupations du siècle, *Cantiques spirituels* (1694). **P. 221** (paragraph 2): **Léon Bloy,** Le lépreux, *Un brelan d'excommuniés* (Paris: Albert Savine, 1899). **P. 230** (paragraph 1): **Blaise Pascal,** Letter II to Mademoiselle de Roannez, October 1656, in *Thoughts, Letters and Minor Works*, The Harvard Classics 48 (New York: P. F. Collier & Son Company, 1938). **P. 235: François Mauriac,** *Life of Jesus*, translated by Julie Kernan (London: Longmans, Green, 1937). **P. 240** (last paragraph): **Blaise Pascal,** "Submission and use of reason," 20 and 17 *Pensées* (1669-1670), selections 265 and 263 in *Thoughts, Letters & Minor Works*, ed. Charles W. Eliot (1910). **P. 241: Denise Levertov,** from *A Door in the Hive* © 1989 by Denise Levertov. Reprinted by permission of New Directions Publishing Corp. **P. 246: Giorgio de Chirico,** © Adagp, Paris, [2021]. **P. 274** (art history commentary, col. 2): **André Suarès,** Letter to Georges Rouault cited by Jean-Pierre Jossua, Sur le seuil de la foi: André Suarès d'après sa correspondance et son oeuvre ultime, *Revue des sciences philosophiques et théologiques*, 93/3 (2009). **P. 281: André Malraux,** © Éditions Gallimard. **P. 282: Charles Baudelaire,** "Correspondences," *Les Fleurs du Mal* (1857); English translation by Roy Campbell, *Poems of Baudelaire* (New York: Pantheon Books, 1952).

Publisher : Romain Lizé
Editor: Jean de Saint-Chéron
Iconography: Isabelle Mascaras
Graphics and page composition: Marine Bezou
Proofreading: Samuel Wigutow and Sr. Myriam-Therese

Original French edition

www.magnificat.com

Photo engraving : IGS-CP
Printed in PRC in 2022
ISBN : 978-1-63967-006-2